'996

Subjects
and
Citizens

Subjects and Citizens

Nation, Race, and Gender from *Oroonoko* to Anita Hill

Edited by

Michael Moon

and

Cathy N. Davidson

Duke University Press

Durham and London

1995

With the exceptions of the introduction by Michael Moon and
Cathy N. Davidson; "Constructing the Black Masculine:
Frederick Douglass, Booker T. Washington, and the Sublimits
of African American Autobiography," by Maurice Wallace;
"Border Subjects and Transnational Sites: Américo Paredes's
The Hammon and the Beans and Other Stories," by Ramón
Saldívar; and "The Body Politic," by Karla F. C. Holloway,
these articles have appeared previously in *American Literature.*

Library of Congress Cataloging-in-Publication Data
Subjects and citizens : nation, race, and gender from Oroonoko
to Anita Hill / edited by Michael Moon and Cathy N. Davidson.
p.   cm.
Includes bibliographical references and index.
ISBN 0-8223-1539-4. — ISBN 0-8223-1529-7
1. American literature—History and criticism—Theory, etc.
2. National characteristics, American, in literature.   3. Politics
and literature—United States—History.   4. Literature and
society—United States—History.   5. Authors, American—
Political and social views.   6. Gender identity in literature.
7. Ethnic relations in literature.   8. Race relations in literature.
9. Sex role in literature.   I. Moon, Michael.   II. Davidson,
Cathy N., 1949–
PS169.N35S83   1995
810.9—dc20   95-10297

Contents *810.9 M818*

Michael Moon and Cathy N. Davidson • Introduction   1

156,837

Michael   Introduction
Moon
and
Cathy N.
Davidson

Subjects and Citizens: Nation, Race, and Gender from *"Oroonoko" to Anita Hill* takes on one of the most vexed issues in American literary studies: American exceptionalism. Beginning in the latter part of the nineteenth century, scholars such as Moses Coit Tyler began to formulate the boundaries of American literature along nationalist lines by debating what was truly "American" about American literature. The nation's literature, according to the exceptionalist view, would represent uniquely American values. But what values and whose? As Nina Baym has shown, Edgar Allan Poe was left out of most late nineteenth-century anthologies and schoolbooks of American literature because he was considered too Southern, too eccentric, and too "effeminate." The regional, aesthetic, gender, and (hetero)sexual prejudices implicit in Poe's exclusion emphasize how national identity is always an ideological construct.

Poe, of course, is now part of the canon of American literature. Other figures and groups have had a more precarious place, notably women of all races and people of color of both genders, many of whom appeared in anthologies during the Thirties only to disappear again until the revisionary inclusiveness of the 1980s. In *Subjects and Citizens*, we start from the premise that what constitutes a canon at a particular moment reflects current assumptions about what or who represents the nation. More to the point, these essays show how issues of race and gender challenge nationalist paradigms and realign the borders of both the nation and the field of American literary history.

In juxtaposing the terms "subject" and "citizen" in the title, we have chosen to emphasize some of the historical and political continuities between the traditional political and social meanings of "subject" (one who is placed under the authority of a monarch and governed by his law, as well as the wife who was enjoined to be "subject" to her husband as servants—or slaves—were to their masters) and the term "subject" in its contemporary sense (a person considered as the sum of the psychic effects of his or her interactions with the laws of language and other institutions that are formative of culture). We also intended that the title point up the interplay in many of these essays between various forms of traditional political "subjection" and the more nearly reciprocal obligations that are supposed to obtain between a citizen and the state in a democracy.

Three of the essays in this collection appear here for the first time while seventeen have been selected from the last four years of *American Literature*. Just as definitions of what constitutes American literature have changed in this century, so too has *American Literature* changed continually since its founding in 1929. This collection exemplifies the kinds of issues being addressed by the journal and the profession today.

The volume is united by three interrelated questions: where does "American literature" begin? (the question of origin); what does *"American* literature" mean? (the question of nation); and what does "American literature" include and exclude and how? (the question of race and gender). The essays in part 1 (by Annette Kolodny, Stephanie Athey and Daniel Cooper Alarcón, Julie Ellison, and Lora Romero) all challenge our myth of origins, the official story of the birth of the nation. In the opening essay Kolodny describes an encounter in 1553 between a Spanish adventurer and an elder from the Yaqui nation. The old man "drew a line on the ground as a demarcation, threatening death to any intruder who dared cross it." The line in the dirt demarcates one boundary of a nation now known as the "United States," and the meeting (recorded by a Spanish scribe) serves as a counter-myth to the celebratory story of conquest epitomized by the landing at Plymouth Rock. It is a paradigmatic instance of what Ramón Saldívar calls "border subjects and transnational sites." The other essays in part 1 pose other sites of origination—England and its seventeenth-century colony, Surinam; white women patriots of the American Revolution; and James Fenimore Cooper (once considered the "father" of American literature). All question the traditional domination of the canon by the Puritan forefathers and their New England descendants.

The question of origins leads inevitably to our second concern—the idea of nationhood—since where we find our origins is always a matter of how we define ourselves. *Subjects and Citizens* provides a range of perspectives on the many different things that "nation" has meant in the early-modern and modern periods, and the many different behaviors and attitudes nationalism has been called on to sanction. These essays situate questions of nationalism and its meaning in a broad historical terrain: How have nationalist practices differed in Europe and the Americas? How have various nationalisms affected the populations of the Americas? How many different nations can be said to inhabit the United States right now? How many can be said to have been inhabiting it in 1861? in 1790? How can we better understand the struggles of native peoples in the Americas, including in the United States, to maintain their own claims to national sovereignty? How can we most productively relate the histories of various old and new "nationalist" formations within the U.S.— from the various African American and pan-Indian nationalisms to the recent emergence of Queer Nation—to the history of successive American federal nationalisms?

The writers formulate related questions as problems for a general theory of the politics of subject formation as well as for the case histories of specific texts, moments, and locales. Working alongside influential scholars of nationalisms in other academic fields, such as Benedict Anderson and Homi K. Bhabha, a number of Americanists have enriched our appreciation of the roles of nation and nationality as one of the key determinants of identity and affiliation. For example, Lauren Berlant's essay, "The Queen of America Goes to Washington City," instructs us that nationalism is also a question of degree: despite the differences among the testimonies of Harriet Jacobs, Frances Harper, and Anita Hill, she writes, "each author went public in the *most national* medium available to her" (our emphasis). So, too, in dealing with figures who have remained better known and more widely read, if seldom read alongside each other (William Wells Brown, Abraham Lincoln, and Herman Melville), Russ Castronovo is able to provide his reader with an illuminating reconstitution of the complex dynamics of antiracist struggle as it permeated national self-definition and redefinition in the late antebellum period. This struggle was effectively shaking what had long been held to be the unshakeable foundations of the nation at a fateful historical moment.

As the essays of Berlant and Castronovo suggest, myths of origins and myths of national identity are inextricably bound up with the third concern of this volume: race and gender. Considered together as components of the national psyche, race and gender unsettle each other in historically precise ways. As Maggie Sale notes in her essay, "Critiques from Within:

Antebellum Projects of Resistance," literary critics have tended to pose questions of race and gender simultaneously only when considering writings by women of color. This practice tacitly assumes—to borrow from the title of the 1982 landmark collection of black women's studies by Gloria T. Hull, Patricia Bell Scott, and Barbara Smith—that all the women are white and all the blacks are men. White, masculine, middle-class heterosexuality is the norm; everything else is Other. Groups designated as Other are always susceptible to discrimination and exclusion from full citizenship within the nation or deprived of their constitutional rights, as is the case now for gay men and lesbians in the U.S.

"Race" and "gender," viewed together, destabilize one another as fixed categories. Each term both constructs and deconstructs the other. No longer monolithic and self-explanatory, "race" and "gender" can be examined as complex, contradictory, changing, malleable, and manipulable— the stuff of literature. The most canonical of canonical figures were all, as the essays in this volume show, variously obsessed, repulsed, and inspired by the twisted permutations of racism, sexism, xenophobia, and homophobia within their culture and within themselves. As we see in essays by Joan Dayan, Lori Askeland, Sander L. Gilman, and Barbara Ladd, for writers such as Poe, Stowe, Twain, and Faulkner (as well as for the less canonical authors analyzed in this volume), writing—making literature—was one way to contain and make sense of (for better or worse) the nation's roiling problems. Those critics who argue that discussing such issues as race and gender "politicizes" literature miss the point, for, with few exceptions, American authors have always been political. Indeed, it is hard to think of writers for whom the most pressing social and political issues of the day did not serve as the motor that drove their work.

As Nancy Bentley shows, domestic fiction of the mid-nineteenth century was almost as preoccupied with race as with gender. In "White Slaves: The Mulatto Hero in Antebellum Fiction," Bentley explores the standard concatenation of blacks-and-women by showing how in domestic fiction white women as well as black men and women are subjected and subjugated by a power that simply gets rationalized away. Their violation is typically portrayed as leading to "transcendent grace or enriched dignity and identity." Yet suffering is not a route to transcendence for all in these texts, for the physical punishment or humiliation of white men is represented as "obscene."

Several authors in this collection invite us to re-examine how the force of gendering has interacted with the violences of race and nation. For example, following such distinguished African American feminist scholars as Hazel Carby and Hortense Spillers, Elizabeth Young returns us to Frances Hopkins's *Iola Leroy* to reconsider what she calls "the color of gender" in that text, while Michele A. Birnbaum contrastingly places Kate Chopin's much-acclaimed protofeminist writing in what turns out to be the highly relevant context of racial conditions in the New Orleans writer's milieu (in effect, to examine the gender of color). The combined violence of sexism, racism, and imperialism is revisited in contemporary America with Kristin Carter-Sanborn's essay on Bharati Mukherjee. The violence is both physical and psychological, individual and international, since Mukherjee's *Jasmine* is an examination of "the contemporary complexities of 'first' and 'third' world relations." Commenting on the reviews of Mukherjee's novel, Carter-Sanborn notes that there is a "simultaneous interest in both Jasmine's alterity and her suitability for naturalization to an 'American' way of life." The values implicit in that dubious concern with immigrant "suitability" are, once again, reminders that what is "American" is both gendered and racialized.

Perhaps because race and gender, considered in tandem, raise so many important issues about what is "natural" or "essential," a number of essays in this volume also concern themselves with categories that are usually considered transparent: namely, "masculinity" and "whiteness." These categories overlap in complicated ways, with masculinist assumptions often inhering in racist ideologies of whiteness. Starting from Paula Gunn Allen's argument that genocide against Native Americans was motivated by patriarchal as well as racist values, Timothy Sweet, in "Masculinity and Self-Performance in the *Life of Black Hawk*," shows the ways in which ethnography as a genre both undermined and redefined Native American ideas/ideals of masculinity by effectively eliminating the Sauk "warrior's cultural position." Siobhan Senier (who also starts with Allen's pioneering work) reaches similar conclusions about the ways in which Zuni gender roles are effaced by the very form of "as told to" narratives which variously render (and undermine) the Zuni story of Junco and Coyote.

What we see in these essays on Native American writing is how ideas of masculinity are related to ideas of white supremacy. Maurice Wallace addresses similar concerns in "Constructing the Black Masculine: Frederick Douglass, Booker T. Washington, and the Sublimits of African American Autobiography." Wallace asks how is (and is not) a black man a "man"? By looking across the categories of race and gender, we can see the ways in which definitions of race, gender, and sexuality have been inextricably interlinked with definitions of what is or is not "American."

We have chosen to end this volume with Karla F. C. Holloway's essay, "The Body Politic," a title that evokes all the concerns of this collection. As Holloway notes, to speak out against a national consensus imperils the speaker: "The cost of voice remains high." To recognize how that remains as true today for Anita Hill or for a gay or lesbian member of the U.S. armed forces as it was for Aphra Behn's royal slaves Oroonoko and Imoinda impels us to join in an effort of intellectual and imaginative recovery of the commonalities that cross and recross the histories under examination in this volume.

Nations within nations, nations within citizens as well as citizens within nations, nationality as a segmentable and comparative quality rather than either an absolute possession or lack: such are some of the at times jarring reperceptions or reorientations these essays require us to make in our habitual modes of thinking. But we have much to gain—as subjects, as citizens, and as students of our chosen field of study—from joining in making the kinds of resitings these essays invite.

Part I

Annette Kolodny

Letting Go Our Grand Obsessions: Notes Toward a New Literary History of the American Frontiers

Situada entre fronteras, en los problemáticos intersticios culturales y lingüísticos creados en el choque e interacción de varias culturas en tensión . . .—Carmen M. Del Río, "Chicana Poets: Re-Visions from the Margin"

A history may be conceptualized as an ideologically or imaginatively governed catalog of figurative elements. The catalog is inconceivable in the absence of ideology, and a shift, or rupture, in ideological premises promotes strikingly new figurations.—Houston A. Baker Jr., "Archeology, Ideology and African American Discourse"

Those societies which cannot combine reverence to their symbols with freedom of revision must ultimately decay either from anarchy, or from the slow atrophy of a life stifled by useless shadows.—Alfred North Whitehead, *Symbolism: Its Meaning and Effect*

On the sunny morning of 4 October 1553, in a gesture meant to translate physical borders into cultural and political boundaries, an old man carrying " 'his bow and arrows, and a wooden staff with a very elaborate handle' " "drew a line on the ground as a demarcation, threatening death to any intruder who dared cross it." Impressive in his " 'black robe . . . studded with pearls, and surrounded by dogs, birds and deer,' " the old man nonetheless faced a formidable adversary: an exploratory expedition dispatched by the Spanish adventurer, Nuño Beltrán de Guzmán, notorious for pillaging the villages of the Indies and enslaving all captives. Tracing the first contacts between Europeans and the Yaqui nation, historian Evelyn Hu-DeHart has translated the anonymous first-person expedition report. "'Aiming our heaviest cannon at them,'" the Spaniards attacked the warriors who accompanied their robed leader and, in the words of the Spanish scribe, quickly concluded that "'These Indians fought as well and as energetically as any Indians I have seen since I have been in the Indies, and I have seen none fight better than they.'" Deciding that they could not afford to sustain additional heavy losses, "the Spaniards turned back," according to Hu-DeHart.[1]

While one motley band of Spanish slavers was driven off, however, the mark intended to inscribe inviolable borders finally came to denote permeable margins. By the 1620s, Jesuit missionaries had established churches and schools within Yaqui enclaves and translated rituals, the Mass for the Dead, and various prayers into the Yaqui language. As anthropologist Edward Spicer has noted, "the ideas in these prayers were therefore a part of Yaqui thought in the Yaqui language."[2] At the same time, *maehtom*, Yaqui lay priests, were developing a species of priestly literacy that preserved elements from distinctly precontact religious beliefs and involved writing in Spanish, Latin, and Yaqui. The old man's line, in short, was quickly contained within a zone of successive interpenetrations which—on all sides—were variously hostile, welcomed, policed, suppressed, acknowledged, and subversive.

To recover and reconstruct the linguistic and textual encodings of seriate interpenetrations such as these would allow us, at last, to embark on a long-overdue literary history of the American frontiers. My aim here is to initiate just such a project. Building on the work of Norman Grabo, William Spengemann, Francis Jennings, William Cronon, Carolyn Merchant, Tzvetan Todorov, and Howard Lamar and Leonard Thompson,[3] I propose extending the implications of their investigations beyond European colonial beginnings; and, in the case of the historians, I want to reinforce their debt to concentrated textual analysis—all in an effort to reconceive what we mean by "history" when we address literary history and to reconceptualize what we mean by "frontier" when we intend the Americas. My strategy is to offer an approach that allows for a more inclusive interdisciplinarity, mitigates the condescension with which we have traditionally treated the impact of region on the construction of literary texts, and at the same time frees American literary history from the persistent theories of continuity that have made it virtually impossible to treat frontier materials as other than marginalia or cultural mythology. For scholars of early American literature—the field in which I was trained—my approach necessarily complicates the notion of *earliness* but, at the same time, promises liberation from the stultifying habit

of regarding that literature merely as precursor to an authentic literature yet to follow or as transition pieces between British forebears and
American identities.

   To effect this project will require that we let go our grand obsessions with narrowly geographic or strictly chronological frameworks and
instead recognize "frontier" as a locus of first cultural contact, circumscribed by a particular physical terrain in the process of change *because of*
the forms that contact takes, all of it inscribed by the collisions and interpenetrations of language. My paradigm would thus have us interrogating
language—especially as hybridized style, trope, story, or structure—
for the complex intersections of human encounters and human encounters with the physical environment. It would enjoin us to see the ways
in which the collision of languages encodes the physical terrain as just as
much a player in the drama of contact as the human participants, with the
landscape variously enabling, thwarting, or even evoking human actions
and desires.

   The Yaqui "Testamento" provides an apt example. As Larry Evers and
Felipe Molina speculate in the introduction to their forthcoming translation, "some time perhaps long after the Yaqui elder inscribed that line on
the earth before the Spanish slave-traders, other Yaquis wrote a narrative on paper as a way of re-inscribing the same boundary."[4] Describing
the origins of what the Yaquis have come to call the Holy Dividing Line,
the "Testamento" represents what Evers and Molina call "a layered discourse in a combination of Spanish and Yaqui," with inflections from Latin
and Hebrew. At the heart of the "Testamento" is the authorizing of Yaqui
land boundaries and the threats to their security. Prophets, or originating
elders, sing "the Holy Dividing Line" into being and then predict that

> . . . "in the course of some years will come
> some wicked men from
> Gethsemane, that is New Spain, those men,
> the image of Lucifer, are
> invaders and enemies of our life and they do not respect
> others and they will keep these properties."
>
> . . . .
> They will ask you: "Whose land is this
> kingdom?"

Clearly, as Evers and Molina point out, establishing the boundaries of
Yaqui lands has become "part of a story that evokes the Bible as much
as any aboriginal Yaqui narratives." It thus participates in a long tradition

"of cross-cultural interpretation" in which the Yaquis write and rewrite "their own culture in a dialogue with . . . European history and Christian religion"—and, I would add, in dialogue with European concepts of ownership and landholding.

In asserting a mythic history for legalistic claims to "our poor inheritance, the earth that was given," the Yaqui "Testamento" renders the landscape ardently, albeit passively, possessed. In other texts that I would designate as integral to a literary history of the frontiers, by contrast, the physical terrain becomes an "active partner" in Carolyn Merchant's terms, "acquiesc[ing] to human interventions through resilience and adaptation or 'resist[ing]' human actions through mutation and evolution." In the works of Willa Cather, just as in Leslie Marmon Silko's *Ceremony*, "nature . . . is not passive, but," as Merchant describes it, "an active complex that participates in change over time and responds to human-induced change."[5] Indeed, Alexandra Bergson confronts the palpably sentient presence of the Nebraska prairies in Cather's *O Pioneers!* (1913), while what Tayo comes to understand as part of his healing in *Ceremony* is that he loves, and is loved by, the mountains that surround his New Mexico pueblo: "They were close; they had always been close. And he loved them then as he had always loved them, the feeling pulsing over him as strong as it had ever been. They loved him that way; he could still feel the love they had for him. . . . This feeling was their life, vitality locked deep in blood memory, and the people were strong, and the fifth world endured, and nothing was ever lost as long as the love remained." When the bond between the people and their land is threatened by uranium mining, by atomic testing laboratories "deep in the Jemez Mountains, on land the Government took from Cochiti Pueblo," and by the Los Alamos installations fencing off the "mountain canyon where the shrine of the twin mountain lions had always been,"[6] Silko provides story and symbol for Merchant's insistence that "the relation between human beings and the nonhuman world is . . . reciprocal."[7]

Although the figurative elements of such contacts do not concern them, historians Howard Lamar and Leonard Thompson similarly "regard a frontier not as a boundary or line, but as a territory or zone of interpenetration between . . . previously distinct societies." For them, "there are three essential elements in any frontier situation . . . . : territory; two or more initially distinct peoples; and the process by which the relations among the peoples in the territory begin, develop, and eventually crystalize."[8] My own definition incorporates theirs, asserting that there always stands at the heart of frontier literature—even when disguised or repressed—a physical terrain that, for at least one group of participants, is newly encountered and is undergoing change because of that encounter; a currently indigenous population and at least one group of newcomers or "intruders"; and the collisions and negotiations of distinct cultural groups as expressed "en el choque e interacción" of languages and texts.[9] Whether written or oral, the texts that comprise this new literary history of the frontiers would be identified by their articulation of these initial encounters. Thus, the literature of the frontiers may be identified by its encoding of some specifiable first moment in the evolving dialogue between different cultures and languages and their engagement with one another and with the physical terrain.

The materials that qualify as the primary or proto-texts of frontier literary history would be those that themselves participate in that first moment of contact—for example, the Eskimo legends of the Tunnit, the strangers who came from afar and erected stone buildings;[10] Christopher Columbus's "Letter to Lord Sanchez . . . on His First Voyage"; Amerigo Vespucci's *Mundus Novus*; Gaspar Pérez de Villagrá's *Historia de la Nueva Mexico*; William Bradford's *History of Plimmoth Plantation*; Mary White Rowlandson's captivity narrative; and Daniel Boone's putative autobiography. The secondary—but no less important—texts of frontier literary history would be those composed after the fact, reworking for some alternate audience or future generation the scene and meaning of original contact, or "recovering" the primary texts so as to give them new readings in a newly imagined and reconstructed past. Examples in English include Joel Barlow's *Columbiad* (1807) and even J. N. Barker's high-pitched melodrama "The Indian Princess; or, La Belle Sauvage" (1808), the first play by a United States author to focus on Indian characters. Reworking incidents from John Smith's *General History of Virginia* (1624), a primary text in my schema, "The Indian Princess" is also the first play to utilize the story of Pocahantas. Among novels that represent examples of significant secondary texts in English, I would certainly include James Fenimore Cooper's Leatherstocking series, Willa Cather's *Death Comes for the Archbishop*, and Leslie Silko's *Ceremony*— with its subtext evoking a twentieth-century nuclear culture intruding itself into the sacred sites of the Indian Southwest.

What makes the paradigm so appealing, however, is that English texts, by themselves, could never constitute a sufficient history. Indeed, the new frontier literary history that I envisage might well begin with a comparative analysis of the Eskimo legends of the Tunnit and the Icelandic and Greenland versions of Norse sagas detailing the discovery and attempted colonization of Vineland, on the North American coast, by Scandinavian explorers from Greenland and Iceland about the year 1000. Recording clashes between Vikings and "Skraellings" (indigenous peoples who may well have been an Eskimo people migrating south), the sagas describe "a fair, well-wooded country" and the appeal "of all the valuable products of the land, grapes, and all kinds of game and fish." The dramatic elements center on the frustrated attempts of the Skraellings to barter with the Europeans and the Europeans' frustration at the fact that "neither (people) could understand the other's language."[11]

Without question, a revised literary history of the frontiers would also include the foundational corpus of the Hispanoamerican written tradition, the *crónicas de Indias*, with texts by *criollo* and mestizo authors alike.[12] Examples include not only the letters and diaries of the more notorious explorers and conquistadores from Columbus on but, as well, the journal of Cabeza de Vaca's wanderings from Florida to Texas (1555), Bartolemé de las Casas's *Historia de las Indias* (1527–61), and Gaspar Pérez de Villagrá's *History of New Mexico* (1610), arguably the first epic poem composed in what is now the United States.[13] A key text for examining the way in which frontiers inevitably give rise to hybridized forms would be the massive two-volume *Royal Commentaries of the Incas and General History of Peru* (published in Spain in separate segments in 1609 and 1616–17). Claiming noble Spanish blood from his father and descent from the royal Inca line on his maternal side, Garcilaso de la Vega, El Inca, intentionally took on the name of the great medieval Spanish warrior-poet Garcilaso de la Vega (ca. 1502–36) in order to compose a text that at once justifies and mourns the demise of the Inca empire. By employing narrative structures from Incan *haravi* (oral verse histories), chivalric romance, and European discovery narratives, the Inca Garcilaso pits the narrative impulse of the Quechua *haravi* chants to celebrate the victories and glories of the ancestors against a distinctly Spanish Golden Age impulse to retell epic victories and reveal epic betrayals:

> When the Spaniards saw how generously Titu Atauchi and his companions had treated them while in confinement, and how attentively they had been cared for and given their freedom, gifts of gold, silver, and precious stones, and provided with a large escort of natives to accompany them back to Spanish quarters, though the Indians might easily have cut them to pieces out of rage and indignation at the death of their

king, and finally how the Indians asked for negotiations on such fair and reasonable terms, they were confounded and amazed.[14]

Moreover, like the (presumably) later and much shorter Yaqui "Testamento," Inca Garcilaso de la Vega's *Royal Commentaries* demonstrates the dynamic and reciprocal relationship between a prior oral tradition and the intrusion of a written literature. The oral (or folkloric) elements have not been simply appropriated or incorporated into the European structures. Rather, their inclusion has fundamentally altered the narrative patterns that previously governed the written genres.

Similarly, the moral dialogues composed by Mendicant friars in the Nahuatl language would become frontier texts. In the years following the Spanish conquest, from Mexico through the present day Southwest, missionaries rendered catechistic texts into language and terminology by which (they hoped) Old World Catholicism might convert New World Aztec thought. Resembling no catechism then available in Latin or Spanish, but decidedly influenced by the traditions of Aztec "flower songs," these texts offer a rich body of proto-literary material that amply plays out—for both Spanish and Nahuatl—the consequences of the encounter of the two languages and the confrontation of two widely variant systems for constructing a cosmology of spiritual meaning and responding, on its basis, to the physical environment.

But the interplay between European and indigenous traditions is also inadequate to any comprehensive understanding of the literary history of the American frontiers. There were, after all, as Leonard Thompson and Howard Lamar remind us, "frontier processes in precolonial America . . . as when Pueblo-dwelling agriculturalists and Apachean hunter-collectors confronted one another in present-day New Mexico and Arizona."[15] With perhaps 550 different languages and dialects in use north of the Rio Grande, rooted in at least nine distinct linguistic stocks, the peoples of precolonial North America repeatedly engaged in exchanges of vocabulary, stories, and oral lore as they traded with or invaded one another, or simply migrated into another group's territory. This hybridizing process was only accelerated when, under pressure from land-hungry Euro-Americans, native peoples withdrew—or, more often, were forcibly removed—from traditional territories to new areas or reservations. In some instances, as with the Delawares, previously separate peoples came together for the first time, postcontact, forging wholly new cultural patterns.

Additionally, the encounter of African languages with English-, Dutch-,

French-, and Spanish-speaking slaveholders must certainly figure into any meaningful understanding of the songs, narrative play, and captivity (or slave) narratives which recall African Americans' original forced removal to a frontier defined by chattel slavery. The hybridized vernacular traditions that Houston Baker Jr. and Henry Louis Gates Jr. have identified as intrinsic to African American literary expression enjoy linguistically complex frontier antecedents. Baker's proposition that any "shift, or rupture, in ideological premises" necessarily "promotes strikingly new figurations" in the historical catalog underscores my point here.[16] When "frontier" is reconceptualized in terms of initial encounters between distinct peoples and the accompanying environmental transitions, then neither the black cowboys nor the Black Seminoles of the nineteenth century are any longer anomalous.[17] And the engagement of fiction writers—from Charles Chesnutt onward—with recapturing the voices and cadences of antebellum landscapes emerges clearly as successive projects to reconstitute for later generations an oral tradition's remembered meaning of first contact.

Equally important, because neither chronology nor geography define the historical frame, an entire corpus of what we now loosely term "immigrant literature" might be given fresh analysis because it could, on the one hand, be uncoupled from the imputed continuities of a New England "errand," and, on the other, be anchored to a landscape in the process of change, regardless of what kind of landscape is involved. Thus, some of the "American" materials in Yiddish by Sholem Aleichem (the pen name of Solomon Rabinowitz), Mary Antin's original Yiddish *From Plotzk to Boston* (which she edited and translated into English for publication in 1899), and the work of Anzia Yezierska would enter a literary history that recognized the concept of urban frontiers. Yezierska's *Bread Givers* (1925) could profitably be read as an anticipation of Edward Rivera's 1982 fictionalized autobiography of growing up Puerto Rican in Harlem, *Family Installments: Memories of Growing Up Hispanic,* while Aleichem's World War I–era evocation of fledgling Jewish communities newly removed from rural *shtetls* in eastern Europe to teeming tenements on Manhattan's Lower East Side might resonate with new meanings when compared to Carlos Bulosan's World War II–era revulsion at fleeing the Philippines only to find in America

> . . . the city where
> The streets scream for life, where men are hunting
> Each other with burning eyes, mountains are made of sand,

Glass, paper from factories where death is calling
For peace; hills are made of clothes, and trees
Are nothing but candies.[18]

In a related move, to get at yet another set of complex frontier responses, scholarship would seek to recover letters, diaries, poems and
fictions composed by Chinese and other Asians brought to labor in the
silver mines or on the railroads in the nineteenth century. Here we
could study the Asians grappling both with their own preconceptions of
America as well as with the language and conceptual patterns of the Euro-
Americans who employ them, even as they help to transform the dominant culture's already mythologized agrarian landscape into an industrial
frontier.

There are, of course, other examples, but for the most part, I think
I've made my point: to establish a truly comprehensive frontier literary history, both geography and chronology must be viewed as fluid and
ongoing, or as a continuously unfolding palimpsest that requires us to include Old Norse, Papago, Nahuatl, Quechua, Spanish, Yaqui, Tewa, Gul-
lah, French, Dutch, Chinese, Japanese, German, Yiddish, and so on—as
well as English—within our textual canon. Hybridized forms and tropes
constitute the focus of textual analysis, and the resultant attentiveness to
"code switching" radically alters our understanding of style and aesthetics. As Gloria Anzaldúa announces in *Borderlands/La Frontera* (itself a
study in intercultural hybridized forms), "the switching of 'codes' in this
book from English to Castillian Spanish to the North Mexican dialect to
Tex-Mex to a sprinkling of Nahuatl to a mixture of all of these, reflects
my language, a new language—the language of the Borderlands. There,
at the juncture of cultures, languages cross-pollinate and are revitalized;
they die and are born."[19]

In effect, in my reformulation the term "frontier" comes to mean what
we in the Southwest call *la frontera*, or the borderlands, that liminal
landscape of changing meanings on which distinct human cultures first
encounter one another's "otherness" and appropriate, accommodate, or
domesticate it through language. By concentrating on frontier as an inherently unstable locus of (generally unacknowledged—at least at the
outset) environmental transitions and cultural interpenetrations, however, I have purposefully dropped two features which previously were
assumed: population scarcity and either primitive technology or a site
where a more developed or superior technology overwhelms an inferior
one. Both are wilfully ahistorical.

The population densities of precontact peoples in the New World are now being radically reassessed as the full implications of European diseases are better understood. Recent evidence suggests that the imported diseases not only decimated native populations but, more crucially, may have left a portion of the survivors sterile or infertile. As a result, many European colonizers encountered dramatically diminished numbers of indigenous inhabitants, the diseases often traveling the native trade routes well ahead of actual direct contact. The immediate consequences were exaggerated reports back to Europe of an empty "wilderness" there for the taking and the tenacious grip of a mythology of sparsely settled frontiers. In fact, the Black Death that swept Europe in the fourteenth century, killing as much as three quarters of the population in some areas, probably left Europe with a population density roughly equivalent to that of North America at the same period. In any event, the precontact population north of the Rio Grande alone has recently been revised upwards from estimates of four million to twelve million or more.

That population had developed extensive and sophisticated trade routes with major trade centers established from South America to the present-day Middle West—the intricate road system branching out from Chaco Canyon (in north-central New Mexico) being only one example. The frontier contacts of these peoples included constant exchanges of technology, from building techniques to basket weaving and pottery. Moreover, in the first recorded contact with European peoples, the Skraellings effectively repulsed the Norse colonizing effort, forcing the Scandinavians to abandon the Vineland settlement after only three years. As Wilcomb Washburn observes, at this point "the technological levels of the two peoples were not far apart." "Even Columbus and his followers did not arrive with overwhelming technological superiority," Washburn continues. "The native inhabitants of the New World had the same bow-and-arrow technology from which Europeans had only recently graduated to crude firearms. Both sides had shields and protective clothing, but Europeans had iron, which gave their sharp weapons and durable household utensils . . . a decisive advantage."[20] Even so, the Spanish chronicles of conquest are filled with awe at the accomplishments of Incan stonework (which even today cannot be replicated); and the letters and diaries of seventeenth- and eighteenth-century English colonists contain repeated references to the Indians' ability to produce rich harvests with only a digging stick as compared to the meager crops that resulted from metal tools. Soon enough, of course, Europeans learned to adapt Indian fertilizing techniques, while the Indians appropriated iron cooking pots, firearms, and metal instruments useful for hunting, gathering, and planting. Therefore, rather than defining a frontier as a site of primitive or disparate technologies, it might prove more useful to think in terms of competing *appropriate* technologies and rapid technological exchange and innovation. This allows us to encompass all frontiers—"wilderness," agricultural, urban, and industrial alike. And it prevents us from ignoring, as part of our frontier equation, the impact of technological exchange on the physical environment.

■ ■ ■

For critics and scholars, for historians of literature, and even for those who create literature out of them, borderlands are never "a comfortable territory to live in." Too often, "the prominent features of this landscape," as Gloria Anzaldúa attests, are "hatred, anger and exploitation."[21] Nonetheless, there are compelling reasons to adopt the reformulation I have outlined here. First, by understanding the frontier as a specifiable first moment on that liminal borderland between distinct cultures, we forever decenter what was previously a narrowly Eurocentric design. As such, we constrain the continuing assertion of vast unsettled or uninhabited areas, no matter how powerfully that notion permeates the texts we would analyze; we afford ourselves the scholarly occasion to examine a variety of contacts between native peoples; and we inhibit the tendency to develop frontier models that exclude certain groups from their rightful place in an ongoing pioneering process on a variety of landscapes.[22] Second, we engage energizing interdisciplinary challenges that demand comparative cultural and literary analyses in which anthropology, geography, ecology, and literary history can work together in new ways. At the very least, in Paul Lauter's view, literary scholars will come "to appreciate a broader range of conventions, to set form more fully into historical and functional context[s], and to comprehend how audience expectation and assumption mandate formal priorities."[23] And third, by acknowledging the many different configurations of indigenous peoples, immigrants, and emigrants who came in contact over time on a variety of landscapes, we allow the literatures of the frontiers to stand—accurately, at last—as multilingual, polyvocal, and newly intertextual and multicultural. In consequence, we find ourselves better able to understand the meanings and trace the genesis of hybridized forms and usages—whether they occur as a borrowing of vocabulary from indigenous peoples, as in John Smith;

as an adaptation by mestizo generations of European discovery tracts, as in Garcilaso de la Vega, El Inca; or as an incorporation by native peoples of European religious narratives, as in the Yaqui "Testamento."

What most appeals to me in this reformulation, however, is that it necessarily destabilizes easy assumptions about centers and margins in the construction of literary history. As I stated at the outset, the persistence of theories of continuity in the study of American literary history has repeatedly distorted its capacity to treat frontier texts as anything other than marginalia or cultural mythology, because the frontier is displaced always to the geographical edges, regarded as transitory, and its texts scoured for signs of hegemonic purposes or anxieties.[24] Obsessed with its own myth of origins, the scholarship that comprises most literary histories is always seeking some defining beginning (usually Puritan New England, sometimes Virginia Plantation, in rare instances the European voyages of discovery) in whose texts may be discerned something peculiarly or characteristically "American"—American by current measure, of course.[25] Understandably, "the stakes are high in this struggle for the defining origins of the American temperament." As Donald Weber explains, "whoever can follow the reverberations of the American voice from the seventeenth century to the nineteenth and beyond can claim an authorizing vision of the culture, and thus impose a compelling paradigm."[26]

But the limitations of this kind of literary history are obvious: the works produced are patently ahistorical, tacitly reading some version of the present back into the past. They are univocal and monolingual, defining origins by what later became the tropes of the dominant or conquering language. And, by imputing "profound continuities between early American literary expression and the classic literature of the United States in the mid-nineteenth century," they necessarily obscure any text that cannot be accommodated to whatever are currently accepted as the features of the mature national literary consciousness. It is notions like these, moreover, adds Philip Gura, that give rise to "the concomitant belief in American 'exceptionalism,' both literary and cultural."[27] Furthermore, in terms of their adequacy to accommodate a literary history of discontinuous frontiers, these studies tend to characterize all productions outside major urban cultural centers as *merely regional* and to underestimate the influence of place and physical environment on any writer's construction of reality.

Although we have only recently marked the one-hundredth anniversary of the supposed closing of the frontier, I am recommending that we reopen it, thematizing frontier as a multiplicity of ongoing first encounters over time and land, rather than as a linear chronology of successive discoveries and discrete settlements. Noting the passionately contested meanings of this year's five-hundredth anniversary of Columbus's first landing, I am asking that we once and for all eschew the myth of origins— with its habits of either fetishizing or marginalizing race, place, and ethnicity—and, by returning to serious study of the frontiers, adopt a model of literary history that privileges no group's priority and no region's primacy. In the frontier literary history I have projected here, there can be no Ur-landscape because there are so many borderlands, and, over time, even the same site may serve for seriatim first encounters. There can be no paradigmatic first contact because there are so many different kinds of first encounters. And there can be no single overarching story.

To be sure, no literary history of the frontiers will fail to note resonances, affinities, semantic and symbolic resemblances across texts. But at the same time, by its very definition, no literary history of the frontiers will naively conflate the Spanish search for cities of gold, the Chinese belief in the Golden Mountain, and the sale of human beings in the trade to supply Europeans with the New World's golden rum into a flattened narrative of unproblematic discovery, settlement, and progress. Similarly, the crush of languages and cultures on a single day at Ellis Island in 1905 represents a frontier with features—and consequences—radically different from the landing at Plymouth Rock. The texts that attempt to delineate these frontier moments—like the literary histories generated to accommodate them—will tell many different stories. Indeed, the study of frontier literary history—like American literary history in general— should properly be marked by endlessly proliferating, multiple, competing narrative designs. The singular identities and unswerving continuities that Americanists have regularly claimed for our literary history are no longer credible.

Nevertheless, the scope of the project outlined here will make many literary historians nervous because it appears to beg the question of "literariness." In asking that we study Norse sagas and the Yaqui "Testamento" as assiduously as we study texts by James Fenimore Cooper and Willa Cather, I threaten to sustain the premise, always suspected by William Spengemann, that American literature *is* "an altogether imaginary subject." But only by opening up the question of literariness can we ever take on Spengemann's "task of reconstructing the foundations on

which our collective enterprise rests."[28] In elaborating a literary history
of the frontiers, the challenge is not to decide *beforehand* what constitutes literariness but rather to expose ourselves to different kinds of
texts and contexts so as to recover the ways they variously inscribe the
stories of first contact. Inevitably, the interdisciplinary and multilingual
skills required for such an undertaking will tend, in Cary Nelson's words,
to "destabilize distinctions between quality and historical relevance by
making them self-conscious."[29]

The same Norse sagas whose stylistic conventions were lauded in my
literature courses at the University of Oslo in 1961, for example, had
been available to me previously (in bad translations and excerpted, to be
sure) only in my high school and college world history courses to signify
the exploits of the Vikings. Similarly, Larry Evers and Felipe Molina's
examination of "conventional Yaqui rhetorical pattern[s]" and the evidence of an ever-evolving written text "in a dynamic relation with Yaqui
oral tradition" invite literary treatments of the Yaqui "Testamento" in the
ways we generally define such procedures. By contrast, for the Yaquis
themselves, as one of Evers and Molina's consultants explains to them,
"a 'testamento' is sacred word that is continually affirmed by the community as it goes about the day-to-day business of its governance, a sacred
word that provides authority in what non-Yaquis might factor out as legal,
moral, and theological realms." Of course, none of these textual usages
is incompatible with any other. They are merely functionally variable and
context-dependent. The point here is that what we commonly think of
as "literariness" may be too narrow to encompass—or may even wholly
distort—the functionally variable roles of texts in different societies. By
forcing us to become self-conscious about how we distinguish the literary from the "merely" historical or ethnographically relevant, the project
of frontier literary history (to quote Cary Nelson again) can eventually
"establish varied cultural roles for literariness—as opposed to a single,
dominant notion of literariness overseen by the academy." And this, in
turn, could produce "different, even contradictory, subject positions from
which literariness can be valued."[30]

Finally, while I would not argue that a literary history of the frontiers
could adequately account for the many different kinds of literature and
literary forms produced in the United States (or in its precolonial past),
I would suggest that such a project will radically alter both what we recognize as "literature" and how we define its historical processes. The

literature of the frontiers may not be the only kind of literature produced in the Americas, but it is surely inherent in all the rest.

Too little of what I have outlined here can come to fruition, however, as long as American literary specialists remain trapped within Departments of *English*. For if we are ever to have what Andrew Wiget calls "a new literary history that is both just and useful,"[31] then American literary specialists must move beyond the training that prepares us to analyze only texts written in English or to recognize only European (or "Western") antecedents. And we must become the intellectual colleagues of those, from a variety of disciplines, who can teach us to read across cultural boundaries. In order to properly study a literature that for so long has been formed and reformed "en el choque e interacción de varias culturas en tensión," American literary scholars must begin to create their own new frontiers, openly declaring their agenda as radically comparativist, demandingly interdisciplinary, and exuberantly multilingual. We must, in short, propose an endlessly proliferating diversity over which no school or theory, no ethnic, racial, or cultural enclave, and no political or scholarly party could ever again take control.

Notes

1   Evelyn Hu-DeHart, *Missionaries, Miners, and Indians: Spanish Contact with the Yaqui Nation of Northwestern New Spain, 1533–1820* (Tucson: Univ. of Arizona Press, 1981), 15–16.

2   Edward H. Spicer, *The Yaquis: A Cultural History* (Tucson: Univ. of Arizona Press, 1980), 326. See also Spicer's *People of Pascua*, ed. Kathleen M. Sands and Rosamond B. Spicer (Tucson: Univ. of Arizona Press, 1989).

3   In conference papers too numerous to list here, in personal correspondence and conversations, Norman S. Grabo has generously shared his study of the first European writings produced within what is now the continental United States, examining works in Spanish, French, and Dutch, as well as English; the only segment so far to have appeared in print is Norman S. Grabo, "Villagrá: Between a Rock and Other Hard Places," *Ideas '92: A Journal to Honor 500 Years of Relations among Spain, Latin America, and the United States* 6 (Spring 1990): 85–92. See also William C. Spengemann, *A Mirror for Americanists: Reflections on the Idea of American Literature* (Hanover, N.H.: Univ. Press of New England, 1989); Francis Jennings, *The Invasion of America: Indians, Colonialism, and the Cant of Conquest* (Chapel Hill: Univ. of North Carolina Press, 1975); William Cronon Jr., *Changes in the*

Land: Indians, Colonists, and the Ecology of New England (New York: Hill and Wang, 1983); Carolyn Merchant, *Ecological Revolutions: Nature, Gender, and Science in New England* (Chapel Hill: Univ. of North Carolina Press, 1989); Tzvetan Todorov, *The Conquest of America: The Question of the Other*, trans. Richard Howard (New York: Harper and Row, 1984); and Howard Lamar and Leonard Thompson, eds., *The Frontier in History: North America and Southern Africa Compared* (New Haven: Yale Univ. Press, 1981).

4   Throughout this essay, all discussion of the Yaqui "Testamento" is indebted to Larry Evers and Felipe S. Molina, "The Holy Dividing Line: Inscription and Resistance in Yaqui Culture" and to "Don Alfonso Florez Leyva's 'Testamento': Holograph, Transcription, and Translation," prepared by Larry Evers and Felipe S. Molina, *Journal of the Southwest* 34, 1 (Spring 1992): 3–46 and 72–106, which, together, offer a comprehensive introduction to the text, a transcription of the handwritten Yaqui document provided to them, and a full English translation. I am enormously grateful to Evers and Molina for giving me a typescript in advance of publication, and I thank Larry Evers for his generosity in discussing this material with me.

5   Merchant, *Ecological Revolutions*, 23, 8.

6   Leslie Marmon Silko, *Ceremony* (New York: Signet/New American Library, 1978), 230, 257.

7   Merchant, *Ecological Revolutions*, 8.

8   Leonard Thompson and Howard Lamar, "Comparative Frontier History," in *The Frontier in History*, 7, 8.

9   Carmen M. Del Río, "Chicana Poets: Re-Visions from the Margin," *Revista Canadiense de Estudios Hispánicos* 14 (Spring 1990): 431.

10   See G. M. Gathorne-Hardy, *The Norse Discoverers of America: The Wineland Sagas* (1921; rpt., London: Oxford Univ. Press, 1970), which makes the provocative suggestion that Eskimo legends of the people they call the "Tunnit" refer to contacts with Vikings from Greenland, viii–ix.

11   Quoted in Edward F. Gray, *Leif Eriksson: Discoverer of America, A.D. 1003* (New York: Oxford Univ. Press, 1930; rpt., New York: Kraus Reprint, 1972), 46, 59; Gray offers serviceable translations from both Greenland and Icelandic versions of all extant texts dealing with the Vikings in Vineland. His comparison of the different versions is useful, and his argument that Vineland was actually in the vicinity of Cape Cod is tantalizing.

12   The best recent overview of this material is José Promis, *The Identity of Hispanoamerica: An Interpretation of Colonial Literature*, trans. Alita Kelley and Alec E. Kelley (Tucson: Univ. of Arizona Press, 1991), to which I am much indebted for my discussion here.

13   Like much of the material listed here, Gaspar Pérez de Villagrá's *History of New Mexico* is available only in a limited edition inadequate prose translation by Gilberto Espinosa (Los Angeles: Quivira Society, 1933). An *en face* edition with verse translation and an updated scholarly and critical introduction is long overdue.

14   Garcilaso de la Vega, El Inca, *Royal Commentaries of the Incas and General*

History of Peru, trans. Harold V. Livermore (Austin: Univ. of Texas Press, 1966; 2nd printing, 1970), Part Two, 745.

15 Thompson and Lamar, "Comparative Frontier History," 11.

16 Houston A. Baker Jr., "Archeology, Ideology, and African American Discourse," in *Redefining American Literary History*, ed. A. LaVonne Brown Ruoff and Jerry W. Ward Jr. (New York: Modern Language Assoc., 1990), 165.

17 See Kenneth W. Porter, *The Negro on the American Frontier* (New York: Arno Press, 1971); Daniel F. Littlefield Jr., *Africans and Seminoles: From Removal to Emancipation* (Westport, Conn.: Greenwood, 1977); and Edwin C. McReynolds, *The Seminoles* (Norman: Univ. of Oklahoma Press, 1957).

18 Carlos Bulosan, *Letter from America* (Prairie City, Ill.: Decker, 1942), 20. For an analysis of the poem and its provenance, see Oscar V. Campomanes and Todd S. Gernes, "Two Letters from America: Carlos Bulosan and the Act of Writing," *MELUS* 15 (Fall 1988): 15–46.

19 Gloria Anzaldúa, *Borderlands/La Frontera: The New Mestiza* (San Francisco: Spinsters/Aunt Lute, 1987), Preface, n.p.

20 Wilcomb E. Washburn, "Epilogue," in *The Smithsonian Book of North American Indians: Before the Coming of the Europeans*, ed. Philip Kopper (Washington: Smithsonian Books, 1986), 269.

21 Anzaldúa, Preface, n.p.

22 An example of this kind of exclusionary model appears in Robert E. Spiller, "The Cycle and the Roots: National Identity in American Literature," in *Toward a New American Literary History*, ed. Louis J. Budd, Edwin H. Cady, and Carl L. Anderson (Durham: Duke Univ. Press, 1980), 3–18. Although Spiller acknowledges their "great importance to the American literary identity today," he nonetheless excludes "three kinds of ethnic groups" from "the main frontier movement. These are the immigrant groups which came to this country comparatively late; the blacks who were brought to this country under special circumstances; and the Jews who in all their history have mingled with, but rarely become totally absorbed into, any alien culture." As Spiller explains, "only immigrations from European countries other than Great Britain followed a course close enough to our model to suggest inclusion here" (15). Spiller eliminates any discussion of Asian immigrants by ignoring the mining, urban, and industrial frontiers; he appears ignorant of the numbers of blacks who escaped their "special circumstances" to relative safety on the frontiers (see note 17 above); and he appears equally ignorant of the Ladino-speaking Spanish Jews (or Sephardim) who escaped the long arm of the Inquisition by fleeing to the New World as *conversos* and establishing communities in what is now the United States Southwest. For a useful introduction, see Frances Hernández, "The Secret Legacy of Christopher Columbus in the Southwest," in *Password* 35 (Summer 1990): 55–70.

23 Paul Lauter, "The Literatures of America: A Comparative Discipline," in *Redefining American Literary History*, 29.

24 Warren I. Susman illustrates this process succinctly in his examination of

post-Turnerian intellectual debates over the meaning and import of the frontier in "The Frontier Thesis and the American Intellectual," in his *Culture as History: The Transformation of American Society in the Twentieth Century* (1973; rpt., New York: Pantheon, 1984), 27–38.

25 Until quite recently, a similar tendency ruled the study of Latin American literary history. As Rolena Adorno points out in "New Perspectives in Colonial Spanish American Literary Studies" (*Journal of the Southwest* 32 [Summer 1990]: 173–91), "Following Alfonso Reyes and Pedro Henríquez Ureña, the goal has been to attach a 'literary vocation' to the historiographical writings about the conquest of America, seeking 'to place the literary origins of Latin American literary discourse in the chronicles of the conquest of America'" (175).

26 Donald Weber, "Historicizing the Errand," *American Literary History* 2 (Spring 1990): 102.

27 Philip F. Gura, "The Study of Colonial American Literature, 1966–1987: A Vade Mecum," *William and Mary Quarterly*, 3d Ser., 45 (April 1988): 309.

28 Spengemann, *A Mirror for Americanists*, 2, 3.

29 Cary Nelson, *Repression and Recovery: Modern American Poetry and the Politics of Cultural Memory, 1910–1945* (Madison: Univ. of Wisconsin Press, 1989), 41.

30 Nelson, *Repression and Recovery*, 41.

31 Andrew Wiget, "Reading Against the Grain: Origin Stories and American Literary History," *American Literary History* 3 (Summer 1991): 228.

**Stephanie
Athey and
Daniel
Cooper
Alarcón**

Oroonoko's Gendered Economies of
Honor/Horror: Reframing Colonial
Discourse Studies in the Americas

> Like the colonized country itself, the women, both African
> and European, become representative objects of desire, and
> their conditions are to some extent parallel. Nonetheless, it
> is the singular and significant exception of their continued ac-
> cess to language in these works which clearly distinguishes
> the European from the African woman, no matter what the
> similarities.—Abena P. A. Busia

> Any critique of strategic exclusions should bring analytical
> presuppositions to crisis.—Gayatri Spivak

Since Octave Mannoni's 1948 delineation of the
"Prospero Complex" and poet George Lamming's 1960 equation of Caliban and Caribbean identity, *The Tempest*—and the Caliban-Prospero relationship in particular—has assumed an increasingly important position
in anticolonialist writings.[1] In fact, studies of colonial discourse over the
last decade have established *The Tempest* as an important analytical paradigm. Yet by the end of the decade both Abena P. A. Busia and Ania
Loomba had countered the masculinist implications of the paradigm by
focusing attention on *The Tempest*'s female figures, Miranda and Sycorax,
and by critiquing the play's representation of black male and female sexuality.[2] In bringing the complicity of race and gender to bear on a familiar
text, Busia and Loomba, among many others, have (in Spivak's terms)
brought "analytical presuppositions to crisis." These critics suggest that
the "deliberate *unvoicing*" of the African female in colonial literature has
been seconded by the strategic exclusion of gender analysis from colonial
discourse studies. Their work insists that in order to study the operation

of gender and sexuality under colonization we must first *see* the white and black women who mediate the exchange between male antagonists. Busia and Loomba demonstrate the importance of deciphering the symbolic function women play in colonist texts, although both critics operate from the assumption that these same female characters lack practical power in a patriarchal and colonial landscape.

Aphra Behn's *Oroonoko; or, The Royal Slave* (1688) throws even this emerging feminist paradigm into crisis. Set in the seventeenth-century British colony of Surinam, *Oroonoko* examines the intersection of three cultures (South American, African, and English) involved in the building of empire and the practice of slavery. Behn's novel not only intervenes in the colonizing discourse of her day but also raises a pointed challenge to contemporary feminist and colonial discourse studies in the Americas. The text questions the presupposition that women mediate between male antagonists, and it raises troubling questions about the lack of power attributed to white and black females in the colonial setting. With few exceptions, the academic study of colonial discourse has given virtually no attention either to the ways in which different sexual, economic, and literary discourses work together to construct women as "white" or "black," or to how women operate relative to each other in the colonial economy.

Interpreters of the Oroonoko story have been most likely to hesitate when confronted with two specific plot elements that bear directly on constructions of power and sexuality in Behn's text: the different concepts of honor circulating throughout the narrative and the character of Imoinda—a black African female who embodies the ideal of white European womanhood. For example, at a crucial moment in Thomas Southerne's 1695 stage adaptation of *Oroonoko*, the black slave hero for whom the play is named is surprised by the entrance of his good friend Aboan, who has just been mortally wounded. Seeing that Aboan is dying, Oroonoko responds:

> My eyes are turned against me and combine
> With my sworn enemies to represent
> This spectacle of honor. Aboan!
> My ever faithful friend![3]

The editors of the authoritative edition of Southerne's play, Maximillian E. Novak and David Stuart Rodes, offer a footnote to this speech which tells the reader: "Many later editions and versions of the play accept the [1736 sexto] reading of 'horror' for 'honor,' among them are the following:

Dublin, 1731; Hawkesworth revision, 1759; anonymous revision, 1760; Gentleman revision, 1760. . . . Inchbald omits the entire sentence."[4] While we might be amused at Inchbald's solution to the frustrating problem (erase it altogether), there is something very revealing in her action. This textual dilemma underscores a central truth about the genre of heroic tragedy: there is no easy distinction between honor and horror. Behn's original text presents the same problem in a different form. Despite the careful mirroring created by the novel's structure, most critics are likely to divide the story into two mismatched parts: the first half driven by the generic dictates of romance and its code of honor; the second, by a graphic realism and the colonial horror of slavery.

As for Imoinda, in rendering the Oroonoko story as heroic tragedy, Southerne converts the black African female into a white European. We view this gesture and other elements of Southerne's adaptation in the same light as Inchbald's editorial decision—an attempt to smooth the fractures in the original text by erasing the site of textual contradictions, Imoinda herself. This erasure persists in contemporary feminist readings of Behn's novel that specifically address race and gender. Imoinda's character is either omitted from discussion, made into an allegory for the plight of white womanhood, or saved for the last and thereby positioned as a final enigma.[5]

Whether delineating codes of honor/horror or the construction of black/white female sexuality, the desire to make an opposition out of a paradox is emblematic of the long-standing debate over whether Behn's novel is an antislavery tract or a slavery apology.[6] Though *Oroonoko* clearly endorses English colonization, it nonetheless fractures at key points in the narrative, revealing not only the horror of the slave system but also the links between codes of male and female honor and the institution of slavery itself.[7]

This essay, then, brings *Oroonoko* into the context of American literature and colonial discourse study in order to examine the relationship between colonial codes of honor/horror and the black female body. We review the critical paradigms that *Oroonoko* unsettles and read the text in such a way as to promote consideration of at least three neglected areas of analysis in colonial discourse studies: the (at least) three-way mediation of racial exploitation in the Americas as European peoples negotiate domination via both African and American populations; the ways in which white, black, and indigenous females are deployed and deploy themselves in relation to each other as well as in support of slavery and other colonial institutions; and the threat and practice of rape as a form of political, discursive control over entire populations—not simply individuals.

■ ■ ■

In one of two strains within the history of anticolonial *Tempest* appropriations, the play is recreated through the literature of resistance and political activism. Anticolonial intellectuals such as Frantz Fanon, George Lamming, Roberto Fernández Retamar, and Houston Baker Jr. focus on Caliban, lifting him out of the play and retaining only those aspects of the Shakespearean context which are analogous to their own historically specific situations. Caliban's cursed relationship to the oppressor's language, his perceived deformity, and his revolt against domination receive particular emphasis. Caliban becomes an archetype for resistance, a name uniting a group around a common status and history. For instance, Fernández Retamar extends Caliban's identity to all "mestizo America." Houston Baker compares him to "a maroon in the Jamaican hills or Nat Turner preparing his phaneric exit from the Great Dismal Swamp or the American South"; Caliban eventually represents Baker's own sphere, that of African American male academics.[8] The symbolic and political use of the Caliban archetype in this arena is clear, as is the importance of Caliban's masculinity. In his survey "Caribbean and African Appropriations of *The Tempest*," Rob Nixon notes that the waning force of the *Tempest* story for political struggle in the late eighties is due precisely to "the difficulty of wresting from it any role for female defiance or leadership in a period when protest is coming increasingly from that quarter."[9]

The work of Stephen Greenblatt, Peter Hulme, and Paul Brown has been influential in shaping a second, explicitly Western and academic, strain of colonial discourse studies, and *The Tempest* has been central to their work. This scholarship employs detailed textual explication to reveal Prospero and Caliban as archetypal combatants in the colonial struggle; Shakespeare's master/slave duo captures, for whatever reasons, the dynamics of colonial relationships and discourse in a way that is in effect "characteristic" and "paradigmatic."

Such analysis, like much analysis of colonial discourse, elevates two specifically male terms from a larger system of actors and positions. The representative interplay between figures is most carefully treated in its psychological aspect, with special emphasis granted to the psychology of the colonizer, in this case "Prospero." Yet, archetypes that pit colonizer against colonized in this way can too easily become static models for misreading. When complex operations of power are exemplified in a psychologized exchange between individuals, the resulting paradigm—however psychologically nuanced—both prematurely simplifies broader forces which work on populations and assumes certain historical transformations are already complete. For instance, the paradigm does not encourage investigation of the role of colonialism in the rise of the "individual," in the creation of "psychology," or in the construction of masculinity in the early modern world.

Similarly, though all of the critics in this tradition insist on historicizing Shakespeare by reading the play together with other contemporaneous texts, all eventually privilege the explanatory power of *The Tempest*. When the author has successfully presented a rereading of *The Tempest* for its colonial meanings, the work of the essay is done, a habit illustrated by the fact that, although the points of departure in these articles are various, their conclusions are synonymous and simultaneous with the conclusion of their explication of Shakespeare. The result is that, despite the call to historicize, the archetypal relationship between colonizer and colonized emerges as rather ahistorical, and the terms "characteristic" and "paradigmatic" take on shades of timelessness.

Thus Peter Hulme situates *The Tempest* at the core of his research on "colonial encounters" between Europe and the native Caribbean from 1492 to 1797: he calls the play "a crucible in which the essentials of the colonial paradigm are laid bare," and deems it "a paradigmatic text for the writing of this book. Not only—as has often been pointed out—can Prospero and Caliban be seen as archetypes of the colonizer and the colonized, but Prospero is also the colonial historian, and such a convincing and ample historian that other histories have to fight their way into the crevices of his official monument."[10] These lines hint at the essay's investment in what Hulme refers to as "Prospero's private psychodrama."[11] They also suggest the extent to which the dual combatant paradigm of colonial antagonism exerts a control over Hulme's own method and structures his analysis of other colonial encounters.

This is not to say that paradigms are in themselves nefarious; nor is it to suggest that such interpretations of *The Tempest* are inevitable; they are, nonetheless, persistent.[12] This being the case, we need to beware our uncanny ability to produce academic studies of colonial discourse which enable us to locate texts against a particular historical background but allow us to maintain the disconnection between one moment in colonialist discourse and another.

Paul Brown, who delivers the most sophisticated argument in this school, would seem directly to oppose the use of *The Tempest* as a paradigm that assimilates diverse colonial histories into itself. According to Brown, colonial discourse criticism has too readily espoused *The Tempest*: "sustained historical and theoretical analysis of the play's involvement in the colonialist project has yet to be undertaken." He thereby separates his work from earlier studies, declaring the play "a radically ambivalent text which exemplifies not some *timeless* contradiction internal to the discourse . . . [but] a struggle to produce a coherent discourse adequate to the complex requirements of British colonialism in its initial phase."[13] Yet Brown also fails to sustain the effort; his conclusion reasserts the importance and paradigmatic status of the play, and thus again makes its meaning for colonial discourse effectively "timeless": *The Tempest* "serves as a limit-text in which the characteristic operations of colonialist discourse may be discerned." In similarly sweeping language, Brown locates within the play a radical ambivalence which is "at once the apotheosis, mystification and potential erosion of the colonialist discourse."[14] Most notable here is how Brown himself performs the "characteristic operations" of academic appropriations of *The Tempest*: although he is resolute about locating the play historically, the text ultimately represents the contradictions of its historical moment in terms characteristic of *all* phases of colonialism and colonial discourse. So too, Brown's preoccupation with ambivalence/doubleness and his later references to the "dreamwork" and "political unconscious" of the play reveal a familiar fascination with the psychology of some generalized and transhistorical colonizer.

Abena Busia and Ania Loomba extend their analyses beyond the confines of the text, situating the play within an African and an Indian context, respectively. Each traces the parallel constructions of gender in Shakespeare, colonialist fiction, and anticolonial discourse theories. In so doing, both scholars retool the *Tempest* paradigm for the examination of gender and race in the play and in contemporary critical theory. Moreover, the work of each corrects the myopic preoccupation with Miranda in Western feminist readings of *The Tempest* and carefully investigates the construction of black female and black male sexuality.[15] Yet while Busia and Loomba revise the Prospero-Caliban paradigm to accommodate an investigation of gender and race, their revisions promote a focus on white and black women in their subordination to patriarchy and discourage an exploration of the power women exercise vis-à-vis each other.

For example, Busia's "Silencing Sycorax: On African Colonial Discourse and the Unvoiced Female" notes that *The Tempest* establishes the paradigm" and, like Conrad's *Heart of Darkness*, has become a seminal text in which "the authors' treatment of their female subjects makes manifest the 'problem' of female representation and subjectivity within colonial discourse."[16] Busia concentrates on the African female and the "construction of her inactive silence" that distinguishes the black from the white female in colonial literature, a focus significant for any reading of *Oroonoko*. However, *Oroonoko* challenges feminist readings of colonial literature which, like Busia's, observe that the white woman possesses little practical authority despite the fact that she is aligned with the colonizing male and invested with great symbolic power. For Busia, the female colonizer's symbolic power is somehow undercut by the fact that she too is a "representative object of [male] desire."

Ania Loomba, like Busia, expands the male colonizer/colonized duo into a quartet of players. Loomba notes that the female positions "prope[l] the narrative even when posited as an absence."[17] Yet for Loomba these females seem to function merely as alibis for the males. She pays particular attention to Miranda in this respect. Miranda is the obedient, chaste participant in colonization and therefore the perfect contrast to "the witch" Sycorax. Sycorax, Caliban's absent mother, exemplifies the "construction of the promiscuity of non-European women [which] served to legitimise their sexual abuse and to demarcate them from white women."[18] But according to Loomba, Miranda's chastity and obedience represent her father's power, not her own; under Prospero's careful tutelage, she is *taught* to pity and despise Caliban and to submit herself to the demands of white patriarchal institutions. Loomba concludes, "Miranda thus conforms to the dual requirements of femininity within the master-culture: by taking on aspects of the white man's burden the white woman only confirmed her own subordination."[19] As the shadow of her father, Miranda serves as the "ideological legitimation of each of Prospero's actions."[20] However, because Loomba offers no prolonged consideration of what Miranda may stand to gain by "confirming her own subordination," she appears as a secondhand colonizer, not an actor in her own right.

Busia and Loomba represent a larger body of feminist colonial discourse scholarship which demonstrates that females in colonial texts symbolize a profound nexus of sexual and racial tension. Yet this scholarship also maintains that these females play out minor variations on the dominant male positions, emerging only as they advance the archetypal

struggle between colonizing and colonized males. The females complicate the mechanism of oppression and resistance, but they do not alter the
fundamental antagonism, which is retained as male against male.[21] Such
readings carry the assumption that gender differences are well established by the early modern period, promoting the further assumption that
gender—over and above racial or economic classifications—functions as
the primary mode of social organization and personal identification at this
moment in colonial expansion. To read in this way, it would seem, is to
avoid looking at the impact of racial constructions and colonization on the
very formation of gender.

This is precisely where *Oroonoko* complicates matters. The novel is
told in the first person by a white female narrator, a member of the colonial gentry, who becomes close friends with Oroonoko, the royal slave.
Her account is as much about the attempt to create her own narrative
authority and to manage her shifting allegiances as it is about Oroonoko
himself. Behn's text engages emergent discourses of race, gender, and
mercantile capitalism, representing the role of females as both consumers
and commodities in the colonial enterprise.[22] The novel's constellation of
African royalty, white colonial male gentry, white female narrator, royal
slave male, royal slave female, slave masses, Amerindian villagers, and a
single Indian mistress demands a fluid notion of colonial power. "Gender
identity" is a nascent or submerged identity at best in a text that reveals many ways to calculate interest or alliances in a New World colonial
setting, calculations which must take account of geographic and cultural
origins, varying roles in the economic process, and relative relationships
between enslaved, free, maroon, male, and female.

Behn's novel turns on two overlapping and carefully mirrored plots.
The first takes place in Oroonoko's West African nation, Coramantien.
The narrator relates information she has gathered from "the Hero himself, who gave us the whole Transactions of his Youth."[23] "Transactions"
is an appropriate pun; throughout the Coramantien section Behn emphasizes that Oroonoko's aristocratic lifestyle is supported by constant warfare and his trade in slaves. Behn focuses on the power struggle between
Oroonoko and his grandfather the king as they fight for sexual control
of Imoinda. Although Oroonoko "ravishes" Imoinda before the king does
and is therefore the victor in this contest, the king proves his ultimate
control over Imoinda's body by selling her into slavery. Oroonoko, on the
other hand, is duped into slavery. In his eagerness to observe the operations of a slaveship firsthand, the prince is kidnapped and taken as a slave

to Surinam. There, in keeping with the conventions of heroic romance, he is reunited with Imoinda.

While the other slaves are confined to shantytowns on the English plantations, Oroonoko's rank as African prince and his European manners and education secure him a life of relative ease. Promised his freedom when the absent Lord Governor returns, Oroonoko spends his time hunting, fishing, and making short expeditions in the company of the white female narrator. The dishonest colonial government, fearing Oroonoko will eventually rebel, enlists the narrator as diplomat and spy. Though Oroonoko vows never to harm her or the colonists, the narrator remains convinced of the need for her close surveillance, and she occupies Oroonoko and Imoinda with stories and excursions.

The major event of the novel's second half is Imoinda's pregnancy and Oroonoko's subsequent decision to lead a slave rebellion. Oroonoko's mutiny takes the slaveholders by surprise, and the English women, fearing Oroonoko will cut their throats, choose to "fly down the River to be secured." Meanwhile, the English men hasten to intercept Oroonoko and his band of fugitives. In the ensuing battle, Imoinda fights at Oroonoko's side, while other slave wives urge their men to surrender.

After the rebellion fails and Oroonoko is brutally tortured, he decides to kill the colonists in revenge, though he knows it will cost him his life. He determines that he must murder Imoinda before he takes vengeance in order to spare her a worse fate: "Perhaps (said he) she may be first ravished by every Brute; expos'd first to their nasty Lusts, and then a shameful Death" (71). As soon as he kills her, however, Oroonoko cannot bring himself to take any action whatsoever. Too weak even to kill himself properly, Oroonoko is captured and dismembered by the colonists.

While it may be entirely possible to read *Oroonoko* as a paradigmatic conflict between male colonizer and male colonized, to do so one must accept the narrator's construction of events without questioning her role as informant and participant. The contest between the English and Oroonoko in colonial Surinam is not simply a struggle between men in which the black female is victim or the white female a minor accomplice and subordinate. Rather, the events in Surinam produce an antagonism which the white female narrator organizes; she withdraws from open conflict in order to occupy a position of reflection and moral judgment. Imoinda is killed, Oroonoko can achieve no honor, the colonial government is exposed as corrupt. Only the narrator retains honorable status as the teller of the tale.

By creating a self-conscious white female narrator to mediate events, and by depicting the African female Imoinda as well as indigenous Americans, the text uses slavery, rape, and dismemberment to foreground an economic competition for the black female body and to outline an implicit competition between black, white, and indigenous females. In examining the multiple identifications of *Oroonoko*'s narrator, one sees that this white female colonizer's command of language can structure oppositions and relations among African, Amerindian, English, male, and female. The way in which this narrator's discourse inflects relations of power between white and black females reveals Imoinda's central role in the text's economy of colonial honor and horror.

■ ■ ■

As in the early travel literature Behn mines, the narrator depicts the New World as an exotic realm of human and animal variation. Amidst this profusion of species, the narrator works to draw meaningful distinctions—ones that will constitute and defend the allegiances among groups, peoples, and individuals. Her account of the English alliance with the Surinamese Indians opens the novel and indicates that the primary lines of distinction are those between commodities and consumers: "With these People, as I said, we live in perfect Tranquility, and good Understanding, as it behoves us to do; they knowing all the places where to seek the best Food . . . and for very small and unvaluable Trifles, supply us with that 'tis impossible for us to get. . . . they being on all occasions very useful to us, we find it absolutely necessary to caress 'em as Friends, and not to treat 'em as Slaves, nor dare we do other, their numbers so far surpassing ours in that Continent" (4–5). By revealing the economic interests underlying the colonists' goodwill toward the Indians, the narrator implicitly invokes and justifies the English-African slave trade. Thus, from the start, the novel establishes an economic and cultural triangle. Food, slaves, and "unvaluable Trifles" circulate throughout this passage, but the racial distinctions that arise in this trade are not inscribed as a self-other antagonism between colonizer and colonized. Here and throughout the text, race is written instead as a three-way negotiation; English supremacy in this region depends upon varied forms of domination and on crucial distinctions between Amerindian and African.

The narrator reveals that all three cultures—English, African, and Amerindian—trade in slaves. For the English alone, slaves are capital and the means of production, not trophies taken in war. The English dare not enslave the Surinamese Indians, the reader is told—"their numbers so far surpassing ours in that Continent." As Behn distinguishes between English, Indian, and African, the focus is not on the physiological or cultural characteristics of single bodies. Nor does Behn emphasize a psychological encounter between individuals. Instead, the distinctions that regulate the circulation of bodies emerge as economic ones, transactions between large groups or populations. The passage emphasizes the size of the Amerindian population, their skill in trade, and the importance of secure Amerindian-English trading patterns.

Behn has inscribed this three-way exchange among populations in the character of Oroonoko himself. Although in this novel he is the most likely candidate for the role of the archetypal colonized male, Oroonoko is not easily read as a psychological portrait, single individual, or even the product of a single culture or continent. Commenting on the title character's unusual name, Peter Hulme says that "in some ways the oddest detail, never explained in the novel, is Oronooko's [*sic*] name. It is not clear what kind of irony or parallel is implied by the arrival just down the coast from the mouth of the Orinoco (spelt 'Oronooko' in English until the nineteenth century) of an African bearing such an evocatively American name."[24] Hulme's puzzle becomes even more intriguing when one notes that the word "orinoco" also designates a type of tobacco. The title character is a black African possessing the best European schooling and manners, and named not only for a South American river but also for a prime American export good.[25] The triangular trade in mercantile goods is written into Oroonoko's name; he is both producer and commodity— slave trader, slave labor, and cash crop. The novel plays on these meanings when describing Oroonoko's execution. Oroonoko is tied to a post "and a great Fire made before him." The narrator notes, "he had learn'd to take Tobacco . . . he desir'd they would give him a Pipe in his Mouth, ready lighted." He is slowly dismembered with "an ill-favoured Knife," his severed parts tossed into the fire. While parted from his "members," ears, nose, and arms, he "still smoak'd on, as if nothing had touch'd him." Finally, "his Head sunk, and his Pipe dropt and he gave up the Ghost, without a Groan, or a Reproach" (77).

William C. Spengemann refers to this moment in the text as one example of Oroonoko's accommodation to his savage surroundings; he has "gone native," adopting the Indian-associated practice of pipe-smoking.[26] But the arresting image of Oroonoko taking tobacco while his own body burns makes literal the analogy between enslaved slave trader and the commodity for which he is named; he signifies a transatlantic conjunction of consumer, producer, and commodity, and—more profoundly—he represents the human beings who are themselves consumed by slavery.[27]

Alongside these complicated trade alliances and overlapping relations of production and consumption, the narrator's protean "we" shows her consolidating her own various identities—gendered, racial, political, and economic. As a royalist, the narrator shares a common sensibility with Oroonoko, the prince who traded slaves before he himself was captured. Both she and Oroonoko are critical of the dishonorable conduct of the bourgeois colonial government. The conflict between aristocratic and bourgeois values here is extremely important. While the narrator is in favor of colonization and regrets the eventual loss of the colony to the Dutch, she finds the mode of government under Lieutenant Governor Byam and his men to be dishonorable and therefore reprehensible. This is no condemnation of the imperial venture itself, however; both Oroonoko and the white female narrator believe that the "noble" are the rightful rulers of "brutes and slaves"; both she and Oroonoko openly admire a more "honorable" and ancient white slaveholding empire—Rome.[28] It is no coincidence that Behn gives Oroonoko the slave name Caesar; nor is it by chance that the narrator entertains Oroonoko and Imoinda "with the Loves of the Romans, and great Men, which charmed him to my Company" (46). Both she and Oroonoko become the emblems of good imperial government in this text. Yet as one who self-consciously offers her "history" to the English market and who is a member of the plantation-owning, slaveholding class in this colony, the narrator's interests are tied to those of the crass British mercantilists she disdains.[29]

In the face of an overt conflict in the narrator's allegiances—that is, conflict between Oroonoko and the English slaveholders—the narrator merges with yet another group, a rather nebulous collection of white females who remove themselves from scenes of mutiny or slave torture. The narrator deftly attributes these departures to threats or sentiments that seem to affect white females exclusively. Thus the crucial moments when gender arises as a mechanism for social organization or individual identity are moments in which the white female is gendered distinctly from the black or native female. At these moments, the role of each woman in the colonial economy is defined by casting each in relationship to the other women, as well as to the men.

An example points this out nicely. In the midst of the climactic slave rebellion and ensuing battle, the narrator describes the Lieutenant Governor's rescue from certain death by the native art of his Indian mistress. The moment is remarkable in that the body of the white colonial governor becomes the focus of an exchange between the pregnant Imoinda and the nameless native female: "Heroick Imoinda, who grown big as she was, did nevertheless press near her Lord, having a Bow and a Quiver full of poisoned Arrows, which she managed with such dexterity, that she wounded several, and shot the Governour into the Shoulder; of which Wound he had like to have died, but that an Indian Woman, his Mistress, sucked the Wound, and cleans'd it from the Venom" (64–65). Both Imoinda and the Amerindian female engage in acts of survival. In Imoinda's attack on the Lieutenant Governor and the Indian mistress's attempt to sustain him, we see a version of a broader economic exchange across African, English, and indigenous populations. But inasmuch as the women's actions are at odds—one shoots to kill, the other provides the cure—their survival would also seem to be at odds. This is the only capacity in which we see the "Indian Woman." In this passage, she alone is sexualized, both by the nature of her cure and her description as "Mistress." Her sexual relationship with the governor is the only interracial sexual liaison which the novel permits.

In the battle scene between Imoinda and the Indian mistress, Behn not only re-presents the Amerindian-English-African trade as an exchange among individuals but also rewrites English economic exploitation and dependence in gendered terms. Furthermore, the gender distinctions separate women from each other as well as from men. While the "Mistress" and Imoinda are opposed, they are both present as active and material bodies with the capacity to reproduce or sabotage colonial relationships. The pregnant Imoinda will either breed new slaves or kill the masters; the Indian mistress can provide or withhold medicinal skill. The white female body alone has fled the scene, effectively removing itself from the scene of colonial struggle and leaving the white male to personify colonial power.

Motivated by the "extreme Fear" that Oroonoko would "cut all our Throats," the narrator has left the site of armed conflict. This fear makes "all the Females of us fly down the River, to be secured" (68). The "Females" she speaks of are, of course, the white females. The vague "Apprehension" she names in and of itself creates a body which is distinct from other female bodies. In the midst of this battle, only the white female body must be "secured"; this body alone is worthy of protection. The same "Apprehension" which distinguishes the white female body allows that body to disappear "down the River," thereby enabling her to acquire an even more powerful presence; she reappears as narrative consciousness and moral judge, the voice that structures the entire scene.[30]

Both Spengemann and Margaret W. Ferguson have commented on the narrator's peculiar absences and her multiple political allegiances within the text. Spengemann notes that "the narrator shifts her position repeatedly," but he attributes the vacillations to a clash between romance and realism: "These rapid shifts in narrative attitude create an ambiguity of tone that enhances the novelistic effects already produced by the collision of Behn's romantic theme with her historical narrative form. Neither romance nor Brief True Relation, her narrative has become a rhetorical blending of heroic ideals and brute reality into a symbolic expression of the narrator's conflicting allegiances to her civilized audience and her savage art."[31]

For Spengemann, the narrator's ambiguity is explained by the incompatible requirements of conflicting genres. Ferguson, on the other hand, suggests that an analogy between gender and race oppression provokes the narrator's realignments: "an opposition drawn along lines of gender within the British community allows—in the peculiar circumstances of colonialism—for an unusual alliance to flourish between white females . . . and the black slave Oroonoko: a community of the unjustly oppressed is thus formed." Ferguson thereby argues that the narrator and Oroonoko are intermittently "allied in a multifaceted league of potential subversion."[32] But rather than read the narrator's ambiguity as a by-product of conflicting genres—where the horror of colonization disrupts a would-be romance—and rather than read some potentially subversive affinity between the white female and the black male, one might focus on the exchange between females and suggest that those moments when the narrator genders herself as white woman are the very moments which elaborate, not subvert, colonial authority. Abdul JanMohamed has suggested that "evident 'ambivalence'" in colonialist discourse can be read as "a product of deliberate, if at times subconscious, imperialist duplicity."[33] To read Oroonoko as just such a case of imperialist duplicity forces an examination of the role of colonial discourse in producing modern gender itself. Although the novel calls frequent, seemingly apologetic attention to the "female pen" transmitting the material, the text makes it clear that the narrator's position as female colonizer with leisure ensures both a particularly effective control over Oroonoko and Imoinda and, eventually, an equally effective control over their narrative. While seeming to document the antagonism between the English men and Oroonoko, male colonizer and colonized, this white female narrator creates and recreates colonial identities and antagonisms as she sees fit and in doing so exhibits her own brand of colonial mastery.

■ ■ ■

Writing in the late seventeenth century, Behn draws on a large body of discourse attempting to produce the white female. Captivity narratives, travel accounts, British political documents, and conduct books are all defining and promoting certain qualities of gender, race, and nation by displaying these qualities in the figure of a single white English woman. Behn scholars have consistently pointed out that the body of her work contributes to the growing seventeenth-century dialogue on British womanhood, but few have noted that this dialogue must construct the modern British woman within the immediate context of British colonialism and its discourse on native female others. *Oroonoko* is of particular interest because the novel manipulates the contemporary rhetorics both of English womanhood and of colonization in order to create a white and female voice of authority, but in so doing it reveals the English lady at work creating herself. That self-production not only requires the "lady" to distinguish herself from indigenous and black females as well as males, but it also requires the "lady" to engage with a discourse of rape that can set value on her bodily integrity—that is, endow her with "honor" and therefore make her worthy of protection.

Elaine Hobby discusses the increase in civil petitions written by women between the 1640s and the 1680s, petitions that attempt to justify a female presence in politics as well as in print. Over the same period a growing body of conduct books begins to define and redefine the qualities most desirable in English women. Moira Ferguson notes that these conduct books—written by both men and women—elaborate "a certain profile in print" that connected and promoted "a matrix of values": piety, duty, honesty, modesty, chastity, honor.[34]

While students of these conduct books agree that this "profile in print" somehow helped forge a link between women and a newly emerging "private sphere," scholars disagree as to whether the transformation of gender roles then underway was ultimately empowering or disempowering for English women. Nancy Armstrong has argued that, beginning in the late seventeenth century and throughout the eighteenth, these conduct books and the domestic fiction they spawned were in effect empowering

an entirely new economic "class." According to Armstrong, nonaristo-
cratic people with otherwise divergent economic and political allegiances
increasingly found themselves bound together within a "community of
common domestic values" that the conduct books so ably invented.[35]

Conduct book representations of an ideal domestic woman were predicated on a larger vision that enabled a reorganization of the social world
into marketplace and household. Where formerly the major lines of distinction separated highborn aristocrats from the rest of the population,
a new social map proposed a world divided into gendered spheres of activity. The British middle class could displace the aristocracy in a world
that reorganized production into masculine enterprise and feminine duty:
the marketplace (firmly located in the world of power and politics) and the
household (seemingly outside that economic and political world). Armstrong argues that, as members of this rising class, British women were
gaining power over cultural institutions—power which was cloaked because it seemed increasingly detached from the world of economics and
politics. This power that seemed not to be power at all took the form of
efficient management, surveillance, and speech.

Thus the new desirable domestic woman assembled in the conduct
books and domestic fictions of the seventeenth and eighteenth centuries
efficiently and inconspicuously managed people and households, and did
so by means of frugality, vigilance, and—most importantly—the power
of discourse: "the rhetoric of the conduct books produced a subject who
in fact had no material body at all. This rhetoric replaced the material
body with a metaphysical body made largely of words, albeit words constituting a material form of power in their own right."[36] This argument
offers a near perfect description of *Oroonoko*'s vigilant, voluble narrator.
Yet Behn's text qualifies Armstrong by relocating the historical moment
and complicating the political conditions under which this sort of female
subject would seem to emerge.

While Armstrong's work is essential to our reading of *Oroonoko*, it is
important to read her argument in light of the fact that both the ideal
of the domestic woman and the class interests she promotes arise during the same period in which nationalist discourse and mercantile wealth
are being consolidated through colonial expansion. For instance, Behn's
narrator anticipates the emergence of the domestic woman and the seemingly apolitical feminine sphere she governs, but this particular narrator
claims moral and verbal authority in order to remove herself from political culpability and simultaneously to claim the power of political speech.

She passes terse judgment on the poorly run British colony and then positions herself as likable ambassador to African and Amerindian, the exemplar of good imperial government. Likewise, Behn's Imoinda is of particular interest for the way the character joins the dialogue about the desirable female while simultaneously forcing us to consider the role of imperialism and race in the construction of that ideal. Put more bluntly, definitions of aristocratic or domestic womanhood do not contend in an already white and English space; that is, race and nation enter as variables in the equation that produces the domestic woman and the British middle class.

Imoinda's skin is black and bears the raised scars that decorate elite female bodies in her West African nation. Her dancing surpasses that of all other captives in the king's seraglio. Yet this markedly exotic body has not prevented her complete acquisition of white European culture; in many ways, Imoinda represents the height of virtuous white maidenhood. Despite the alien trappings, Imoinda embodies precisely those traits which, by the late seventeenth century, English women are being encouraged to cultivate. She is identified not only by her aristocratic bearing but also by her domestic virtues: her honor, modesty, and reticence—qualities which enrapture Oroonoko when she first receives him in her Coramantien home.

Imoinda's blend of aristocratic and domestic qualities is easily maintained in the first half of the novel. Yet as the story moves her from one continent to the next, one economy to another, her character becomes the site of competing definitions of femininity and race. Behn eventually marks certain feminine qualities as white and English and transfers them to the female narrator, while other feminine qualities are marked as alien and African and come to dominate Imoinda's character. By casting Imoinda in relationship to another female, Behn creates a filter through which this mix of femininity is separated and clarified until, finally, Imoinda is associated only with her material body. Yet if it is against the material body that Behn must establish the metaphysical female subject, Behn's attempt to distinguish the narrator from Imoinda shows that her move to consolidate a modern female subject is a move to consolidate womanhood, whiteness, and Englishness simultaneously. Thus the womanhood particular to each female is defined by an exchange between women that simultaneously inscribes "womanhood" as either "black" or "white."

It is no coincidence that attributes of gender and race are worked out and assigned within a colonial setting. The moment Imoinda arrives in a colonial slave economy is the very moment when the white female narrator materializes as a character as well as a narrating voice. Only at this juncture and in this economy does the novel begin to insist upon the contradiction between an African female body and white female sensibilities. Once enslaved, Imoinda comes to be valued entirely for the (re)productive capacity of her body, and our narrator comes to be valued for her *meta*physical qualities, her discourse and her moral sense.

Furthermore, the changing values ascribed to female bodies in this text are registered in part through a colonial discourse of rape. While in the first half of the novel rape appears as a practice that makes the female an object in a struggle between men, in the context of colonial Surinam Behn presents a discourse of rape which actually establishes one female as subject and one as object. Inasmuch as that discourse of rape is marshaled and manipulated by the white female narrator herself, one must view the discourse of rape in this text as part of a textual transaction between women. A closer look at Imoinda—both Coramantien princess and pregnant slave—is essential to understanding the connections Behn forges between rape, honor, and protection; this discourse of rape, in turn, is essential to a reading of the interdependence of the colonial economy on the relative values of female bodies.

■ ■ ■

In both Coramantien and Surinam, Oroonoko takes significant action when he comes to fear that Imoinda may be raped by rivals. In each case, Oroonoko protects his honor by protecting Imoinda. Ironically, Oroonoko's "defense" against these threats of rape means that he must violate Imoinda's body before others do so. Clearly, to define a particular act of violence as an act of duty, defense, or rape, Oroonoko must invoke a set of socially and historically specific sanctions and prohibitions. Again and again Oroonoko calls on his code of honor to distinguish acceptable violence from what is unacceptable.

Let us contextualize and clarify the argument here. In her discussion of the so-called Indian Mutiny or Sepoy Rebellion of 1857, Jenny Sharpe addresses "the historical production of rape within a system of *colonial relations.*" She argues, as we would concerning *Oroonoko*, that "what it means to be rapable" itself has a history.[37] Sharpe here pinpoints the aspect of meaning and interpretation that is crucial to the concept and practice of rape. Some acts of violence that resemble rape are not always defined as rape; "rape" in this seventeenth-century text is implicitly a struggle over social definitions of violation, a struggle which inherently depends on social codes of honor and protection.[38] To pursue this thinking then, the discourse of rape actually structures and reinforces relations of power among bodies—which bodies can be violated and with what social impact, by whom and with what level of impunity; these particulars are fought out in the social arena as well as on a proto-individual or psychic level. In Behn, the discourse of rape and "what it means to be rapable" become one mechanism which distinguishes the black female body from the white female body, organizing social power simultaneously in terms of gender and race.

Behn's description of Coramantien society grants honor a pivotal role in all economic, political, and sexual transactions. In his comparative study of slave societies, Orlando Patterson has argued that honor, power, and slavery are intimately linked: "wherever slavery became structurally very important, the whole tone of the slaveholders' culture tended to be highly honorific."[39] Patterson's data reveal the "strong sense of honor the experience of mastership generated, and conversely, the dishonoring of the slave condition."[40] Significantly, Oroonoko experiences the interdependence of honor and dishonor as both master and slave. As a prince in Coramantien society, his power and prosperity—and, therefore, honor—are directly related to his participation in the slave trade. Yet even as Behn outlines an economy of honor that relies on the trade in bodies, she sketches the difference between male and female bodies in that economy. Her plot turns on the contrast between masculine and feminine forms of honor: in Coramantien, the prince's honor demands success in the competition for slave bodies in general and Imoinda's body in particular. Because Imoinda's hymen marks both female honor and male honor, it registers their impossible coexistence; the woman's honor must give place to the man's.[41]

In Coramantien, king and prince have each laid public claim to Imoinda, but neither has managed to write that claim on her body. Oroonoko has married Imoinda but not consummated the marriage. His impotent grandfather has claimed her for his harem but can assail her only with limp embraces. Social custom and political rank typically govern the sexual exchange, but in this case the king's rights are at odds with the husband's; both the king and Oroonoko suspect that the other's claim to Imoinda takes priority over his own.

As each man attempts to rape Imoinda before the other does, Behn is clearly not concerned with Imoinda's safety or bodily integrity. Her rape is culturally sanctioned and eminently social in its ramifications. Since the sexual rivalry threatens to redistribute political power, Behn's focus is on the role the woman's virginal body plays in securing each man's political position.[42] In this scenario the hymen is a form of currency and a token of honor, valuable only in its potential for exchange. Whoever "possesses" the hymen—Imoinda, Oroonoko, or the king—possesses honor but leaves the other two dishonored. To retain her virtue—that is, to avoid permanent dishonor in the exchange—the female must receive something in return—either the sanction of honorable marriage or the honor of being mistress to the king.[43]

Losing the "prize" to his hyperpotent grandson, the king still exercises ultimate control over Imoinda's body; he sells her into slavery, even though "death would be more honorable for a maid of that quality." The statement concludes Imoinda's role in the Coramantien plot sequence even as it points ahead to the events in Surinam. The assertion that "death would be more honorable" indicates the romance formula for female honor and anticipates two lessons about honor that Oroonoko will learn in Surinam. As Orlando Patterson has argued, the generalized dishonor of slavery is akin to social death: "Those who do not compete for honor, or are not expected to do so, are in a real sense outside the social order."[44] First, Oroonoko and Imoinda discover that romance notions of female honor (virginity or sanctioned marriage) are impossible under slavery; and second, as a slave, Oroonoko, who can "do nothing that honor does not dictate," finds himself trapped in the economy of dishonor that Patterson describes.[45]

In both Coramantien and Surinam, Imoinda is a unit of exchange, yet the value assigned to her body changes. When finally both Oroonoko and Imoinda are relocated in colonial Surinam, the aristocratic contest over Imoinda's hymen becomes an interracial struggle over the African female body. For Oroonoko, this change in meaning begins to register when Imoinda becomes pregnant: "This new Accident made him more impatient of Liberty . . . he began to suspect them of Falshood, and that they would delay him till the time of his Wife's Delivery, and make a Slave of that too: for all the Breed is theirs to whom the Parents belong" (45). Once pregnant, Imoinda has increased her worth and that of Oroonoko in the slave economy. While in the Coramantien romance plot Imoinda's value resides only in her hymen and its one time rupture, in the slave economy her greater value resides in her womb and in the potential for multiple, repeatable reproduction of the labor force.[46] In a system that shifts the value of the African female body from hymen to womb, Oroonoko's sexual use of Imoinda's body can only reproduce dishonor by increasing their value to the system. When Imoinda "began to shew she was with Child," she "sighs and weeps," believing "if it were so hard to gain the liberty of two, 'twould be more difficult to get that for three" (59). This fact compels Oroonoko to lead a rebellion.

When the rebellion fails, Oroonoko suffers the brutal indignity of torture for the first time. He is whipped ferociously and "to compleat his Rage, he saw every one of those Slaves, who but a few days before ador'd him . . . now had a Whip to give him some Lashes." Oroonoko is then put in irons and "Indian pepper" is rubbed into his open wounds; finally, he is left tied "so fast to the Ground, that he could not stir, if his Pains and Wounds would have given him leave" (67).

In this extremity, Oroonoko's honor would seem to demand two contradictory feats. He must avenge his torture and, therefore, resolves "not only to kill [Lieutenant Governor] Byam, but all those he thought had enraged him"; yet he must also protect Imoinda from the "nasty Lusts" of "the enraged Multitude" (71). The understanding that he cannot accomplish both comes upon him all at once. Regardless of whether he succeeds or fails in his plot of revenge, Imoinda may be subject to repeated rape. Oroonoko's choices are mutually exclusive; in either case—whether he avenges himself or protects Imoinda—his action will result in dishonor.

For Oroonoko, the threat of rape in this instance is an "Apprehension too insupportable to be borne" because the meaning of rape itself is transformed. In the colonial setting rape does not simply mean that he will lose Imoinda's body to a superior rival but also that she will be subject to the widest possible sexual circulation. Imoinda will be available to multiple violation by "every Brute" on the plantation (71). This thought eventually overwhelms Oroonoko and brings about his murder of Imoinda.

In Surinam, as in Coramantien, the discourse of rape, honor, and protection is written on the black female body; it affirms her physical value with violent results. However, when the configuration of rape, honor, and protection established in Coramantien recurs in Surinam, it is altered by the intrusion of white and Amerindian players and a colonial economy. For instance, in Surinam Oroonoko is at times called upon to "protect" white women, especially in the excursion to an "Indian Town." At other times he himself is deemed the threat. In either case, the discourse affirms the white female's metaphysical value. Thus, in the colonial setting concepts such as rape, protection, and honor work to draw and redraw alliances, especially those among the white female narrator, the black male, and the black female.

In its account of Imoinda's murder, the novel carefully echoes her earlier "ravishment" in Coramantien. Imoinda's pregnant body becomes the site of a critical linkage between the aristocratic code of honor and the codes of honor and dishonor that govern colonization: "the lovely, young and ador'd Victim lays her self down before the Sacrificer; while he, with a hand resolved and a heart-breaking within, gave the fatal Stroke, first cutting her Throat, and then severing her yet smiling Face from that delicate Body, pregnant as it was with the Fruits of tenderest Love" (72). This "sacrifice" parallels the Coramantien conflict over Imoinda, the taking of female "virgen-honour" for male. Yet while the scene symbolically re-enacts the taking of Imoinda's hymen, the action renders it gruesome, even macabre. Where the threat of rape in the early part of the novel leads to the taking of Imoinda's maidenhead, by the end of the novel Oroonoko severs her "face" in a gory decapitation. Behn dwells on the details: Oroonoko covers the body, keeping the "severed face" to look on. He lies next to the decaying corpse for eight days, until the slaveowners track him by the "loathsome" smell: "for Stinks must be very noisom, that can be distinguished among such a quantity of natural Sweets, as every Inch of that Land produces" (74).

As the "Fruits of tenderest Love" rot in this otherwise fertile setting, and the "noisom" stench of Imoinda's spoiling flesh rises over the New World landscape, the language of the travel narrative reasserts itself. The narrative consciousness intrudes on the scene to remind us that the ruined productivity of the enslaved female body points directly back to the transcendent productivity of the land, every inch yielding "natural Sweets." In so doing, the passage highlights the exchange between the black female's body and the white female's voice. Not only does this bizarre dismemberment replay the earlier conjunction of rape, honor, and protection, but the act also invokes the discourse of rape in its necessary relation to the colonial economy and the trade in goods and bodies, a trade in which all three cultures—African, Amerindian, and English— are implicated and over which the narrator presides.

■ ■ ■

This essay has argued that Behn places her narrator and Imoinda in a relationship of exchange; they take part in a textual transaction in which both are feminized, but in which the white female gathers metaphysical traits unto herself and inscribes the black female with physical value only. Behn thus endows her narrator with moral, political, and narrative authority; and she does so by fashioning a distinctly white female subjectivity, a "gendered identity," if you will. But in Behn we also see multiple contemporaneous discourses at odds; economic, racial, and gender divisions all vie for the power to organize populations and describe individual bodies. Gender does not stand apart from or prior to these conflicting modes of social classification.

In Behn's late-seventeenth-century strategy, we see that through the narrative itself the narrator—a woman without husband or father—is able to take her own body out of economic and sexual circulation and to substitute instead the value of her words and watchfulness. In representing the circulation of bodies and body parts among British, Amerindian, and African, the narrator appears to control that circulation and to profit from it by removing herself from it. Throughout the novel she wields a subtle rhetoric of allegiance that enables her to be against mutiny but for Oroonoko; against the corrupt colonists and the Lieutenant Governor but for colonization; against having her own throat cut but for the "honorable" decapitation of Imoinda. Behn's depiction of colonial slavery constitutes the narrator as simultaneously white and metaphysically feminine; the narrator claims the power of political speech and the protections of citizenship for her person.

The legacy of *Oroonoko* can be read in the discourse on race in the Americas, its impact traced in primitivist fiction and the slave narrative, as well as in sentimental abolitionist fiction in the United States and Britain. *Oroonoko* raises provocative and politically charged questions with which to examine the American lines of descent. For instance, Behn's seventeenth-century narrator employs a discourse of rape to distinguish herself from indigenous and black females and thereby achieves political immunity while justifying her own political speech. How, then, might the discourse of rape codify race and gender at different historical moments, and what is the investment of "white" females in manipulating that discourse? What is the investment of white females in various systems of colonial power? How are females gendered vis-à-vis other females, and males vis-à-vis other males through colonizing discourse? How do texts encode and support domination via multiply "raced" and gendered "others"? Such questions seem pressing if our object is to investigate the sexual and racial ideologies supporting colonial interests and, most importantly, if we would, as Benita Parry urges, trace the permutation of those ideologies at different points in time down to present day imperialist conflicts.[47]

Notes

The epigraphs to this essay are taken from Abena P. A. Busia, "Silencing Sycorax: On African Colonial Discourse and the Unvoiced Female," *Cultural Critique* 14 (Winter 1989–90): 94; and Gayatri Spivak, "A Literary Representation of the Subaltern: A Woman's Text from the Third World," in *In Other Worlds: Essays in Cultural Politics* (New York: Routledge, 1987), 249. An earlier version of this essay was presented at the first Congreso Internacional de Conflictos Culturales en la Literatura Contemporánea, held at the University of Puerto Rico, Mayagüez, in February 1991. We would like to thank Marty Roth and Christy Brown for their comments on early drafts.

1   See Octave Mannoni, *Prospero and Caliban: The Psychology of Colonization*, trans. Pamela Powesland (New York: Praeger, 1956); George Lamming, "A Monster, a Child, a Slave," in *The Pleasures of Exile* (London: Allison & Busby, 1984), 95–117.

2   Busia, 81–104; Ania Loomba, "Seizing the Book," in *Gender, Race, Renaissance Drama* (New York: Manchester Univ. Press, 1989), 142–58.

3   Thomas Southerne, *Oroonoko*, ed. Maximillian E. Novak and David Stuart Rodes (Lincoln: Univ. of Nebraska Press, 1976), 113.

4   See note in Southerne, 113.

5   We refer here to three texts to which this essay is indebted: Laura Brown's "The Romance of Empire: *Oroonoko* and the Trade in Slaves," in *The New Eighteenth Century: Theory, Politics, English Literature*, ed. Felicity Nussbaum and Laura Brown (New York: Methuen, 1987), 41–61; Moira Ferguson's chapter, "*Oroonoko*: Birth of a Paradigm," in her *Subject to Others: British Women Writers and Colonial Slavery, 1670–1834* (New York: Routledge, 1992); and Margaret W. Ferguson's "Juggling the Categories of Race, Class and Gender: Aphra Behn's *Oroonoko*," *Women's Studies* 19 (1991): 159–81. In fact, Margaret W. Ferguson speculates provocatively on Southerne's conversion of black female into white and discusses the cover of the Norton edition of Behn's text, which depicts a white Imoinda and her black husband, who gestures at her with a knife. Rather than taking their scholarship to task, we mean to point to the tendency that excludes black females from analysis or pushes them to the background of studies in race and gender, as if the nexus of the two were better or more interestingly realized in the intersection of black male and white female. Nancy Stepan's work

prompts our speculation that antiracist cultural studies have been too quick to borrow the analogy between black male and white female as a metaphor for disempowerment. The analogy may only serve to distract from investigations of white women's power or from examinations of race-and-gender as a different conjunction for black women than it is for white women. See Nancy Leys Stepan's "Race and Gender: The Role of Analogy in Science," in *Anatomy of Racism*, ed. David Theo Goldberg (Minneapolis: Univ. of Minnesota Press, 1990), 38–57.

6   The move to sanction slavery condemns it at the same time, and the ease with which Behn's novel was converted in the eighteenth century into popular abolitionist dramas illustrates this phenomenon. Anthony Gerard Barthelemy comments: "The stage history of *Oroonoko* and of its various adaptations clearly demonstrates this point, for as each generation of audiences required a stronger abolitionist statement, the play was altered to meet that need" (*Black Face, Maligned Race: The Representation of Blacks in English Drama from Shakespeare to Southerne* [Baton Rouge: Louisiana State Univ. Press, 1987], 181). Wylie Sypher discusses the Oroonoko history in detail in his *Guinea's Captive Kings: British Anti-Slavery Literature of the Eighteenth Century* (New York: Octagon, 1969), 108–21.

7   For a study of honor and dishonor in slave societies, see Orlando Patterson, *Slavery and Social Death: A Comparative Study* (Cambridge: Harvard Univ. Press, 1982). What *Oroonoko* adds to his discussion is a notion of honor as necessarily gendered and economic. This gendered economy of honor/dishonor not only supports and unites the two halves of Behn's novel but also makes monarchy, rape, empire, and slavery consistent practices.

8   Roberto Fernández Retamar, *Caliban and Other Essays*, trans. Edward Baker (Minneapolis: Univ. of Minnesota Press, 1989), 4; Houston Baker Jr., "Caliban's Triple Play," in *"Race," Writing, and Difference*, ed. Henry Louis Gates Jr. (Chicago: Univ. of Chicago Press, 1985), 391.

9   Rob Nixon, "Caribbean and African Appropriations of *The Tempest*," *Critical Inquiry* 13 (Spring 1987): 577.

10   Peter Hulme, *Colonial Encounters: Europe and the Native Caribbean, 1492–1797* (New York: Methuen, 1986), 123, 125.

11   Hulme, 123.

12   The Shakespearean canon has long been the testing ground for any new critical approach to literary interpretation, particularly any that would gain ascendancy within humanist disciplines. The history of Shakespeare studies as an academic proving ground may indicate that the real contest here is not between Prospero and Caliban, but rather "old" and "new" textual approaches. In the broader context of postcolonial studies, this criticism raises a more curious question: to what extent does anticolonial criticism perform an ironic reinstitution of Shakespeare—and through it British culture—as a primary (paradigmatic) lens through which to understand colonial culture? Only Loomba, writing from within the Indian education system, is acutely

conscious of Shakespeare's continuing role as interpreter of the experience of both imperialists and colonial subjects, as was exactly the case in the initial phases of English literature as a colonial discipline. Her introductory chapter is particularly good at connecting the use of Shakespeare and English literature in a colonial and postcolonial context, demonstrating how English literature continues to jointly serve the needs of imperialism as well as the indigenous elite.

13   Paul Brown, "'This thing of darkness I acknowledge mine': *The Tempest* and the discourse of colonialism," in *Political Shakespeare: New Essays in Cultural Materialism*, ed. Jonathan Dollimore and Alan Sinfield (Ithaca: Cornell Univ. Press, 1985), 131–32.

14   Paul Brown, 151.

15   Laura Donaldson's work on "The Miranda Complex" is perhaps the most recent example of feminist reading that, while contributing to a critique of white women and colonization, accepts at face value the reading of Caliban as attempted rapist and fails to consider Sycorax altogether (*Decolonizing Feminisms: Race, Gender, and Empire-Building* [Chapel Hill: Univ. of North Carolina Press, 1992]).

16   Busia, 84.

17   Loomba, 153.

18   Loomba, 152.

19   Loomba, 156.

20   Loomba, 153.

21   Hazel Carby's formulation of this is emblematic: "The white woman's body within colonial discourse was the preserve of a white patriarchal order. . . . At the nexus of imperial relations the white woman's body became symbolic of colonial oppression and is thus often represented in colonial fiction as a central figure in the struggle between colonizing and colonized males" ("Proletarian or Revolutionary Literature: C. L. R. James and the Politics of the Trinidadian Renaissance," *New Formations* 10 [1990]: 105).

22   For a discussion of white women as consumers in the text, see Laura Brown, 41–61.

23   Aphra Behn, *Oroonoko; or, The Royal Slave* (New York: Norton, 1973), 1. Subsequent citations from Behn will appear parenthetically in the text.

24   Hulme, 241.

25   The *OED* defines "oroonoko" (a variant of oronooko) as a type of tobacco and speculates that the term of "uncertain origin" is apparently "a proper name connected with the river Oronoco in South America" (2nd ed., vol. X [Oxford: Clarendon Press, 1989]).

26   Spengemann also points to an earlier moment of "going native," Oroonoko's desperate and confused actions at the novel's climax: after killing Imoinda, Oroonoko, uncertain whether to attempt to destroy his oppressors or to destroy himself, finally attempts both and succeeds at neither. In Oroonoko's final moments, Behn has him borrow a tactic from the Surinamese Indians—

self-mutilation—to defy the English colonists. He lops off pieces of his throat and throws them at the colonists, then disembowels himself (75). Of this native practice the narrator says, "It's by a passive Valour they shew and prove their Activity, a sort of courage too brutal to be applauded by our Black Hero; nevertheless, he express'd his Esteem of 'em" (58). In adopting this practice—which he previously thought too full of rage and malice, too horrible—Oroonoko is engaging a native, non-European code of honor and aligning himself with the only people he has seen who have successfully resisted the treacherous colonists. See William C. Spengemann, "The Earliest American Novel: Aphra Behn's *Oroonoko*," *Nineteenth-Century Fiction* 38 (1984): 384–414.

27 His smoking also reinforces Behn's portrait of the New World as a region of extremities. Just as the "Indian pepper" was ground into his wounds to heighten his suffering, so too the smoking induces Oroonoko's impossible calm in the midst of his own dismemberment. Also noteworthy is the fact that the economic conjunction discussed here is further emphasized in Oroonoko's transformation from trophy taker to trophy: in Coramantien he presents Imoinda with captured slaves and, later in Surinam, presents the narrator with a "tyger cub" after killing its mother. After his own execution, Oroonoko's severed limbs are distributed as trophies amongst the plantation owners in order to display before their slaves, presumably in the hopes of frightening them into submission. Even in death, Oroonoko cannot escape furthering the slave economy.

28 That Oroonoko shares this attitude is made clear in his rebellion speech, in which he states that had he and the other slaves been "vanquished . . . nobly in Fight" they would have no cause to rebel (61).

29 Behn thus creates what will become a standard structure for primitivist narrative. Her narrator, like Conrad's Marlowe, apparently stands apart from the "civilized" colonial rulers in order to judge them corrupt. The narrator retains the economic benefits and protections of imperialism, while proving herself more civil, more moral than either the colonial government or the enslaved or indigenous populations. This cunning stance of ambivalent observation creates a moral hierarchy within her own culture: by displaying moral sensitivity, the narrator can distinguish herself from the barbaric capitalists. The imperialist's critique of imperialism itself becomes testimony to the moral superiority available through "civilization."

30 The relationships between females established in this battle episode are replayed in Oroonoko's torture scene. As Oroonoko is whipped, Imoinda is carried away from the spectacle, "not in kindness to her, but for fear she should die with the sight, or miscarry, and then they should lose a young Slave, and perhaps the Mother" (67). While Imoinda's absence draws attention to the reproductive value of her material body, the narrator's absence draws attention to her emotional sensitivity; she has removed herself yet again, this time due to a fit of melancholia. The narrator chooses precisely

this moment to repeat her account of the governor's wound and the mistress's cure. Thus the Indian mistress also reappears and performs the same function she had before. The repetition of the Indian mistress incident itself is curious. The first time it appears, it is told as part of the account of the slave rebellion, so the rescue seems to occur at the very moment the governor is shot. Yet the second time the narrator refers to the timely rescue, we learn that the cure is worked long after the governor is wounded. It isn't until Oroonoko has been captured and is being whipped that the governor grows faint and the poison is discovered. In both cases, the narrator has fled the scene.

31   Spengemann, 402–03.

32   Margaret W. Ferguson, 165–66.

33   Abdul R. JanMohamed, "The Economy of Manichean Allegory: The Function of Racial Difference in Colonialist Literature," in *"Race," Writing, and Difference*, 80.

34   Hobby claims that this matrix constituted a "web of words" so closely associated that one such quality, for instance honor, would consistently bring all the others to mind. See her *Virtue of Necessity: English Women's Writing, 1649–1688* (London: Virago, 1988), 9; and Moira Ferguson, 21.

35   Nancy Armstrong, *Desire and Domestic Fiction: A Political History of the Novel* (New York: Oxford Univ. Press, 1987).

36   Armstrong, 95.

37   Jenny Sharpe also implicates the discourse of rape in the production of race and gender categories: "The demand on contemporary feminism, then, is to disrupt the taken-for-grantedness of such categories through an excavation of the histories that produce racial and sexual difference" ("The Unspeakable Limits of Rape: Colonial Violence and Counter-Insurgency," *Genders* 10 [Spring 1991]: 26).

38   Susan Jeffords uses the phrase "scenario of protection." She traces a "rhetoric of rape" which has been crucial to the development of American nationalism, and she links the contemporary rhetoric surrounding the 1991 Persian Gulf War and the "rape of Kuwait" to early nationalist fantasies promoted by captivity narratives and the literature of the American Revolution. We borrow her emphasis on protection but work toward a different end. Where she sees the scenario of protection inventing a villain and a protector, we emphasize the creation of the victim, a body (national or individual) worthy of protection. We are also attempting to argue that the discourse of rape in Behn's text, and in the captivity narratives from which she borrows, works to codify race, gender, and nation simultaneously; hence rape is preeminently a social act. Jeffords writes, "The rhetoric of rape and the scenario of protection have little room for discussion of rapes except as they can be metaphorized to stand for a threat to a community at large." We argue that rape is quite literally—not simply metaphorically—a threat to a community at large as well as an act that constitutes a particular body as violable. See

Susan Jeffords, "Rape and the New World Order," *Cultural Critique* 19 (Fall 1991): 203–15.

39 Patterson, 79.

40 Patterson, 11.

41 Behn's depiction seems to fit with Patterson's data on slavery and honor in West African society: "In the struggle for prestige, what was critical in *all* African societies was the number of dependents an ambitious man could acquire. Kinship and the affinal alliances were the two major techniques for accumulating dependents, but a third important means was the institution of slavery. Among many African tribes this was often the sole reason for the acquisition of slaves, there being little or no economic difference between the condition of slaves and their masters and no such thing as a slave class" (Patterson, 83).

42 Beverle Houston notes that "the threatened rape is narrativized in its significance for Oroonoko, the man, not for the woman herself; the woman functions as a token of power exchange among the men" ("Usurpation and Dismemberment: Oedipal Tyranny in *Oroonoko*," *Literature and Psychology* 32 [1986]: 32).

43 The exchange that generates honor here is necessarily an exchange between male and female, each with a specific role to play. Ultimately, however, one's place in the aristocratic hierarchy, not one's gender, defines the transaction. The manifest signs of rank—king, prince, general's daughter—and not the manifest signs of masculinity or femininity determine one's amount of power in the exchange. The Royal Veil is a ceremonial substitute for the hymen; the king "sends the Lady he has a mind to honour with his Bed, a Veil, with which she is cover'd, and secur'd for the King's use" (12). For the female, the veil replaces the honor of virginity with the "honor" of service to the crown.

44 Patterson, 79.

45 He literally "can do nothing" at the end of the novel. Nearly paralyzed beside the dismembered body of Imoinda, he neither fights nor runs. Movement is only possible when he alters his very definition of honor and adopts the "passive valour" of self-mutilation that he has learned from the Surinamese Indians.

46 Imoinda's pregnancy is the first literary characterization of the pregnant female slave, a figure of increasing significance throughout the history of African American women's writing. In this literature, the pregnant female slave is a potent sign of the reproducibility of slave economics. In one moment the figure conveys the nexus of white desire/exploitation/reproduction which is rewritten onto her body.

47 Benita Parry, "Problems in Current Theories of Colonial Discourse," *Oxford Literary Review* 9 (1987): 27–58.

Julie Ellison

Race and Sensibility in the Early Republic: Ann Eliza Bleecker and Sarah Wentworth Morton

O ne could argue, citing the tone of recent American politics, that we are in the midst of a new age of sensibility. Political events now turn on representations of suffering, of which the Rodney King videotape is the premier example. Campaign rhetoric bears witness to pain, as in Albert Gore's account, while accepting the Democratic vice-presidential nomination, of the transforming effect of his son's near-fatal accident. Susan Sontag composes a historical "romance." Economic debates question the value of sympathy as embodied in the welfare state. Academics have repoliticized themselves by defending marginal or minority positions. The political right has counterattacked, charging academics with an overinvestment in victimage. Meanwhile, conservatives themselves use "the culture of pain" to draw sympathy away from groups identified with liberal or radical causes (women, gays and lesbians, racial minorities) and toward the unborn—as in Pat Boone's pro-life music video, "Let Me Live," in which he dreams of infant voices that sing to him of "experiencing life."[1] The former U.S. attorney general, Dick Thornburgh, pushed for the legal validity of victims' testimony and victims' rights in the judicial process. Journalists comment dryly on the current emphasis on male sensitivity across the political spectrum. Everywhere, it seems, we perform the intimate connections between feeling, gender, and otherness.

In this era of politicized emotion, it is not surprising that the history of ideology ("cultural criticism") and the history of feeling ("emotion criticism") are both receiving new scholarly scrutiny.[2] The topic of emotion was ushered into literary studies by the feminist renovation of sentimental genres. In our post-poststructuralist moment, subjectivity has gained in prestige as the route to historical concreteness and agency at the same time that emotion has been redefined as a set of social and cultural practices. But looking at these trends in the context I have sketched out above suggests that the connection between political self-consciousness and sensibility cannot be accounted for simply in terms of shifting academic orientations. Taking advantage of our position within the troubled sensibility of post–Cold War politics and relying on the historical temper of the humanities, we can look again at past relationships between otherness and care, alienation and sympathy. These configurations have always been operative and occasionally dominant in the political culture of the U.S. Our style of political emotion acquired its role as a crucial modern formation in the eighteenth-century idioms of Anglo-American societies, and the predicaments of vicarious relationships in public life have been with us ever since. The intention that I bring to this essay— to map the literary history of emotional politics—is therefore symptomatic of the long-standing conjunction between ideological stress and the language of sympathy. Such efforts as mine arise from precisely the conditions they examine, so that the sentimental habits of the present make the political role of sensibility in the past more visible to us.

Looking at the history of sentimental politics from this perspective means redefining the "Age of Sensibility." This term has been a narrowly literary one, used most often for the melancholy literature of the British "man of feeling" in the later eighteenth century.[3] While the late-eighteenth-century texts of masculine melancholia and sympathy are central to the phenomenon of sensibility, our received view needs to be extended temporally and geographically and made more complex. The "Age of Sensibility" begins much earlier than standard usage permits. One can trace the prestige of manly tears from the political plays of the Exclusion Crisis, through Addison's *Cato* (1713), to the pamphlet literature of the American Revolution.[4] The project of sympathy takes shape in and through the historical stresses of racial and cultural difference in European empires. As early as Addison's treatment of Juba in *Cato* or Steele's "Inkle and Yarico" essay in *The Spectator*—two of the most contagious texts in eighteenth-century literature—race relations and sexual relations in the empire are represented in terms of sympathetic transactions.[5] Sensibility becomes an international style, both in the sense of being exportable (especially, in the American instance, to white colonial literati) and also in the sense of being about race, about what we now call multicultural experience.

Sensibility, then, is not simply a taste for pathos, but a complex discourse of emotional action. Sensibility is sophisticated. Its genres can reflect on their own conventionality. Its conventions register an awareness of the connections between emotion and history, between spectatorship and the suffering body—especially the body of the victim of color. The literature of victimage and pity, tears and melancholia, can be knowledgeable about the market for pain and troubled by early modern forms of liberal guilt. Such writing is composed by writers who understand themselves to be participants in a system, or a web of systems, although no author is conscious of every system simultaneously. Frequently the author understands that trade and colonization are potentially violent practices and that violence can be reflexive or catching, turning back on the dominant society. He or she realizes, too, that sensibility itself can be a means of degradation. In this tradition, melancholy combines with otherness to give mood a historical location.

Sensibility, as Dana Nelson demonstrates, served careerist purposes as well as reformist ones. "Do [women writers] utilize [sentiment] simply as an effective strategy to gain authorial advantage in Anglo-American culture or do they also employ it to proffer an alternative social vision?" she asks. "What are the implications of their sympathetic readings of 'race'?"[6] Nelson applauds the sentimental tradition of white women's writing as it is asserted in some portions or on some levels of the text, while showing how the quest for "authorial advantage" and the staging of middle-class civility as a universal norm shape other aspects of its construction. Sympathy was a paradigm for literary reception, and emotionality—then as now—was a route to the reader. But we should not be too quick to categorize certain texts of sensibility as naive on the basis of their interested relationship to the marketplace, opposing them to sophisticated works that are committed to sympathy as a means of reform. A text may be self-conscious about the connections between gender and genre but defend the feminine by relying on unexamined racial categories, as is the case with the poems of Ann Eliza Bleecker (1752–1783) of upstate New York. Bleecker's poems are reactionary and nonreflective on the issue of race but are nonetheless politically and rhetorically complicated. Her ambivalent desire to stop time at the moment of maternal loss and also to locate that loss in the history of the war for independence is not progressive, but it is not simple either. And a work may sustain a vision of racial harmony but do so only within the framework of an imaginary, premodern masculinity, as in *Ouabi* by Sarah Wentworth Morton (1759–1846) of Boston.

Most crucial to the meaning of sensibility in this period is its role in social or intersubjective encounters, its status as an idiom that specializes in inside-outside transferences. It is precisely this option, the possibility of modulating from the interior fluctuations of fancy to the prospects of historical time and space, that most attracted women poets. The treatment of gender in poetry by women is by no means directed entirely to modalities of the feminine. Gender is always relational, so that a poet of maternal grief like Bleecker both presents white men of her own class as absent in moments of crisis and enhances Indian terror by evoking an aura of masculine predation. Morton, closer to the tradition of Whig sentimentalism and its scenes of male bonding, attributes to masculine friendship a depth of interpersonal transparency not present in heterosexual encounters. For her, the scene of racial concord requires two men, since sexual difference supersedes racial difference in contacts between men and women.

For Bleecker and Morton, the conjunction of melancholia and race provided occasions for significant literary achievement.[7] In looking closely at their work, I want to set forth the thematic and affective dynamics of their poems in terms of the culture of sensibility as I have described it, a culture preoccupied with racial others and with the vexed, often contradictory possibilities for sympathy in the contexts of gendered nationality. I want also to establish the connection between sentimental treatments of race and the development of women's poetry.[8] We need to place Bleecker's and Morton's verse within Anglo-American sensibility and to expand our idea of that culture to include their publications. The study of early American poetry cannot advance by isolating poetry in a generic or territorial preserve. The poetry of national prospects in the tradition of Thomson and Goldsmith, for example, makes historical prophecy possible for American women poets. The classical or scriptural allusion translated into the language of female lament engages certain aspects of high culture, while adaptations of the Indian death song—a genre with a British as well as a North American career—are coded differently. The poems of Bleecker and Morton are full of transatlantic prose influences, too: the captivity narrative, the oriental romance, epistolary conventions, and dramas of sentimental male friendship. So the first step in establishing the importance of these texts for any argument about Anglo-American sentimental culture is the act of generic, or polygeneric, description.

■ ■ ■

Although the poems of both Bleecker and Morton exhibit the defining qualities of North American sensibility, their attitudes about race are markedly dissimilar. Stories of interracial encounter leading to affective crises are common to both. Bleecker—writing as the Revolutionary War churned through her upstate neighborhood and in the midst of exceedingly complex interactions among the Six Nations of the Iroquois, British regulars, indigenous Loyalists, and assorted rebel units—demonizes the Native Americans that Morton glamorizes a decade later.[9] Bleecker laments that she has been doomed to maternal grief by the assaults of male "savages." Indeed, the strength of feminine rage and grief which constitutes the most impressive feature of her poetry is persistently motivated by the chaotic violence of the racial other. She draws heavily on the conventions of captivity narratives, a genre revived (and revised) during the French and Indian War and then during the Revolution. In Bleecker's work, the captivity narrative reveals not only its susceptibility to both pathos and anger but also its investment in powerful feminine mourning that takes the form of an attachment to place. Bleecker's poems reread the Bible, the *Aeneid*, and English landscape poetry in terms that give women's indignant mourning both literary ambition and historical meaning.

Though Morton, too, went on to publish poems of motherly mourning, her first major publication, the long narrative poem *Ouabi* (1790), generously distributes high-minded pathos among a love triangle comprised of one European and two Native American protagonists.[10] The almost equal success in *Ouabi* of the virtuous European's assimilation into the life of the Illinois tribe and the Illinois sachem's convenient death after the white man proves himself worthy to be his successor suggests that heroes of different races may be sentimentally bound to one another in an archaic revenge culture that constructs them as peers. In Morton's vision of racial concord, masculine friendship depends on a primitive social frame. Morton was a committed abolitionist as well as a defender of Native American culture. Bleecker's letters, by contrast, suggest that she accepted the subordination of her family's black servants unquestioningly, if sometimes sentimentally, and she is troubled by race only insofar as she wishes to "give . . . some idea of savage cruelty" in order to "justify our fears."[11] One has to conclude from the comparison that the affinity between racial others and melancholy pleasure in eighteenth-century poetry prevails whether persons of color are heroicized or detested.

Bleecker is characterized by her daughter (and editor) as having always been prone to fluctuations between delight and suffering. Margaretta Faugeres, herself a poet, writes that her mother periodically turned against her own work in the grip of mood swings that catapulted her from "flights of fancy" to "dejection": "she was frequently very lively, and would then give way to the flights of her fertile fancy, and write songs, satires, and burlesque: but, as drawing a cord too tight will make it break, thus she would no sooner cease to be *merry*, than the heaviest *dejection* would succeed, and then all the pieces which were not as melancholy as herself, she destroyed" (xv). With the onset of the war, terror intervened between fancy and melancholia. History's intrusion shattered the self-delighting inventiveness of the retired family. Or at least this is the tale of loss told by the poet in her role as suffering subject.

Though Bleecker was a precocious writer as a girl growing up in a comfortable Manhattan merchant family, her career as a serious but non-publishing author began with her marriage in 1769 at age seventeen. She and her husband John Bleecker, a wealthy lawyer from New Rochelle, moved after a year to a new estate on inherited land at Tomhanick, twelve miles north of Albany. He encouraged Bleecker to preserve her poems for the first time, though they were published only posthumously. The move to Tomhanick not only exposed Bleecker to the traumas that become the subject of her subsequent poetry but also, through the representational options associated with "retirement," affected the choice of poetic genres that she henceforth favors.

The Bleeckers' privileged rural domesticity soon found itself both committed to and at risk from the politics of independence. This predicament is reflected in Bleecker's use of poetic convention. The Tomhanick estate is the central figure in Bleecker's poetry, or rather, the place from which figuration flows. John Barrell has described the "prospect" as a class-inflected view of the landscape in the English poetry of sensibility, an aestheticized vista that signifies leisure.[12] In both English and American contexts, the prospect also permits a view, beyond the present horizon of historical time, of the progress or ruin of empires and nations. Furthermore, the prospect requires a malleable subjectivity or intersubjectivity. The speaker links poetry to history by offering a play-by-play account of the mind's faculties and moods—fancy, imagination, dejection, ambition, prophecy—and their various itineraries at home and abroad, then, now, and in future time. Bleecker's prospective poetry is altered from its British precedents by the fact that war, racial conflict, and national destiny do not observe their habitual remoteness on the poet's horizon. Rather, they break through the frame of leisured sensibility and require different kinds of representation.

Bleecker's writing darkens into elegy, indignant complaint, and anxious topographical surveys after the assaults of Iroquois and British forces around Tomhanick in 1777. With her two children and "a young mulatto girl" (almost certainly a slave), she joins the precipitous retreat from "the infatuated Burgoyne" and his "savages." First her daughter Abella and then, shortly afterwards, her mother and sister die of sickness (v). Under these pressures, the poetry of prospect incorporates the topoi of the captivity narrative.

Bleecker's *History of Maria Kittle*, written in 1779 and published three times posthumously in the 1790s, contains the alternately visceral and refined language of the genre in its later incarnations; "Personifications and mythological references contrast strangely with events: 'Ceres' presides over fields through which screaming Indians run, killing and tearing off scalps. The tomahawking of the pregnant Comelia, with details of her cleft white forehead, the dead staring of her 'fine azure eyes,' and the ripping out of her fetus and dashing it to pieces are unusually concrete, if grim, visualizations. Purple passages describe Maria's sorrows as her abductors drag her to their allies in Montreal."[13] Though set during the French and Indian War (1754–63), the *History of Maria Kittle* conveys Bleecker's sense of the alien terror unleashed upon white women in 1777. Her treatment of Native Americans as instigators of violence against mothers suggests that the popularity of captivity narratives during and immediately after the Revolution was motivated in part by the genre's attention to female victims. The late-eighteenth-century boom in captivity narratives was not caused simply by the settlers' desire to stage an "empowering" assimilation of Native American regions.[14] Nor is it solely the result of the wish to define "the American character by proclaiming the rejection of British culture."[15] The popularity of the genre arises also from the need to express the cultural superiority, physical exposure, and political entanglements of white women. The republication of Rowlandson's 1682 *Narrative* in Boston six times between 1770 and 1773 does suggest, as Sieminski proposes, that feminine captivity could represent the colonies' overall enslavement to the British tyrant as well as Boston's particular status as the victim of a British "massacre," a term for Indian attacks.[16] But the conflation of tyrants and savages as enemies of North American domestic sanctuaries reinforces the republic's civility as well as its capacity for resistance. Unlike some other practitioners of captivity rhetoric, Bleecker does not use the association with the Indians to demonize the British, whom she regards as still capable of politeness. Rather, she locates the whole terror of war in the Iroquois. Because

Bleecker does not write as a former captive but as a virtual, vicarious, or potential victim only, she treats Native Americans as a mobile strike force, as embodied panic, and as an antidomestic energy that frightens families out of their homes, then makes them fall ill.

Faugeres's memoir tells the story of Ann Bleecker's escape from Tomhanick in terms derived from Bleecker's own accounts. The "perfect tranquillity" of an extended family in the "green valley" with "fair prospects . . . opening on every side" had already been disturbed by the looming risk of Burgoyne's attack. While her husband was in Albany looking for another place to live, Bleecker "received intelligence that the enemy were within two miles of the village, burning and murdering all before them." From this moment on the sense of maternal action and maternal anguish pervades the account: "Terrified beyond description she rose from the table and taking her Abella on her arm, and her other daughter (about four years old) by the hand she set off on foot with a young mulatto girl, leaving the house and furniture to the mercy of the approaching savages. The roads were crowded with carriages loaded with women and children, but none could afford her assistance—distress was depictured on every countenance, and tears of heartfelt anguish moistened every cheek" (v–vi). During this phase of the retreat, Bleecker repeatedly sought help—a ride, a room—but was turned away. Finally reunited with her husband in Albany, they joined a group traveling downstream on the Hudson until Abella became too ill to travel.

Then, in 1781, a raiding party of Tories, British regulars, and Hessians (one bearing a tomahawk) seized John Bleecker, an elderly male slave or servant named Merkee, and an unnamed "white servant" while they were harvesting the Bleeckers' crops. Although this was not an Indian attack, the terror of the event confirms Bleecker's sense of the racial horror of the haunted woods. Her revulsion persists despite her appreciation of British sensibility as it manifested itself during John Bleecker's week of captivity. Merkee, an "old Negro," invokes Bleecker's feminine anguish at the very moment of capture while testifying to his own emotional negligibility. "I am an old Negro—no matter for me," Merkee is reported to have said, but "my dear mistress will break her heart" (135–36). Playing off one race against another, Merkee's awareness of her sensibility against enemy savagery, Bleecker goes on to admire the Anglo-American male bonding made possible by the image of her suffering as articulated by the empathetic slave. As the raiding party and its captives travel through the woods, sensibility transcends politics.

Merkee is not mentioned again, but "the British were humane, and wept whenever my sad spouse deplored the mournful fate of his wife and child" (136). John Bleecker is unexpectedly liberated by Connecticut troops six days later. But, as in 1777, the consequence of familial trauma and dislocation is maternal loss. "Soon after I fell into premature labour, and was delivered of a dead child," Ann Bleecker tells her correspondent. "Since that I have been declining" (178).

The instantaneous change from domestic idyll to domestic tragedy in 1777, repeated in 1781, shaped Bleecker's subsequent poetry. Whether she represents herself thereafter as the victim of interludes of deranged violence unleashed by historical events, a mourner whose grief and anger are reactions to a shattered New World pastoral, or a commentator whose personal calamities are located in a narrative overview of the war, Bleecker treats Abella's death as pain cherished in proportion to the horror of its shockingly alien cause. Bleecker regards Abella as the immediate victim of the "cruel savage," of "conflagration in the blooming wild" (221). Abella died because Ann Bleecker had to flee her home, and recovering Tomhanick's groves becomes the trope of completed mourning.

Bleecker's poems center, then, on the "Abella topos," the loss that structures the speaker's relation to all other events and texts. In addition to the many lyrics that respond directly to the child's death, two other kinds of writing reveal the full scope of this trauma. Interweaving characterizations of the Tomhanick estate before and during the fighting, Bleecker describes the war's effect on her Hudson River idyll, presenting the war from the point of view of the domestic female of the landed merchant or professional class.[17] Her spouse, politically engaged and committed to the militia, is mostly absent, and during the war she feels her home to be surrounded by aliens. From this perspective, the fighting becomes a contest over who rules the "shade," the "woods," and the "groves." Abella dies because the forces of darkness take over the woods and issue forth in a rush that becomes Bleecker's figure for the temporality of shock: "Down rush'd the tawny natives from the hill" ("A Pastoral Dialogue," 258).

These prospects, or moments of geographical survey, modulate into personal chronicles of the war which, along with occasional poems such as "Elegy on the Death of Montgomery," narrate the progress toward American independence in terms of the alternation between violence and tranquillity. The pastoral-cum-war-poem becomes a figure for the state of poetry itself, for cultivated genres incongruously called upon to describe terror. The rural sanctuary has already been constructed, by Bleecker herself and by prior poetic convention, as the place that is neither urban nor savage. In these texts, North American captivity narratives by and about women intersect the British poetry of meditative retirement; the poet speaks as the victim, aesthetician, and caretaker of an exposed estate. Britain's ministerial conspiracy is also subsumed under the image of the invisibly-lurking-then-frantically-rushing Indian. The Revolutionary War will purge the woods of all sorts of aliens. Remembering Abella means memorializing and renovating the Bleeckers' groves through the poet's own patriotic elegies.

Bleecker's "Written in the Retreat" declares itself throughout to be written after the retreat, after Abella's death, and in defiance of "relief." The question that Wordsworth will later ask about Nature's intent in the first book of *The Prelude*—"Was it for this?"—calls attention here to the mother's tragic overinvestment in the daughter:

> Was it for this, with thee a pleasing load,
> I sadly wander'd thro' the hostile wood;
> When I thought fortune's spite could do no more,
> To see thee perish on a foreign shore? (215)

The rhetorical question, or protest, is interrupted by the first of several bursts of apostrophe that convey lamentation's resistance into the text of the poem:

> Oh my lov'd babe! my treasure's left behind
> Ne'er sunk a cloud of grief upon my mind;
> Rich in my children—on my arms I bore
> My living treasures from the scalper's pow'r:
> When I sat down to rest beneath some shade,
> On the soft grass how innocent she play'd.
>
> . . . .
>
> Unconscious of her danger, laughing roves,
> Nor dreads the painted savage in the groves. (215–16)

The journey defers but does not evade the threat of the "hostile wood." The maternal power to carry children bodily out of danger—a feminine strength that depends on the catalyzing presence of an embowered enemy—proves temporary, though its force will revive in Bleecker's obstinate grief. When "fallacies" of maternal rescue collapse, the speaker is at first silent before Abella's corpse ("sorrow chain'd my tongue"), then finds her voice in a defense of mourning:

> Then—then my soul rejected all relief,
> Comfort I wish'd not for, I lov'd my grief:
> "Hear, my Abella!" cried I, "hear me mourn,
> "For one short moment, oh! my child return." (216)

The poet becomes fully articulate when she finds an antagonist in the banalities of consolation, which she parodies:

> My friends press round me with officious care,
> Bid me suppress my sighs, nor drop a tear;
> Of resignation talk'd—passions subdue'd,
> Of souls serene and Christian fortitude;
> Bade me be calm, nor murmur at my loss,
> But unrepining bear each heavy cross. (217)

She furiously relegates these false comforters back to the hostile wood, where death dwells in the shape of the savage. Grief frees her from conventional pious submission and permits a newly resistant poetic authority. She rewrites the New Testament to defend a feminine Christ:

> "Go!" cried I raging, "stoick bosoms go!
> "Whose hearts vibrate not to the sound of woe;
> "Go from the sweet society of men,
> "Seek some unfeeling tyger's savage den,
> "There calm—alone—of resignation preach,
> "My Christ's examples better precepts teach."
> Where the cold limbs of gentle *Laz'rus* lay
> I find him weeping o'er the humid clay;
> His spirit groan'd, while the beholders said
> (With gushing eyes) "see how he lov'd the dead!"
> And when his thoughts on great *Jerus'lem* turn'd!
> And sad *Gethsemene's* nocturnal shade
> The anguish of my weeping Lord survey'd:
> Yes, tis my boast to harbour in my breast
> The sensibilities by God exprest. . . . (217)

"*Gethsemene's* nocturnal shade" redeems the hostile wood. Bleecker's woe holds others to the test of sensibility. "Society" comprises the small circle of the dead, the principle mourner, and the "beholders," whose "gushing eyes" confirm their understanding of her love. In a letter of December 1777, Bleecker moves similarly from exasperation to the demand for sympathy: "Curst be the heart that is callous to the feelings of humanity, and which, concentered in itself, regards not the wailings of affliction!" Although she apologizes for her "enthusiasm" or anger, her curse validates her loss. She was "concentered" in Abella, and human community should form itself to her lamentation: "I have supported every shock with tolerable fortitude, except the death of my Abella—She indeed had wound herself round every fibre of my heart—I loved, I idolized her. . . . I could . . . have beheld with less anguish the dissolution of Nature than the last gasp of my infant" (viii–x). Bleecker can move from the testimony of personal suffering to active political assertion and back, but not without relying on the unexamined catalyst of the demonized racial other. Less obvious but also important in this early American version of "the female complaint" is the shadowy "good" otherness of the sympathetic slave or servant (Merkee and the "mulatto girl"), the poet's affective double.[18]

In "On Reading Dryden's Virgil," Bleecker's complaint authorizes her to revise the classics as she has reinterpreted the New Testament. She is audacious in her willingness to plant herself squarely in Virgilian narrative. After casting herself as the weeping reader, she writes herself succinctly into epic loss, retold as the cyclical fate of sensibility. Bleecker's formulaic "scenes of horror"—the fiery vista surveyed from a distance, the yelling savage who represents terror close at hand—establish the connection between the history of the war and the history of the family:

> Now cease these tears, lay gentle *Vigil* [Virgil] by,
> Let recent sorrows dim the pausing eye:
> Shall *Aeneas* for lost *Creusa* mourn,
> And tears be wanting on *Abella's* urn?
> Like him I lost my fair one in my flight
> From cruel foes—and in the dead of night.
> Shall he lament the fall of *Illion's tow'rs*,
> And we not mourn the sudden ruin of *our's*?
> See *York* on fire—while borne by winds each flame
> Projects its glowing sheet o'er half the main:
> Th'affrighted savage, yelling with amaze,
> From *Allegany* sees the rolling blaze.
> Far from these scenes of horror, in the shade,

I saw my *aged parent* safe convey'd;
Then sadly follow'd to the friendly land,
With my *surviving infant* by the hand.
No cumb'rous houshold gods had I indeed
To load my shoulders, and my flight impede;
The hero's idols sav'd by *him* remain;
My gods took care of me—not *I* of *them*!
The Trojan saw *Anchises* breathe his last,
When all domestic dangers he had pass'd:
So my lov'd *parent*, after she had fled,
Lamented, perish'd on a stranger's bed.
—*He* held his way o'er the Cerulian Main,
But *I* return'd to hostile fields again. (230–31)

Bleecker focuses on the moment in Book II of the *Aeneid* when Aeneas—having led his small son, his father, and his wife Creusa out of the fires of Troy—realizes that Creusa is lost. Distraught and disoriented, he returns to Troy to look for her. The ghost of Creusa appears to him and accepts her role as a sacrifice to the Roman future—a consolation perhaps available to but disregarded by Bleecker. Bleecker sympathizes with the hero who mourns his own inattention sufficiently to return home for his wife; she measures her difference from him by staying there.[19] In her poem, the "hostile fields" are sought out as the place of mourning and are still contested through the energy of maternal, as opposed to patriarchal, attachment.

Bleecker's several poems of female dialogue, pastorals in a time of war, show clearly how her sufferings during the Revolutionary War connect local and national perspectives. In "To Miss Ten Eyck," one of two poems addressed in an epistolary vein to her half-sister, Bleecker imagines her distant correspondent in an idealized pastoral of feminine pleasure replete with "sylvan bow'rs," "salubrious flow'rs," and moonlit reflections: "[You] view your blushes mant'ling in the stream, / When Luna gilds it with her amber beam." If "Kitty" blushes in New Jersey, the poet blanches in New York: "The brazen voice of war awakes our fears, / Impearling every damask cheek with tears." The story she tells here resembles the captivity related in the *History of Maria Kittle*, complete with the captivity narrative's mandatory scene of the mutilated baby. In such poems as these, Bleecker participates in the adaptation of the captivity narrative to the purposes of anti-British propaganda but also uses patriotic resistance to

Britain to fuel demonic representations of Native Americans, so that race and nationality are conflated to form the enemy of rural mothers. In dramatizing the rape of the pastoral, Bleecker's images tumble over one another, and it is briefly unclear whether the savage is terrifying a human or animal couple:

> The savage, rushing down the echoing vales,
> Frights the poor hind with ill portending yells;
> A livid white his consort's cheeks invest;
> She drops her blooming infant from her breast;
> She tries to fly, but quick recoiling sees
> The painted Indian issuing from the trees
>
> . . . .
>
> Oh horrid sight! her partner is no more;
> Pale is his corse, or only ting'd with gore.
> Her playful babe is dash'd against the stones,
> Its scalp torn off, and fractur'd all its bones.
> Where are the dimpling smiles it lately wore?
> Ghastly in agony it smiles no more!
> Dumb with amaze, and stupify'd with grief,
> The captur'd wretch must now attend her chief. . . . (231–32)

This assault leads Bleecker to an apocalyptic prospect. "Half the land" and the entire sky are filled with the "conflagration" set by the enemy. The device of the vista, so productive of emotional responses to history in this period, returns Bleecker to the mode of epistolary lament: "Such are our woes, my dear." The moon accentuates "Albania's [Albany's] sons" who "every street patrole": "thro' the night / Their beamy arms reflect a dreadful light." The poem ends abruptly with an apology for "this plaintive strain," acknowledging the way pastoral, under duress, can "transgress" its conventions and turn into complaint (232).

When Bleecker celebrates the end of the war in "Peace," she focuses on exorcising the woods, whose natural shade must dispel associations with racial otherness and terror. "The groves we now safely explore, / Where murd'ring banditti, the dark sons of treason, / Were shelter'd and aw'd," she exults, once again reversing "the aspect of the land" to its proper serenity. The "swain with his oxen" gives thanks "that *Britain's* black ally / Is chas'd to *Canadia's* deep woods." With the Indians relegated to someone else's woods, Bleecker reappropriates the trees for the purposes of republican panegyric:

Echo no longer is plaintively mourning,
  But laughs and is jocund as we;
And the turtle ey'd nymphs, to their cots all returning,
Carve "WASHINGTON," on every tree. (252)

The recurring scene of the Indian issuing from "his dark recess / With fell intent" reappears in Bleecker's most overtly political poem on the war, "A Pastoral Dialogue." "Pastoral dialogue," a genre designating the conversational ethic of women, describes attacks on, precisely, the pastoral. Pastoral, however, has the last word. Because it is capable, finally, of telling the story of the Revolution from the point of view of the winners, it narrates its own victory. Two large prospects are at work in this poem. The allegorized history of political events leading up to the Revolution—in which the protagonists are *"Columbia," "George," "Virtue," "Oppression,"* and *"Freedom"*—alternates with a more sensuous, descriptive account of the Hudson River Valley as the figure of *"Desolation"* storms through it.

The dialogue (between "Susanna" and "Eliza") begins with the dilemma of its own composition at the point when an American victory was likely but not yet achieved: "these hostile shades refuse / Admission to the lute or peaceful Muse." The "awkward swain" carries a musket, not a crook, and the poet protests that, under the circumstances, she is not up to the pastoral genre: "From undissembled grief my numbers flow, / And few the graces that attend on woe." Urged to "sing" despite (or because of) her melancholy frame of mind, Eliza summarizes the history of European settlement in North America, recites the causes of the war, and recounts British onslaughts on American abundance. The settlers "with incessant toil" created a landscape of cottages, "golden harvests," and "harbours open'd wide" to "wealthy ships." Then Bleecker's middle-class utopia of industrious citizens encountered the "ambitious homicide," George III, egged on by "the hydra Envy" to restrict American freedoms and successes. The colonies are conventionally portrayed as an emotional suppliant or victim: *"Columbia* weeps, she kneels before the throne, / But plaints, and tears, and sighs, avail her none" (254–56). Mourning is inseparable from resistance for Bleecker, however, and Columbia (abruptly, but logically, according to Bleecker's habitual link between tears and defiance) rallies and fights.

Bleecker's narrative of the war focuses on the depredations carried out in the Hudson River Valley. The title, "A Pastoral Dialogue," is followed by quasi-dramatic designations of time and place: "scene—Tomhanick.

1780." When the figure of the Iroquois—*"Britannia's ally,"* who "from his dark recess / With fell intent invades the shades of Peace"—enters, the "scene" shifts away from the general history of the colonies to Bleecker's own position. "Look from this point," the speaker directs her companion, "where op'ning glades reveal" the prospect that is about to be assaulted: "The glassy *Hudson* shining 'twixt the hills; / There many a structure dress'd the sleepy shore, / And all beyond were daily rising more." After a lengthy passage lauding cultivated and natural abundance, terror strikes: "Down rush'd the *tawny natives* from the hill." The difference between white women and the combined forces of the "dark sons of Treason" (Tories) and their "black" allies (Indians) becomes the difference between peace and war. "Every place" is filled "with fire and murder" distributed by natives or nativized assailants "Arm'd with the hatchet and a flaming brand." The consequence is topographical; the attackers

> reverse the aspect of the land:
> Observe, *Susanna*, not a bird is there,
> The tall burnt trees rise mournful in the air,
> Nor man nor beast the smoking ruins explores,
> And *Hudson* flows more solemn by these shores. (257–58)

The poet, who referred to her own mourning earlier, now sees the effects of her poem on her "Echo," Susanna: "ah! I see thee turn away and mourn, / Thy feeling heart with silent anguish torn." But pathos again leads to defiance, and melancholia to martial vigor. If mourning leads Bleecker in some poems to resist false comforters and in others to revise the masculine epics of imperial history, here Susanna's "silent anguish" provokes partisan noise. "Cheer up," says Eliza, and shifts from lament over a lost pastoral to fervent personifications insisting that paradise can be regained. She points to divine intervention ("His obvious arm how lately interpos'd, / To render Britain's *northern phalanx* vain") and then to the invincible team of Freedom and Conquest ("For *Conquest* loves to be on *Freedom's* side"). The poem ends abruptly with a vision of Britain's "disappointed navy" in retreat and with the racket of victory: "acclamations fill the region round, / And from their hollow ships loud shouts rebound" (259).

"A Pastoral Dialogue" links pastoral ground to the fluctuating voice of the female poet. It develops a topography that accommodates suffering and aggression. Both moods, terror leading to melancholia and melancholia leading to indignation, rely on the figure of the Indian for their affective charge. When mourning turns to anger, the "aspect of the land" can be reversed once more, this time in favor of the white woman poet. Sadness is transformed into energy once it finds an enemy. Bleecker revises the relationship between sensibility and otherness, so that victimage produces revenge. Her vision of winning means both coming home—"all hail my well-known trees!"—and thinking nationally—"I told them I could not see how they dared break through the confederacy while they were sensible all America's happiness depended upon the union" (260, 153). Her version of sensibility leads not to an ideology of republican motherhood but to one of republican mourning. The nation appears where the child once was, as a figure of memory and compensation.

■ ■ ■

Bleecker juxtaposes the racist terror of the captivity narrative to feminine sanctuaries in order to accentuate women's risk and exposure. Sarah Wentworth Morton's celebration of the link between melancholia and virtue transforms into narrative romance another genre that was doing well during the late eighteenth century, the Indian death song. Morton, in Boston, had greater access to and sympathy for the idealizations of liberal ethnography. Along with Mercy Otis Warren and Judith Sargent Murray, Morton was prominent in the literary renaissance among liberal privileged women in revolutionary and early national Boston. She is certainly the most sentimental of the three, and, not surprisingly, the most absorbed in "writing race."[20]

Werner Sollors and others have documented the conjunction of white courtship narratives and Indian death songs or tales of Indian suicide, a configuration that became popular in the 1780s and lasted until about 1840. The fascination with Native American melancholia, part of the widespread "vanishing Indian" topos, was a transatlantic phenomenon. The "Son of Alknomook," the song performed in Royall Tyler's *The Contrast* (1787) by "our profound and republican heroine . . . alone and 'disconsolate,'" had a wide American circulation.[21] But the English poet Ann Hunter (1742–1821)—the aunt of Joanna Baillie, known for her dramatizations of "the Passions"—published perhaps the earliest version of this text in 1782. The fact that "Son of Alknomook" can be traced back to Ann Hunter, who published her first poem in 1765, suggests that the Indian death song was not an exclusively North American genre but one that emerged in the North Atlantic poetry of an Anglo-American sensibility deeply preoccupied with race.[22]

Sollors offers a persuasive rationale for the North American variants of the "surprising conjunction of romantic love, arranged marriage, and Indian melancholy" in melodrama and other art forms. As he argues, this thematic mixture helps justify white republicanism: "As cursing-blessing elders the Indians conveyed a sense of chosen peoplehood to the sentimental heroines and heroes as well as to the weeping readers and viewers of these fictions. As melancholy figures they reminded white Americans of the passage of time and of the march of empires. As Saturnine characters they seemed to promise the return of the golden age in the new world while dreaming the power dream that is so characteristic of melancholy. The noble chieftains thus conveyed a sense of legitimacy to whites who imagined them."[23] But two things are missing from Sollors's account of "Indian melancholy": the importance in Britain—and thus in sensibility's larger imperial context—of the conjunction of melancholy and racial difference, and the importance of gender. The literature of sensibility relies on sorrow to connect gender to race. Race and gender become figurations of each other. Suffering maternity can be a way of intensifying scenes of racial violence, as in Bleecker's texts, and sympathy toward the racial other becomes a way of demonstrating the idealistic scope of the white woman poet, as in the case of Morton.[24]

Under her pen name "Philenia," Sarah Wentworth Morton published three long narrative poems in the genres of sentimental politics: *Ouabi, Or the Virtues of Nature, An Indian Tale in Four Cantos* (1790); *Beacon Hill, a Local Poem, Historic and Descriptive* (1797), which moves from topographical prospects to the history of the war, to end with a "Prophetic Apostrophe to the Progress of Freedom"; and *The Virtues of Society: A Tale Founded on Fact* (1799), the story of an Englishwoman's pursuit through American lines of her captured husband. *Ouabi*, then, which develops an already operative cultural connection between sentiment and Native Americans, marks the self-conscious beginning of a female career.

Prior to this first publication, Morton had arrived on the American literary scene through an ordeal of embarrassment. As a consequence of her husband's attraction for her younger sister, who later committed suicide, Morton saw herself written into "The Story of Ophelia," the "incestuous" subplot of William Hill Brown's *The Power of Sympathy* (1789). Cathy N. Davidson has pointed out the way in which *The Power of Sympathy* conflated "truth" and exposé, a strategy most evident in Isaiah Thomas's marketing strategy, which foregrounded the novel's link to the

Apthorp-Morton scandal.[25] A year after the publication of *The Power of Sympathy*, Morton dedicated *Ouabi* to James Bowdoin. The former governor of Massachusetts and a family friend, Bowdoin had conducted (with John Adams) the official investigation of Fanny's suicide. Morton's personal response to the scandal combined dignified public loyalty to her husband with significant personal estrangement.[26] Her literary response was indirect but pointed.

Ouabi defines the "virtues of nature" as the qualities that make possible the honorable negotiation of extramarital love. Celario, "Europe's fairest boast," rescues the radiantly innocent Illinois woman Azâkia from rape at the hands of a Huron enemy. A triangular dilemma ensues. Celario lusts after Azâkia from the moment he sees her, while also bonding passionately with Ouabi, her spouse. Ouabi, the Illinois sachem, is tender to his friends but perpetually and vengefully at war with the Hurons. Azâkia is powerfully attracted to Celario but unambivalently loyal to Ouabi. Ouabi generously understands the dynamics between the two of them and finally permits Celario to earn Azâkia through heroic demonstrations, on the field of battle, of loyalty to himself. The terms of Native American "marriage," as described by Morton, are flexible enough to permit the satisfaction of both desire and honor. Thus *Ouabi* is in some ways the pointed antithesis of the novel of seduction. But its affective commitments—to high-minded eroticism that crosses the boundaries of cultural difference, to tormented male friendship, to female fantasy, and to the ever-present option of suicide—clearly belong to the discourse of seduction in the early republic.[27] They show how closely related sentimental seduction plots and narratives of race relations could be, and how together these elements provide a way for female authors to explore the psychology of power.

In this context, anthropology is a masculine discipline that women study. Morton's introduction and footnotes contain the poem's most self-conscious rhetoric, in both senses of the word "self-conscious": at once embarrassed and sophisticated. The volume opens with the dedication to Bowdoin of Morton's "wholly American" production, signed "Philenia." This is followed by a constipated letter from Bowdoin thanking Morton for the dedication and chiding her on her pseudonym: "In room of Philenia, he thinks it would be best the real name of the fair author should be substituted."

Morton's own "Introduction" is really a set of acknowledgments in which she enumerates her sources, especially Major General Benjamin Lincoln, whose "obliging communications" on "local rites and customs" constitute the "best information" available, and William Penn, who attests to the Indians' "comely, European-like faces" and their capacity for friendship, self-control, and self-government. She introduces anecdotal proof that "an amiable and polished European" can become an assimilated Native American under the influence of love.[28] She took the story of *Ouabi*, she says, from a prose tale in "Mr. Carey's entertaining and instructing Museum" (*The American Museum*, Carey's Philadelphia magazine), which she does not hesitate to criticize and improve. Ethnography, Morton suggests, conducted in a "liberal" but patriotic spirit, is the woman writer's best defense against charges of enthusiasm. Relying on anthropological "authorities" allows her to tell a tale of spouse-switching and sentimental friendship between men of different races in terms of Native American rituals:

> Sanctioned by such authorities I flatter myself, allowing for the justifiable embellishments of poetry, that I shall not be considered an enthusiast in my descriptions. The liberal reader will, I trust, make many allowances for the various imperfections of the work, from a consideration of my sex and education; the one by education incident to weakness, the other from duty devoted to domestic avocations. And I am induced to hope, that the attempting a subject wholly American will in some respect entitle me to the partial eye of the patriot; that, as a young author, I shall be received with tenderness, and, as an involuntary one, be criticized with candor. (viii)[29]

Indian lore provides a screen for idealism. Or rather, respect for the racial other is assimilated to national loyalty, a shift that legitimates one set of idealizations by invoking another.

Celario, having fled Europe after a duel or other accidental murder, has wandered into the North American interior where, "in hopeless exile," he "mourn[s] the tedious day" (10). One wonders whether Celario catches the habit of auto-elegiac reflection from the Native Americans he encounters or whether he transmits sadness to them from the Old World. Having come to America afflicted with guilt and disenchantment, looking for a native cure, Celario would seem to bring melancholia to the Illinois. But Ouabi, the singer of the "Death Song" who concedes Azâkia to Celario and then dies, makes virtuous suicide look more indigenous than imported. And Azâkia, driven by folkloric authority to interpret her dreams literally, is only restrained from killing herself by the strength of her promise to Celario to postpone such drastic action. All three take turns offering to die for one another, showing repeatedly that suicide is proof of natural virtue, as well as providing an ostensibly nonaggressive way for the white male to win.

Ouabi is largely about sentimental homosocial dilemmas. Morton celebrates the bond between a European fleeing a duel gone wrong and a Native American sachem dedicated to a culture of hand-to-hand combat and personal revenge (19). This masculine primitivism allows Morton implicitly to criticize contemporary Anglo-American masculinity, with its adulterous insincerity and antiheroic attention to business. It also lets her favor a blend of sentiment and aggression in a way quite different from the connection between mourning and energy in Bleecker's poems. In *Ouabi*, sensibility leads to action, and masculine suffering is catalytic, not receptive. The passionate terrain reflects the emotional velocity of its inhabitants, and even their death songs react passionately to "the flames":

Where MISSISSIPPI rolls his *parent flood*
With slope impetuous to the surgy main,
The desert's painted chiefs explore the wood,
Or with the thund'ring *war-whoop* shake the plain.

There the fierce *sachems* raise the battle's din,
Or in the stream their active bodies lave,
Or midst the flames their fearless songs begin—
PAIN HAS NO TERRORS TO THE TRULY BRAVE. (10)

By contrast, the feminine melancholia that afflicts Azâkia produces the mental hyperactivity of suffering that has no outlet in action. In the opening episode of the poem, Celario draws "the deathful tube" (thereby introducing firearms into mid-America) and saves Azâkia from rape at the hands of a Huron brave. Her stance as a "soft captive" who "sickens with alarms" and calls on someone who is not there (Ouabi) positions her as the one who suffers vicariously with and on behalf of male protagonists. Her suicidal desires, when she is later convinced that Ouabi has died, stem from dreams and fantasies that are shown to be erroneous (34, 41). Azâkia, whose experience is imaginative and figurative, dramatizes the connection between stasis, suffering, and poetry. Only through negotiations between the two men can her desire for Celario be fulfilled. Her feelings have the same transparent integrity as theirs and her psychological life is far richer, but she is never instrumental.

Celario's Italianate masculinity is marked by a similar proneness to mental torments. The poem implies that he has been unfairly punished, "banish'd" from his "native shore" after an honorable fight. Though he is disgusted now by Europe's "perfidious vice" and "the glare of wealth" (15), he is still looking for a place where he can fight unimpeded. He explains: "Far beyond the orient main, / By my rage a youth was slain; / He this daring arm defied, / By this arm the ruffian died" (12). Celario is delighted to discover that the North American interior is dominated by feuds between the Illinois and the Hurons and governed by an enthusiastic ethic of revenge. Indeed, the Hurons, as "bad Indians," are not very different from Bleecker's "scalpers." "Revenge," Morton specifies in one of her many ethnographic footnotes, is cultivated by the Indians as "one of their first virtues," but one taught "rather [as] a deliberate sentiment of the mind, than a rash ebullition of passion" (15, 29).

Given to choleric and sexual passions, Celario suffers from guilty feelings that do not afflict the Native Americans for whom revenge is a system, not a mood. Celario's guilt—especially the guilt that follows his erotic stares at Azâkia—is a sign of the European decadence that Ouabi heals. When Ouabi enters while he is trying unsuccessfully to seduce Azâkia, "*Celario's* cheek betrays the conscious glow"; he stands "with averted mien, / Struck to the soul, by secret guilt oppress'd" (26). Ouabi proves his wisdom by entrusting his tribe, and particularly Azâkia, to the wounded Celario's care while he goes off to war. Overcome by Ouabi's generous trust, Celario launches into a rhapsodic hymn to masculine sensibility and homosocial friendship:

Native reason's piercing eye,
Melting pity's tender sigh,
Changeless virtue's living flame,
Meek contentment, free from blame,
Open friendship's gen'rous care,
EV'RY BOON OF LIFE IS HERE! (27)

In response to Ouabi's earlier questions about what ails Europeans, Celario itemizes the "traitors of the mind": terror, guilt, envy, fear, suspicion, affectation, passion, and more (17). Ouabi treats guilt, not desire, as Celario's problem, a diagnosis with which Celario concurs much later, confessing his "guilty flame" and "perfidious art" (43–44):

Thus great *Ouabi* sooths with gentle care
The guilty anguish of *Celario's* breast,

Dissuades his purpose from the coming war,
And calms his stormy passions into rest. (28)

The relationship between guilt and homosocial bonding is very strong here, as it is throughout the literature of sensibility. Moral differentials, as well as power differentials, frequently organize scenes of masculine affection. One man becomes emotionally transparent to another when his guilt is perceived and forgiven. Morton's focus on masculine love is pertinent both to her defense of Native Americans and to her concern with how men treat women. Ouabi dramatizes the moral rescue of European manhood by means of Indian friendship. And Celario's ability to restrain his impulses toward seduction, with Ouabi's help, advances him toward a noncoercive marriage with Azâkia.

After Celario and Ouabi have been saved by each other, the two friends are briefly poised in moral equality. But Ouabi quickly removes himself from competition with Celario, bowing out not once but several times over. He renounces his "marriage" to Azâkia so that she and Celario can finally become the couple they were always meant to be. Ouabi vows to pursue a career of revenge but quickly selects another woman in a spirit of sexual pragmatism and formal symmetry: now there can be a double wedding. Finally, during the celebratory dance, he collapses and dies (47). Morton thus gives Ouabi two death scenes: the earlier one in which he sings a "Death Song" while being tortured by the Hurons and his actual last words delivered near the end of the poem. In this final speech, Ouabi interprets the meaning of his demise and completes Celario's assimilation into the tribe by sending him off to war in his stead: "*Celario!* thou my place sustain, / The chiefs expect thee on the plain" (48).

Ouabi's exit conforms to the plot of the "Vanishing American" syndrome in texts by white writers, according to which Indians die bravely at each other's hands or sing themselves to death alone in the forest.[30] The structural convenience of this device, of course, lies in the way North America depopulates itself to make room for white settlement. Morton downplays the sense of pathetic belatedness that pervades some versions of the Indian death song. Ouabi is not unhappy in love but drawn to war. His proleptic death song refuses the stoicism featured in *The Contrast* ("the son of Alknomook will never complain") in favor of defiance: "*Rear'd midst the war-empurpled plain, / What Illinois submits to pain!*"[31] Still, Ouabi's song ends by confronting the problem of succession: "*Think not with me my tribe decays, / More glorious chiefs the hatchet raise; / Not unreveng'd their sachem dies"* (37). The new sachem is Celario. Having thought he was about to enjoy "pleasure, wealth, and fame" with Azâkia (47), Celario finds himself slated to re-enact the energizing but endlessly repetitive contest with the Illinois's peers, the Hurons.

Ouabi ends with a double coda. The first, within the frame of the Indian tale, focuses on the "spot" where Ouabi is buried and its transformation into a monument where his "NATIVE VIRTUES shine." The three stanzas dedicated to the "sacred pile" honored by "each lonely *Illinois*" are heavily glossed. One footnote comments on Native Americans' visitations to the "sepulchres . . . of their chiefs" and to "rites and ceremonies" performed there, rites "not precisely known to the Anglo-Americans." Another note describes the physical appearance of the burial pile and likens it to ancient structures of England and Wales (50), a comparison that prepares the way for the parallels between Anglo-Saxon and Native American virtue claimed in the poem's concluding lines. A typographical ornament isolates the last two stanzas of the book. Here Morton addresses the republic:

> Let not the CRITIC, with disdainful eye,
> In the weak verse condemn *the novel plan*;
> But own, that VIRTUE beams in *ev'ry sky*,
> Tho wayward frailty is the lot of man.
>
> Dear as ourselves to hold each faithful friend,
> To treat the path, which INNATE LIGHT inspires,
> To guard our country's *rites*, her soil defend,
> Is all that NATURE, all that HEAV'N requires. (50–51)

In juxtaposing these two concluding passages, Morton implies that "our country's *rites*" are analogous to, not destructive of, the Native American practices of piety and war to which Celario has been converted. By eliding the difference between the "rites" of Anglo-American and Indian cultures, Morton shows her occasional ability to regard her own culture anthropologically. Both the Illinois nation and the United States, these stanzas suggest, must honor their dead, bring marriage in line with desire, and defend their territories. This parallelism works only as long as the Americans are thought of defending themselves against the British, not against the Illinois. For once Native and white Americans want to defend the same soil against each other, therapeutic parallels break down. Morton, sensing this, lets Ouabi withdraw before he is beaten.

Morton, like Bleecker, relies on the connection between emotion and historicity. Racial issues are experienced, in the poems of both writers, as collective, national, or public realities. Race is inseparable from the politics of war, whether war occurs in the context of the Iroquois alliance that haunts Bleecker or the Huron-Illinois rivalry that structures Morton's *Ouabi*. At the same time, emotion takes the form of longing, and melancholia becomes a figure for subjectivity itself. If race is a historical theme and if subjectivity is inseparable from melancholy, then the Age of Sensibility can be defined by its focus on the moments when consciousness dilates to historical horizons and when history is compressed into consciousness. The "rites" of grief—Bleecker's mourning for Abella, inseparable from her Indian-hating commitment to national unity, and Morton's admiration for both Native American and Anglo-American memorials, inseparable from her liberal urban patriotism—are central to the careers of both. Eighteenth-century American poetry, if properly located in the culture of sensibility, becomes an allegory of why we cannot explain the relationships between gender, genre, feeling, and race in terms of the distinction between public and private spheres. Even as the notions of such spheres were being formulated in Anglo-American gender ideology, the literature of sensibility challenged the distinction by showing how history and feeling engage in mutual transformations.

Notes

I am grateful to my colleague Kerry Larson for his helpful comments on this essay.
1   See David Morris, *The Culture of Pain* (Berkeley: Univ. of California Press, 1991). Lauren Berlant showed "Let Me Live" during her lecture, "America, 'Fat,' the Fetus," delivered under the auspices of CSST (Comparative Study of Social Transformations), University of Michigan, 1 April 1992.
2   I first encountered the term "emotion criticism" in an unpublished manuscript by Keith Opdahl.
3   For an overview of the term, see Janet Todd, *Sensibility: An Introduction* (New York: Methuen, 1986).
4   This lineage for masculine sensibility descends through scenes between stern fathers (or father figures) and weeping sons in Whig "Roman plays." These plays include Nathaniel Lee's *Lucius Junius Brutus*, suppressed in 1680; Lucius Junius Brutus plays by Gildon (1703), Bond (1733), and Duncombe (1734); Addison's *Cato* (1713); and Thomson's *Sophinisba* (1730).

On the connection between *Cato, Cato's Letters*, and American revolutionary pamphlets, see Bernard Bailyn, *The Ideological Origins of the American Revolution* (Cambridge: Harvard Univ. Press, 1967), chap. 2. "Whig Sentimentalism" is Kenneth Silverman's term for the curiously overwrought tone of the writings first of English Opposition Whigs and later of colonial pamphleteers (*A Cultural History of the American Revolution* [New York: Columbia Univ. Press, 1976], 82–87). For more on masculine affect in early American contexts, see Jay Fliegelman, *Prodigals and Pilgrims: The American Revolution Against Patriarchal Authority* (New York: Cambridge Univ. Press, 1982).

5   Lawrence M. Price documents the proliferating treatments of the Inkle and Yarico story in numerous languages, and in genres ranging from verse to ballet in his *Inkle and Yarico Album* (Berkeley: Univ. of California Press, 1937). For more recent treatments see Felicity Nussbaum's "Introduction" to the special issue on "The Politics of Difference" of *Eighteenth-Century Studies* 23 (1990): 375–86; and Peter Hulme, *Colonial Encounters: Europe and the Native Caribbean, 1492–1797* (New York: Methuen, 1986), 225–63.

6   Dana D. Nelson, *The Word in Black and White: Reading "Race" in American Literature, 1638–1867* (New York: Oxford Univ. Press, 1992), 67, 145.

7   Bleecker and Morton are representative of a general preoccupation with race among women writers. For a detailed discussion of antislavery poetry by women, see Moira Ferguson, *Subject to Others: British Women Writers and Colonial Slavery, 1760–1834* (New York: Routledge, 1992). On race relations during the American Revolution, see David Brion Davis, *The Problem of Slavery in the Age of Revolution, 1770–1823* (Ithaca: Cornell Univ. Press, 1975); Gary B. Nash, *Race, Class, and Politics: Essays on American Colonial and Revolutionary Society* (Urbana: Univ. of Illinois Press, 1986), esp. chap. 11, "Forging Freedom: The Emancipation Experience in the Northern Seaports, 1775–1820"; Roger Bruns, *Am I Not A Man and a Brother: The Anti-Slavery Crusade of Revolutionary America, 1688–1788* (New York: Chelsea, 1977); Duncan J. MacLeod, *Slavery, Race, and the American Revolution* (New York: Cambridge Univ. Press, 1974). See also Sidney Kaplan and Emma Nogrady Kaplan, *The Black Presence in the Era of the American Revolution*, rev. ed. (Amherst: Univ. of Massachusetts Press, 1989).

8   The on-line MLA Bibliography shows no entries for either Bleecker or Morton other than the facsimile edition of Morton's *My Mind and Its Thoughts in Sketches, Fragments, and Essays*, ed. William K. Bottorff (1823; Delmar, N.Y.: Scholars' Facsimiles and Reprints, 1975). Several recent books have provided valuable readings of eighteenth-century poetry by (mostly British) women; see Marlon Ross, *The Contours of Masculine Desire: Romanticism and the Rise of Women's Poetry* (New York: Oxford Univ. Press, 1989); Donna Landry, *The Muses of Resistance: Laboring-Class Women's Poetry in Britain, 1739–1796* (New York: Cambridge Univ. Press, 1990); and Ferguson, *Subject to Others*. Pattie Cowell's *Women Poets in Pre-Revolutionary America, 1650–*

1775: An Anthology (Troy, N.Y.: Whitston, 1981) is a good resource, helped along by *The Heath Anthology of American Literature*. Cheryl Walker's new anthology, *American Women Poets of the Nineteenth Century* (New Brunswick: Rutgers Univ. Press, 1992) provides selections from the period immediately after the one I am concerned with here. *The Collected Works of Phillis Wheatley*, edited by John Shields for the Schomburg Library of Nineteenth-Century Black Women Writers (New York: Oxford Univ. Press, 1988), is invaluable.

9   See Barbara Graymont, *The Iroquois in the American Revolution* (Syracuse: Syracuse Univ. Press, 1972); Isabel Thompson Kelsay, *Joseph Brant, 1743–1807: Man of Two Worlds* (Syracuse: Syracuse Univ. Press, 1984); *Chainbreaker: The Revolutionary War Memoirs of Governor Blacksnake as told to Benjamin Williams*, ed. Thomas S. Abler (Lincoln: Univ. of Nebraska Press, 1989); and Nash, *Race, Class, and Politics*. See also Thomas J. Davis, *A Rumor of Revolt: The 'Great Negro Plot' in Colonial New York* (New York: Free Press, 1985), chaps. 1–3; and Stefan Beilinski, "Episodes in the Coming of Age of an Early American Community: Albany, N.Y., 1780–1793," in *World of the Founders: New York Communities in the Federal Period*, ed. Stephen L. Schechter and Wendell Tripp (Albany: New York State Commission on the Bicentennial of the United States Constitution, 1990), 117–19.

10   *Ouabi, Or the Virtues of Nature, An Indian Tale in Four Cantos* (Boston: I. Thomas and E. T. Andrews, 1790). All subsequent references to *Ouabi* will be cited parenthetically in the text. Morton's poems of maternal mourning appear in *My Mind and Its Thoughts*: "Stanzas / To my late lovely and beloved daughter Charlotte, at the age of fifteen," 67–68; "Memento, / For my Infant, who lived but eighteen hours," 255–56; "Lamentations / of an unfortunate mother, over the tomb of her only son (1)," 260–61; "Stanzas, / occasioned by the question of a friend, 'What has preserved you?'" 263; "Lines / enclosing the beautiful ringlets of my son," 264; "Apostrophe / to the memory of my beloved daughter Charlotte, / Fragment," 264–65; "Lines, / to those who have said, 'You are tranquil,'" 265–66.

11   *The Posthumous Works of Ann Eliza Bleecker in Prose and Verse. To which is added, A Collection of Essays, Prose and Poetical, by Margaretta V. Faugeres* (New York, 1793), 146. All subsequent references will be cited parenthetically in the text. Published by Faugeres in 1793, Bleecker's *Posthumous Works* includes poems; correspondence; *History of Maria Kittle*; and "The Story of Henry and Anne," the tale of a poor couple's emigration to America from quasi-feudal Europe. The citation is from a letter that accompanies a manuscript of *History of Maria Kittle*. "I take the freedom to trouble you with a little history," Bleecker explains, "written some time ago for Susan [Susan Ten Eyck, Bleecker's half-sister], which being altogether a fact, may give you some idea of savage cruelty, and at the same time will justify our fears in your opinion" (146). It would be necessary to delve into local records to ascertain definitely if the black men and women Bleecker refers to as "old

Merkee" and "a young mulatto girl" were slaves, but the prevalence of slave-holding in upstate New York late into the century and Bleecker's locutions suggest that this is the case. In one letter she refers to Merkee and the white servant together as simply "two servants," which may suggest that Merkee is not a slave (179). But on the names of slaves and freed African Americans in northern cities, see Nash, *Race, Class, and Politics*, 294–98. "Merkee" resembles what Nash identifies as slave names rather than the names of free blacks.

12 John Barrell, *English Literature in History, 1730–80: An Equal, Wide Survey* (New York: St. Martin's, 1983), chap. 1, "An Unerring Gaze: The Prospect of Society in the Poetry of James Thomson and John Dyer."

13 L. W. Koengeter, entry on Bleecker, in *American Women Writers*, ed. Lina Mainiero (New York: Frederick Ungar, 1979).

14 Richard Slotkin, *Regeneration Through Violence: The Mythology of the American Frontier, 1600–1860* (Middletown, Conn.: Wesleyan Univ. Press, 1973). Slotkin's reading of eighteenth-century captivity narratives in terms of "a representative of the kind of heroism that natural, uncultivated, American man is capable of" (189) is distinctly unhelpful with regard to captivity narratives by and about women.

15 Captain Greg Sieminski, "The Puritan Captivity Narrative and the Politics of the American Revolution," *American Quarterly* 42 (March 1990): 36. Mitchell Breitwieser, in *American Puritanism and the Defense of Mourning: Religion, Grief, and Ethnology in Mary White Rowlandson's Captivity Narrative* (Madison: Univ. of Wisconsin Press, 1990), deals with an earlier text organized by female mourning and racial difference. Breitwieser's emphasis on the relationship between Puritan religious ideology and the shock of "the real" in Rowlandson's narrative has some parallels to Bleecker's response to trauma. See also Annette Kolodny, *The Land Before Her: Fantasy and Experience of the American Frontiers, 1630–1860* (Chapel Hill: Univ. of North Carolina Press, 1984), 27–28; and Rafia Zafar's "Capturing the Captivity: African-Americans among the Puritans" in *MELUS* 17 (Summer 1991–92): 19–35.

16 Sieminski, 37–39.

17 Landry provides a useful summary of the relationships between class, gender, and genre in eighteenth-century pastoral and georgic poetry in *The Muses of Resistance*, 22–29.

18 Lauren Berlant, in "The Female Complaint," calls attention to the vexed relationship between complaint and resistance or critique (*Social Text* 19/20 [Fall 1988]: 237–59).

19 Dryden's version reads as follows:

> Alas! I lost *Creusa*: hard to tell
> If by her fatal Destiny she fell,
> Or weary sate, or wander'd with affright;
> But she was lost for ever to my sight.

· · · · · · · · · · ·
What mad expressions did my Tongue refuse?
Whom did I not of Gods or Men accuse?
This was the fatal Blow, that pain'd me more
Than all I felt from ruin'd Troy before.
Stung with my Loss, and raving with Despair,
Abandoning my now forgotten Care,
Of Counsel, Comfort, and of Hope bereft,
My Sire, my Son, my Country Gods, I left. (11.1002–05, 1010–17)

The Works of John Dryden, Vol. 5, ed. William Frost and Vinton A. Dearing, et al. (Berkeley: Univ. of California Press, 1987), 379–414.

20 Also operative in Morton's cultural politics is her distaste for new styles of commercial wealth, dramatized in her indignant opposition when her husband, Perez Morton, converted her family's ancestral home into a bank. See "Lines to the Mansion of My Ancestors, on Seeing it Occupied as a Banking Establishment," *My Mind and Its Thoughts*, 30–31.

21 Werner Sollors, *Beyond Ethnicity: Consent and Descent in American Culture* (New York: Oxford Univ. Press, 1986), 104. Thomas Tanselle, according to Sollors's reference, tracks down twenty-six printings of "Son of Alknomook" (*Newberry Library Bulletin* 6 [May 1979]: 389–401). I have not been able to confirm this citation.

22 Ann Hunter, "North American Death Song, Written for, and Adapted to, An Original Indian Air," in *Eighteenth Century Women Poets: An Oxford Anthology*, ed. Roger Lonsdale (New York: Oxford Univ. Press, 1989), 363–64. The link between the conventions of sensibility and lyric treatments of slavery by female poets was already clear. Mary Deverell had included a eulogy to Phillis Wheatley in her *Miscellanies in Prose and Verse* of 1781, the same year that Anna Laetitia Barbauld—whose first volume of poetry was published in London in 1773, the same year as Wheatley's *Poems on Various Subjects*—published "Hymn," centered on the figures of a slave woman and her child. See Moira Ferguson, "British Women Writers and an Emerging Abolitionist Discourse," *The Eighteenth Century: Theory and Interpretation* 33 (Spring 1992): 3.

23 Sollors, 104, 128–29.

24 Christina Zwarg reads a later text dealing with Native Americans, gender, and emotional topographies—Margaret Fuller's *Summer on the Lakes* (1844)—in terms that provide a useful corrective to Sollors by showing how representations of women in American landscapes become inseparable from the history of race relations. See "Footnoting the Sublime: Margaret Fuller on Black Hawk's Trail," forthcoming in *American Literary History*.

25 Cathy N. Davidson, *Revolution and the Word: The Rise of the Novel in America* (New York: Oxford Univ. Press, 1986), 289 n. 32. See also 85, 90, 96, 101–02.

26 Morton, *My Mind and Its Thoughts*, 7–9.

27 Davidson, 106.
28 "There is now a living instance of a like propensity. A gentleman of fortune, born in America, and educated in all the refinements and luxuries of Great Britain, has lately attached himself to a female savage . . . and in consequence of his inclination, has relinquished his own country and connections, incorporated himself into the society, and adopted the manners of the virtuous, though uncultivated Indian" (vi).
29 Morton is an "involuntary" author because she publishes "in compliance with the solicitations of . . . friends" (v).
30 On the discourse of the "Vanishing American," see Brian W. Dippie, *The Vanishing American: White Attitudes and U.S. Indian Policy* (Middletown, Conn.: Wesleyan Univ. Press, 1982); and Slotkin, 357–69.
31 The same preference for a spirit of resistance over one of resignation comes through in Morton's "The African Chief," in *My Mind and Its Thoughts*, 201–02.

Lora Romero   Vanishing Americans: Gender, Empire, and New Historicism

Cultural historians have identified James Fenimore Cooper's *The Last of the Mohicans* as one of approximately forty novels published in the U.S. between 1824 and 1834 that together suggest the existence of a virtual "cult of the Vanishing American" in the antebellum period. Requisite to membership in this cult was a belief that the rapid decrease in the native population noted by many Jacksonian-era observers was both spontaneous and ineluctable.[1] Cooper would seem to betray his indoctrination in the cult of the vanishing American when he states in the introduction to the 1831 edition of his novel that it was "the seemingly inevitable fate of all [native tribes]" to "disappear before the advances . . . of civilisation [just] as the verdure of their native forests falls before the nipping frost."[2] The elegiac mode here performs the historical sleight-of-hand crucial to the topos of the doomed aboriginal: it represents the disappearance of the native as not just natural but as having already happened.[3]

In the novel itself, of course, Cooper's Indians "vanish" in somewhat more spectacular fashion than the introductory invocation of forest and frost leads us to anticipate. However pacific the introduction's simile, in the narrative proper individual representatives of the *doomed* race expire in utterly sensational ways. Indeed, the frequency with which Cooper's Indians plunge to their death from great heights is positively dumbfounding.

The most memorable instance of this is the villainous Magua's spectacular demise at the end of the novel. Evading pursuit by Cooper's white hero Hawk-eye, Magua attempts to leap from the brow of a mountain to an adjacent precipice, but he falls "short of his mark" and finds himself dangling from a "giddy height," clinging desperately to a shrub growing from the side of the precipice. Bent on destroying his enemy, Hawk-eye fires. The wounded Magua's hold loosens, and "his dark person [is] seen cutting the air with its head downwards, for a fleeting instant . . . in its rapid flight to destruction" (p. 338).

To claim that Cooper earlier *foreshadows* Magua's Miltonic fall would grossly understate the case. Indeed, the fall of dark persons from on high is a virtual *theme* in *The Last of the Mohicans*. Similar rapid flights to destruction abound, for example, in an early confrontation between whites and enemy Indians that takes place in the vertiginous topography of a huge cavern. One Indian plunges "into [a] deep and yawning abyss" (p. 69). A second hurls "headlong among the clefts of [an] island" (p. 70). A third tumbles down an "irrecoverable precipice" (p. 71), while yet another drops "like lead" into the "foaming waters" below (p. 75).

Mere sensationalism does not quite account for Cooper's fascination with the precipitous dark person. The figure sometimes surfaces in relatively banal forms—for example, when the noble savage Uncas at one point darts "through the air" and leaps upon Magua, "driving him many yards . . . headlong and prostrate" (p. 113), or later when, in his fatal attempt to save Cora Munro's life, Uncas leaps between her and Magua in an act of what Cooper calls "headlong precipitation" (p. 336). And perhaps the most banal reiteration of the figure occurs when the novelist describes a Huron, tomahawk in his hand and malice in his heart, rushing at Uncas. A quick-witted white man sticks out his foot to trip the "eager savage" as he passes, and the Huron is "precipitated . . . headlong" to the ground (p. 238). Etymologically considered ("precipitation" is from *praeceps* or "headlong"), the phrase is as peculiarly reiterative as the headlong aboriginal it describes.

I would like to suggest that the redundancy of both phrase and figure in Cooper's novel signals that text's participation in and instantiation of a larger antebellum cultural discourse in which the ethnographic and pedagogic overlap. Cooper at one point refers to an enemy Huron who is about to plunge down a precipice as a "prodigy" (p. 69). An educational treatise written by a doctor and appearing six years after *The Last of the Mohicans* discusses the phenomenon of precocity and provides a compelling if unlikely analogue to Cooper's precipitous native. In his *Remarks on the Influence of Mental Cultivation and Mental Excitement Upon Health*, Dr. Amariah Brigham records the case of a white prodigy, one William M., born in Philadelphia on the Fourth of July, 1820. While still a toddler,

William M. astonished those around him with his musical talents, his conversational skills, and his lofty moral sentiments.

According to Brigham, "the heads of great thinkers . . . are wonderfully large." At birth William M.'s head "was of ordinary size," but "very soon, after an attack of dropsy of the brain, it began to grow inordinately." Indeed, by the time the child learned to walk, his head had grown so large that "he was apt to fall, especially forwards, from readily losing his equilibrium." This tendency proved to be more than a minor annoyance. At eight years of age he suffered a precipitous demise—a death both untimely and literally headlong. Losing his balance one day, he fell headfirst against a door, bruised his forehead, "became very sick, and died the next evening." William M.'s fatal loss of equilibrium evinces the thesis advanced in this section of Brigham's treatise, namely, that "mental precocity is generally a symptom of disease; and hence those who exhibit it very frequently, die young." A "passion for books" and other mental excitements may, in the doctor's opinion, presage early death.[4]

The ethnographic subtext of Brigham's thesis (and hence the treatise's relevance to Cooper's novel) becomes more legible when William M.'s story is juxtaposed against Margaret Fuller's discussion of equilibrium and race in her account of a journey into Indian territory in *A Summer on the Lakes* (1844). In fact, the case of William M. reads like a curiously materialist interpretation of what Fuller calls "civilized man['s] larger mind." Fuller sees the difference between "civilized" and "savage" as in part a matter of proportions, a difference of relative development of mind and body. Civilized man "is constantly breaking bounds, in proportion as the mental gets the better of the mere instinctive existence." In the process, however, "he loses in harmony of being what he gains in height and extension; the civilized man is a larger mind but a more imperfect nature than the savage." What Fuller calls "civilized man['s] larger *mind*," Brigham translates into civilized man's larger *head*—but even Fuller's analysis has a materialist component. She asserts that Indian tribes subjugated by whites cease to bear physical resemblance to members of their race as yet uncontaminated by civilization. Unlike other natives, members of conquered tribes, she writes, are "no longer strong, tall, or finely proportioned."[5]

Whereas Fuller imagines that physical degeneration in the form of disproportion is desirable because it fosters spiritual development, Brigham believes in "the necessity of giving more attention to the health and growth of the body, and less to the cultivation of the mind . . . than is now given." But Brigham's concern extends beyond individual bodies and their well-being. Educational treatises published in the U.S. in the antebellum period slide easily from the individual to the race. Brigham's preface declares, "The people of the United States ought to become the most vigorous and powerful race of human beings, both in mind and body, that the world has ever known."[6] William M.'s significant birthplace (Philadelphia) and birthdate (the Fourth of July) render him the local instance of an alleged racial defiance of Brigham's imperialist imperative.

The same entanglement of child-rearing and empire-building surfaces in the work of Catharine Beecher—whose popular advice to housewives and whose former position as head of the prestigious Hartford Female Seminary guaranteed her pedagogy both domestic and institutional influence.[7] Like Brigham, Beecher worried that Anglo-American children were "becoming less and less healthful and good-looking" and that they were every year producing children even "more puny and degenerate" than themselves. Beecher contrasts puny Anglo-Americans with the robust ancient Greeks, who, she asserts, were of a stock so vigorous that they "conquered nearly the whole world."[8] This last comment suggests the way in which early nineteenth-century educational treatises—characteristically if not constitutionally—traverse the discursive registers of home and empire. The figure of the prodigy, one may conclude, organizes into a single discursive economy two distinct cultural arenas expressed through binarisms of feminine and masculine, private and public, suburbia and frontier, sentiment and adventure.[9] Expressing these binarisms in somewhat different terms, I would claim that the prodigy illuminates the affiliations of the micro- and the macro-political.

■ ■ ■

Michel Foucault supplies a model for uncovering the connections between micro- and macro-politics when (in anticipating objections to his characterization of modern government as "power organized around the management of life rather than the menace of death")[10] he concedes that the modernity of the genocidal might seem to suggest that the life-destroying power of the sovereign not only survived his decapitation but actually *escalated* in the nineteenth and twentieth centuries. Conceiving of modern power as the power to administer life rather than the power to inflict death would seem to require ignoring the genocidal animus which has characterized Western interaction with both Jews and people of color in the modern era. By emphasizing production, Foucauldian theory would seem unable to account for the racial holocausts that have punctuated the modern era and hence would seem necessarily to marginalize (if not to erase altogether) an important part of the history of Jews and the Third World.

Yet, even if race remains a largely undeveloped category of analysis in the history it traces, still *The History of Sexuality* does theorize interracial conflict as an inevitable component of modernity. Foucault asserts that precisely inasmuch as power legitimates and incarnates itself through "the right of the social body to ensure, maintain, or develop its life," racial holocaust becomes "vital" to its expression. Arguing for the simultaneity of productive technologies that promote the well-being of the individual and deductive technologies that ensure the well-being of the race, he writes that in eighteenth- and nineteenth-century Europe "precocious sexuality was presented . . . as an epidemic menace that risked compromising not only the future health of adults but the future of the entire society and species." [11] Modifying Foucault's analysis slightly, I will be locating antebellum representations of the prodigy—a less explicitly sexualized relative of the precocious child—on the discursive axis of two distinctive forms of power in modern Western societies.

Foucault's remarks on genocide unsettle the thumbnail literary history proposed earlier in *The History of Sexuality*. There Foucault proposes that the rise of the micro-political corresponds roughly with the displacement of narratives of adventure by narratives of sentiment: "we have passed from a pleasure to be recounted . . . centering on the heroic . . . narration of 'trials' of bravery . . . to a literature ordered according to the infinite task of extracting [truth] from the depths of oneself." [12] Perhaps one consequence of this statement is that Foucauldian criticism has concentrated on domestic, realist, and sentimental fictions to the neglect of adventure fictions (which, because they so often unfold on borders between "civilized" and "savage," frequently engage questions of the survival of races). Foucauldian New Historicist critics writing about the nineteenth century—particularly, Richard Brodhead, Nancy Armstrong, and D. A. Miller—have constructed the home and its narratives as, in Miller's words, the domain of an "extralegal series of 'micro-powers'" and hence the proper sphere for Foucauldian inquiry. [13] But if we take seriously Foucault's comments about the involution of micro- and macro-powers around questions of race, then we would expect to uncover not the superannuation of heroism by sentiment but rather their simultaneity and co-implication. The ease with which educational treatises like

Beecher's and Brigham's oscillate from the individual to the race suggests the pertinence of Foucauldian analysis to race relations. Similarly, analysis of the figure of the precipitous aboriginal whose precocity signals his *inevitable* demise in *The Last of the Mohicans* suggests that this type of analysis is as relevant to imperial fictions as it is to domestic ones.

Such a reading of the relation between home and frontier, however, suggests more than the need for simple expansion of the domain of New Historicism. I would like to use this reading as an occasion to interrogate the politics of Foucauldian analysis itself. Uncovering the interaction between micro- and macro-political concerns raises some questions about the gender and racial politics of the Foucauldian "shift" from which New Historicist criticism on the nineteenth century proceeds. A shift from an economy of punishment to one of discipline is not just passively evidenced but rather *actively deployed* in early nineteenth-century U.S. representations of the prodigy. It is not simply that antebellum texts like *The Last of the Mohicans* either prefigure or preempt contemporary theoretical and critical developments (although I *would* claim that New Historicism of the Foucauldian variety has in its discussion of power recapitulated more than it has analyzed an important component of nineteenth-century discourse). More importantly, I would argue that a reading of antebellum texts demonstrates that narratives of the shift from punishment to discipline (like the one Foucauldian New Historicism has given us) have, historically, operated to the detriment of both white middle-class women and people of color. Whatever its politics within its own cultural setting, Foucauldian knowledge does not encounter a political vacuum when it enters contemporary U.S. critical discourse. Instead it meets with a history extending back to the antebellum period in which intellectuals have deployed narratives of a shift in the nature of power toward politically suspicious ends. For this reason contemporary intellectuals in the U.S. whose work has been influenced by Foucault (myself included) need to historicize their own discourse by reconstructing its genealogy and inquiring into the rhetorical work performed by the Foucauldian shift that supplies their work with its hard historical foundations.

■ ■ ■

Just as Brigham encodes in William M.'s brief life the ethnographic logic supporting an account of the decline of Anglo-Americans, compacted within Cooper's precipitous aboriginal is a logic ensuring the ideological transformation of Native Americans into Vanishing Americans. Despite the spectacular nature of their individual deaths, Cooper's natives, every bit as much as his introductory reference to the "verdure . . . fall[ing] before the nipping frost," expunge imperialist conflict from the Jacksonian cultural memory. They do so by foregrounding issues of proportion and equilibrium so crucial to antebellum accounts of the *disappearance* of races.

Cooper incorporates the racial other as an earlier and now irretrievably lost version of the self. Perhaps this is part of the reason why our culture has come to regard *The Last of the Mohicans* and other nineteenth-century Anglo-American frontier fictions as "children's literature." Just as Freud in his essay on "The Sexual Aberrations" collapses the "primitive" or "archaic" and the infantile,[14] Cooper conflates racial difference and temporal distance on an evolutionary continuum of human history. In other words, it is as though for him aboriginals represent a *phase* that the human race goes through but which it must inevitably *get over*. Regardless of whether the ethno-pedagogic text celebrates equilibrium (in the case of Cooper and Brigham) or disequilibrium (in the case of Fuller), in equating the savage and the juvenile it starts by assuming that certain Americans must vanish.

Cooper's concern with proportion registers his debt to ethnopedagogic thinking. The novel's white characters marvel over the "perfection of form which abounds among the uncorrupted natives" (p. 53), and the narrator himself praises what he calls Uncas' "beautiful proportions" (p. 275). Uncas is "an unblemished specimen of the noblest proportions of man" and resembles "some precious relic of the Grecian chisel" (p. 53). In the Western tradition the ancient Greeks had long represented the ideal of physical beauty, but in the antebellum U.S. their beautiful proportions had become the *sine qua non* of a call for educational reform. Beecher, for example, launches her critique of the U.S. educational system with the observation that the Greeks "were remarkable, not only for their wisdom and strength, but for their great beauty, so that the statues they made to resemble their own men and women have, ever since, been regarded as the most perfect forms of human beauty." "Perfect forms" here conveys roughly what "beautiful proportions" connotes in Cooper: a balance of intellectual and physical culture—hence Beecher's interest in the Greek educational system as a model for contemporary times. According to her, the Greeks' perfection of form derived from the fact that "[t]hey had two kinds of schools—the one to train the minds, and the other to train the bodies of their children."[15]

Whatever nostalgia Cooper expresses for savage equilibrium in his description of Uncas, he imagines that civilization necessarily spells the end of archaic proportions. Hence Cooper contrasts Uncas' "beautiful proportions" with the white man David Gamut's "rare proportions" (p. 17). Gamut, writes the novelist, possesses "all the bones and joints of other men, without any of their proportions." While Cooper reassures us that Gamut is not actually physically "deformed," his description of Gamut does little to assuage his reader's anxiety on that score: "His head was large; his shoulders narrow; his arms long and dangling; while his hands were small, if not delicate. His legs and thighs were thin nearly to emaciation, but of extraordinary length; and his knees would have been considered tremendous, had they not been outdone by the broader foundations [i.e., his feet] on which this false superstructure of blended human orders, was so profanely reared" (p. 16).

Gamut's peculiar proportions are just one sign that he is the vehicle by which civilization is carried into the wilderness. Around him also accrue linked images of language, femininity, and power. Referring to Gamut's annoying habit of bursting into song whenever the proximity of enemy Indians demands absolute silence (Gamut is a psalmodist by profession), Hawk-eye laments the fact that, as he puts it, although the "Lord never intended that the man should place all his endeavours in his throat," Gamut had "fallen into the hands of some silly woman, when he should have been gathering his education under a blue sky, and among the beauties of the forest" (p. 224).

While perhaps Cooper, like Hawk-eye, believes that God never intended that *man* privilege language at the expense of the development of the body, both seem to believe that the Supreme Being intended that *woman* do so. This is suggested by Cooper's habitual association of feminine control over education in the settlements with both the proliferation of words and with precipitous behavior. For example, as darkness begins to settle on his party's search for clues to the whereabouts of the captive Munro sisters, Hawk-eye advises his companions to abandon the trail until morning. "[I]n the morning," he insists, "we shall be fresh, and ready to undertake our work like men, and not like babbling women, or eager boys" (p. 189).

Hawk-eye's association of loquacious femininity and headstrong boys has antecedents in Rousseauvian notions of noble savagery. In *Émile* women's control over the education of children threatens the survival of the white race: "[P]uberty and sexual potency," according to Rousseau, "always arrive earlier in learned and civilized peoples than in ignorant and barbarous peoples," and this explains why Europeans (unlike noble savages) are "exhausted early, remain small, weak, . . . ill-formed" and die young. "Man's weakness," he writes, proceeds from "the inequality between his strength and his desires."[16] Only in boyhood and savagery is there an equilibrium of body (what we can get) and mind (what we want), and for Rousseau equilibrium is synonymous with nobility—a quality whose residual existence in civilized societies boyhood guarantees.

Émile's anti-feminism derives from Rousseau's belief that, because their lack of physical strength prevents them from attaining self-suffi-ciency, women inevitably want more than they can get. The satisfaction of even a woman's most basic wants necessarily requires that she defraud her constitutional destiny by using words to persuade others to do for her what she cannot do for herself. Women, Rousseau feels, must and should rely upon men to get what they want. The problem arises when women are given unsupervised control over the education of boys. Whereas the father can discipline the child through simple physical coercion (which Rousseau heartily recommends), the mother must resort to complex sen-timental manipulations expressed in words. Individual pedagogical errors are revenged upon the race as the son discovers that the efficacy of the verbal tool obviates the necessity of bodily vigor. The boy too learns how to defraud the body through "feminine" acts of representation, de-stroys the juvenile balance of needs and strength, and thereby becomes a prodigy. Put in Cooper's terms, in *Émile* babbling women yield eager boys.

Cooper's Rousseauvian subtext emerges when one of his noble sav-ages asserts that "Men speak not twice" (p. 314). Real men do not need words because they have physical strength. Women and precocious sons, however, require verbal prosthetics to get what they want. Furthermore, for Cooper as well as for Rousseau, words represent a whole economy of power marked as feminine. Thus, after declaring himself a warrior not a reader, Hawk-eye asserts that he, unlike Gamut, is no "whim-pering boy, at the apron string of one of your old gals" (p. 117). Free of books, Hawk-eye liberates himself from the power that nineteenth-century domesticity gave to women—liberates himself from what Leslie Fiedler calls the "gentle tyranny of home and woman."[17] Hence when Gamut demands that Hawk-eye buttress one of his numerous philosophi-cal speculations with some authoritative textual prop, the enraged scout demands: "[W]hat have such as I, who am a warrior of the wilderness . . .

to do with books! I never read but in one [that is, the book of nature], and the words that are written there are too simple and too plain to need much schooling" (p. 117). I would argue that the fiction of the "plainness" of the book of nature in this passage supports another fiction: that of the legibility of paternal power imagined as simple physical force. Cooper attempts to differentiate between knowledge gained from experience on the trail and "bookish knowledge" (p. 189) in order to create the fiction of power relations "plain" as nature itself.

Both the disregard for books and the association of them with the newly-empowered antebellum woman are staples of the period. Although *the book* is usually associated with the reign of the father, in the antebellum period *books* seem to be associated with the reign of the mother. The pervasiveness of this association is suggested by Thoreau's chapter on "Reading" in *Walden*. There the author expresses his disgust not just over the *quality* of popular books but also over their *quantity*. Embedded within Thoreau's anxiety about multiplicity lies an anxiety about the mother's assumption of the educational duties formerly administered by the father—or so Thoreau's confusion of mechanical production and female sexual reproduction leads one to suspect.

Thoreau confuses the printing press with the womb when he derides the "modern cheap and fertile press." Machine-like literary mothers produce not only insubstantial volumes (like the popular series called "Little Reading," which the author came across one day in his local library); they also produce insubstantial people. Thoreau characterizes the readers of "Little Reading" as themselves little, like the "modern puny and degenerate race" described by Beecher. They are "pygmies and manikins" and "a race of tit-men." Thoreau distinguishes this modern race from the archaic, athletic, and robust race of men nurtured by literary fathers before the age of mechanical reproduction. According to "Reading," in a heroic age long past it "require[d] a training such as the athletes underwent" to read literature. Whereas the modern press is "fertile," "the heroic writers of antiquity" produced works which were "solitary."[18]

Thoreau's opposition of the feminine, the diminutive, and the multiple against the masculine, the massive, and the singular services a Rousseauvian distinction between power conceived of as a physical force and power conceived of as verbal and sentimental manipulation. The *solidity* of the paternal book in "Reading" symbolizes the visibility of power relations under the patriarch, and the robustness of the (male) reader of the (male) classics denotes his ability both to see and to fight whatever threatens his autonomy. Hence Thoreau writes that, even if read in translation (in what he calls "our *mother* tongue") the massive "heroic books" are written in a language alien to the modern reader. They "will always be in a language dead to degenerate times," and therefore they require their readers to seek "laboriously . . . the meaning of each word and line." The laboriousness of the reading preserves the autonomy of the subject. The classics speak in a "*father* tongue, a reserved and select expression" that does not compromise volition because, rather than lulling the reader to sleep, it demands that he "devote [his] most alert and wakeful hours" to reading. By contrast, we learn our "mother tongue . . . unconsciously" and hence read popular books like sleepwalkers. In "Reading" the smallness of books written by women suggests not just their trivial contents, but also the microscopic scale of maternal power. Thoreau's comment that readers of little books are "machines" anticipates the Foucauldian anxiety over a power whose invisibility (accomplished through domestication, decentering, and proliferation) only augments its efficiency.[19]

Although Thoreau's chapter reads like an attempt to disempower the domestic woman, the same disparaging association of mass-production and female generativity made by Thoreau surfaces even in the texts apparently most instrumental in instituting the reign of the mother. Domestic ideology's demonic double, what Michael Paul Rogin dubs "momism,"[20] is if anything even more evident in the work of Hannah More, the British author generally credited with the founding of domestic ideology. Her influential treatise on female education was reprintd in numerous editions in the U.S. between 1800 and 1826 and helped determine the shape of domesticity in this country as well as in Britain.

In *Strictures on the Modern System of Female Education*, More, like Thoreau, expresses anxiety about the quantity of "little books" on the market. "Real" knowledge and piety, she writes, have suffered from "that profusion of little, amusing, sentimental books with which the youthful library overflows."[21] After questioning the pedagogical value of multiplying the number of books students read, More is overcome by a proto-Malthusian vision of the uncontrollably generative popular press. She writes: "Who are those ever multiplying authors, that with unparalleled fecundity are overstocking the world with their quick-succeeding progeny? They are the novel-writers; the easiness of whose productions is at once the cause of their own fruitfulness, and of the almost infinitely numerous race of imitators, to whom they give birth." More's nightmare vision collapses the mechanical production increasingly characterizing the book industry with female sexual reproduction. Mass-production of children (the creation of a "race of imitators") is the evil twin of domestic ideology's attempt to standardize child-rearing practices. The hysteria over the abundance of books in the antebellum period both represents and creates an anxiety over the violation of the independence of the subject by disciplinary methods directed at the interior rather than at the body. An anxiety over the decorpo-realization of power compels the advice offered time and again in educational treatises in the early nineteenth century: more emphasis should be placed upon the cultivation of the juvenile body and less upon the development of the juvenile mind. The excessively cerebral Anglo-Saxon in More's text stands on the verge of disappearing as power disappears. The Anglo-Saxon race, she writes, is threatened with the same "quick succession of slavery, effeminacy, . . . vice, . . . and degeneracy" that overtook the inhabitants of ancient Rome.[22]

For Cooper, to read in the book of nature is to be educated through the paternal apprenticeship system rather than the maternal representational system. Cooper suggests this when at one point in the narrative Chingachgook and Hawk-eye lose Magua's trail. Uncas, who has long since uncovered the proper path, nevertheless assumes a "calm and dignified demeanour" suggestive of "dependen[ce] on the sagacity and intelligence of the seniors of the party" (p. 213). Savage society, in Cooper as in Rousseau, does not produce prodigies. According to the novelist, when members of Indian tribes convene to confer on matters important to the whole community, "there is never to be found any impatient aspirant after premature distinction, standing ready to move his auditors to some hasty, and, perhaps, injudicious discussion, in order that his own reputation may be the gainer. An act of so much precipitancy and presumption, would seal the downfall of precocious intellect for ever. It rested solely with the oldest and most experienced of the men to lay the subject of the conference before the people" (p. 292). Indian society then offers a highly visible version of power. According to the narrator, the power of the Indian leader is the power of physical force: "the authority of an Indian chief [is] so little conventional, that it [is] oftener maintained by physical superiority, than by any moral supremacy he might possess" (p. 92).

If basing power on physical superiority prevents aboriginal precocity, it also makes the patriarch's control over the tribe tenuous. Even Cooper's most noble savages seem barely restrained by the father. Uncas' "dignified and calm demeanor" disappears at a moment's notice. As soon as Chingachgook solicits his help, Uncas bounds "forward like a deer" and directs his elders to the proper trail (p. 213). The young Mohican's sudden shift from rock-like self-restraint to frenetic activity is one that characterizes natives whether represented individually or in groups. Such fluctuations in Indian demeanor suggest what Cooper imagines as the fundamental exteriority to the self of power legitimated by physical superiority. Despite its patriarchal nature, Indian government permits radical independence because, like the authority exercised by Foucault's sovereign, that restraint is imagined to be of a strictly corporeal nature.

Fiedler's "gentle tyranny," on the other hand, would subvert radical native independence and undermine native proportions. This is in fact what happens to Uncas. Aware at some level of Uncas' admiration of her, Cora gains an "intuitive consciousness of her power" over the young Mohican (p. 79). Like the ethnologists of his day, Cooper believed Indians experienced no romantic passion.[23] Hence he calls Uncas' enamored ministrations to Cora both a "departure from the dignity of his manhood" and an "utter innovation on . . . Indian customs" (p. 56). His love "elevate[s] him far above the intelligence, and advance[s] him . . . centuries before the practices of his nation" (p. 115).

It seems that Cooper imagines that Cora's gentle tyranny "seal[s] the downfall" of Uncas' "precocious intellect." Falling under Cora's power, educated without his knowledge, Uncas dies a racial prodigy. Hawk-eye notes the Mohican's uncharacteristic precipitancy during their search for the captive Munro sisters. He chastises Uncas for suddenly becoming "as impatient as a man in the settlements" (p. 185). The noble savage turned eager savage repeatedly puts himself at risk in pursuing the captive Cora Munro: "In vain Hawk-eye called to him to respect the covers; the young Mohican braved the dangerous fire of his enemies, and soon compelled them to a flight as swift as his own headlong speed" (p. 334).

Significantly, it is this precocious development under woman's invisible tutelage that makes Uncas the *last* of the Mohicans. At the end of the novel, he stands upon a ledge overlooking Magua who is threatening Cora with a tomahawk. The impassioned Mohican leaps "frantically, from a fearful height" and falls between Magua and his intended victim, but only to fall victim himself to his enemy's tomahawk (p. 337). Cooper reports Magua's headlong death at Hawk-eye's hands on the very next page of the novel and the language of precipitancy, the reiteration of the image of the headlong Indian, encourages us to confuse the two red

men. Invoking the antebellum figure of the prodigy, Cooper's text replaces Hawk-eye's rifle with the middle-class woman's apron strings.[24] It
translates firepower into mother power.

The Last of the Mohicans deflects attention from the macro-political
realm represented in the text by the army (for which Hawk-eye is a
scout), and upon women falls the responsibility for the *disappearance* of
the native. But the prodigy's presence does more than deflect. The threat
that woman's invisible power poses to the male subject produces the need
for some space (the frontier) to elude her miasmic influence and hence
makes imperative the macro-political controls effecting Indian removal
from contiguous territories. In other words Cooper's "discovery" of the
discipline deployed against his white men legitimates the technologies of
punishment deployed against his red men.

■ ■ ■

Antebellum discourse, I have argued, uses images of the modern proliferation of words as a sign that feminine words have replaced masculine
muscle as the basis of authority. Momist imagery of the loss of autonomy
resulting from this feminization of power expresses nostalgia for a form
of power whose lack of psychic consequence guarantees that it does not
compromise the autonomy of the male subject. Yet neither this subject
nor this form of power ever existed. Because it is administered and experienced by human agents, even "simple" brute force must have psychic
consequences and must produce subjectivities particular to it.

The myth of simple brute force in antebellum discourse generates what
Renato Rosaldo calls "imperialist nostalgia." "When the so-called civilizing process destabilizes forms of life," writes Rosaldo, "the agents of
change experience transformations of other cultures as if they were personal losses."[25] Developing Rosaldo's point, Amy Kaplan suggests that
such nostalgia makes aggression against Third World peoples the logical
consequence of anti-feminism directed against First World women because in it "the empire figures as the site where you can be all that you
can no longer be at home—a 'real live man'—where you can recover the
autonomy denied by social forces of modernization, often aligned in this
way of thinking with feminization."[26]

Following Rosaldo and Kaplan, I would argue that in our own time
scholarship on the alleged feminization of society itself participates in the
imperialist nostalgia of the discourse it analyzes. Traditionally, momist

texts like Cooper's were seen as evidence of a historical "feminization of American culture" in which expanded female leisure and literacy permitted Hawthorne's "scribbling women" to usurp the cultural offices once occupied by less prolific but more profound male authors.[27] More recently, New Historicist criticism of the Foucauldian variety has encouraged us to regard the feminization of culture as a symptom of a larger feminization of power. Yet, the novelty of New Historicism does not reside in its emphasis on power. Earlier cultural analysis also equated feminization with normalization. Richard Brodhead's recent characterization of the modern ideal of maternal love as a power whose "silken threads are harder to burst than the iron chains of authority" employed by "old-style paternal discipline" recalls Fiedler's analysis of the rise of a "gentle tyranny of home and woman" in the nineteenth-century.[28] D. A. Miller's revelation of a nineteenth-century "field of power relations" masquerading as a "domesticating pedagogy" harkens back to Ann Douglas' discussion of the "manifold possibilities" offered by Victorian maternal influence for "devious social control."[29] Nancy Armstrong's assertion that domestic ideology provided the "logic" that permitted women to enter the world of work through social services and thereby extended "subtle techniques of domestic surveillance beyond the middle-class home and into the lives of those much lower down on the economic ladder" mirrors Christopher Lasch's claim that the "rise of the 'helping professions'" allowed "society in the guise of a 'nurturing mother' [to invade] the family, the stronghold of . . . private rights."[30]

Neither the poststructuralist upheaval that divides the cultural analysis of the 1960s and 1970s from that of the 1980s nor the feminist critiques to which these analyses have been subjected have altered the basic narrative: normalization is still women's work. What is even more startling is that this narrative appears to date back to antebellum times. Yet, the failure of New Historicists to articulate a genuinely novel reading of the nineteenth century troubles me far less than their apparent obliviousness to the rhetorical content of what they present as historical facts.[31] Even if exposing the rhetorical work of Foucauldian history does not *in and of itself* undermine the facticity of New Historicist claims (all facts require human interpreters and so all truth is necessarily rhetorical), still its practitioners cannot possibly hope to direct their own rhetoric toward progressive ends without first inquiring into the gender and race politics perpetuated by their use of Foucauldian knowledge.[32]

New Historicists' dependence upon Foucault's narrative of modernization would seem to account for their apparent obliviousness to the way in which they have been engaged in the retelling of a politically suspect nineteenth-century narrative of modernization. Despite the emphasis I have put on it, Foucault's assertion that the West's commitment to managing the life of its own population also entails a commitment to massive destruction of populations designated as "other" is parenthetical to the history outlined in the first volume of *The History of Sexuality*. Whereas his brief comments on modern racial holocausts suggest the simultaneity of deductive and productive manifestations of power, Foucault's larger historical narrative (as represented by both *The History of Sexuality* and *Discipline and Punish*) is founded upon a temporal distinction between them such that the deductive (punishment) represents the pre-modern and the productive (discipline), the modern form of power. Hence Foucault's own narrative is subject to the same critique to which I have subjected antebellum narratives of modernization. Inasmuch as he defines modernity as the decorporealization of power, he participates in the construction of an utterly mythic time in which authority represented simple physical superiority (an era personified in *Émile* by the father who governs by means of the lash). Foucault's temporalization of the difference between discipline and punishment suggests that even contemporary images of modernity collaborate in the production of the imperialist nostalgia I have been describing.

Notes

1   Brian W. Dippie, *The Vanishing American: White Attitudes and U.S. Indian Policy* (Middletown, Conn.: Wesleyan Univ. Press, 1982), p. 2. Dippie borrows the phrase from G. Harrison Orians, *The Cult of the Vanishing American: A Century View* (Toledo, Ohio: H. J. Chittenden, 1934).

My own essay grows out of talks I gave in 1988 at the University of California at Los Angeles, Northwestern University, Princeton University, the University of Rochester, and at the annual meeting of the American Studies Association in Miami Beach, Florida. The current version is based on talks delivered at the University of Texas, Austin, in 1989 and at a conference sponsored by The Center for the Critical Analysis of Contemporary Culture at Rutgers University in 1990. I wish to thank Ann Cvetkovich, Walter Michaels, Jeff Nunokawa, Michael Rogin, Eric Sundquist, and Lynn Ward-ley—each of whom offered indispensible advice on one of the multitude of earlier drafts of this essay.

2 *The Last of the Mohicans: A Narrative of 1757* (Albany, N.Y.: State Univ. of New York Press, 1983), pp. 6–7. Hereafter quotations will be taken from this edition and cited parenthetically in the text.

3 In fact, the rise of the cult of the Vanishing American corresponds roughly with the rise of the U.S. government's policy of Indian Removal, a massive military campaign of systematic dispossession and effective extermination begun in the late 1820s. According to Francis Paul Prucha in *The Great Father: The United States Government and the American Indians* (Lincoln: Univ. of Nebraska Press, 1984), "the military phase of Indian relations" would not end until the early 1880s (p. 560). Thus we see just how much effort went into effecting the "inevitable."

4 *Remarks on the Influence of Mental Cultivation and Mental Excitement Upon Health*, 2nd ed. (Boston: Marsh, Capen & Lyon, 1833; rpt. New York: Arno, 1973), pp. 49, 42, 36, 45.

5 *Summer on the Lakes, in 1843* (Boston: Charles C. Little and James Brown; New York: Charles S. Francis, 1844), pp. 221, 182.

6 Brigham, pp. vii, viii.

7 For a relevant discussion of the intersecting rhetoric of domesticity and imperialism see Amy Kaplan, "Romancing the Empire: The Embodiment of American Masculinity in the Popular Historical Novel of the 1890s," *American Literary History* 2 (1990), 659–90.

8 *Letters to the People on Health and Happiness* (New York: Harper & Row, 1855), pp. 8, 10, 8.

9 The criticism on the Leatherstocking tales has played a crucial role in establishing for us a sense of ideological distance between the frontier and the home. Since D. H. Lawrence's famous analysis of Cooper's Leatherstocking series appeared in 1923, Cooper criticism has taken as one of its perennial themes the anti-feminine (if not outright misogynist) sensibility compelling Natty Bumppo's flight from the civilized society of women into the savage society of the red man. See, for example, Lawrence's *Studies in Classic American Literature* (Garden City, N.Y.: Doubleday, 1951) and Leslie A. Fiedler's *Love and Death in the American Novel* (New York: Meridian, 1960).

10 *The History of Sexuality, Volume I: An Introduction*, trans. Robert Hurley (New York: Vintage, 1980), p. 147.

11 Foucault, pp. 136–37, 146.

12 *Ibid.*, p. 59.

13 *The Novel and the Police* (Berkeley and Los Angeles: Univ. of California Press, 1988), p. viii.

14 Freud writes, "In inverted types, a predominance of archaic constitutions and primitive psychical mechanisms is regularly to be found." See "The Sexual Aberrations" in *Three Essays on the Theory of Sexuality*, trans. and

revised by James Strachey (New York: Basic Books, 1962), p. 12n. My belief in the relevance of the Freudian developmental narrative to genocidal thinking grows out of discussions with Jeff Nunokawa about his work on the figure of the doomed male homosexual in British Victorian literature.

15 Beecher, p. 8.

16 *Émile, or On Education*, trans. Allan Bloom (New York: Basic Books, 1979), pp. 215, 216, 165.

17 Fiedler, p. 189.

18 *Walden* in *Walden and Civil Disobedience*, ed. Owen Thomas (New York: Norton, 1966), pp. 72, 68.

19 Thoreau, pp. 67 (my italics), 68 (my italics), 70, 68, 71.

20 "Momism" is Rogin's term for a "demonic version of domestic ideology" that expresses anxiety over the "maternal power generated by domesticity." Whereas Rogin discusses momism as a twentieth-century response to the revival of the domestic ideal in the 1950s, I am suggesting that domesticity and its demonic double arose simultaneously in the antebellum period. See Michael Paul Rogin, "Kiss Me Deadly: Communism, Motherhood, and Cold War Movies," *Representations*, No. 6 (1984), 6–7.

21 *Strictures on the Modern System of Female Education*, 3rd American ed. (Boston: Joseph Bumstead, 1802), p. 97. My argument here has been influenced by Mark Seltzer's analysis of the deployment of gender in literary naturalism in his "The Naturalist Machine" in *Sex, Politics, and Science in the Nineteenth-Century Novel*, ed. Ruth Bernard Yeazell (Baltimore: Johns Hopkins Univ. Press, 1986), 116–47.

22 More, pp. 104, 48.

23 In *White Over Black: American Attitudes Toward the Negro, 1550–1812* (Chapel Hill: Univ. of North Carolina Press, 1968), Winthrop D. Jordan notes that early U.S. ethnographers frequently represented the Native American as "deficient in ardor and virility" (p. 162). Cooper's contemporary Henry Lewis Morgan claimed that "the passion of love was entirely unknown" among the Iroquois. See Morgan's *League of the Iroquois* (1851; rpt. New York: Corinth, 1962), p. 322.

24 My identification of Cora with the middle-class woman is complicated by the fact that, even though she has been raised white, she is in fact mulatta—the product of the British imperialist effort in the West Indies. It might be more accurate to say that Cora represents the Third World woman through whose agency the colonial power exerts its influence. In Frantz Fanon's analysis of "the colonialist program" in Algeria, "it was the woman who was given the historic mission of shaking up the Algerian man." One could argue that Cora performs a similar function for Uncas. Fanon's analysis appears in *A Dying Colonialism* (New York: Grove, 1965), p. 39, and is quoted in Kaplan, 673.

25 Renato Rosaldo, "Imperialist Nostalgia," in *Culture and Truth: The Remaking of Social Analysis* (Boston: Beacon Press, 1989), p. 70.

26 Kaplan, p. 664.

27 The classic statement of this position is, of course, Ann Douglas' *The Feminization of American Culture* (New York: Avon, 1977). For a more developed critique of claims for the feminization of U.S. culture in this period, see my essay "Novels and Domesticity" in *The Columbia History of the American Novel*, ed. Emory Elliott (forthcoming, Columbia Univ. Press).

28 "Sparing the Rod: Discipline and Fiction in Antebellum America," *Representations*, No. 21 (1988), 87. Actually, this characterization of maternal love appears in an antebellum publication entitled *Mother's Magazine*, which Brodhead quotes; however, it is clear in context that Brodhead regards the quote as an accurate description of maternal authority.

29 Miller, p. 10; Douglas, p. 81.

30 *Desire and Domestic Fiction: A Political History of the Novel* (New York: Oxford Univ. Press, 1987), p. 93; Christopher Lasch, *Haven in a Heartless World: The Family Besieged* (New York: Basic Books, 1977), p. 18.

31 I admit that "obliviousness" is probably too strong a word to use in Armstrong's case. On p. 26 of the introduction to her book she manifests a good deal of self-consciousness about the gender politics of her own claims, even if she seems not to recognize the way in which they implicate her in the historical discourse she analyzes.

32 Previous feminist critiques of New Historicism include Judith Lowder Newton, "History as Usual?: Feminism and the 'New Historicism,'" in *The New Historicism*, ed. H. Aram Veeser (New York: Routledge, 1989), pp. 152–67 and Carolyn Porter, "Are We Being Historical Yet?" *South Atlantic Quarterly*, 87 (1988), 743–86. For reasons I explain in my article "Bio-Political Resistance in Domestic Ideology and *Uncle Tom's Cabin*" (*American Literary History* 1 [1989], 715–34), I do not endorse the view shared by Newton and Porter that by subscribing to theory that (in Newton's words) "den[ies] the possibility of change and agency" (p. 118) New Historicism disallows the possibility of political resistance.

Part II

Joan Dayan   Amorous Bondage: Poe, Ladies, and Slaves

> The *order of nature* has, in the end, vindicated itself, and the dependence between master and slave has scarcely for a moment ceased.—Thomas R. Dew, *Review of the Debate in the Virginia Legislature* (1832)

In October 1989 I presented the Annual Poe Lecture at the Enoch Pratt Library in Baltimore. As part of the memorial to Poe's death, we walked to the grave and put flowers on the ground—wondering if Poe was really there, for some say the body has been removed. We then proceeded to the Library where I was to deliver the Sixty-Ninth lecture on Poe. I had titled the talk "Poe's Love Poems." In writing it, in thinking about those difficult last poems of Poe—unique in the history of American poetry—I turned to what I called "his greatest love poem," the much-contested review of Paulding's *Slavery in the United States* published in the *Southern Literary Messenger* in April 1836.[1] Traditionally these lectures are published as monographs by the Poe Society of Baltimore. A month after my talk, I received a letter from the Society saying that they wanted to publish the proceedings but advised that I limit the paper to the "fine analysis of the love poems" and cut out the dubious part on slavery.

I realized then that the process of how we come to read or understand our fondest fictions results from a sometimes vicious cutting or decorous forgetting. I have not been allowed to forget my attempt to talk about the "peculiar institution" behind Poe's most popular fantasies. I have received letters from male members of the Poe Society arguing that Poe did not write the proslavery review. Three years ago, after I spoke on Poe at the Boston Athenaeum, an unidentified man appeared before me, saying: "I enjoyed your talk, but Poe had nothing to do with such social issues as slavery." He then referred to an ongoing communication he had had with another Poe critic following my talk in Baltimore, adding that I had "overstepped the bounds of good taste and discretion by contaminating the purest love poems in the English language."[2]

As these continuing confrontations demonstrate, the very questioning of authorship raises questions about Poe, property, status, superstition, and gentrification, questions that put Poe quite squarely in dialogue with the romance of the South and the realities of race. Just as the ideology of Southern honor depended upon fantasies of black degradation, racist discourse needed the rhetoric of natural servility to confirm absolute privilege. As I will argue, for Poe the cultivation of romance and the facts of slavery are inextricably linked.

I don't want to sound like Poe in his protracted discussion of his infamous performance at the Boston Lyceum in *The Broadway Journal* for nearly two years, but I do want to draw our attention to the coercive monumentalization of certain writers—specifically, how necessary Poe (and "his ladies") remain as an icon to the most cherished and necessary ideals of some men. Here is Floyd Stovall writing on "The Women of Poe's Poems and Tales": "They are all noble and good, and naturally very beautiful. . . . Most remarkable of all is their passionate and enduring love for the hero."[3] It is perhaps not surprising that some Poe critics— the founding fathers of the Poe Society, for example—sound rather like the proslavery ideologues who promoted the ideal of the lady as elegant, white, and delicate. Poe's ladies, those dream-dimmed, ethereal living dead of his poems, have been taken as exemplars of what Poe called "supernal Beauty"—an entitlement that he would degrade again and again. Think about Lady Madeline Usher returning from the grave as a brute and bloodied thing, reduced from a woman of beauty to the frenziedly iterated "*it*" of her brother Roderick. Many of the dissolutions and decays so marked in Poe's tales about women subvert the status of women as a saving ideal, thus undermining his own "Philosophy of Composition": the "death of a beautiful woman is, unquestionably, the most poetical topic in the world." No longer pure or passive, she returns as an earthy—and very unpoetical—subject.

It doth haunt me still

Let us take my experience as prelude to a rereading of Poe that depends absolutely on what has so often been cut out of his work: the institution of slavery, Poe's troubled sense of himself as a southern aristocrat, and, finally, the precise and methodical transactions in which he revealed the threshold separating humanity from animality. As I will demonstrate, his most unnatural fictions are bound to the works of natural history that are so much a part of their origination. Read in this way, Poe's sometimes inexplicable fantasies become intelligible. Poe's gothic is crucial to our understanding of the entangled metaphysics of romance and servitude. What might have remained local historiography becomes a harrowing myth of the Americas.

When we read about masters and slaves in the justifications of slavery which proliferated following the Nat Turner rebellion in Virginia on 21 and 22 August 1831, called by most Southerners the "insurrection" or "servile insurrection," women are very often absent from the discussion. Yet the Southern lady, pure, white, and on her pedestal, remained the basis out of which developed the proslavery philosophy. It was she, that amorphous yet powerfully contrived vessel of femininity, who represented the refined and artificial wants of civilized society. The patriarchal defense of the intimate relation between master and slave found itself coordinate with the insistence on the subordination of women. Here is George Fitzhugh, writing in 1850 what would become part of his acclaimed *Sociology for the South*: "A state of dependence is the only condition in which reciprocal affection can exist among human beings. . . . A man loves his children because they are weak, helpless and dependent. He loves his wife for similar reasons. When his children grow up and assert their independence, he is apt to transfer his affection to his grand-children. He ceases to love his wife when she becomes masculine or rebellious; but slaves are always dependent, never the rivals of their master."[4]

I now turn briefly to the disputed review of James Kirke Paulding's *Slavery in the United States* and William Drayton's *The South Vindicated from the Treason and Fanaticism of the Northern Abolitionists*. Here, Poe explicitly makes philosophy out of color: turning the negro inside out, he makes metaphysics out of a biological trait. The mark of blackness compels him to elucidate the propriety of possession, a belief that underlies his most popular rituals of terror. Poe begins his review with the French Revolution, arguing that "property" is what everyone wants most, and that such desire is dubiously called the "spirit of liberty." He calls this Revolution—which made its first triumph "the emancipation of slaves"—"this eccentric comet," nearly the same words used by Thomas Jefferson in *Notes on the State of Virginia* to describe the negro's imagination.[5]

But the crucial section of the Paulding review remains Poe's analysis of the "patriarchal character." His strangely sober take on "moral influences flowing from the master and slave" depends on what he calls "the peculiar character (I may say the peculiar nature) of the negro."[6] We can go further. Poe suggests that the enslaved want to be mastered, for they love—and this is the crucial word for Poe—to serve, to be subservient. Dependence is necessary to reciprocal affection, yet note that Poe does not comment on Paulding's excursus on women as "guardian angels," whose "appropriate sphere is their home, and their appropriate duties at the cradle of the fireside." Indeed, Poe says nothing about what preoccupies the conclusion of Paulding's book: his disquisition on women abolitionists who have "prostituted" (his word) themselves by "assuming the character of a man."[7] What Poe does do, however, before getting back to Paulding, is to describe the "essential" negro. He notes an inscrutable power "which works essential changes in the different races of animals." Like Jefferson he faces the conundrum of color, pausing to consider "the causes which might and should have blackened the negro's skin and crisped his hair into wool."[8]

Poe then turns to that well-worn familial argument, which he describes as the "loyal devotion on the part of the slave" and "the master's reciprocal feeling of parental attachment to his humble dependent." These "sentiments in the breast of the negro and his master," Poe explains, are stronger than they would be under like circumstances between individuals of the white race: "That they [these sentiments] belong to the class of feelings 'by which the heart is made better,' we know. How come they? . . . They grow by the habitual use of the word 'my,' used in the language of affectionate appropriation, long before any idea of value mixes with it. It is a term of endearment. That is an easy transition by which he who is taught to call the little negro 'his,' in this sense and *because he loves him*, shall love him *because he is his*."[9] It seems at first that the language of affectionate appropriation says simply that you love most what you own. But Poe goes further: he suggests that you own what you love. For unlike George Fitzhugh, Thomas Dew, or Beverley Tucker, Poe is not simply speaking of desirable and ready submission, he is busy making convertible love and possession.

Mud and spirit

I might have titled this essay "Mud and Spirit," for Poe's textual cruxes have always to do with conversions between matter and spirit, between the utmost carnality and absolute ideality. The debate in *Eureka* about the suspension in cosmic rhythms between matter and not matter is grounded in enlightened disquisitions on the physiognomies of man and brute and, more precisely, in the character of a man and the nature of the negro. In most natural histories—for example Buffon's *Histoire Naturelle* or those other strangely unnatural "natural histories" of the Caribbean—as in the works of Southern theologians and proslavery advocates, the negro approximated the most destitute and most needy of all animals. For Edward Long in his extraordinary *History of Jamaica* (1774), negroes, excluded from the rest of mankind, were signal for a particular kind of exaltation. According to Long, from these degradations, from "mere inert matter," we can ascend "into the animal and vegetable kingdoms," until finally we proceed "from analogy" to "matter endued with thought and reason!"[10]

What is most striking and of course most infamous in Long's meditation is that the word *negro* calls up a disturbingly minute analysis of body parts and gradations of being, until finally he draws an analogy between the negro and the orangutan. "The oran-outang's brain," he claims, "is a senseless *icon* of the human; . . . it is meer matter, unanimated with a thinking principle."[11] Thomas Dew, Poe's friend and professor of political economy at William and Mary College, warned that even with "the free black . . . the animal part of the man gains the victory over the moral, and he, consequently, prefers sinking down into the listless, inglorious repose of the brute creation."[12]

When Long wrote about what he called the progression "from a lump of dirt to a perfect human being," he meant the move from matter to man. But what is the relation between those "creatures" constituted as brute exemplars of matter and the rarified vessels of spirit, those species of "true womanhood" who haunt the learned discourse on race as the absolute perfection so antithetical to—and yet as subordinated as—that lump of dirt? What do we gain by forcing proximity on those categories and claims the naturalists so rigorously separated?

Perhaps all of Poe's work is finally about radical dehumanization: You can de-materialize—idealize—by turning humans into animals or by turning them into angels. As Poe proves throughout *Eureka* and in his angelic colloquies, matter and not matter are convertible. Further, both processes, etherealization or brutalization (turning into angel or brute), involve displacement of the human element. We are dealing with a process of sublimation, either up or down. Animality, after all, emerges for most nineteenth-century phrenologists, theologians, and anthropologists in those beings who are classified as both human and beast: lunatics, women, primates, black men, and children. What remains unmentioned, and uncoded, is the manhood at the center of these operations. It is this powerfully absent construction that Poe intentionally probes. He, the white epistemologist of the sublime, the enlightenment "universal man," haunts Poe's writings. It is his divisions, as well as his projections, that Poe confounds.

Thus the unbelievable overturning of the law of identity and contradiction that I have argued to be central to Poe's work can now be considered as more than a fable of mind. Poe's reconstructions depend upon experiences that trade on unspeakable slippages between men and women, humans and animals, life and death. Poe deliberately undermines the taxonomic vocations of male supremacy and thus attributes to it a troubling, ambiguous vitality.

"My tantalized spirit"

Poe's tales about women—"Morella," "Ligeia," "Berenice," "The Fall of the House of Usher," and "Eleonora"—are about the men who narrate the unspeakable remembrance: not the gun-toting, masterful cavaliers or gentlemen of southern fictions of the gentry, but the delicate acolytes of erudite ladies or the terrified victims of the lady revenants. In these tales, possession, multiple hauntings, and identity dissolutions suspend gender difference as a component of identity. The memorial act demands a willing surrender to an anomalous atmosphere where one thing remains certain: the dead do not die. They will not stay buried. In Poe's tales these awfully corporeal ghosts are always women. As we read the compelling narratives of the men who wait and watch for the inevitable return, we sense how much the terror depends on the men's will to remember, their sorcerer-like ability to name and to conjure the beloved, who is, of course, the exemplar for later "white zombies."

Poe's ideal of "indefinitiveness," his turn to the "ethereal," "ideal," "breath of faery," or "mystic," is most weirdly disrupted in his poetry. The three poems that trouble me most are the second "To Helen," "For Annie," and "To——." Terms such as "saintliness," "sweet," "ideal," or "feminine perfection" (often used by critics to describe the women of Poe's poems) obscure how deliberately Poe fragments and dissolves conventional images of "womanliness." In these poems Poe reveals the progress of perfection: its absolute dependence on the imperfect. In "To Helen," we move from a lady's "upturn'd" face in a landscape of dying, smiling roses, with faces also "upturn'd," to the progressive elimination of the world of nature: "The pearly lustre of the moon went out: / The mossy banks and the meandering paths, / The happy flowers and the re- pining trees, / Were seen no more." Every part of the lady is obliterated, except for her eyes: *"Only thine eyes remained.* / They *would not* go— they never yet have gone / . . . . / They follow me—they lead me through the years. / They are my ministers—yet I their slave."[13]

There is something less than ideal or sanctifying about these eyes. They recall the eyes of the Lady Ligeia or Berenice's teeth forever im- printed on the narrator's mind. In the process of abstraction, once every piece of nature named is blotted out, no woman remains but only what Poe calls "less than thou." Woman, "the fair sex," and the "romance" she bears can only be experienced as fragment. Freed from marriage, domesticity, and any possible relation to property, the beloved is reduced to a haunting remnant. But what happens to the poet? Yielding himself passive to the lovelight, as does the death-obsessed imaginist of "For Annie," Poe renders himself up as "slave" to those omniscient eyes: "Their office is to illumine and enkindle— / My duty, *to be saved* by their bright light" (96–97). The bereaved lover thus figures himself through a servitude articulated as salvation.

As a way to read the surrender of these love poems, I want briefly to recall the rhetoric of redemption in Poe's Paulding-Drayton Review. In the scenes of suffering that conclude the review, Poe appreciates the all-consuming etiology of possession. As the master weakens, the ser- vant remains fixed in a relentless, nearly superhuman deathwatch. How different are such spectacles of feeling from Poe's representation of the compulsive lover in these poems, or in the bedside vigils of "Ligeia" and "Morella"? For Poe, adoration is always a deadly business. When he wrote his review, Poe merely reiterated the sentimental decor necessary for maintaining the illusion of mastery. But by the time he composed these late poems, he had apprehended the ruse of sentiment and not only exposed, but satirized the inalienable bond between the illusions of reverent attachment and the matter of human bondage.

In "To———" written to Marie Louise Shew in 1848, Poe fantasizes about being swallowed up by the object of his affections. A strange turn takes place midway through the poem. He takes the name that he will not name, "two foreign soft dissyllables"—Lady "Marie Louise"—(she remains unnamed in the published version) as prod to his undoing:

> . . . And I! my spells are broken.
> The pen falls powerless from my shivering hand.
> With thy dear name as text, though bidden by thee,
> I cannot write—I cannot speak or think,
> Alas, I cannot feel; for 'tis not feeling,
> This standing motionless upon the golden
> Threshold of the wide-open gate of dreams,
> Gazing, entranced, adown the gorgeous vista,
> And thrilling as I see upon the right,
> Upon the left, and all the way along
> Amid empurpled vapors, far away
> To where the prospect terminates—*thee only*. (88)

Here we have another strange vanishing ritual, which like that of "To Helen" seems to mock the progress of corporeality from matter to man. The more closely Poe analyzes and purifies his notions, the more he tries to establish a solid foundation, the more he loses himself in fantasy. Poe's unlinked Great Chain completely mixes men, nature, women, reason, and dreams. Not only does feeling summon dissolution, but Poe takes heartfelt affection and turns it into lust. What Southerners dignified by the name love, Poe rather unceremoniously presents as fierce, inhuman desire. In "To————" he animates not feeling or thought, but instead wildly physicalized passion that has far from salutary effects on the soul.

The poet trades his subjectivity, his very power to speak or write, for the most fleshly part of his beloved, looking into her heart of hearts. Poe has coerced feeling into image; as in "To Helen," we are left with a strangely fetishized kernel of womanhood, those scintillant "star eyes." Here, "thee" is implicitly the "heart" that can be reached only through penetration "adown the gorgeous vista" into a tunnel-like space that thrills as it constrains, "upon the right / Upon the left, and all the way along / Amid empurpled vapors, far away / To where the prospect terminates—."

Why does Poe so often present himself in these later poems as a "slave" to the images he has created? What does he mean by this posture of enfeeblement, his claim of impotence? What I will suggest is that Poe articulates a specific relation of domination, where the speaker who has defined himself as possessor is in turn defined by his possession. I quote two passages of variously willed passivity: a stanza from "To Annie" and a passage from a letter to Sara Helen Whitman.

> Sadly, I know
>   I am shorn of my strength,
> And no muscle I move
>   As I lie at full length—
> But no matter!—I feel
>   I am better at length. (98)

Oh God! how I now curse the impotence of the pen—the inexorable *distance* between us! I am pining to speak to *you*, Helen,—to you in person—to be near you while I speak—gently to press your hand in mine—to look into your soul through your eyes—and thus *to be sure* that my voice passes into your heart.[14]

To gain a voice necessitates the writer's becoming the beloved. Getting into her mind will ensure that his voice gets into her heart. To want to be in the place of another is to be possessed. Or put another way, if you can't have her, then you can become her. Poe understands the law of the heart, the power in the word *my*. And in nearly all of Poe's dealings with ladies, whether in letters (recycled to various "real" beloveds), poems, or tales, he has possessed all the others so fully that they become the same, not only interchangeable with each other, but with Edgar Poe.

Yet if we put "To Helen" or "For Annie" in their Southern context, we can go further. Nathaniel Beverley Tucker, proslavery apologist and professor of law at William and Mary, who befriended Poe and was his greatest supporter when Poe edited the *Southern Literary Messenger* in 1835–36, wrote much about "obedience to the law of Love." In his "Moral and Political Effect of the Relation between the Caucasian Master and the African Slave," the terms of contrast are again limited to the benevolent master and grateful servant paradigm. But in *George Balcombe*, a romance of Missouri and Virginia, published in 1836, Tucker included women—and especially "genuine feminine devotion"—in his philosophy of feeling. He asked his male readers to seek those women who reject the "'ologies' of female radicals," and prefer "to learn the housewifely duties and plain old fashioned sense of a Virginia lady." Referring to unmarriageable "learned ladies," George Balcombe warns that there are "'secrets in heaven and earth not dreamed of in their philosophy.'" Instead, the uncorrupted—and "uncultivated"—woman will beware "*intellectual distinction,* or *distinction* of any kind," for such "a feeling unsexes her." This *real* woman "reads her Bible, works her sampler, darns her stockings, and boils her bacon and greens together." [15]

Before turning to Poe's review of Tucker's *George Balcombe*, I want to emphasize that Tucker's portrayal of the lady depends for its effect on another favorite subject of the gentleman George Balcombe: the zealous and appreciative negro. Balcombe's most lengthy disquisitions concern wives and slaves. What is the "noblest of God's works"? Balcombe has the answer: "a *right woman*—a *genuine unsophisticated woman.*" [16] The "established order of the universe," Balcombe's magisterial hierarchy, depends absolutely on distinguishing superior and inferior beings: "I see gradations in everything. I see subordination everywhere." Within this created order, rising in a climax of subordination, white men are on top. Men of "delicacy" marry only women who know their place. Only these women can enjoy the bonds of matrimony, and only grateful negroes can be graced with "that strong tie . . . spun out of the interchange of service and protection." Those born slaves actually "feel themselves inferior," and that sentiment alone is "the *rationale* of the filial and parental bond." [17] Finally, Balcombe clinches his argument about negroes, tradition, and "inextinguishable affection" by joining women with blacks in happy servitude: "Is gratitude abject? Is self-abandoning, zealous devotion abject? If the duties of heaven require these sentiments, and its happiness consist in their exercise, which of us is it that is but a little lower than the angels— the negro or the white man? . . . Let women and negroes alone, and instead of quacking with them, physic your own diseases. Leave them in their humility, their grateful affection, their self-renouncing loyalty, their subordination of the heart, and let it be your study to become worthy to be the object of these sentiments." [18]

Poe reviewed *George Balcombe* in *The Southern Literary Messenger* in 1837. Most of the review is plot summary. Although Poe says nothing about Tucker's theory of servitude, he does pay attention to the women characters. The ever-blushing Mary Scott, who was "'beautiful and intelligent—gay, sprightly and impassioned,'" Poe praises as "imbued with the spirit of romance." Remarking on Elizabeth, whom he describes as "the shrinking and matronly wife of Balcombe," he concludes: "She is an exquisite specimen of her class, but her class is somewhat hacknied." Poe's favorite character is Ann, the proper Virginia lady, who in Balcombe's words is "'wise, generous, and delicate.'" Poe concludes his judgment of Tucker's ladies by asserting: "Upon the whole, no American novelist has succeeded, we think, in female character, even nearly so well as the writer of George Balcombe." [19]

Like women characters in the works of John Pendleton Kennedy and William Gilmore Simms, Tucker's proper ladies are passive and accommodating, utterly dependent on the men who regulate their destiny. In *George Balcombe*, Tucker's portrayal of the ideal wife reflects the character of her husband: "while her husband's light was above the horizon, [she] hid herself beneath it, or if she appeared at all, modestly paled her lustre in his presence." [20] But when Poe yields himself up to the "bright light" of Helen, he shifts the entire patriarchal argument to the domain that seems relevant to him, namely, the reversibility of supremacy. In Poe's mechanics of love, heartfelt men become vague and impotent, while beloved women become shadowy or reduced to pieces of prized and sexualized symbolic matter. In a time when many argued for sharper categorizations and more hierarchy, when ladies, slaves, and men endured ever more difficult trials of definition, Poe managed to confound and denaturalize the so-called "natural order" of things. In prostrating himself before the fetishized women of his poems or creating powerful intellects, mystics, and witches like Ligeia and Morella, Poe worked changes on the subservient women praised by his fellow Southerners.

As we have seen, Poe is preoccupied with repeated and varied postures of enfeeblement: a deliberate weakness that leaves only feeling, an obsession with the heart that links the white male writer, the white woman of his dreams, and the ungendered, unmentioned black. Without mentioning blacks, Poe applies the accepted argument on the "nature" of negroes and the "spirit" of women—both feeling, not thinking things— to the white men usually excluded from such categorization. [21]

When Poe dwells repeatedly on the extremes of savagery and cultivation, brute possession and tender affection, he refers to a long history of racialist writings, including those by natural historians such as George Buffon and Edward Long. Buffon described "Negroes" as "naturally compassionate and tender." [22] Edward Long discussed at length the "courteous, tender disposition" of the orangutan, debasing black women in the process. Long tells his readers that orangutans "sometimes endeavour to surprize and carry off negroe women into their woody retreats." He then turns to these negroes, to whom he grants not a trace of affectionate feeling, describing them as "libidinous and shameless as monkies, or baboons." Entertaining no question as to whether or not a black female would accept an ape for a husband, Long assures his readers that "hot" negro women seek out these animals to "embrace." [23]

If white women were imaged by advocates of slavery as emptied of all qualities that could attach them to physical reality while black women became vessels for the carnality that was expelled from icons of pure womanhood, Poe takes the blushing belle and makes her both passionate and suspiciously white, with a deathly, unnatural pallor that makes whiteness as negative and opaque as what Jefferson had described in *Notes on the State of Virginia* as an "immoveable veil of black." Further, Poe's voice as poet reconstitutes itself, the male lover in nineteenth-century America, as a wholly negative consciousness, obeisant to the law of the heart.[24] The law, as Poe defines it, however, has more to do with lust than propriety, and he substitutes monomaniacal frenzy for the delicately modulated feelings of the "civilized" Southerner.

There is a two-pronged program here. First Poe plays with the possibility of one thing passing into another and vice versa—the *convertibility* so much a part of his project. The superior male mind erected over the bodies of women continuously purified or defiled, and blacks alternately sentimentalized or cursed, turns into the very objects once posited as external to it. Second, Poe repeats, exaggerates, and transforms the immutable, romanticized attributes white women are granted by men. He dramatizes the fact of appropriation, and thereby undefines the definitions that mattered to civilized society. It is not surprising, then, that one Poe reviewer writing in 1856 reflected: "In perusing his most powerful tales, the reader feels himself surrounded by hitherto unapprehended dangers; he grows suspicious of his best friends; all good angels appear turning to demons." [25]

Dying to serve

To read much of nineteenth-century literature is to encounter conceits of servitude. From Caleb Williams's anguished and ambiguous declaration to Falkland, "Sir, I could die to serve you!" to Jane Eyre's "I'd give my life to serve you," to a Bartleby who quite literally dies to serve while refusing to do so, readers who thought they would escape to fictions, or romances, found themselves treated to scenes of mastery and servitude. Even the supernatural in many gothic tales had its real basis in the language of slavery and colonization, put forth as the most natural thing in the world. One has only to read the 1685 *Code noir* of Louis XIV, that collection of edicts concerning "the Discipline and Commerce of Negro Slaves in the French Islands of America," to understand how what first seems phantasmagoric is locked into a nature mangled and relived as a spectacle of servitude. Its surreal precisions in human reduction (how best turn a man into a thing), like Long's anatomical permutations on monkey, man, horse, and negro, demonstrate how unnatural the claims to right and property actually were.

The *Code noir* or *Black Code* is a document of limits.[26] Unlike the racist disquisition on blacks as lacking the finer feelings of a tender heart, the Code is not concerned with the tangled semantics of charitable servitude or lurking debauchery. We read instead sixty articles that take us into a chilling series of qualifications: prohibitions that permit, limitations that invite excess, and a king's grandiloquence that ensures divestment. There is no time for discussions of innate inferiority, natural difference, or nightmares of contamination. For the blacks and slaves in French America are introduced not as persons, but as a special kind of property: a "thing," according to Roman law, juridically deprived of all rights. Once acquired by a planter, legally divested of their self and removed from their land, slaves became the planter's possession. Alternately defined as chattels and as real property, they were sometimes movable assets (part of the planter's personal estate) and sometimes unmovable, disposed of as if real estate, or in especially macabre cases, as if garbage.

If the *Black Code* turned a human into a thing, a piece of movable property, it could be argued that "the law of the heart" accomplishes the same end. For the law of the heart remains inseparable from the fact of property. Southern proslavery apologists appreciated the special privileges that accompanied possession, as did some abolitionists, who could never quite liberate their objects of pathos from domination. The acclaimed dispossession of Stowe's *Uncle Tom's Cabin* works only as long as the "negro" is kept forever separate in essence from the Anglo-Saxon, locked in the precincts of affectionate service, impressionable spirituality, and childlike simplicity. Stowe's fantasy, brimful of just pity, remains entirely affirming and satisfying to the "superior" white ego. How different, after all, is Stowe's representation of Tom stretched out supine on the veranda in order to be close to the dying Eva—what Miss Ophelia calls "sleeping anywhere and everywhere, like a dog"—from Poe's portrayal in the Paulding-Drayton Review of the bond between master and servant?

Poe's dramatizations of possession—a reciprocal devouring of self and other—reminds us of the force of language, especially literary language, to allow the covert continuation of domination. Fictions of sentiment and idealizations of love, the special realm of right-minded women and domesticated blacks, are linked in unsettling ways to the social realities of property and possession. Poe knew how the sanctifying of women depends upon a more sinister brutalization, or spectralization. His narrators in "Ligeia," "Berenice," and "Morella," for example, demonstrate how the language of love can animate and sustain utter servility.

Sentiment, as Poe confirmed in "The Black Cat," is not only coercive but also despotic. The rare and special love between slave and master, man and wife, based on the law of property, becomes the medium by which perfect submission becomes equivalent to a pure but perverse love. A slave, a piece of property, a black pet, once loved in the proper domestic setting, effects an excess of devotion, an inextricable bond that proslavery apologists—and even Captain Delano in Melville's *Benito Cereno*—argued can never be felt by two equals. Of course, Poe writes "The Black Cat" to demonstrate how destructive is the illusion of mastery: just as the pet of perfect docility turns into *"a brute beast,"* "a man, fashioned in the image of the High God," is dependent on and utterly enslaved by the very thing he has so lovingly brutalized (603).

No place of grace

We need to reread Poe's romantic fictions as bound to the realities of race, keeping "every thing . . . within the limits of the accountable—of the real," as he urged in "The Philosophy of Composition." There is a logic to his excessive attention to blood, things dirtied, and bodies mutilated. Lurking in every effusion of ennobling love is the terror of literal dehumanization: not only the Burkean sublime or the Calvinist's rhetoric of sensation, but that most terrific conversion, the reduction of human into thing for the ends of capital.

Think about the degradation and rot, the "premature burial" in the confines of the Grampus in *The Narrative of Arthur Gordon Pym* in terms of the slave ship: the "close atmosphere of the hold" where Pym hides; drinking water "putrid and swarming with vermin"; Augustus's body "loathsome beyond expression," reduced finally into a "mass of putrefaction." When Pym describes the ship of the dead, he uses rhetorical strategies characteristic of an apocalypse, but the ultimate disclosure here is the stench of a slaver (a return to the "skeleton ship" of Coleridge's *The Ancient Mariner*): "Of a sudden, and all at once, there came wafted over the ocean from the strange vessel (which was now close upon us) a smell, a stench, such as the whole world has no name for—no conception of—hellish—utterly suffocating—insufferable, inconceivable" (1085). In reconsidering Poe's relentlessly circumscribed settings, the pits of unspeakable crimes, we recall the holds of slave ships, those " 'dens of putrefaction' " as C. L. R. James described them in *The Black Jacobins*, his history of the revolution in Saint-Domingue.

I take as parable for the late-in-coming recognition of the African American ever present though unrecognized in Poe's gothic, "Morning on the Wissahiccon," his strange meditation on the hidden though "real Edens" of the United States. Those ignored areas, less travelled than those on the northern and eastern seaboard, are located in "the gorgeous interior . . . of some of our western and southern districts" (939). Poe finally chooses a "pedestrian tour" along the Wissahiccon, "a brook . . . which empties itself into the Schuylkill, about six miles westward of Philadelphia" (942).

After describing the typical walk, he recounts his own visit to the stream, where, enwrapped in dreams of the " 'good old days'," he sees "or dreamed that I saw" an elk from the days when "the red man trod alone." His fantasies of those idyllic days before the land had been marred "by the stern hand of the utilitarian" are interrupted by a curious intrusion. He suddenly hears a furtive " 'hist! hist!' " and says: "In an instant afterwards, a negro emerged from the thicket, putting aside the bushes with care, and treading stealthily." The "noble animal" does not escape, but attracted by the offering of salt by the negro, bows, stamps, and "then lay quietly down and was secured with a halter." So, he ends his "romance of the elk" (944). The Native Americans have vanished, but their elk is now kept as a pet, domesticated by a wealthy family, whose black servant retrieves the animal into bondage. The romance of the Americas, as Poe knows, depends upon a sequence of subordinations, variously called love, care, or devotion. An entire history of violence, genocide, and slavery, it could be argued, is hidden in Poe's apparently tame and visionary landscape sketch.

The facts of race intrude almost imperceptibly, yet persistently into Poe's romance. "God's plan for securing the hearts of his creatures," to quote George Balcombe, Poe insists is analogous to the polemicist's plot to justify human bondage. But he reserves his greatest scorn for those who condemn slavery while continuing to restrict blacks to the status of objects: recipients of the charity of white men who continue to be masters. As "critical reader of the transcendentalist ideologies of his time," Poe's compulsive satire on the "pundits," on their mystifying language and cant, was fueled by the abolitionist leanings of those he called the "Frogpondians": Emerson, Thoreau, Lowell, and especially Longfellow.[27]

Emerson's 1844 address on the tenth anniversary of the emancipation of the negroes in the British West Indies preceded Poe's Lyceum debacle by about a year. For Emerson, the mettle of white men has been proved by their largesse on "behalf of the African": "Other revolutions have been the insurrection of the oppressed; this was the repentance of the tyrant. It was the masters revolting from their mastery."[28] Not only is Emerson idealizing, and decontextualizing, a far more disturbing history, but what he calls "elevation and pathos" keeps whites quite secure in their superiority while blacks, though no longer called slaves, remain inferior. Invited to the Boston Lyceum, Poe deliberately insults his audience by reading "Al Aaraaf" (which he introduced by saying he wrote it at nineteen years old), renamed "The Messenger Star of Tycho Brahe" for that "drunken" spectacle.[29] Poe's blustering and offensive performance no doubt had its sources not only in envy, insecurity, and aesthetic debate, but in his disapproval of Emerson's high-minded celebration of West Indian emancipation as a "piece of moral history."

Poe's attack in *Eureka*, carrying further his condemnation of those he called the oracles of "higher morality," those "thinkers-that-they-think," who wander "in the shadowy region of imaginary truth," remained grounded in his disdain for those he condemned in his reviews as "the small coterie of abolitionists, transcendentalists and fanatics in general." After all, what he attacked as "the frantic spirit of generalization" was one of the major accusations of proslavery advocates in the South who called the Northern abolitionists fools of abstraction who knew nothing of the particulars of Southern slavery. In order to understand Poe's unceasing condemnation of the Bostonians as a "knot of rogues and madmen," we need to reread literary history as regional debate.

Poe's obsessive attacks on Longfellow—and especially his critique of the poem "The Slave in the Dismal Swamp" in his 1845 review of Longfellow's *Poems of Slavery* (1842)—come not only from envy or aesthetic discretion, as some have suggested, but the acute knowledge of the facts behind Longfellow's romantic sentimentalism. The Dismal Swamp, sometimes called "the Great Dismal," was for a long time the receptacle of runaway slaves in the South. Poe no doubt read Samuel Warner's "Authentic and Impartial Narrative," an account of Nat Turner's "Horrid

Massacre," published in 1831. Warner's description of the "very large bog, extending from N. to S. near 30 miles, and from E. to W. at a medium about 10 miles," where cypress and cedar cast an "everlasting shade," could well be a source for Poe's ghastly landscape of "Silence— A Fable" (composed in 1832 and published in 1835). Even birds do not fly over this gloomy swamp, "for fear of the noisome exhalations that rise from this vast body of filth and nastiness. These noxious vapors infect the air round about." Warner then exclaims, "It is within the deep recesses of this gloomy Swamp, 'dismal' indeed, beyond the power of human conception, that the runaway Slaves of the South have been known to secret themselves for weeks, months, and years, subsisting on frogs, tarrapins, and even snakes!"[30]

Poe must have known about the scouring of the swamp in pursuit of slaves, of the hounds that scented unsuccessfully after Nat Turner. Yet, as so often in his writings, Poe misrecognizes or disavows the facts he knows, condemning Longfellow for writing "a shameless medley of the grossest misrepresentation. When did Professor LONGFELLOW ever *know* a slave to be hunted with bloodhounds in the *dismal swamp*? Because he has heard that runaway slaves are so treated in CUBA, he has certainly no right to change the locality."[31] But some of what Poe says matters, for Longfellow's poem purifies the place. He cleans up the mire. The vessel for squalor, the bearer of putrefaction in "The Slave in the Dismal Swamp" is his "poor old slave, infirm and lame," who hides in an unreal landscape:

Where will-o'-the wisps and glowworms shine,
    In bulrush and in brake;
Where waving mosses shroud the pine,

.   .   .   .

All things above were bright and fair,
    All things were glad and free;
Lithe squirrels darted here and there,
And wild birds filled the echoing air
    With songs of Liberty![32]

Longfellow's picture of the "hunted Negro," like other portraits of the pathetic hero so popular in the North, allows the reader pity but also distance from the poeticized object of emotion.[33]

Poe did not accept Longfellow's translation of the Dismal Swamp into an Edenic scene contaminated by one spot of deformity, the slave. Indeed, Poe's dark, stagnant waters, the "morass" and "wilderness" in "Silence—A Fable," at "the boundary of the dark, horrible, lofty forest," reiterates the locale of the hunted. It is "The Island of the Fay," however, that communicates something of the terror felt by those Southerners who read accounts of black "monstrosity" and feared insurgent slaves hiding in the shadows of the Dismal Swamp. Poe's voyager observes "in a single view both the eastern and western extremities of the islet." The two ends mark two extremes of landscape and two myths of the South: one a "radiant harem of garden beauties," a piece of heaven, filled with flowers, butterflies, and sun; the other "whelmed in the blackest shade." The voyager dreams about the dark side. In the gloom of the cypress he forces a merger between his idyll of innocence and an unrelenting dirge. Seen after "the light," the shadow upon shadow on this end of the island move Poe to fancy a place of enchantment. But what kind of enchantment? "This is the haunt of the few gentle Fays who remain from the wreck of the race." As in *Pym*, the narrative depends upon a crisis of black and white, but here what was white becomes utterly imbricated in and absorbed by blackness.[34] And yet the shadows that overtake the imagined "Fay," identified by Poe as "Death," are part of her very substance, what had made her "magic": "her shadow fell from her, and was swallowed up in the dark water, making its blackness more black" (937–38).

In what should be reread as Poe's fantasy of the South, the shadows of those who once lived "sweet lives" gradually dissolve "into the ebony water" and become "absorbed into its blackness," until finally, "the Fay, now the mere ghost of her former self, went disconsolately with her boat into the region of the ebony flood—and that she issued thence at all I cannot say,—for darkness fell over all things, and I beheld her magical figure no more" (938). The spirit's magic, her enchanted beauty, is hybrid, an amalgam of black and white. Poe rewrites the cult of purity central to Southern romance. All that remains of "the master race" are these spirits. But in this fable of color, the white fays, in getting back their bodies, merge into blackness. No longer pure, they disappear, blending with what had been construed as their antithesis in the "natural" order of things.

When we note varying denigrations of blacks in Poe's early works, it becomes even more unsettling that issues of race, like those of gender, have not figured significantly in Poe criticism.[35] But then, much that is necessary to the sanctification of something called "literariness"—those texts that are praised as art not politics—is risked if we put Poe in his place, if we avoid the romantic image of a genius in "Dream-Land," "Out of SPACE / out of TIME" (79). For instance, in "The Journal of Julius Rodman," the "faithful negro" Toby is described "as ugly an old gentleman as ever spoke—having all the peculiar features of his race; the swollen lips, large white protruding eyes, flat nose, long ears, double head, pot-belly, and bow legs" (1242). And of course, there is the orangutan in "Murders in the Rue Morgue," whose strange gibberish at first sug-gests "primitive" vocables: "it might have been the voice of an Asiatic—of an African" (416).[36] In Poe's review of Robert Bird's *Sheppard Lee*, a story of metempsychosis, lost bodies, and wandering spirits—an obvious source for Poe's "The Gold Bug"—Poe discusses the "negro servant, Jim Jumble . . . a crabbed, self-willed old rascal, who will have every thing his own way." In Bird's story, as Poe represents it in his review, Jim Jumble "conceives that money has been buried by Captain Kid, in a certain ugly swamp, called the Owl-Roost. . . . The stories of the negro affect his master to such a degree that he dreams three nights in succession of finding a treasure at the foot of a beech-tree in the swamp."[37] Sheppard Lee's failure to find the treasure, falling dead, and then turning into a ghost and looking for yet another body to inhabit (briefly possessing the corpse of a "miserable negro slave" called "Nigger Tom"), will be revised in Poe's tale of Legrand, who does the conceiving, and the manumitted black servant Jupiter, who knows (*nose*) nothing—unable to tell his left eye from his right—concluding with a final, successful treasure hunt.[38]

Yet even though Poe used racist stereotypes in stories like "The Man That was Used Up," "The Gold Bug," or "Murders in the Rue Morgue," I suggest that he exercised these images in order to tell another story. Let us take as example "The Man That Was Used Up: A Tale of the Late Buga-boo and Kickapoo Campaign" (1839). Not only does Poe describe the dis-memberment and redemption of Brigadier General John A. B. C. Smith, but he writes the "other" into the white hero's tale, putting those called "savages" or "things" into the myth of Anglo-Saxon America. Reduced to "an odd looking bundle of something" by the Bugaboo and Kickapoo Indians in a "tremendous swamp-fight away down South" (doubtless, an allusion to the Dismal Swamp), the General is put together every morn-ing by Pompey, his black valet. With each successive body part replaced, the General regains the voice of the consummate Southern gentleman while remaining utterly dependent on the "old negro" he debases. He calls Pompey "dog," then "nigger," then "scamp," and finally, once all his parts are reassembled, "black rascal" (315–16).

When Poe was "dying" for "Annie," he was writing his most horrible tale of retribution, "Hop-Frog; or, The Eight Chained Ourang-Outangs" (1849). What Mabbott regards as "a terrible exposition of the darkness of a human soul" is Poe's envisioned revenge for the national sin of slavery.[39] As we have seen, orangutans were deemed the most appropriate analogues for blacks. Here Poe literalizes what natural historians perceived as bestial similitude and prophesies the apocalypse of "servile" war so feared by Southerners. In the fiery climax of "Hop-Frog," eight cruel masters get turned into orangutans by an enslaved dwarf "from some barbarous region . . . no person ever heard of" (900). Just as the unidentifiable "gibberish" of the orangutan murderer in the Rue Morgue "might have been the voice of an Asiatic—of an African," this unheard of place refers implicitly to Africa. Tarred and flaxed, the masters are burned to "a fetid, blackened, hideous, and indistinguishable mass" (908). The blind spot of most critics to slavery and its justifications as ground for the turn in "Hop-Frog" is exemplifed when Mabbott reflects: "The manner of chaining apes described is not mentioned by any authorities consulted."[40]

The dependence of much gothic fiction on Calvinist theology and apocalyptic text can be particularized as the relation between a "suffering"—alternately degraded and idealized—"servant" and an omniscient master. In Poe's narrations of domination, enslavement compels convertibility, where, as Hegel argued in his *Phenomenology*, the distinction between master and slave is transformed: "just as lordship showed its essential nature to be the reverse of what it wants to be, so, too, bondage will, when completed, pass into the opposite of what it immediately is."[41] Aware of the perils of mastery, Poe repeats the conversion narrative so much a part of material possession. As with Poe's tales about avenging women—those beloveds who haunt and possess the lover—"Hop-Frog" inverts and reconstitutes what Orlando Patterson has called "the idiom of power."[42]

"When ladies did not walk but floated"

Poe's "ladies," once returned to their home in the South, urge us to think about the way rituals of purity depend on reminders of dirt. In the fantasy of dissolution that concludes "The Island of the Fay," the fairy reveals her essence in dying. Her gist is black, and hence her death is a darkening. In this final spectralization, Poe responds to racial taxonomies that depend for their effect on precariously rarified white women. This spirit exudes the shadows that had always filled her. In 1852, three years after Poe's death, George Frederick Holmes reviewed *Uncle Tom's Cabin* in the *Southern Literary Messenger*. Holmes moves from the descent of the novel "from its graceful and airy home" to "a more vulgar mission," thus, he believes, tainting its "robe of ideal purity" to "that sex," who must be protected by "'the lords of creation,'" unless she, like her fiction, "deliberately steps beyond the hallowed precincts—the enchanted circle—which encompasses her with the halo of divinity."[43]

What Poe called the "circumscribed Eden of dreams" he knew to encompass more than just maiden purity. Women can be granted "spirit" by men only because these men delimit ceremonies of subordination that include women, blacks, dogs, and children. Just as slaves earn benefits when they labor and obey, women deserve gallantry as long as they are inert or inactive vessels. But if these privileged women interact with their maker, get too close to the men who act on them, men could be threatened with the foul contamination they feared. In love stories that become ghost stories, Poe's narrators first look upon, idealize, and feel with the mind, hollowing out the beloved image, and then turn on the object of their affections, only to suffer retribution for their conversion, or "alternation," as the narrator of "Berenice" puts it.

In "Our Cousin, Mr. Poe," Allen Tate writes that Poe's "exalted idealization of Woman" was "more intense, than the standard cult of Female Purity in the Old South." Tate suspects that Poe "was not quite, perhaps, a Southern gentleman." For he turns his dead ladies into vampires, and most important, these erudite women could never be part of the social and economic needs that undergirded antebellum Virginia. After all, Virginia perpetuated itself "through the issue of the female body, while the intellect, which was public and political, remained under the supervision of the gentlemen."[44]

What then is the nature of Poe's intensity in writing about women? In his "private" dealings with women, Poe was excessively polite, if not chivalric in courtly, Southern style. In his personal life, he appreciated the value of recycling terms of endearment, the more romantic the better. It did not matter what he did to his ladies—whether he courted more than one at the same time, lied, or betrayed—as long as he remained genteel. Yet Poe's objects of affection should not blind us to Poe's serious attention to women writers, nor to his awareness of society's mechanisms of control. Writing about Elizabeth Barrett Browning, he laments that a false code of gallantry prohibits the serious critique women deserve as well as men. Poe as critic did not want to subject women to "the down-right degradation of mere puffery," and when he turns to Barrett's *The Drama of Exile*, he does not spare her his critique. He praises her for "very extraordinary resources," but condemns her for representing Eve not as "a woman" but instead as "a mystical something or nothing, en-wrapped in a fog of rhapsody about Transfiguration." Unlike his cloying and sentimental reviews of Frances Sargent Osgood and Lydia Huntley Sigourney, Poe is tough on Barrett, no doubt because her "obscurity" reminds him of "the cant of the transcendentalists."[45]

Like those Southern gentlemen who kept "black wenches" and "white ladies" neatly categorized, Poe does not explicitly connect the idea of race to that of gender, yet he suggests such a coupling in his fictions and poetry. Although he reviews both Margaret Fuller and Lydia Maria Child, he never mentions their essays against slavery or their comparison of violated slaves to women subordinated in marriage. Only once in a review does Poe link the institution of marriage and that of slavery. Reviewing Longfellow's *Poems on Slavery*, he describes "the Quadroon Girl" as "the old abolitionist story—worn threadbare—of a slaveholder selling his own child." He adds, "a thing which may be as common in the South, as in the East, is the infinitely worse crime of making matrimonial merchandise—or even less legitimate merchandise—of one's daughter."[46]

What Poe seldom did in his criticism, he accomplished in his fictions. Let us recall that in "Ligeia" Poe's blond Lady Rowena of Tremaine is married off for money: "Where were the souls of the haughty family of the bride, when, through thirst of gold, they permitted to pass the threshold of an apartment *so* bedecked, a maiden and a daughter so beloved?" A "lady" like Ligeia becomes the site for a crisis of racial identity. In life, Ligeia "came and departed as a *shadow*," and before her bodily "return," the narrator envisions "a *shadow* . . . such as might be fancied for the shadow of a shade." That Ligeia would not tell her lover about her family, or ever reveal her "paternal name" makes this lady sound as if she might well be Poe's rendition of the favorite fiction of white readers: the "tragic mulatta" or "octoroon mistress."[47]

In "Ligeia," Poe signals the same physiognomic traits as did taxono-mists of color in the Caribbean and the South: hair, eyes, and skin. Ligeia has "the raven-black, the glossy, the luxuriant and *naturally-curling tresses*" also used by Stowe when describing Harry in *Uncle Tom's Cabin* and by Child in her portrayal of Rosabella in *A Romance of the Re-public* and Rosalie in "The Quadroons," with her "glossy ringlets of . . .

raven hair." In *A Romance of the Republic* miscegenation is safely re-inscribed as nature's delightful caprice and the charming ability to speak many languages, to be mixed up or "polyglot." The female products of white and black coupling are represented as compounds of flowers blended, shaded, or striped in "mottled and clouded" hues and color natu-ralized as an "autumnal leaf" or the color of a pear made golden by the sun. Here, the origin myth for the mulatta is a "tropical"—never African—"ancestry." [48]

Ligeia's eyes, like those of the sensuous Creole beauties described by numerous observers, are large and expressive. But Poe goes further: "far larger than the ordinary eyes of *our own race*. They were even fuller than the fullest of the *gazelle eyes* of the tribe of the valley of Nourjahad." Mabbott notes that Poe alludes "to *The History of Nourjahad* by 'Sidney Biddulph' (Mrs. Frances Sheridan)" and then quotes from this text that describes Nourjahad's "seraglio" as "adorned with a number of the most beautiful female slaves, . . . whom he purchased at vast expense." [49] Ligeia's sirenlike voice, the reiterated " 'strangeness' " in her beauty, and her passion all suggest a racial heritage that would indeed be suspect, but Poe's rhapsodic and tortured circlings around the *whatness* of eyes that are linked to those of a dark tribe suggest how masterful had be-come the euphemisms for marks of blackness in a land preoccupied with construing purity out of impurity. If we recall Poe's elaborate, phantas-magoric decor of the bridal chamber wrought for the new bride Rowena with its "few ottomans and golden candelabra, of Eastern figure," we are reminded that the scene for Ligeia's resurrection is indeed a harem de-voted to the memory and perpetuation of a submission far more grounded in a particular and "peculiar" institution than has previously been noted.

Could a white lady of sufficient piety be described as having such "wild eyes," "wild desire," and "wild longing"? [50] Ligeia's "skin rivalling the purest ivory" links her further to the dubious status of women of color. How can you detect color in a white "suspect"? As colors faded and hair and eyes became closer to those of "pure" whites, new distinctions had to be invented. The attempt to name, label, and classify the degrees of color in between the extremes of black and white resulted in fantastic taxonomies of a uniquely racialized enlightenment. The epistemology of whiteness, absolutely dependent for its effect on the detection of black-ness, resulted in fantasies about secret histories and hidden taints that would then be backed up by explicit codes of law. And since it was not always possible to detect black blood in lightened skin, natural historians assured their readers that the tone of whiteness was different: unnatural, less animated, dull or faded, white but pale or closer to yellow, with a tint ranging from grayish yellow to yellowish white like ivory. This gothic obsession with identity and origins—for example, the indeterminacy of Isabella with "dark, olive cheek" in Melville's *Pierre* ("I seem not of woman born")—gets its metaphors and the myth of its ambiguities from the mottled discourse of racial identity.

Further, if matrimony remains a woman's sole purpose, even a Southern writer like Tucker in *George Balcombe* suggests, though indirectly, the horrific slippages that Poe deliberately intensifies. According to Tucker's gentlemen, a proper woman is endowed with primitive qualities that civilized society hones into generous sentiments. Docile, she learns to cherish her husband's superiority and subordinate herself to the "master feeling of her heart." A turn to God, "the great King above all gods," clinches these bonds of affection. God loves and asks nothing in return from "us helpless worms" except "our hearts."[51] Poe takes this fiction and exposes it as coordinate with the most terrifying possession. In Poe's tales about women, marriage turns what was cherished into what is scorned. In this process of reciprocal repulsions, the "Conqueror Worm" gets into the heart, "seraphs sob at vermin fangs," and as beastliness reveals itself to be the true if concealed ground of immaculate femininity, the Great House collapses.

Poe demonstrates that if justifications of slavery depended on making the black nonhuman and unnatural, women were also subject to the mind of man. They would always remain on the side of the body, no matter how white, how rarified or ethereal, or how black, earthy, and substantial. They can be hags or beauties, furies or angels. They are nothing but phantasms caught in the craw of civilization, and Poe's gothic literalizes the way that racialist terminology—and the excesses of a system that depended on discourses of gender purity for its perpetuation—generated its own gods and monsters.

Getting back to Richmond

Though Poe left Richmond in 1827, he returned home in 1835 and became editorial assistant, principal book reviewer, and finally editor of *The Southern Literary Messenger*. In 1830 the total population of Virginia was 1,211,405, of whom 694,300 were white, 47,348 were "free persons of color," and 469,757 were black slaves. Further, the 1820 census figures for Richmond demonstrate the high percentage of African Americans in the city of Poe's youth: about two-thirds of the households owned slaves.[52] So, Poe's Virginia could be argued to be a very African place.

Nat Turner's 1831 rebellion—in Southampton, some seventy miles below Richmond—along with accounts of butchery and, very often, stories of "unoffending women and children" victims were summoned whenever the question of emancipation was raised. And since emancipation in the British West Indies had been finalized in 1834, a year before Poe's return, we can imagine that many proslavery advocates found themselves faced with a double bind: rebellion or emancipation. It could be argued that folks in the Virginia Tidewater knew more about the revolution in Saint-Domingue than many in the Northern states, since proslavery newspapers and pamphlets compared "General Nat's" failed insurrection to the successful working of blood by Dessalines in Haiti in 1804, "when in one fatal night more than 1000 of the unfortunate white inhabitants of the island of St. Domingo (men, women and children) were butchered by the Negroes!"[53]

Some Virginians even feared that some of the refugees of Saint-Domingue who settled in Southampton had brought their negroes with them. "Over ten thousand émigrés from that island fled to the southern States, bringing with them new elements of fear of slave uprisings."[54] The *Virginia Gazette and General Advertiser*, for example, published frequent accounts of women tortured by black insurgents, their eyes gouged out with corkscrews and bellies ripped open to reveal unborn children to their dying mothers.[55] Although Southern newspapers tended to underplay white-sponsored atrocities during the last years of the war for independence, they did report General Rochambeau's use of bloodhounds from Havana, Cuba to disembowel black prisoners in his spectacular arena set up on the grounds of the old Jesuit monastery at Cap Français. Most of the French colonists—nearly 25,000—seeking refuge in the United States ended up in Philadelphia, Baltimore, Charleston, New Orleans, and Norfolk. As the exiled white Martiniquan lawyer and historian Médéric Louis Elie Moreau de Saint-Méry noted, Norfolk was especially attractive, since "the inhabitants of this place have shown a constant affection for the French."[56]

Poe returned to Richmond as fear of black terror and retribution spread. Note that in the review of *Slavery in the United States*, though Poe refers to "recent events in the West Indies" and talks of "the parallel movement here," he nowhere refers to the Nat Turner insurrection.

Perhaps Poe knew that his readers would too readily recall the Turner rebellion and white vengeance in southeastern Virginia, the inhuman carnage that finally cost many innocent blacks—some estimate about 200—their lives. As Poe worked on the *Southern Literary Messenger*, increasing circulation from five hundred to about thirty-five hundred, what became known as the Great Southern Reaction of the 1830s and 1840s created a closed, nearly martial society intent on preserving its slave-based civilization.

Slave trading in the city of Richmond was frequent and had reached its height in Virginia during the 1830s. Some have argued that Virginia slave traders enjoyed an affluence rivaled only by tobacco merchants of the previous century: "Prior to 1846, the Bell Tavern, on the north side of Main just below Fifteenth, was the scene of a great many of these deplorable spectacles."[57] Poe must have frequently walked past the Richmond slave market, which was only two blocks away from the offices of the *Southern Literary Messenger*. He doubtless witnessed slave auctions and experienced the terror of those led through the streets, chained in slave coffles, readied for their journey to the Deep South.

We have evidence of Poe's relationships with the leading proslavery advocates in Virginia, but what about his relationship to those variously represented in the Virginia Slavery Debate of 1831–1832 as "pets," "playmates of the white children," "the merriest people in the world," "valuable property," or "monsters"? How can we begin to think about those who left no written records but were a constant presence, whose existence though distorted or erased informed Poe's unique brand of gothic narrative in ways that have been ignored?

Poe's guardians, the Allans, had at least three household servants (all slaves, but at least one of these was owned by someone else and bonded to Mr. Allan). On 1 January 1811, Mr. Allan hired a woman named Judith from Master Cheatham for 25 pounds, "to be retained and clothed as usual under a bond of £50."[58] According to some accounts, Judith was Edgar's "Mammy," perhaps the "Juliet" or "Eudocia" mentioned by receipts and the bills of sale as being in John Allan's household. Whatever her name, she sometimes took him to the "Old Church on the Hill" grounds where he spent many late afternoons. After all, his foster mother Fanny Allan was often too ill to attend to Poe. Though we hear about Poe's dead mother Eliza and all those subsequent, surrogate pale mothers (especially Jane Stannard and Fanny Allan in Richmond), we are never reminded of the black woman in the house. When Poe was awaiting entry into West

Point in 1829, living with Maria Clemm in Baltimore, he sold a slave. In April 1940, *The Baltimore Sun* published the record of the bill of sale of "a negro man named Edwin," calling it an "Item for Biographers." The article begins: "While examining some entries in an underground record room at the Courthouse a few days ago a Baltimore man who wishes his name withheld quite by chance came across an old document relating to Edgar Allan Poe, which seems thus far to have entirely escaped the poet's biographers."[59]

Many Virginia accounts of the Nat Turner rebellion blamed its occurrence on superstition and religious fanaticism. But these written accounts of the "extraordinary" beliefs of negroes, shared by many whites, probably mattered less to Poe than his daily encounters with slaves in his own house or on the plantations he visited. Poe's gothic, his unique tools of terror, finally have less to do with "Germany" or the "soul," as he once proclaimed in the Preface to his "Tales of the Grotesque and Arabesque," than with African American stories of the angry dead, sightings of teeth, the bones and matter of charms, the power of conjuring. Let me add that such stories, merging with early Christian folk beliefs transplanted to the South, as well as the frenzy of revivals with whites and slaves caught up in the Holy Spirit, might also have encouraged the strangely sentient landscapes of Poe, his obsession with the reciprocities between living and dead, human and animal, the possessions and demonic visitations of his most well-known tales.[60]

Dialogue with the dead

In writing *Fables of Mind: An Inquiry Into Poe's Fiction*, I struggled with the philosophical and religious cruxes in Poe's tales. Philosophy meant Locke. Religion meant Calvin and Edwards. The path to enlightenment was clear. I could explain the dark hauntings, the spectral return of a Ligeia who took possession of the physical Rowena by looking at Calvin's insistence on visibility in the flesh, by Locke's paradoxes on identity, and even Newtonian mechanics. Yet what if we turn to the equally critical ground in Poe's past, that of African American belief? In "Unspeakable Things Unspoken," Toni Morrison notes the presence, the shadow, the ghost from which most critics have fled.[61] In a world where identities wavered between colors, where signs of whitening and darkening were quickly apprehended by all inhabitants, enlightenment depended on shadows. The gods, monsters, and ghosts spawned by racist discourse redefined the supernatural. What the white masters called sorcery was rather an alternative philosophy, including spiritual experiences shared by both blacks and whites. The most horrific spirits of the Americas were produced by the logic of the master filtered through the thought and memory of slaves.

After "Ligeia" was published in 1839, Poe sent it to Philip Cooke and asked whether or not the ending was intelligible. What most dismays Cooke about the ending is the way "the Lady Ligeia takes possession of the deserted *quarters* . . . of the Lady Rowena." He explains, "There I was shocked by a violation of the ghostly proprieties . . . and wondered how the Lady Ligeia—a wandering essence—could, in quickening *the body* of the Lady Rowena . . . become suddenly the visible, bodily, Ligeia."[62] Consider the ending: Ligeia with her "huge masses of long and dishevelled hair" and "wild eyes" enters and takes the place of the "fair-haired, the blue-eyed Rowena." Seeing the quickening, risen flesh, the narrator thinks, "Can it be Rowena?" only to recognize Ligeia. Familiar with stories of the returning dead, Poe worked them into the tale he called his "best." The spirit so fills the living body that no trace remains of the once-alive vessel; taken by the spirit, the body reacts. Its gestures and lineaments conform to ghostly demands. We are no longer dealing with a narrator in trance, a madman who hallucinates, a drugged murderer, but the scene of possession. Not by a white master—the affectionate appropriator of Poe's disputed review—but by a spirit, conjured and rising up, like Ligeia, from quiescence to revenge.

I grew up in the South and recall the terrors that constitute knowledge, the awful concreteness of the spirit and theories that needed no John Locke to reveal wandering souls or shape-shifting identities. Who are the ghosts to drag you down? Blood on the carpet, a look at the moon that could kill you, circumscribed by fear of women who left their skin at the door—haints more present than the living. The question is how to bring what has been constituted as mere foolishness or worse into the study of a literary text without turning practice into cliché, without turning African American belief into a trope in yet another scholarly exercise. I conclude with two slave stories recorded by Moreau de Saint-Méry before he left Saint-Domingue for the United States. These stories of genesis suggest that cosmologies of color were not the property of whites alone:

According to them, God made man and he made him white; the devil who spied on him made another being just the same; but when he finished the devil found him black, by a punishment of God who did not want his work to be confounded with that of the Evil Spirit. The latter was so irritated by this distinction, that he slapped the copy and made him fall on his face, which flattened his nose and swelled his lips. Other less modest negroes say that the first man came out black from the hands of the Creator and that the White is only a negro whose color has deteriorated.[63]

Poe's racialized gothic—the terrors of whiteness in Poe's *Pym*, the shadows and shades in fairyland, the blurring of privilege and perversion in tales about ladies who turn into revenants and lovers who turn into slaves—requires that we rethink the meaning of color and the making of monsters, as well as question the myths of the masters who still haunt the halls of the academy.

Notes

An early version of this essay was presented at the University of Arizona, 18 December 1991. I am grateful to Edgar Dryden and Drexel Woodson for their sharp questions.

1   Edgar Allan Poe, review of *Slavery in the United States* by J. K. Paulding and *The South Vindicated from the Treason and Fanaticism of the Northern Abolitionists* by William Drayton, *Southern Literary Messenger*, April 1836. Reprinted in *Complete Works of Edgar Allan Poe*, ed. James A. Harrison (New York: Thomas Y. Crowell & Co., 1902), 8:265–75. Although the review is often noted as the "Paulding Review," Bernard Rosenthal argues that it is more accurate to refer to it as the "Paulding-Drayton Review," since the other book under review (*The South Vindicated*) once thought to be anonymous is now known to be by William Drayton, to whom Poe dedicated his *Tales of the Grotesque and Arabesque, 1839–40*. See Rosenthal, "Poe, Slavery, and the *Southern Literary Messenger*: A Reexamination," *Poe Studies* 7, 2: 29–38. Here I refer only to Paulding's *Slavery in the United States* since I believe that Poe responds primarily to that text. For my full analysis of Poe's review, see "Romance and Race" in *The Columbia History of the American Novel*, ed. Emory Elliott (New York: Columbia Univ. Press, 1991), 94–102.

2   Not until 1941, when William Doyle Hull claimed in his doctoral dissertation at the University of Virginia that Nathaniel Beverley Tucker wrote the Paulding review did scholars question Poe's authorship. See William Doyle Hull, "A Canon of the Critical Reviews of Edgar Allan Poe in the *Southern Literary Messenger* and *Burton's Gentleman's Magazine*, with an examination

of his relationships with the proprietors" (Ph.D. diss., University of Virginia, 1941). Previous to Hull's work, the review was included in James A. Harrison's Virginia edition of Poe's work, and both Hervey Allen in *Israfel* (1929) and Arthur Hobson Quinn in his *Critical Biography* (1941) discuss the Paulding review as Poe's work. After Hull, the institutional erasure of Poe, slavery, and the South has continued in the Library of America edition of Poe's *Essays and Reviews* (1984), which omits the review. I cannot rehearse the arguments for and against Poe's authorship of the review here, but direct the reader to the excellent, still unsurpassed analysis by Bernard Rosenthal cited in note 1. A marvel of restorative historiography and detection, Rosenthal's essay remains the most convincing unraveling to date of the enigmatic review. Besides emphasizing Poe's friendship with proslavery apologists like Thomas Dew and Nathaniel Beverley Tucker and his attachment, even if vexed, to the idea of Virginia aristocracy, Rosenthal demonstrates that the letter of 2 May 1836, used by Hull and others to prove Tucker's authorship of the review, must refer to a different essay. Among the many other details he adduces to question Hull's contention, Rosenthal demonstrates that there remains a "basic chronological inconsistency in relation to the letter and the appearance of portions of the April *Messenger* in the *New Yorker*" (31–32). See also John Carlos Rowe, "Poe, Antebellum Slavery, and Modern Criticism" in *Poe's "Pym": Critical Explorations*, ed. Richard Kopley (Durham: Duke Univ. Press, 1992), 117–41, which came to my attention after this essay was completed.

3   Floyd Stovall, "The Women of Poe's Poems and Tales," *Texas Studies in English*, no. 5 (1925): 197.

4   Originally published as "Slavery Justified by a Southerner," later included in *Sociology for the South, or The Failure of Free Society* (1854). Cited here from *Slavery Defended: The Views of the Old South*, ed. Eric L. McKitrick (Englewood Cliffs: Prentice Hall, 1962), 45.

5   Thomas Jefferson, in *Notes on the State of Virginia*, talks about the "wild and extravagant" imagination of the negro which, "in the course of its vagaries, leaves a tract of thought as incoherent and eccentric, as is the course of a meteor in the sky" (ed. William Peden [New York: Norton, 1954], 189).

6   Poe, review of Paulding, 270.

7   James Kirke Paulding, *Slavery in the United States* (New York: Harper and Brothers, 1836), 309.

8   Poe, review of Paulding, 270–71.

9   Poe, review of Paulding, 271–72.

10 Edward Long, *The History of Jamaica, or General Survey of the Antient and Modern State of that Island* (London, 1774; reprint, New York: Arno, 1972), 2:356, 372.

11 Long, 2:30.

12 Thomas Dew, *Review of the Debate in the Virginia Legislature*, in *Slavery Defended*, 30. After the Nat Turner rebellion, Virginia's legislators debated

openly during January and February 1832, with antislavery spokesmen arguing for colonization of the blacks in Liberia and stressing the destructive effects of slave labor. In the end, most delegates accepted the proslavery argument that colonization was too costly to implement. It is generally agreed that Dew's expert analysis of the debates with his conclusions and recommendations defeated once and for all western Virginia's gradual emancipationists and ushered in a decade of repressive slave controls (the "black laws") and expanded patrol and militia systems.

13 Edgar Allan Poe, *Poetry and Tales*, ed. Patrick F. Quinn (New York: Library of America, 1984), 95–96. All subsequent quotations from Poe's poetry and tales are from this edition and are cited in the text.

14 Edgar Allan Poe, *The Letters of Edgar Allan Poe*, ed. John Ward Ostrom, vol. 2, rev. ed. (New York: Gordian, 1966), 396.

15 Nathaniel Beverley Tucker, *George Balcombe, A Novel*, 2 vols. (New York: Harper & Brothers, 1836), 1:88, 277, 275, 278.

16 Tucker, 1:273.

17 Tucker, 2:164–65.

18 Tucker, 2:166.

19 Edgar Allan Poe, review of *George Balcombe. A Novel*, by Nathaniel Beverley Tucker, in *Essays and Reviews*, ed. G. R. Thompson (New York: Library of America, 1984), 956, 975–76.

20 Tucker, 1:275.

21 Some proslavery advocates, however, deprived the black even of feeling. William Beckford Jr. (not the Beckford of Fonthill, author of *Vathek*), in his *Remarks Upon the Situation of the Negroes in Jamaica* (London: T. and J. Egerton, Military Library, 1788), arguing against emancipation in the West Indies, wrote: "A slave has no feeling beyond the present hour, no anticipation of what may come, no dejection at what may ensue: these privileges of feeling are reserved for the enlightened" (84).

22 George Louis Leclerc Buffon, *A Natural History of the Globe, of Man, of Beasts, Birds, Fishes, Reptiles, Insects, and Plants*, ed. John Wright, trans. W. Kendrick, 3 vols, new edition with improvements from Geoffrey, Griffith, Richardson, Lewis, Clark, Long, Wilson (Boston: Gray and Brown, 1831), I:163.

23 Edward Long, 2:360, 364, 361, 383.

24 Besides Hegel's elaboration on "The Law of the *Heart*, and the Frenzy of Self-Conceit," 391–400, his concept of the "Beautiful Soul" in his *Phenomenology of Mind*, trans. J. B. Baillie (New York: Harper and Row, 1967) is also useful here. For Hegel the "identity" of the "Beautiful soul" comes about "merely in a negative way, as a state of being devoid of spiritual character." The " 'beautiful soul' . . . has no concrete reality" (676).

25 *North American Review*, 83 (October 1856): 432.

26 Note that in three hundred years the *Code Noir* has not been translated into English. Most significantly, this codification of methodical divestiture re-

mains so difficult to find that it has vanished from historiography. I first read the *Code Noir* in a collection that included the additional royal edicts, 1699–1742: *Recueils de règlements, édits, declarations et arrêts . . . concernant le commerce, l'administration de la justice, la police des colonies françaises de l'Amérique . . . avec Le Code Noir et l'addition au dit Code* (Paris: Chez les libraires associés, 1745).

27   I am referring throughout to Poe's argument against the transcendentalists as elucidated in my *Fables of Mind* (New York: Oxford, 1987).

28   Ralph Waldo Emerson, "Emancipation in the British West Indies," *The Complete Works of Ralph Waldo Emerson* (Cambridge: Riverside Press, 1904), vol. 11:146.

29   Poe then retold the story in two consecutive articles of *The Broadway Journal*. For an account of this episode, see Arthur Hobson Quinn, *Edgar Allan Poe: A Critical Biography* (New York: Cooper Square Publishers, Inc., 1969), 487ff.

30   Samuel Warner, "Authentic and Impartial Narrative of the Tragical Scene Which Was Witnessed in Southampton Country (Virginia) on Monday the 22nd of August" in *The Southampton Slave Revolt of 1831: A Compilation of Source Material*, ed. Henry Irving Tragle (Amherst: Univ. of Massachusetts Press, 1971), 296–98.

31   Edgar Allan Poe, review of *Poems on Slavery* by Henry Wadsworth Longfellow, in *Essays and Reviews*, 763.

32   Henry Wadsworth Longfellow, *Poems on Slavery* (Cambridge: John Owen, 1842), 1:285.

33   No one has demonstrated more powerfully than Winthrop D. Jordan in *White Over Black* how excessive sentimentality diminished the possibility of action or ethics in the antislavery program: "A romantic sentimentalism was a symptom of, and perhaps a subtle yet readily intelligible social signal for, a retreat from rational engagement with the ethical problems posed by Negro slavery" (New York: Norton, 1977, 370–71).

34   For a discussion of color in *Pym*, see Dayan, "Romance and Race," 107–09.

35   Dana D. Nelson's *The Word in Black and White: Reading "Race" in American Literature 1638–1867* (New York: Oxford Univ. Press, 1992) came to my attention after I completed this essay. Her rigorous redefinition of "race" in both fictional and nonfictional works of Anglo-American writers is crucial to understanding the metaphysics of whiteness, the rewriting of race as aesthetics, and the connections in America between race, romance, and nation. See especially "Ethnocentrism Decentered: Colonial Motives in *The Narrative of Arthur Gordon Pym*," 90–109. In yet another turn on Poe and race, Toni Morrison in *Playing in the Dark: Whiteness and the Literary Imagination* (Cambridge: Harvard Univ. Press, 1992), claims Poe as crucial "to the concept of American Africanism" (32).

36   As I have argued in "Romance and Race," Poe's Dupin knows how to detect

unadulterated barbarism, and the descriptions of the affectionate, yet easily enraged ourangutan who loves to mimic his master and violate women refer readers to the familiar fantasies of consanguinity between black men and apes. As Edward Long puts it in his *History of Jamaica*: "an oran-outang . . . is a human being . . . but of an inferior species . . . he has in form a much nearer resemblance to the Negroe race, than the latter bear to white men" (103).

37 Edgar Allan Poe, review of *Sheppard Lee: Written by Himself* by Robert Bird, in *Essays and Reviews*, 390–91.

38 See Robert Montgomery Bird, *Sheppard Lee* (New York: Harper and Brothers, 1836), 1:36–38, and esp. 2:156–77, where Sheppard Lee enters the body of Tom, saying, "If thou art dead, my sable brother, yield my spirit a refuge in thy useless body!" Awakening as Tom in the chapter "In which Sheppard Lee finds every thing black about him," Lee, expecting to be "the exemplar of wretchedness," finds instead the surprise of humane and gentle treatment by a "good-natured" and " 'right-born master,' " thus replicating the hyperbolized scenes of plantation life so dear to the postslavery argument.

39 See discussion of "Hop-Frog" in Dayan, "Romance and Race," 103–04.

40 Thomas Ollive Mabbott, ed., *Collected Works of Edgar Allan Poe* (Cambridge: Harvard Univ. Press, 1978), 3:1344.

41 Hegel, 237.

42 See Orlando Patterson, *Slavery and Social Death: A Comparative Study* (Cambridge: Harvard Univ. Press, 1982), 17–34.

43 George Frederick Holmes, "Uncle Tom's Cabin," *Southern Literary Messenger* (December 1852): 721–31.

44 Allen Tate, "Our Cousin, Mr. Poe," *Collected Essays* (Denver: Allan Swallow, 1959), 459. I thank Stephen Rachman for drawing my attention to Tate's essay.

45 Edgar Allan Poe, review of *The Drama of Exile and Other Poems*, by Elizabeth Barrett Browning, in *Essays and Reviews*, 116, 118, 119.

46 Poe, review of *Poems on Slavery*, in *Essays and Reviews*, 285.

47 Note that the offspring of a "misalliance" between a white man and a black female slave followed the condition of the mother. In laws trying to curb interbreeding, light-colored women were prohibited from using the name of the father. Especially problematic is the use of the term *mulatto*. Virginia Domínguez writes in *White by Definition: Social Classification in Creole Louisiana* (New Brunswick, N.J.: Rutgers Univ. Press, 1986), that "Limited lexical options meant that the term *mulatto* was used to denote anyone who did not appear all white *or* all black" (49). In Europe and the United States, and in most of the Caribbean by the late 1700s, the general term mulatto was used to metonymize varying nuances of skin color and extent of blood mixture. Note, however, that colonial taxonomies were far from lexically limited

but bear witness to a frenzied nomenclature of color. According to Moreau de Saint-Méry's theoretical taxonomies of color in *Description de la partie française de l'Isle Saint-Domingue*, mulatto was one of eleven categories of 110 combinations ranked from absolute white (128 parts white blood) to absolute black (128 parts black blood), pushing the invisibility of color differentiation to fantastic extremes. Such a system not only displaced the human element from the hybrid offspring of colonial coupling, but became a desperate attempt to redefine whiteness. This analysis of rituals of color and black codes is elaborated in my *Haiti, History, and the Gods* (forthcoming, Univ. of California Press, 1995).

48 Surely one of the most problematic uses of women by well-intentioned abolitionists was their conversion of the racist portrayal of a demonic and lascivious ape-woman into a sentimental heroine, processed as the refined, potentially salvagable, but ever fallen "tragic mulatta."

49 Mabbott, 2:332.

50 I am indebted here to my student Jennifer Ellis's analysis of Ligeia in her paper, "Rereading Poe's Textual Body in 'Ligeia', and Ligeia's Body as Text: Doubling and the Racial Unconscious" (December, 1992).

51 Tucker, *George Balcombe*, 2:51–52; 1:71–72.

52 Richard C. Wade, *Slavery in the Cities: 1820–1860* (New York: Oxford Univ. Press, 1964), 20.

53 Warner, 293–94.

54 Clement Eaton, *The Freedom of Thought Struggle in the Old South* (1940; reprint, New York: Harper and Row, 1964), 90.

55 See Alfred N. Hunt, *Haiti's Influence on Antebellum America: Slumbering Volcano in the Caribbean* (Baton Rouge: Louisiana State Univ. Press, 1988), 38–40, and Winthrop Jordan, *White Over Black*, 375–80, for excellent summaries of white reactions in the United States to the black revolution in Saint-Domingue.

56 Moreau de Saint-Méry, *Voyage aux Etats-Unis de l'Amérique, 1793–1798*, ed. Stewart L. Mims (New Haven: Yale Univ. Press, 1913), 55–56.

57 Virginius Dabney, *Richmond: The Story of a City* (New York: Doubleday & Company, 1976), 111.

58 I am grateful to Jean M. Mudge for this information.

59 I thank Jeffrey Savoy of the Poe Society of Baltimore for sending me this article.

60 The biography that deals most with the contact between the young Poe and slaves is Hervey Allen's *Israfel: The Life and Times of Edgar Allan Poe*, 2 vols. (London: Brentano's Ltd., 1927). Note that the revised, one-volume edition of *Israfel* published in 1934 excludes these discussions of Poe and his African American surround.

61 Toni Morrison, "Unspeakable Things Unspoken: The Afro-American Presence in Literature," *Michigan Quarterly Review*, 28 (Winter 1989), 12.

62 Philip Cooke to Poe, 16 September 1839, in *Complete Works of Edgar Allan Poe*, 50.

63 Moreau de Saint-Méry, *Description topographique, physique, civile, politique et historique de la partie française de l'isle Saint-Domingue* (1797; reprint, Paris: Société de l'Histoire des Colonies Françaises et Librairie Larose, 1984), 1:58.

Maggie Sale   Critiques from Within:
Antebellum Projects of Resistance

Recent scholarship has proposed the importance of (re)evaluating writing by white women and women and men of color— such as the novels of Susan Warner and Catharine Maria Sedgwick, and the narratives of Harriet Jacobs and Frederick Douglass—that has been excluded from the traditional canon of the antebellum period. For example, Jane Tompkins has argued for the importance of the cultural work of writing by (white) antebellum women, Susan Harris has proposed a new method for evaluating nineteenth-century "American women's fiction," Hazel V. Carby has mapped the emergence of black women novelists from the slave narrative tradition, Frances Smith Foster has examined the specificity of personal narratives by black women, and Henry Louis Gates Jr. and Houston A. Baker Jr. have explored racial identity formation in the writing of Frederick Douglass and other African American writers of the period.[1]

Typically this scholarship is structured so that either gender or race is brought to the fore, while the other factor is suppressed. Questions about gender are considered most often in the writing of white women or women of color, and questions about race in writing by people of color, both women and men. When questions of race and gender are posed simultaneously, it is almost always in response to writing by women of color; the studies of Carby and Foster, for example, consider both race and gender. This pattern of questioning has occurred, I think, because the importance of gender or race is most readily identified and argued for when either factor has been the implicit if not explicit means of exclusion or marginalization, either from the canon or from "mainstream" society, that is, when a writer's gender or race differs from that which is asserted as "the norm." Thus there are few studies that analyze either the writing of men, of any race, in terms of gender, or the writing of white people, of any gender, in terms of race. David Leverenz's study of "classic American writers" in terms of class-based models of manhood and Richard Yarborough's evaluation of race and masculinity in the work of Frederick Douglass are two of the few examples of scholarship that attempts to make visible the suppressed factor of gender in writings by men.[2] The few analyses that take "whiteness" as their subject have made little impact on literary studies.[3]

This masking of either gender or race is facilitated by the operation of ideological constructs that present that which is white, masculine, middle-class, and heterosexual as the norm, and everything else as different or other (and therefore marked by race, gender, etc.). It is the role of these constructs to present themselves as universal, natural, inevitable, and unchanging, and thereby to mask the ways in which they support the interests of a particular group. Thus their very success makes it difficult to identify them as constructs and to map their operation. At the present moment, one place where this masking of whiteness and masculinity can be identified is in how studies of the so-called "American Renaissance" rarely consider the notion of an innate, immutable, and gendered hierarchy of races that was developed during the Jacksonian period and was central to the cultural logic of the antebellum United States.[4]

In mainstream Americanist criticism of this period, traditional and revisionist, progressive writers like Thoreau and Melville are most often chosen for study, and their work is not the most representative of the depth and pervasiveness of the logic of masculine white supremacy, although it does participate in that logic. The choice of these writers is made in part, I think, because critics do not wish to give authority to texts that are obvious proponents of masculine white supremacy. For those of us who are white, it is difficult and embarrassing to acknowledge assertions of our own racial "superiority" in nineteenth-century texts, and we think, perhaps, that we can best overcome this legacy by excluding it from our curricula and from our vision of the past. We make it easier on ourselves by repressing what we do not want to acknowledge and by focusing on writers whose sensibilities are perhaps closer to our own. Yet too often this exclusion facilitates the operation of the very ideological constructs we are attempting to subvert by masking their presence—and thus their power—but not eliminating their operation. In addition, we often repress rather than analyze the gendered, racialist attitudes of the progressive writers we do choose to study. For white feminist critics this can mean analyzing the ways in which white women writers addressed and subverted the limitations of their culture's construction of gender, while ignoring these same writers' reproduction of their culture's assumption of white supremacy. For scholars of African American literature this can mean examining how black male writers developed strategies of resistance to the white supremacist assumptions of antebellum culture but not questioning how many of these writers invoked the notion of a common masculinity as the premise of their right to citizenship.

This essay proposes that we return simultaneously the repressed contexts of gender and race to the study of antebellum writers. First, it sketches out one strategy for rematerializing the context of masculine white supremacy in order that its operation may be examined. Next, the essay explores how three African American writers and activists—Frederick Douglass, Frances Watkins Harper, and Harriet Jacobs—created differently gendered discursive sites of resistance to this cultural logic. As I have suggested, these projects of resistance can be most fully appreciated when read against the background of what they were formed in opposition to. Although I argue that these projects necessarily use and manipulate dominant discourses, it should be emphasized that such actions are not merely derivative but are formative of new positions. The importance of rematerializing the context in order to explore projects of resistance is based on the theoretical view of language as a site of struggle between differently empowered groups and is predicated on the notion that meaning cannot be divorced from the cultural and historical context in which these groups interact.[5] My goal is to restore the context in which the challenges of Douglass, Harper, and Jacobs not only made sense but were deeply disruptive of various hegemonic attempts to define all black men and women as voiceless non-subjects. While informed both by Gramsci's formulation of hegemony and Foucault's notion of discourse, this essay also asserts the importance of the racial and gendered position of the speaking/writing subject: the doctrine of natural rights has a different meaning when asserted, for example, by John Calhoun, Angelina Grimké, or Maria Stewart. The essay argues that Douglass, Harper, and Jacobs disrupted assertions of the innate and immutable inferiority of Africans and their descendents by transforming the rhetoric of the Revolution and by invoking certain cultural assumptions about gender while challenging others.

■ ■ ■

The myriad assertions of the United States as a white man's country that appeared in the early nineteenth century were not monolithically formulated but rather came from a variety of sources that were themselves vying for hegemonic control. Reginald Horsman notes that while the term "Anglo-Saxon" has a long history, after 1815 it was ethnically but not ideologically shorn from its roots in pre-1066 Britain and was used increasingly in the United States to describe almost any person of European descent who was willing to identify with the label.[6] For example, an article from the *Democratic Review* entitled "The Course of Civilization"[7] figures these "Anglo-Saxons" as descended from the Puritans and as having been chosen by Providence to lead the world to a higher form of civilization based on republican institutions. The text erases the context of slavery and the genocide of the indigenous populations in order to promote the North American continent as an empty land set aside by God for this teleological development. Written during a period of increasing sectional tension over the extension of slavery into the territories, this discursive erasure of slavery serves the interests of those wishing to exclude both slavery and blacks from the territories, interests that were later organized into the Free Soil party. Thus this mythology of white supremacy does not include representations of Africans and their descendents in any form.

In contrast, John Van Evrie's *Negroes and Negro "Slavery": The First an Inferior Race, the Latter their Normal Condition*[8] centralizes racial slavery in the United States and argues that the presence of a "naturally inferior and subordinate race" is that which makes freedom among white men possible. Van Evrie asserts that all great civilizations, Ancient Greece and Rome in particular, have relied on slave labor so that the elite are relieved of ordinary labor in order to pursue higher learning, which is the foundation of true freedom. He concludes that the ancient system has been improved upon in the southern United States because the condition of slavery has been relegated only to those for whom it is a natural or "normal" condition, that is, Africans and their descendents. Written when sectional tension was nearing its height, this text is one of the many defenses of slavery proposed by Southerners in opposition to both the doctrine of free-soil and the challenges of abolitionists.

In "The Course of Civilization," the myth of American freedom and democracy functions ideologically to shear the master narrative of freedom from the material conditions of slavery and race oppression; in *Negroes and Negro "Slavery,"* the dependence of freedom on slavery is both the foundation and the point of the argument. By making the appropriation of the North American continent by white men in the contrived absence of all ethnic others (in the first case) or the freedom of white men and the enslavement of blacks (in the second) appear natural and inevitable, each text asserts the specific sectional interest of its author. Yet despite their important differences, these assertions inform and support one another in their assertion of Anglo-Saxon superiority. This allegiance, based on the supposedly natural category of race despite certain political differences, was meant to ensure that whatever else happened, the United States would remain a white man's country. Eventually democracy and an innate desire for liberty came to be defined by various dominant groups not as political or historical constructs but as "racial" in origin, as parts of an Anglo-Saxon essence, and therefore as realizable only by people with those hereditary traits.[9]

In a converse relation to the Anglo-Saxon within this hierarchy of races, there arose both popular assertions and scientific theories of the innately and immutably inferior nature of African Americans.[10] Earlier, during the Revolutionary period, there had developed in some intellectual circles a rhetoric of regeneration that cast people of African descent and indigenous people as "less civilized" races that were capable of eventual equality with enough moral and intellectual education.[11] This rhetoric posited differences between the races as environmental rather than biological, and therefore as changeable with proper training (it is important to note, however, that such "training" was never provided by the United States government, even during the nineteenth-century expansion of the educational system). But this notion of possible regeneration was soon discarded within the discourse of most dominant groups in favor of the theory of an innate and immutable hierarchy, such as this one from the *Southern Quarterly Review*: "How well is the vigilant, active, white man, contrasted with the drowsy, slothful black man, while the copper-coloured race holds the intermediate ground between them."[12] Where the rhetoric of regeneration had once represented Africans as capable of eventual equality, dominant discourses in the South in particular presented them as forever inferior.

This discourse of a forever inferior role, developed to its full extent in the context of slavery but referred to in both the North and West, represented Africans and their descendents as naturally savage and unpredictable but capable of becoming docile, contented, and childlike under the influence of the "civilized" Anglo-Saxon race. The *Southern Quarterly Review* comments that "To begin to civilize the African, it seems absolutely necessary first to subdue him to the bit of bondage to a civilized race" (85). The rhetoric of regeneration differs from this notion of a permanently inferior role in that the process of proposed regeneration, while slow, does not limit the amount of advancement possible, while the construct of permanent inferiority strictly does. This forever inferior role took the dualistic form of the contrasted figures of Sambo and Nat for men [13] and Mammy and Jezebel for women;[14] dutiful Sambos and Mammies were always in danger of reverting to their supposedly more natural and savage state as Nat and Jezebel.[15] This precarious relation within the dualistic form meant that the dutiful positions of Sambo and Mammy were the highest achievement possible by African Americans within this schema. Various dominant discourses throughout the growing nation now represented the processes of mental and moral uplift as beyond the scope of possibility for people of color, who were destined to remain in perpetual submission if they were "good" or in perpetual savagery if they were "bad."

This new hierarchy of races was also gender-coded. Francis Parkman's comment that "The Germanic race, and especially the Anglo-Saxon branch of it, is peculiarly masculine, and, therefore, peculiarly fitted for self government"[16] adds masculine gender to the notion of democracy as part of an Anglo-Saxon essence. It makes explicit a contemporary assumption about the masculine nature of the republican subject and indicates how this articulated assumption about gender may then be used to bolster an argument for white supremacy. Similarly, "The Course of Civilization" argues that in the development of republican institutions, the highest form of civilization, "the men sufficient to accomplish the work needed to be peculiar men," not "striplings made effeminate by the luxuries of courts," but men with "the manly spirit of courage and endurance" (211). This notion of "manly spirit" takes on an especially aggressive and acquisitive quality when viewed in the context of Andrew Jackson's Florida campaigns of "removal" of the indigenous populations and the formulations of Manifest Destiny that appeared in the context of war with Mexico.

Constructed in opposition to this masculine Anglo-Saxon model, Africans and their descendents were cast as feminine in nature. Southern slaveholders asserted that blacks' (reported) "unwillingness" to fight for their freedom marked them as a feminized race lacking an innate desire for freedom and therefore deserving of enslavement.[17] T. B. Thorpe, writing for *Harper's New Monthly Magazine,* characterizes enslaved people as prone to the feminine faults of imitation, jealousy, and "wrangling." Some abolitionists, on the other hand, assigned positive connotations to supposedly innate racial characteristics by drawing an analogy between the "essential natures" of men and women of color and white women. This view, popularized by Harriet Beecher Stowe's *Uncle Tom's Cabin* in 1852, asserted the spiritual superiority of these groups by positing within them an innate sense of morality, religion, and compassion, and an increased capacity for Christian martyrdom. Thorpe agrees that "the religious feelings of the negro are easily touched and excited," but he cautions that they can lead to superstition if not firmly directed,[18] a fate to which women are purportedly prone. Although Stowe's text values the feminine traits it assigns to blacks and presents a broader range of possible positions for blacks than the dualistic forms of Mammy/Jezebel and Sambo/Nat, it nevertheless represents a complex hierarchy based on essentialized race and gender characteristics in which agency is generally assigned in proportion to whiteness.

Dominant groups both sympathetic and hostile to slavery participated in the (re)production of the notion of an innate, gendered hierarchy of races that privileges what is masculine and Anglo-Saxon. This production occurred in cultural and social, as well as political and economic, arenas. This hierarchy operated through the assertion of stereotypical images of both men and women of African descent, and of white women, all of which were represented as natural and for the most part unchanging; only white men were constructed as capable of continual improvement. The hegemonic functioning of this hierarchy served the interests of various groups of white men—and the white women who aligned themselves with them—who were themselves struggling for economic, social, cultural, and political control.

■ ■ ■

In their struggle to disrupt hegemonic assertions of the inferiority of Africans and their descendents, Frederick Douglass, Frances Watkins Harper, and Harriet Jacobs turned to various aspects of the rhetoric of the Revolutionary period, such as the notions of an innate desire for liberty

residing in all people and of the right to revolt against an unjust oppressor. This rhetoric, while originally developed in the service of dominant
colonial groups then emerging into empowerment (land-owners, slaveholders, merchants, etc.), nevertheless provided these writers/activists
with a language that still had wide influence at the historical moment
in which they were writing and that they could reinscribe with different
meanings for their own purposes. For example, the rhetoric of regeneration, which was originally used by dominant groups to support notions of
their "superior" European culture and society, could be used by African
Americans to argue for their rights to education and opportunities for
employment. Similarly, in order to resist the (re)figuring of "liberty for
all" as the sole property of the Anglo-Saxon men, these writers/activists
posited a desire and willingness to struggle for freedom as innate in both
enslaved and free people of color and therefore as justification for various
kinds of rebellion.

This strategy does more than reproduce the rhetoric of an earlier age,
because as that rhetoric is used in the service of people other than those
for whom it was originally developed its meaning changes. At the time of
the Revolution this rhetoric, while proclaiming that "all men are created
equal," acted primarily in the service of men with property. The use of
this rhetoric by Douglass, Harper, and Jacobs inscribes it with the new
meaning of equality for all rather than merely for land-owners. This of
course was the promise of the Jacksonian period. But the extension of the
franchise to all men of European descent occurred simultaneously with
the insertion of the word "white" in most Northern state requirements
for the vote; all states added to the Union between 1815 and the Civil
War called for universal *white* manhood suffrage.[19] So the empowerment
of non-elite white men was inextricably linked to the disfranchisement
of black men. Thus Douglass's, Harper's and Jacobs's uses of the rhetoric of the Revolution in order to refigure themselves as members of the
republic—with inalienable rights to liberty—also attempts to transform
their racist society into an egalitarian one. Because of their differently
gendered subject positions, Douglass and Harper and Jacobs use and reinscribe different aspects of the revolutionary rhetoric available to them.
Whereas Douglass invokes this rhetoric in the service of black men,
Harper and Jacobs use it to authorize the struggles of black women as
well.

In "The Heroic Slave" (1853), a fictionalized slave narrative that recounts a successful slave mutiny, Frederick Douglass offers an exemplary

model of heroic manhood in slave revolt leader Madison Washington. Douglass describes Washington as "*one* of the truest, manliest, and bravest of [Virginia's sons] . . . a man who loved liberty as well as did Patrick Henry—who deserved it as much as Thomas Jefferson—and who fought for it with valor as high, an arm as strong, and against odds as great as he who led all the armies of the American colonies through the great war for freedom and independence."[20] Here Douglass invokes the rhetoric of the Revolution by asserting that Madison Washington's "strike for liberty"[21] is within a tradition established by the Founding Fathers. Because this Washington has shown himself to be made of the same stuff as the famous George, the passage implicitly argues, his full humanity and natural rights should be generally acknowledged. Douglass disrupts the operation of dominant notions of who is authorized to be a citizen by appropriating an earlier model of the republican subject, one that, although explicitly gendered—"all men"—is not explicitly marked by race. But whereas Patrick Henry, George Washington, and Thomas Jefferson were all slaveholders, Douglass transforms this earlier model by reinscribing it in the service of slave revolt as opposed to revolt among white men.[22] Thus Douglass appeals to traditional notions of masculinity, such as valor and strength, in order both to destabilize the gendered racial hierarchy in his own time and to recast the heroic figure of the Revolution. Douglass's argument implicitly challenges Parkman's comment that the Anglo-Saxon race "is peculiarly masculine" because here a similarity in gender characteristics is used to transcend a dissimilarity in constructions of race.

In addition, Douglass's Washington rejects the Andrew Jackson model of masculine aggression and acquisition in favor of a different masculine model that incorporates moral restraint and respect for other peoples. For example, Washington prevents the revengeful killing of the white sailors because it is unnecessary for the slaves' victory, and he responds indignantly to the sailors' accusations of his savagery with the assertion, "I am not a murderer. God is my witness that LIBERTY and not *malice*, is the motive for this night's work. . . . We have done that which you applaud your fathers for doing, and if we are murderers, *so were they!*" (66). Douglass uses the revolutionary rhetoric of revolt against an unjust oppressor to validate Washington's act of mutiny. Yet Washington's bravery, physical prowess, and ability to fight for his freedom are tempered by a moral restraint that recognizes the natural rights of his opponents, regardless of their race. Thus Douglass's heroic model insists that moral and ethical considerations must transcend racial distinctions. Implicitly then, this manly model critiques those hegemonic representations of Anglo-Saxon manhood that supported and exalted an unrestrained aggressiveness toward peoples of color.

Douglass's model of masculinity operates in two other important ways. First, it contests the martyrdom of Uncle Tom and other models of "feminine" resistance in Stowe's novel (which was published just one year prior to "The Heroic Slave") by supporting the use of violence, if only when necessary.[23] And second, it offers a notion of patriarchal connection to family and community that modifies any individualistic valorization of personal freedom.[24] In contrast to the protagonists of male-authored slave narratives, which generally represent the strongest and most resourceful of black men in individual escapes to the North, Douglass's Washington returns to the South with the intention of rescuing his wife Susan. She, however, is shot in the attempt, and he is recaptured as he stands guard over her dead body. Washington's next and more dramatic escape frees not only himself but an entire ship full of enslaved people. This patriarchal model of fighting for the freedom of one's family and one's community disrupts the dominant discourse of masculine white supremacy that defines these people of color as lacking in agency and—in connection to one another—as voiceless, inferior non-subjects.

Yet Douglass's model of rebellious manhood is constructed in opposition to a notion of passive womanhood. Although Douglass's Susan joins Washington when he returns to rescue her, she is assigned no agency independent of her husband; there is no indication, for example, that she attempted or contemplated escape during Washington's absence. The implication is that she, unlike her husband, is unable or unwilling to fight for her own freedom. Neither is there any suggestion, as there is, for example, in Jacobs's *Incidents in the Life of a Slave Girl* or in "The Fugitive's Wife" by Harper, that Douglass's Susan did not attempt to leave her condition of enslavement in order to ensure the safety of her children.[25] In failing to present an escape designed and executed by Susan, Douglass's text reproduces a norm of its time: women of any race were not considered to have the same natural rights, desires, and abilities attributed to "all men." The lack of any exploration of Susan's thoughts or concerns is more problematic, I think, as is her complete voicelessness in a text that is so much about the *articulation* as well as the execution of revolt. Although Douglass wrote elsewhere of his support for women's suffrage, "The Heroic Slave" does not represent Susan (or any woman) as having any qualities that might qualify her for membership in the republic. Thus,

while "The Heroic Slave" contests an ideology of race that would construct African American men as unfit for membership in the republic, this
text does not present a similar critique of gender ideologies.[26]

Like Douglass, Frances Watkins Harper and Harriet Jacobs disrupt
the operation of hegemonic theories of racial difference, but they do so
in ways that also question the gender biases of abolitionist discourse by
presenting women as central to the struggle for freedom, abolition, and
equal protection under the law, and by complicating traditional notions
of what constitutes heroism and resistance. Both Harper's and Jacobs's
writings and Harper's activities as an orator represent women of African
descent as active and articulate historical agents.

In one of her published speeches, "Could We Trace the Record of Every
Human Heart,"[27] Harper asserts that "the law of liberty is the law of God,
and is antecedent to all human legislation" (100). In contrast to Douglass's dependence solely on the rhetoric of the Revolution as justification
for Washington's revolt, Harper invokes a discourse of Christianity by
appealing to the giver of natural rights, God, in order to circumvent any
notion of the construction or limitation of these rights by human beings.
This appeal authorizes Harper, as it did Phillis Wheatley, Maria Stewart,
and Angelina Grimké before her, to claim and discuss natural rights as
a Christian rather than as a republican subject. Because women were
supposedly more empowered as moral and Christian than as political and
republican subjects, this strategy enables Harper to challenge successfully social and cultural prohibitions both against women addressing such
"masculine" issues as the Fugitive Slave Law and the Dred Scott Decision
and against their addressing them in public forums.

Harper uses this authorization to unmask the hypocrisy of the Republic's acceptance of slavery and the North's complicity in it by recounting
the flight of "a man escaped from bondage" who, "from Boston harbour,
made memorable by the infusion of three-penny taxed tea . . . Boston
almost beneath the shadow of Bunker Hill and almost in sight in Plymouth
Rock, . . . is thrust back from liberty and manhood and reconverted into
a chattel" (101). Like "The Heroic Slave," this passage disrupts dominant discourses of masculine white supremacy by invoking the memory
of the Revolution in order to show how this memory is dishonored by
current laws that deny rather than support liberty. Like Douglass's story,
it acknowledges a connection between liberty and manhood, but unlike
it, the passage also complicates this acknowledgment by asserting that
damages inflicted upon manhood are likewise inflicted upon womanhood.

When discussing the danger to free blacks unleashed by the Fugitive Slave Law, Harper draws this scene: "A man comes with his affidavits from the South and hurries me before a commissioner; upon that evidence *ex parte* and alone he hitches me to the car of slavery and trails my womanhood in the dust" (102). Here the gendering of the rhetorical persona operates in at least two important ways. First, this scene, which represents one way that black women are affected by the institution of slavery, differs dramatically from the pervasive abolitionist vision of enslaved women's oppression, in which helpless and weeping but voiceless victims are either brutally separated from their children on the auction block or whipped into unconsciousness at the whim of their masters. It reminds us that there are free black women in the North and that they, like Anthony Burns[28] and other escaped slaves, are endangered by this infamous provision of the Compromise of 1850. This scene differs from Douglass's representation of Susan as well, for it presents a female speaking subject who feels the sting of her stolen liberty and who articulates her outrage at this offense. Second, this passage is representative of a standard rhetorical strategy of Harper's in which she uses the word "womanhood" or makes other references to women in a discussion that is otherwise not gender specific in order to make women's presence and participation explicit.[29] Given the common use of "men" and "manhood" in black abolitionist discourse to represent all black people—and in this Douglass's "The Heroic Slave" is representative—Harper's rhetorical strategy complicates the notion that the exclusive representation of black men serves black women as well. The purpose of this strategy is not to undermine abolitionist discourse or the authority of black men, but to correct at least one aspect of common gender biases and so to create a more inclusive, and perhaps more promising, foundation for solidarity among black women and men.[30]

Having made this correction, Harper's rhetorical persona identifies the common cause of men and women of color as race oppression in this recasting of the Dred Scott decision: "I stand at the threshold of the Supreme Court and ask for justice. . . . Upon my tortured heart is thrown the mocking words, 'You are a negro; you have no rights which white men are bound to respect!'" (102). On one level, Harper's skill as a writer disrupts dominant discourses of masculine white supremacy that define her as a member of an inferior species; on another level, the rhetorical persona's outrage and indignation at having her rights violated indicates the depth of her personal claim to them. Clearly the rights of the per-

sona in this context are denied on the basis of race rather than gender—
"You are a negro"—although the persona's oppressor is marked by both
race and gender—"white men." What is important to emphasize here
is that it makes a difference that these words are spoken by a female
persona, even though she is speaking words that could be spoken by a
persona of any gender. This particular gendering matters because in this
instance the much more common situation of a male persona representing
all black people is reversed so that a female persona stands for the whole.
In addition, the gender of the persona matters because a woman even
discursively pleading her case "at the threshold of the Supreme Court"
occupies a very different position from that of a man; even though the
rights of both men and women of African descent were denied by the
Dred Scott decision, the general proscription against women dealing with
political and therefore masculine issues made a black woman's eminently
public claim to legal justice all the more problematic.

In "Could We But Trace" Harper extends the jurisdiction of her authority from simply criticizing the return of "a man escaped from bondage" to describing a legal outrage perpetrated against someone like herself, to making her own public claim for justice. At the historical moment
in which it was produced, the rhetorical progression of this argument was
all the more forceful and shocking because it was not simply published
and read but delivered as a speech and heard by mixed audiences. Even
though Harper did not explicitly claim her rights *as a woman* in the last
passage quoted, that fact would have been obvious to any person who saw
her speak. Rather than being a retreat from or a denial of her rights to ask
for justice or speak publicly, Harper's strategy of first gendering her rhetorical persona ("trails my womanhood in the dust") and then promoting
solidarity among black women and men by noting their common source
of oppression ("You are a negro") was very effective at a time when the
explicit assertion of women's rights, done most often by white abolitionist women, was contributing to the factionalizing of abolitionist forces.
While not explicitly demanding her rights to speak as a woman,[31] Harper
nevertheless succeeds in presenting herself as being just as capable and
authorized to contest dominant discourses of masculine white supremacy
as, for example, Madison Washington.

Like this speech of Frances Harper's, Harriet Jacobs's *Incidents in the
Life of a Slave Girl* disrupts discourses of masculine white supremacy by
asserting the articulate expression and agency of the narrative's pseud-
onymous protagonist Linda Brent. And like Douglass in representing

Madison Washington, Jacobs calls upon the rhetoric of the Revolution by casting Brent's plight as within the tradition of the Founding Fathers. Written in first person, Brent presents herself as struggling against tyrannical and unjust oppressors when she describes the years she spent eluding the lecherous advances of her aged master and the jealous punishments of his much younger wife. Her master's claims to her body— "He told me I was his property; that I must obey him in all things" (27)— are reminiscent of the aggressive and acquisitive tone of masculine white supremacy, evident in "The Course of Civilization," that defines the invasion of the North American continent as the Manifest Destiny of the new republic. Brent challenges these claims by reinscribing a notion of revolutionary resistance in the service of her own agenda. She states soon after beginning her seven years of concealment, "When I started on this hazardous undertaking, I had resolved that, come what would, there should be no turning back. 'Give me liberty, or give me death,' was my motto" (99). Just as Douglass's appropriation of the authority of the Founders presents a shift in the terms of discourse, Jacobs's appropriation of this famous phrase infuses the words of Patrick Henry with a new meaning, that of a commonality among all peoples in their desire for liberty. While both Douglass's Washington and Patrick Henry made their "strikes for liberty" in traditionally masculine ways, Jacobs presents a new vision of heroism as Brent wages a primarily discursive battle for the liberty of her children and herself from the attic of her grandmother's home; it is through her letter writing that Brent eventually manages the sale of her children to their father. Jacobs's vision thus challenges the masculine assumption that physical battle is the most effective and heroic.

In addition, Jacobs and Harper develop matriarchal models of resistance that call for responsibility and connection to others, children in particular.[32] These models stretch the possibilities of acceptable behavior for all women by appealing to certain cultural assumptions about gender in order to contest others. Figures of active maternity allowed for an assertion and acceptance of female resistance that did not trouble too deeply cultural assumptions about woman's nature and role, because the need and desire to protect children against any kind of danger was assumed to be innate in all women. Yet it is important to remember that the stereotypical figure of Jezebel, the savage and sexual being who cared little for family or children (the converse stereotype of Mammy), was commonly used by dominant groups to justify the separation of enslaved families by pointing to the supposed lack of familial connection among enslaved people. In this context, Harper's and Jacobs's assertions of a fundamental bond between mother and child take on a different meaning than that for white women. In the following poem by Harper, the female protagonist claims her child's rather than her own right to freedom; in *Incidents*, Jacobs modifies Brent's bold appropriation of Henry's words by prioritizing her children's delivery.

In "Eliza Harris" Harper retells the story of a familiar figure from Stowe's *Uncle Tom's Cabin*. Like Stowe's novel, Harper's poem presents the mother's difficult flight to freedom as support for the child's: "For she is a mother—her child is a slave." Yet unlike Stowe's merely charismatic heroine, Harper's Eliza is motivated by the same commitment to liberty or death articulated by Henry and Jacobs's Brent: "And she'll give him his freedom, or find him a grave!"[33] In Harper's schema, the child is not old enough to fight for his own freedom, so his mother takes on the role of liberator for him. In Stowe's novel, there is no suggestion of either Eliza's or her child's desire for *liberty*; Eliza's concern is that her child not be sold away from her; there is no indication that she would have ever left the Shelby household had her relationship with her son not been threatened.[34]

Moreover, the following lines from Harper's poem construct an explicitly *heroic* female protagonist:

Oh! poverty, danger and death she can brave,
For the child of her heart is no longer a slave! (62)

While Harper's poem does not cast Eliza as a figure claiming her own right to liberty, it does present her as sharing the values of the Revolution in her desire and willingness to struggle for her son's liberation. Furthermore, that "she can brave" "poverty, danger and death" in this struggle earns for her the status of historical agent. This representation of Eliza offers thereby an alternative to Douglass's (and others') problematic representations of passive womanhood, and it further contests the negative association of feminization with passive acceptance or non-resistance. It thus problematizes gender in two important respects: in the way it disrupts both disempowering characteristics assigned to women and in the gender coding of dominant representations of African Americans.

As with Harper's Eliza, the claim of Jacobs's Brent to personal freedom is complicated by a responsibility and connection to others. The affection and contact between Brent and her grandmother, who raised her after the early death of her mother, is presented throughout the text as central to Brent's identity formation. Similarly, Brent's psychic, if not physical, freedom is consistently represented as tied to the condition of her children; for example, the immediate motivation for her escape is that her son and daughter are to be brought to the farm where she has been working in order for them all to be "broke in" (94). And when she finally succeeds in manipulating her master into selling her children into apparent freedom, she remarks, "The darkest cloud that hung over my life had rolled away. Whatever slavery might do to me, it could not shackle my children" (109). This success, among others, asserts Brent's moral and mental capability in contrast to that of her depraved and manipulative master, that "prominent member" of the community. Whereas Douglass's patriarchal model combines the typically masculine qualities of physical prowess with the typically feminine qualities of moral restraint, Harper's and Jacobs's heroic models combine the typically masculine features of a willingness to struggle for freedom with the typically feminine feature of responsibility and connection to others.

Of the three examples of resistance considered here, Jacobs's goes the furthest in contesting the very notion of innate gender and racial characteristics. Her text is peopled with women of all shades who choose either to adopt or to reject the values of responsibility and connection to others. Jean Fagan Yellin argues that "a sisterhood of mothers," both enslaved and free, "supports Brent in her insurgency," while a "failed community"[35] of primarily white women denies any connection to the enslaved women who nurtured and care for them. The women of this failed community, her jealous mistress chief among them, in fact exhibit behavior authorized by masculine white supremacy and typified by Andrew Jackson and Brent's master. Conversely, Jacobs characterizes Brent's uncle Phillip and brother William as adopting the values of responsibility and connection to others that characterize the "sisterhood of mothers." Thus, rather than appealing to an essentialized notion of either manhood or womanhood in order to claim authority, Jacobs's text rejects the notion of specific characteristics as assigned to either gender or race and asserts the importance of acquired attitudes that value equally a respect for and the protection of personal freedom *and* community. As such it offers a significant reinscription of the project of revolutionary rhetoric in the United States.

When comparing the projects of Jacobs and Harper, it is important to remember that the degree of their public visibility differed greatly.[36] Harper, then Frances Watkins, was a young, unmarried woman on the abolitionist lecture circuit, speaking sometimes more than daily before audiences of both men and women. Her extant writing needs to be considered in relation to her position as an eminent public figure who was continually open to sexist as well as racist attacks. Jacobs's *Incidents* was written, as Jacobs herself says, in moments stolen from her full-time duties as servant and governess;[37] it was originally published without her name as author. It is very possible that Jacobs's relative anonymity allowed her to take positions more explicitly critical of the gender biases of her and Harper's shared culture than were feasible for the more public and popular Harper. Still, I would argue that Harper's presence and excellence as an orator represented a kind of challenge to these biases that was not possible with print alone. Rather than judging the relative significance of their different strategies, my point here is to emphasize the importance of rematerializing the context in which these strategies were originally produced and articulated.

■ ■ ■

The cultural and political work of the writing of Douglass, Harper, and Jacobs disrupts the notion of a rigid and gender-coded hierarchy among races. Reading this work against a background of various dominant discourses that developed and supported notions of masculine white supremacy makes the importance and magnitude of these disruptions, these projects of resistance, more apparent. In an effort to combat race oppression, Douglass redefined the rhetoric of the Revolution by invoking a notion of masculine solidarity among white and black men. Some contemporary scholars have argued that Douglass's strategy is compromised by its alliance to an inherently oppressive system.[38] While it is certainly the case that Douglass argued for the access of men of African descent to the economic and political structures of the United States rather than for the development of a completely different political and economic organization, I would argue that if black men had obtained full access to political and economic power in the antebellum United States—and Douglass wanted nothing less—that access would necessarily have constituted a reconstruction of the entire oppressive system because it would have served to transform a decidedly racist society into a more egalitarian one. Furthermore, this criticism of Douglass's strategies rests on the notion that one can exist, indeed one can think, in a place outside of culture, outside of the language systems through which we make sense of the physical world and the material conditions in which we all live. Even if such a place did exist—and I do not believe it does—how effective would an analysis be, how persuasive would a proposition be, that emanated from such a place, which shared no foundation, no common culture? In order for Douglass and others like him to create effective projects of resistance to the pervasive and varied discourse of masculine white supremacy, they had to use a language that was shared with those they were trying to persuade. The rhetoric of natural rights and struggle against an unjust oppressor offered a discursive site where their oppositional voices could enter a discourse used by dominant groups and reinscribe it with a different meaning, and the power of their reinscriptions is evident in the magnitude of the repressive measures that were called for in response to them.

Yet just as Douglass's use of the rhetoric of the Revolution transformed its meaning from that intended by the Founding Fathers, Harper's and Jacobs's use of that same rhetoric transformed the meaning inscribed in it by Douglass. Harper and Jacobs also recognized the authority granted the rhetoric of the Revolution, and like Douglass they claimed authority for themselves by making use of and redefining a language that had been developed and used in the service of white land-owning men. On one level, their use of this rhetoric transforms it in a fashion similar to that of Douglass, because Harper, Jacobs, and Douglass share similarly racialized subject positions and similarly radicalized political and conceptual agendas, such as the abolition of slavery, greater civil rights for free people of color, and the allocation of agency and authority to people of color. But on another level, Harper and Jacobs transform the meaning posited in this rhetoric by Douglass—that of a common gender as the basis of solidarity among black and white men—by using the rhetoric of the Revolution in the service of the struggle of enslaved and free women of color. While maintaining a sense of racial solidarity, Harper and Jacobs also perceived limitations in the way the rhetoric of the Revolution was used to support only the claims of black men to natural rights, and their writings challenged these limitations by replacing representations of women as passive and voiceless, such as Douglass's, with ones of black women's articulate expression and agency.

I find Harper's and Jacobs's implied critique of Douglass's strategy—a strategy followed by many black men—more compelling than those proposed by many contemporary scholars because Harper's and Jacobs's critiques were developed from within the same imagined community.[39] In my view, because women like Harper and Jacobs shared positions within a discourse and within a culture similar to those of Douglass and other black men, they had clearer access to what it was possible to think and speak and write within their imagined community than we have now. It is their ability not simply to conceive of but *to represent* black women as complex actors that is the most challenging to the biases and prejudices of those who figured black women as passive and inarticulate. The work of Harper and Jacobs illustrates that while all three of these writers/activists may have used the rhetoric of the Revolution, they did not equally contest its exclusionary biases. While the rhetoric of the Revolution may no longer hold the potential for progressive change that it once did for Harper, Jacobs, and Douglass, in our own historical moment the manipulation of dominant discourses in the service of oppositional agendas, together with constant modifications of those agendas from within a given imagined community, continues to be a most useful strategy.

Notes

1   Jane Tompkins, *Sensational Designs: The Cultural Work of American Fiction, 1790–1860* (New York: Oxford Univ. Press, 1985); Susan Harris, " 'But is it any Good?': Evaluating Nineteenth-Century American Women's Fiction," *American Literature* 63 (1991): 43–61; Hazel V. Carby, *Reconstructing Womanhood: The Emergence of the Afro-American Woman Novelist* (New York: Oxford Univ. Press, 1987); Frances Smith Foster, "Adding Color and Contour to Early American Self-Portraitures: Autobiographical Writings of Afro-American Women," in *Conjuring: Black Women, Fiction, and Literary Theory*, ed. Marjorie Pryse and Hortense Spillers (Bloomington: Univ. of Indiana Press, 1985), 25–38, and her forthcoming *African American Women Writers, 1750–1892*; Henry Louis Gates Jr., *Figures in Black: Words, Signs, and the "Racial" Self* (New York: Oxford Univ. Press, 1987); Houston A. Baker Jr., *Blues, Ideology, and Afro-American Literature* (Chicago: Univ. of Chicago Press, 1984).

2   David Leverenz, *Manhood and the American Renaissance* (Ithaca: Cornell Univ. Press, 1989); Richard Yarborough, "Race, Violence, and Manhood: The Masculine Ideal in Frederick Douglass's 'The Heroic Slave,' " in *Frederick Douglass: New Literary and Historical Essays*, ed. Eric J. Sundquist (Cambridge: Harvard Univ. Press, 1990), 166–88.

3   bell hooks's recent article, "Representing Whiteness in the Black Imagination," in *Cultural Studies*, ed. Lawrence Grossberg, Cary Nelson, and Paula Treichler (New York: Routledge, 1992), 338–46; and Richard Dyers's "White," *Screen* 29 (1987): 44–65, are informative and provocative analyses

of the subject. In historical studies, Reginald Horsman's *Race and Manifest Destiny: The Origins of American Racial Anglo-Saxonism* (Cambridge: Harvard Univ. Press, 1981) is a comprehensive and accomplished study of the construction of the "Anglo-Saxon" race in both European and U.S. thought and popular culture; see also George M. Frederickson's *The Black Image in the White Mind: The Debate on Afro-American Character and Destiny, 1817–1914* (Middletown, Conn.: Wesleyan Univ. Press, 1987), especially chapter five on "White Nationalism."

4   There are exceptions to this, especially among critics of African American literature; one important essay is Toni Morrison's "Unspeakable Things Unspoken," *Michigan Quarterly Review* 27 (1989): 1–34. Yet within African American studies there is usually a greater emphasis on how black writers challenged hegemonic constructions of their inferiority. My point here is that those challenges can be appreciated more deeply, especially by white critics and readers who may not be as aware of racism, if read against the background of masculine white supremacy.

5   My sense of language and meaning production is developed from Carby's *Reconstructing Womanhood*. See in particular 16–18. My efforts to rematerialize the context of masculine white supremacy are in part a response to her comment that "We need more feminist work that interrogates sexual ideologies for their racial specificity and acknowledges whiteness, not just blackness, as a racial categorization" (18).

6   Horsman, *Race and Manifest Destiny*, 94.

7   *Democratic Review* 6 (1839): 208–17.

8   *Negroes and Negro "Slavery": The First an Inferior Race, the Latter their Normal Condition*, 3rd ed. (1853; New York: Van Evrie, Horton, 1863). Van Evrie's was only the most extended of many texts that expounded upon the virtues created for white men by the presence of an enslaved subordinate race. The ideas considered here can be found much earlier in, for example, "Domestic Slavery," *Southern Literary Messenger* 5 (1839): 677–87. See also Edmund Morgan, "Slavery and Freedom: The American Paradox," *Journal of American History* 59 (1972): 5–29, for a discussion of the interdependence of freedom and slavery.

9   Frederickson, *Black Image in the White Mind*, 100–01.

10   See Horsman, *Race and Manifest Destiny*, 116–57, for an overview.

11   Samuel Stanhope Smith is perhaps the best-known proponent of this thesis. See *An Essay on the Causes of the Variety of Complexion and Figure in the Human Species*, ed. Winthrop Jordan (1787; rpt., Cambridge: Harvard Univ. Press, 1965); Horsman, *Race and Manifest Destiny*, 99; and Frederickson, *Black Image in the White Mind*, 72.

12   *Southern Quarterly Review* 10 (1854): 74.

13   John W. Blassingame, *The Slave Community: Plantation Life in the Antebellum South* (New York: Oxford Univ. Press, 1979), 224.

14   Deborah Gray White, *Ar'n't I a Woman?: Female Slaves in the Plantation South* (New York: Norton, 1985), 27–61.

15   Frederickson, *Black Image in the White Mind*, 52–55.

16   Quoted in Horsman, *Race and Manifest Destiny*, 184.

17   See Frederickson, *Black Image in the White Mind*, 97–129, for an overview of the gendering of the African race, both positive and negative.

18   Both quotations are from "Cotton and Its Cultivation," *Harper's New Monthly Magazine* 8 (1854): 461.

19   Leon F. Litwack, *North of Slavery: The Negro in the Free States, 1790–1860* (Chicago: Univ. of Chicago Press, 1961), 76 and 79.

20   Douglass, "The Heroic Slave," in *Autographs for Freedom*, Vol. 1, ed. Julia Griffiths (Boston: Jewett and Co., 1853); rpt. in *Three Classic African-American Novels*, ed. William L. Andrews (New York: Mentor, 1990): 25; all further references to this text are to the 1990 edition.

21   This phrase was often used in the abolitionist press to describe mutiny by enslaved people. Douglass's short story develops a life story for one of the instigators of a mutiny on board the brig *Creole* in 1841. For an analysis of the newspaper accounts of this and the *Amistad* mutinies see my "The Slumbering Volcano: Recasting Race, Masculinity, and the Rhetoric of the Revolution," Ph.D. diss., University of California, San Diego, 1992.

22   William L. Andrews is skeptical about how much of an exemplar Madison Washington can be if his models are slaveholders. This position assumes that the assertions of liberty by Henry, Jefferson, and Washington are contradictory or hypocritical, which would invalidate their claims to freedom. That is, Andrews questions the value of Madison Washington's making claims to liberty on the same basis as these Founding Fathers. I would suggest that Douglass's appeal to the Founders has a different purpose, which is to authorize his own exposition on the subject of liberation and at the same time transform their discourse by questioning its very premise, the dependency of freedom on slavery. Rather than suggesting that Washington occupies the same position as Henry et al., Douglass simultaneously invokes and undermines their position. See Andrews, *To Tell a Free Story: The First Century of Afro-American Autobiography, 1760–1865* (Urbana: Univ. of Illinois Press, 1986), 187.

23   Challenging the nonresisting image of Uncle Tom, who has often been considered unmanly, was at the time and has been since an important project for many African American men. See, for example, James Baldwin, "Everybody's Protest Novel," *The Price of the Ticket* (1955; rpt., New York: St. Martin's, 1985), 27–34; Ishmael Reed, *Flight to Canada* (1976; rpt., New York: Atheneum, 1989); and Richard Wright, *Uncle Tom's Children* (New York: Harper & Row, 1940).

Robert Stepto argues that Douglass's Washington revises Stowe's Tom and that "Douglass won his debate with Stowe [about appropriate abolitionist action], for he could claim some role in inducing her to write about a black revolutionary [in *Dred*]. But she won, too: When she wrote about a rebel, she wrote about one—from Virginia—who failed [i.e., Nat Turner]" ("Sharing the Thunder: The Literary Exchanges of Harriet Beecher Stowe, Henry Bibb, and Frederick Douglass," in *New Essays on "Uncle Tom's Cabin,"* ed. Eric J. Sundquist [New York: Cambridge Univ. Press, 1986], 152).

24   Yarborough argues that the function of Douglass's Susan is simply to re-inforce the heroic isolation of the protagonist by her loss. While I would agree that this representation of Susan is problematic in a number of ways, as will become clear shortly, I would also want to emphasize the importance of Douglass's gesture toward the importance of family and community when considered in the context of other male-authored slave narratives, including his own. See "Race, Violence, and Manhood," 176.

25   Harriet A. Jacobs, *Incidents in the Life of a Slave Girl, Written by Herself*, ed. Jean Fagan Yellin (1861; rpt., Cambridge: Harvard Univ. Press, 1987); and "The Fugitive's Wife," rpt. in *A Brighter Coming Day: A Frances Ellen Watkins Harper Reader*, ed. Frances Smith Foster (New York: Feminist Press, 1990), 72–73.

26   This criticism of "The Heroic Slave" needs to be considered in conjunction with Douglass's genuine and lifelong support of women's rights. Douglass was, of course, the only man to support the Declaration of Sentiments at the Women's Rights Convention in Seneca Falls in 1848, and he wrote and published others in support of women's rights. See *Frederick Douglass on Women's Rights*, ed. Eric S. Foner (Westport, Conn.: Greenwood, 1976). Yet Douglass, like most nineteenth-century people, believed in essential-ized gender characteristics and in appropriate roles for men and women. Waldo E. Martin Jr. notes that "there were radically egalitarian marriages among Douglass's feminist-abolitionist contemporaries," but "the reforma-tion of sex roles certainly did not extend into the private sphere of the Douglass home" (*The Mind of Frederick Douglass* [Chapel Hill: Univ. of North Carolina Press, 1984], 147).

27   Frances Foster notes that this "was one of several addresses delivered dur-ing the Fourth Anniversary Meeting of the New York Anti-Slavery Society, May 13, 1857. Harper's inclusion in the program and the subsequent publi-cation of her remarks show that she was now considered a major abolitionist spokesperson" (*A Brighter Coming Day*, 96). This speech was originally published in the *National Anti-Slavery Standard*, 23 May 1857. It is reprinted in *A Brighter Coming Day*, 100–02; all textual references are to this edition.

28   Foster proposes that Harper is probably referring to the Anthony Burns case, in which Burns was returned from Boston to slavery. This event set off a major riot in which federal troops had to be called in (*A Brighter Coming Day*, 96).

29   Harper consistently includes figures of women in her general discussions, uses "womanhood" and other references to women alongside "manhood"

and other references to men, and explores the subjectivity of black women. Some examples include the following: "and in my own southern home, I see women, whose lot is unremitted labor, saving a pittance from their scanty wages to defray the costs of learning to read" ("The Colored People in America," in *A Brighter Coming Day*, 100); "Our greatest need is not gold or silver, talent or genius, but true men and true women," and "If this government has no call for our services, no aim for your children, we have the greater need of them to build up a true manhood and womanhood for ourselves" ("Our Greatest Want," in *A Brighter Coming Day*, 103 and 104).

30 James Oliver Horton describes the complex situation facing free black women who sought to confront the gender biases of their male contemporaries. Horton notes that black men supported the reform efforts of black women as long as they focused on race rather than gender oppression, and recalls that Maria Stewart was forced to leave Boston because her criticisms of black men so outraged her audiences ("Freedom's Yoke: Gender Conventions Among Antebellum Free Blacks," *Feminist Studies* 12 [Spring 1986]: 63).

31 The amount of scholarly attention paid to the arguments of such feminist abolitionists as Susan B. Anthony, Angelina and Sarah Grimké, Maria Stewart, Elizabeth Cady Stanton, and Fanny Wright has overshadowed the less explicit but no less important feminist strategies of figures like Frances Harper. From a late-twentieth-century Euro-American viewpoint, Harper's writings may not seem as "feminist" as these other figures because she does not privilege gender over race; when forced to make a decision over whether or not to support the Fifteenth Amendment, for example, she chose to "let the lesser question of sex go." Yet this set of priorities should not be emphasized to the point where the importance of her consistent inclusion of women and their concerns in abolitionist discourse is obscured. See Elizabeth Cady Stanton, Susan B. Anthony, and Matilda Joslyn Gage, *History of Woman Suffrage*, Vol. 2 (1875; rpt., New York: Source Book Press, 1970).

32 Harper and Jacobs both present matriarchal models that differ fundamentally from the notion of republican motherhood proposed by white women after the Revolutionary period. Harper and Jacobs present their female protagonists as actively engaged in a struggle for personal and communal freedom, whereas republican motherhood is primarily concerned with the education of young male republicans. For a contemporary source see, for example, Catharine Maria Sedgwick, *Means and Ends, or Self-Training* (Boston: Marsh, Capen, Lyon, and Webb, 1839); see also Linda K. Kerber, *Women of the Republic: Intellect and Ideology in Revolutionary America* (Chapel Hill: Univ. of North Carolina Press, 1980), 265–88.

33 Versions of this poem appeared in *The Liberator* and in *Frederick Douglass' Paper* in December 1853, and in Harper's *Poems on Miscellaneous Subjects* (Boston: J. B. Yerrinton & Son, 1854); rpt. in *A Brighter Coming Day*, 61; all further references to this poem are from this edition.

34 When Mrs. Bird questions Eliza about why she ran away, Eliza answers that

she had both a kind master and a kind mistress, but that "'I have lost two [children], one after another . . . and I had only this one left. I never slept a night without him; he was all I had . . . and, ma'am, they were going to take him away from me,—to sell him,—sell him down south, ma'am, to go all alone, . . . I couldn't stand it, ma'am. . . . I took him and came off in the night and they chased me" (*Uncle Tom's Cabin; or, Life Among the Lowly* [1852; rpt., New York: Collier, 1962], 138).

35 Jean Fagan Yellin, *Women and Sisters: The Antislavery Feminists in American Culture* (New Haven: Yale Univ. Press, 1989), 90 and 91.

36 Although Jacobs wrote letters to the abolitionist press, knew many prominent abolitionists of her day (including Frederick Douglass, Julia Griffiths, and her brother John Jacobs), and became an agent for the Philadelphia and New York Quakers both during and after the Civil War, she did not attain, nor probably desire, the public status of Harper. See the Appendix to *Incidents* for references to her letters to the press, 237, 256 n. 34, and the Introduction to *Incidents*, xxv.

37 Jacobs writes to Amy Post that "it was hard for me to find much time to write as yet I have not written a single page by daylight"; in her instructions to Post regarding Post's authenticating note to *Incidents*, Jacobs writes, "mention that I lived at service all the while that I was striving to get the Book out." (Appendix to *Incidents*, 237 and 242).

38 Although Yarborough admits that it is difficult to imagine how Douglass could have extricated himself from this conceptual "briar patch," he emphasizes that "his celebration of black heroism is subverted from the outset by the racist, sexist, and elitist assumptions upon which the Angle-American [*sic*] ideal was constructed and that so thoroughly permeated the patriarchal structure of slavery." My emphasis here is somewhat different, which is that in order to appreciate Douglass's project of resistance we have to consider the possibilities as defined by the collective activity of his own imagined community. See "Race, Violence, and Manhood," 182. William L. Andrews argues that Douglass justifies the violence of the mutineers by "an appeal to the authorizing mythology of an oppressive culture," but he also suggests that an emphasis on either the authorizing or compromising aspect of this strategy is a matter of a critic's personal perspective. See *To Tell a Free Story*, 185–87.

39 I use Benedict Anderson's phrase loosely here to indicate a group of people who may never meet but who nevertheless imagine relations among themselves because of their common positions within a discourse. See *Imagined Communities: Reflections on the Origins and Spread of Nationalism* (London: Verso, 1983).

Russ Castronovo   Radical Configurations of History in the Era of American Slavery

Writing in 1849, critic Theodore Parker notes one spot of originality amid what he deems the bleakness of the American literary landscape: "There is one portion of our permanent literature, if literature it may be called, which is wholly independent and original. . . . So we have one series of literary productions that could be written by none but Americans, and only here; I mean the lives of the Fugitive Slaves. But as these are not the work of men of superior culture they hardly help to pay the scholar's debt. Yet all the original romance of Americans is in them, not in the white man's novel."[1] Parker's praise is undercut by the consideration that the slave narrative diminishes America's stature in two ways: the very existence of slave narratives indicts the principle of freedom that makes America exemplary among the nations of the world; and slave narratives, because they are "not the work of men of superior culture," hardly seem monuments of national triumph for entry onto the world literary stage. Narratives which reveal severely compromised democratic principles fail to provide foundations stable or patriotic enough for a swaggering cultural monumentalism. Instead of signifying a cornucopia of originality—consistent with a limitless landscape or an unparalleled experiment in democracy—the testimony of fugitive slaves exposes the hollowness of freedom and the failure of white American writers.

To safeguard the purity of national literature, Parker implies that an inseparable gulf lies between the slave narratives and the writings of white Americans, but I would argue that such a demarcation is false. Slavery pervades nationalism as an ever-present reminder of political sin, a repressed context always threatening to return and unsettle the foundations of a monumental American culture.[2] Abolitionists cited founding principles in their denunciations of political immorality. Even slaves inscribed radical selves with appeals to the words and actions of original American patriots, thereby assuring that racial politics entered into dialogue with a legacy ironically authorized by American history itself. In short, as Toni Morrison has insisted, "miscegenation" informs rather than detracts from a sacred body of American texts. Interpreters of texts, writes Morrison, have "made wonderful work of some wonderful work," finding in the novels of Melville, Twain, and others a pure aesthetic that transcends race and culminates in a monument of "'universal'" literature. But an awareness of miscegenation argues against any imagined purity of literary tradition, reinvesting American literature with "unspeakable things unspoken," suggesting how words, images, metaphors—in short, meaning—derive from an African American presence that has been repressed through the wonders of interpretation.[3]

Encouraging critics towards a "re-examination of founding literature of the United States,"[4] Morrison's strategy seems a not-too-distant echo of mid-nineteenth-century works whose commitment to republican theorizing reconceives the founding principles of a nation. In sharp contrast to both abolitionists and proslavery thinkers who used juxtaposition to lament the present as a degradation of a coherent past, republicans do not seek to explain how an ordered past indicts the present; for they do not accept the idea of an ordered or consistent past. Rather, republicans understand that contradiction invests the very moments of founding, that the meaning of American history is found in a legacy already riddled with irony and inconsistency. William Wells Brown, Herman Melville, and Abraham Lincoln all act as republicans, not by ironically positioning nineteenth-century slavery against the legacy of 1776 but by reading slavery into that legacy. In the same way that Machiavelli in the *Discourses* writes a republican history by not shrinking from states' origins in bloodshed and deceit, Brown's autobiographies, Melville's tale "The Bell-Tower," and Lincoln's most famous speeches all acknowledge the impurity and imperfection of American origins. Each re-examines the political traces of race within the foundations of America and discovers a set of national origins permanently disfigured by freedom coupled with slavery, by political sin cloaked with civic virtue, and by a conception of liberty shot through with rapacity. Their critical approach does not simply bemoan the degeneration of the virtue of the past into the vice of the present; instead the republican criticism of Brown, Melville, and Lincoln configures America's origins within a radical irony by juxtaposing founding history not against the corrupt present but against itself. These American republicans decry national origins that are their own moral aberration, a history at variance with its own sanctified authority.

■ ■ ■

Before pursuing these thinkers' ironic construction of national history, it is necessary to examine the racial dimensions, often repressed, of America's monumentalism. Jasper Cropsey painted a sublime Niagara Falls to evoke the tremendous and savage beauty of Nature, and Herman Melville heard within Hawthorne's writings "the far roar of his Niagara." Along with engravings and lithographs of Virginia's Natural Bridge, popular representations of Niagara Falls provided the antebellum public with grand, powerful images of their country. When ex-slave Austin Steward stopped at the Falls, he—like Jefferson awed by the Natural Bridge— experienced an inspirational contact with the *terribilita* of the sublime. Listening to "the ceaseless thundering of the cataract," Steward mused in *Twenty-Two Years a Slave* (1856), "How tame appear the works of art, and how insignificant the bearing of proud, puny man, compared with the awful grandeur of that natural curiosity." Although the natural power that dwarfs humans paradoxically elevates Steward to a conventional meditation on existence, his narrative re-implants itself in the social world to structure an accusation. Unlike art patrons who purchased images of Niagara Falls, and unlike Melville who made the cataract a sign of native literary talent, Steward's thoughts contain no ether of national pride. He does not find himself impelled to a transcendental appreciation of republican institutions; instead, he returns to consider humanity in an even more debased manifestation:

> There [at Niagara Falls] you will find the idle, swaggering slaveholder blustering about in lordly style; boasting of his wealth; betting and gambling; ready to fight, if his slightest wish is not granted, and lavishing his cash on all who have the least claim upon him. Ah, well can he afford to be liberal—well can he afford to spend thousands yearly at our Northern watering places; he has plenty of human chattels at home toiling year after year for his benefit . . . and should his extravagance lighten [his purse] somewhat, he has only to order his brutal overseer to sell—soul and body—some poor creature; perchance a husband, or a wife, or a child, and forward him the proceeds of the sale.

Once slavery enters the big house of monumentalism, a culture's sublime pretensions reveal themselves vulnerable to contradiction. Steward's slaveholder struts across the Falls, sullying its greatness, leading the citizen not to a rhapsodic tribute to America but to a more archaic history that supposedly had been left in the Old World among dissolute aristocrats. Steward's slaveholder shows embarrassing continuity with a tradition of seigneurial privilege which America believed itself to have escaped forever in 1776.[5]

Concerned with attacking business rivals and with the political imbroglios of a Negro settlement in Canada, Steward does not elaborate his portrait of an American sublime whose magnificent splendor harbors licentious tyranny. Monumentalism met with a more extended and severe critique in the lectures, memoirs, and fictions of William Wells Brown. The sublime, for Brown, could never transcend slavery. Even though the virgin character of the landscape seemed to invest national history with innocence, Brown saw that both the land and the patriarchal mythos suffered the corruptions of race slavery. Drawing upon that common image of the sublime, Niagara Falls, Brown asked in an 1848 verse entitled "Jefferson's Daughter,"

> Can the tide of Niagara wipe out the stain?
> No! Jefferson's child has been bartered for gold.

In the same way that Emerson in "The American Scholar" pursues "the sublime presence" in that "one design [which] unites and animates the farthest pinnacle and the lowest trench," so too Brown conjoins the lofty cataract with a mundane newspaper notice announcing that Jefferson's slave daughter fetched $1000 at a New Orleans auction. Whereas Emerson uncovers an underlying principle of unity, Brown's conjunction emphasizes disjunction within American monumentalism. The "tide of Niagara," though it inspires sublime paintings from the Hudson River School, is ineffectual in washing away the stain of slavery.[6]

In both speeches and writing Brown argued against slavery and racial prejudice, not by appealing to religious tenets—as many white abolitionists and slave narrators did—but by manipulating the discourses of American politics and history. His slave narrative and memoirs rival Douglass's classic autobiographies, recalling how he bribed white schoolboys with candy to teach him to read, thus linking, as Douglass does, literacy and freedom. Brown continued to improve his literacy, producing histories of African Americans' cultural contributions and, with the publication of *Clotel; or, The President's Daughter* (1853), becoming the first African American novelist. Soon after his escape from slavery, Brown emerged as an articulate spokesman for black emancipation, suggesting that just as white revolutionaries demanded liberty in 1776, so too would black patriots demand theirs. Hesitant to cater to the complacent pacifism of many Northern whites, Brown used American founding principles to advocate violent overthrow of the slave power. In *St. Domingo: Its Revolutions and its Patriots* (1855), he no doubt both thrilled and shocked audiences with graphic scenes of Haitian blacks killing so many whites that "the waters [were] dyed with the blood of the slain." He concluded the work by forecasting a similar scene south of the Mason-Dixon line: "Who knows but that a Toussaint . . . may some day appear in the Southern States of this Union? That they are there, no one will doubt. That their souls are thirsting for liberty, all will admit. The spirit that caused the blacks to take up arms, and to shed their blood in the American revolutionary war, is still amongst the slaves of the south; and, if we are not mistaken, the day is not far distant when the revolution of St. Domingo will be reenacted in South Carolina and Louisiana."[7]

While these not-so-subtle whisperings of slave rebellion assailed the present by exploiting white fears of Babo-like patriots armed with cunning and razors, Brown also staged an insurrection against the monumental past. Throughout his writings, he critically remembers the sacred founding principles of America. He pledges himself to civic virtue without paralyzing himself with a docile acceptance of ideological consensus. Brown understands the lesson of Melville's *Israel Potter*—that a citizen must actively interrogate America's monumental legacy if the ideals of participation and independence are to be preserved. Yet, unlike Israel, who took up arms in the name of American independence and had his actions on the battlefield sanctified by the Bunker Hill Monument, Brown has no legacy from the founding fathers. As a slave, the fact that his father "was a white man, a relative of [his] master, and connected with some of the first families of Kentucky" only circulates as rumor, a spurious form of history.[8] Genealogy, for the slave, confers little more than an illegitimate legacy. Brown nevertheless authorizes himself as a historical subject able to comment upon the history of a nation that has denied him history from the outset.

Brown's autobiographical prefaces to *Clotel* and *The Black Man: His Antecedents, His Genius, and His Achievements* (1863) accord him a personal history that authorizes him to construct both fiction and history about slavery and the position of blacks in the United States. Although the audiences of slave narratives demanded that they adhere to the historical truth—a concern that led to doubts about their authenticity—Brown's autobiographical sketches serve a larger function than merely satisfying a readership's demands for accuracy. In constructing his own past, Brown constructs national history as well, demonstrating how shibboleths of monumentalism validate racial injustice. Details vary in Brown's memoirs of slavery and his escape to freedom; for instance, he records three different birthdates and gives contradictory accounts of his family genealogy, one claiming his mother was Daniel Boone's daughter.[9] The various narratives highlight different scenes from Brown's life in slavery and afterwards. *The Narrative of William W. Brown* records the author's quest for freedom and a name; the autobiographical preface to *Clotel* shifts the drama in order to focus on a slave bribing children to teach him how to read; the memoir of the author introducing *The Black Man* documents the slave's ingenuity in surviving, and his greater ingenuity in escaping. These diverse autobiographical accounts do not so much constitute a complete life, inviolable in the authority of its own experiences, as they subtly reconstitute history, implying its mutable and selective aspects.

Having formulated an autobiographical narrative from privileged instances of memory, Brown suggests how a similar logic of construction shapes narratives of American history. *The Black Man* devotes a chapter to Crispus Attucks, "the first martyr to American liberty," who ignited a crowd and emboldened resistance to British soldiers in a riot memorialized as the Boston Massacre. This episode glorifying the past concludes by censuring the present, whose faculty of memory is impaired by an ethic of historical construction that resists incorporation of nonwhite elements: "No monument has yet been erected to him. An effort was made in the legislature of Massachusetts a few years since, but without success. Five generations of accumulated prejudice against the negro had excluded from the American mind all inclination to do justice to one of her bravest sons. When negro slavery shall be abolished in our land, then we may hope to see a monument raised to commemorate the heroism of Crispus Attucks."[10] Brown practices a strategy which pits history against itself, disrupting the narratives it tells. Monumental history touches up, alters, or omits segments of the past, as Brown was not the first to discover. Nor is his perception that such alterations follow a race-biased logic particularly revolutionary. Rather, the comments of this fugitive slave are critically republican, articulating from within a counter-narrative to historical monumentalism.

A sly addition from the mouth of a fugitive slave can dispel the sublime sanctity of tradition. While Brown complains of Crispus Attucks's omission from monumental history, he elsewhere fills the American heroic tradition with instructive touches of irony: "Some years since, while standing under the shade of the monument erected to the memory of the brave Americans who fell at the storming of Fort Griswold, Connecticut, I felt a degree of pride as I beheld the names of two Africans who had fallen in the fight, yet I was grieved but not surprised to find their names colonized off, and a line drawn between them and the whites. This was in keeping with American historical injustice to its colored heroes."[11] Certainly, Brown repeats his criticism of a legacy that denigrates blacks either by exclusion, as with Attucks or, as here, by grudging inclusion. Still more significantly, this passage unearths the ideological foundations of America's projects to fabricate a national history. Brown's use of the word "colonized" reveals how a consideration of race wrests monumental history from its nativist innocence and situates it within another unacknowledged and destabilizing past. Two different connotations reside within "colonized," echoing the oppositions which constitute the monument as well as monumental history. On the one hand, within the context of revolutionary remembrance "colonized" elicits the Colonies' struggle for independence; on the other, in the antebellum era "colonized" meant not simply to settle a new land in quest of greater freedom but to separate, and it was applied to the "Negro question" when discussing plans to transport emancipated blacks to Africa.[12] Brown mocks the staggering mass of the monument, pointing to subtle fractures that threaten the coherent narrative it encodes. In Brown's representation, the monument's double meanings—its promise of inclusive freedom and its practice of exclusive injustice—bear a mutinous relation to the narrative it presents.

Just as Brown's search for personal freedom causes him to flee to England, so too his search for a foundational history that is critical rather than blindly monumental sends him abroad.[13] In London Brown visits Nelson's Column, which depicts a heroic black man at the admiral's side, and reflects, "How different, thought I, was the position assigned to the colored man on similar monuments in the United States." That a comparison to English public monuments prompts his analysis is especially damaging to America's efforts to remember a national history unconnected and superior to Old World traditions. In fact, for Brown a consideration of the narratives encoded on ancient Roman monuments further illustrates the irony of American historical construction: "I once stood upon the walls of an English city, built by enslaved Britons when Julius Caesar was their master. The image of the ancestors of President Lincoln and Montgomery Blair, as represented in Britain, was carved upon monuments of Rome, where they may still be seen in their chains. Ancestry is something the white American should not speak of, unless with his lips to the dust." Brown prefaces his conclusions with an ironic apology, "I am sorry that Mr. Lincoln came from such a low origin." Such conclusions question nationalist exceptionalism, which basks in declarations of America as the stage of a new historical era, a *novus ordo seclorum*. The history of the fugitive slave here denies that any rupture has ever occurred, and within the continuity Brown uncovers a foundational history of an older republic, Rome. His archaeological endeavor denies the myopic American construction of history by resituating national origins within a larger historical context which reveals the American citizen to be descended from slaves.[14]

Brown thus challenges not the past which America remembers but the ways in which it remembers that past. Like Nietzsche, Brown understands the role monuments play in forging a national consciousness. The word "monument" is derived from *monere* meaning "to remind" or "to warn," and monuments have an instructive purpose, ensuring that America's post-Revolutionary sons do not lapse into the irreverence of forgetfulness. Again like Nietzsche, Brown sees that forgetfulness inevitably accompanies the monument's admonition to remember. The root *monere* also implies "to say with authority"—and it is this authority Brown questions by reminding America how its monumental history, sanctioned by nationalism, both emerges from ignoble origins and effaces the contradictions in its legacy. In writing his autobiographical history, Brown intimates that America's monumental history forgets that it has strayed from aspects of its foundations. Near the close of his 1848 autobiography, he reflects: "While the people of the United States boast of their freedom, they at the same time keep three millions of their own citizens in chains; and while I am seated here in sight of Bunker Hill Monument, writing this narrative, I am a slave, and no law, not even in Massachusetts, can protect me from the slave-holder."[15] Here, *The Narrative of William W. Brown* rebels against the narrative of American history. The statement, "I am seated here in sight of Bunker Hill Monument," is immediately followed by qualifications that imply syntactically the fugitive slave's attitude toward monumental history by modifying the original statement. The reader must negotiate the contradiction which structures not simply the sentence but the fugitive slave's tenuous hold upon freedom. At first glance, the sentence defines Brown's physical position relative to that icon of freedom, the Bunker Hill Monument; yet his act of "writing this narrative" is an act of historical remembering sharply opposed to the mode of history embodied by the Monument. Though he can see Bunker Hill, Brown is "colonized off" from the securities the Monument symbolically promises. Brown makes his segregation part of the American narrative; he divisively integrates his autobiography into the legacy encoded by the Bunker Hill Monument, an edifice Melville in *Israel Potter* suspiciously termed "the Great Biographer" of American history. Inscribing his separation into the architecture of the past, Brown makes inequality and contradiction part of America's monumental history. National narratives rise up triumphantly, only to be discredited by an unmasking of the chain of inconsistencies and exclusionary clauses feebly supporting the structure.

■ ■ ■

Although Brown critically evaluated how racial politics fractured monumentalism's configuration of history, not all post-Revolutionary sons were perceptive—or ideologically motivated—enough to note the fissures in the past. While Brown juxtaposed American foundations with his own slave history and artifacts from classical antiquity, George Lippard published a lengthy patriotic volume, *The Legends of the American Revolution*. As Brown did repeatedly throughout his career, Lippard inscribed a black figure into the revolutionary past. He tells the story of Black Sampson, who comes upon a "hideous object among the embers"—the burned body of his master—and swears vengeance against the British regimentals who committed the murder. Further incensed by the rape of his young mistress, Black Sampson takes up his scythe, calls his faithful dog, and wreaks havoc among the British lines at Brandywine: "The British soldiers saw him come—his broad black chest gleaming in the sun—his strange weapon glittering overhead—his white dog yelling by his side, and as they looked they felt their hearts grow cold, and turned from his path with fear." [16]

Lippard understands that the inclusion of a black figure into the sacred history of the Revolution may appear inappropriate and shock his audience. He advises the reader, "Start not when I tell you, that this hero was—a Negro!" Although Black Sampson fights for the memory of white patriarchy and the honor of white womanhood, the narrator fears that the miscegenation of a slave within a tradition of freedom may blemish the patriotic legacy and call attention to the political contradictions of the present. These fears are not allayed by Lippard's invocation of racist physiology, making Black Sampson a "white" negro descended from African kings: "A Negro, without the peculiar conformation which marks whole tribes of his race. Neither thick lips, flat nose, receding chin or forehead are his." A direct and lengthy address from the author, intended to dispel any unintentionally subversive implications, is needed:

> Do not mistake me. I am no factionist, vowed to the madness of trea-son, under the sounding name of—Humanity. I have no sympathy—no scorn—nothing but pity for those miserable deluded men, who in order to free the African race, would lay unholy hands upon the Ameri-can Union.
>
> That American Union is a holy thing to me. It was baptized some seventy years ago, in a river of sacred blood. No one can count the tears, the prayers, the lives, that have sanctified this American Union, making it an eternal bond of brotherhood for innumerable millions, an altar forever sacred to the Rights of Man. For seventy years and more, the Smile of God has beamed upon it. The man that for any pretence, would lay a finger upon one of its pillars, not only blasphemes the mem-ory of the dead, but invokes upon his name the Curse of all ages yet to come. . . .
>
> So the American Union may be the object of honest differences of opinion; it may be liable to misinterpretation, or be darkened by the smoke of conflicting creeds; yes, it may shelter black slavery in the south, and white slavery in the north. Would *you* therefore de-stroy it?"[17]

This authorial intrusion seeks to guard against a racial fracturing of America's monumental narrative by "colonizing off" with a series of apolo-gies and explanations any trace of blackness within the Revolutionary legacy. Sensing that his introduction of Black Sampson into the "sanc-tified" Union may inadvertently perpetrate a subversive irony, Lippard fortifies his narration by appealing to the Union as a transcendental entity. Convinced that race slavery is unjust, he nevertheless refuses to urge its abolition and thereby to jeopardize the "baptized" body politic. The memory of the fathers in the legend of Black Sampson narrates a foun-dational structure stable enough to contain sectional crisis. Yet the span of temporal continuity between 1776 and the 1850s degenerates into an unbridgeable gap of temporal alienation. What Lippard omits is that the "seventy years and more" that link a people to its legacy also act to divide a people from its legacy.

Although Lippard convinces himself this address to the reader has warded off the specter of "feverish philanthropy," making it safe to proceed with the narrative of Black Sampson, he nevertheless calls attention to the fractures he has covered with rhetoric and patriotic zeal. In the background of his denunciation of those who would repeat "the leprosy of Arnold's Treason," one can hear the voice of more militant proponents of abolition who hold the patriotic legacy as a mere shibboleth. In 1844, William Lloyd Garrison pronounced a sentiment that must have sounded like blasphemy to Lippard: "If the American Union cannot be maintained, except by immolating human freedom upon the altar of tyranny, then let the American Union be consumed by a living thunderbolt, and no tear be shed over its ashes. If the Republic must be blotted out from the roll of nations, by proclaiming liberty to the captives, then let the Republic sink beneath the waves of oblivion, and a shout of joy, louder than the voice of many waters, fill the universe at its extinction." In contrast to Lippard, Garrison could not proceed with the narrative of American Union. Whereas God told Lippard to honor the creation of his fathers at all costs and contradictions, Garrison was instructed to slay the unfaithful. The range between these two passages alarmingly illustrates how God, like William Wells Brown, could also speak with an irony inimical to historical continuity. While some Americans like Lippard ritually reaffirmed the Puritan promise of a blessed community, others, perhaps not all as extreme as Garrison in his call for heavenly retribution, looked at the present and doubted the future. Or, as Lincoln did in 1861, they saw an "almost chosen people." [18]

■ ■ ■

The divine teleology of an America born to conquer a New Canaan now ironically threatened to unravel. The antebellum present seemed an exception, a political and moral aberration. In terms of rhetoric, we can understand this aberration within the national narrative by the trope of parenthesis. [19] In *The Estrangement of the Past*, Anthony Kemp uses the term "parenthesis" to describe a temporal consciousness in which the immediate past stands as an abyss between the distant past and the present. [20] The structure of parenthesis Kemp applies to religious history can describe the political culture of the antebellum era as well; 1776 became the pure, originary past, allowing America to remain in continuous

temporal and ideological harmony with its own genesis.[21] So close was
that unassailable past, a citizen could count with certainty back to the moment of founding; as Lincoln began at Gettysburg, "Fourscore and seven
years ago our fathers brought forth on this continent, a new nation, conceived in Liberty." Yet in the context of increasing talk of disunion, unity
with 1776 seemed illusory; 1776 ceased to form part of the recent past
and retreated into a mythically pure distant era. Parenthesis cordoned off
the factional slaveholding present and thereby preserved historical foundations, ensuring that the contaminated 1850s did not infect either the
past or the future *telos* of America. Although "Fourscore and seven years
ago" indicated a connection with the past, it also marked the dimensions
of the temporal abyss.

Parenthesis asserts that the origins remain pure precisely because it
places the present in an ideological, temporal quarantine. Parenthesis
deems the past virtuous and the present politically impure; America sup-
poses its past a political virgin, refusing to see that it has spawned an
ignoble present. Here, parenthesis resonates with the meaning of irony
as ignorance purposefully affected. Bred with careful regard for their
legacy, social reformers decried the incongruity of a nation at odds with
its own founding. Few critics, however, evaluated how scorn and outrage over present practice acted as an ideological buffer insulating the
founding ideals from censure. The present absorbed all of the abolitionists' contempt; the present became a scapegoat in order to preserve the
unsullied reputation of 1776. In this sense, then, criticism of the present
merely reinforces the foundations of America; or, as Sacvan Bercovitch
has written, dissent actually acts as consent. Yet Brown, Melville, and
Lincoln, as critical republicans, dissent from the foundings, not simply
the present. Their acts of dissent evade the containment of the dissent/
consent relation which for Bercovitch is so pervasive. Both Melville and
Lincoln not only perceive that proclaiming a disjunction between past and
present safeguards the past but also make their way beyond an ideological dissemblance that centers all dissent around the present in order to
interrogate American foundings.[22]

While Brown's sketches of American monumentalism critique the present's remembering of the past and not the past itself, Melville's "The
Bell-Tower" resolutely examines the origins from which monumentalism
erects itself. Just as Brown implies that the colonizing off of Negro patriots on a revolutionary battle monument is inconsistent with the ideals
they died for, Melville's story begins within an ironic disjunction: "In the

south of Europe, nigh a once-frescoed capital, now with a dark mould cankering its bloom, central in a plain, stands what, at a distance, seems the black mossed stump of some immeasurable pine, fallen, in forgotten days, with Anak and the Titan." In addition to implications of decline and ruin, the structure of the sentence parallels the image of the crumbling tower. The sentence falls from "once" to "now," an empty, poisonous gulf separating the two eras. Lincoln repeatedly adopts this structure in his "Address Before the Young Men's Lyceum" of 27 January 1838 in order to forecast the imminent erosion of America's political foundation. He tells his audience that the foundational principles "are a legacy bequeathed us, by a *once* hardy, brave, and patriotic, but *now* lamented and departed race of ancestors." The echoes of Titanic greatness on the Italian plain Melville imagines dwindle to a castrated stump; for Lincoln, a vigorous patriotic presence lapses into absence. In each instance, the parenthesis of present forms a vacuum of incongruity and intervenes between the "once" and the "now."[23]

This ironic incongruity, however, performs an instructive political function as an admonition to recuperate a vanishing past. Lincoln hopes to rededicate his audience to his ancestors' republican faith; for example, consideration of Washington's greatness can lead to an act of *monere*, of reminding or warning those of the present generation not to backslide into civic forgetfulness. Although not designated as a monument, the bell-tower of Melville's story—in its present state of decay—similarly returns the narrator to the history of a once resplendent small Italian republic. Imbued with an air of magical realism anchored by political allusions to Melville's America, the story promises to deliver a satirical allegory reminiscent of *Mardi*. Just as *Mardi's* narrator Taji witnesses the severe contradictions within the liberty-loving nation of Vivenza which enslaves the tribe of Hamo, "The Bell-Tower" transmits a critique of a republic that authorizes the erection of an overtopping edifice adorned with a mechanical slave named Haman.[24] But rather than shuttling between past principles and the present monumental project, Melville keeps his attention focused upon the founding moments, refusing to digress from his interrogation of the past with a denunciation of the present. That is, he does not succumb to the dissembling nature of parenthesis; he does not affect a purposeful ignorance about the foundations of a legacy in order to conserve its sanctity.

First published in August 1855, Melville's story narrates the prideful demise of the architect Bannadonna. Commissioned to construct "the

noblest Bell-Tower in Italy," Bannadonna watches the edifice rise, resolving to "surpass all that had gone before" (819, 821). He constructs
a mechanical figure representing a manacled slave that advances along a
track and strikes the bell upon the hour. On the consecration day of the
tower, absorbed in some final adjustments to the bell, Bannadonna forgets the time, and at one o'clock the slave advances to strike the hour and
smites and kills its creator instead. This homicide echoes an earlier murder in the narrative of the monument. As further proof of his ingenuity,
Bannadonna creates a "great state-bell" destined for the top of the tower;
the narrator thus designates him a "founder," accenting his dual role as
one who establishes the foundation of the republic's tower and one who
melts the metals and casts the bell (820).[25] Yet, at the moment of founding a murderous taint infects the design: "The unleashed metals bayed
like hounds. The workmen shrunk. Through their fright, fatal harm to the
bell was dreaded. Fearless as Shadrach, Bannadonna, rushing through
the glow, smote the chief culprit with his ponderous ladle. From its smit-
ten part, a splinter was dashed into the seething mass, and at once was
melted in" (821). From this original sin, a host of other offenses against
the spirit of republicanism emerge. Not wishing to compromise the glory
that the great bell will bring to the republic, the magistrates and citizens
ignore the homicide. Once the bell is finished, the civil authorities grow
restless, pressing Bannadonna to determine the day when the republic can baptize the tower in a public ceremony. The magistrate tells the
architect the city officials are "anxious to be assured of your success. The
people too—why they are shouting now. Say the exact hour when you
will be ready" (824). The republic shares in both the guilt of the founder's
crime and the glory of his creation. It forgets the scandal of the past to
triumph in the ritual of the present. Caught up in a narrative of denial,
the republic ineluctably continues to erase the flaws within its history; it
accords the murderer-founder a state funeral while, under the cover of
night, it hustles the "rebellious slave" out of its dominions and sinks it in
the depths of the ocean. The republic, intent on conserving the nobility
of foundations that were never noble, effaces the blemishes in its representation of the past. Indeed it literally re-presents the past, altering its
composition and structure, exiling unpleasant memories to the realm of
amnesia by repairing the ruined tower and recasting the defective bell.

   Melville's story acts against the body politic and records a genealogy
of sin which the populace seeks to deny through specious historical constructions. Wishing to obscure Bannadonna's crimes as well as its own

complicity, the public discards uncomfortable memories in the abyss of purposeful amnesia; it declares it knows nothing about any crimes in order to fabricate an unadulterated legacy. Yet the narrator counteracts and exposes the bad faith of the community's dissembling ignorance by sketching a repressed connection between the "once" and the "now" and illuminating how the republican pomp of the city-state stems from the "cankering" bloom of Bannadonna's tyrannical license. Incongruity in the narration causes history to rupture against itself, laying bare how the magistrates and citizens place the sins of their own history in the paren-thesis of forgetfulness to deny a temporal continuity that would indict their state.

The community's fraudulent representation of history coincides with Bannadonna's fraud in concealing a defect in the bell's composition. The fragment from the murderous ladle thrown into the molten mass spawns a hardly noticeable but significant defect in the bell's composition: "Next day a portion of the work was heedfully uncovered. All seemed right. At length, like some old Theban king, the whole cooled casting was disin-terred. All was fair except in one strange spot. But as he [Bannadonna] suffered no one to attend him in these inspections, he concealed the blemish by some preparation which none knew better to devise" (821). Bannadonna certainly acts in his own self-interest; and, at the same time, he performs a civic duty by insulating the community from any memory of the homicide they have condoned. Using "some unknown compound," the architect smooths over his defective founding, forging a monumental history whose key element is forgetfulness (833). Standing on the Floren-tine plain, the tower promises to acquire symbolic prominence, to serve as an icon of republican openness. This promise, however, is as false as Bannadonna's bell is imperfect. Although the state bell perched atop the campanile could serve as a monument and recall a past laced with the flaw of the slain artisan, Bannadonna forestalls such an act of *monere*. The republic sees no reminder of past injustice in the bell, but only confirma-tion of its own affluence. The narrator works against Bannadonna's and the republic's construction and again insists on temporal continuity, even though that continuity jeopardizes ideological cohesion. A legacy of vio-lence resonates within a tradition of republican glory. Although Melville asserts continuity, linking the splintering of the bell with the homicidal splintering of the ladle, the community resolves to place history in an alembic of amnesia and refine away any impurities. Soon the bell and the campanile require repair, but rather than follow Bannadonna and hide the defect, the republic improves upon his methods and re-founds the bell as though nothing—not the artisan's murder, the architect's "accidental death," or the mechanical slave's revolt—had taken place: "The remolten metal soon reassumed its place in the tower's repaired superstructure" (833).

We can better understand the significance of "The Bell-Tower" for the American republic if we restore the story's context in the antebellum era and trace its allusive import. The defective bell evokes another icon of public freedom, the Liberty Bell.[26] Like Bannadonna's creation, the State House bell in Philadelphia cracked during its founding, was recast, and then, according to tradition, fractured irreparably as it tolled for Washington's birthday 22 February 1846.[27] Even though the crack in the bell might on some metaphoric level suggest the distance between the Founding Fathers' generation and its descendants, for much of antebellum America the Liberty Bell served as a relic of a patriotic legacy, bringing together the fathers and sons in a paternal embrace. The same volume containing the story of Black Sampson, Lippard's *Legends of the American Revolution*, initiates a sacramental status for the Liberty Bell by narrating a story that would be construed as fact by thousands of Americans.[28] Lippard's most famous legend begins when on 4 July 1776 an old bell-ringer tries to make out the inscription on the bell of the State House. His tired eyes fail him, so he calls, "Come here, my boy; you are a rich man's child. You can read. Spell me those words, and I'll bless ye, my good child!" Reading the verse from Leviticus, "Proclaim liberty to all the land and all the inhabitants thereof," the boy invokes a democratic spirit that levels the class distinctions between himself and the bell-ringer. The old man requests another favor from the youth, asking him to wait in the street and listen for the decision of the Congress debating the resolution for independence. As though he were part of the expectant citizen mob described in Bannadonna's republic, the old man waits anxiously, doubting that the boy has remembered his promise: "Moments passed, yet still he came not. The crowds gathered more darkly along the pavement and over the lawn, yet still the boy came not. 'Ah!' groaned the old man, 'he has forgotten me! These old limbs will have to totter down the State House stairs, and climb up again, all on account of that child.'" Much as Lincoln does in his speech to the Young Men's Lyceum, the bell-ringer distrusts the sons, suspecting a weakness in their civic faith that will cause them to become distracted by the present and ignore their obligations to the past. The stakes of this legend are enormous;

liberty is jeopardized if gaps arise between generations. As Lincoln put it in 1838, if America forgets the "task of gratitude to our fathers, justice to ourselves, duty to posterity," then the national fabric of founding principles could well unravel.[29]

Since Lippard was more fortunate than Lincoln and could rely upon conventions of narrative closure to dispel the threat of amnesia, the rich man's son, of course, dutifully awaits the outcome of the Congress's deliberations. Hearing the acceptance of the Declaration of Independence, the boy, "swelling his little chest . . . raised himself on tip-toe, and shouted a single word—'RING!'" Only a reverential civic memory can realize the verse inscribed upon the Liberty Bell. Later versions of Lippard's tale stress the importance of genealogical continuity by discovering a blood relation between the boy and the old man and culminate in the cry, "Ring! Grandpa, ring!" The boy's shout disproves Lincoln's admonition "that the scenes of the revolution . . . must fade upon the memory of the world, and grow more and more dim by the lapse of time." As the old man translates the boy's "RING!" into the "terrible poetry in the sound of that State House Bell," his body is rejuvenated with the honest Yankee resilience of independence. Liberty does not fall into the abyss of forgetfulness but is rescued by a tenacious link between the bell-ringer and the boy, between founding fathers and their sons. Liberty is renewed, made eternal, as young as the fathers once were: "Do you see that old man's eye fire? Do you see that arm so suddenly bared to the shoulder, do you see that withered hand, grasping the Iron Tongue of the Bell? The old man is young again; his veins are filled with new life. Backward and forward, with sturdy strokes, he swings the Tongue. The bell speaks out! The crowd in the street hear it, and burst forth in one long shout!"[30]

In contrast, "The Bell-Tower" hardly acquiesces in the assertion of republican renewal ensured by the genealogical continuity Lippard's legend evokes. Although the republic refurbishes the tower and remelts the bell, the renewal lasts only until the first anniversary of the tower's completion, when an earthquake reduces the edifice to an impotent stump. The campanile does not resonate with the lusty sounds of liberty that echo through the Philadelphia State House; instead, Bannadonna's death muffles the peal, emitting only "a dull, mangled sound—naught ringing in it; scarcely audible, indeed, to the outer circles of the people—that dull sound dropped heavily from the belfry" (827). The orchestrated ritual to inaugurate the bell-tower merely renews the cycle of violence begun when Bannadonna's "esthetic passion" took the life of the workman. It is not the slave who deadens the sound; he faithfully performs his office. The founder himself, Bannadonna, impedes with his skull the execution of the design. The monumental history of the fathers slays itself in its own contradictions. Absorbed in concealing the murderous flaw in the bell of liberty, the founder forgets to watch his back and looks up to see his slave bludgeon him. Intimations of slave insurrection dropped by Brown reappear in Melville's tale; and yet the rebellion staged is not simply one of slave against master but of founder against himself. Melville adopts the logic of the fugitive slave: like Brown's subversion of nationalist historical narrative through the exposing of contradictions embodied in the Fort Griswold battle monument, "The Bell-Tower" discloses the fissures that belie monumental representations of republican foundings. In the hands of the narrator, the trope of parenthesis no longer protects the past; nor does the decayed tower stir up idealized memories of a glorious founding. Rather, the narrative of "The Bell-Tower" focuses critically on the founding moments and insists on the continuity of political history, even at the cost of uncovering atrocities within sacred origins. The fissures, cankers, and ruin that mark the tower are nothing new; murder, fraud, and contradiction disfigure the republic's self-representation from its inception. Melville's skeptical re-examination of the past removes national origins from their dignified and unassailable foundation and regrounds the noble republic in deception and forgery. Such ironic historiography cripples monumental narrative, for a generation cannot inherit a coherent legacy if that legacy was never coherent in its origin.

Only forgetting can fashion a narrative stable or coherent enough to support the accumulated layers of history from the origins to the present. The citizens of "The Bell-Tower" contract to remember the past, but— desirous of erecting a monumental body politic—they also contract to forget the past. In the *Second Treatise of Government*, John Locke acknowledges the necessity of political memory, declaring that citizens "begin to look after the history of their founders and search into their original when they have outlived the memory of it." Lincoln echoes this point in his speech to the Young Men's Lyceum, registering Americans' befuddlement as they sit at the crossroads of memory and forgetting. Whereas the previous generation once embodied "a *living history*" in the memories of those patriots who stood as a "forest of giant oaks" and witnessed Revolutionary triumphs, the post-Revolutionary sons find their forebears' memories destroyed by death and time: "the all-resistless hurricane has swept over them, and left only, here and there, a lonely trunk, despoiled of its verdure, shorn of its foliage; unshading and unshaded, to murmur in a few more gentle breezes, and to combat with its mutilated limbs, a few more ruder storms, then to sink, and be no more." Memory replaces "*living history*," but it seems to be a paltry substitute. As Lincoln looks around the American republic, he notices mob violence and racial bigotry, indications that memory fails to adhere to the revolutionary legacy. Lincoln hopes to stave off an apocalypse of amnesia by imploring the current generation to restore its weakened legacy with sober reverence for the Declaration of Independence and the Constitution designed to protect it.[31]

After describing the search for origins, Locke checks any enthusiasm for it by issuing a caution: citizens "would do well not to search too much into the original of governments" or else they might find a foundation whose secrets and instabilities would de-authorize their current government's legitimacy. But unlike Locke, Lincoln does not include a measure of amnesia in his political faith. Lincoln insists on remembering the foundations of liberty, even if uncovered ironies make that liberty appear contradictory and incongruous; he does not acquiesce in a strategy of bad faith in which the citizens of a republic overlook the flaws in the founding just so they can erect a bell-tower or state that will "surpass all that had gone before." Objecting to the small print in Locke's contract that sanctions amnesia within the project of memory, Lincoln resembles the narrator of "The Bell-Tower" who retells the history of a republic, including events and rumors the citizens would rather had sunk into the sea with the rebellious slave. Both renounce a parenthetical version of memory that would forget the sins of the past by concentrating on the "dark mould" of the present. While many opposed to slavery decried America's flagrant disregard for its sacred origins, both Lincoln and the narrator of "The Bell-Tower" unflinchingly question that sacredness. Surveying the history of the ruined capital, the narrator does not shrink from representing a founding contaminated by murder, fraud, and slavery, but undertakes a genealogical investigation bearing him back to the origins. And Lincoln, examining the history of a prosperous republic, steadfastly confronts the principles of the founding fathers. Acknowledging that the origins of American republicanism contain sanctified principles, Lincoln nevertheless understands that many of these principles are flawed. Imperfection resides within the tradition of liberty begun in 1776; a genealogy of sinful continuity, not political virtue, links the "once" and the "now."

Speaking in Baltimore on 18 April 1864, Lincoln praises the soldiers marching through the city and observes "that three years ago, the same soldiers could not so much as pass through." Lincoln's words create a parenthetical structure in which the Civil War's past is "colonized off" both from its present and from what preceded it, the distant days of antebellum harmony. Parenthesis would render the war a bad memory, a hiatus better forgotten in a temporal quarantine protecting the purity of the past. Lincoln, however, undercuts the very parenthesis he has set up by subtly betraying America's complicity with its past: "But we can see the past, though we may not claim to have directed it." Despite the present republic's predilection for affecting innocence about past cultural chaos, Lincoln's remark exposes the desire to deny temporal continuity (and thus ideological responsibility). Foreclosing the possibility of a reassuring parenthesis, he discourages a reverential view of an untouchable past and announces his findings even though they unsettle hallowed foundations. His representation of the past discovers a founding, like Bannadonna's, fractured in its origins:

> The world has never had a good definition of the word liberty, and the American people, just now, are much in want of one. We all declare for liberty; but in using the same *word* we do not all mean the same *thing*. With some the word liberty may mean for each man to do as he pleases with himself, and the product of his labor; while with others the same word may mean for some men to do as they please with other men, and the product of other men's labor. Here are two, not only different, but incompatible things, called by the same name—liberty.[32]

Never, even within its origins, has America had an uncontested definition of liberty. When "liberty" authorizes some people to dominate others, it is divided against itself, engendering an inconsistent narrative which lapses into forgetfulness in order to guarantee a coherent *telos* for the nation. In the same way that "The Bell-Tower" erects a history ruptured by the ironies it houses, Lincoln's America rests upon a fractured cornerstone. Though heralded as a sacred new order with a unitary ideological foundation, America, as Lincoln reveals, has always been politically schizophrenic, marked by an element of the "incompatible," and in debate about its fundamental, authorizing principles.

Acknowledging the inconsistencies of founding narratives can radically alter our conception of national history. Lincoln opens the Gettysburg Address by remembering the birth of the American republic: "Fourscore and seven years ago our fathers brought forth on this continent, a new nation, conceived in Liberty, and dedicated to the proposition that all men are created equal." Here, the newborn nation seems whole, immaculately conceived in a liberty which Lincoln does not mark as inherently fractured or contradictory. Still, Lincoln does not call for a rebirth of this liberty; instead, he resolves that America "shall have a new birth of freedom." Though subtle, the difference between a rebirth and a "new birth" implies that citizens should not strive to replicate the past. Nor is the project to restore and refurbish the past as the citizens of "The Bell-Tower" do, devising a strategy even more effective at concealing the murderous crack in the bell. A "new birth" would not establish itself as pure and uncontaminated or invent ways to forget and recast imperfection as perfection; it would devote itself to its own memory, even though that memory may record division and contradiction.

Without memory, any founding has as little legitimate authority as Bannadonna's design for a mechanical slave and any conception of liberty will accrue as much suspicion as the liberty achieved by Babo in "Benito Cereno." Murder infects Bannadonna's founding much as a history of bloodshed stains the liberty formulated by Babo aboard the *San Dominick*. The political message of both stories is that once authority effaces its past it can only be subject to the debilitating mistrust of all citizens, even ones as obtuse as Amasa Delano or as blindly patriotic as the populace of "The Bell-Tower." Melville could not conceive of a "new birth" of liberty; he could only see monstruous re-births in which the recessive traits of violence become increasingly dominant with each generation. Lincoln's "new birth" is articulated at a cemetery, a grisly site of memory ensuring that the liberty engendered will engage in none of the historical evasions and cover-ups of the Italian republic or Babo. A "new birth" of liberty must have none of the parenthetical bad faith that would characterize a "re-birth." Political hope for a severely tested republicanism appears in Lincoln's understanding of the solemn moments of Gettysburg. From a memory of cultural conflict and "incompatible" ideologies, he brings forth a sketch of civic faith committed to a narrative of foundations which, ironically, may be inconsistent, incongruous, even bloody. Such a narrative remembers the founder George Washington as well as the founder Bannadonna, and acknowledges the blood of the father in the face of the son, even if the son is a slave, even if that blood stains the father's hands.

Notes

I am indebted to Michael Cowan, John Schaar, Hayden White, and the editorial board of *American Literature* for criticisms, suggestions, and support in writing this essay.

1   Theodore Parker, *The American Scholar*, ed. George Willis Cooke (Boston: American Unitarian Association, 1907), 44. Despite Parker's claim that slave narratives are "original," these works often adapted and cunningly manipulated more established literary forms, among them the picaresque tale, the sentimental novel, and the travel narrative.

2   A study of the intersection of monumentalism and race could also examine the United States government's attitude toward Native Americans. Beginning with the Hudson River School, art and literature portrayed Native Americans relinquishing the grandeur of nature to the white settler. Their actual dispossession from the land coincided with the symbolic inclusion of Native Americans within an iconic history. Treaties with Native tribes were often ratified with peace medals engraved with the president's image. (See, for instance, the medallion emblazoned with an image of Washington that Chingachgook wears in *The Pioneers*.) In addition, representatives from tribes took part in the formal ceremonies consecrating the Washington Monument, and some of its stones, whose inscriptions face inside, were donated by tribes.

3   Toni Morrison, "Unspeakable Things Unspoken: The Afro-American Presence in American Literature," *Michigan Quarterly Review* 28 (Winter 1989): 6, 12–13, 11, 13.

4   Morrison, 14.

5   Herman Melville, "Hawthorne and His Mosses," in *Pierre, or the Ambiguities; Israel Potter, His Fifty Years of Exile; The Piazza Tales; The Confidence-Man, His Masquerade; Uncollected Prose; Billy Budd, Sailor (An Inside Narrative)* (New York: Library of America, 1984), 1165; Austin Steward, *Twenty-Two Years a Slave, and Forty Years a Freeman: Embracing a Correspondence of Several Years, while President of Wilberforce Colony, London, Canada West* (1856; rpt., New York: Negro Universities Press, 1968), 303–04.

6   William Wells Brown, *The Anti-Slavery Harp: A Collection of Songs for Anti-Slavery Meetings, Compiled by William W. Brown, a Fugitive Slave* (1848; rpt., Philadelphia: Rhistoric, 1969), 23; Ralph Waldo Emerson, "The American Scholar," in *Essays and Lectures* (New York: Library of America, 1983), 69.

7   William Wells Brown, *The Narrative of William W. Brown, A Fugitive Slave, Written by Himself*, in *Four Fugitive Slave Narratives*, ed. Robin W. Winks, et al. (Reading, Mass.: Addison-Wesley, 1969), 43; *St. Domingo: Its Revolutions and its Patriots; A Lecture Delivered Before the Metropolitan Athenaeum,*

London, May 16, and at St. Thomas' Church, Philadelphia, December 20, 1854 (1855; rpt., Philadelphia: Rhistoric, 1969), 25, 32.

8   Brown, *Narrative*, 1.

9   For the different editions and changing details of Brown's autobiography, see Larry Gara's introduction to *The Narrative of William W. Brown*, xi.

10   William Wells Brown, *The Black Man: His Antecedents, His Genius, and His Achievements* (1863; rpt., New York: Johnson Reprint, 1968), 109–10.

11   William Wells Brown, "A Visit of a Fugitive Slave to the Grave of Wilberforce," in *Autographs for Freedom*, ed. Julia Griffiths (1853; rpt., Rochester: Wanzer, Beardley, 1854), 71.

12   William A. Craigie cites two examples particularly relevant to this latter meaning. In 1863, Thomas Prentice Kettel wrote in *History of the Great Rebellion*, "The President alluded to the efforts he had made in relation to emancipation, and also in relation to colonizing the emancipated blacks." In 1854, Maria Cummins wrote in the sensationally popular *The Lamplighter*, " 'The house is pretty considerable full just now, to be sure, but maybe you can get colonized out.' . . . 'One room, in the next street!' cried the doctor. 'Ah, that's being colonized out, is it?' " (*A Dictionary of American English on Historical Principles*, 4 vols., ed. William A. Craigie, et al. [Chicago: Univ. of Chicago Press, 1960], 1:558–59).

13   On ideas of critical and monumental history, see Nietzsche's *The Use and Abuse of History*.

14   Brown, "A Visit of a Fugitive Slave," 71; *The Black Man*, 34.

15   Brown, *Narrative*, 46.

16   George Lippard, *The Legends of the American Revolution, or, Washington and His Generals* (1847; rpt., Philadelphia: Leary, Stewart, 1876), 360, 368.

17   Lippard, 361–62. This passage nicely illustrates Lippard's understanding of the ideological contradictions posed by the figure of the black slave, but even more contradictory for him was the figure of the white slave of industrial labor. David S. Reynolds writes, "Though painfully conscious of the southern Negro's plight, Lippard was more concerned with the white slavery in northern factories than with black slavery on southern plantations" (*George Lippard* [Boston: Twayne, 1982], 59).

18   Lippard, 361; William Lloyd Garrison, "No Compromise with Slavery," in *The Liberty Bell. By Friends of Freedom* (Boston: Massachusetts Anti-Slavery Fair, 1844), 216; Abraham Lincoln, *The Collected Works of Abraham Lincoln*, 9 vols., ed. Roy P. Basler, et al. (New Brunswick: Rutgers Univ. Press, 1953–1955), 4:236.

19   Parenthesis—from the Greek meaning "to put in beside"—implies a passage having no grammatical connection to the text into which it is inserted. Often the lack of connection is contextual as well, in the sense that the digression steps outside the supposed process of the discourse. Within a sentence, parenthesis destroys unity, producing a dislocation that interrupts the ex-

pected progress of the sentence from beginning to end. Hugh Blair writes, "I proceed to a third rule for preserving the Unity of Sentences; which is, to keep clear of all Parentheses in the middle of them. . . . for the most part, their effect is extremely bad; being a sort of wheels within wheels; sentences in the midst of sentences, the perplexed method of disposing of some thought, which a writer wants art to introduce in its proper place" (*Lectures on Rhetoric and Belles Lettres*, 2 vols., ed. Harold F. Harding [1783; rpt., Carbondale: Southern Illinois Univ. Press, 1965], 1:222).

20 Anthony Kemp, *The Estrangement of the Past: A Study in the Origins of Modern Historical Consciousness* (New York: Oxford Univ. Press, 1991). See especially 82–83.

21 For instance, during his presidency James Monroe used to appear on ceremonial occasions dressed in his Revolutionary War uniform, even though the heroic days of 1776 had been past for nearly a half-century. See George B. Forgie, *Patricide in the House Divided: A Psychological Interpretation of Lincoln and His Age* (New York: Norton, 1979), 49. Forgie's book furnishes many examples of attempts to either preserve or throw off the founding past.

22 See Sacvan Bercovitch, *The American Jeremiad* (Madison: Univ. of Wisconsin Press, 1978).

23 Herman Melville, "The Bell-Tower," in *Pierre or, The Ambiguities . . .*, 819 (all subsequent references are to this edition); Lincoln, 1:108. Lincoln's Lyceum speech is motivated by outbreaks of mob violence which seem to indicate the present's distorted understanding of democracy. It is not insignificant that he takes as one of his examples the lynching of a black man in St. Louis.

24 Various critics have noted the dimensions of both wage slavery and race slavery in "The Bell-Tower." See especially Carolyn Karcher, *Shadow over a Promised Land: Slavery, Race, and Violence in Melville's America* (Baton Rouge: Louisiana State Univ. Press, 1980); Marvin Fisher, *Going Under: Melville's Short Fiction and the American 1850s* (Baton Rouge: Louisiana State Univ. Press, 1977), as well as his "Melville's 'Bell-Tower': A Double Thrust," *American Quarterly* 18 (Summer 1966): 200–07.

25 Earlier in his career, Bannadonna participates in another "founding." He reminds one of the magistrates, "Some years ago, you may remember, I graved a small seal for your republic, bearing, for its chief device, the head of your ancestor, its illustrious founder" (825).

26 Other commentators have noted the correspondence of Bannadonna's bell and the Liberty Bell. See, for instance, Karcher, 156; and Fisher, "Melville's 'Bell-Tower,'" 206.

27 Historical legends present dates other than Washington's birthday in 1846 for the cracking of the Liberty Bell. Among them are the arrival of Lafayette in 1824, the Catholic Emancipation Act of 1828, the death of John Marshall in 1835, and Washington's birthday in 1835. See Justin Kramer, *Cast*

in America (Los Angeles: Justin Kramer Inc., 1975), 77; Rev. John Baer Stoudt, D.D., *The Liberty Bells of Pennsylvania Presented to the Pennsylvania German Society at the Annual Meeting in the Pennsylvania Building at the Sesqui-centennial on Friday, October 8, 1926* (Philadelphia: William J. Campbell, 1920), 120–21.

28   David S. Reynolds discusses the veracity of Lippard's creations in *George Lippard*, 49.

29   Lippard, 392; Lincoln, 1:108.

30   Lincoln, 1:115; Lippard, 392, 393.

31   John Locke, *Second Treatise of Government*, ed. C. B. Macpherson (Indianapolis: Hackett, 1980), 54; Lincoln, 1:115.

32   Lincoln, 7:301–02.

Nancy   White Slaves:
Bentley   The Mulatto Hero
               in Antebellum Fiction

Although *Uncle Tom's Cabin* champions righteous suffering and its paradoxical power, embedded in Stowe's novel is a brief moment radically at odds with this ethos. When Augustine St. Clare foretells the "San Domingo hour" that will erupt if ever the slaves on Southern plantations revolt against their masters, he describes the imagined scene in heroic terms. The ringing tones of the passage owe more to European *Sturm und Drang* romanticism, with its celebration of defiance and revolt, than to the poetics of domestic fiction: "If ever the San Domingo hour comes, Anglo Saxon blood will lead on the day. Sons of white fathers, with all our haughty feelings burning in their veins, will not always be bought and sold and traded. They will rise, and raise with them their mother's race."[1] At the heart of the novel, Stowe has included a glimpse of parricidal violence that echoes the grandeur invested in Byron's heroes or Blake's prophetic books. It is an odd moment in a novel that otherwise seems to condemn any active aggression.

Of course the image of heroic revolt plays a very different role in Stowe's domestic novel than it does in Blake's epic poems. In *Uncle Tom's Cabin* the scene of violent rebellion is precisely what the novel is meant to prevent. The possibility of an uprising, pictured only briefly and obliquely, is crowded out by two alternatives: the Christian transformation of hearts by a black martyr (Uncle Tom) or the geographical relocation of slaves by a black nationalist (George Harris). Rebellion is the scandal of domestic poetics. It violates the domestic worldview: that social relations can and should be patterned after family relations and that the family, far from being the field of original conflict as portrayed in classical myth (and later in Freudian science), is governed instead by compassion and sacrifice. Furthermore, Stowe's imagined revolt clashes with domestic ideology not only because it presents violence in heroic terms but because it focuses on a racial scandal in the antebellum family. A true portrait of the American family would have to include sons and daughters who were the legal slaves of their fathers. In creating St. Clare's prophecy of a "San Domingo hour," Stowe combined what were to whites the two most volatile images in antebellum America, North and South: the terrorism symbolized by the Haitian revolution and the racial mixing symbolized by the Mulatto.[2] Her brief vision is an antitype of nineteenth-century domesticity, a scene of sexual/racial transgression confounding the culture's fundamental categories of kinship and race. This disorder has to be excluded to ensure the coherence of domestic ideology.

Yet Stowe was compelled to include this glimpse, however brief, of a scene of heroic violence. Why in this one moment does Stowe become a Byronic poet who writes lyrically of bloody revolt? The puzzle is not that the novelist is a woman; men are not the only sex capable of visions of glamorized violence (think of Julia Ward Howe). Rather the question is one of genre: by what logic would a domestic novel give way to such a drastically different mode? Here gender is crucial, as is race. What makes a difference in the San Domingo passage, I would argue, is that it represents slaves as white men, with white men's blood "burning in their veins." As Stowe knew from her Bible, God is no respecter of persons, and in Christ there is neither male nor female, bond nor free; but the domestic novel *is* finally a respecter of persons, structured by different rules of representation for women and men, for black and white. These rules are most apparent when it comes to narrating violence inflicted upon a body, for the color and gender of that body determine what happens when violence erupts and what that violence means.

The tacit rules of the domestic novel, I will argue, are these: for women's bodies and black bodies the infliction of violence or abuse can be a means by which the individual achieves a transcendent grace or enriched dignity and identity. But for the body of the white male, this law does not hold. Certainly evil white men can be beaten, humiliated, assaulted; this is imaginable within the poetics of the sentimental novel. But the idea that violence to a white man's body would enhance his selfhood is nonsensical or heretical—despite the fact that the model for the passive power of martyrdom, Jesus Christ, was a white man. Put another way, the physical humiliation of a white man is obscene in the domestic novel; the representation can only degrade, never redeem. Understanding these tacit rules helps to explain the strange passage in Stowe's novel when the idiom of domestic fiction gives way to a romantic sublimity. At the moment when the novel represents slaves as white men with "Anglo Saxon blood," the discourse of domestic fiction is transformed into an antithetical language of sublime terror as the "white slave" becomes the heroic agent of violence.

This narrative logic, latent but determinate in the domestic novel, can be illuminated by comparing Stowe's narrative with other antislavery texts that share similar features. In Richard Hildreth's *Archy Moore, The White Slave*, for instance, the Mulatto achieves identity through violent retribution on anyone who would trespass his manhood—his body, his sexual rights, his will to power. In contrast to Stowe's George Harris, who becomes the novel's surviving African American hero, Archy Moore in effect achieves full selfhood as a white man, represented through the literary codes of the white hero. Examining these and other antebellum novels can help to explore the corporeality of selfhood in antislavery fiction, the "links between one's identity and one's body," as Karen Sánchez-Eppler has described it.[3] The figure of the Mulatto hero has received less critical attention than the "tragic" Mulatta, in part because he appears less frequently and with greater attendant anxiety. But this imbalance is itself a symptom of the fact that the fictional Mulatto is the figure who most distinctly locates the internal contradictions of domestic ideology and its subtext of the body. By comparing Stowe's portrait with Hildreth's, and with the response of African American novelists such as William Wells Brown, I will argue that the fictional Mulatto exposes the ultimate significance of bodily difference even in a genre which seeks to unveil the sameness of (worthy) souls. Examining that corporeal difference, moreover, reveals a surprising symbiosis between the seemingly opposed literary modes of domestic sentimentalism and heroic adventure. I will argue further that the rules of representation in fiction have an analogous force in social life as well: Frederick Douglass was far from the fictional Mulatto type in the pages of antislavery novels, but as a biracial man his story nevertheless displays the particular cultural calculus of body and identity that governs the antebellum novel.

■ ■ ■

The Mulatto has a potentially disruptive position in the antebellum American novel, for the biracial person splits apart the imagined synthesis between nature and society in bourgeois domesticity. While U.S. law denied their existence—in legal terms Mulattoes were identical with blacks—white anxiety came from knowing what law and the social order would not recognize: that blood relations bound Africans and Europeans and subverted the idea of a natural boundary between black and white. Repressed in social laws, this knowledge produced in whites a combination of sympathy, revulsion, and fascination for the figure of the Mulatto. The person of mixed black and white parentage stood precisely at the place where nature and culture could come unbound. The Mulatto figure was a scandal—not only a sexual but an intellectual scandal, confounding as it did the racial categories that were as fundamental to social life in the North as in the South.[4]

Given the right conditions, however, scandals can be eminently useful. The scandal of the Mulatto was of use to antislavery fiction writers, anyway: both African American and white authors focused on biracial characters in their narratives, and "miscegenation provides an essential motif of virtually all antislavery fiction."[5] Where the law averted its eyes, fiction gazed obsessively. Biracial characters were made the symbols of an inescapable history of Southern guilt. And the miscegenation crimes of the slavocracy were not sins of sexual violation only; the scandal of race "confusion" was an odious crime in itself, and white writers often had their characters express this confusion as a painful lived experience. "I'm afraid to die; yet I am more afraid to live," proclaims Dion Boucicault's Zoe, the Mulatta heroine in his play *The Octoroon; or, Life in Louisiana* (1859).[6] But significantly, writers had a distinct preference for the stories of Mulattas. Judging simply by the numbers, it would appear that the biracial woman was more easily absorbed into the existing categories of the novel than the biracial man.[7] Critics have pointed to the obvious racism that made light-skinned characters the slaves of choice for the white antislavery audience.[8] But racism alone does not account for the fact that Mulatta heroines not only outnumber their male counterparts but present a wholly different character type than the "white slave" hero. The difference, I would argue, is a product of the difference attributed to male and female bodies: not the different morphology but the different *mythology* of flesh separating the bodies of men and women.

In the case of the Mulatta heroine, if the problem of racial identity could not be resolved it could be displaced. For her, miscegenation lead to a special species of slavery. As the logic of antislavery fiction has it, the sexual oppression that produces her Europeanized "beauty" also makes her the victim of the next cycle of abuse. A "handsome woman, who is a slave," Lydia Maria Child remarked of a Mulatta heroine, "is constantly liable to insult and wrong, from which an enslaved husband has no power to protect her."[9] Yet the multitude of wrongs to which she was subjected in these tales provided proof of the fundamental substance of spirit that transcends the body altogether, even for those "ruined" women whose abuse made them objects of pity only. As Sánchez-Eppler has written, the domestic conventions of most antislavery fiction invoke a "spiritual code that devalues bodily constraints to focus on the soul."[10] It is here, in the notion of selfhood as soul, that the domestic tradition echoes the Pauline principle that God is no respecter of persons: the inviolability of the soul is independent of any specific kind of body. It is also independent of any damage to the body. From Paul's violent leveling on the Damascus road to Jesus' passion and crucifixion, Scripture offered textual models of a life for the soul freed from its body.

Keeping body and soul together, as it happens, is never the first priority in antislavery fiction (in marked contrast to the lives of most real enslaved African Americans). In fact, the idea of the inviolate soul in this fiction modulates all too easily into the notion of a soul that thrives upon, or even requires, the humiliation of the body. By definition, the tragic Mulatta is granted her most pronounced symbolic power by virtue of her worldly suffering—her sexual exploitation and the betrayals and abuse she endures usually find physical expression in suicide or fatal illness. By jumping into the Potomac, William Wells Brown's heroine Clotel gives the most poignant proof of her "unconquerable love of liberty."[11] The same logic defines the spiritual power of Uncle Tom; the greatest sign of the victory of the soul is the destruction of the body. Legree asserts his ownership of Tom through violence: " 'An't yer mine, now, body and soul?' he said, giving Tom a violent kick with his heavy boot; 'tell me!' In the very depth of physical suffering, bowed by brutal oppression, this question shot a gleam of joy and triumph through Tom's soul. . . . 'No! no! no! my soul an't yours, Mas'r! You have n't bought it,—ye can't buy it!' "[12] The worthy soul is inviolate, whatever the body's condition, treatment, or race. If anything, the soul is empowered by the oppression of the body. For tragic Mulattas, as for Tom, the violence they suffer confirms the value of the soul in a spiritual realm wholly distinct from the body. The problem of racial identity—in fact any problem of the body, such as sexual defilement—is effaced. White women and girls are also subject to this sacrificial logic in antislavery fiction. In *Uncle Tom's Cabin*, Little Eva's death anticipates the martyrdom of Tom. The unexplained wasting

away of her body is presented to us as the inevitable, almost natural result of her pure spirituality. Similarly, Georgiana Peck in Brown's *Clotel*
has her empathy for the "injured negro" sanctified through her death
by consumption. In the deathbed scene, Brown contrasts the power of
Georgiana's spiritual authority with her own "emaciated" body ("death
stamped upon her countenance") and with the "torn and gashed" backs
of the newly freed slaves. Brown's diction reflects the sense of a sentimental exchange between spirit and flesh, whereby the moral efforts of
liberation extract an equal and opposite mortality from the body of the
white heroine: "In less than a week after her emancipated people had
started for Ohio, Mrs. Carlton was cold in death!" [13]

But in contrast to this pattern, few if any such soul-confirming wounds
are inflicted upon a white man's body in the pages of antislavery fiction.
On the surface we might explain this as the result of the prevailing conventions of the "feminized" domestic novel that made it logical to cast
white men as the oppressors and obstacles to emancipation rather than
the victims. And historically, of course, the slave owners and politicians
were, with few exceptions, white men. But the most prominent white
abolitionists were men, too. When the Reverend P. Elijah Lovejoy was
murdered by a mob in 1837, his death became a powerful symbol for the
antislavery movement, and yet no such violence against a white man, it
would seem, could be translated into the imagery of fiction. In antislavery
fiction, narrators avoid portraying the violation of even half-white men.
The enslaved Mulatto is radically ambiguous in the role of victim, as if
writers wished to veil his humiliation—even though they relished the
tragic perils of the Mulatta and iterated countless scenes of her shock,
abuse, and betrayal. We can see this contrast, for instance, in the different treatment of two characters in Brown's *Clotel*. When the heroine
Clotel is first presented to the reader, her body is displayed on the auction block where (like Jesus) her physical humiliation is simultaneously a
spiritual victory: "There she stood, with a complexion as white as most
of those who were waiting with a wish to become her purchasers; . . . her
form tall and graceful, and her whole appearance indicating one superior
to her position." [14] But when a light-skinned slave hero—George Green—
is publicly displayed in the novel, it is in the theater of the courtroom,
where (unlike Jesus) as a prisoner he nevertheless commands the scene
as the most powerful orator in the room. Green invokes the American
Revolution to claim for slaves the right to an armed struggle for liberation: "Did not American revolutionists violate the laws when they struck

for liberty? They were revolters, but their success made them patriots—
we were revolters, and our failure makes us rebels."[15] Faced with his
American Pontius Pilate (a judge "amazed" not as Pilate was at the prisoner's silence but at his speech), George Green not only speaks in grand
defiance but also reduces his white listeners to the tears that usually are
shed by the tragic Mulatta and the black slave.

Brown resolves his novel through an even more telling contrast between the female and male Mulattoes. As a white slave hero, George
Green is spared physical degradation and an "ignominious" death through
a literal substitution of the body of Clotel's daughter Mary, who allows him
to escape from prison disguised in her clothes and remains in his place.
Upholding George's white heroism in this manner, however, creates a
notable narrative strain: George must refuse this offer of rescue from a
woman before finally being won over to her plan, and after the escape
his physical transformation into a "woman" (never described directly) is
immediately remedied—"he had walked but a short distance before he
felt that a change of his apparel would facilitate his progress." But even
risking this feminization, the body of the Mulatto ("as white as most
white persons") is protected and freed—at the cost of the enslavement of
his Mulatta counterpart, a willing sacrificial victim. Ultimately, the novel
does not require Mary's death or torture; perhaps Clotel's suicide in the
preceding chapter ("Death is Freedom") carries enough symbolic power
to save her daughter from the Mulatta's scripted fate. But significantly,
Mary is prepared to "suffer in his stead." Presenting two otherwise identical bodies ("as George was of small stature, and both were white, there
was no difficulty in his passing out [of the prison] without detection"),
the novel traces a fault line of gender. White male bodies are spared and
female bodies sacrificed: "I was willing to die if you could live," Mary
announces.[16]

Brown's George Green was probably modeled after Stowe's George
Harris, a Mulatto hero who had similarly blurred the boundary between
violent rebellion and liberation: "You say your fathers did it; if it was right
for them, it is right for me!" With this language of romantic defiance,
George is poised for heroic action. But it is precisely at this point that
George is supplanted by Tom, who is somehow more fit for the cultural
work at hand. There is a passing of the baton, which George will possess
again only after Tom's ritualized death. In essence, George is too white
to play the role of martyr. Counterintuitive as this may sound, the logic
is borne out when we compare Stowe's portrait of George Harris with

Richard Hildreth's biracial protagonist Archy Moore. Prompted by the phenomenal success of *Uncle Tom's Cabin*, Hildreth published in 1852 a new, longer version of his fictional slave narrative, originally called *The Slave* (1836).[17] But where Stowe had shifted the role of male protagonist from George to Uncle Tom, in *The White Slave* Hildreth keeps his mixed-race character Archy squarely at the center of the narrative (Archy is also the narrator). In doing so, Hildreth, as we will see, is finally compelled to transgress the domestic mode that he invokes throughout the narrative. Representing the oppression of a "white slave" hero seems irresistibly to convert the tenets of domesticity into a counterpoetics of violent revolt, and almost compulsively Hildreth turns to the kind of agonistic romanticism we saw in Stowe's brief glimpse of heroic slave rebellion.

Like George Harris with his "high, indomitable spirit," Archy Moore is a slave who is said to have inherited a "proud spirit, sensitive feelings and ardent temperament" from his white father (10). In *Uncle Tom's Cabin*, the predominantly feminine vocabularies of domestic and Christian love keep in check the spirit of radical rebellion the Mulatto son typically represents. When Stowe's George Harris has a foretaste of family happiness in the Quaker household, his "misanthropic, pining, atheistic doubts, and fierce despair, melted away before the light of a living Gospel."[18] In this way Stowe manages to have domestic love overcome the Mulatto hero's "natural" desire for vengeance.

Hildreth makes use of these domestic idioms as well. Like Stowe's narrative, *Archy Moore* draws on the sentimental tradition of domestic love for its moving portrayal of families broken apart by the slave system. But the novel also offers moments of bitter cynicism about the slave family. Archy remarks that "slaves yield to the impulses of nature, and propagate a race of slaves;—but save in a few rare instances, slavery is as fatal to domestic love as to all other virtues" (34–35). In fact Hildreth makes a point of merging domestic love with the taboos of incestuous passion. The sincere conjugal love between Archy and his common-law wife Cassy is mixed with sensational moments that capitalize on their incestuous relation as half-siblings. Cassy does not know that her white master/father is Archy's father as well, and Archy decides not to tell her in order to avoid troubling himself with what he deems her "unnecessary scruples." Her horror at the master's incestuous advances, then, brings to the novel a painful ambiguity. Archy tells us, "her breathing became short and quick—she clung to me, . . . and, bringing her lips close to my ear, she exclaimed in a trembling and scarcely audible whisper—'Oh Archy!—and he my father!' " (42). When her father later attempts rape, Cassy confronts him: "Master,—Father, . . . what is it you would have of your own daughter?" (129). In most domestic fiction, any hint of incest— though clearly aiming to titillate as well as outrage—primarily used the taboo to draw a doubly-powerful condemnation from the audience. The incest theme is everywhere in miscegenation stories, and for Mulatta heroines the real or threatened incest is a tragic force that is usually condemned and contained by her suicide.[19] But since Archy is the narrator and approves the love between Cassy and himself, the subject of incest is presented at cross purposes here. On one hand, the polemic against the slave master depends on condemning incest as a heinous violation of family sentiment; but on the other, Hildreth condones—flaunts, really— the transgressive passion of the sibling lovers. Creating an ardent Byronic lover, Hildreth diverts the theme of love from domestic piety to the kind of narcissistic celebration of the hero's sexuality found in the poetics of high romanticism. Part of the heroic manhood that Hildreth constructs for Archy, then, appears to require the boundary-defying sexuality of the romantic mode. The more restricted male sexuality of the domestic ethos is secondary at best. At worst, it is undermined by the novel's fascination with illicit passion, as domestic feeling merges indiscriminately with sexual passion. What has happened to domestic ideology when a father is a rapist and a brother a husband?

Despite these transgressions, Hildreth is careful to invoke the fundamental principles of domesticity. Echoing one of the doctrines of sentimentalism, Archy points to the special capacity for sympathy in women and children. "Pity," he says, is too quickly banished from the man's soul and "seeks refuge in the woman's heart; and when the progress of oppression drives it even thence . . . still it lurks and lingers in the bosom of the child!" (217). Sympathy is the bedrock of domestic poetics, and it can convert hearts where coercive force is powerless. But while Hildreth pays homage to the household gods of pity and compassion, his own aim is not to prompt empathy but to effect instead the "remorse of tyrants": "let the story of my wrongs summon up, in the mind of a single oppressor, the dark and dreaded images of his own misdeeds, and teach his conscience how to torture him with the picture of himself" (5). Stowe, we know, also based her narrative on the power of images: "There is no arguing with pictures," she wrote her editor, "and everybody is impressed with them, whether they mean to be or not."[20] But whereas the "dreaded images" Archy presents are meant to torture the conscience, the canonized images from *Uncle Tom's Cabin*—Little Eva's death, the aftermath of Tom's beating—are moments of stilled, nonviolent suffering. Hildreth, in contrast, tries to grasp the power to *inflict* pain by holding a mirror up to the oppressor. In giving the master a "picture of himself," Hildreth forces him to experience his own violence.

This shift in strategy changes the whole narrative texture of the sentimental race melodrama. The language of *Archy Moore* aims to capture the fullest sensations of violent abuse and humiliation. When Archy and Cassy are returned after an escape attempt, Archy presents experiential details of his whipping that make the reader share the slave's field of vision: "the blood ran trickling down my legs and stood in little puddles at my feet" (88). Where Stowe gives us the after-effects of violence—suffering, mourning, recovery—Hildreth focuses on dramatically staged moments of active aggression. The novel presents multiple hangings, beating, slavehunts, a fatal knifing, even death by fire at the stake. Interestingly, however, Hildreth cuts short the scene of Archy's beating through a "fortunate fainting-fit" that dissolves Archy's description of his abuse. When Hildreth subjects Archy to another familiar scene of slave humiliation, the display of his body upon the auction block, he allows Archy to deflect the abuse, turning the scars from his whipping into a badge of insubordination: "Abundance of questions were put to me, as to where I was raised, why I was sold, and what I was fit for. To all these inquiries I made the shortest and most indefinite answers. I was not in a humor to gratify this curiosity; and I had none of that ambition to bring a high price, so common among slaves. . . . [One] expressed the opinion that I was an unruly fellow and 'mighty hard to manage.' The scars on my back tended to confirm these suspicions" (73–74).

Deflected away from Archy's body, the violence in the narrative is increasingly located in acts of resistance or retribution against white tyrants. One of the most dramatic occurs when a fellow slave named Thomas kills an overseer, a deed Archy calls a "just retribution" (206). After prolonging the overseer's agony, the narrative cuts off the white man's plea for mercy just as the bullet does: "'Spare me, spare me!— one half hour longer—I have much—' He did not live to finish the sentence. The gun flashed; the ball penetrated his brain, and he fell dead without a struggle" (205). As this last example shows, violence in *Archy Moore* is not always portrayed from the point of view of the one who receives it; the experiential style can convey the sensations of one who inflicts violence as well. Philip Fisher makes the point that "phenomenal descriptions [of violence] rarely occur within sentimental fiction because they violate its moral purpose in covertly identifying the reader with the aggressor."[21] Hildreth, violating the poetics of the sentimental narrative, makes just such an identification: through Thomas's act of murder, readers are drawn into looking through the eyes of the agent of violence. Archy is a spectator at this execution. But the strategy of evoking the "remorse of tyrants" through a narrative of violence eventually converts Archy from the role of victim to avenger: he evolves from being one who receives attacks (whippings), to one who watches violence approvingly (Thomas's revenge killing), to become finally one who inflicts violence himself. When he meets a rival in a high seas fight, Archy has become the executioner: " '—a wretch like you deserves no mercy!' and as I spoke I plunged the weapon to his heart, and felt thrilling to the very elbow-joint, the pleasurable sense of doing justice on a tyrant!" (230). Archy pulls back from the "thrilling" exaltation of violence and remarks that "justice ought never to be sullied by passion"; but that passion is nonetheless channeled into what is very nearly a call for radical slave revolt: "Yet from what I then felt, I can well understand the fierce spirit and ferocious energy of the slave, who vindicates his liberty at the sword's point, and who looks upon the slaughter of his oppressors almost as a debt due to humanity" (231).

It is easy to see from this scene why Stowe prefers a rhetoric of tears to a poetics of violence. The poetics of violence have a concomitant politics: Hildreth's Mulatto story is about the making of an avenger rather than a martyr or mediator. It converts sentimentalist sympathy to a rationale for revolt. Moreover, the ease with which the one is replaced by its seeming opposite can be explained by recognizing the gender-race physiology at play in the opposition between empathy and revenge. Archy praises sympathy but delimits it: "pity" has a corporeal home in the woman's "heart" and the child's "bosom." At the same time we can see from Hildreth's description of the shipboard sword fight that a very different rhetoric of corporeality upholds an ethos of male revenge: the "pleasurable sense of doing justice on a tyrant." Like the highly physicalized discourse of sentimental empathy where tears and heartache literally embody a humanitarian doctrine,[22] this vivid phenomenology of revenge—the sensation of "thrilling to the very elbow-joint," a feeling of "ferocious energy"—similarly yokes (male) bodily experience to a pious principle. The "slaughter" of oppressors is offered as "a debt due to

humanity." The ideology of sacrifice and passive submission is naturalized in the body of the woman; her empathy and suffering are bred in the
bone. But so localized, the sentimental ethos can coexist with another
principle—also expressed in the language of the body—that "vindicates"
liberty through the masculine pleasures of inflicting righteous violence.
What Archy calls the "birthright" of the white man is in part a sanctioned
and even sanctified corporeal power. Hence when Archy, like St. Clare,
warns of a coming apocalypse, his ominous prophecy tells of an inevitable
violence which will follow from the whitening of the flesh of male slaves:
"In vain do your laws proclaim that the children shall follow the condition
of the mother. The children of free fathers are not thus to be cheated
of their birthright [as] your oppressed victims, becoming, as they do,
day by day, not by a figure of speech, merely, or by a pedigree derived
from Adam, but as a matter of notorious and contemporary fact, more
and more your brethren, flesh of your flesh, and blood of your blood"
(405–06).

In biblical cadences, the passage announces a day of righteous wrath.
But Archy's most dramatic act of heroic vengeance is a rather curious
event for a narrative of slavery. Strictly speaking, the shipboard sword
fight is only an allegory of a slave revolt. To dramatize Archy's violent
vindication, Hildreth has cast the scene as a swashbuckler, a pirate duel
on the open seas. The Mulatto's vengeance, then, takes the form of the
kind of romance plot we find in a Dumas novel. He is fashioned after the
familiar European hero who combines force with highborn eloquence,
brandishing swords and stylized phrases in the same instant. Discursively, the heroic body here is a white body. (Is it a historical coincidence
that Dumas, himself of both black and white descent, helped to establish
the nineteenth-century symbolics of heroism by inventing the consummate choreographies of glamorized violence for the white male body?) In
suggesting that Hildreth makes Archy white, I am not arguing that this
New England historian was unable to imagine the Mulatto as a heroic
character. But I am arguing that in creating the image of a Mulatto hero
he drew from a literary language that encoded the hero as a European
nobleman-outlaw or Byronic avenger. The moment Archy achieves his
greatest stature is also the moment Hildreth has swerved into an idiom
of pure romance, leaving behind both the Southern setting and the flavor
of rough realism he borrowed from the genre of the slave's narrative.

In contrast to Hildreth's romanticism, Stowe found a way to represent the Mulatto hero to antebellum audiences without painting him in white-face. By recognizing slaves as families and members of a universal Christian family, she absorbs them into the domestic novel and its sanctified kinship relations. The Mulatto remains a problem in her scheme, though, since one cannot undo transgressive paternity. The biracial family, though it earns full dignity and humanity in Stowe's narrative, nevertheless mars the nation-as-family model that undergirds *Uncle Tom's Cabin*. Stowe's Liberian solution marks her desire not only to return the slaves to their African home but also to return them to being Africans. Within her sentimental cultural vision, national and racial categories are still covertly identified. When George Harris chooses to identify with his mother's race and to return to Africa, Stowe has the Mulatto "solve" the riddle of miscegenation through his own free will: "It is with the oppressed, enslaved African race that I cast in my lot; and, if I wished anything, I would wish myself two shades darker, rather than one lighter."[23] George's role as a Christian African obviates the scandal of the Mulatto. But to accomplish this Stowe sacrifices the Mulatto's complex identity (*com-* together + *plexus* plaited, *OED*) in her attempt to reconstruct the black family along status quo boundaries of nation and race.

Stowe gives us the Mulatto son turned black family patriarch; Hildreth, the Mulatto as the heroic oedipal son of a white father. These portraits seem like opposite literary types, drawn from antithetical modes, but the two very different representations are in reality the obverse of one another because both adhere to the logic of corporeal identity that governs antebellum fiction. One drop of African blood may have determined a man's legal identity as a negro, but—at least as fiction writers portrayed him—the male Mulatto possessed a white man's body ("His hair was straight, soft, fine, and light; his eyes blue, nose prominent, lips thin, his head well formed, forehead high and prominent," we are told of George Green).[24] Inhabiting that body, he is unable to gain his identity as a full subject or soul through the Christ-like self-sacrifice required of the black Uncle Tom or the Mulatta. To be redeemed the male body required either a new, literally displaced identity as an African or the inviolate identity of the white man with the power to wield physical force. If Stowe had sent George Harris on the journey into Southern slavery that she fashioned for Uncle Tom, would the narrative have ended with a San Domingo scene writ large? That outcome is implicit in the novel's logic of race, though Stowe was determined to preclude it. The picture of the white slave's rebellion could not be represented fully in Stowe's poetics of domesticity without converting a system of sentimental signs to oedipal scenes of violent redress.

Surveying antislavery fiction, Carolyn Karcher suggests that the presence or absence of violent rebellion in this literature can be explained by the writer's gender: male writers are more likely than women to represent scenes of revolt.[25] Comparing Hildreth's novel with Stowe's appears to confirm this idea. But the pattern might be misleading unless we recognize that both Hildreth and Stowe created their narratives out of the same general codes of representation, as did African American writers like Brown. Whatever differences there may have been between male and female experience or consciousness, novelists wrote with a shared lexicon of literary signs. We can better understand the different representations in antebellum novels, I would argue, if we look not to the gender of the writer but the gender of those who are written, the specific bodies of characters in the works. For both Stowe and Hildreth, representing a white-skinned man introduced an ethos that was likely to contradict the key principles of sufferance and bodily sacrifice, principles that conferred worth and identity on black slaves and white women. The ethos of revolt, inscribed as the rebellion of "Anglo Saxon blood" in male veins, coexists with the ethos of sentimentalism in the broader poetics of nineteenth-century fiction. True, they coexist uneasily (as uneasily, we might say, as did the era's construction of masculinity and femininity per se), and we can see the same contrasting modes yoked together in works that have little to do with race or slavery, works such as Melville's novel *Pierre*. But the source of difference between these modes is not to be found in distinct sensibilities of men and women writers but in the built-in, transpersonal, contradictory but complicit literary codes which contained (even as they revised) the informing mythologies differentiating color and sex. Because they feature different species of protagonists—Stowe's feminized black slave and Hildreth's Europeanized white slave—the surfaces of their narratives appear antithetical, but in fact each is implicated in the other. That both domestic fiction and heroic romanticism are finally mutually supporting confirms the recent arguments of scholars like Lora Romero and Amy Kaplan who show that the nineteenth-century narrative of sentiment ultimately worked in concert with the supposedly premodern narratives of heroic adventure. It did so most pointedly by retaining for white men, in the domestically regulated discipline of the modern world, a preserve or an island of legitimate corporeal power that could be exercised against savages and other dark people at the imperial frontier.[26]

In comparing two of the most prominent early antislavery texts by Stowe and Hildreth, then, we have seen a bifurcation which splits the slave hero into Black Christian and Europeanized Avenger. In response to these polarized types, African American writers like Frederick Douglass, Martin Delany, and William Wells Brown sought to create a forceful black protagonist of full African descent. Douglass's Madison Washington and Delany's Henry Blake are black men of valor who refute the race mythology that would attribute an "indomitable" spirit to a white inheritance. Even Stowe, in her later antislavery novel *Dred*, tried her hand at creating a black revolutionary—though for Stowe the rebellious slave, however heroic, was ultimately doomed. The black rebel hero, then, might well count as a third version of the Mulatto hero, a protest version in which color and descent are wholly transformed. But while the problematics of color were erased by making the hero black, the project of portraying a forceful dark hero ready to commit violence for liberty had, as Richard Yarborough notes, its own "conceptual briar patch": "Black men were viewed as unmanly and otherwise inferior because they were enslaved; at the same time, they were often viewed as beasts and otherwise inferior if they rebelled violently."[27]

Brown's first 1853 version of *Clotel* reflects this dilemma in portraying black heroism, even as it reflects the deep-seated taboo against depicting any redeeming violence to the white male body. While the "white" George Green manages to avert his scheduled hanging after performing a bold act of rescue from a burning building ("the white men took him up in their arms, to see if he had sustained any injury"), the leading role for the black male body in this edition is as the victim of horrific violence. A chapter called "The Negro Chase" tells a story designed to unveil "the inhumanity and barbarity" of the inhabitants of Natchez, Mississippi. But the chapter's focus of narrative energy is "the body of the Negro," a representative, even reified figure—never named—who is hunted, chained to a tree and burned, and finally shot when he breaks out of his chains in agony: "The body of the Negro fell a corpse on the ground. He was picked up by some two or three, and again thrown into the fire, and consumed, not a vestige remaining to show that such a being ever existed."[28] White men hold up the body of George Green in awe and respect, while the unnamed black man is cast down by white men in an act of total physical violation. The passage, rendered in shocking detail, is probably the novel's most sustained, serious portrait of a proud dark-skinned male slave, in this case one who dared "to raise his hand against a white man." In return for his physical rebellion, the black man has his very existence denied and "consumed" in the violence that follows. Brown includes the scene for its power to shock, but the dehumanized portrait wipes out any possibility of offering readers a surviving black hero.

Significantly, though, the actual description of the murder is not Brown's but rather the language of a newspaper report that he grafts onto his fictional plot. It is the discourse of the Natchez *Free Trader* that reduces the potential black hero to a powerless body ("the body was taken and chained to a tree . . . [and faggots] piled around him") and then a corpse. In a later edition of the novel, Brown reclaims the black male body by transforming his Mulatto hero: virtually white in the first edition, George Green is rebaptized in a 1864 edition (*Clotelle; A Tale of the Southern States*) not only with a new name—Jerome Fletcher—but with a new skin color: "perfectly black."[29] The transformation illustrates an important protest by African American writers against the dominant descriptions of black men. Of special significance for this essay, though, is the fact that the revisionist fictions featuring dark slave heroes represent another instance of the pressure—now coming from within the African American community—to resolve the Mulatto figure into a man of unambiguous color. Yet the same gravitational pull toward an unmixed race identity was not exerted upon the fictional Mulatta heroine in these novels. Like the revised hero Jerome Fletcher, both Madison Washington and Henry Blake marry light-skinned women who resemble the conventional imperiled Mulatta slave. Since the possibility of selfhood won through passive suffering obtained for black and white women alike, there was not the same pressure to transpose the figure of the Mulatta. Thus the black writers' revisionism—which redescribed the slave hero but not the slave heroine—is further evidence of the different set of rules for defining the humanity of men and women, rules which black writers were no more able to escape entirely than were progressive white writers.

■ ■ ■

I have attempted to suggest dominant patterns within prewar fiction, what I have called the rules of corporeal representation for white and black bodies. But how relevant are such fictional rules to the perceptions and actions of living people in this period? The mimetic exchanges between life and art are of course far too complex for any formal resolution, but the extraordinary autobiographical narratives of Frederick Douglass offer an intriguing test case of the fictional poetics we have seen in Stowe, Hildreth, and Brown. In Douglass's narratives the question of male identity and its relation to the body is thrown into relief: Douglass, whose father was white, explicitly links his selfhood to his manhood and the inviolate power of his body. "A man, without force," Douglass asserts, "is without the essential dignity of humanity."[30]

Douglass's narratives share a complex kinship with Stowe's popular novel. The self-portrait Douglass had composed in his 1845 *Narrative* is part of the archival record out of which Stowe created George Harris. What is more, she actively sought Douglass's help as she was composing the novel, writing that she wanted to "make a picture that shall be graphic & true to nature in its details." In turn the novel that Douglass called the *"master book* of the nineteenth century" became a silent presence in his own later narratives and in his fictional work *The Heroic Slave*, which Robert Stepto has described as a "countercomposition" to *Uncle Tom's Cabin*.[31] Scholars have begun to analyze in detail the many textual links that unite this body of writing.[32] Of special interest here is the way that Douglass's representation of his own identity and body makes visible the same limits to sentimental empathy we have seen in antislavery fiction— and makes visible as well the textual "signs of power," as Douglass calls them, that are the evidence of the male subject.

In representing his "career as a slave," Douglass saw the "turning point" as his two-hour fight with the overseer Covey. In both the 1845 and 1855 narratives, Douglass does not often dwell on the bloodier scenes of slavery. Brutal episodes like the whipping of his Aunt Hester are stark but few; he is more apt to dilate when describing the existential miseries of slavery, as he does in his apostrophe to the sailboats in the Chesapeake Bay. But in the fight scene with Covey, Douglass renders details of the struggle—literally, a blow-by-blow narration—with the same magnification of the gestures of violence that we saw in Hildreth: "I held him uneasy, causing the blood to run where I touched him with the end of my fingers."[33] In recasting this line in his later 1855 narrative, Douglass altered "fingers" to "nails." But the original phrasing may have been deliberate, giving the sense as it does of a superior force within Douglass that draws blood simply by laying hands on Covey. For Douglass's narration makes it altogether clear that the physical fight itself is continuous with the agonistic struggle of a more essential strength and weakness. We get a glimpse of this underlying struggle again when Douglass writes that he kicked the man Covey had summoned to his aid: "This kick had the effect of not only weakening Hughes, but Covey also. When he saw Hughes bending over with pain, his courage quailed" (*N*, 112). The fight is a physical expression of Douglass's simultaneous struggle for the intangible currency of identity. In addition to whatever pain he may have inflicted, Douglass's actions are a vocabulary through which he pronounces a more fundamental mastery over Covey and a concomitant possession of his own identity as a man. A balance of power has shifted, but more than that is at stake. As if selfhood were a zero-sum commodity, Douglass seems to win his dignity or what he calls his "humanity" at the expense of the body of the man who had denied it. The exchange is expressed in an equation of blood: "he had drawn no blood from me, but I had from him" (*N*, 113).

Covey never charges Douglass with the crime of striking a white man. In 1845 Douglass is puzzled at this fact. But in the 1855 description of the fight, Douglass's explicit reflections on the question of color can be said to supply an answer: "The fighting madness had come upon me, and I found my strong fingers firmly attached to the throat of my cowardly tormentor; as heedless of consequences, at the moment, as though we stood as equals before the law. The very color of the man was forgotten" (*MB*, 149). The battle effects a change in Douglass's ascribed race identity, and the change is recognized by both men. The proof: both ignore the legal distinction that dictated that a black man could not strike a white one. While the men were fighting, Douglass was temporarily a "white" man— that is, they were "equals before the law." Douglass does not deny an African identity, but he does claim white manhood, a manhood conditioned upon an inviolate body. Covey never touches him again, and Douglass, though a "slave in form," will never again be a "slave in fact." Although Douglass here and elsewhere employs sophisticated analyses of different levels of slavery, we should not overlook the primal sense in which he declares himself emancipated in this passage; from now on no man can violate his body: "I did not hesitate to let it be known of me, that the white man who expected to succeed in whipping me, must also succeed in killing me." Douglass even acknowledges what Archy Moore described as the physical "pleasures" of fighting a tyrant, sensations which Douglass describes as the "gratification" and "deep satisfaction" of having "repelled by force the bloody arm of slavery" (*N*, 113).

It is startling, then, when Douglass goes on to interpret the scene in emphatically spiritual terms: "It rekindled the few expiring embers of freedom, and revived within me a sense of my own manhood. It recalled the departed self-confidence, and inspired me again with a determination to be free. . . . It was a glorious resurrection, from the tomb of slavery, to the heaven of freedom. My long-crushed spirit rose, cowardice departed, bold defiance took its place; and I now resolved that, however long I might remain a slave in form, the day had passed forever when I could be a slave in fact" (*N*, 113). Like Stowe, Douglass brings a Christian typology to the story of American slavery. But unlike the spiritual transcendence of Tom's plantation crucifixion, Douglass's "glorious resurrection" is not a triumph *over* the body but most emphatically *in* the body. Freedom is not a release from the bondage of mortal flesh but a reclaiming of its physical powers. By insisting upon his body's integrity and force, Douglass claims no more than what Hildreth and even Stowe require for the white man's fullest identity as a subject. Douglass insists upon this not because he wishes to be white, I would argue, but because he recognizes what is at stake in allowing the black man's selfhood to be severed from his body: that to all eyes but God's it would be a racially marked manhood never comparable to the subjectivity possessed by white men.

Douglass's evangelical language of the spirit, then, is not wholly paradoxical here. The bloody fight is a conversion experience in the most profound way possible because it changes, at the site of the body, Douglass's spiritual status or selfhood. In *My Bondage and My Freedom*, Douglass even more starkly describes the battle as effecting an almost ontological change: "I was a changed being after that fight. I was nothing before; I was a MAN NOW. It recalled to life my crushed self-respect and my self-confidence, and inspired me with a renewed determination to be a FREEMAN." What follows is perhaps the most explicit statement of the differentiating rules which govern the representation of selfhood for male bodies: "A man, without force, is without the essential dignity of humanity. Human nature is so constituted, that it cannot *honor* a helpless man, although it can *pity* him; and even this it cannot do long if the signs of power do not arise" (*MB*, 151). It is an ex-slave, born of mixed race parentage, who is able to articulate most directly the tacit principles of male identity in this period. He correctly unveils the limits of pity, limits which are present even in Stowe's epic of sentimental power. And he correctly identifies the necessary "signs of power"—the body and its capacity for force over others—that are the tokens of "humanity" for men in antebellum culture.

Douglass knew the power of sentiment, and his later autobiographical narratives expand his treatment of family themes and other topoi from domestic fiction. But he knew, too, that the redemptive power of empathy was not monolithic. Like Stowe and Hildreth, Douglass understood that the antithetical languages of passive suffering and heroic violence were coextensive, strange but necessary bedfellows in the ideology of the dominant culture that Douglass both resists and repeats. It is fitting, then, that Douglass ends his "conversion" chapter not with any evangelical image from sentimental poetics but with a signature of high romanticism, a speech from Byron's *Childe Harold*:

> Hereditary bondmen, know ye not
> Who would be free, themselves must strike the blow? (*MB*, 153)

Notes

1   Harriet Beecher Stowe, *Uncle Tom's Cabin; or, Life Among the Lowly*, ed. Kathryn Kish Sklar (New York: Library of America, 1982), 315. My primary concern is with literary representations of violence in the antebellum fiction of slavery, but a historical context—the Haitian rebellion and other uprisings—is fundamental to understanding this topic. Eric Sundquist's "*Benito Cereno* and New World Slavery," in *Reconstructing American Literary History*, ed. Sacvan Bercovitch (Cambridge: Harvard Univ. Press, 1986), 93–122, includes Stowe's image of a "San Domingo hour" in a study that beautifully integrates history and fiction.

2   I use the terms "Mulatto" and "Mulatta" with a capital letter in this essay to refer to the specific literary and ideological representations of people of biracial descent that were constructed and circulated in antebellum America.

3   Karen Sánchez-Eppler, "Bodily Bonds: The Intersecting Rhetorics of Feminism and Abolition," *Representations* 24 (Fall 1988): 49.

4   Werner Sollors argues that this scandal to American categories, often rendered in melodramatic terms, has been used by African American and white writers alike as "the subject for a tragic construction of the conflict between real blood ties of family relations and the social barriers of slavery and the color line (often based on fake 'blood' imagery)" ("'Never Was Born': The Mulatto, An American Tragedy?" *The Massachusetts Review* 37 [1986]: 305).

5   Sánchez-Eppler, 40.

6   Dion Boucicault, *The Octoroon; or, Life in Louisiana* (1859; rpt., Upper Saddle River, N.J.: Gregg, 1970), 36.

7   The figure of the Mulatta, for instance, is often elided with the "tragic octoroon" heroine, whom Jules Zanger describes as "a beautiful young girl who possesses only the slightest evidences of Negro blood" patterned after "the

conventional ingenue 'victim' of sentimental romance" (Jules Zanger, "The 'Tragic Octoroon' in Pre–Civil War Fiction," *American Quarterly* 18 [1966]: 63). The titles of some antislavery works show the centrality of the Mulatta heroine in much of this literature; other examples are Longfellow's "The Quadroon Girl" (1842); William Wells Brown's *Clotel; or, the President's Daughter* (1853); Mayne Reid's *The Quadroon* (1856); and H. L. Hosmer's *Adela the Octoroon* (1860).

8   Sterling Brown's critique is one of the earliest and most often cited arguments about the racist implications of the popular Mulatta theme. See his *The Negro in American Fiction* (New York: Atheneum, 1969), 133.

9   Lydia Maria Child, "Madison Washington," in her volume *The Freedmen's Book*, ed. James M. McPherson (1865; rpt., New York: Arno, 1968), 147. Child is speaking of Madison Washington's wife Susan in Frederick Douglass's novel *The Heroic Slave*.

10   Sánchez-Eppler, 49.

11   William Wells Brown, *Clotel; or, The President's Daughter* (1853; rpt., New York: Macmillan, 1970), 177.

12   Stowe, 415.

13   Brown, 190, 192.

14   Brown, 14.

15   Brown, 226.

16   Brown, 228, 339.

17   In an 1856 edition of the longer 1852 text, Richard Hildreth's "Introduction" sketches a history of the reception of the first 1836 version, describes the book's two English publications and foreign language translations (French, Italian, and German), and, while acknowledging Stowe's novel as the enabling condition for a second publication, stakes his claim to the "invention, (as applicants for a patent say in their specifications)" of "the first successful application of fictitious narrative to anti-slavery purposes" (*Archy Moore, The White Slave; or, Memoirs of a Fugitive* [1852; rpt., New York: Negro Universities Press, 1969], xxi). All further references will be cited by page numbers in the text. Despite Hildreth's claim to hold a narrative "patent," the 1852 text is certainly a reinvented novel: it contains close to two hundred pages of additional material, and Stowe's novel must be considered as much an influence upon this second version as Hildreth's 1836 narrative was for *Uncle Tom's Cabin.*

18   Stowe, 170.

19   Sollors writes that "the themes of incest and miscegenation, of inner and outer boundaries to sexual choices, easily get confused in American race melodrama, merging two fears into a single, overpowering one" (302). He also notes that European mulatto stories often ended in interracial marriages, while "the mulatto suicide is the cultural given in American settings" (300).

20   Stowe, cited in E. Bruce Kirkham, *The Building of "Uncle Tom's Cabin"* (Knoxville: Univ. of Tennessee Press, 1977), 66–67.

21 Philip Fisher, *Hard Facts* (New York: Oxford Univ. Press, 1988), 115.

22 Sánchez-Eppler observes that reading sentimental fiction is a "bodily act," and that "the success of a story is gauged, in part, by its ability to translate works into pulse beats and sobs" (36). Also see Fisher, 108.

23 Stowe, 501.

24 Brown, 224. For a discussion of Brown's dual use of and resistance to the racism of the fictional types he reproduces in *Clotel*, see Richard Yarborough, "Race, Violence, and Manhood: The Masculine Ideal in Frederick Douglass's 'The Heroic Slave,'" in *Frederick Douglass: New Literary and Historical Essays*, ed. Eric J. Sundquist (New York: Cambridge Univ. Press, 1990), 166–88, a collection which brings together some of the best recent work on Douglass.

25 Carolyn L. Karcher, "Rape, Murder and Revenge in 'Slavery's Pleasant Homes': Lydia Maria Child's Antislavery Fiction and the Limits of Genre," *Women's Studies International Forum* 9 (Fall 1986): 323.

26 See Amy Kaplan, "Romancing the Empire: The Embodiment of American Masculinity in the Popular Historical Novel of the 1890s," *American Literary History* 2 (1990): 659–90; and Lora Romero, "Vanishing Americans: Gender, Empire, and New Historicism," *American Literature* 63 (1991): 386–404.

27 Yarborough, 174.

28 Brown, 81.

29 William Wells Brown, *Clotelle; A Tale of the Southern States* (1864; rpt., Hamden, Conn.: Archon, 1969), 57.

30 Frederick Douglass, *My Bondage and My Freedom* (1855; rpt., Urbana: Univ. of Illinois Press, 1987), 151.

31 Robert Stepto, "Sharing the Thunder: The Literary Exchanges of Harriet Beecher Stowe, Henry Bibb, and Frederick Douglass," in *New Essays on "Uncle Tom's Cabin,"* ed. Eric J. Sundquist (New York: Cambridge Univ. Press, 1986), 137. Stowe is quoted in Stepto, 137, and Douglass in the same source, 144.

32 In a study responding to several of the essays in *Frederick Douglass: New Literary and Historical Essays*, Robert S. Levine examines the reception of *Uncle Tom's Cabin* among contemporary African American writers, in *"Uncle Tom's Cabin* in *Frederick Douglass' Paper*: An Analysis of Reception," *American Literature* 64 (1992): 71–93.

33 Frederick Douglass, *Narrative of the Life of Frederick Douglass, an American Slave* (1845; rpt., New York: Penguin, 1982), 112, hereafter cited in the text as *N*. References to Douglass's later 1855 narrative, *My Bondage and My Freedom*, will be cited in the text as *MB*. David Leverenz analyzes this fight scene in detail and places the topic of manhood in a larger literary context in *Manhood and the American Renaissance* (Ithaca: Cornell Univ. Press, 1989). He illuminates the significant differences between the 1845 and 1855 descriptions of the fight with Covey, but for the purposes of uncovering the corporeal logic of Douglass's sense of identity both versions can be treated together.

Part III

Timothy Sweet   Masculinity and Self-Performance in the *Life of Black Hawk*

> Traditional tribal lifestyles are more often gynocratic than not, and they are never patriarchal.—Paula Gunn Allen, *The Sacred Hoop*

> It is not customary for us to say much about our women, as they generally perform their part cheerfully, and never interfere with business belonging to the men!—Black Hawk, *Life of Black Hawk*

In *The Sacred Hoop*, Paula Gunn Allen articulates the need to recover the original feminine traditions of American tribal peoples as part of a general critique of white Western patriarchy. Traditional tribal lifestyles, according to Allen, underwent an incomplete but significant transformation from gynocratic to patriarchal modes as a result of contact with Europeans who enforced their own values, especially Christian misogyny, in their dealings with Native Americans. Whether or not "the physical and cultural genocide of American Indian tribes is and was mostly about patriarchal fear of gynocracy," it is certainly true that the European conquest of the Americas brought about significant alterations in the gender structures of Native American cultures, as it did in every other facet of tribal life.[1] Yet if femininity was altered, so was masculinity. Thus Allen's project of "recovering the feminine," articulated in the subtitle of her important study, must be complemented by an endeavor to recover the masculine in order to attain a full understanding of gender in American tribal societies. The feminine roles that Allen valorizes did not exist in isolation but rather in mutually enabling relations with various masculine roles such as shaman, healer, hunter, politician, and defender of the tribe, all of which were altered in some way by the European conquest.[2]

A good place to begin investigating these concerns is the autobiographical *Life of Black Hawk*.[3] Here we read the personal narrative of a Sauk war chief, a man who in 1832 led a small band in the only violent resistance to Indian Removal in the old Northwest. Threatened by soldiers who were coming to force his people from the village of Saukenuk on the Rock River in Illinois, which had been ceded by a suspect treaty in 1804 (discussed below), Black Hawk moved his band of men, women, and children to the north, attempting to rendezvous with the Winnebago and Potawatomi in Wisconsin, and, as he thought, British forces in Canada. He then intended to return and retake Saukenuk. But he had been deceived by a Sauk chief, Neapope ("Broth"), and a crossblood Sauk-Winnebago, Wabokieshiek ("White Cloud" or "Prophet"), about the possibility of an alliance with the British.[4] After the discovery of this deception, the war took the form of a strategic retreat to the west, with Black Hawk attempting to protect his band from massacre by the Illinois Mounted Volunteers on the one hand and attack by the Sioux on the other. The majority of the Sauk and Fox did not participate in the war; they had been persuaded by Black Hawk's political rival Keokuk to remove west of the Mississippi as the treaty specified. The war marked a turning point in Sauk political and cultural history. Through subsequent negotiations they lost all of the land west of the Mississippi that had been granted to them (in perpetuity, of course) by the treaty of 1804. Once a powerful force in the Mississippi Valley, by 1845 they were confined to a tiny reservation in Kansas, ironically at the headwaters of a river named for their traditional enemies, the Osage.[5]

While other traditionally masculine tribal roles, such as hunter, were also altered by white conquest, the significance of the *Life of Black Hawk* consists in its representation of the collision between the specific Sauk tradition for the masculine gendering of the self as a warrior and the U.S. government policy, also enacted by "warriors," that sought to eliminate the Native American warrior tradition in order to control and ultimately eradicate tribal cultural wholes. This government policy is exemplified in the treaty of 1804, which Black Hawk regarded as invalid since he did not think the signers represented the Sauk interest. The primary intent of the treaty was, of course, the acquisition of Sauk and Fox land (bounded by the Mississippi and Illinois Rivers) and the removal of the tribes west of the Mississippi. But it held other, deeper cultural implications as well, in specifying that the tribes could no longer be responsible for their own defense. The treaty stipulated that the tribes must place themselves "under the protection of the United States, and of no other power whatsoever," that they must not take "private revenge or retaliation" for violations of the treaty but instead appeal to a judicial process administered by the United States government, and that they must "put an end to the bloody war which has heretofore raged between their tribes and those of the Great and Little Osages."[6] Strict adherence to these conditions would alter the gender economy of the tribe by minimizing the importance of warriors. The defeat of the Sauk in the Black Hawk war confirmed this alteration, ensuring that warriors no longer had a legitimate cultural role to play. In the face of white military and political efforts to emasculate the tribal warrior, the *Life of Black Hawk* emerges as an attempt to preserve his traditions.

Black Hawk's story was translated into English and published in late 1833, the year after the war. The actual oral narratives of the war that Black Hawk told to his Sauk contemporaries are unavailable. But we can assume that the conventions governing such narratives would have shaped his telling of the story to a white audience. Given both the social relations surrounding the traditions of Sauk men's personal narratives and the circumstances determining the production of the *Life of Black Hawk*, Black Hawk appears to us primarily as a defender of the tribe, a warrior, and not as a hunter or a seeker of visions or other possible subject-positions. In the partiality of that representation vis-à-vis whatever his "whole" sense of self might have been, we will find a fundamental connection between personal narrative and the construction of masculinity in Sauk society. This connection is put into question by the context of Black Hawk's defeat and the telling of his story to the victors, but it is nevertheless available to a careful reader of the *Life*.

The *Life of Black Hawk* is told by an unassimilated Sauk. The telling is mediated by two men. Antoine LeClair, a crossblood (French-Canadian and Potawatomi) who was fluent in several tribal languages as well as French and English and had been employed by the U.S. government since 1818 as an interpreter, reported that in August of 1833 Black Hawk approached him at the Rock Island Indian Agency and "express[ed] a great desire to have a History of his Life written and published" (*L*, 35). LeClair enlisted the editorial assistance of John Patterson, a newspaper editor. Patterson provided no account of the nature and extent of his editing, and it is not clear whether he ever spoke to Black Hawk in person.

All manuscripts and correspondence surrounding the collaboration have been lost.[7] However, prefaces to the *Life* by both LeClair and Patterson attest to the text's fidelity to Black Hawk's actual words.

It was not unusual in the nineteenth century for tribal leaders to want representations of themselves produced for white audiences. While "as told to" personal narratives were rare—for reasons related to logistics and the literary marketplace—painted portraits were common. The usual itinerary of a tribal delegation to Washington included sitting for portraits, which were then displayed in the Indian Gallery at the War Department. The men were usually gratified that their images were thus preserved and publicized; some demanded copies to take home with them. One writer describing the Winnebago delegation in 1850 remarked that "nothing pleased them so much as to tell them that their likenesses were in the War Department, and that their fame was spread through the world."[8] While Black Hawk's desire for fame is evident, his motivations go beyond this and he takes a more active role in self-representation than merely sitting for a portrait (although, as I will discuss below, he did this as well).

The immediate audience for Black Hawk's narrative is the United States government as represented in the person of the interpreter LeClair and the physical space of the Rock Island Agency—a situation in some ways analogous to delegation portraiture. However, according to LeClair's preface, Black Hawk envisioned a wider audience, desiring "(as he said), 'that the people of the United States, (among whom he had been travelling, and by whom he had been treated with great respect, friendship, and hospitality,) might know the *causes* that had impelled him to act as he had done, and the *principles* by which he was governed'" (*L*, 35). Supposing the accuracy of LeClair's story and translation here, we can see that Black Hawk believed in both the possibility of cross-cultural communication and the interest of white readers in his story. That is, Black Hawk demonstrated his awareness that the *Life* would be what Arnold Krupat calls a "bicultural composite composition."[9]

The most theoretically sophisticated treatment of "bicultural composition" is given in Krupat's *The Voice in the Margin: Native American Literature and the Canon*, which provides a useful framework for understanding the relation between the textual structures and social contexts of Native American literature by analyzing textual production in terms of Mikhail Bakhtin's *The Dialogic Imagination*.[10] Krupat, who has provided the only substantial readings to date of the *Life of Black Hawk*, identifies a tension in the text between genuine cross-cultural dialogue, evidenced by its autobiographical form (the fact that Black Hawk speaks for himself rather than being represented as the subject of a historical narrative), and white monologue, evidenced by Patterson's editorial procedure. In following the chronological imperative of European autobiography, Patterson made Black Hawk's words conform to the dominant discourse for dealing with Indians—"savagism"—which "claimed as a necessity of nature the accession of Indian savagery to white civilization."[11] This discourse, Krupat argues, produced a generic narrative structure of "decline and fall in the comic mode."[12] That is, the overall Jacksonian-progressivist ideological narrative of westward expansion determined the textualization in English of any story of Indian-white interaction, no matter who narrated it originally, as a comedy in which "the red-skinned 'blocking characters' are overcome" to produce the "happy ending" of white settlement.[13] Alternatively, such a narrative could be read as a tragedy of a noble people doomed by the "flaw" of Indianness without distorting the Jacksonian-progressive master narrative. The difference between these modes lies in nineteenth-century white attitudes toward the master narrative—Western Indian-hating or Eastern philanthropy.[14] We will need to read from neither of these positions if we hope to recover tribal tradition from a text that seems, in its overall narrative structure, to be so completely co-opted.

Bakhtin's later work on "speech genres" provides an additional analytical frame for investigating the questions of gender that I raised at the beginning of this essay. Speech genres are "relatively stable types of utterance" ranging in verbal complexity from primary genres, such as the conventional "short rejoinders of daily dialogue" or "the brief standard military command," through secondary genres such as "the diverse forms of scientific statement and all literary genres."[15] Secondary genres are composed of strings of primary genres which are "absorb[ed] and digest[ed]" in various conventional ways.[16] The concept of speech genre can be used to theorize both H. David Brumble's empirical catalogue of pre-literate autobiographical traditions—coup tales, informal autobiographical tales, self-examinations, self-vindications, educational narratives, and stories of the acquisition of powers—and the English textualization of these traditions.[17] If we understand the *Life of Black Hawk* as merely an assemblage of utterances in various complex speech genres translated by LeClair and organized by Patterson, we can watch the teleological narrative dissolve into more localized sets of verbal conventions, some of which function to construct and maintain gender roles in Sauk culture.

Before investigating gender roles, however, we must understand the cross-cultural speech genre of ethnography which is essential to an identification of Black Hawk's subject position in the text.[18] The *Life* contains a good deal of ethnographic material, which is placed between Black Hawk's criticism of the dubious treaty of 1804 (the conditions of which compel Black Hawk to go to war) and the account of the war itself; this placement is probably due to Patterson's desire to heighten the dramatic impact of the narrative through a contrast of genres. Regardless of its placement, it is interesting in itself as an example of the cross-cultural dialogization of speech genres. The ethnographic description is oriented toward whites (since Black Hawk would not need to explain these things to his own people), and yet it depends on a "native informant." Further embedded within the ethnographic description are various traditional tribal genres; for example, Black Hawk's account of the ceremony celebrating the new corn leads him into telling a story that might be told at this ceremony: "When the corn is fit to use, another great ceremony takes place, with feasting, and returning thanks to the Great Spirit for giving us corn. I will here relate the manner in which corn first came. According to tradition, handed down to our people, a beautiful woman was seen to descend from the clouds . . ." (*L*, 93). When the story of the woman who brings beans, corn, and tobacco is told within the context of ethnography, it becomes dialogized toward its white audience. As such, the story becomes alienated from its original, tribal orientation; for although LeClair and Patterson textualize it in a way that registers Black Hawk's consciousness of the continuity of oral transmission, the story's traditional social context has been radically altered by virtue not only of its appearing in print for white readers, but, even prior to this, by Black Hawk's telling it to the government employee LeClair rather than to the Sauk.

Black Hawk himself is aware of the cross-cultural situation of this particular telling of the story of Corn Woman. He concludes by acknowledging the dialogic frame without vitiating the legitimacy of the place of the story within the Sauk worldview, which is attempting to come to terms with the presence of whites in America: "The two first [corn and beans] have, ever since, been cultivated by our people, as our principal provisions—and the last used for smoking. The white people have since found out the latter, and seem to relish it as much as we do" (*L*, 94). The story's contextualization transforms it into ethnographic information, while demonstrating how one speech genre (ethnography) can operate on another (sacred story) to produce a cross-cultural text that does not destroy the legitimacy of the original, monologic story. Enabling the dissemination of the story by telling it within this context, Black Hawk builds a cultural bridge to the whites based on a common appreciation for tobacco. White readers are of course free to make their own assessment of the story as "myth"—and in so doing would be operating on it with their own speech genres (for example, theological or scientific discourses)—but nothing in the text itself especially encourages them to do so. Black Hawk thus represents himself as one firmly grounded in tribal tradition, implicitly emphasizing not his uniqueness or individuality (conventions of modern, white autobiography), but his cultural sameness with other Sauks and his qualification to explain Sauk ways to the whites.

Black Hawk's sense of his cultural sameness with other Sauks is fundamentally important, for his credibility and honor with respect to the main events of the *Life*—his self-identification as warrior and his conduct in the war—depend on his ability to represent himself as following the way of the Sauk, always in comparison with his political rival Keokuk, who is from Black Hawk's perspective too much under the influence of whites. Black Hawk attempts to discredit Keokuk, who agreed to abide by the treaty of 1804, by suggesting that he does not possess the qualities of a warrior. Thus Keokuk, as he comes to be represented in the *Life of Black Hawk*, would not have been entitled to tell the kind of personal narrative that Black Hawk tells. Yet the U.S. government chose to regard Keokuk as "chief" of the Sauks, and he became powerful and influential among his own people even before Black Hawk's defeat in 1832.[19]

Black Hawk's sense of social position is heavily invested in his self-representation as a Sauk who makes no gestures toward assimilation. In this way he is unlike "civilized Indians" such as Samson Occom and William Apes, who in their autobiographies voice the dominant white discourses of salvationism and progressivism in attempting to produce narratives of assimilation. Black Hawk does not write in his own "voice" but has his words transcribed and translated for him, a situation that embroiled contemporary readers in questions of the text's "authenticity"[20] but that interestingly preserves the integrity of Black Hawk's status as an unassimilated Sauk. Patterson makes a point of including on facing pages both a phonetic transcription and a translation (the English version is labeled a "Dedication") of Black Hawk's opening address to the victorious General Atkinson. This address calls on Atkinson to "vouch for the facts contained in my narrative, so far as they came under your observation" (*L*, 37). The facing-page layout would have been far too cumbersome to carry through the entire book, but its use here indicates a desire to represent the voice of the text as Black Hawk's own. Thus, despite the Jacksonian-progressivist context, a Native American (in this instance, Sauk) worldview is acknowledged through language, as it is not when Native Americans such as Occom and Apes write in English in the eighteenth and nineteenth centuries. Unlike John Neihardt's treatment of Black Elk's voice in *Black Elk Speaks*, there is no reason to believe Patterson edited out any evidence of assimilation to white culture.[21] For example, the accounts of trading with whites and descriptions of the impact of that trade (such as the increasing use of alcohol) are integrated without comment into the section of the text describing "our customs, and the manner we live" (*L*, 87). Indeed, in 1833 the newspaperman Patterson would have had every political incentive to preserve or even to fabricate such evidence, which would demonstrate an Indian's acknowledgment of the superiority of white ways. Black Hawk is instead seen to acknowledge only the superiority of white military force, and on his own terms—the terms of a Sauk warrior. As he states at the beginning of his address to Atkinson, "The changes of fortune, and vicissitudes of war, made you my conqueror" (*L*, 37).

In attempting to imagine what the terms of the Sauk warrior might be, we must bear in mind recent caveats about the difficulties of regarding any printed text as an "Indian autobiography" while hoping that the project of coming to some understanding of the warrior Black Hawk and his world is not impossible. An analysis of two categories of speech genre is relevant to developing such an understanding: first, the textual presentations directed toward a white audience, which belong to the "ethnographic" genre described above; second, the oral presentations by means of which Black Hawk's Sauk identity is established and maintained in his own society. Of course, the latter are necessarily mediated for us by the former. To put it another way, Black Hawk's Sauk identity must be seen to influence the textualized, translated (self-)presentation of "Black Hawk" in an important way—if not in terms of overall narrative structure, then in terms of topics or speech genres.

Black Hawk's self-representation as a warrior evokes two traditional, preliterate speech genres: the coup tale and the self-vindication narrative. Brumble characterizes the entire *Life of Black Hawk* as a self-vindication narrative and argues that in telling such a story Black Hawk was "acting in a perfectly traditional manner."[22] Equally important, however, is the coup tale—or, more precisely, the warrior's self-defining performance. Chronologically, the first life event of Black Hawk's narrative occurs at age fifteen (in contrast to Western autobiography, in which childhood is often assumed to be significant in the formation of character). Along with his father, he joins a war party against the Osages and kills his first enemy:

> Standing by my father's side, I saw him kill his antagonist, and tear the scalp from his head. Fired with valor and ambition, I rushed furiously upon another, smote him to the earth with my tomahawk—run [*sic*] my lance through his body—took off his scalp, and returned in triumph to my father! He said nothing, but looked pleased. This was the first man I killed! . . . Our party then returned to our village, and danced over the scalps we had taken. This was the first time that I was permitted to join in a scalp-dance. (*L*, 47)

The killing itself is important in two ways: of course it contributes to the Sauk victory in this battle, but it also enables Black Hawk to establish a new position in the community. He is formally acknowledged as a warrior for the first time by means of his participation in the scalp dance. Whites might miss the full significance of this narrative for Black Hawk's self-presentation if not for the apparently ethnographic orientation of the last sentence.[23]

This first act of self-performance authorizes Black Hawk to consolidate his new identity in further action (he reports, for example, that a subsequent successful raid "gained for me great applause" [*L*, 47]). Yet further ceremonies are at least equally important in the construction and maintenance of identity. One such ceremony, the "national dance," is described in some detail in a later ethnographic passage which clearly shows the fundamental link between warrior identity and self-performance in Sauk culture:

> The large square in the village is swept and prepared for the purpose. The chiefs and old warriors, take seats on mats which have been spread at the upper end of the square—the drummers and singers come next, and the braves and women form the sides, leaving a large space in the middle. The drums beat, and the singers commence. A warrior enters the square, keeping time with the music. He shows the manner he started on a war party—how he approached the enemy—he strikes, and describes the way he killed him. All join in applause. He then leaves the square, and another enters and takes his place. Such of our

young men as have not been out in war parties, and killed an enemy,
stand back ashamed—not being able to enter the square. I remember
that I was ashamed to look where our young women stood, before I
could take my stand in the square as a warrior.

What pleasure it is to an old warrior, to see his son come forward
and relate his exploits—it makes him feel young again, and induces
him to enter the square, and "fight his battles o'er again." (L, 91–92)

With this information, the reader is in a position to understand the importance of self-performative activity in the establishment and maintenance
of a particular configuration of masculine identity in Sauk culture: the
moment of (communally validated) self-definition as a warrior is simultaneously the moment of (again, communally validated) self-definition as
self-definer.[24] The warrior is necessarily an autobiographer. This moment
is repeated periodically throughout the warrior's life. There would, of
course, be other contexts in which masculinity is defined in other terms,
such as the ceremony following a young man's first successful hunt, but
these would not necessarily admit repeated performative validation.[25]

An important component of this performance is the possibility of meeting the gaze of those whom the tribe acknowledges as sexually available
women. Males who cannot participate in this dance are defined only nega-
tively, as not warriors and not fully masculine in this context; they are
"ashamed to look where our young women stood." About Black Hawk's
life before his first kill the text is utterly silent, mirroring the noniden-
tity of these unfortunate youths. This silence indicates that the self-
presentation of the warrior configuration of masculinity is linked with the
very possibility of self-presentation itself. The sexual competition implied
in Black Hawk's account of the national dance suggests that the moment
of self-definition contains an element of sexual self-objectification. This
moment, in which the warrior becomes both masculine subject and sexual
object, suggests that gender is constructed according to a paradigm more
complex than that of traditional Western patriarchy, in which "woman" is
marked (only) as object and "man" (only) as subject: for the Sauk man,
both subject and object positions are occupied at once. Additionally, it is
not merely the moment of self-objectification before the female gaze that
is significant, but the other warriors' observation of this moment as well.
The entire community is fully involved.

The sexual politics surrounding the perception of men by women, however, remain unexamined in the context of Black Hawk's situation as

narrator of the *Life*. The printed narrative emerges as a textual trace of Black Hawk's attempt to recover the original oral-performative definition of identity not primarily in relation to Sauk women but rather in relation to white soldiers and Sauk warriors, now that the war and Keokuk's accession to power seem to put his masculinity into question. At this point the originary relation between masculinity and formal self-presentation in Sauk culture, like the story of Corn Woman, is mediated by the ethnographic frame of the text. This mediation, the crossing of cultural boundaries, holds potential consequences for the gendering of the subject that Black Hawk attempts to overcome. He is describing the "national dance" for white readers, placing it within the context of events that take place after the corn is planted and within the larger context of his general description of Sauk life. Thus, while we can recognize how Black Hawk, like most Sauk men, established and maintained a gendered identity by means of personal narrative embodied in a ceremonial performance of his warrior role, we must also recognize the possibility that this gendered identity is alienated from him by the nonceremonial context of the interviews with the translator LeClair and by the medium of print technology. Without full communal authorization, accounts of wartime exploits may be mere idle boasts.

Black Hawk is no doubt aware of the difference in the production of identity between participating in a tribal ceremony and describing this participation to an agent of the U.S. government. Yet he knows that to present his already actualized, gendered self to whites who do not share this ceremonial context he must go through the discourse of ethnography and the medium of print, so that whites "might know the *causes* that had impelled him to act as he had done, and the *principles* by which he was governed" (*L*, 35). The "causes" of the war were the 1804 treaty of cession and Keokuk's inability or unwillingness to renegotiate; the "principles" were those of the Sauk warrior who, since he did not personally recognize the treaty, felt compelled to prevent the expropriation of the lands of the people for whom he took responsibility. In this narrative he attempts a cross-cultural authorization of his status as warrior, which embroils him in political controversy with Keokuk, whom he knows the whites regard as the "chief" of the Sauks and Foxes.

Black Hawk's descriptions of Keokuk typically mark the latter as a nonwarrior and, more generally, as one who violates Sauk tradition at crucial moments—in contrast to Black Hawk himself, who always demonstrates his centeredness within the traditional tribal worldview. Here, for example, is his assessment of the political situation on the eve of the war:

> We were a divided people, forming two parties. Ke-o-kuck being at the head of one, willing to barter our rights merely for the good opinion of the whites; and cowardly enough to desert our village to them. I was at the head of the other party, and was determined to hold on to my village, although I had been *ordered* to leave it. But, I considered, as myself and band had no agency in selling our country . . . that we could not be *forced* away. I refused, therefore, to quit my village. It was here, that I was born—and here lie the bones of many friends and relations. For this spot I felt a sacred reverence, and never could consent to leave it, without being forced therefrom. (*L*, 107)

Black Hawk argues that "my reason tells me that *land cannot be sold*. . . . Nothing can be sold, but such things as can be carried away" (*L*, 101). Keokuk had, in Black Hawk's view, both affirmed the white idea of land ownership and denigrated the warrior tradition in his negotiations with the whites:

> Ke-o-kuck came to the village; but his object was to persuade others to follow him to the Ioway [i.e., to the Iowa River where a new village site had been specified by the U.S. government]. He had accomplished nothing towards making arrangements for us to remain, or to exchange other lands for our village. There was no more friendship existing between us. I looked upon him as a coward, and no brave, to abandon his village to be occupied by strangers. (*L*, 101)

As Black Hawk clarifies the political situation, he impugns Keokuk's masculinity and thus questions his qualifications to assume such a position of leadership.

Keokuk had not always held precisely this view of the treaty, but Black Hawk had long suspected his political qualifications. Black Hawk had returned from the War of 1812 (in which he had fought on the side of the British) to find that Keokuk had been named "war-chief of the braves then in the village" (*L*, 72). Black Hawk's report of how this had happened in his absence is tinged with irony. U.S. soldiers had been spotted in the vicinity and a council had been called, which decided that the people ought to leave the village temporarily: "Ke-o-kuck, during the sitting of the council, had been standing at the door of the lodge, (*not being allowed to enter, having never killed an enemy*,) where he remained until old Wa-co-me came out. He then told him that he had heard what they had decided upon, and was anxious to be permitted to go in and speak, before the council adjourned!" (*L*, 72, emphasis added). Keokuk persuaded the council to appoint him war-chief, possibly (although Black Hawk does not say so) because there were few experienced warriors currently in the village, most having been for some time at the war.[26] Again, inflecting the entire political-historical discourse is the sense of Keokuk's not having achieved a tribally confirmed status as warrior. This war party might provide Keokuk with the opportunity to achieve this status, as Black Hawk had long since done, through ceremonial self-performance. Black Hawk's historical account continues: "He marshalled his braves— sent out spies—and advanced with a party himself. . . . They returned without seeing an enemy. The Americans did not come to our village. All were well satisfied with the appointment of Ke-o-kuck. He used every precaution that our people should not be surprised. This is the manner in which, and the cause of, his receiving the appointment. I was satisfied, and then started to visit my wife and children" (*L*, 73). Although Black Hawk himself professes to be "satisfied," he does not say whether it is with the fact that no enemies attacked the village, with Keokuk's appointment in general, or with the fact that Keokuk got no opportunity to prove himself a warrior (thus confirming Black Hawk's view of him as "no brave"). The reminder that Keokuk was not yet formally recognized as a warrior indicates Black Hawk's suspicion and makes it seem as if Keokuk was merely lucky that no enemies were near. The odd conclusion of the story—the reiteration of the topic—marks it as somehow questionable, as if the insistence that this is the complete explanation covers some incompleteness; perhaps it is meant to cast suspicion on Keokuk's credentials. By the time of the war twenty years later it is still not clear whether Keokuk has ever engaged an enemy in battle. All subsequent mentions of him in the *Life of Black Hawk* characterize him, with historical accuracy, as a protreaty spokesman, while none refer to any exploits in battle.[27]

Keokuk's position gained him favorable portrayal by whites, which contrasts interestingly with Black Hawk's view of him and with the whites' view of Black Hawk. For George Catlin, it is Keokuk, not Black Hawk, who represents the epitome of Sauk manhood at this historical moment— the pacified and potentially civilizable warrior. One of Catlin's portraits, made during a visit to "Kee-o-kuk's village of Sacs and Foxes" on the Des Moines River in 1835, shows Keokuk holding a tomahawk in the right

Figure 1   George Catlin, *Keokuk (The Watchful Fox), Chief of the Tribe*. National Museum of American Art, Smithsonian Institution, gift of Mrs. Joseph Harrison Jr.

hand and a feathered staff in the left (fig. 1).[28] Catlin insists on the authenticity of this representation. Keokuk, he writes, "is the present chief of the tribe, a dignified and proud man, with a good share of talent, and vanity enough to force into action all the wit and judgement he possesses, in order to command the attention and respect of the world. . . . In this portrait I have represented him in the costume, precisely, in which he was dressed when he stood for it, with his shield on his arm, and his staff (insignia of office) in his left hand."[29] Linked with this portrait is a verbal image of Keokuk as the supposed true defender of the tribe—but one who uses means approved by the whites: "There is no Indian chief on the frontier better known at this time, or more highly appreciated for his eloquence, as a public speaker, than Kee-o-kuk; as he has repeatedly visited Washington and others of our Atlantic towns, and made his speeches before thousands, when he has been contending for his people's rights, in their stipulations with the United States Government, for the sale of their lands."[30] The tomahawk had appeared in the portrait by both Keokuk's own choice and Catlin's approval.[31] Catlin's verbal description omits any mention of this sign of warrior status, implying new limits on Sauk masculinity in the postsubjugation period: only the role of politician, a role easily managed by the U.S. government and military, is relevant. However, the tomahawk is clearly depicted, suggesting the form that Keokuk's masculinity could take under freer circumstances.

In contrast, Catlin emasculates the public image of Black Hawk both verbally and visually. Black Hawk sat for Catlin in late 1832 or early 1833, while he was imprisoned at Jefferson Barracks south of St. Louis.[32] The conventional bust-length portrait made at this time would be unremarkable but for the tail feathers of a black hawk held in the right hand (fig. 2).[33] Where Keokuk's tomahawk could be taken to mark him as a potential warrior, Black Hawk's pose seems feminine, as if he were an elegant lady holding a fan. Thus Catlin takes the man's very name and uses it as a device to re-gender his identity for a white audience. Catlin's verbal description of Black Hawk, included in his account of his visit to "Kee-o-kuk's village" in 1835, does not emphasize the feminine connotations of the 1832–33 portrait. Nevertheless, the description serves to cast doubt on Black Hawk's credentials as a warrior:

> [Black Hawk] was defeated by General Atkinson, and held a prisoner of war, and sent through Washington and other Eastern cities, with a number of others, *to be gazed at.*
>
> This man, whose name has carried a sort of terror through the country where it has been sounded, has been distinguished as a speaker or counsellor rather than as a warrior; and I believe it has been pretty generally admitted, that "Nah-pope" and the "Prophet" were, in fact, the instigators of the war; and either of them with much higher claims for the name of warrior than Black Hawk ever had.[34]

Catlin's assault on Black Hawk's masculine identity is threefold. If he was a warrior, then he was defeated and exhibited as a prisoner of war. But in fact he was not really a warrior and did not instigate the war.

Figure 2 George Catlin, *Black Hawk, Prominent Sauk Chief*. National Museum of American Art, Smithsonian Institution, gift of Mrs. Joseph Harrison Jr.

Moreover, as a statesman he was not nearly so impressive, by comparison, as Keokuk. Where Catlin describes Keokuk's presence among the whites in terms of action, speaking for his people's rights, he describes Black Hawk as passive, occupying the conventionally feminine position (in Western tradition) of the object of a "gaze"—a position emphasized by the particular pose of the portrait. However, it is doubtful that Sauks, unfamiliar with the conventions of the nineteenth-century drawing room,

Figure 3   George Catlin, *Keokuk on Horseback*. National Museum of American Art, Smithsonian Institution, gift of Mrs. Joseph Harrison Jr.

would have read the same feminine connotations into Black Hawk's pose, because to them the feathers would signify the man's name and thus connote all the deeds performed under that name. Their reading of the portrait would depend on their opinion of the man, an opinion that would be formed communally, in the contexts of warfare and ceremony.

Catlin's second portrait of Keokuk (fig. 3) more strongly represents him as a warrior than does the first, and thus provides an emphatic contrast to Catlin's feminized representation of Black Hawk. Although this pose can be said to represent a tribal warrior, Catlin's models are European baroque monuments of military officers reining in powerful, spirited horses, on their way to performing heroic, liberating deeds. It is, perhaps, the archetypal image of the warrior in white Western culture. However, Catlin's verbal description also establishes Keokuk's legitimacy as a warrior in Sauk terms by remarking that "his scalps were attached to the bridle-bits." [35] At the same time, Catlin reminds us that the status of warrior among the Sauk is now merely ornamental. He says that it is

Keokuk's "vanity" in his "fine appearance on horseback" (rather than any fame that Keokuk has gained as a warrior) that convinced him to paint this second portrait. Catlin's remark that "the horse that he rode was the best animal on the frontier; a fine blooded horse, for which he gave the price of 300 dollars, a thing that he was quite able to, who had the distribution of 50,000 dollars annuities, annually, amongst his people" reminds us that the enabling condition of Keokuk's particular pose on this magnificent horse is U.S. government patronage and administrative control.[36]

Black Hawk describes a similar pose, connoting the heroic warrior but without the subtext of white control, at a key moment of the war: "I was mounted on a fine horse, and was pleased to see my warriors so brave. I addressed them in a loud voice, telling them to stand their ground, and never yield it to the enemy" (*L*, 134). But, as always, his band is woefully outnumbered. Black Hawk admits that he is simply directing a strategic retreat, defending women and children from potential massacre with a loss of six men. As he often does, he here hopes that an understanding of the warrior code will vindicate his actions: "I would not have fought there, but to gain time for my women and children to cross to an island. A warrior will duly appreciate the embarrassments I labored under—and whatever may be the sentiments of the *white people*, in relation to this battle, my nation, though fallen, will award to me the reputation of a great brave, in conducting it" (*L*, 135). This is one of the clearest instances of the "self-vindication" speech genre, encapsulating what Brumble argues is the intention of the entire narrative. In this passage Black Hawk is more concerned with his status among the Sauks than among the whites, but the reference to a generic "warrior" does not exclude whites—not, at least, the whites who matter to him, the soldiers such as General Atkinson who would be in the best position to understand him.

Applying the warrior code as a single standard that he believes ought to be universal, Black Hawk is highly critical of instances in which Indians or whites do not behave in a manner he considers honorable.[37] Throughout the text we see Black Hawk appealing to the idea that the values of the warrior ought to transcend cultural differences. Being told of West Point, "the place where the Americans dance their national dance," Black Hawk infers a commonality with the self-performance of warriors in the Sauk "national dance"; West Point, in his interpretation, is "where the old warriors recount to their young men, what they have done, to stimulate them to go and do likewise. This surprised me, as I did not think the whites understood our way of making braves" (*L*, 92). Black Hawk's conflation of West Point with the "nation" may be every U.S. Army officer's fantasy, but it is a drastic misunderstanding of the narrow way in which a white soldier's identity is established in a "nation" that is basically non-communal. Yet it is in this context that we must interpret Black Hawk's argument that white "war chiefs"—rather than the usual notoriously corrupt and avaricious merchants—ought to serve as Indian agents (*L*, 151). Such an idea may strike us as naive, but it demonstrates a non-Western conception of politics that is at the core of Black Hawk's understanding of himself and his place in Sauk society. The Sauks never waged war with the intention of violently imposing their own social, economic, and political structures on another people—in contrast to the whites, who in the nineteenth century engaged in warfare primarily as a means of imperial conquest (and arguably still do).

Contemporary whites formed a better opinion of Keokuk, the politician who conformed to U.S. policies and avoided war, than of Black Hawk, the warrior who followed the Sauk way and felt honor bound to fight. Catlin also implies that many Sauks thought quite highly of Keokuk in the years following the war. At this time, of course, the ability to collect government money—at which Keokuk excelled—was of paramount importance, while traditional Sauk conceptions of warfare were impossible to implement in any serious way. Catlin describes an incident in the late 1830s that illustrates these issues. He reports that Keokuk and several other Sauk and Fox men had an opportunity to view the portrait of Keokuk on horseback when they attended one of Catlin's lectures on "Customs of the Indians" during a visit to New York City: "During the Lecture, I placed a series of portraits on my easel before the audience . . . and at last I placed this portrait of Kee-o-kuk before them, when they all sprung up and hailed it with a piercing yell. After the noise had subsided, Kee-o-kuk arose, and addressed the audience in these words:— 'My friends, I hope you will pardon my men for making so much noise, as they were very much excited by seeing me on my favorite war-horse, which they all recognized in a moment.'"[38] Here we see a staging of communal validation apparently similar to that reported by Black Hawk, in which members of the tribe formally acknowledge the status of a warrior. The situation differs, however: the event to which the men respond is not a living ceremony, but a static image. The effect may be similar, but it is Catlin's performance, rather than Keokuk's, to which the men respond: they see in the image of the mounted warrior a potential for the defense of the tribe that, in not having been tested as Black Hawk's had been, retains its ideological power.

This episode confirms the white intervention into the gendering of the Sauk male enacted by the war. Black Hawk, potentially emasculated by his defeat, must employ traditional speech genres—now necessarily mediated by nontraditional ones—in order to reaffirm his identity. Keokuk, in contrast, has gained his elevated position by virtue of his role as subaltern for the U.S. government. The Sauk men who saw Catlin's painting in New York were not Black Hawk's partisans, of course, but followers of Keokuk. Even so, it is not clear that they cheered for the specific image of Keokuk as warrior; as Keokuk himself reports it, they cheered not simply for him but for his horse (which was, ironically, paid for by the government that oppressed them). They may, more generally, have been cheering for any white acknowledgment of the Sauk warrior tradition which could no longer occupy an integral place in their society.

Arnold Krupat points out that Black Hawk's defeat (and the Jacksonian master narrative of Native American defeat more generally) was the "enabling condition" of the production of the *Life of Black Hawk*.[39] But it is highly unlikely that Black Hawk himself came to think in Jacksonian-progressivist terms. There is nothing in Black Hawk's opening address to General Atkinson that can be interpreted as an admission of the justness of Indian Removal, while there is a great deal in the narrative, such as Black Hawk's views on land tenancy and treaties, which is openly critical of U.S. policies (and we will never know if he said more). The narrative does end with Black Hawk's proclamation of friendship for his former enemies: "from my heart I assure them, that the white man will always be welcome in our village or camps, as a brother. The tomahawk is buried forever! We will forget what has past—and may the watchword between the Americans and Sacs and Foxes, ever be—'*Friendship!*'" (L, 153–54). We must recall that it is the editor Patterson, and not Black Hawk, who places these words at the end of the narrative, thus implying that they bear a teleological significance. Having been defeated in war with no practical hope of revenge, having spent some time in an Army prison camp, and now like the rest of his tribe dependent on government annuities for his livelihood, Black Hawk has something to gain—or at least nothing to lose—by professing "friendship" somewhere in the course of his narrative. In any case, Black Hawk hopes that the "friendship" will be structured in terms of the mutual respect of one warrior for another. That is, even in his overt concession of defeat (burying the tomahawk—

which leaves open the possibility that it can be dug up again) he never fully surrenders his warrior identity. While a prisoner in the East after his defeat, he witnesses a militia exercise in Baltimore, his account of which is placed near the conclusion of the text: "The chiefs and men were well dressed, and exhibited quite a warlike appearance. I think our system of military parade far better than that of the whites—but, as I am now done going to war, I will not describe it, or say any thing more about war, or the preparations necessary for it" (*L*, 147). The *occupatio* here reiterates the warrior theme of the entire text and reminds us that the terms of the "friendship" as Black Hawk conceives it depend on the mutual respect of warriors.

Ironically, Black Hawk's identity is preserved not despite but because of textual mediation. Traditional conditions for the preservation of that identity no longer exist in Sauk culture, having been vitiated by the defeat and containment of the tribe, which eliminated the warrior's cultural position. In response to this drastic re-ordering of Sauk society, Black Hawk enjoins his white readers to validate his identity. The methods of cross-cultural textual production—the transcription, translation, and editing of Black Hawk's narrating voice—embroil us in questions about the text's "authenticity"; yet a preoccupation with "authenticity" may mislead us. The necessary interventions between voice and text, explicitly indicated for us by the phonetic transcription and accompanying English translation of the opening address to General Atkinson, identify Black Hawk as a tribal warrior who is not assimilated to the Jacksonian master narrative but who nevertheless hopes for some translatability of the warrior code in order to promote an understanding and dissemination of the terms of his identity.

Notes

I would like to thank Timothy Dow Adams and Dennis Allen for their helpful comments on this essay.

1   Paula Gunn Allen, *The Sacred Hoop: Recovering the Feminine in American Indian Traditions* (Boston: Beacon, 1986), 3.

2   This is not to say that there was an absolute binary division between "masculine" and "feminine" as single paradigms for identity; not every man or woman played every culturally available role. For example, among the Ojibwa, warriors were usually not simultaneously civil leaders; see Basil

Johnston, *Ojibway Heritage* (New York: Columbia Univ. Press, 1976), 67–69. The role of the *berdache*, still evidently an integral part of Sauk and Fox culture when George Catlin visited them in 1835, indicates some fluidity in the relation of sex to gender. Catlin's account reveals the whites' desire to eliminate an indeterminacy that they found unsettling: the *berdache* is "a man dressed in woman's clothes, as he is known to be all his life, and for extraordinary privileges which he is known to possess, he is driven to the most servile and degrading duties. . . . [He] is looked upon as *medicine* and sacred, and a feast is given to him annually. . . . This is one of the most unaccountable and disgusting customs that I have ever met with in the Indian country . . . and for further account of it I am constrained to refer the reader to the country where it is practised, and where I should wish that it might be extinguished before it be more fully recorded" (George Catlin, *North American Indians*, 2 vols. [1841; rpt., Edinburgh: John Grant, 1926], 2:243–44). Allen argues that homosexual practices and identities generally were socially valorized in a great number of tribes prior to white contact but later became increasingly subject to white repression, which tribal peoples themselves internalized (197–200).

3   *Life of Ma-ka-tai-me-she-kia-kiak, or Black Hawk . . . Dictated by Himself* (Cincinnati, 1833), in *Black Hawk: An Autobiography*, ed. Donald Jackson (Urbana: Univ. of Illinois Press, 1964), 33–154. All quotations from this work will be documented parenthetically in the text using the abbreviation *L*.

4   A remark on names is in order here. It seems to be conventional to use the English translation "Black Hawk," but to use phonetic spellings of other Sauk names rather than translations, especially in the case of Keokuk ("Watchful Fox"). I continue this practice to avoid confusion. As will become apparent, there are variant spellings of "Keokuk"; I have chosen the simplest.

5   For a more detailed history, see William T. Hagan, *The Sac and Fox Indians* (Norman: Univ. of Oklahoma Press, 1958).

6   Jackson, 157, 158, 159–60. Jackson provides the entire text of the treaty.

7   Jackson, 26.

8   Herman J. Viola, *The Indian Legacy of Charles Bird King* (Washington: Smithsonian Institution, 1976), 65.

9   Arnold Krupat, *For Those Who Come After: A Study of Native American Autobiography* (Berkeley: Univ. of California Press, 1985), 31. This idea is central to all treatments of the genre. See H. David Brumble III, *American Indian Autobiography* (Berkeley: Univ. of California Press, 1988); Hertha D. Wong, "Pre-literate Native American Autobiography: Forms of Personal Narrative," *MELUS* 14 (1987): 17–32.

10 Arnold Krupat, *The Voice in the Margin: Native American Literature and the Canon* (Berkeley: Univ. of California Press, 1989), 135–43. See also Hertha D. Wong, "Pictographs as Autobiography: Plains Indian Sketchbooks of the Late Nineteenth and Early Twentieth Centuries," *American Literary History* 1 (1987): 296.

11 Krupat, *Voice*, 149, 150.

12 Krupat, *For Those*, 116.

13 Krupat, *For Those*, 48.

14 An elegiac mode—evident, for example, in *The Last of the Mohicans*—also seems prevalent. Since the inevitability of death is an important elegiac topos, the application of this topos to the supposed death of an entire culture, allegorized in a single Indian character, would also be consistent with the Jacksonian master narrative.

15 M. M. Bakhtin, "The Problem of Speech Genres," in *Speech Genres and Other Late Essays*, ed. Caryl Emerson and Michael Holquist (Austin: Univ. of Texas Press, 1986), 60–61.

16 Bakhtin, 62. Although Bakhtin (who was surprisingly uninterested in traditional oral cultures) discusses only written complex or secondary speech genres, it is clear that oral genres such as oratory, legend, historical narrative, and the like are built of combinations of primary genres in much the same way as their written counterparts. The concept of "*speech* genre" need not be taken to imply the logocentric privileging of speech as somehow prior to writing, given Derrida's argument that oral speech acts are already culturally encoded—already "written"—and thus their position with respect to the individual subject is as mediated as acts of writing are; see Jacques Derrida, "Signature Event Context," in *Margins of Philosophy* (Chicago: Univ. of Chicago Press, 1982), 307–30. Bakhtin's and Derrida's positions are similar in this respect, since Bakhtin stresses the conventional nature of speech genres. However, since I am not performing a merely linguistic analysis, it is finally only complex speech genres, especially various forms of narrative, that will interest me here.

17 See Brumble, 21–47.

18 I am using the term "ethnography" loosely here to refer to material that we would now recognize as bearing ethnographic significance, regardless of the original process of collecting and presenting the information. Krupat points out that Patterson would have considered himself a historian rather than an ethnographer and speculates that "the cultural material . . . probably was Black Hawk's voluntary contribution" (*Voice*, 153).

19 Black Hawk was never a civil chief, as distinct from a war chief, nor was Keokuk a civil chief until the U.S. government made him one. Keokuk had been a client of Indian Agent William Clark since 1820. Clark's generous patronage contributed to the growth of Keokuk's influence (and the consequent waning of Black Hawk's) among many of the Sauk, whose traditional economic base was by this time seriously eroded; see Hagan, 89.

20 On the question of authenticity, see Jackson, 24–30. Some contemporaries thought it a hoax; others believed it was genuine. Hagan, Jackson, Brumble, and Krupat do not doubt that the story originated with Black Hawk, although only Krupat ponders the theoretical implications of terms such as "authenticity" and "origin."

21 See Thomas Couser, "Black Elk Speaks with Forked Tongue," in *Studies in Autobiography*, ed. James Olney (New York: Oxford Univ. Press, 1982), 73–88. Couser argues that in editing out evidence of Black Elk's assimilation—e.g., his conversion to Catholicism and role on the reservation as catechist—Neihardt was "trying to make [the story] more Indian" but as a consequence "made it less autobiographical" (88).

22 Brumble, 39.

23 While the specification of what is "permitted" would go without saying among the adults of the Sauk community who witnessed Black Hawk's first participation in the scalp dance, it is possible that this apparently ethnographic sentence has its origin in precontact tribal speech genres as well. Such an explanation might be offered to a member of another tribe who was unfamiliar with Sauk ways (another sort of ethnographic function) or to young members of the tribe who were being formally or informally instructed about appropriate behavior.

24 Wong points out the importance of communally oriented "dramatic" forms of "self-expression" among plains tribes as well (29).

25 Johnston describes the first hunt ceremony among the Ojibwa, a neighboring people of the same Algonquin language and culture group as the Sauk, although he does not specify a self-presentational aspect of the ceremony that would parallel the Sauk national dance (142). Unlike the first hunt ceremony, which is enacted only once, the Sauk scalp dance and national dance offer the opportunity to renew and reaffirm identity.

26 There is no way to confirm this story. Hagan's only source for his account (57) appears to be Black Hawk's narrative.

27 Hagan, whose only source for tribal origin is the *Life of Black Hawk*, does not record any instance of Keokuk's fighting against the whites. It seems likely that he fought against other tribes—an important issue in view of his position in Sauk politics.

28 Catlin, 169.

29 Catlin, 238.

30 Ibid.

31 According to Catlin, Keokuk "brought in all his costly wardrobe, that I might select for his portrait such as suited me best; but at once named (of his own accord) the one that was purely Indian. . . . In it I painted him at full length" (170). It is likely that Keokuk frequently presented this self-image to white painters. A portrait by Charles Bird King painted in Washington in 1829 shows a similar pose and props, except that the shield is missing and Keokuk wears only a loincloth; this painting is reproduced in Andrew J. Cosentino, *The Paintings of Charles Bird King* (Washington: Smithsonian Institution, 1977), 171. A portrait by J. O. Lewis painted at the Prairie du Chien Indian Agency in 1825 shows Keokuk holding a similar feathered staff in his right hand (in this case the staff is tipped with a spear point) but no tomahawk (reproduced in Hagan, 50).

32 Jackson, 8.

33 Jackson identifies Black Hawk's namesake as a "sparrow hawk" (2).

34 Catlin, 239, emphasis added.

35 Catlin, 240.

36 Catlin, 240–41.

37 For example, both the whites and the Sioux come in for criticism by this standard when Black Hawk reports surrendering only to find that "a large body of Sioux had pursued, and killed, a number of our women and children who had got safely across the Mississippi. The whites ought not to have permitted such conduct—none but *cowards* would ever have been guilty of such cruelty—which has always been practiced on our nation by the Sioux" (*L*, 140).

38 Catlin, 241.

39 Krupat, *For Those*, 48.

Maurice Wallace   Constructing the Black Masculine: Frederick Douglass, Booker T. Washington, and the Sublimits of African American Autobiography

I suspect I must have been born somewhere and at some time.—Booker T. Washington, *Up from Slavery*

Although Hortense Spillers's seminal essay "Mama's Baby, Papa's Maybe: An American Grammar Book" aims most directly at advancing an epistemology of black feminism, this particular project of hers would seem to be useful for, if not essential to, the development of a black masculinist critical theory. "The African-American male," she remarks, "has been touched by the mother, handled by her in ways that he cannot escape—and in ways that the white American male is allowed to temporize by a fatherly reprieve. . . . Legal enslavement removed the African-American male not so much from sight as from *mimetic* view as a partner in the prevailing social fiction of the Father's name, the Father's law."[1] Implicitly, Spillers's discourse deconstructs the univocality of black phallocentric literary production to the same degree that it explicitly pursues a unique line of black feminist inquiry. Undoubtedly, if there is to be an enduring theory of black male identity construction in the West, it will be significantly indebted to a careful synthesis of post-Freudian psychoanalysis and the epistemological work of black feminism, as Spillers's language clearly suggests.[2]

Even if black feminist discourse like that of Spillers proves perfectly congenial to black masculine identity ("Tell us what it is to be a woman so we may know what it is to be a man," Toni Morrison recently said), there are distinct risks one runs by adding psychoanalytic theory to the project. Some African-Americanist scholars hold the systematic application of

Freudian psychoanalysis to African-American cultural production in low esteem, dismissing the field of psychoanalysis as "bourgeois and conservative."[3] To impose Freud on the "sable mind," some argue, is to extend European hegemony grievously far. This resistance to the psychoanalytic critique is the inevitable consequence of American conservatism's scandalous (mis)appropriations of psychoanalysis to construct a demeaning narrative of African American historiography.

Like psychocriticism's detractors, I too am cautious about bringing psychoanalysis to bear on black subjectivity.[4] Clinical terms such as "disorder," "neurosis," and "complex" might well represent cultural "contingencies," to use Barbara Herrnstein Smith's apt lexeme, rather than transcendent or universal pathologies which, "warding off [hegemonic notions of] barbarism and the constant apparition of an imminent collapse of standards," the Freudians have used at odd moments to serve their own egoistic fantasies and to "justify the exercise of their own normative authority."[5] Such terms as these, therefore, can be dangerously marginalizing, effecting in their worst ethnocentric formulations cultural xenophobia whenever they are assigned outside the context of contingencies that established them. They ought always to be regarded with healthy suspicion. But to abandon the principles of psychoanalysis categorically is to throw the baby out with the bathwater. Post-Freudian psychoanalysis, eclectically and responsibly deployed, affords black literary criticism a usable polygraph for discerning those persistent, visceral impulses lurking beneath the black subject's ego. In other words, Frantz Fanon's psychoanalytic diagnosis of "the unbearable insularity" of black identity can only be confirmed or rejected in African American letters according to the principles of psychoanalysis which generated it.[6] Moreover, critics and theorists of African American literary production do well to recall, as Arnold Rampersad reminds us,[7] that not a few of the major figures in twentieth-century African American cultural studies—including W. E. B. Du Bois, Richard Wright, and Ralph Ellison—were influenced by the ubiquity of Freudian thought early in the century.[8] It would seem worthwhile, therefore, to begin with the psychoanalytic imperative of black literary theory and criticism by bringing it into dialogic relation with that "literary genre which presumably offers one of the most revealing and 'real' portraits of the self: autobiography."[9]

Despite the repeated claim that autobiography is an inherently dishonest literary genre because of the autobiographer's intense efforts to present for public view a polished portrait of him- or herself, this is precisely the reason black male autobiography, and autobiography generally, lends itself so generously to psychocriticism. Since, as Michael Cooke argues, black autobiography "is the *coordination* of the self as content and the self as *shaped*,"[10] the authorial construction of the autobiographical subject, fully formed and self-conscious, is achieved only at the expense of the exhausting effort required by the author to repress the fragmentary, duelling impulses of a divided consciousness normally kept in the reserve of the unconscious. Psychoanalytically considered, autobiography depends on more than "everything available in memory, perception, understanding, imagination, [and] desire"[11] suitable for public discourse. It rests also upon the autobiographer's success in repressing "everything that . . . in some way or other [is] painful . . . alarming or disagreeable or shameful by the standards of the subject's personality."[12] These splits of consciousness unearthed by the psychoanalytic critique of black male autobiography invest the subject with a representational complexity— in this essay, an essential polymorphous libidinality—which makes him marvelously human. To put it another way, from this theoretical vantage point, the black self becomes supremely *text-ured*.

My efforts in this essay are guided by a desire to explore in Frederick Douglass's *Narrative of the Life of Frederick Douglass, An American Slave* and Booker T. Washington's *Up from Slavery* that vast area of repression which the self-conscious autobiographical subject is always skirting, to trespass into "those serpentine caves," as Virginia Woolf said, "where one goes with a candle peering up and down, not knowing where one is stepping."[13] More to the point, this essay is concerned with the early, developmental stage of African American male identity formation characterized in black male autobiography by *preliminal* racial and sexual ambivalence which I see as corresponding biologically to the pre- and post-pubescent stage of boyhood. This developmental stage distinguishes itself from the subsequent stage of *liminal* or self-conscious racial and sexual identification by a nervous panic, a pediatric "neurosis" (Fanon's word) that propels the black manchild headlong into a crucible of identity negotiations.[14]

■ ■ ■

The line of black masculinist autobiography in which the panic I am describing can be detected begins most notably with Douglass's 1845 *Narrative* and its literary offspring in the tradition, Washington's 1901 *Up from Slavery*. Though both begin with formulaic birth narratives, ironically, neither autobiographer can state precisely the date or the circumstances of his birth. The problem of racial being and nothingness is perhaps nowhere more poignantly expressed than by Washington in the epigraph to this essay: "I suspect I must have been born somewhere and at some time" (9). Bastard sons of enslaved black mothers and obscure white fathers/masters, Douglass and Washington fashion *non*-oedipal dramas of slavery in which nuclear relations matter less in the slavocracy than the bourgeois imperatives of ownership, dominance, commodity, and (re)production. Over and above the problems posed by the strained primal configurations immanent in these autobiographical accounts, the bastard/mulatto status of Douglass and Washington figures as a trope of the national illegitimacy felt by both nineteenth- and twentieth-century African American authors.[15] It is a trope that for the black writer, I suspect, has its origins in the biblical themes of bondage, lineage, and inheritance.[16] Metaphorically, the enslaved mulatto is the illegitimate, banished son of the American Abraham and the patriarch's black handmaiden, the American Hagar, casting about for existential determinacy from within the elemental indeterminacy ("born somewhere and at some time") of the slave condition.

Gates's chapter, "Binary Oppositions in Chapter One of *Narrative of the Life of Frederick Douglass, An American Slave Written by Himself*" in his *Figures in Black: Words, Signs, and the "Racial" Self*, proposes a veritable catalogue of bipolar identities (nature/culture, beast/human, barbaric/civilized) between which the autobiographical African American manchild is freely and aimlessly conveyed as through a sublime "oceanic" middle passage of identity formation.[17] Eventually, however, the gentle tide of psychological passage becomes a furious surge and the helpless manchild, surprised by the storm, is tossed ashore onto the strange banks of racial and sexual consciousness. This sudden and violent landing, I affirm, is the moment of identity panic when the distressed pubescent discovers his polymorphism as destitute of cultural relevance or social legitimacy.[18] In short, Gates's catalog of binarisms suggests that the most immediate inheritance of the enslaved manchild is a fragile universe of confounded indeterminable identities which recognizes neither temporal nor geographical specificity; neither racial singularity nor familial cohesion; nor, as I hope to prove forthwith, gender differentiation, which, in the interest of Culture, was among the first endowments of white children in the antebellum era.

In a stringently Freudian analysis of Douglass's autobiography entitled

" 'Called into Existence': Gender, Desire and Voice in Douglass's *Narrative* of 1845," George Cunningham argues from this remarkable premise: "Within the domain of slavery, gender or culturally derived notions of man- and womanhood do not exist [for the enslaved]."[19] Cunningham's hypothesis points plainly to what Eugene Genovese calls "the annihilating implications of chattel slavery."[20] Because the historical American slave belongs primarily to the commercial order of livestock, his or her sex is not the same cultural determinant of power or protection that it is in the society of slaveholders. It is, rather, merely a commercial feature of the slave's being, a convenient accessory for the master. Wholly devoid of cultural import, the slave's gender, insofar as the slaveholder cares, matters only to the extent that it brings value to plantation (re)production. It follows, dialectically, that the slave's struggle for political freedom is also an effort to be freed from the condition of social and cultural nothingness. This struggle is, finally, the crisis of the autobiographical black manchild upon *liminality*—that is, upon his awakening to sexual consciousness. Symptoms of the impending crisis tend to surface early in the naive impulses of pubescent sexuality that occasionally leap forward indiscriminately in *Narrative* and *Up from Slavery* where neither autobiographer seems to have intended.

■ ■ ■

In recounting the "most terrible spectacle" of Aunt Hester's rape by Captain Anthony, Douglass seizes, apparently unaware, upon his own undifferentiated sexual subjectivity at the time of the incident. He describes Captain Anthony's brutalization of Aunt Hester as Anthony pornographically strips his victim "from neck to waist, leaving her neck, shoulders, and back entirely naked. [Captain Anthony] then told her to cross her hands, calling her at the same time a d——d b——h. After crossing her hands, he tied them with a strong rope, and led her to a stool under a large hook in the joist, put in for the purpose. He made her get upon the stool and tied her hands to the hook. *She now stood fair for his infernal purpose*" (52, emphasis mine). With this, and sparing any more horrible details, Douglass turns away from the self-implicating triangularity of the scene, wanting to escape this shameful and painful reality. "Heart rending shrieks from [Hester] and horrid oaths from [Anthony]" serve, by their contrast, to make pronounced the quiet of Douglass's flight from language. That is to say, it is precisely Douglass's silent terror, his inability to "commit to paper," as he says not much later, a fuller disclosure of his feelings while witnessing the "exhibition" that signals an early instance of the kind of repression described above. That Douglass is withholding a more private, unrepresentable reaction to this scene, one that diverges substantially from the decidedly masculine self-portrait sustained throughout the text, is incontrovertible: "I was so terrified and horror-stricken at the sight, that I *hid myself in a closet*, and dared not venture out. . . . *I expected it would be my turn next*" (52, emphasis mine).[21] Certainly gay and lesbian studies has made the closet a classic symbol of sexual coverture in a way that is harmonious with the suggestion in the preceding passage of an erotics of slavery which, forsaking gender difference, puts the enslaved biological male and the enslaved biological female equally within reach of the master's wanton hand. In this context, the potential is great for a suppressed/repressed psychosexual voice belying Douglass's fear that he might suffer the same sexualized violence inflicted upon Hester. Douglass's introduction in this scene to the barbarous "hell of slavery" (51) is simultaneously his introduction to human sexuality ("I expected it would be my turn next").

I wish to resist the argument advanced by David Van Leer that the youthful Douglass did not understand "the gender specificity of [Aunt Hester's] beating." Van Leer wrongly denies that there are grounds for Douglass's sexual panic:

> [Douglass] rightly labels the scene as one of the horrors of slavery. What he does not understand is that this particular horror is not and never will be his. Not only does the boy's 'turn' never come—at least not quite in this way—but the sexual undercurrents in the [Aunt Hester–Captain Anthony] passage clearly indicate the narrator's implicit understanding of the different power dynamics in male and female beatings. His failure to comment more directly on the difference marks his tacit admission that as a male he is shut out from a knowledge of this uniquely female experience.[22]

Van Leer, I contend, gives the slavocracy too much credit. While it is almost certain that homosexual assault was never as prevalent as the heterosexual abuses perpetrated by white male slaveholders, incidents of homoerotic assaults in out-of-the-way places along coffle routes going south and on some plantations are not entirely unheard of.

The problem with Van Leer's conclusion about the gender specificity of plantation rape is twofold. First, it depends on an uncritical, modern conception of rape as a heterosexual violation of women's bodies and fails to comprehend that the slave's rape was motivated not simply by the economic advantage whereby property under force reproduced itself without costs but just as often by antebellum white racialist fantasies about black eros. It is not at all unlikely, therefore, and rather to be expected, that, in light of popular myths about the extraordinary size and potency of the black phallus and slaveholders' absolute control over black bodies, the sexual urges of male slaveholders would seek out now and then black male slaves for their gratification. There is little doubt that same-sex desire was as real in the nineteenth century as the heterosexual impulse.[23]

The second failing of Van Leer's argument is its tacit assumption that the dearth of evidence on this count demonstrates the non-occurrence of violent homoerotic behavior by white men visited on the bodies of their powerless black male slaves. Admittedly, precious little of the literature of the slave era confesses to homosexuality in general, much less homosexual abuse across the color line. That homoerotic violence could have indeed posed a genuine threat to young Douglass, however, and did in fact occur is corroborated in at least one female-authored slave narrative.

In an obscure and often overlooked passage from Harriet Jacobs's *Incidents in the Life of a Slave Girl* (1861), Jacobs recalls a fugitive friend named Luke whom she meets by chance along the streets of free New York shortly after her own escape. Before his successful flight to freedom, Luke belonged to a young man Jacobs describes as having become "a prey to the vices growing out of the 'patriarchal institution'" (504). The unnamed slaveholder, having been "deprived of the use of his limbs by excess dissipation," shows all of the worst symptoms of sexual deviance according to certain pre-Freudian medical theories current in America from the 1830s until Freud. Dissipation and palsy occurring in otherwise healthy young men were considered by nineteenth-century medical experts to be the consequences of such sexual excesses as onanism and homosexuality, the usual prognosis for which was progressive dementia. Accordingly, Luke's young master, Jacobs says, "took into his head the strangest freaks of despotism" (504). Her indictment of the maniacal slaveholder reflects the popular medical opinion of her day that homoerotic desire was produced by a "strange order of ideas" in the mind.[24] And euphemisms like "vice," "excess," and "dissipation" all signify in nineteenth-century sexual discourse a pathological deviation from the cultural norms of the human sexual economy.[25] In the end, Luke's master takes to bed, "a mere degraded wreck of manhood," brought down in mind and body by sexual excess.

Neither decorum nor literary convention would have permitted Jacobs (or Douglass) to depict blatant homoeroticism. But the image of poor Luke having to "kneel beside the couch . . . [and] *not allowed to wear anything but his shirt*" (504, emphasis mine) is amply suggestive. Nevertheless, Jacobs leaves only the simplest conclusions for the prurient reader to draw: "Some of these freaks were of a nature too filthy to be repeated. When I fled from the house of bondage, I left poor Luke *chained to the bedside of this cruel and disgusting wretch*" (505, emphasis mine). It is evident that Jacobs's reticence ("too filthy to be repeated") intentionally suppresses details too impolite to name publicly. Her evasion recalls Douglass's vituperation of Captain Anthony in *My Bondage and My Freedom* (1855). In this, Douglass's second autobiography, he denounces Captain Anthony for committing "outrages, deep, dark and nameless."[26] For both Jacobs and Douglass, neither of whom had great difficulty representing miscegenation in their texts, few "perversions" other than onanism and homosexuality remained unrepresentable.

Reflecting on Luke's sexual degradation, Jacobs says somewhat more plainly what Douglass approximates by close association and identification with Aunt Hester: both male and female enslaved black bodies are vulnerable to the sexual impositions of the master who intends to fulfill his "infernal purpose." One need no longer question *if* sexual subjectivity exists in *Narrative*; one only wonders *how much* primal sexuality is buried in Douglass's rememory of the Aunt Hester–Captain Anthony drama: "It was the first of a long series of such outrages, of which I was doomed to be a witness and a *participant*" (51, emphasis mine), Douglass confesses.

Watching the rape from a distance and yet equally vulnerable, the young Douglass turns Freud's oedipal model on its head by rejecting the role of the entranced child taken in by the coital activity of his oblivious parents. Instead the panic-stricken slaveboy retreats, impotent to injure the primal father as the oedipal script directs. Identifying with the ravished body of a female, Douglass's fear of also being raped by Captain Anthony instantiates a fluid pubescent libidinality located intermediately between the libidinal masculine and the libidinal feminine.[27] It is within that abstract zone where the space surrounding the one libidinal pole intersects the space of the other that all boys eventually live. His is a field of both struggle and play, the self-satisfied intersection of dual instincts, a "location in self (*reparge en soi*)," following Cixous, "which doesn't annul [sexual] differences but stirs them up, pursues them, increases their number."[28] But because he has learned from Aunt Hester's beating the primacy of the phallus ("I shall never forget it whilst I remember any thing" [51]), Douglass must hasten, in spite of himself, to extinguish his polymorphic nature, finally and completely, for the sake of gaining "phallic monosexuality"[29] if bodily freedom, political or sexual, is to be his. The psychosocial exigency of the subject's having been prematurely thrust into sexual consciousness is to follow the way of culture by differentiation.

The mature Douglass's preoccupation with the masculine ideal in *Narrative* is coterminous with his fear of the feminine, of being regarded, in other words, as also woman. Perhaps he knows the risk of being classed with the sentimental subject of nineteenth-century white women's writing by virtue of his powerlessness to resist sexual assault. To concede a feminine division of consciousness in the public medium of literature is for Douglass to jeopardize his claim in *Narrative* to the virile perfectibility of black men. It is this phobic posture toward a dynamic sexual identity which, I argue, ultimately provokes Douglass's sudden retaliation against Covey later on, an act punishable by death.

In accord with Fanon's axiomatic faith that "[we] know how much sexuality there is in all cruelties, torture, [and] beatings,"[30] I maintain that Douglass's violent retaliation against Mr. Covey is fundamentally a psychosexual response to the whipping/rape of Hester indelibly inscribed in Douglass's memory as well as to the immediate danger in Mr. Covey's whip.[31] I mean to say that the threat to young Douglass posed by Mr. Covey is the same threat realized by Captain Anthony on Aunt Hester. Viewed this way, the climactic standoff between overseer and slave which transformed Douglass into a man shows that Douglass's achievement of manhood represents much more than a mere physical triumph for the slave. It represents just as profoundly a counterattack of psychosexual virility signifying physiological phallic consciousness. Douglass's age at the moment of his conversion from slave to self-made man—sixteen—places him at the threshold of full biological maturity and marks a critical stage of human sexual development. Douglass's transformation is also, then, his psychic passage from boyhood (and sexual impotency) into phallic manhood (and sexual virility). Thus, what slavery is to freedom, boyhood is to manhood.[32]

Although many critics have paid special attention to Douglass's heroic

efforts to achieve mastery and power over Covey in this episode (arguably the narrative's most important), few, if any, seem to have recognized
the "interchangeability between power [or force] and sexuality"[33] in the
nineteenth century: "The *gratification* afforded by the triumph was full
compensation for whatever else might follow, even death itself" (113,
emphasis mine). Douglass's violent reaction to the threatened beating
checks the otherwise unrestrained power of master over slave, including
the "deepest, most mysterious, most fearful [power] of all: sexuality."[34]

In a curious footnote, Van Leer remarks: "During the beating that
opens the tenth chapter [of *Narrative*] there is some indication of a submerged homosexual threat . . . in Covey's repeated orders—and Douglass's repeated refusals—to strip."[35] Unmistakably, the narrative picture
of Covey, enraged by the slave's recalcitrance, ripping the clothes from
the slaveboy's body "with the fierceness of a tiger" (102), serves as a
graphic reminder of Captain Anthony's brutalization of Aunt Hester. If,
as feminist critic Jenny Franchot has argued, "Douglass's narrative construction of [Hester's punishment] privileges it as its originating moment,
and thus lodges a memorial urge inside his rhetoric of indictment aimed at
exposing slavery's 'foul embrace,' "[36] then the eroticized version of Douglass's punishment which I am positing may be a more tactical maneuver
on Douglass's part than a repressed one.

I wish to pursue this line of interpretation in further considering the
contest between Douglass and Covey. To do so, it is necessary to cite a
substantial portion of the episode.

> As soon as I found what he was up to, I gave a sudden spring, and
> as I did so, he holding to my legs, I was brought sprawling to the
> stable floor. Mr. Covey seemed to think he had me, and could do what
> he pleased; but at this moment—from whence came the spirit I don't
> know—I resolved to fight; and, suiting my action to the resolution, I
> seized Covey hard by the throat; and as I did so, I rose. He held on
> to me and I to him. . . . He trembled like a leaf. This gave me assur-
> ance, and I held him uneasy, causing the blood to run where I touched
> him with the ends of my fingers. Mr. Covey soon called out for help.
> Hughes came, and while Covey held me, attempted to tie my right
> hand. (112)

The narrative rehearsal of Covey thinking to "do what he pleased" and
Hughes helping to "tie [Douglass's] right hand" recalls and recasts Captain Anthony's binding of Aunt Hester strong and fast in order to exe-

cute his lascivious deeds. Thus framed, Douglass's previous references to Covey as "the snake," simultaneously evoking sex and Satan, seems scarcely coincidental. Undaunted by Covey's determined struggle for corporal dominance, the adolescent strikes back with a virile exhibition of his own, cowing Covey into a physical, even "female," submission reminiscent of the romance. In the second autobiography, Douglass kicks hard at Hughes's groin when Hughes tries to help Covey. The avenging blow to Hughes's groin underscores the sexual threat a whipping (re)presents in Douglass's psychic universe. The rhetorical turn signalled by "I rose" in the passage above, marks, too, a reversal of dialectical positionality for Douglass from defensive sexual object to virile phallic agent. It is by physical confrontation that Douglass is "made a man." Violence is matched with violence and one phallus, as it were, *over-comes* another. The normal plantation relationship of black to white, master to slave, is, in this special moment, inverted. If Douglass, in this scene, is a slave made a man, then Covey is a man made a slave.

The Narrative of the Life of Frederick Douglass is not merely the record of "how a slave was made a man" in the universal sense of "human being"; it also documents how a male slave is *not* made a woman. Douglass's private, preliminary reaction to the violence of the American slave experience subverts the black masculinist pretense of public self-representation. For Covey's insistence in chapter 10 that the slaveboy "strip" off his clothes also signifies the threat to the ex-slave of having his hard-fought identity as an actor in "the prevailing social fiction"—if only marginally—stripped away. Even if Douglass's self-identity is, in the last analysis, not much more than an imitation of the fiction of white masculinity, the broken promise of gaining cultural capital by way of gender leaves the denied victim dispossessed, just as if he were sexually violated, of the privileges of his own body, his own sex. We must believe, therefore, that Douglass's success at resisting Covey was no small victory. By bodily dominating Covey, escaping the tempestuous libidinality engendered by bodily subjugation in a sexually repressed society, Douglass squashes his polymorphism and, desiring to move past the stage of the vulnerable, self-conflicted pubescent, wrests his manhood from Covey as if for his life.

■ ■ ■

Frederick Douglass's vivid, sometimes painfully enduring anamnesis of the power of slavery in *Narrative* and *My Bondage and My Freedom* differs widely in spirit from the "dim recollections of childhood," as Du Bois once described them, in Booker T. Washington's *Up from Slavery*. Washington's happy version of his passage into liminal adulthood lacks the sense of bitterness evident in Douglass's reflections. This stance on the part of Washington seems to me a function of his social and economic philosophy of accommodationism rather than a manifestation of his anxiety about Douglass's aesthetic influence (as we in literary studies might desire).[37] Not until his third autobiographical effort, *My Larger Education*, does Washington acknowledge the impact of Douglass's life and career upon his early development:

> Even before I had learned to read books or newspapers, I remember hearing my mother and other colored people in our part of the country speak about Frederick Douglass' wonderful life. I heard so much about Douglass when I was a boy that one of the reasons I wanted to go to school and learn to read was that I might read for myself what he had written and said. In fact, one of the first books that I remember reading was his own story of his life, which Mr. Douglass published under the title of "My Life and Times." This book made a deep impression upon me and I read it many times. (103)

If David Dudley is right that intergenerational conflict is the key problem in the black male autobiographical tradition, the success of this curiously oedipal thesis, mapping out as it does hard and fast genealogical lines within the broad tradition of African American literature, depends on our being able to name the Father, intertextually. It is virtually inconsequential that Douglass's and Washington's texts show plainly that "geneological trees do not flourish among slaves . . . [and the role of] father is literally abolished in slave law and practice."[38] In his own oblique manner, Washington, who like Douglass could not name his biological sire with surety, *names* Douglass his literary Father. Just as Douglass "heard whispers" that his father was a white man, Washington remembers "*hearing* [his] mother and other colored people . . . speak about Frederick Douglass' wonderful life," much as most any slaveboy could only *hear* about his paternal lineage.

That Washington, then, removed from Douglass by one generation, misnames the book (the Father's master narrative) he claims to have read and reread lends Dudley support on psychoanalytic grounds. Along these lines, Washington's error bespeaks a breach in the seams of consciousness bursting with the fullness of unconscious repression. Put differently, Washington's confusion about what he claims to remember clearly and what he has mistakenly remembered implies a collision between the conscious and the unconscious in the autobiographical subject. Dudley explains that *My Life and Times* is actually a conflation of the titles of Douglass's second and third autobiographies, *My Bondage and My Freedom* and *Life and Times of Frederick Douglass*. This conflation, however, does not necessarily refute those critics who view *Narrative* as the direct antecedent to *Up from Slavery*. Other than Washington or his scribbling ghostwriter, Max Bennet Thrasher, who can know which of Douglass's two texts was foremost in Washington's mind? The greater concern for this paper raised by the inconsistency between the consciously remembered ("I remember hearing," "I remember reading") and the forgotten (or repressed) is the question of authorial trustworthiness and the superficiality of autobiography, a theoretical issue which interests me much more than determining which Douglass text Washington did or did not remember.

Because Washington's subject is doubly shaped (once by the function of genre, once by signification on Douglass) the critical task of deconstructing Washington's autobiographical pretenses is a peeling away of densely layered ego. Just as Douglass's protective closet conceals his libidinal relation to the feminine (because he identifies with Hester there), Washington's childhood home in the slave quarters ("a poorly built cabin" not larger than "about fourteen by sixteen feet square") joins him to the libidinal feminine insofar as his mother's memory issues from there. Because she was the plantation cook at Hale's Ford and their one-room shanty both kitchen and bedroom, the narrow cabin with its paradoxical "open" fireplace locates for Washington the domestic center of the text— the architectonic source of origins which appears as equivalent both to Douglass's closet and to Harriet Jacobs's famous garret-space. By contrast, the open space of the fields, the woods—the outdoors—is, in *Up from Slavery*, a distinctively masculine domain. "During the period I spent in slavery," Washington writes,

> I was not large enough to be of much service, still I was occupied most of the time cleaning the yards, carrying water to men in the fields, or going to the mill. . . . The road [from the mill] was a lonely one and often led through dense forests. I was always frightened. The woods

were said to be full of soldiers who had deserted the army and I had been told that the first thing a deserter did to a Negro boy when he found him alone was to cut off his ears. (13–14)

The outdoors, full of "men in the fields" and "soldiers who had deserted from the army," names the site where, by surviving its ravages, physical strength, rugged individualism, and mobility validate manliness—a formidable challenge to a small boy, as Washington's example confirms. In his early trials at these masculine rites, Washington's fear of the outdoors, of (men roaming) the woods, overwhelmed him to the point that, often, he quit the effort midway "to wait, sometimes for hours, till a chance passer-by came along" (14) to help him, crying, back to his mother's cabin.

Despite culturally imposed assignments of gender to the indoors and outdoors, to restricted and unrestricted spaces, private and public spheres, Washington belongs exclusively to neither side of this grand division but slips in and out of both discursive universes comfortably, and— for the moment—unproblematically. It is only later, when the slaveboy reaches liminality, finally confident that he can manage outdoors, that he is called peremptorily away from his station to domestic work in the "big house." Here gender fixity, suddenly vital to the pubescent, eludes him. In that moment of self-discovery, the subject, aware for the first time of the rigid, extragendered white world he is enslaved to, suddenly recognizes his own undifferentiated identity; that is, his sexual formlessness, the "undecideability" (Spillers's term) of his gender. His reaction is a mad dash to satisfy the culturally prescribed role of the masculine prepared for him but denied him in the "big house."

As a structural and discursive universe unto itself, the "big house" contrasts sharply, in its enormity, with the narrowness of the slave cabin. Yet, the comparative expansiveness of the "big house" can in no way match the vastness of the fields, the woods, or the outdoors generally. However sizeable or privileged a space it is, the "big house" has in common with the cabin the structural and discursive restrictedness that characterized the writerly postures of nineteenth-century women authors appropriating for themselves, as Jacobs's remarkable phrase goes, "loopholes of retreat" from *their* restricted spaces (i.e., the attic, the pigeon-house, the garret, the parlor). The "big house," then, is also women's space. Accordingly, few men in Washington's account occupy the "big house"; the Civil War, the historical moment of Washington's autobiography, has taken them away. On the rare occasion when (white) men are remembered by Washington to have occupied the "big house," they did so only as disabled soldiers sidelined from a war they promptly returned to after being nursed back to health. Their powerlessness to govern, control, or otherwise dominate the plantation in the manner of a master approximates a bourgeois brand of white male emasculation leaving, by default, the white mistress to oversee the plantation. And yet at Hale's Ford, Washington's mistresses shun the master's sovereignty over the plantation that the privilege of whiteness offers them in his absence, in order to maintain the privileges of ladyhood (leisure, indulgence, protection) that their white femaleness has provided. By this means of double default (and only this means), the male slaves become pseudo-patriarchs, viceroys of the plantation, with one hope of proving their masculine potential by following the Father in protecting his wife and daughter: "The slave who was selected to sleep in the 'big house' during the absence of the males was considered to have a place of honor. Anyone attempting to harm 'young Mistress' or 'old Mistress' during the night would have had to cross the dead body of the slave to do so" (20). What appears by this time in Washington's discourse about effete soldiers and dauntless slaves as a clever inversion of white male strength/potency and black male powerlessness/impotency, turns out instead to be merely a clever illusion betrayed by the honored slave's eunuchism, the slave being coolly devoted to the protection of the chaste respectabilities of white women while "the males" (the black slave presumably excluded from this gender category) tested and proved their virile selves in the outdoors at war. Strategically, the black male slave, coming indoors, is rendered by Washington a nonthreat in the most dreaded sexual arrangement imaginable in the collective consciousness of the white slaveholding South. In the "big house," male virility—black or white—is nonexistent. Under the conditions of domestication, the maturing, pubescent Washington is confronted squarely by the alarming contradiction of an extragendered free white society and the virtual impossibility of stable gender identity within the slave community. His consequent experience of self-alienation is worthy, if inversely, of the primordial dehiscence which precedes Lacan's mirror stage of identity formation.[39]

■ ■ ■

In the canon of black male autobiography in which boyhood figures prominently, there is ample evidence of sexual anxiety. The instant of identity

panic in which Washington rushes to escape the psychic vertigo characterizing his preliminal stage is not, however, as easy to pinpoint as it is in
Douglass's *Narrative*. If there is indeed a single instance of sexual panic
to be found in the boyhood chapters of *Up from Slavery*, it lies buried
somewhere between the lines of chapter 1 ("A Slave among Slaves"),
in the realm of the unspeakable. Because the innocent boy lacks the
adult's virtually unlimited access to language, the child's experience of
what might be called hegemonically a sexual hysteria is usually unspeakable, as Douglass's case bears out. Like the excitable mute frustrated in
his attempt to articulate his delight, the naif is capable only of sporadic,
scarcely intelligible, "ejaculations." Even the mature autobiographer, for
whom language poses no impediment, is reticent with respect to the
sexual feelings of the naif—if Douglass's withdrawal into the closet says
anything at all about his authorial fears. Since self-conscious black male
narrative seems to have observed the traditional constraints of cultural
and literary propriety in order to correct the image of the black male
as hypersexual, black male writers (Washington among them), despite
their mastery of language, for the greater part eschew anything like a full
disclosure of their essential psychosexual constitution.[40]

Regardless of what are either narrative evasions by the mature narrator or punctuated instances of juvenile ineffability, the struggle to manage
silences and keep sexuality at bay sometimes fails. There is, for instance,
a quietly transgressive *je ne sais quoi* disrupting the romantic southern
idyll in chapter 1 of *Up from Slavery*, which describes "two young [white]
mistresses and some lady visitors eating ginger cakes in the yard" (17).
The language used by Washington to relate this edenic scene is so suggestive that the readerly tendency Eve Kosofsky Sedgwick describes
as "knowing" that the unspeakable is necessarily a codification of erotic
meaning (the heuristic "We Know What That Means") becomes entirely
irresistible:[41] "[Those] cakes seemed to me to be absolutely the most
tempting and desirable things that I had ever seen and I then and there resolved that if I ever got free, the height of my ambition would be reached
if I could get to secure and eat ginger-cakes in the way I saw those ladies
doing" (17). I am postulating (and pretending to "know" in the Sedg-
wickian sense) that contrary to what is said, young Washington's hunger/
hankering is not for ginger-cakes at all but rather, like that for the forbidden fruit of Eden, the more profound, nameless desire for white women
which, as the discussion above suggests, the enslaved manchild cannot
articulate, or alternatively, the adult autobiographer dares not confess

to. It is revealing that this coded episode lies seductively juxtaposed to Washington's deep sense of his own corporeality, of his own pubescent bodiliness.

Washington's "most trying [childhood] ordeal," he claims, was the acute suffering caused him by a flax shirt worn on his "soft and tender" body "like a dozen or more chestnut burrs or a hundred small pin-points, in contact with his flesh" (18). Even as the slaveboy's "soft and tender" skin recalls the sentimental subject Douglass feared, it further affords the male subject a sensuality typically unacknowledged in conventional models of masculinity. "I had to wear the . . . shirt or none; and had it been left to me to choose, I should have chosen to wear no covering" (19), Washington complains.

One can only speculate about the genuineness of Washington's sexual naïveté when he expresses an unabashed preference for "no covering" to the compulsory flax shirt worn by virtually all enslaved boys who wore anything on the plantation. It is plausible that Washington's innocence here is really authorial subterfuge, the mature autobiographer skillfully throwing his voice in a performance of rhetorical ventriloquism to say what any nineteenth-century adult black male writer knows he cannot acceptably write. This other, provisional image of the boyish servant innocently exposed and indulging the delicate and fanciful Victorian sensibilities of three white maidens is as much a part of the autobiographer's erotic economy, I believe, as his titillating confession of "ginger-cake" reverie.

Contemporary cultural historians and cultural theorists have not failed to explore the intense libidinal anxieties engendered by the proximity of black- and white-skinned people in controlled spaces (the nation, the region, the "big house," the yard). American historian Winthrop Jordan's *White over Black: American Attitudes toward the Negro, 1550–1812* may constitute the most thoughtful documentation of the kind of interracial libidinality produced by the white master/mistress–black slave relation I am interrogating. What Jordan's historiography reveals about the domestic services of "Negro boys" to American Victorians is both instructive, given Washington's experience in that role, and vital to my project of specifying potential moments of gender obfuscation in autobiographies by African American men.

Jordan's discussion of the popular eighteenth-century practice of Negro boys serving at the dinner table in the "big house" and "wearing only a shirt not always long enough to conceal their private parts," is, in connection with Washington's complaints about the flax shirt, telling to say the least.[42] That the complete nudity Washington wishes for might be displaced in his reality only by a semi-nudity Jordan cites as "commonplace" is not a remote possibility: "Until I had grown to be *quite a youth* this single garment was all that I wore" (19, emphasis mine). For the domesticated slaveboy, whose education outdoors has been frustrated by his duties indoors, the unremarked exposure of his private parts before a white (women's) audience mocks—indeed negates—the psychophysiology of phallic development. Jordan quotes one traveler observing this domestication of "Negro boys": "I am surprized this [nudity] does not hurt the feelings of the fair Sex to see these young boys of about Fourteen and fifteen years old to Attend them. these whole nakedness Expos'd and i can Assure you It would Surprize a person to see these d——d black boys how well they are hung [*sic*]."[43] The irony in this situation is that the slaveboy cannot enter the "big house" until he is of "sufficient size" ("When I had grown to a sufficient size, I was required to go to the 'big house'" [17]), but when, finally, he *is* of "sufficient size" anatomically (double entendre intended), his bodiliness and his developing sex must be treated as invisible by the very persons who would substantiate and authenticate them if they did not fear them.

■ ■ ■

In black male autobiography from Douglass onward, the problem of paternity and mixed birth complicates for the African American manchild a process which for his white counterpart is usually unproblematic. Since the traditional rites and laws of patrilineal inheritance assume that a masculine code has been or will be transferred from father to son, the panic-stricken white son is met halfway by the willing white father in the son's haste to embrace a culturally meaningful identity. For young male slaves, however, the "mimetic" invisibility of adult African American men as legitimate players in the "prevailing social fiction" of patriarchy and their status as the objects, never the agents, in the patrilineal transfer, cause the black manchild's fateful angst:

> I used to take a great deal of satisfaction in the lives of men who had risen by their own efforts from poverty to success. It is a great thing for a boy to be able to read books of that kind. It not only inspires him with the desire to do something and make something of his life, but

it teaches him that success depends upon his ability to do something useful, to perform some kind of service that the world wants.

The trouble in my case, as in that of other coloured boys of any age, was that the stories we read in school were all concerned with the success and achievements of white boys and men. Occasionally I spoke to some of my schoolmates in regard to the characters of whom I read, but they invariably reminded me that the stories I had been reading had to do with members of another race. Sometimes I tried to argue the matter with them, saying that what others had done some of us might also be able to do, and that lack of a past in our race was no reason why it should not have a future.

They replied that our case was entirely different.[44]

I am arguing that Washington's notion of success is not only materially based but also phallocentric. His ideas about success depend fundamentally on one's demonstrating virility sufficient "to do something" that presumably the impotent (the boy) cannot do. The successful person must, as all phallists worry, "perform." Oddly, though, Washington's schoolmates seem to have known better than he that the "lack of a [patrilineal] past" presented more than a small stumbling block in a black boy's pathway to a mature masculine future. Washington's idealism about the matter in *My Larger Education*, however, is not a feature of the earlier *Up from Slavery*. In fact, Washington's optimistic indifference to having a patrilineal past here is at odds with his initial concern for history that the want of paternal validation represents in *Up from Slavery*. The contrast in sentiment between *My Larger Education* and *Up from Slavery* is striking. In the latter, Washington expresses sore regret about his lack of a past:

I used to picture myself in the position of a boy or a man with an honoured and distinguished ancestry which I could trace back through a period of hundreds of years, and who had not only inherited a name, but a fortune and a proud family homestead (43). . . . I used to envy the white boy who had no obstacle placed in the way of his becoming a Congressman, Governor, Bishop or President by reason of the accident of his birth or race. I used to picture the way I would act under such circumstances. (45)

Yet, it only *seems* that the crisis of illegitimacy felt in the 1901 *Up from Slavery* had been resolved by 1911 when the narrative of *My Larger Edu-*

cation was completed. Although his envy of "the white boy" in *Up from Slavery* pretends to reflect a fatuous childishness ("I used to picture," "I used to envy") which the more stolid Washington would later mock good-humoredly, his jealousies are not as fully absent from *My Larger Education* as Washington wants to imply, despite the tone of confidence expressing it ("I used to take . . . satisfaction in . . ."). In the later book, Washington's earlier anxieties do not disappear but are ascribed instead to "other coloured boys," not to his own sensibilities. That Washington abandons the earlier disquieted self of *Up from Slavery* for an air-brushed portrait of childhood that refuses to acknowledge his earlier acute envy suggests a classic case of denial and displacement—Washington straining to kill the memory of longing and envy because it is the memory of dashed hopes. The "lack of a [Fatherly] past" insures that Washington, whatever his individual material gains, will always lack the capacity to evince traditional manliness and, therefore, self-legitimation.

Because of the slaveholder's practice of trading male slaves more regularly than females, Spillers's idea of the "mimetic" absence of enslaved black males as fathers finds its realization in *Up from Slavery*. Although a slave from another plantation became Washington's stepfather, "he seldom came to the plantation [near Hale's Ford, visiting] . . . perhaps once a year" (31) until Emancipation. (Even following Emancipation, he did not have so much as a surname to bequeath Washington, as the laws of patrilineage require.[45]) And, if it is indeed true that the outdoors constituted the fin-de-siècle proving ground for masculinity, as the American Naturalists urged in their fiction, then the paucity of black male field literature in which boyhood is figured as a fundamental stage of character development means that in the literature of the male "house Negro" like Washington or Douglass, the only acceptable model for masculinity is white and fiercely phallocentric.

Washington's veneration for Hampton president General Samuel C. Armstrong, "the noblest, rarest human being . . . a perfect [white] man" (59–60), is also a signal that the search for legitimacy has been satisfied by a surrogate. It is General Armstrong, not Washington's stepfather (nor even Douglass, whom Washington revered in his youth) who teaches Washington the principles of the masculine. In the context of General Armstrong's mentorship to him, Washington states: "The older I grow, the more I am convinced that there is no education . . . that is equal to that which can be gotten from *contact* with great men and women. Instead of studying books so constantly, how I wish that our [black] schools and colleges might learn to study men and things" (60, emphasis mine). But *contact* in the slavocracy is a relative experience. For the cultural elite, it may signify the patrilinear interface between men and boys as between benefactors and beneficiaries of the great masculinist code. In this vein, the function of contact is to facilitate inheritance. For the slave-boy living outside this culture, contact undergoes semantic dislocation, no longer signifying the prerequisite intimacy of father and son in the patrilineal transfer, as it does for free white boys of wealth and privilege. Rather, it represents a nameless intimacy of another order. Contact, I mean to suggest, "is also the basic schematic type of initiating sexual action (touching, caressing—sexuality),"[46]—which is, as I have argued, Douglass's predicament. That Washington's use of the term "contact" falls into the former denotative category (contact as patrilinear transfer) is hardly a paradox. In the first place, it is consistent with both his early envy of white boys and his post-emancipation adoption of General Armstrong as father figure. In the second place, it seems almost elementary that contact with General Armstrong failed to excite the sexual anxieties of the pubescent/adolescent—as in the case of Douglass facing Covey—because the general, contrary to Washington's portrayal of him as "a perfect man" and despite his wielding absolute power at Hampton, suffered from severe bodily paralysis. Washington's "perfect" white man is a disabled white man—less a model for black masculinity than a reassurance that Washington, in his own socially/politically enforced posture of eunuchism, is not really impotent. Incapable of the sexual aggression played out in *Narrative*, Armstrong, nonetheless, "touched" Washington with the heroism and dogged individualism which have come to signify the masculine ideal in American culture.

Paralysis notwithstanding, General Armstrong's enormous agency over countless bodies of color under his superintendency at Hampton is one of the central ironies of Washington's schoolday reminiscences. "General Armstrong made a personal inspection of the young men in ranks" (65), Washington reports admiringly. Erotic inferences aside, the greater value of Washington's relation to Armstrong, for my purposes, is the correlation between the general's corporeal powerlessness and the impotency of the panic-stricken slaveboy undifferentiated in his self-conscious. Conversely, Armstrong's exceptional fortitude accords with the inevitable triumph of phallic primacy over the last gasps of sexual formlessness in black male self-identity.

However much Washington and black male autobiographers might try to resist white masculinist codes of being and behavior ("In later years, I confess that I do not envy the white boy as I once did" [45]), a good deal of the effort to prove black masculinity in black autobiography has tended not only to be imitative ("what others had done some of us might also be able to do") but sometimes overcompensatory, precisely because the terms "black" and "man" have been historically opposed and therefore mutually combusting units in the lexicography of European anthropology and ethnography. The corollary to this idea suggests that black machismo is the angry effort to overcome the self-combustion of a subaltern identity.

To its credit, black male autobiography has accomplished the notable feat of overcoming black (mis)representation in generations of hegemonic discourse. But I fear that the concomitant strategy of black phallist writers to assert agency through the romanticization of masculinity is a trap. The ends of black male autobiography have been noble and necessary. But occasionally the means have been self-defeating. As black feminist theory and psychoanalytical critiques like Peter Walker's portrait of Douglass have shown us,[47] the glorification of one split of consciousness and the suppression/repression of another do not en-gender the discursive potency black masculinist production desires for itself. To the contrary, such activity yields little more than the epistemological frigidity of the black male body in bondage.

Notes

1   Hortense J. Spillers, "Mama's Baby, Papa's Maybe: An American Grammar Book," *Diacritics* 17 (1987): 80.

2   Kaja Silverman's recent *Male Subjectivity at the Margins* (New York: Routledge, 1992) skillfully demonstrates some of the psychoanalytic interrogations which might be brought to bear on conventional paradigms of masculinity. Notwithstanding a few important, yet regretfully brief exceptions by gay black writers (Marlon Riggs, Essex Hemphill), a work analogous to Silverman's which attempts to answer for the contradictions, deviations, and sudden, extraparadigmatic ruptures presented by black masculinity to the dominant model has yet to emerge.

3   Earle E. Thorpe, "*The Slave Community*: Studies of Slavery Need Freud and Marx," in *Revisiting Blassingame's "The Slave Community": The Scholars Respond*, ed. Al-Tony Gilmore (Westport: Greenwood Press, 1978), 56.

4   For a brilliant discussion and demonstration of the limits of psychocriticism

vis-à-vis African American literature, see Hortense Spillers, "The Permanent Obliquity of an In(ph)allibly Straight," in *Changing Our Own Words: Essays on Criticism, Theory, and Writing by Black Women*, ed. Cheryl Wall (New Brunswick: Rutgers Univ. Press, 1989), 127–49.

5   Barbara Herrnstein Smith, "Contingencies of Value," *Critical Inquiry* 10 (1983): 18.

6   Frantz Fanon, *Black Skins, White Masks*, trans. Charles Lam Markmann (New York: Grove Press, 1967), 50.

7   Arnold Rampersad, "Biography and Afro-American Culture," in *Afro-American Literary Studies in the 1990s*, ed. Houston Baker and Patricia Redmond (Chicago: Univ. of Chicago Press, 1989). Also discussed in Rampersad's "Biography, Autobiography, and Afro-American Culture," *Yale Review* 73 (1983) and "Psychology and Afro-American Biography," *Yale Review* 78 (1988).

8   In the preface to a 1954 edition of his 1896 work, *The Suppression of the African Slave Trade to the United States of America*, Du Bois remarked about the critical reception of his book in 1896, demonstrating how deeply concerned he was about the relevance of psychoanalysis to his own intellectual pursuits, "As a piece of documented historical research, [the original work] was well done and has in the last half century received very little criticism as to accuracy and completeness. One area of criticism which I have not seen . . . but which disturbs me is my ignorance in the waning 19th c. of the significance of Freud. . . . [The] work of Freud . . . [was] not generally known when I was writing the book, and consequently I did not realize the psychological reasons behind the trends of human action which the African trade involved."

9   Bruce Mazlish, "Autobiography and Psychoanalysis: Between Truth and Self-Deception," *Encounter* 35 (1970): 30.

10 Michael Cooke, "Modern Black Autobiography in the Tradition," in *Romanticism: Vistas, Instances, and Continuities*, ed. David Thornburn and Geoffrey Hartman (Ithaca: Cornell Univ. Press, 1973), 273. Also quoted in Henry Louis Gates's *Figures in Black: Words, Signs, and the "Racial" Self* (New York: Oxford Univ. Press, 1987), 95. Emphasis added.

11 Ibid.

12 Mazlish, "Autobiography and Psychoanalysis," 30.

13 Virginia Woolf, *A Room of One's Own* (San Diego: Harcourt Brace Jovanovich, 1957), 88.

14 "Preliminal" and "liminal" belong to anthropologist Arnold van Gennep. His study of "life-crisis ceremonies," *Les rites de passage* (1909), taking up among its other discursive streams "the critical problems of becoming male and female" in various societies, accords fruitfully with my own efforts in this essay. Although van Gennep foregrounds the communal or tribal ceremonies (*rites*) that accompany "life-crises" (i.e., death, birth, marriage, adoption, remarriage), rather than the progressions of gender development

I am examining, his communal *rites*, subdivided into preliminal rites (rites of separation), liminal rites (rites of transition), and postliminal rites (rites of incorporation)—the totality of which symbolize the passage of a life cycle—conform very nearly to the stages of gender development I am arguing for as experienced nonceremonially in the individual subjects of *Narrative* and *Up from Slavery*. I deal in this essay only with the first two stages or *rites*.

15   For example, William Wells Brown's *Clotel* (1853) and Martin Delaney's *Blake: or, the Huts of America* (1859) in the nineteenth century, and James Weldon Johnson's *Autobiography of an Ex-Colored Man* (1912) in the twentieth. In each novel, America represents the "strange land" of Old Testament Egypt where Jehovah's chosen nation, Israel, has been forced into bondage. Political freedom for black Americans, these three writings seem to say on one level or another, may not be realizable except abroad.

16   It is no accident that the Bible, the archetypal Western text in some respects, was also the first (if not only) reader for many black Americans before and following Emancipation. Many scholars (Gates, for example) also credit the European picaresque for its typologization of the trope of mixed lineage inherited by black writers. See Gates, "Binary Oppositions in Chapter One of *Narrative of the Life of Frederick Douglass, An American Slave Written By Himself*" in *Figures in Black: Words, Signs, and the "Racial" Self*. For a history of black literacy and the Bible, refer to Janet Duitsman Cornelius, *When I Can Read My Title Clear: Literacy, Slavery, and Religion* (Univ. of South Carolina Press, 1992); Renita Weems, "Reading *Her Way* through the Struggle: African American Women and the Bible"; and David Wimbush, "The Bible and African-Americans: An Outline of an Interpretive History." Weems and Wimbush are collected in *Stony the Road We Trod: African-American Biblical Interpretation*, ed. Cain Hope Felder (Minneapolis: Fortress, 1991).

17   I am freely borrowing the notion of "oceanic" identity from Spillers.

18   By "identity (racial and/or sexual) panic," I mean to evoke simultaneously Fanon's discourse of the "neurotic" native and Eve Sedgwick's "homosexual panic." Sedgwick's "homosexual panic" is called, alternately, the subject's "blackmailability." It is much too tempting not to consider the special brand of *racialized* sexual panic which is foregrounded here as the black subject's *blackmaleability*.

19   George Cunningham, "'Called into Existence': Gender, Desire, and Voice in Douglass' *Narrative of 1845*," *Differences: A Journal of Feminist Cultural Studies* 1 (1989): 108.

20   Eugene Genovese, *The World the Slaveholders Made* (Middletown: Wesleyan Univ. Press, 1988), xvi.

21   In *My Bondage and My Freedom*, the 1855 version of Douglass's autobiography, the slaveboy's hiding place is described as a "little, rough closet, which opened into the kitchen; and through the cracks of its unplaned boards, [Douglass] could distinctly see and hear what was going on, without being

seen by old master" (87). The modern equivalent to this architecture would likely be a simple broom closet.

22   David Van Leer, "Reading Slavery: The Anxiety of Ethnicity in Douglass' *Narrative*," in *Frederick Douglass: New Literary and Historical Essays*, ed. Eric Sundquist (New York: Cambridge Univ. Press, 1990), 131.

23   Homosocial, if not homosexual, desire figures noticeably in Douglass's own novella, *The Heroic Slave*. Although ostensibly representing a political alliance, the transracial male bonding between Madison Washington, the "black but comely" slave protagonist whose "appearance betokened Herculean strength," and Mr. Listwell, the white abolitionist sympathizer who "long desired to sound the mysterious depths of the thoughts and feelings of a slave," deserves more critical attention as an early construction of homosocial/homoerotic desire.

24   Robert A. Nye, "Sex Difference and Male Homosexuality," *Bulletin of the History of Medicine* 63 (1989): 41.

25   Ibid.

26   Frederick Douglass, *My Bondage and My Freedom* (New York: Dover Publications, 1969), 79.

27   "Libidinal masculine" and "libidinal feminine" are Hélène Cixous's terms in "Laugh of the Medusa," collected in *Critical Theory Since 1965*, ed. Hazard Adams and Leroy Searle (Tallahassee: Florida State Univ. Press, 1989).

28   Ibid., 314.

29   Ibid.

30   Fanon, *Black Skins*, 159.

31   Earle Thorpe, *The Old South: A Psychohistory* (Durham: Seeman, 1972), 127.

32   The most casual reader of Douglass's autobiography cannot fail to recognize Douglass's sense that achieving manhood is inextricable from achieving freedom. That boyhood parallels slavery is somewhat less obvious but not an esoteric connection. "I am but a slave," says Douglass at the midpoint of *Narrative*, "and all boys are bound to someone" (113).

33   Ronald G. Walters, "The Erotic South: Civilization and Sexuality in American Abolitionism," *American Quarterly* 2 (1973): 186.

34   Ibid., 180.

35   Van Leer, "Reading Slavery," n. 33.

36   Jenny Franchot, "The Punishment of Ester: Frederick Douglass and the Constitution of the Feminine," in *Frederick Douglass: New Literary and Historical Essays*, 150.

37   Knowing that it is by now a quite common view among African Americanist literary critics that Washington's *Up from Slavery* constitutes a formal revision of Douglass's *Narrative*, one writer has called Washington's text "a corrective rewrite" of Douglass's, viz., David Dudley, *My Father's Shadow: Intergenerational Conflict in African American Men's Autobiography* (Philadelphia: Univ. of Pennsylvania Press, 1991), 41.

38   Washington, *My Bondage and My Freedom*, 34–35.

39   Lacan's mirror stage is precipitated by the fragmentation of the body and its image—"a certain dehiscence . . . , a primordial Discord betrayed by the signs of uneasiness and motor uncoordination of the neo-natal months." It is as if both Douglass and Washington experience a second birth into subjectivity, once the dehiscence of race and gender becomes liminal. See Jacques Lacan, "The Mirror Stage as Formative of the Function of the I as Revealed in Psychoanalytic Experience," in *Ecrits*, trans. Alan Sheridan (New York: Norton, 1977).

40   For a substantive discussion on this point, see Gloria Naylor, "Love and Sex in the Afro-American Novel," *Yale Review* 78 (1988): 19.

41   Eve Kosofsky Sedgwick, *Epistemology of the Closet* (Berkeley: Univ. of California Press, 1990), 204.

42   Winthrop Jordan, *White over Black: American Attitudes toward the Negro, 1550–1812* (Baltimore: Penguin, 1969), 161.

43   Ibid., 159.

44   Booker T. Washington, *My Larger Education* (New York: Doubleday, Page and Co., 1911), 103. Emphasis mine.

45   The autobiographer, we recall, adopted the surname Washington years past his slavery days on the plantation. His adoption of the surname belonging to "America's first great leader" may have inclined Booker T. Washington toward the self-made masculine construction of *Up from Slavery*. This point I owe to Michael Moon.

46   Fanon, *Black Skins*, 56.

47   Peter Walker, *Moral Choices: Memory, Desire, and Imagination in Nineteenth Century Abolition* (Baton Rouge: Louisiana State Univ. Press, 1978).

Sander L. Gilman	Mark Twain and the Diseases of the Jews

> In estimating the position of Israel in the human values we
> must remember that the quest for righteousness is oriental,
> the quest for knowledge occidental. With the great prophets
> of the East—Moses, Isaiah, Mahomet—the word was "Thus
> saith the Lord"; with the great seers of the West, from Thales
> and Aristotle to Archimedes and Lucretius, it was "What says
> Nature?" They illustrate two opposite views of man and his
> destiny—in the one he is an "angelus sepultus" in a muddy
> vesture of decay; in the other, he is the "young light-hearted
> master" of the world, in it to know it, and by knowing to
> conquer.—William Osler, "Israel and Medicine" (1914)

Twain's Travels

There has been increased interest recently in Mark Twain's essay "Concerning the Jews," which appeared in the September 1898 issue of *Harper's Magazine*.[1] Indeed, there has even been speculation that Sigmund Freud's last public statement on the nature of anti-Semitism was a paraphrase of Twain's work.[2] Twain's essay responded to a reader's inquiry following Twain's ironic account in the August *Harper's* of the anti-Semitic rhetoric of the "debate" in the Austrian parliament concerning the bill mandating Czech as the official language of Bohemia. Twain's reasoned answer and the addendum concerning the role of the Jew as soldier make up one of the most complex documents written against anti-Semitism in late nineteenth-century America. Yet it bears the hallmark of a set of presuppositions concerning the special nature of the Jew which were noted even by Twain's contemporaries, such as M. S. Levy, who wrote in 1899 that "from the many statements Mark Twain makes regarding the various traits of the Jews, it is plain that they are not only tinged with malice and prejudice, but are incorrect and false."[3] It is clear that Twain's intent in writing his 1898 essay was to counter the growing anti-Semitism following the increase of Eastern European Jewish immigration to the United States. The shifting, sometimes contradictory positions concerning the Jews which Twain espoused were recognized by his contemporaries. What is important and has not been noted by the critics, both contemporary and contemporaneous, is that Twain shifts the underlying rhetoric of his argument about the Jews from one which sees the nature of the Jews as immutable to one which understands it as socially constructed. This essay will examine three interrelated topics: 1) Twain's image of the Jew in his earliest writing and its affinity to the model of the "diseased Jew," 2) the various racial models of the diseased Jew which existed in European and American thought through the nineteenth century, and 3) the similarities and differences between Twain's later views and his earlier ones. To understand the differences and continuities in Twain's image of the Jew, the reader must comprehend that there was an earlier, as yet unread image of the Jew in Twain's work published decades before the more widely cited essay "Concerning the Jews."

Thus my discussion will begin not with this late, "liberal" essay (though I shall be making reference to it later in this analysis) but with Twain's first extended representation of the Jews in his most popular book, *The Innocents Abroad, or The New Pilgrims' Progress*.[4] I shall be examining Twain's pattern of representing illness in this work and the relationship of this model to contemporary discussions of the illnesses of the Jews. This travel account, published in 1869, represents a specific debate concerning the Jew's body which occurred during Reconstruction. It reveals a set of presuppositions about the meaning of racial identity and the inheritability of such an identity which were widely debated at the time. *The Innocents Abroad* recounts Twain's journey to Europe and the Holy Land during 1867. One of its central themes is the meaning of disease in the traveler's life and experience. Disease is a concept closely linked to religion and the exotic. This theme quickly becomes one of the structuring principles furnishing a philosophy of history that underlies Twain's account of his journey as moving backward in time as he and his friends travel ever eastward in space. And, as we shall see, no people is more ancient or remote or diseased than the Jews. For Twain, the tracing of disease becomes a commentary on the role of the Jews in Western civilization. Such underlying views would seem to run counter to the stated intentions of Twain's essay of 1898.

The Innocents Abroad begins with the reprinting of the announcement for the tour. This list of particulars notes, as the fourth item following the description of the steamer "Quaker City," the fact that "an experienced physician will be on board" (18). It is, of course, not unusual that such provisions for medical care be made for extended cruises. But the theme of ubiquitous illness and disease is made an intrinsic part of the fabric of the trip. The relationship of the American visitors to the disease and death they experience as inherent in the exotic locales they visit in Europe and the Middle East defines the Americans as the curable, if not the healthy, and a "white" United States as that place where there may be illness but there is also modern "scientific" medicine and the potential for remedy. (Twain, as we shall see, assumes that the Native American is predisposed to illness.) For, even with all of the minor illnesses experienced by the American travelers, there is no parallel in their experiences (at least on this trip) to the ever-mounting roll call of horrors seen on their trip. Medicine is on their side, as is an unencumbered belief in that science. It is the reality of disease and death which haunts Twain's representation of his travels eastward.

Earlier American travelers on the Grand Tour had recounted their own fascination with the specter of disease, but always within the frame of the aesthetic. Among the standard stops on the Grand Tour were the exhibitions of anatomical figures in the museums of Bologna, Florence, Rome, and Vienna.[5] Florence especially—and specifically the "Royal and Imperial Museum of Physics and Natural History" (founded in 1775 and called "La Specola" because of its observatory)—became the mecca for travelers fascinated by the world of decay. Represented in the collection of the Florentine school were a number of the great masters of wax casting, especially the famed Sicilian wax modeler Gaetano Giulo Zummo. He, like many of the sculptors, was responsible both for many of the anatomical exhibitions and for religious art work in this medium found throughout Italy and France. The traveler experienced these traditions as one, linking the anatomized body and that of the martyred saint through the use of the same aesthetic devices cast in wax.

These collections of anatomical art became a focus for the visits of Americans on the Grand Tour. They were offered a sense of the "sublime," the emotion of overwhelming sensation to be had through nature. This was nature frozen in the aesthetic form of the wax cast rather than in the stinking cadavers of the anatomical theater. Henry Wadsworth Long-fellow, in the 1830s, saw these figures on his Grand Tour of the Continent and sensed both their reality and the unreality which one must ascribe to the medium of the wax sculpture:

> Zumbo [*sic*] . . . must have been a man of the most gloomy and satur-nine imagination, and more akin to the worm than most of us, thus to have reveled night and day in the hideous mysteries of death, corrup-tion, and the charnel house. It is strange how this representation haunts one. It is like a dream of the sepulcher, with its loathsome corpses, with "the blackening, the swelling, the bursting of the trunk,—the worm, the rat, and the tarantula at work." You breathe more freely as you step out into the bright sunshine and the crowded, busy streets next meet your eye, you are ready to ask, Is this indeed a representation of reality?[6]

The dream of the real—or perhaps the nightmare of death, of the body corrupt, of the body putrefied—is "real" only because it tricks the high-est sense, sight; it is "unreal," a false representation, because it lacks the other senses. Longfellow's vision was of the permanence of corruption, of the immutability of mutability, all images so contradictory that they lead to a questioning of the very body itself. But Longfellow saw all of this in the work of art representing death and decay.

The world of exotic religion as experienced by these American trav-elers was also closely associated, through the wax cast, with the erotic and death. As late as 1858, Nathaniel Hawthorne (on his Grand Tour) sensed the close relationship between the religious use of such wax sculp-tures and erotic imagery: "And here, within a glass case, there is the representation of an undraped little boy in wax, very prettily modelled, and holding up a heart that looks like a bit of red sealing-wax. If I had found him anywhere else, I should have taken him for Cupid; but being in an oratory, I presume him to have some religious signification."[7] Twain's fascination, perhaps because of his Western exposure to public images of disease and physical corruption, was not with this type of aestheticized corpse but with the dreary realities to be found in European daily life. For Twain, it is not the image of decay and the body which fascinates but the dead and decaying body itself.

In Paris, one of their first stops in Europe, Twain's travelers in *The Innocents Abroad* first visit Notre Dame, where they are shown Church relics similar to Hawthorne's little wax figure. But here they include the "bloody robe" of the Archbishop of Paris, assassinated on the Parisian barricades in 1848, as well as "the bullet that killed him, and the two vertebrae in which it was lodged." Twain's comment that "these people have a somewhat singular taste in the matter of relics" links (as do the comments of Longfellow and Hawthorne) the representation of the body within the rituals of Christianity (here, especially Catholicism) and the barbarous dismemberment and display of the body. Little surprise that from the Cathedral the travelers next stop is "the Morgue, that horrible receptacle for the dead who die mysteriously and leave the manner of their taking off a dismal secret" (105). There they see the body of a drowned man—"naked, swollen, purple"—which is gawked at by the passersby, "people, I thought, who live upon strong excitements, and who attend the exhibitions of the Morgue regularly, just as other people go to see theatrical spectacles every night. When one of these looked in and passed on, I could not help thinking: 'Now this don't afford you any satisfaction—a party with his head shot *off* is what you need' " (106). Such a body would have been the body of the Archbishop of Paris as exposed in the Cathedral of Notre Dame. Twain has established the relationship between religion, especially exotic religions such as Catholicism, and the dead or dying body.[8]

Twain's sense of the horrors associated with the representation of disease and its relationship to the exotic is heightened as he travels farther East. Thus in entering Constantinople he is reminded of the "dwarfs" and "cripples" he had seen on the streets of Genoa, Milan, and Naples. But his Italian experience was nothing compared to the "very heart and home of cripples and human monsters" which is Constantinople. There Twain sees in the very flesh the deformed and mutilated—a woman with three legs, two of them withered; a man with an eye in his cheek. The normally mutilated, "a mere damaged soldier of crutches would never make a cent. It would pay him to get a piece of his head taken off, and cultivate a wen like a carpet sack" (285). All of these horrors of the flesh are seen by the travelers on their way to the Mosque of St. Sophia. Again the association between the diseased and the religious is made, but here exponentially. For in Paris the association was made between two isolated places in the city, which Twain linked to provide his readers with an association between religion and disease; in Constantinople disease, deformity, and dirt are everywhere, invading—indeed defining—the very presence of the Mosque itself (286).

The closer Twain and his party get to the Holy Land, the more the metaphors of disease and religion are linked. It is in Damascus—on the way to the Holy Land—that the very sight of the city causes Twain to begin to quote from what is his (and his companions') true guidebook on this journey—the Bible. For the travels of the innocents in Twain's account are a disguised account of a pilgrim's progress, but the progress of a pilgrim already doubting the veracity of his own faith. The sight of Damascus evokes Paul's sojourn there and the origins of Pauline Christianity, "that bold missionary career which he prosecuted til his death" (365). Twain's own ambivalence toward religion in general takes on the coloration of his anxiety about the link between disease, death, and belief. Twain no longer sees this process as taking place in isolation or at a distance from himself. Rather, he slowly comes to understand that his own Christian belief system, the cultural perspective which forms his vision, is itself a product of a religious worldview, and that this worldview is that of the Jews. It is therefore not in the New Testament that Twain finds the appropriate vision by which he can comprehend the Holy Land.

The image Twain uses to close this chapter and to introduce us to the Holy Land is taken not from the New Testament but from the Old. He quotes from 2 Kings 5 the words of Naaman, who praised the waters of Damascus as "better than all the waters of Israel. May I not wash in them and be clean?" For Naaman, "the favorite of the king," was a leper, and his house in Damascus has been turned into a leper hospital whose "inmates expose their horrid deformities and hold up their hands and beg for buckseesh when a stranger enters." Twain's response is one of horror: "One can not appreciate the horror of this disease until he looks upon it in all its ghastliness, in Naaman's ancient dwelling in Damascus. Bones all twisted out of shape, great knots protruding from face and body, joints decaying and dropping away—horrible!" (367). To this point Twain had distanced the horrors of death. They were the fascination of others—of the visitors to Notre Dame or the Rue Morgue, of those unfortunates who exposed their mutilations in Catholic Italy or Muslim Turkey. Here the horrors seen are immediately internalized. It is in Damascus, in the city of Naaman the Leper, that Twain is struck ill.

After visiting the leper's hospital, Twain spent his final day in Damascus suffering from "cholera, or cholera morbus" (368). Given his symptoms, it is clear that his intestinal complaint is what we would call today "turista" or, perhaps, Naaman's Revenge. It was hardly cholera as understood in the late nineteenth century.[9] His response to his symptoms was hysterically to apostrophize his healthy American audience—as if his stomach cramps were the sign of his own corrupt nature. His association of the world he has entered with disease has now infiltrated into his very being, into his innermost sense of self. Twain comes to realize that his association of death, illness, and religion is not merely characteristic of exotic practices (Catholicism) or religions (Islam) or of spaces which are unrelated to his sense of self (Paris, Naples, Constantinople). Rather, he now has to struggle with the image that this association belongs to his world, the world of backwoods Christianity as represented by the book which formed his sense of self, the Bible. But Damascus, the gateway to the world of the Bible, becomes retrospectively—in contrast to the generally diseased nature of the Holy Land—his "one pleasant reminiscence of this Palestine excursion." [10] The loathing Twain comes to feel for the diseased world of the Bible confuses his text. His hysterical discovery that the disease attributed to others was part of his own sense of self creates physical symptoms (revulsion and nausea) and moves the text between the ancient past (which is part of Twain's present world) and the present (which reveals itself to be a continuation of the past). What was external and seen in Constantinople has now become internalized as a symbolic representation of the means by which Twain belongs to this world. Illness is real and it exists in the very fabric of the world around him; it infiltrates into the very essence of his being. But illness is tied closely to religious belief, to "superstition," which the ironic Twain and his appreciative reader must see as remote from themselves. In this frame of mind, Twain sets off for the Holy Land. The very first experience he has—"just stepping over the border and entering into the long-sought Holy Land" (372)—is that of disease.

On 17 September 1867 Twain entered the Holy Land with seven companions. There he finds that the very ground on which the Savior walked, "that Jesus looked on in the flesh" (373), is the land of disease.[11] "Standing on ground that was once actually pressed by the feet of the Savior," Twain sees himself surrounded by "the usual assemblage of squalid humanity," which in its passive suffering evoked in him the image of the Native Americans: "They remind me much of Indians, did these people. . . . They sat in silence, and with tireless patience watched our every motion with that vile, uncomplaining impoliteness which is so truly Indian, and which makes a white man so nervous and uncomfortable and savage that he wants to exterminate the whole tribe. These people about us had other peculiarities, which I have noticed in the noble red man, too: they were infested with vermin, and the dirt caked on them till it amounted to bark"

(374–75). The children are covered with flies, and they suffer from sore eyes which eventually lead to blindness in many of them. And in their passivity and acceptance of illness they are the very antithesis of the white American: "And, would you suppose that an American mother could sit for an hour, with her child in her arms, and let a hundred flies roost upon its eyes all that time undisturbed? I see that every day" (375). Twain's "sight" is a mark of his American health, as opposed to the blindness of the inhabitants of the Holy Land.

Once the waiting multitudes learn that among the travelers is a physician, Dr. J. B. Birch of Hannibal, Missouri, they come in droves: "The lame, the halt, the blind, the leprous—all the distempers that are bred of indolence, dirt, and iniquity—were represented . . ." (375). (Are they not attracted by exactly that same faith that moved the steamship line back in the United States to advertise so prominently the presence of a physician on board the "Quaker City"?) And the doctor ministered to them with his "dread, mysterious power" and "phials . . . of white powder." For these diseased individuals "he was gifted like a god" (376). The physician as "god" is a mirror of one of the central metaphors of Christianity, that of Christ as physician: "and great multitudes came together to hear, and to be healed by him of their infirmities" (Luke 4:15).

And here Twain pulls out the card he has been waiting to play from the moment he and his companions left the United States. For it is the despair of these individuals which makes the wonders of the historical Christ comprehensible, a factor understood in the abstract in Western religion but written on the very skin of the inhabitants of the Holy Land:

> Christ knew how to preach to these simple, superstitious, disease-tortured creatures: He healed the sick. They flock to our poor human doctor this morning when the fame of what he had done to the sick child went abroad through the land. . . . The ancestors of these—people precisely like them in color, dress, manners, customs, simplicity—flocked in vast multitudes after Christ, and when they saw him make the afflicted whole with a word, it was no wonder that they worshipped Him. No wonder His deeds were the talk of the nation. No wonder the multitude that followed Him was so great that at one time—thirty miles from here—they had to let a sick man down through the roof because no approach could be made to the door; no wonder His audiences were so great at Galilee that he had to preach from a ship removed a little distance from the shore; no wonder that even in the desert places about Bethsaida, five thousand invaded His solitude, and He had to

feed them by a miracle or else see them suffer for their confiding faith and devotion; no wonder when there was a great commotion in a city in those days, one neighbor explained it to another in words to this effect; "They say that Jesus of Nazerath is come!" (376)

Here is the secret of Christ's historical mission—he cured the diseased in a world tormented by infirmity. His miracles mirrored the needs of the world in which he found himself. But his audience were persuaded only by the reality of their experience of their own disease. They were materialists who could only understand the transcendental (if transcendental he was) if it were literally internalized and then written on their skins.

But Twain's mid-nineteenth-century Palestinian Arabs (whether Moslem or Christian is unstated) were not biblical Jews. He stresses the fact that he is speaking in the present about the Arabs of the Holy Land, for one of the children treated by his traveling companion the physician is the daughter of the local Sheikh. Nevertheless, Twain sees "this poor, ragged handful of sores and sin" now inhabiting the Holy Land as identical in all respects with the Jews who dwelt there at the time of Jesus (377). Their physiognomy is unchanged, and this is also reflected in the unchanged nature of their diseased bodies. Christ preached to the biblical Jews whose sorry state made them believe in him. Seeking the most efficacious way of persuading them of his mission, he cured them of their afflictions. But the Jews remain essentially uncured, as they remain unconverted to Christianity. The "blindness" which marks the inhabitants of the Holy Land is both an explanation of a perceived reality (the relationship between flies and blindness) as well as the reified antithesis of a health which emanates from the American and is represented by the Twain's Christian insight. This is the central Christian trope about the nature of the Jew, for those who "lacketh" knowledge of our Lord Jesus Christ are "blind, and cannot see afar off, and hath forgotten that he was purged from his old sins" (2 Peter 1:8–9). For "that blindness in part is happened to Israel, until the fulness of the Gentiles be come in" (Romans 11:25). Jews are blind; Christians see.

For Twain, the image of Jesus is linked to his ability to heal. He ironically imagines the young Jesus in these terms: "Recall infant Christ's pranks on his schoolmates—striking boys dead—withering their hands." [12] Jesus as a child does precisely what the adult Jesus undoes—he strikes his playmates with illness and death. One can think of the account of the first Jews Twain ever saw in Hannibal, the Levin boys, and the "shudder" which went through all of the other boys in town as they discussed whether they should crucify the Levin boys.[13] Jews were automatically associated with the act of crucifixion and were seen as literally defiling the Christian world by their presence. But for Twain these Jews "were clothed in the damp and cobwebby mold of antiquity. They carried me back to Egypt, and in imagination I moved among the Pharoahs."[14] The present evoked the past. In 1853 Twain could still speak of Jews "desecrating" two historical houses in Philadelphia.[15] This image of pollution is closely linked to the world of the Jews. Twain can and does draw a clear distinction between the Jews and himself—they are corrupt and he (like all other Protestant Christians) is not. And yet in entering into the Holy Land he must face an inescapable fact, understood in the abstract but here suddenly writ large for even Twain to see: all of those beloved figures of the Old and the New Testament were Jews—Jesus as well as Naaman. But they were Jews like the present-day inhabitants of the Holy Land. They were diseased just as Twain himself was in Damascus. Twain needs to separate his Christian-American identity from the image of the Jew which was part of his cultural inheritance. Everyone (including Mark Twain) has the potential to become ill, but the Jews are illness incarnate.

Thus the central question which Twain presents in his image of the Jews, reaching from the biblical leper Naaman to their contemporary surrogates, is their diseased nature and its relationship to their essence. It mirrors Twain's own questioning of his internalization of the Judeo-Christian presuppositions of the Bible. Disease and religion are indeed linked, but they are linked in the very essence of the Jew. The racial identity of the Jew is unchanged across centuries, even though the religious identity of the people inhabiting the Holy Land may have shifted. Twain reads this not merely as a reflex of the space in which the Jews are located. There is a fin-de-siècle school of thought, best represented by the German anthropologist Friedrich Ratzel, which argues that the nature of a race is a reflex of the geographical space in which it is to be found.[16] The nature of the Jews is tied to the space they "naturally" inhabit. For Twain the movement into the Holy Land is also a movement back in time. The world he finds does not shape the peoples found in it; rather, it reflects their inherent nature. The nature of the Jews is tied not only to their space but also to their historical times. The Arabs of the Holy Land are merely unchanged biblical Jews in disguise. This view of Jewish immutability is a commonplace of late nineteenth-century anthropological and medical science. In Richard Andree's 1881 study of Jewish folklore, the central question is the relationship between ideas of who the Jews are and what their bodies mean. Andree's discussion centers on the permanence of the Jewish racial type, but more importantly on its implications. Concerning the conservative nature of the Jewish body and soul he observes:

> No other race but the Jews can be traced with such certainty backward for thousands of years, and no other race displays such a constancy of form, none resisted to such an extent the effects of time, as the Jews. Even when he adopts the language, dress, habits, and customs of the people among whom he lives, he still remains everywhere the same. All he adopts is but a cloak, under which the eternal Hebrew survives; he is the same in his facial features, in the structure of his body, his temperament, his character.[17]

And it is the body of the Jew which is the sign of this immutability. This thesis of the immutability of the Jew is linked in the discourse of the late nineteenth century to the unchanging relationship of the Jew to the world of disease, pathology, and death. Twain is responding to a debate about the diseased nature of the Jews which was part of Western culture and which took a striking turn in the latter half of the nineteenth century.

Jews are Diseased

The signs of disease had long marked the Jew as different. The earliest modern images evoked their decrepitude as an essential aspect of their nature. It was seen as the physical sign of their guilt for the Crucifixion. Johannes Buxtorf, writing for a fearful Christian audience about the inner nature of the Jews in an account of their nature and practices, catalogued their diseases (such as epilepsy, the plague, leprosy) in 1643.[18] Johann Jakob Schudt, the late-seventeenth-century Orientalist who was *the* authority on the nature of the difference of the Jews for his time, cited their physical form as diseased and repellent: "among several hundred of their kind he had not encountered a single person without a blemish or other repulsive feature: for they are either pale and yellow or swarthy; they have in general big heads, big mouths, everted lips, protruding eyes and bristle-like eyelashes, large ears, crooked feet, hands that hang below their knees, and big shapeless warts, or are otherwise asymmetrical and malproportioned in their limbs."[19] Schudt's view saw the diseases of the Jews as a reflex of their "Jewishness," of their stubborn refusal to acknowledge the truth of Christianity. What is striking about Schudt's early comment is the tradition of seeing the diseased Jew as "swarthy." The Jews are black in their illness.

How intensively this image of the black Jew haunts the imagination of European society can be seen in a description by the "liberal" Bavarian writer Johann Pezzl, who traveled to Vienna in the 1780s and described the typical Viennese Jew of his time:

> There are about five hundred Jews in Vienna. Their sole and eternal occupation is to counterfeit (*Mauscheln*), salvage, trade in coins, and cheat Christians, Turks, heathens, indeed themselves. . . . This is only the beggarly filth from Canaan which can only be exceeded in filth, un-cleanliness, stench, disgust, poverty, dishonesty, pushiness and other things by the trash of the twelve tribes from Galicia. Excluding the Indian fakirs, there is no category of supposed human beings which comes closer to the Orang-Utan than does a Polish Jew. . . . Covered from foot to head in filth, dirt and rags, covered in a type of black sack . . . their necks exposed, the color of a Black, their faces covered up to the eyes with a beard, which would have given the High Priest in the Temple chills, the hair turned and knotted as if they all suffered from the *plica polonica*.[20]

The image of the Viennese Jew is of the Eastern Jew, suffering from the diseases of the East such as the *Judenkratze*, the fabled skin and hair disease also attributed to the Poles under the designation of the *plica polonica*.[21] The Jews' disease is written on the skin. It is the appearance—the skin color, the external manifestations—which marks the Jew as different. Here Pezzl argues by analogy—the Jews are like the blacks. When this tradition is transferred into American culture during Reconstruction, the questions of the analogy between the Jew and the black has an even greater salience. For if the Jews are to be understood to be black, how does the Christian white reader, especially the Christian white physician, relate to the idea of the marked nature of the Jew's body? The image of the Jews in *The Innocents Abroad, or The New Pilgrims' Progress* can be best placed in the tradition of this complex American reading of the Jew's body.

The very charge of the diseased nature of the Jews—whether dis-eased because of their essence or because of their experience—was hotly debated in the United States following Reconstruction, when the racial question was differently constructed. If the Jews were equated with blacks within the European tradition, in the United States they were clearly not blacks, even though they were understood as different. Twain's early image of the diseased Jew—along with its relationship to models of Jewish "infiltration" into other arenas of modern life such as the economy—is reversed for his contemporary American readers. In an exchange of letters in 1874 in the prestigious Philadelphia *Medical and Surgical Reporter*, Madison Marsh, a physician from Port Hudson, Louisiana, put forth the argument that Jews had a much greater toleration for disease than the general population. He based his view on the supposed Jewish immunity to tuberculosis. Marsh argued that the Jews "enjoy a wonderful national immunity from, not only phthisis [pulmonary tuberculosis] but all disease of the thoracic viscera." The Jew does not suffer from tuberculosis because "his constitution has become so hardened and fortified against disease by centuries of national calamities, by the dietetics, regimen and sanitas of his religion, continuing for consecutive years of so many ages." [22] This view was generally held during the latter half of the nineteenth century. Lucian Wolf, in a debate before the anthropological Society of Great Britain and Ireland in 1885, stated categorically that "figures could also be given to prove the immunity of Jews from phthisis"; Dr. Asher, in that same debate, observed that "Jews had an extraordinary power of resistance to phthisis." [23] Jews (at least Jews in the Diaspora) live longer, have a lower child mortality, and are generally healthier than Christians. The Jew's "high average physique . . . is not less remarkable than the high average of his intelligence." Jews are the "purest, finest, and most perfect type of the Caucasian race." [24]

This view was one widely espoused by American Jews in the late nineteenth century. Rabbi Joseph Krauskopf informed his Reformed congregation in Philadelphia that "eminent physicians and statisticians have amply confirmed the truth: that the marvelous preservation of Israel, despite all the efforts to blot them out from the face of the earth, their comparative freedom from a number of diseases, which cause frightful ravages among the Non-Jewish people, was largely due to their close adherence to their excellent Sanitary Laws. Health was their coat of mail, it was their magic shield that caught, and warded off, every thrust aimed at their heart. Vitality was their birthright. . . . Their immunity, which the enemy charged to magic-Arts, to alliances with the spirits of evil, was traceable solely to their faithful compliance with the sanitary requirements of their religion." [27] Marsh added one new twist to this equation: Jews are healthier, live longer, are more immune to disease, are more intelligent because of their healthful practices, such as diet—and because they belong to the "white" race. Or at least so the Jew was seen from the standpoint of a rural Louisiana physician during Reconstruction.

A month after this report was published, it was answered in detail by Ephraim M. Epstein, a Jewish physician practicing in Cincinnati who had earlier practiced medicine in Vienna and in Russia. He rebutted Marsh's argument point by point. Jews have no immunity from tuberculosis or any other disease, including those long associated with Jewish religious practices: "I am sure I have observed no Jewish immunity from any diseases, venereal disease not excepted."[26] Jews do not have "superior longevity"; they have no advantage either because of their diet or because of their practice of circumcision. But Jews do possess a quality lacking in their Christian neighbors. What makes Jews less at risk is the network of support, the "close fraternity, one Jew never forsaking the material welfare of his brother Jew, and he knows it instinctively." What preserves the Jew's health is indeed his "common mental construction," as well as the constitutional stamina which that nation inherited from its progenitor, Abraham of old, and because it kept that inheritance undeteriorated by not intermarrying with other races."[27] Group dynamics and racial purity are the source of Jewish health, such as it is.

Here the battle was joined: the Southern, Christian physician saw in the Jews' social practices and their race a key to universal health. He, of course, defines race in terms of his own ideological understanding of the primary difference between the "Negro" and the "Caucasian" races. The Jews, according to the standard textbooks of the period, such as that of the Viennese biologist Carl Claus, are indeed "Caucasians."[28] But in American terms, following the close of the Civil War, this concept was given a special, intensely political association. Whites have the potential, with good diet and the fortitude to bear oppression (such as Reconstruction), to be healthier, more intelligent, more immune from disease— and here Marsh's readers would understand—"than blacks." The Eastern European Jewish physician saw any limited advantage accruing to the Jews lying in their inherited nature and sexual practices to which non-Jews could have absolutely no access, indeed which by definition exclude them.

Marsh's intense, vituperative response came in August of 1874.[29] Initially, he called upon the statistical evidence from Prussian, French, and British sources to buttress his argument about Jewish longevity. He then dismissed Epstein's argument about Jewish risk for disease completely and turned to the question of the role which Epstein ascribed to "the moral cause that had prevented intermarriage of the Jews with other nations, and thus preserved intact their health and tenacity of life." It was circumcision as a sign of the separateness and selectivity of the Jews that Epstein evoked as the proof for his case about Jewish difference. Circumcision for Marsh is a "sanitary measure and religious rite . . . in practice by the ancient Egyptians. . . . It never became a Hebrew institution until friendly relations had been established between Abraham and the Egyptians. Then it was initiated by the circumcision of Abraham and Isaac by the express command of God." Circumcision was an Egyptian ritual, and "Moses, the great champion, leader and lawgiver of the Hebrew race, was himself an Egyptian priest, educated in all the deep research and arts of the Chaldean Mage and mystic philosophic development of Egyptian and Oriental science, and all that was then known of the science of medicine, in its general principles and in its application of details for the preservation of health and prevention of disease." It is through the impact of this philosophy with "a slight tinge of Egyptian and Indian, or Asiatic philosophy, and shadow of its teachings [which] pervade all the books of Moses" (133) that Jews enjoy good health. The ritual practices of the Jews are but an amalgam of the combined knowledge of the West. They are in no way the special product of this inbred and haughty people. And indeed Marsh, like Mark Twain, is immediately brought back to Egypt, to the "damp and cobwebby mold of antiquity" in which the Jews continue to be understood.

What could Epstein know about real medicine? Marsh dismisses Epstein as merely a Jew whose authority is drawn solely from his Jewishness: "What evidence or authority does he bring to support his pretensions to superior knowledge? His being himself a Jew, per se" (134). And Marsh affirms his view that the Jews possess the secret to greater health which they are unwilling to share with the rest of the world. The subtext to Marsh's argument is that the Jew has a special immunity that is the result of accident and that protects them from disease. But the true secret is that this gift is not theirs at all; it was taken from the peoples among whom they lived. Jews like Epstein are charlatans who try to disguise their true nature. It is the Jewish body which lies at the heart of anti-Semitism. In the late nineteenth century it was the claim of the special nature of the Jewish body which evoked the anger of the non-Jew toward the Jew's sexual selectivity or *amixia*.[30] Marsh reversed this because he too wished to share in the special status of the "healthy" Jewish body.

Circumcision had become a major issue within the medical practice of

the United States. Indeed, the American physician Peter Charles Remondino, writing in the 1870s, could note that "circumcision is like a substantial and well-secured life annuity; . . . it ensures them better health,
greater capacity for labour, longer life, less nervousness, sickness, loss
of time."[31] And indeed by the 1890s an American association had begun
to be made between "uncircumcised" and "uncivilized."[32] In this context
it is not surprising that circumcision, an intervention which could be made
by the physician, came to have a function in the definition of "hygiene."
But it is in no way to be understood as a Jewish practice in the terms
which Epstein had outlined. The debates about the "health" or "illness"
of the Jews centered on the inherent nature or social practices of the
Jews. The image of the Jew as different was always juxtaposed with the
unstated understanding of the diseased and inferior nature of the African American. Twain's views about the diseased nature of the Jews in
biblical times can be placed within this long-standing and complex debate
about where the true boundary of inferiority is to be placed. Twain's
focus on the religious aspects of disease and the corrupt body reflects the
parameters of this debate. Like Marsh, Twain sees the world through
the model of a Christian understanding of the nature of the Jew. The Jew
is different from the Christian in terms of his understanding of the world
as exemplified by the very nature of his body.

Twain Sees the Diseased Jew

The contrast between the Jews Twain represents in his essay of 1898
and those he saw in 1867 is striking. In the *Adventures of Huckleberry
Finn* he had parodied the assumptions of the relationship between African Americans and mental illness which dominated the medical discourse
about African Americans from the 1840s on through Reconstruction.[33] In
his 1898 essay on the Jews, written in the heat of anti-Semitic outbreaks
in the United States and in the light of the debates he had experienced
in Vienna, there seems to be a more liberal, more benign view of the
Jews. Indeed, the late 1890s mark the high point of both anti-Semitic and
anti-African American hysteria.[34] Certainly Jews, like Nigger Jim, are in
no way associated with images of disease. Or at least not overtly. For
Twain's concern in the 1890s is to present a positive image of the Jew
in terms of the Jew's awareness of his civic responsibility. For Twain the
Jews may still be diseased, like other peoples, but at least they take care

of their own. The Jews are never beggars; indeed they create "charitable institutions" like hospitals (14) to take care of their afflicted. They are quite unlike the diseased multitudes who flocked to the tent of the Western doctor in Palestine some three decades earlier.

These Jews are the victims of society. As Susy Clemens recorded in her notebook, Twain "decided that the Jews had always seemed to him a race much to be respected; also they had suffered much, and had been greatly persecuted, so to ridicule or make fun of them seemed to be like attacking a man who was already down."[35] The debate between those who believed that illness was an essential aspect of the Jewish race and those who saw it as a reflection of the social status of the Jews is worked out in Twain's own texts. At the fin de siècle, Twain saw the nature of the Jew as a reflection neither of space nor race but of the oppression inflicted upon the Jews by Western culture. The rationale for writing his essay on the Jews in 1898 was a letter from a Jewish-American lawyer who asked Twain about the cause of anti-Semitism. The Jews are seen as the victim, especially in the context of his experience in Vienna. Twain sees contemporary Jews as little different from all the other inhabitants of Europe and the United States, except that they are self-consciously aware of their status as victims. Some thirty years later, when Twain moved from the past to the present, the argument shifted from the origins of Christianity to the nature of late-nineteenth-century capitalism and the role of the Jews. But Christianity and capitalism are linked, as we have seen in the arguments about the Jew's nature in the eighteenth and nineteenth centuries. Initially the Jews were for Twain the afflicted and superstitious Jews of the past—Naaman the Leper incarnate in Twain's experience entering into the Holy Land. These Jews are the originators of Christianity. But the miracles of Christ, recounted in detail in Twain's commentary, seem not to have helped them very much over time. For they seem still to be in the same diseased state they were in two thousand years before Twain arrived in the Holy Land. It seems to be American science which the sufferers in the Holy Land need today, rather than the mysteries of the past.

Twain differentiated between the corrupt Jews of the Bible and contemporary Jewry. But he also unconsciously linked them. Twain found it impossible to hold these two categories apart. In his essay of 1898 Twain evoked his own Southern image of the Jew and noted that "religion [i.e., Christianity] had nothing to do with" the hatred of the Jew. During Reconstruction the Jew had opened "shop on the plantation, supplied all the Negro's wants on credit, and at the end of the season was proprietor of the Negro's share of the present crop and of part of the share of the next one. Before long, the whites detested the Jew, and it is doubtful if the Negro loved him" (18). The category "Jew" has nothing to do with religion, as Marsh noted, but is a racial designation. In his system, Twain, like Marsh, can differentiate between "whites," "Negroes," and "Jews." Jews are designated as different from "whites" and "Negroes" on the basis of their racially marked character and practices. Here the question was whether the Jew was white or not, a question which reappeared in the debate about the social position of the Jew in the South during the Leo Frank case.[36] This distinction is important. For just as Twain needed to separate his identity from that of the diseased Jews and their progeny in the Holy Land, so too does he need to see himself as different from the corrupt Jews in America. For as Clara Clemens commented, Twain's "defense of Christ's race" was so "eloquent" that "it was rumored at one time Father himself was a Jew."[37] Indeed in Vienna, while he was observing the debates which triggered the essay on the Jews, he was labeled by the anti-Semitic press as the "Jew Mark Twain."[38]

The Jews are diseased, but their infection is the desire for capital. Twain's answer to anti-Semitism returns to the central theme of his earlier writing, to the image of the Jews in the context of the Holy Land. Twain supports the political aims of Theodor Herzl, but he ironically fears the ingathering "in Palestine, with a government of their own—under the suzerainty of the Sultan, I suppose." For "if that concentration of the cunningest brains in the world was going to be made in a free country (bar Scotland), I think it would be politic to stop it. It will not be well to let that race find out its strength. If the horses knew theirs, we should not ride any more" (27). It is this cunning which marked the Jews in the South and which Twain sensed in the origins of Christianity. And this cunning is a sign of the inherent difference of the Jews as a race, a mark of their corruption and disease. For in the science of the late nineteenth century, this corrupt genius is as certain a pathological sign as the physical symptoms of the leper.[39] Twain's rhetoric about physical disease has been transformed into rhetoric about psychological predisposition, which is as far as he was able to go in rethinking the meaning of the diseases of the Jews. Twain sees the diseases of the Jews as markers for the Jews' difference but also for the difference which they (as individuals who have experienced death and disease in their own world) see in themselves.

And yet, in his own estimation, he is not as "ill" as the Jews—and that redeems him.

Notes

1   Mark Twain, *Concerning the Jews* (Philadelphia: Running Press, 1985). All quotations are from this edition, which has a good historical introduction. See also Carl Dolmetsch, "Mark Twain and the Viennese Anti-Semites: New Light on 'Concerning the Jews,'" *Mark Twain Journal* 23 (1985): 10–17; Guido Fink, "Al di qua della paroia: Gli ebrei di Henry James e di Mark Twain," in *Il recupero de testo: Aspetti della letteratura ebraico-americana*, ed. Guido Fink and Gabriella Morisco (Bologna: Cooperative Lib. Univ. ed. Bologna, 1988), 29–50. The general background in Twain's work can be judged by the extracts in *Mark Twain on the Damned Human Race*, ed. Janet Smith (New York: Hill & Wang, 1962) and *Mark Twain and the Three R's: Race, Religion, Revolution*, ed. Maxwell Geismar (Indianapolis: Bobbs-Merrill, 1973). The best overall discussion of Mark Twain's attitude toward the Jews is still to be found in Philip S. Foner, *Mark Twain, Social Critic* (New York: International Publishers, 1958), 288–307, which documents in great detail the critical reception of this piece, including its use in the anti-Semitic propaganda of the early twentieth century. On the overall question of the image of the Jew in nineteenth-century American culture, see Louis Harap, *The Image of the Jew in American Literature from Early Republic to Mass Immigration* (Philadelphia: Jewish Publication Society, 1974).

2   Marion A. Richmond, "The Lost Source in Freud's 'Comment on Anti-Semitism': Mark Twain," *Journal of the American Psychoanalytic Association* 28 (1980): 563–74.

3   Cited by Foner, 300.

4   All references are to Mark Twain, *The Innocents Abroad/Roughing It* (New York: Library of America, 1984). On the historical background for this volume see Dewey Ganzel, *Mark Twain Abroad: The Cruise of the "Quaker City"* (Chicago: Univ. of Chicago Press, 1968); and Franklin Dickerson Walker, *Irreverent Pilgrims: Melville, Browne, and Mark Twain in the Holy Land* (Seattle: Univ. of Washington Press, 1974).

5   See L. Belloni, "Anatomica plastica: The Bologna Wax Models," *CIBA Symposium* 8 (1960): 84–87; François Cagnetta, "La vie et l'oeuvre de Gaetano Giulio Zummo," *Cereoplastica nella scienza e nell'arte series: Atti del 1 congresso internazionale. Biblioteca della Revista di storia delle scienze mediche e naturali 20* (1977): 489–501. On the religious background to this tradition, see the general historical introductions of these two catalogues: Benedetto Lanza et al., *La cere anatomiche della Specola* (Florence: Arnaud Editore, 1979) on the Florentine collection, and, on the Viennese collection, *Kata-*

log der josephinischen Sammlung anatomischer und geburtshilflicher Wach-spräparate im Institut für Geschichte der Medizin an der Universität Wien, ed. Konrad Allmer and Marlene Jantsch (Graz-Köln: Hermann Böhlaus Nachf., 1965).

6   Henry Wadsworth Longfellow, *Outre Mer: A Pilgrimage beyond the Sea* (London: C. Routledge, 1853), 224–25.

7   Nathaniel Hawthorne, *Passages from the French and Italian Note-Books* (Boston and New York: Houghton, Mifflin, 1871), 380.

8   One must note that such a specific use of death and decay is quite different from Twain's metaphoric use of death. See Stephen Cooper, "'Good Rotten Material for a Burial': The Overdetermined Death of Romance in *Life on the Mississippi*," *Literature and Psychology* 36 (1990): 78–89.

9   Patrice Boudelais and Andre Dodin, *Visages du Cholera* (Paris: Belin, 1987).

10 *Mark Twain's Notebooks and Journals: Volume 1 (1855–1873)*, ed. Frederick Anderson, Michael B. Frank, and Kenneth M. Sanderson (Berkeley: Univ. of California Press, 1975), 438.

11 On Twain's theology, see Susan K. Harris, *Mark Twain's Escape from Time: A Study of Patterns and Images* (Columbia: Univ. of Missouri Press, 1982).

12 Quoted by Ganzel, 222.

13 Quoted by Harap, 349.

14 *The Autobiography of Mark Twain*, ed. Charles Neider (New York: Harper and Row, 1975), 3.

15 See the discussion in Foner, 288–89.

16 Friedrich Ratzel, *The History of Mankind*, 3 vols., trans. A. J. Butler (London: Macmillan, 1896), 3:183. The German edition appeared between 1885 and 1888. For a more detailed discussion see my *Jewish Self-Hatred: Anti-Semitism and the Hidden Language of the Jews* (1986; rpt., Baltimore: Johns Hopkins Univ. Press, 1990), 216–17.

17 Richard Andree, *Zur Volkskunde der Juden* (Leipzig: Velhagen & Klasing, 1881), 24–25; translation from Maurice Fishberg, "Materials for the Physical Anthropology of the Eastern European Jew," *Memoirs of the American Anthropological Association* 1 (1905–1907): 6–7.

18 Johannes Buxtorf, *Synagoga Judaica* . . . (Basel: Ludwig Königs selige Erben, 1643), 620–22.

19 Johann Jakob Schudt, *Jüdische Merkwürdigkeiten*, 2 vols. (Frankfurt am Main: S. T. Hocker, 1714–18), 2:369. On the later ideological life of this debate see Wolfgang Fritz Haug, *Die Faschisierung des bürgerlichen Subjekts: Die Ideologie der gesunden Normalität und die Ausrottungspolitiken im deutschen Faschismus* (Berlin-West: Argument Verlag, 1986).

20 Johann Pezzl, *Skizze von Wien: Ein Kultur- und Sittenbild as der josephinischen Zeit*, ed. Gustav Gugitz and Anton Schlossar (Graz: Leykam-Verlag, 1923), 107–08.

21 On the meaning of this disease in the medical literature of the period, see the following dissertations on the topic: Michael Scheiba, *Dissertatio inauguralis medica, sistens quaedam plicae pathologica: Germ. Juden-Zopff, Polon.*

Koltun: quam . . . in Academia Albertina pro gradu doctoris . . . subjiciet defensurus Michael Schieba . . . (Regiomonti: Litteris Reusnerianis, [1739]); and Hieronymus Ludolf, *Dissertatio inauguralis medica de plica, vom Juden-Zopff . . .* (Erfordiae: Typis Groschianis, [1724]).

22 Madison Marsh, "Jews and Christians," *Medical and Surgical Reporter* 30 (1874): 343–44, esp. 343.

23 See the debate following the presentation of Joseph Jacobs, "On the Racial Characteristics of Modern Jews," *Journal of the Anthropological Institute* 16 (1886): 23–63, esp. 56 and 61.

24 Marsh, 344.

25 Joseph Krauskopf, *Sanitary Science: A Sunday Lecture* (Philadelphia: S. W. Goodman, 1889), 7.

26 Ephraim M. Epstein, "Have the Jews any Immunity from Certain Diseases?" *Medical and Surgical Reporter* 30 (1874): 440–42, esp. 440.

27 Epstein, 441.

28 Carl Claus, *Grundzüge der Zoologie zum Gebrauche an Universitäten und höheren Lehranstalten sowie zum Selbststudium,* 2 vols. (Marburg: N. G. Elwerts Universitäts-Buchhandlung, 1872), 2:123.

29 Marsh, "Have the Jews any Immunity from Certain Diseases?" *Medical and Surgical Reporter* 31 (1874): 132–34.

30 On the history of this concept see *Anti-Semitism in Times of Crisis,* ed. Sander L. Gilman and Steven T. Katz (New York: New York Univ. Press, 1991), 29.

31 Peter Charles Remondino, *History of Circumcision from the Earliest Times to the Present. Moral and Physical Reasons for its Performance, with a History of Eunuchism, Hermaphroditism, etc., and of the Different Operations Practiced upon the Prepuce* (Philadelphia: F. A. Davis, 1891), 186. Remondino's book was only published in 1892, but he notes in his introduction that it had been written decades earlier.

32 Stuart Creighton Miller, *"Benevolent Assimilation": The American Conquest of the Philippines, 1899–1903* (New Haven: Yale Univ. Press, 1982), 75.

33 Sander L. Gilman, "On the Nexus of Madness and Blackness," in my *Difference and Pathology: Stereotypes of Sexuality, Race, and Madness* (Ithaca: Cornell Univ. Press, 1985), 131–49.

34 See George Frederickson, *The Black Image in the White Mind: The Debate about Afro-American Character and Destiny, 1817–1914* (New York: Harper and Row, 1971).

35 Cited by Foner, 290.

36 See Eugene Levy, "'Is the Jew a White Man?': Press Reaction to the Leo Frank Case, 1913–1915," *Phylon* 35 (1974): 212–22.

37 Clara Clemens, *My Father, Mark Twain* (New York: Harper & Brothers, 1931), 203–04.

38 Dolmetsch, 14.

39 Sander L. Gilman, "The Jewish Genius," in my *The Jew's Body* (New York: Routledge, 1991), 128–49.

Elizabeth Young   Warring Fictions:
Iola Leroy and the Color of Gender

Criticism of American Civil War fiction has produced
a literary history that, despite the remarkable quantity of its subject
matter—there are more than two thousand Civil War novels alone—is
marked by a series of mysterious absences. In particular, the black experience of a war whose profound result was to end slavery drops out
of this criticism and, by implication, seems nowhere to be found in the
fiction itself. For example, in the two classic surveys of Civil War fiction,
Edmund Wilson's *Patriotic Gore* and Daniel Aaron's *The Unwritten War*,
black authors seldom appear, while the white authors under discussion,
as Aaron notes, focus on white characters.[1] As for women, some—specifically, white women—fare slightly better in critical texts, although a
recent assessment of Civil War fiction asserts unironically that "for most
Americans, war represented the ultimate test of manhood."[2] But black
women are rendered doubly invisible in this scheme: excluded from the
Civil War literary canon by virtue of both race and gender, their wartime
stories would seem—to use Aaron's term—remarkably "unwritten."

Invisibility may depend on where one looks, however; for Frances
Harper's 1892 novel, *Iola Leroy; or, Shadows Uplifted*, offers a powerful
vision of the Civil War years as seen by this prominent activist for black
rights, feminism, and temperance. At sixty-seven, Frances Ellen Watkins Harper was an experienced lecturer, essayist, short-story writer,
and poet when her only novel was published. *Iola Leroy* is the story of
a woman, the novel's eponymous heroine, raised as a privileged white
daughter of the antebellum South who discovers on the eve of the Civil
War that she is of mixed-race ancestry, and who is then sold into slavery.
Rescued by the Union army, she eventually reunites with her family when

the war is over. Black feminist criticism has recently brought new attention to *Iola Leroy*. Hazel Carby, for example, argues in a persuasive reading of the novel that Iola's journey from orphaned youth to family-filled adulthood both recalls the mid-nineteenth-century domestic "woman's novel" and recasts its plot in the context of the black family. Iola's triumphant claim of family at novel's end applies "not only to the individual heroine but also to the entire race," for it serves, Carby argues, as the vehicle for Harper's observations on the black diaspora and the emerging postwar role of black intellectuals.[3]

We may take the politics of domesticity in another direction, however, by viewing *Iola Leroy* as a domestic novel about a domestic political crisis: the Civil War. Far beyond simply supplying a prelude to the novel's Reconstruction plot, the war profoundly affects the novel's formal and thematic concerns. As a reading of history, *Iola Leroy* rewrites the conventions of war narrative, foregrounding black heroism in combat. Black women are central to this effort, not only as wartime actors but also as mothers whose presence in the narrative frames its war sections. Indeed, Harper embeds the war in a narrative trajectory of maternal quest and reunion, simultaneously feminizing war narrative and using this literary form to represent the importance of maternal and familial structures in the black community.

This use of the Civil War, intercutting the axes of race and gender, is also specific to its meaning as an *internal* conflict. Harper uses "civil war" as a metaphor to describe a variety of conflicts outside the formal battlefield, among them Iola's resistance to the dynamics of interracial rape and her decision, as a light-skinned mulatta, not to pass for white. Engaging and interweaving a variety of antinomies—black/white, male/female, North/South—Harper shows individual identity to be decisively marked by both gender and race. The formations of war, in other words, serve in *Iola Leroy* as a model for the construction of subjectivity.

What complicates this portrayal further is that by the time Harper wrote the novel, the Civil War had already been structured by literary conventions as a series of novelistic plots about sexuality and marriage. Reading Harper's novel against D. W. Griffith's overtly racist 1915 film *The Birth of a Nation*—which elaborates and epitomizes these conventions—suggests the extent to which metaphor determined the politics of Civil War discourse and, consequently, the extent to which Harper's use of metaphor acts as a strategic political intervention. That is, the novel's use of metaphor is reciprocal: *Iola Leroy* simultaneously employs the war as a metaphor for identity and offers a novelistic plot of individual identity that metaphorically restages the Civil War itself. *Iola Leroy*, in short, sets race and gender at battle with war, history at war with metaphor, and representation—political and literary—in conflict with itself.

■ ■ ■

How does *Iola Leroy* construct the historical moment of the Civil War? To answer this question, we might begin by tracing both the participation of black women in the war itself and the transformation of that experience into nonfictional prose. In this double context—war history and the history of war narrative—*Iola Leroy* gains specificity as a black woman's perspective on the war, one rooted in maternal and familial dimensions of black experience.

At the beginning of the Civil War, slavery was an entrenched institution in the American South; by its end, abolition had been secured through both legislation and a set of economic and social changes that made its continuation impossible.[4] In the four years from 1861 to 1865, black slaves and free blacks in the North were a vital part of the wartime effort. Black men participated en masse in the Union army, despite the racism that initially prevented them from enlisting as soldiers. By 1865, nearly 200,000 black soldiers had served in the Northern armed forces.[5]

The trajectory of black women's wartime efforts is more difficult to reconstruct, since most black women experienced the war outside of formal military activities. Jacqueline Jones cites three disparate examples of Southern slave women's activity during the war: a seventy-year-old woman who escaped along with her twenty-two children and grandchildren in the war; a woman whose plantation was so isolated from news that she lived on in servitude until the 1880s; and a woman who stayed at a plantation even after she was freed, midwar, because the plantation afforded security for herself and her children.[6] For slave women, the possibilities of freedom were often gauged in the context of the risk to family members, especially children. As Jones writes, "Amid the dislocation of Civil War . . . black women's priorities and obligations coalesced into a single purpose: to escape from the oppression of slavery while keeping their families intact."[7]

For some black women, this escape coincided with the opportunity to help the war effort directly. Black women aided the Union army in a variety of capacities. Harriet Tubman, for example, worked within the ranks of the army as soldier, scout, and spy, and was known as "General

Tubman"; another ex-slave, Susie King Taylor, was part of the Union army's first black regiment. Taylor's example is a particularly important one, for as one of many black commentators upon the war she later wrote a memoir, *Reminiscences of My Life in Camp* (1902), which describes at length her experience within the Union army.[8] Taylor worked first as cook and laundress—services for which she was paid—and then taught reading and writing to the soldiers. As the war went on, she "learned to handle a musket very well while in the regiment, and could shoot straight and often hit the target," which she thought "great fun."[9] After the war, she helped to found a relief organization. Her efforts thus encompassed a range of activities, from the male preserve of gun-shooting to the all-women's postwar "Relief Corps." Her account helps to undo the silence in which, as she says, "many people . . . do not know what some of the colored women did during the war. . . . These things should be kept in history before the people" (141–42).

In offering a record of these experiences, Taylor's narrative also re-shapes the formal contours of the literary representation of war. Her first chapter, "A Brief Sketch of My Ancestors," begins "My great-great-grandmother was 120 years old when she died. She had seven children, and five of her boys were in the Revolutionary War" (25). Following this intertwined genealogy of women and wars, Taylor moves on to her great-grandmother, a noted midwife and "the mother of twenty-four children, twenty-three being girls" (25), and then to her grandmother, a free woman who lived by selling produce, doing laundry, and taking care of some "bachelors' rooms" (27). The second chapter expands this web of matrilineal relations to include the topic of literacy, as Taylor's grandmother orchestrates her education by sending her to two women teachers. Taylor, in turn, passes on her skills literally by writing passes for her grandmother, "for all colored persons, free or slaves, were compelled to have a pass" (31).

The two opening chapters, then, frame the text in such a way that when war does appear in Taylor's narrative, it is against the background of a black matrilineal legacy and a female tradition of literacy. Taylor's work as a laundress for groups of male soldiers recalls her grandmother's activity cleaning "some bachelors' rooms"; her teaching evokes the lessons her own grandmother sponsored so that she might read. Her great-great-grandmother's household—a woman and five boys off to the American Revolution—is echoed in this description of the gratitude of Union soldiers toward Taylor: "You took an interest in us boys ever since we have been here, and we are very grateful for all you do for us" (67). Finally, the Women's Relief Corps activities that close the war are balanced by the opening matrix of women that includes her midwife-grandmother and her dozens of girls. In short, it is as though the war itself were one event on a continuum of mothering, repeated in a range of activities over generations.

This complex view of mothering also works to erode the distinction between the battlefield and the homefront. The Civil War challenged this boundary constantly, fought as it was by definition on "home" territory—both within the domestic boundaries of the nation and, at times, literally inside domestic space. Indeed, as Kathleen Diffley has recently argued in reference to Civil War fiction, the nation in wartime seemed a "house invaded," with the disruption of national stability intimately linked to the control of domestic space.[10] Implicating the Civil War in a network of familial relations, Taylor too links homefront and battlefront, as conceived in terms of maternal and military service.[11] Her memoirs stand both as gripping evidence of the experience of black women in the war and as an important example of how the perspective of a black woman writer could reshape the paradigms of the traditional wartime plot.

Susie King Taylor's *Reminiscences* were not published until ten years after *Iola Leroy*, although it is quite possible that Harper, a tireless campaigner for black rights, was aware of Taylor's participation in the war.[12] But the depiction of war in Harper's novel participates to a striking degree in the same double movement as Taylor's text—foregrounding the role of black men and women in the narrative of war, and, in turn, altering war narrative itself by plotting it in the context of black family life. *Iola Leroy* opens in the midst of the war, on a North Carolina plantation in which a close-knit slave community eagerly awaits news of the Union army. The arrival of the army means a chance for several of the male slaves, including Robert Johnson and Tom Anderson, to participate in the Union cause; it also means the rescue from slavery (by a Union general) of the light-skinned Iola Leroy, a woman of beauty and virtue to whom Tom and others have been attracted. A sequence of chapters focuses on life in the army, depicting Robert's commitment to a black regiment despite the light skin that would enable him to pass, Tom's heroic death in the service of the cause, and the growing friendship between Iola—now a nurse in the army—and a white Northern doctor named Gresham.

At this point the action shifts back twenty years in time, and we learn the story of Eugene Leroy, a white Southerner who falls in love with a light-skinned woman, then frees, educates, and marries her, to the horror of his cousin and of the white Southern society that ostracizes her. Feeling this stigma, Eugene and Marie send their children North to be educated. When Eugene dies, his cousin seizes his property and sells Marie Leroy and her children into slavery. Here the action returns to the midwar "present," when Iola rejects the attentions of the white Northern doctor and discovers that Robert Johnson is her uncle; her brother Harry, meanwhile, has enlisted in a black Union regiment. The war over, Robert, Harry, and Iola all search for their families, a quest centered on a search for mothers. United at last in the North, the characters embark on projects of social reform. Iola marries a fellow activist, a mulatto doctor named Latimer, and they return to the South. The novel concludes with the major characters resolutely involved in the black Reconstruction effort to "uplift the race."

As this summary suggests, Harper's presentation of the war explicitly foregrounds the heroism of black men in wartime, a focus that combatted a variety of contemporary misrepresentations. As the first novel to address black participation in the war, *Iola Leroy* paid literary witness to the achievements of black soldiers, whose involvement had been treated with ambivalence from the start and could all too easily fade from cultural memory.[13] Moreover, by the 1880s, Northern representations of the war tended to downplay antebellum slavery and to highlight the positive qualities of white Southerners in the interests of sectional reconciliation.[14] Most immediately important in the context of the novel's publication was its presentation of black male heroism, which directly contradicted the horrific onslaught of negative imagery that motivated and authorized Southern lynching crusades against black men in the 1890s. Rescuing the experience of black men in the war from fictional oblivion, then, Harper's novel intervened in contemporary constructions of race relations shaped most urgently by the racist discourse of lynching.

In *Iola Leroy*, three black male characters exemplify the courage of black soldiers in wartime. Harry Leroy enlists in a "colored regiment" while in the North; Robert Johnson plans to join the Union army when it arrives in the South. Tom Anderson, disqualified from being a soldier because of "physical defects," joins as a helper and scout, and sacrifices his life bravely for the war: " 'You are soldiers and can fight. If they kill me, it is nuthin'.' So Tom leaped out to shove the boat into the water. Just then the Rebel bullets began to rain around him."[15] As Tom's comment suggests, the novel presents black men not only fighting bravely but eagerly welcoming military challenge, since the war provided them with a more organized opportunity to express their hatred of slavery. As Robert reasons, "It would have been madness and folly for him to have attempted an insurrection against slavery" before the war, but now he "waited eagerly and hopefully his chance to join the Union army" (35, 36). The war, that is, offers an arena in which to fight for freedom, one in which a man's personal heroism—a commonplace of war narrative— takes on the representative role of liberating an entire race.

As Harper presents it, black women are central to this war effort. There is no single female character in the novel who, like a Susie King Taylor, fills many wartime functions. Rather, Harper splits the variety of war efforts among different female characters. Aunt Linda, who states at the beginning of the novel, "I ralely b'lieves dat we cullud folks is mixed up in dis fight" (12), ends up selling food to the soldiers as they come through the South, while another black woman, a laundress, serves as a Union spy. And Iola, the protagonist, nurses wounded soldiers for the Union army; with her "gentle ministrations" (40), she is an indispensable member of the hospital. The novel thus simultaneously inserts black hero-ism into a male combat narrative and genders this portrait by highlighting the efforts of black women. Moreover, what is particularly striking about this rendering of history is that—as with Taylor's memoir—the novel redefines the conventions of war narrative itself. The novel's Civil War events, which occupy the first half of the novel and are recounted in remi-niscence throughout the second, are filtered through a black maternal lens. As Taylor's ancestral mothers fortify her in her wartime efforts, so too does Iola align the antislavery crusade leading to war with Marie Leroy: "I know mamma don't like slavery very much. . . . My father does not think as she does" (98).

If Harper and Taylor both stress the conjunction of wars and mothers, there is nevertheless an important difference between their texts. For while the black maternal legacy is strongly present in Taylor's memoirs, *Iola Leroy* frames the war in terms of maternal *absence*. The war enters Iola's life simultaneously with her father's death and her mother's disap-pearance; its presence in her life parallels her quest for reunion with her mother. Nursing Tom, she says, "You are the best friend I have had since I was torn from my mother" (54). When Dr. Gresham proposes marriage to her in the midst of their war experience, he frames it as a maternal recovery: "What is to hinder you from sharing my Northern home, from having my mother to be your mother?" (116). She responds: "Oh, you do not know how hungry my heart is for my mother" (117). The end of the war brings the realization of this desire, as Iola announces "I am on my way South seeking for my mother, and I shall not give up until I find her" (168). When she and her mother are at last reunited, "Marie rushe[s] forward, clasp[s] Iola in her arms and sob[s] out her joy in broken words" (195).

Maternal search defines not only Iola's experience of war but that of the men who fight it. The soldiers in the novel are often portrayed in relation to their mothers. Debating whether to run off to war, Robert asserts early in the novel, "I ain't got nothing 'gainst my ole Miss, except she sold my mother from me. And a boy ain't nothin' without his mother" (17–18). When he wakes up after being wounded, he sees Iola and assumes she is his mother rather than recognizing her as his niece. Meanwhile, Harry has joined a black regiment because it is the one most likely to reunite him with his mother; wounded, he wakes up to find a gentle nurse bending over him, and shouts "Mamma; oh, mamma! have I found you at last?" (191).

The presence of a nurse at this crucial moment in the novel is not coincidental, for in a narrative that links mothering with wartime, the nurse serves as a hinge between the two realms. Harper shows no battle scenes; the major moment of heroic injury—Tom Anderson's martyrdom—is presented only in retrospect, through another soldier's account, and instead we see Tom in the hospital with his nurse, Iola. As Susie King Taylor nurses her "boys," turning the war setting into a domestic space, so Iola, as nurse, feminizes the war; under Iola's care, Tom "couldn't have been more tender if he had been a woman" (50). And as nursing extends the process of mothering, it also forms a link to postwar teaching. Iola's postwar activities, like Taylor's, involve women's groups and relief work, and her own goals for the Reconstruction era emphasize—as she titles a speech to fellow middle-class blacks after the war—the "Education of Mothers." As Elizabeth Ammons puts it, *Iola Leroy* ultimately appeals "to a sisterhood of mothers and argue[s] in favor of maternal values as the ethical alternative and logical corrective to racial injustice in America." [16]

As Ammons herself notes, however, she is discussing *Iola Leroy* in the context of a set of white women writers, especially Harriet Beecher Stowe. The maternal ideology in Harper's novel is certainly linked to white women's fashionings of the war. Middle-class white women were prominent as nurses in the war, especially in the Union army. They, too, worked to erode the distinction between male and female wartime arenas, expressing a "complicated urge to make the front truly a home-front, to replace the captain with the mother, the doctor with the nurse, and even to out-soldier the soldiers."[17] What distinguishes such women from Iola, however, is that the "home-front" is already a given for the white nurse-mother of the war; it is already a category which she inhabits, and whose boundaries she wishes to expand. Iola, by contrast, has been denied family: as she states, "Instead of coming into this hospital a self-sacrificing woman, laying her every gift and advantage upon the altar of her country, I came as a rescued slave, glad to find a refuge from a fate more cruel than death" (113). The black nurse who brings the "boys" of the wartime hospital to life does not simply step into the white role of nursing and take on its features. Rather, she transforms the category into a specific analogue for the black mother who finds in wartime an opportunity to seek both freedom and family.

In this context, she also stands more generally for the familial dis-location which often characterized the slave experience, and which the fighting of the war was meant to end. Hortense Spillers has theorized that a central, defining effect of slavery, in its transformation of human beings into property, was the enforcement of "kinlessness."[18] The Civil War meant the opportunity to abolish a system that at its core legitimated the separation of children and parents and prohibited affective relations between individuals. Iola's maternal quest is shared by her brother Harry and her uncle Robert, both of whom are seeking their mothers. An important link between the novel's women, the black mother also evokes relationships among members of the entire black community. It is only when she has been found that Reconstruction can truly begin.

As a war novel, then, Harper's text executes a series of complicated generic maneuvers that crosscut race and gender. Most obviously, it recasts white male narratives of combat to foreground black men's heroism; but it goes on to decenter that combat narrative itself, making women central actors in the war. The figure of the nurse, in turn, feminizes the war effort, but that very transformation of traditional wartime gender roles must also be contextualized in terms of race, since—as in Susie King Taylor's memoir—Harper's nurse acts as one of a series of black mothers. Unlike Taylor's story, though, *Iola Leroy* makes the black maternal figure most important in her absence. An elusive figure, she turns the war into a maternal quest for women, a familial quest for the slave community as a whole, and an opportunity to rewrite the fictional forms of war narrative with a black female signature.

■ ■ ■

What does it mean that the war experience *Iola Leroy* records and transforms is not simply any type of battle, but civil war in particular? Margaret Higonnet has offered a provocative formulation for the specific significance of civil wars to gender relations: "Once a change in government can be conceived, sexual politics can also become an overt political issue. . . . Civil war serves as emblem and catalyst of change in the social prescription of sexual roles." The fiction that focuses on such wars, she argues, takes up this double theme, effecting a "metaphoric transfer of civil war from an external, political realm to inner conflict over sexual choice and the proper gender roles." This process works in reverse as well, so that "political relations acquire the color of gender." [19]

Higonnet's paradigm is a helpful one, for *Iola Leroy* indeed pairs political and gender orders, exploring dissent and conflict within and between these realms. Yet as with the novel's exploration of maternal thematics, gender is intertwined with race throughout, giving Higonnet's phrase "the color of gender" a literal meaning. In the novel's complicated map, black and white, male and female are constantly recoloring one another, presenting a variety of "civil wars"—from interracial rape to intraracial marriage—which parallel and intersect the declared conflict of North and South. And as we shall see, the many "civil wars" in *Iola Leroy* have a complex double function, simultaneously providing an historical metaphor for the novel's fictional plots of individual identity and using those fictional plots to inform political discourse about the Civil War itself.

Iola herself stands at the center of each of the novel's "civil wars," beginning with their most violent and oppositional form: interracial rape. For Iola, the war begins with the dissolution of her family, an event which results in her being sold into slavery. She is immediately catapulted into a system that legitimates the rape of female slaves by white owners. She will do everything she can to combat this oppressive system; for example, she is introduced as a woman "held in durance vile by her reckless and selfish master, who had tried in vain to drag her down to his own low level of sin and shame" (38–39). Tom's description a few pages later makes clear that Iola is actively battling with her white master: "One day when he com'd down to breakfas', he chucked her under de chin, an' tried to put his arm roun' her waist. But she jis' frew it off like a chunk ob fire.

She looked like a snake had bit her. Her eyes fairly spit fire. Her face got red ez blood, an' den she turned so pale I thought she war gwine to faint, but she didn't, an' I yered her say, 'I'll die fust' " (41). This passage is suggestive in the congruence of its language with that of battle: the owner strikes a blow; Iola ignites like "fire" and throws it off; and she heroically declares that she would "die fust," as though she were a soldier preparing for death. As the Confederate and Union armies do battle, then, Iola and her white master engage in their own war, no less ferocious for being outside the perimeters of official combat.

If interracial rape marks the endpoint on this spectrum of war, Harper suggests that interracial marriages in a context of slavery mark a potential conflict only slightly less oppressive. Iola's parents, Marie and Eugene, came together voluntarily in an interracial union in which there is no suggestion of rape. When they first marry, Iola's mother is overjoyed: "Instead of being a lonely slave girl, with the fatal dower of beauty, liable to be bought and sold, exchanged and bartered, she was to be the wife of a wealthy planter; a man in whose honor she could confide, and on whose love she could lean" (74–75). Yet the contrast between slave and wife is not absolute, since Marie's acquiescence in the life of a planter's wife, and her willingness to "lean" on Eugene, are ultimately disastrous strategies. After Eugene's death, she is at the mercy of his cousin, and she learns too late that the slave system exercises an all-powerful hold on black women, even though they may hope to insulate themselves from it. Marie's story, in other words, illustrates the risks of not doing battle with the slave system—an attitude exemplified in the indifference of her response to the declared war: " 'A civil war?' exclaimed Marie, with an air of astonishment. 'A civil war about what?' " (87).

Iola, of course, is the result of this marriage: as she fights her own battles against rape, her position as a mulatta marks the contradictions inherent in interracial arrangements like that of her parents. Yet Iola's role is not simply to express the effects of interracial conflicts on the next generation; in a transformation of the conventional topos of the "tragic mulatta," the figure of the woman of mixed-race origin here generates its own separate set of "civil wars."[20] Iola, like her entire family, is light-skinned enough to pass for white; and after she is freed from her war against rape, her next activity—nursing in the Union hospital—coincides with decisions about "passing." Puzzled, Dr. Gresham observes her: "She is one of the most refined and lady-like women I ever saw. . . . Her accent is slightly Southern, but her manner is Northern. . . . I cannot understand how a Southern lady, whose education and manners stamp her as a woman of fine culture and good breeding, could consent to occupy the position she so faithfully holds. It is a mystery I cannot solve" (57). Gresham's comment, which serves ironically to explode the concept of "good breeding," places Iola in an ambiguous position. She appears, at this moment, similar to a Northern lady: she has been at a Northern school, is deeply opposed to slavery, and is now working for the Union army. Yet her accent is "slightly Southern," and her past links her to a succession of Southern ladies, from her mother—a plantation mistress, if a reluctant one—to "ole Miss," who separated Robert from his mother, and to a woman identified as "ole Gundover's wife," in Uncle Daniel's words "de meanest woman dat I eber did see" (27). Iola's wartime experience thus becomes an expression of the conflicts at work in a position of racial liminality.

While Gresham's description suggests that Iola is caught between two racial communities, his marriage proposal also prompts her to make a decision about gender roles. To the doctor, wartime is a brutal setting that makes him want to rescue Iola: "All the manhood and chivalry of his nature rose in her behalf" (59). But the terms of chivalric romance were Marie Leroy's, who looked for a man "on whose love she could lean." Iola rejects these terms, as well as the racial assimilation Gresham represents. Her "civil war" culminates in a victory over the impulse to pass for white and to assimilate to the chivalric, inegalitarian model of marriage that Gresham represents.

If the Civil War prompts civil wars within Iola, then national Reconstruction also represents the reconstruction of her subjectivity as an adult black woman. After the war, Iola refuses a second proposal from Gresham, explaining: "I intend spending my future among the colored people of the South" (234). This allegiance to the black community entails a clear rejection of the role of the white woman, particularly the Southern lady, a refusal that echoes indirectly in Aunt Linda's description of the war: "I wanted ter re'lize I war free, an' I couldn't, tell I got out er de sight and soun' ob ole Miss" (154). Iola further realizes her own distance from "ole Miss" in her friendship with Lucille, a dark-skinned black woman to whom, as sister-in-law, she eventually becomes literal kin.

Lucille, who is "grand, brave, intellectual, and religious" (242), gestures, in addition, to a new configuration of gender roles, and specifically to a model of egalitarian relationships within marriage. Harper is concerned to suggest that gender conflict is not simply an intensified strain of black/white relations; it is its own axis of struggle, circulating within white and black communities. Thus the war frames gender conflicts between white characters and—more important for the novel's focus— gender disputes within black partnerships. As with Aunt Linda's conflict with "ole Miss," the folk community of the novel most overtly enacts such dynamics. Uncle Daniel, a black slave, says of women, "I sometimes think de wuss you treats dem de better dey likes you" (20); after the war's end, Aunt Linda describes a conflict with her husband John in which he "didn't want to let on his wife knowed more dan he did, an' dat he war ruled ober by a woman" (155). Iola, for her part, undergoes a transformation from the "gentle ministrations" of wartime nursing to an assertive mode during Reconstruction that has specific implications for gender relations: "I have a theory that every woman ought to know how to earn her own living" (205).

When Iola does accept a marriage proposal, she chooses Dr. Latimer, who is also light-skinned and middle-class. He woos her with the lines "To prove myself thy lover / I'd face a world in arms"; to which she responds, "And prove a good soldier . . . when there is no battle to fight" (268–69). The military metaphors that structure this language come from the conventions of love poetry, but they are significant nonetheless, since they suggest that the negotiation of this marriage as a partnership is the last civil war Iola will have to face. When Latimer "[pours] into her ears words eloquent with love and tenderness" (270), to Iola's ears this love accommodates a vision of shared political activity. Together they will battle on behalf of the race: "Grand and noble purposes were lighting up their lives; and they esteemed it a blessed privilege to stand on the threshold of a new era and labor for those who had passed from the old oligarchy of slavery into the new commonwealth of freedom" (271).

For all the struggles from which Iola emerges triumphant in her narrative of self-formation, however, there are also some battles "lost." In our first glimpse of Iola, amid early wartime, she is rebellious—in Tom Anderson's word, a "spitfire." Yet postwar, her brother is reunited with a very different sister:

> "Why, Iola," said Harry, "you used to be the most harum-scarum girl I ever knew—laughing, dancing, and singing from morning to night."
> "Yes, I remember," said Iola. "It all comes back to me like a dream. Oh, mamma! I have passed through a fiery ordeal of suffering since then. But it is useless . . . to brood over the past." (195)

Iola's wartime years coincide with a transition between two warring conceptions of behavior: a "harum-scarum" girlhood and a more sedate, "mature" womanhood. As an adult, she will now take her place "going to teach in the Sunday-school, help in the church, hold mothers' meetings to help these boys and girls to grow up to be good men and women" (276). Iola's adult self, in other words, accords far more with the standards of middle-class white womanhood than with any notion of a rebellious black community. Her war of self-formation is in a further sense a "civil" one: she will be as courteous, polite, and gracious as the adjective implies.

This civility extends even further, both to the novel's selective focus upon particular years of the war and, by implication, to the contemporary audience reading *Iola Leroy* itself. *Iola Leroy* concentrates only on the later years of the Civil War, *after* the Union army has begun to welcome black soldiers. This focus conveniently evades the issue of overt, programmatic racism within the Union army and among its white supporters—the same supporters who might now comprise part of the audience for *Iola Leroy*, along with the novel's stated readership among black communities, and particularly black churches.[21] *Iola Leroy*'s evasiveness suggests the novel's negotiation of a complex set of audience expectations. Barbara Christian has argued, for example, that Harper's characterization of Iola responds not only to the needs of an emerging black readership, but also to the demands of a white audience looking for an accessible heroine, preferably a virtuous, refined, light-skinned mulatta.[22] A civil audience, that is, wanted reminders of the successful integration of the army, not of the army's hypocritical exclusion of those black soldiers whom it was ostensibly fighting to free. A civil audience, we may infer, wanted a civil heroine who stressed black education and employment—not one who advocated open insurrection.

Civil war, then, provides a metaphoric figure for internal division in *Iola Leroy*, one whose possibilities the novel exploits in several directions. Iola overtly negotiates many of the internal conflicts that the war represents, particularly those over racial identification and the assumption of gender roles; in these battles she appears as a figure of radical self-assertion. At the same time, however, this transformation has its limits. For with a female protagonist restrained from earlier rebellion, in a war setting purged of its earlier racism, the novel would seem to construct a civil Civil War indeed.

■■■

This interpretation of the way in which the Civil War functions in *Iola Leroy*—as a complex metaphor for struggles about identity—is, however, itself incomplete. For it is crucial to understand that by the time Harper wrote *Iola Leroy* the idea of individual development was already in use to discuss the war, in an intermingling of "historical" and "fictional" registers with immediate consequences for race and gender relations in the postwar nation. In this context, *Iola Leroy*'s plots not only suggest the way history may serve as metaphor for fiction but exemplify—and comment critically upon—this metaphoric transfer in reverse.

In descriptions of war, Elaine Scarry notes, "Each of the two armies periodically becomes a single embodied combatant."[23] While this figurative translation may operate in a variety of ways, what is most relevant in the context of *Iola Leroy* is the extent to which political discourse about the Civil War depicted two bodies that were marked both racially and sexually in a set of distinctions adapted from antebellum political discourse. Before the war, for example, many Northerners viewed the South as radically "other," both feminizing the region and viewing it as "black."[24] Once the war began, these existing rhetorical modes were adapted to the actions of the regional armies with results that were most obvious in terms of gender. As Kathleen Diffley explains, "the operative technique was to realign a sexually coded language with the military opposition the war brought about. The resulting figures of a feminine South, a masculine North, and the threat of violence in their relations shaped histories as early as 1866."[25] This configuration varied, of course, by region: the casting of the South as a woman raped by war, for example, reflected Southern outrage at Sherman's march, an event whose literal progress through Southern homes entrusted to women became the metaphoric epitome of male invasion.

The postwar consequences of such scenarios were profound. In particular, Southern constructions of the war as the "rape of the South" took on explicit force in the context of virulent Southern racism at the turn of the century, when they served to authorize accusations of interracial rape against black men and subsequent lynchings. A variety of Southern authors in this period reinforced the ideological circuitry of this metaphoric transfer, whereby the projection of rapaciousness onto the "male" North became transmuted, more locally, into the accusation of rape against the black man. Bestsellers such as Thomas Nelson Page's

Red Rock (1898) and Thomas Dixon's *The Clansman* (1905), for example, effectively evoked and fostered turn-of-the-century Southern outrage at interracial rape by foregrounding the heroic, newly reempowered Southern white man in his struggle against the hypersexual, evil black villain.[26] This ideological framework reached its height in D. W. Griffith's film adaptation of Dixon's *Clansman, The Birth of a Nation* (1915), which translated from written text to visual spectacle the alignment of race, rape, war, and revenge that had been in circulation since the birth of the Ku Klux Klan in the 1860s. Indeed, *Birth of a Nation* merits close examination here, for it marks the apex of the social anxieties against which antilynching activist Frances Harper, writing *Iola Leroy* in the 1890s, situated herself and her text.

Birth of a Nation is the most fully elaborated, starkly realized, and popularly successful example of a set of postwar representational configurations involving race, gender, violence, and rape. The film chronicles the war and early years of Reconstruction through a focus on two families—the Northern Stonemans and Southern Camerons—beginning in the antebellum era, during which friendships between the families flourish. When the war begins, both families send boys to fight while the women remain tearfully at home. In a juxtaposition of title and text, the film constructs the war as a Northern rape of the South: as Northern soldiers invade the Carolina town of the Camerons, for example, one title announces, "While women and children weep, a great conqueror marches to the sea," and another bemoans the "torch of war against the breast of Atlanta." The second half of *Birth of a Nation* realigns this motif of rape and feminization in racial terms. The film depicts the rapid accession of male ex-slaves to political positions after the war, presenting black male rapists as the inevitable consequence of this development, and proposing to fight interracial rape with a new organization, the Ku Klux Klan, which will save "the South from anarchy, but not without the shedding of more blood than was spilled at Gettysburg." With the "anarchy" in question the rape of Southern white women, the narrative moves from literal rape threats against specific women to a climactic metaphoric rape sequence in which a group of black men struggle to batter down the door of a small cabin, inside which Southern whites—male and female—cower fearfully. Arriving just in time to rescue the whites, the Klan acts as savior. The Klan's triumph at the moment of this second "rape" thus enables the film to fantasize the South—specifically, Southern white men—winning the war it had lost once before.[27]

Like *Birth of a Nation* and much of the earlier Klan propaganda of the Reconstruction Era, *Iola Leroy* intertwines the themes of war and rape. But Harper posits precisely opposite configurations of literal and metaphoric, white and black, and male and female. Griffith's film presents rape as an act metaphorically perpetrated upon the entire white South during the war. Harper, by contrast, foregrounds rape as a literal structure of oppression underpinning the antebellum South. In the novel's terms, the arrival of the Union army signals the North's decision to take up institutionally the battle that black women have already been fighting against rape; as Iola describes her rescue by the army, "The last man in whose clutches I found myself was mean, brutal, and cruel. I was in his power when the Union army came into C——" (196). The war signals that the already ongoing battle between white men and black women is a just one: the "Union had snapped asunder because it lacked the cohesion of justice" (24).

Harper also combats the other half of this equation—the supposed black rapist of the Reconstruction South—by contrasting the image of the antebellum white rapist with that of the novel's black men, for whom the war years bring new opportunities to forge a positive masculine identity. Although "fragile women and helpless children were left on the plantations," the slaves "refrained from violence" (9). A man like Robert waits "eagerly and hopefully his chance to join the Union army," "ready and willing to do anything required of him by which he could earn his freedom and prove his manhood" (36). Harry too is "in the flush of his early manhood" (127) when he enlists. This model of manhood, utterly opposed to the idea of rape, carries over into the Reconstruction era, when Robert wants "the young folks to keep their brains clear, and their right arms strong, to fight the battles of life manfully" (170). Dr. Latimer declares the postwar importance of having "our boys . . . grow up manly citizens" (242), linking this goal to their refusal to strew flowers before Jefferson Davis. The war thus brings not a feminized South, but a training in manhood, one inextricable from the figure of an empowered black woman.

In this context, Reconstruction does appear as a new war, but it is continuous with the values of the Civil War, not—as in the cultural account that Griffith helped to crystallize—an antagonistic reenactment of it. After the war, Gresham describes the arrival of "numbers of excellent and superior women . . . from the North to engage as teachers of the freed people" (145); a page later these women are "a new army that had come with an invasion of ideas" (146). Attending a church meeting, an older black woman recounts how her children were separated from her under slavery, and declares, "I'm on my solemn march to glory" (180). This army expands to include Harry, who "joined the new army of Northern teachers" (192), and other workers in the public sphere, including Iola who, when she begins an office job, "at last found a place in the great army of bread-winners" (211). In contrast to Griffith's army-like Klan, which stands as antagonist to the earlier Civil War, Harper presents a "great army" of united black men and women whose struggles emerge organically from not one but two earlier wars—their antebellum struggles of resistance to slavery and the official battles of the Civil War itself.

As Harper inverts the Southern strategy of using rape plots for racist and misogynist ends, her marriage plots also rework Northern visions of the war. Conventionally in such plots, the war was framed as a thwarted romance between white protagonists; black characters appeared only in smaller roles that generally conformed to racist stereotypes. Usually, the suitor was Northern and male; the wooed, Southern and female. The Northern victory at the end of the war signalled a happy marriage, with the marital union standing in for the newly forged re-Union of the nation. The subsuming of the South into the "national Union" neatly paralleled that of wife into her husband, as the head of both Unions—marital and national—was male. For the woman in this Northern scenario, the overlay of marital metaphor onto regional allegory meant that "Miss South," as it were, became "Mrs. United States."[28]

Iola Leroy initially offers such a plot: the marriage proposal of Dr. Gresham, a Northerner, to the Southern Iola. But the novel twice refuses to fulfill this plot. Harper does not want to reject the triumph of the Northern antislavery forces that such plots inscribe; she stands firmly on the side of the abolitionism of the North. However, she reworks these plots to reject their insistent white and male bias. The marriages she foregrounds are those of two black couples: Iola and Latimer, and Harry and Lucille. These unions, moreover, confuse any straightforward alignment of Northern with male: Iola and Harry are Southerners who go North and return South, while Latimer and Lucille are Northerners who go South. Both couples ultimately return to North Carolina rather than stay in the North. And both feature women who remain relatively autonomous rather than submit to male authority.

In fact, the very center of the reconstructed nation will be, in Rev.

Eustace's words, a "union of women with the warmest hearts and clearest brains" (254). The phrase "union of women" suggests the extent to which the novel resists the conventional dynamics of war metaphor. For national union, like marital control, was traditionally vested in the "male" term ("North" or "husband") which then subsumed its "female" term ("South" or "wife"). Instead, in *Iola Leroy* women not only remain in the (marital and national) union: they form its core "union of women." As it explicitly challenges racist formulations like Griffith's, the novel also carefully rewrites the gender terms of a more sympathetic Northern discourse.

War-formation and self-formation, then, stand in a dialectical relation in *Iola Leroy*. Civil war operates not only as historical ground but as metaphorical figure in the novel, serving as a defining image of Iola's development throughout—from her resistance to rape at the start of the war itself through her happy marriage at its end. But these fictional rape and marriage plots themselves reshape cultural representations of the war already in place at the time, representations that had served to construct this most "historical" of events in sharply literary terms from the outset. Harper, that is, does not simply use history to write fiction; she exposes history as fiction, and reshapes its ideological contours with her own fictional plots.

■ ■ ■

In his survey of American war literature, David Lundberg begins by asking, "What would our literary heritage be without *The Red Badge of Courage* (1895), *A Farewell to Arms* (1929), or *The Naked and the Dead* (1948)?"[29] Lundberg asks this question rhetorically, anticipating that his readers share a set of assumptions that privilege a white patrilineal genealogy (Crane, Hemingway, Mailer) as representative of *the* war experience. By contrast, *Iola Leroy* takes this question seriously, and not only asks what an American literary heritage would be *with* other texts but also challenges the mimetic claims and narrative forms of the war plot. Harper's novel foregrounds the black experience of the war and in so doing turns war itself into an event shaped by the black family—particularly the black mother. Further, this conjunction of war and women in *Iola Leroy* gives new resonance to the idea of "civil war," identifying a variety of civil-war conflicts that might shape black women's subjectivity at the same time that it uses the subject-formations of individual characters to rewrite the fictional construction of the Civil War itself.

The implications of Harper's wartime fiction continue to echo in twentieth-century American Civil War fictional texts. Margaret Walker's *Jubilee*, for example, offers a panoramic recreation of black experiences of the war, while Rosellen Brown's novel and June Jordan's autobiographical essay, both entitled "Civil Wars," employ the concept of internal conflict to explore a range of issues, including race, gender, and civility itself.[30] Working outward from Harper's novel, we might construct an alternative genealogy—matrilineal and multiracial—of Civil War texts, one that provides a striking contrast to the cultural myopia whereby, as Richard Slotkin puts it, "To the extent that our memory of the Civil War is shaped by literary and cinematic fiction, the war is still understood as a moral victory for 'Old South' values and principles."[31] This more capacious literary landscape would both reflect and foster new perspectives on the literature of the Civil War, perspectives that not only bring new texts to visibility but rethink the larger frameworks of analysis that have shaped critical understanding of the war.

As it transforms the literary legacy of the Civil War, this interpretation of *Iola Leroy* intervenes as well in the ongoing reexamination of the American literary canon as a whole. Feminist and African American critiques have formed two strategies for this reassessment, but they have all too often proceeded separately. By contrast, *Iola Leroy* not only stands as an important work in emergent genealogies of writing by women and by African Americans but also offers within its plots a model for the complex interrelation between these genealogies. The portrait that emerges from the novel confirms the centrality of both gender and race as axes of power relations, suggesting the ways in which these paradigms for critical interpretation may be in civil war with each other—as frequent combatants, but also inexorable partners, in the reconstruction of American literary history.

If Harper's *Iola Leroy* illuminates conflicts on the "homefront" of revisionary critique, it also reminds us of the consequences of debates over literature as a whole, both within and outside the academy. In a recent essay, Toni Morrison suggestively frames canon debates in military language:

> I planned to call this paper "Canon Fodder," because the terms put me in mind of a kind of trained muscular response that appears to be on display in some areas of the recent canon debate. . . . What is astonishing in the contemporary debate is not the resistance to displacement of works or to the expansion of genre within it, but the virulent passion

that accompanies this resistance and, more importantly, the quality of its defense weaponry. The guns are very big; the trigger-fingers quick.[32]

Morrison's imagery of "guns" and "trigger-fingers" usefully reminds us that to discuss *Iola Leroy* at all is to intervene in a contemporary struggle in which domestic novels of war are part of a domestic "war" over novels. *Iola Leroy*'s own interrogation of the relation between (female) homefront and (male) battlefront, moreover, helps us to see the ideological constructions uneasily at work in contemporary attacks on literary studies, whereby the university Department of English—normally a feminized realm of "unimportant" domestic affairs—is deemed worthy of the masculine attention ordinarily accorded important foreign policy; thus strenuously, if improbably, transformed into a site for civil war, the English Department becomes an appropriate target for the full assault wartime enemies merit. And finally, this imagery of "defense weaponry" is not simply metaphoric, as Frances Harper, both novelist and activist, clearly realized. As long as governments continue to mobilize public support through elaborate scenarios of rape and revenge—narratives dragged into service for foreign wars and domestic reelection campaigns alike—then "canon fodder" will echo doubly, on literal as well as literary battlefields. In this context too, *Iola Leroy* offers a particularly salient exploration of the process whereby "literary" and "political" discourse continue to make and unmake one another, in an ongoing battle—at once internecine and uncivil—of warring fictions.

Notes

For their helpful comments on earlier drafts of this essay, I would like to thank Elizabeth Abel, William A. Cohen, Laura Green, Carolyn Porter, Mary Ryan, Susan Schweik, and Eric Sundquist.

1   Edmund Wilson, *Patriotic Gore: Studies in the Literature of the American Civil War* (New York: Oxford Univ. Press, 1962); Daniel Aaron, *The Unwritten War: American Writers and the Civil War* (New York: Knopf, 1973). On the issue of race, see Aaron: "A striking feature of the literature I have mentioned in this book is its comparative inattention to what many believe to be the central issue of the War—the Negro" (332). For an introduction to Civil War fiction, see Robert Lively, *Fiction Fights the Civil War: An Unfinished Chapter in the Literary History of the American People* (Chapel Hill:

Univ. of North Carolina Press, 1957); and Albert J. Menendez, *Civil War Novels: An Annotated Bibliography* (New York: Garland, 1986). The figure of two thousand novels is from Helen Taylor, *Scarlett's Women: "Gone With the Wind" and Its Female Fans* (New Brunswick: Rutgers Univ. Press, 1989), 202.

2   David Lundberg, "The American Literature of War: The Civil War, World War I, and World War II," *American Quarterly* 36 (1984): 376.

3   Hazel V. Carby, Introduction, *Iola Leroy; or, Shadows Uplifted* (Boston: Beacon, 1907), xvii; see also Carby, *Reconstructing Womanhood: The Emergence of the Afro-American Woman Novelist* (New York: Oxford Univ. Press, 1987), 62–94. For other recent readings of the novel, see Elizabeth Ammons, "Stowe's Dream of the Mother-Savior: *Uncle Tom's Cabin* and American Women Writers Before the 1920s," in *New Essays on Uncle Tom's Cabin*, ed. Eric Sundquist (New York: Cambridge Univ. Press, 1986), 155–95; Barbara Christian, *Black Feminist Criticism: Perspectives on Black Women Writers* (New York: Pergamon, 1985), 165–70, and *Black Women Novelists: The Development of a Tradition, 1892–1976* (Westport, Conn.: Greenwood, 1980), 3–5, 25–31; Marilyn Elkins, "Reading Beyond the Conventions: A Look at Frances E. W. Harper's *Iola Leroy, or Shadows Uplifted*," *American Literary Realism* 22 (Winter 1990): 44–53; Vashti Lewis, "The Near-White Female in Frances Ellen Harper's *Iola Leroy*: Public Image Versus Private Reality," *Phylon* 45 (1985): 314–22; Deborah McDowell, "'The Changing Same': Generational Connections and Black Women Novelists," *New Literary History* 18 (Winter 1989): 281–302; Claudia Tate, "Allegories of Black Female Desire; or, Rereading Nineteenth-Century Sentimental Narratives of Black Female Authority," in *Changing Our Own Words: Essays on Criticism, Theory and Writing by Black Women*, ed. Cheryl A. Wall (New Brunswick: Rutgers Univ. Press, 1989), 98–126; and Mary Helen Washington, *Invented Lives: Narratives of Black Women Writers* (New York: Anchor/Doubleday, 1987), 73–86. See also the introductions by Hazel Carby and Frances Smith Foster to the editions of the novel published respectively by Beacon Press (1987) and, in the Schomburg Library of Nineteenth-Century Black Women Writers, by Oxford Univ. Press (1988). For a recent overview of Harper's life and career, see Frances Smith Foster's introduction to *A Brighter Coming Day: A Frances Ellen Watkins Harper Reader* (New York: Feminist Press, 1990), 3–40.

4   For a summary of the impact of the war, see Eric Foner, *Reconstruction: America's Unfinished Revolution, 1863–1877* (New York: Harper & Row, 1987), 1–34.

5   See *Freedom: A Documentary History of Emancipation, 1861–67. Series II: The Black Military Experience*, ed. Ira Berlin, Joseph P. Reidy, and Leslie S. Rowland (New York: Cambridge Univ. Press, 1982); statistical information is discussed on 14.

6 Jacqueline Jones, *Labor of Love, Labor of Sorrow: Black Women, Work, and the Family, from Slavery to the Present* (New York: Basic, 1985), 47.

7 Jones, 51.

8 On Harriet Tubman, see *Black Women in White America: A Documentary History*, ed. Gerda Lerner (New York: Pantheon, 1972), 326–29; for a range of black commentary about the war, see *Black Writers and the American Civil War*, ed. Richard A. Long (Secaucus, N.J.: Blue and Grey Press, 1988).

9 Susie King Taylor, *A Black Woman's Civil War Memoirs: Reminiscences of My Life in Camp With the 33rd U.S. Colored Troops, Late 1st South Carolina Volunteers*, ed. Patricia Romero (New York: Markus Wiener, 1988), 61. All subsequent quotations will be taken from this edition; page numbers appear parenthetically in the text.

10 Kathleen Diffley, "Where My Heart is Turning Ever: Civil War Stories and National Stability from Fort Sumter to the Centennial," *American Literary History* 2 (1990): 627–58, esp. 630. See also Drew Gilpin Faust, "Altars of Sacrifice: Confederate Women and the Narratives of War," *Journal of American History* 76 (1990): 1200–28; and Jane Schultz, "Mute Fury: Southern Women's Diaries of Sherman's March to the Sea, 1864–65," in *Arms and the Woman: War, Gender and Literary Representation*, ed. Helen M. Cooper, Adrienne Auslander Munich, and Susan Merrill Squier (Chapel Hill: Univ. of North Carolina Press, 1989), 59–79. For a full-length study that examines a range of ways women authors have reshaped conventional conceptions of the "homefront," see Susan Schweik, *A Gulf So Deeply Cut: American Women Poets and the Second World War* (Madison: Univ. of Wisconsin Press, 1991).

11 I borrow the phrase "maternal and military service" from Nancy Huston, "The Matrix of War: Mothers and Heroes," in *The Female Body in Western Culture: Contemporary Perspectives*, ed. Susan Suleiman (Cambridge: Harvard Univ. Press, 1985), 119.

12 Lewis suggests an affinity between Iola Leroy and Susie King Taylor in "The Near-White Female," 319.

13 Bernard Bell, *The Afro-American Novel and Its Traditions* (Amherst: Univ. of Massachusetts Press, 1987), 57, notes the novel's pioneering status. On the response to black soldiers in the Union army, see *Freedom: A Documentary History*, ed. Berlin, Reidy, and Rowland; and Forrest G. Wood, *Black Scare: The Racist Response to Emancipation and Reconstruction* (Berkeley: Univ. of California Press, 1968), 40–52.

14 See David W. Blight, "'For Something Beyond the Battlefield': Frederick Douglass and the Struggle for the Memory of the Civil War," *Journal of American History* 75 (March 1989): 1156–78.

15 Frances Harper, *Iola Leroy; or, Shadows Uplifted* (Oxford: Oxford Univ. Press, 1988), ed. Frances Smith Foster, 46, 53. All subsequent quotations will be taken from this edition; page numbers appear parenthetically in the text.

16   Ammons, "Stowe's Dream of the Mother Savior," 176–77.

17   Ann Douglas Wood, "The War Within a War: Women Nurses in the Union Army," *Civil War History* 18 (1972): 206.

18   Hortense Spillers, "Mama's Baby, Papa's Maybe: An American Grammar Book," *Diacritics* 17 (Summer 1987): 74.

19   Margaret Higonnet, "Civil Wars and Sexual Territories," in *Arms and the Woman*, 80–81, 87, 81.

20   I draw here on Carby's formulation that "the mulatto, as narrative figure, has two primary functions: as a vehicle for an exploration of the relationship between the races and, at the same time, an expression of the relationship between the races" (*Reconstructing Womanhood*, 89). For discussion of the figure of the "tragic mulatta," see Judith R. Berzon, *Neither White Nor Black: The Mulatto Character in American Fiction* (New York: New York Univ. Press, 1978), 99–116.

21   See William Still's original introduction to the novel: "Doubtless the thousands of colored Sunday-schools in the South, in casting about for an interesting, moral story-book . . . will not be content to be without *Iola Leroy*" (3). Harper's own endnote declares the novel's mission as awakening "in the hearts of our countrymen a stronger sense of justice" and inspiring "the children of those upon whose brows God has poured the chrism of that new era" (282).

22   Christian, *Black Feminist Criticism*, 166–70. For related discussions of the novel's concessions to genre and audience, see McDowell, " 'The Changing Same,' " and Tate, "Allegories of Black Female Desire." McDowell notes that Iola "comes to resemble a human being less and less and a saint more and more" (286); Tate concedes that novels like *Iola Leroy* seem "overly preoccupied with middle-class propriety, civility, domesticity, and commodity consumption," but suggests that this focus may serve to "call deliberate attention to the fact that black people were not categorically poor" (106–07).

23   Elaine Scarry, *The Body in Pain: The Making and Unmaking of the World* (New York: Oxford Univ. Press, 1985), 70. For a recent discussion of *The Body in Pain* in relation to the Civil War, see Timothy Sweet, *Traces of War: Poetry, Photography, and the Crisis of the Union* (Baltimore: Johns Hopkins Univ. Press, 1990).

24   See Carolyn Porter, "Social Discourse and Nonfictional Prose," *Columbia Literary History of the United States*, ed. Emory Elliott (New York: Columbia Univ. Press, 1988), 354–57.

25   Kathleen Diffley, "The Roots of Tara: Making War Civil," *American Quarterly* 36 (1984): 359. For discussion of a variety of gender implications of postwar relations between North and South, see Nina Silber, *The Romance of Reunion: Northern Images of the South, 1865–1900* (Ph.D. diss., Univ. of California, Berkeley, 1989).

26   On Page and Dixon, see respectively Lawrence J. Friedman, *The White Savage: Racial Fantasies in the Postbellum South* (Englewood Cliffs, N.J.:

Prentice-Hall, 1970), 62–76; and James Kinney, "The Rhetoric of Racism: Thomas Dixon and the 'Damned Black Beast,'" *American Literary Realism* 15 (Autumn 1982): 145–54. On the nexus of race and rape in this era, see also Jacqueline Dowd Hall, "'The Mind That Burns In Each Body': Women, Rape, and Racial Violence," in *Powers of Desire: The Politics of Sexuality*, ed. Ann Snitow, Christine Stansell, and Sharon Thompson (New York: Monthly Review Press, 1983), 328–49.

27 For a discussion of *Birth of a Nation*, see Michael Rogin, "'The Sword Became a Flashing Vision': D. W. Griffith's *The Birth of a Nation*," *Representations* 9 (Winter 1985): 150–95. For an overview of the use of the Civil War in early film, see Evelyn Ehrlich, "The Civil War in Early Film: Origin and Development of a Genre," *Southern Quarterly* 19 (Spring–Summer 1981): 70–82.

28 For a summary of these Civil War marriage plots, see Diffley, "The Roots of Tara," 366–68; detailed discussion is provided in Silber, *The Romance of Reunion*. On the specific racial implications of these works, see Kenneth T. Rainey, "Race and Reunion in Nineteenth-Century Reconciliation Drama," *American Transcendental Quarterly* 2 (June 1988): 155–69.

29 Lundberg, "American Literature of War," 373.

30 Margaret Walker, *Jubilee* (New York. Bantam, 1966); Rosellen Brown, *Civil Wars* (New York: Viking Penguin, 1984); June Jordan, "Civil Wars," in *Civil Wars* (Boston: Beacon, 1981), 177–88.

31 Richard Slotkin, "'What Shall Men Remember?': Recent Work on the Civil War," *American Literary History* 3 (1991): 132.

32 Toni Morrison, "Unspeakable Things Unspoken: The Afro-American Presence in American Literature," *Michigan Quarterly Review* 28 (Winter 1989): 1, 5.

Michele A. Birnbaum   "Alien Hands": Kate Chopin and the Colonization of Race

> What intellectual feats had to be performed by the author or
> his critic to erase me from a society seething with my pres-
> ence . . . ?—Toni Morrison

> All along the white beach, up and down, there was no living
> thing in sight.—Kate Chopin

Upon one of the several literal and figurative "awak-
enings" in Kate Chopin's *The Awakening* (1899), Edna Pontellier rouses
herself from a "delicious, grotesque, impossible dream to feel again the
realities pressing into her soul."[1] These waking realities—motherhood,
marriage, Victorian mores—leave Edna heavy-lidded; in the glare of
domestic, religious, and social conventions, she is repeatedly "overcome"
(47, 82, 83) and "overtake[n]" (78) by "sleep" and "drowsiness" (82).
Her husband attempts to force her "thoroughly awake" by reproaching
her with "her habitual neglect of the children" (48), but in the home, as
in church (82), she feels pressed into slumber. Although Edna is touted
as a woman who "refuses to be caged by married and domestic life and
claims for herself moral and erotic freedom,"[2] her feminine liberation is
narcoleptic, a movement in and out of consciousness.

Because the world seems too much with Edna, critics have aligned
Chopin's work with transcontinental "New Woman fiction" preoccupied
with the fin de siècle "desire to throw identity away and live beyond culture."[3] Hence Edna's dozing is seen as an attempt to dispose of "that
fictitious self,"[4] and her ennui as a kind of out-of-culture experience.
The result of such an alignment is the critical reinscription of a traditionally Western conceptual duel (and duality) of self against culture, and

the idealization of the self-sufficient individual.[5] Sandra Gilbert, for instance, implicitly endorses the myth of autonomy by arguing that Chopin institutes a "feminist myth of Aphrodite/Venus as an alternative to the patriarchal myth of Jesus."[6] Just as Venus springs fully formed from the waves, so Edna appears above but not of culture. Represented as a self-made woman and placed in the tradition of an American Adam/Eve, Edna inherits the legacy of what Quentin Anderson termed the imperial self.[7] This characterization, however, tends to preempt investigation of the cultural and, I wish to argue, specifically colonial production of white female selfhood and sexuality in the novel.

In her critical revision of Anderson, Wai-chee Dimock suggests that the imperial self is not a matter of personal character but rather a function of national culture. And as such, the imperial self is also an imperialist: "'imperial' not only in consciousness but in conduct. . . . At once autonomous and impregnable . . . the imperial self is quite literally empire-like, his province akin to national polity."[8] Within this expansionist discourse, the imperial subject is avaricious, colonizing, annexing. To be the "soul that dares and defies," Mlle. Reisz in *The Awakening* points out, "includes much," for "one must possess many gifts—absolute gifts—which have not been acquired by one's own effort" (115). In other words, the independent self cannot acknowledge receipt of gifts it must appear to own a priori; individuality must be a sufficiency unto itself even as it is acquisitive. It is in this context that I wish to interrogate the cultural and racial boundaries of Edna's "solitary soul," for as the "regal woman, the one who rules, who looks on, who stands alone" (145), her sovereignty has gone unimpeached.

Although Edna appears to be the epitome of discrete selfhood—insisting that her sexual "awakening" is the result of "no external" source (79), that she is "self-contained" and feels as though she walks "unguided" (61)—she declares in the same breath that neither does her restlessness derive from any source "within" (79). Rather, she provocatively suggests that she "had placed herself in alien hands for direction" (79). It is this alien touch, a foreign presence that again and again "overcomes" Edna, which goes unnoticed in critical projects that focus only on *The Awakening*'s movements "beyond culture." It did not go unnoticed, however, by Chopin's contemporaries, who commented frequently on her representation of "these semi-aliens,"[9] the diverse residents of Louisiana, remarking that her characters are an "exotic, not-quite-American species."[10] For Chopin and her readers, there were more compelling images than

Aphrodite—no less mythic and much closer to home—in the historical racial types with which she was quite familiar. In other words, Aphrodite was in Chopin's own backyard, for those of the "warmer" races had been long considered "well-vers'd in Venus' school."[11]

Edna locates in racial and ethnic Others a territory necessary for a liberating alterity: in their difference, she finds herself. The white Catholic Creole society is the most apparent but not the only influence upon Edna (a Protestant Kentuckian). Although Edna admits that she is initially attracted to the "excessive physical charm of the Creole" (57) and to the caresses of Mme. Ratignolle in particular, Creole women in *The Awakening* are also described as emphatically chaste. Edna calls Mme. Ratignolle a "faultless Madonna" (54), a "sensuous Madonna" (55), whose "lofty chastity" is in "Creole women . . . inborn and unmistakable" (53). Instead, Edna first discovers the erotic frontiers of the self by exploiting the less visible constructions of sexual difference associated with the blacks, quadroons, and Acadians in the novel.

By returning these repressed Others to considerations of Chopin's possessive individualism, one can better understand Edna's fitful naps. Alternately awake and asleep—sovereign ("unguided" [61]) and subjugated ("overcome" [47])—Chopin's heroine enacts the paradox of the imperial self who appears to rule while being herself ruled. The unbearable contradiction of being both free agent and yet acted upon is characteristic of the colonizer's position. And as the myth of self-authorization must involve the erasure of its own authorizing principle, so must Edna repress that which is both the basis for and a threat to her autonomy. As Albert Memmi argues, the colonizer, unable to accept his or her sovereignty as contingent, must eventually seek to "dismiss [the colonized] from his mind, to imagine the colony without the colonized."[12] In this sense, Edna's sleep is both passive (in its submission to alien influence) and aggressive (in its effective silencing of any conflict within the self). Her paroxysmal sleep can be seen as an unwitting contribution to what George Washington Cable refers to as the "silent South,"[13] part of the collective amnesia regarding the abuses and uses of the color line in the postwar South.

The Erasure of Race

In one sense "alien hands," anatomized and anonymous, simply render domestic services; nameless, speechless, shadowy women manumit

Edna from "responsibility" (79), and, as critics have noted, to that extent her sexual awakening is a white middle-class luxury.[14] But the relation between sex and labor is not simply a matter of economic privilege in *The Awakening*, for Edna's class bias is not her "chief obstacle to freedom of expression."[15] Critics have argued that the hierarchical class relations in the novel limit Chopin's feminist project because they interrupt the circuit of female sympathy for those less privileged; however, it is actually Edna's generalized identification with—rather than her alienation from— the marginalized which both affirms her class position and allows her to critique the sexual constraints associated with it. Equating maternity and slavery, for instance, Edna remarks that her children are her "soul's slavery" (175). Karen Sánchez-Eppler, in her analysis of early- and mid-nineteenth-century feminist abolitionist works, critiques the appropriation of the imagery of slavery for the purposes of feminine liberation, arguing that the strategic likening of white women to black female slaves promoted "the recognition that personhood can be annihilated and a person can be owned, absorbed, and un-named. The irony inherent in such comparisons is that the enlightening and empowering motions of identification that connect feminism and abolitionism come inextricably bound to a process of absorption not unlike the one they expose."[16] Not only does identification elide the particularity of white and black women's exploitations, it actually enables a more subtle form of distancing. By emphasizing and identifying with the subjugation and silencing of the slave, the white woman "asserts her right to speak and act, thus differentiating herself from her brethren in bonds. The bound and silent figure of the slave metaphorically represents the woman's oppression and so grants the white woman access to political discourse denied the slave."[17]

By initiating her escape from gender convention through the rhetoric of racial oppression, Edna reinforces rather than razes class and race differences. In fact, class distinctions reflect the structuring of racial difference which enables Edna's sexual expression. There is no suggestion that she sympathizes with the vague dissatisfaction of the nannies on Grand Isle, who appear "disagreeable and resigned" to their caretaking duties (63).[18] Edna neglects not so much her children, as Mr. Pontellier insists, but the quadroon nursemaid who tends them. When Mr. Pontellier rhetorically asks "if it was not a mother's place to look after children, whose on earth was it?" (48), neither Edna nor her husband seem to recognize the answer revealed by their daily practice: the quadroon's. Not just of no account, but not accounted for, the quadroon cares for the toddlers morning to night. It is she who accompanies the children to Iberville when Edna begins her affair with Arobin, and she who takes them for the day when Edna escapes with Robert to *Chênière Caminada*. Edna's agency is measured against—indeed is contingent upon—the necessarily mute quadroon.

Actually, despite her presence the quadroon is often neither heard nor seen. As Edna awakens, race is rendered narratively invisible.[19] Much of her vacationing on Grand Isle involves the "vacating" of the quadroon, who steps into the narrative ellipses created by Edna's consuming presence. For example, in a rather mundane passage in which the quadroon initially appears, she is inventoried along with the other items of local color as Edna surveys the scene outside her New Orleans house: "The boys were dragging along the banquette a small 'express wagon,' which they had filled with blocks and sticks. The quadroon was following them with little quick steps, having assumed a fictitious animation and alacrity for the occasion. A fruit vendor was crying his wares in the street" (104). Such impressionistic note-taking generates the accumulative description often associated with local color literature. The details are listed rather than ranked, and this leveling of the field of signification (with the concomitant implication of the "objective" reporter) has led critics to call Chopin a "quasi-anthropological" writer with an "almost scientific detachment."[20] Mary Louise Pratt notes that such anthropological portraiture (associated also with travelogue and conquest literatures) "textually produces the Other without an explicit anchoring either in an observing self or in a particular encounter in which contact with the Other takes place";[21] that is, because the perceiving subject is absent (although the authorial and authoritative voice remains), one never witnesses the interaction of "native" and "non-native." Hence, the "neutral" reporting masks the often aggressive physical or textual effacing of the Other.

Similarly, in Edna's account the relationship between the quadroon and herself is made unavailable because it is encoded within established subject positions inherent in the genre. In fact, one begins to understand how the two might function in relation to each other only when Edna recounts her lack of enthusiasm for the world around her, this time ticking off everything but the quadroon: "She felt no interest in anything about her. The street, the children, the fruit vendor, the flowers growing there under her eyes, were all part and parcel of an alien world which had suddenly become antagonistic" (104). When Edna enters the picture, the nanny is, as it were, excused. As an item on a list, the quadroon was never in relief, but her elision in the passage is significant in relation to Edna's entrance and heightened self-consciousness. It is the nanny who first betrays a theatrical estrangement from the world in which she appears; her behavior is "fictitious," she is in but not of the picturesque scene. The quadroon's playacting suggests the kind of epistemological disjunction that provokes Edna's own sense of alienation. In becoming "self-absorbed" (104), Edna absorbs as well the split sensibility of the quadroon. When the narrator comments that Edna was "becoming herself and daily casting aside that *fictitious* self which we assume like a garment with which to appear before the world" (108, emphasis mine), the echo suggests that she has claimed the quadroon's fictive identity even as she rejects the association. Although the quadroon reinspires her childhood sense of the divided self, the "dual life—that outward existence which conforms, the inward life which questions" (57), Edna has no recollection of the quadroon at all as she awakens to her new alien-ated self.[22]

It is no accident that the quadroon is anonymous; she is in effect absented or, perhaps more accurately, displaced by Edna. The "sweet, half-darkness" (102)[23] that Edna seeks is made possible by the partially visible life of the quadroon, a life which may be entered only by remaining unexposed and little understood. After all, Edna does not really want to know the experience of the people of color she sees dimly on the street; her new identity emerges only in the twilight of junctures, in the illicit coupling of her life to theirs. Assuming the "far-away meditative air" (44) which earlier in the novel characterizes her nanny, Edna takes on and takes over the quadroon's distance from the bourgeois life Edna is eager to leave behind. As a "little negro girl" sweeps with "long absent-minded strokes" (79), as "an old *mulatresse*" sleeps "her idle hours away" (163), so Edna is frequently lost in an "inward maze of contemplation or thought" (46) and feels pulled to "lose [her soul] in mazes of inward contemplation" (57). And in direct proportion to her "awakening," she becomes absent-minded—daydreaming in company (60), acting "idly, aimlessly," (61) humming "vacantly" (129).

Thus it is not only that the quadroon's (and the little black girl's and the *mulatresse*'s) physical labor is taken for granted, but that Edna employs as well their tropological potential, their associations with the marginal and, ultimately, with the erotic. In his useful analysis of the figure of the black servant in the visual arts, Sander L. Gilman points out that one of the image's "central functions in . . . the eighteenth and nineteenth centuries was to sexualize the society in which he or she is found."[24] From Hogarth's *A Harlot's Progress* (1731) to Manet's *Olympia* (1863), black servants, signifying sexuality though not necessarily overtly sexual themselves, eroticize white women. As Gilman argues in his discussion of Manet's *Nana* (1877), the "sexualized female [functions] as the visual analogue of the black" even where no blacks are present, for "the black servant is hidden in *Nana*—within Nana. Even Nana's seeming beauty is but a sign of the black hidden within."[25] In Chopin's fiction the quadroon similarly appears divested of subjectivity and, it would seem, of sexuality. And yet like Nana's, Edna's sexuality is brought into relief by the quadroon's literary inheritance of sexual conventions. As Hortense Spillers puts it, the "mulatto in the text of fiction" silently speaks of unsanctioned sex, allowing the "dominant culture to say without parting its lips that 'we have willed to sin.'"[26] The relationship between Edna's willingness to "sin" and the quadroon's is further reinforced by the narrative's own "vocabulary of signs,"[27] signs which provocatively yoke Edna's and the quadroon's mutual distraction, and, thereby, their potential social and sexual deviance.[28]

Oppression by the Oppressed

The racial midwifery of Edna's sexual awakening is not simply repressed; it is refigured. To the children, the silent and static quadroon is simply a "huge encumbrance, only good to button up waists and panties and to brush and part hair" (51); to Edna, the quadroon and the other servants are equally obtrusive. Indeed, such women are not only in the way; they function as stable counters to Edna's flights. When Edna throws her wedding ring to the floor in a pique of frustration, it is not her husband but the maid who returns it to her, reaffirming the established life that Edna has tried to toss aside (100). Servants and nannies, Chopin implies, are the keepers rather than the victims of traditional Southern society; hence Edna can complain, as she moves out of her husband's house, that there are "too many servants" whom she is "tired bothering with" (134). However, Edna does not live entirely on her own, for her independence is made both possible and appealing because "Old Celestine, who works occasionally for me, says she will come stay with me and do my work. I know I shall like it, like the feeling of freedom and independence" (134). Her comments suggest that people of another color and class are, paradoxically, both a hindrance to and yet necessary for her liberation. Celestine is one of the bare essentials in life, but too many like her become a basic part of Edna's oppression.

Color itself, not as it is discriminated against but as it functions to discriminate, becomes oppressive to Edna. The "black," the "mulatto," the "quadroon," and the "Griffe" are subtle indices to social status in the white community. Named according to the ratio of "Negro blood" in their veins, these representative figures function not as indictments of an arbitrary colorline, but as reminders and reinforcements of cultural tiering. At one of many parties that Edna and her husband are obliged to attend, she notes that a "light-colored mulatto boy, in dress coat and bearing a diminutive silver tray for the reception of cards," admits the guests, while a "maid, in white fluted cap, offered the callers liqueur, coffee, or chocolate" (100). The mulatto boy is one of the prestigious minutiae—like the silver tray, the liqueur, the white cap—that constitute the suffocating drawing-room atmosphere Edna loathes; he is visible as a racial marker (not a victim) of social hierarchies. The oppressed become the oppressors as black subordination becomes an element of white victimage.[29]

The reversal has at least two effects, both of which are most evident in an important but overlooked scene between Victor Lebrun and a nameless "black woman" with whom he has a dispute over opening the door for Edna. The incident, an example of the "offensive" behavior of blacks (owing to what Victor calls "imperfect training"), codes sexual initiation as concern over a servant's duty. An interesting gloss on Edna's relationship with the quadroon, the episode suggests the ways in which blacks obliquely structure white sexual experience. Furthermore, because potential debates about civil rights are, in effect, reinscribed as sexual rites, the episode illustrates the process by which race and class conflicts are deflected:

> Before she saw them Edna could hear them in altercation, the woman— plainly an anomaly—claiming the right to be allowed to perform her duties, one of which was to answer the bell. Victor was surprised and delighted to see Mrs. Pontellier. . . . He instructed the black woman to go at once and inform Madame Lebrun that Mrs. Pontellier desired to see her. The woman grumbled a refusal to do part of her duty when she had not been permitted to do it all, and started back to her interrupted task of weeding the garden. Whereupon Victor administered a rebuke in the form of a volley of abuse, which, owing to its rapidity and incoherence, was all but incomprehensible to Edna. . . . [Victor] at once explained that the black woman's offensive conduct was all due to imperfect training, as he was not there to take her in hand. (110–11)

The black woman's resistance is not simply a sign of domestic unrest but a mark of Victor's adolescent incompetence. The argument is potentially threatening to traditional roles, but the debate becomes unrecognizable—"incomprehensible" and "incoherent"—and thus is represented as little more than an entertaining aside: the heteroglossic exchange does not produce social parity, the babble does not level rank. Despite Victor's reference to the woman's need for training, it is her superior knowledge of "natural" hierarchies which eventually reinforces the domestic order as well as an established sexual economy. Although she eventually does go in search of his mother as he asked, she has underlined his social/ physical immaturity, thus emasculating him before Edna.

Described as having a childish crush on Edna, Victor's manhood is put in question by the insubordination of one supposedly "under" him. In this curious triangulation of desire, the boy cannot become a man except by overcoming the mother. The black woman acts as a mammy to the boy, but as the presence of his biological mother upstairs suggests, hers is a symbolic maternity. She also, more provocatively, doubles as the "woman before" Edna (she literally precedes her at the door), as a test case of his masculine authority. The black woman is a sexual stumbling block he must overcome before he is man enough for a white woman; in that sense, Victor's seemingly innocuous attempt at verbal domination evokes the history of rape as boyhood initiation. The black woman is used as so many before her, as the measure of a white boy's political power and sexual prowess. She is not allowed direct speech—we know her words, like those of all the women of color in the novel, only as they are mediated through indirect narration—but she is both social arbiter and sexual measure.

"Strange, New Voices"

This kind of sexual work in the novel is rendered either by domestics, like the quadroon and the "black woman," or by various "servants-at-large." Women of another color or class tend to serve as sexual coaches, their homes as sexual "safehouses." Often older than their pupil—and thus putatively removed from sexual competition—they authorize white sexuality and self-knowledge. In Chopin's fiction, the experienced woman is always of a lower racial or ethnic status than her novitiate: if the heroine is white Creole, her mentor may be Acadian; if she is Acadian, her guide may be "black." The "black as the night" (195) Manna-Loulou in "La Belle

Zoraïde" (1894), for instance, enlightens her mistress about sex beyond the pale. In "Athénaïse" (1896) the quadroon landlord, Sylvie, instructs the Acadian heroine in the ways of sex and motherhood.[30]

Thus it is not altogether unusual that Edna in *The Awakening* names Mme. Antoine, her hostess on *Chênière Caminada,* as the source of an after-dinner tale of adultery (124). A counter to Dr. Mandelet's didactic tale of a woman's errant love "seeking strange, new channels, only to return to its legitimate source" (123), Edna's version of illegitimate sex is ascribed to an author other than herself. Although the story is Edna's and not the Acadian's, she betrays the ethnic precedent of her own narratives.

Arguably, Manna-Loulou's, Sylvie's, and Mme. Antoine's stories are examples of Chopin "giving voice" to these women, granting them, with their supposedly more "worldly" knowledge, conditional authority over white women. Yet Mme. Antoine speaks "no English" (83). And earlier when Edna is napping in the woman's home, she perceives only Mme. Antoine's son's "slow, Acadian drawl" (which she says she does not understand) and Robert's French (which she understands only "imperfectly") among "the other drowsy, muffled sounds" (84). Robert in a sense assumes Mme. Antoine's voice, translating and brokering Edna's exchanges with her. Edna uses her cultural illiteracy to her advantage, however, for Robert's translations (very much like Victor's) stand between her and the natives or servants, performing an enabling interference. In effect, the translation of Mme. Antoine's patois offers Edna the immediacy of the spoken word without the responsibilities and required give-and-take of conversation. Patricia Yaeger points out that "Robert's knowledge of several languages" gives him "the power to control what others hear and speak."[31] Nevertheless, his "attentions, his services, his affection" are, as Cynthia Wolff suggests, "extensions of [Edna's] own will or desire."[32] In this case, Robert's linguistic negotiations both dramatize and sustain Edna's own ambivalent role with the locals by providing, as George Steiner describes it, the "dialectic of impenetrability and ingress, of intractable alienness and felt 'at-homeness'" which remains "unresolved, but expressive" in translation.[33] Erotic in their elusiveness, the strangeness of the languages "lull[s] her senses" (84). The sensual voices are muted, then, but usefully so because the "drowsy" (84), secondhand talk allows her to be both "in" and yet not implicated in a culture which she finds appealing only to a point.

Most important, these narratives precede and are therefore not the result of her romantic longings, as Edna herself seems to suggest when she compares being moved by beautiful music and memories of Robert to an earlier time when she "had wept one midnight at Grand Isle when strange, new voices awoke in her" (116). She is, admittedly, obsessed with "the spiritual vision [of] the presence of the beloved one" (145), but she misses Robert when he leaves for Mexico because she links him with the "brightness, the *color*" (95, emphasis mine) he brings to her life. His attractiveness derives from his status not as a lover but as a guide to this "local color." Critical focus on Edna's male partners rather than the indistinct voices on the islands masks the primacy of the latter in her sexual awakening, for the men function more to mediate than to initiate Edna's "latent sensuality" (163).

The Colonization of Race

Within the codified hierarchies of race and class in post-Reconstruction Louisiana, Acadians were considered "lesser" whites. Their lower class status and rural lifestyle set them apart economically, ethnically, and linguistically from Creole society; in Chopin's fiction, they are often represented as both primitive and passionate.[34] Hence Edna's dozing in Mme. Antoine's house on *Chênière Caminada* reflects, paradoxically, her desire to be one of the "folk" and yet to remain stretched out "in the very center of the high, white bed" (84), the "snow-white" (83) bed. The scene dramatizes Edna's sense, articulated later when she moves from her husband's house, of having "descended in the social scale, with a corresponding sense of having risen in the spiritual" (151)—but what to make of a white "lady" (83) on a whiter bed?

White bourgeois entitlement, reiterated by the white on white iconography, is clearly one tradition Edna does not reject. It is in another's home and in another's bed—the site of both birth and sexuality—that Edna feels "invited . . . to repose" (83). Much later, Edna recalls that she "liked then to wander alone into strange and unfamiliar places. She discovered many a sunny, sleepy corner, fashioned to dream in. And she found it good to dream and to be alone and unmolested" (109). The strange and unfamiliar corners Edna finds, however, are sometimes occupied— a point easily forgotten, for women such as Mme. Antoine are apparently "all eagerness to make Edna feel at home" and (ironically, given who is intruding upon whom) "unmolested" (83). In similar fashion, when Edna shows up unannounced at Victor's house "for no purpose but to rest"

(173), she nevertheless expects to have dinner, and, if they have it, fish in particular. Victor volunteers his own room, although she assures him that "any corner will do" (174).[35]

Mme. Antoine's "strange, quaint bed" (84) is just right for Edna in this erotic fairy tale, and there are no returning bears angry with Goldilock's trespassing. Nevertheless, she is not content with her status as guest; she would rather her host disappear altogether. Upon rising from her own nap, she narrates her own apocalyptic fantasy in which she condemns most everyone else to an eternal sleep: "How many years have I slept? . . . A new race of beings must have sprung up, leaving only you and me as past relics. How many ages ago did Madame Antoine and Tonie die? and when did our people from Grand Isle disappear from the earth?" (85). Edna is not Rip Van Winkle, however, but Snow White, dwarfing those around her in order to live out her fantasy of solitude in the lap of "native hospitality" (83). Like Lyndall in Olive Schreiner's *The Story of An African Farm* (1882), who tells her lover "I will not go down country . . . I will not go to Europe. You must take me to the Transvaal. That is out of the world," Edna perceives *Chênière Caminada* as otherworldly—both primitive and timeless: "How still it was, with only the voice of the sea whispering through the reeds that grew in the saltwater pools! . . . It must always have been God's day on that low, drowsy island, Edna thought" (83). Rendered static, the indigenous land provides at once a stable and ancient site for self-discovery, although Edna must imaginatively purge her utopian world in order to occupy it. Her "narrative of personal progress," as Wai-chee Dimock might term it, allows her to "impose a 'manifest' harmony on what might otherwise appear naked conflict."[36] This progress toward independence both justifies Edna's presence on the "colony" and simultaneously naturalizes any conflict, for she is as welcome as "the sunlight" (83) in Mme. Antoine's cot.

Nevertheless, her bid for the right of self-possession subtly entails native dispossession. The burden her patronage places on others is the less obvious because those obliged are so very compliant. The "fat" Mme. Antoine—who, after all, had only unproductively "squatted" and "waddled" (87) during her years on *Chênière Caminada*—is quite pleased, we are told, to have ventured out during Edna's nap. Robert speculates that she has gone to Vespers and to visit friends (86); hence, Edna's arrival and Mme. Antoine's leaving are presented as acts of mutual liberation. Yet it is noteworthy that Mme. Antoine makes such an effort not for her own sake but because she "thought it best not to awake" Edna (86).[37]

Edna does finally find a place of her own, but even that bears the shadow of the Other. As Spillers argues, in the nineteenth century passion lay beyond the "precincts of the father's house,"[38] usually in the slave cabins with the mulatto/a. Notably it is only after Edna's move from her husband's estate and his "precincts" (140) to the "pigeon-house" around the corner that she begins her affair with Arobin. The pigeon-house resembles the Grand Isle cottages where Edna experiences the first stirrings of rebellion and which Gilbert suggests represent a "female colony."[39] But perhaps more important than the homosocial appeal is a past of racial bondage, for the cottages are ex-slave quarters. The Pontellier's place of summer retreat was a sugar plantation prior to 1866—"the main building" of which is still "called 'the house' " (44). As Frederick Stielow points out in his study of the Louisiana leisure class, Grand Isle "included a selection of buildings dramatically altered from their previous duties. . . . Interestingly, the most prized accommodations were thirty-eight refurbished slave cabins, set in double rows."[40] Lafcadio Hearn, describing a visit to Grand Isle after the war, also notes this peculiar conversion: "It makes a curious impression on me: the old plantation cabins, standing in rows like village streets, and neatly remodelled for more cultivated inhabitants."[41] A new twist on the old plantation as imaginative refuge, Edna leaves the patriarchal house but most certainly not the grounds.[42] The pigeon-house in New Orleans, while not homologous with the Grand Isle cabins, nevertheless recreates the sexual cartography of the plantation: Edna leaves the Big House in town and is subsequently more free to entertain both Robert and Arobin.

The erotics of race not only govern the place but afford the principal basis of Edna's awakening. Although Edna finds the Ratignolles "very French, very foreign" (105), she also decides that they lead a rather "colorless existence" (107). In contrast to Mme. Ratignolle's "embodiment of every womanly grace and charm" (51), Edna's frank arousal leaves her "unwomanly" (165) in her lack of "repression in . . . glance or gesture" (123); at best, she admits, she is a "devilishly wicked specimen of the sex" (138). Her "unwomanly" behavior does not unsex her—quite the opposite, it allies her with the putatively feral and libidinous races. The cult of true womanhood (whose tenets of purity, piety, submissiveness and domesticity, Mme. Ratignolle as a "mother-woman" to some degree represents) sets race against gender; females of the physical and promiscuous race by definition fall outside the bounds of womanhood—as does Edna.[43] Her sexual awakening is couched in the same terms as those conventionally used to define the woman of color in the 1890s. She becomes "some beautiful, sleek animal waking up in the sun" (123); her lover "appeal[s] to the animalism that stirred impatiently within her" (133). Even her dining habits assume a bestial air as she tears at her bread with "her strong, white teeth" (85). Chopin writes of a similar animal in "Emancipation: A Life Fable" (1869), often referred to as a precursor to *The Awakening*. Basking in the sun, a beast with "strong limbs," "handsome flanks," and "sleek sides" (177) escapes its caged and well-fed life. Written only four years after the Civil War, the vignette employs antislavery discourse—rejection of the cage's dubious protection— in order to critique the sheltered confines of the bourgeois marriage. Joining woman and beast, Chopin finds deliverance from Victorian convention in felinity. Edna resembles the quadroon Palmyre in Cable's *The Grandissimes* (1880), a "barbaric beauty" whose "grace and pride was inspiring but—what shall we say?—feline? It was femininity without humanity— something that made her with all her superbness, a creature that one would want to find chained."[44] Awakening to this new and more colorful identity, even Edna's skin is illumined with "myriad living tints" (145), in contrast to the alabaster cast of the more conventional Mme. Ratignolle. The tan which her husband complains at the outset of the novel burns Edna almost "beyond recognition" (44) is not only a rebuttal of the "fair lady" image but a foreshadowing of her awakening into a "native" sexuality.

As Calvin Hernton notes, despite the fact that the "Negro woman is denied virtually all the 'privileges and graces' of American culture . . . according to the myth of Negro sexhood, it is the black woman who is endowed with an irresistible sexual attraction and enjoys the sex act more than any other creature on earth."[45] White women's desire for sexual expression, therefore, may lead to a sympathetic admiration nevertheless predicated upon racialist notions of sexuality: as Manna-Loulou tells her mistress in "La Belle Zoraïde," "you know how the negroes are. . . . There is no mistress, no master, no king nor priest who can hinder them from loving when they will" (198). The famed uprising of *The Awakening*'s Edna, then, cannot be seen as an uncharted move into what Freud tellingly called the "dark continent" of female sexuality.[46] If hers is a radical departure from the repertoire of white women's sexual norms, it is nevertheless quite in keeping with scripted conventions of racial behavior.[47] Given these conventions, some white women may "not only envy Negro females," as Hernton suggests, "but actually want to *be* black."[48]

Edna's racial surrogacy is at once less explicit and more inclusive, for it is not only black women who become representative of alternative sexual experience. She is intrigued, for instance, by Mariequita, a "vulgar" Spanish girl with "pretty black eyes" and "ugly brown toes" (81) who is sexually associated with both Victor and Robert (98). As alter egos, the two women are mutually fascinated and mildly competitive with each other. In fact, Edna moves from her usual indifference to momentary jealousy when she imagines Robert and the "transcendently seductive vision of a Mexican girl" (161).[49] Edna appropriates this vision, however, becoming by the novel's end the transcendently seductive object of *Mariequita's* jealousy (173).

This conversion entails the translation of racial or ethnic difference into the idiom of contested selfhood. Seeing "with different eyes and making the acquaintance of new conditions in herself that colored and changed her environment" (88), Edna turns inside out what W. E. B. Du Bois referred to in 1903 as "double-consciousness, this sense of always looking at one's self through the eyes of others."[50] Du Bois's "second-sight" (364), imposed by the "other [white] world," forces color upon him— he must see himself as others do; Edna's "different eyes," on the other hand, let her see herself as others do not. Her borrowed vision is a lens turned upon the world and herself, but unlike Du Bois she does not look at herself looking. The double vision for both, however, "yields no true self-consciousness" (Du Bois, 364); Edna can only vaguely "realize that she herself—her present self—was in some way different from the other self" (Chopin, 88). Her inner confusion becomes an "indescribable oppression, which seemed to generate in some unfamiliar part of her consciousness, filled her whole being with a vague anguish. It was like a shadow. . . . It was strange and unfamiliar" (49). She assumes this alien presence is simply a "mood" (49), although as something foreign within, her ambivalence reproduces the political stance and emotional tenor of Southerners who first imported and then felt invaded by blacks. Internal colonization—usually a reference to the North American colonization of Native and African Americans—is in Edna's case actually the internalization of the colony.[51] In other words, Edna interiorizes the intimate distance marking most Southern interracial relations, circumscribing within the arena of selfhood the tension of racial and ethnic influence.

White Beaches

The critical emphasis on and frequent celebration of Edna's quest for "solitude" mask these inner struggles as existential angst and thus replicate the character's own fictions of social identity. Yet possessive individualism, with its myth of the inalienable self, is precisely what makes it so difficult to see the investment in race upon which the white female subject capitalizes. Behind her claims to self-sufficiency and "self-contain-[ment]" (61), Edna's authority derives from and is frequently threatened by that which comes "upon her like an obsession . . . independent of volition." This superfluity, the "extraneous" (145), shadows her life as well as her death.

There is no racial or ethnic presence in the final scene on the beach. And yet Edna's image of the "white beach" where there "is no living thing in sight" (175) reveals anxiety about the influence of the Other. "Certain absences are so stressed," argues Toni Morrison, "so ornate, so planned, they call attention to themselves, arrest us with intentionality and purpose, like neighborhoods that are defined by the population held away from them."[52] The population textually held at bay in the last scene is implied by the emphasis on Edna's "white body" and "white feet" on the "white beach" (175–76). (Edna's earlier trial swim shares this preoccupation: as waves like "white serpents" play at her feet, she breathes the scent of "white blossoms" and the "white light" of the moon dispels the "weight of darkness" [73] around her.) This fetishization of whiteness perhaps suggests not only a defensive insistence on racial privilege (such as Mme. Antoine's "high, white bed") but an attempt to blanche her self of those "myriad tints" (145). Her final thoughts of childhood during the fatal swim might suggest this kind of denial, for they predate her arrival on the islands and therefore also her sexual awakening. More likely, though, is the possibility that the overdetermination of color reflects an attempt to resolve the heightening tension between Edna's sexual indebtedness to racial/ethnic difference and her fundamental commitment to the status of whiteness. An extension of her earlier fantasies of solitude, this resolution involves not the imagined death (85), but the total absorption of the "population held away."

Given the sexual logic of the novel, this incorporation of the ethnic and racial Other is to a certain degree predictable. Edna moves back and forth between racial models of womanhood (alternately "tanned" or "tinted" to unequivocally "white"), but liberation is represented, finally, only in terms of a colonizing whiteness. "White" moves from an adjective to an assertion of race in a process of assimilation perhaps most vivid in a later story, "The Storm" (1898). The Spanish Calixta, whose hair is "kinked worse than a mulatto's," (179)[53] becomes suffused with whiteness during lovemaking: with her "white neck," "white throat," and "whiter breasts," she is as "white as the couch she lay upon. Her firm, elastic flesh that was knowing for the first time its birthright, was like a creamy lily. . . . The generous abundance of her passion : . . was like a white flame" (283–84). It is not sex per se but the climax of whiteness which temporarily frees Calixta—as it does Edna. Orgasm is the context for Calixta's freedom, but the realization of her sexual "birthright" (284) is incumbent upon her momentary escalation from a "dark" woman to "white" woman. Albescence, then, represents an attempted resolution of the "antithetical sexual natures of white women and dark women,"[54] a move which in *The Awakening* similarly enables Edna to be "new-born" (175). Although of course transcendent whiteness leads not to *petit mort* but to death for Edna, debatably both sex and suicide are modes of liberatory release.[55]

Edna may be transformed by the white subsumption of the Other, but women like Mariequita or the quadroon or the "black woman" do not and cannot change in the novel. Precisely because Edna's break with gender constraints is dependent upon representations of racial and ethnic difference, those differences—in order to be available in the first place—must remain intact. As sexual "catalyst[s],"[56] the serviceable equations of race and sex make possible a Victorian erotics, but they are also subtly tied to the Jim Crow legalisms predicated on similar constructions of difference[57]—an irony which nevertheless might explain the subtle necessaries and sufficiencies of race for whites in American culture.

My point, then, is not that Edna fails to pierce the veil of stereotypes—a critique which irresistibly dichotomizes ontological categories as well as power structures: real/false, self/other, colonizer/colonized—but rather that racial figuration is intimately involved in the warranty and production of her "self." To the extent such troping is in a sense "productive" as well as repressive, race is constitutive of Edna's new identity. In this light, the racial politics of womanhood in Chopin's novel must complicate, if not compromise, our celebration of a nineteenth-century white woman's sexual liberation.

Notes

I am especially grateful to Johnnella Butler, Amy Kaplan, Mark Patterson, Ross Posnock, and Hortense J. Spillers for their thoughtful responses to earlier versions of this essay.

1 Kate Chopin, *The Awakening*, in *The Awakening and Selected Stories*, ed. Sandra Gilbert (New York: Penguin, 1984), 78. Subsequent citations from this work and Chopin's other short fiction refer to this edition and are parenthetically noted in the essay.
2 Quoted from the backjacket of the cited edition.
3 Linda Dowling, "The Decadent and the New Woman," *Nineteenth-Century Fiction* 33 (1979): 451.
4 *The Awakening*, 108.
5 See Rita Felski for the argument that a liberatory politics, though requiring a subject with agency, need not uncritically enable bourgeois individualism. *Beyond Feminist Aesthetics: Feminist Literature and Social Change* (Cambridge: Harvard Univ. Press, 1989), 66–71.
6 Sandra M. Gilbert, "The Second Coming of Aphrodite," introduction to *The Awakening and Selected Stories*, 20.
7 See Quentin Anderson, *The Imperial Self: An Essay in American Literary and Cultural History* (New York: Vintage, 1972).
8 Wai-chee Dimock, *Empire for Liberty: Melville and the Poetics of Individualism* (Princeton: Princeton Univ. Press, 1989), 8.
9 From a Houghton Mifflin advertisement for Chopin's *Bayou Folk* in *Publisher's Weekly* (17 March 1894), 450; quoted in Emily Toth, *Kate Chopin* (New York: William Morrow, 1990), 223. Chopin's Northern audience included Creoles as well as Acadians and blacks in this category. Southern reviewers, while sensitive to the social and cultural distinctions among ethnic groups, did not consider these populations to be "alien" in this same sense.
10 From the review, "Living Tales from Acadian Life," *New York Times* (1 April 1894), 23; quoted in Toth, 226.
11 Quoted in Winthrop Jordan, "Fruits of Passion: The Dynamics of Interracial Sex" in *Woman and Womanhood in America*, ed. Ronald W. Hogeland (Lexington: D.C. Heath, 1973), 55.
12 Albert Memmi, *The Colonizer and the Colonized* (Boston: Beacon Press, 1965), 66.
13 Cable explains the implications of the "silent South" in "The Freedman's Case in Equity": "It means to recommit [racial inequity] to the silence and concealment of the covered burrow. Beyond that incubative retirement, no suppressed moral question can be pushed" (*The Silent South Together with the Freedman's Case in Equity and the Convict Lease System* [New York: Charles Scribner's Sons, 1889], 3). Cynthia Griffin Wolff similarly suggests that Edna uses sleep and daydreaming as a strategy of repression, arguing that Edna's internalization of the contradicting images of womanhood (the mother-woman and the vixen) is in part what leads her "to produce an 'identity' which is predicated on the process of concealment" ("Thanatos and Eros: Kate Chopin's *The Awakening*" in *The Awakening* by Kate Chopin, ed. Nancy A. Walker [New York: St. Martin's Press, 1993], 235). Wolff's psychoanalytic perspective leads her to the conclusion that this contradiction arises

from the differences between Edna's sisters, Margaret and Janet, rather than from the sexual contradictions established between white women and women of color that Edna also internalizes.

14 See Elizabeth Ammons, *Conflicting Stories: American Women Writers at the Turn into the Twentieth Century* (New York: Oxford Univ. Press, 1991), 75.

15 Shannon Anna Elfenbein, *Women on the Colorline: Evolving Stereotypes and the Writings of George Washington Cable, Grace King, and Kate Chopin* (Charlottesville: Univ. Press of Virginia, 1989), 143.

16 Karen Sánchez-Eppler, "Bodily Bonds: The Intersecting Rhetorics of Feminism and Abolitionism," *Representations* 24 (1988): 31. See also Anne Goodwyn Jones, who suggests that Chopin uses blacks "as an objective correlative for her feelings about oppression" in *Tomorrow is Another Day: The Woman Writer in the South, 1859–1936* (Baton Rouge: Louisiana State Univ. Press, 1981), 151.

17 Sánchez-Eppler, 31.

18 There are many other instances of black labor: Mme. Lebrun has a "little black girl" sit on the floor and work the "treadle of the [sewing] machine" so she need not imperil her "health" (66); "two black women" spend their afternoon making ice cream for a whites-only party (70); Mme. Ratignolle points out to Edna that laundry is "really [the] business" (105) of her black maid, 'Cité. While one may interpret as ironic comment on Creole gentility Mme. Lebrun's insistence on protecting her "health," there is no suggestion elsewhere that white women should assume their servants' labor.

19 "Race" of course is a slippery expression and, and though I invoke it throughout the essay without quotations, it is used with the assumption that its legitimacy lies not in science or biology but in its application as a trope of difference. In the 1890s, race was frequently and loosely applied not only to people of color or to people of a certain class but to people of various religious identifications (especially Catholic) as well. For discussions of the history and debates surrounding this term, see Stephen Jay Gould, *The Mismeasure of Man* (New York: Norton, 1981); Nancy Stepan, *The Idea of Race in Science* (Hamden, Conn.: Archon Books, 1982); and Eric Cheyfitz, *The Poetics of Imperialism: Translation and Colonization from "The Tempest" to "Tarzan"* (New York: Oxford Univ. Press, 1991).

20 Gilbert, 16, 17.

21 Mary Louise Pratt, "Scratches on the Face of the Country; or What Mr. Barrow Saw in the Land of the Bushmen" in *'Race,' Writing, and Difference*, ed. Henry Louis Gates Jr. (Chicago: Univ. of Chicago Press, 1986), 140.

22 Wai-chee Dimock, in "Rightful Subjectivity" (*Yale Journal of Criticism* 4 [1990]: 25–51), argues that the "quadroon's 'off-centeredness' complements the centered subjectivity that is Edna's"; hence the subjectivity of both the quadroon and Edna's husband, Dimock suggests, are similarly "adduced and dismissed" (42). My point is that the quadroon is not simply a foil but fundamental to Edna's sense of self.

23 Gilbert quotes a similarly provocative line from Chopin's travel journal which refers to the "sweet, half-seen pagan life" (33), using it to support her argument that Chopin drew on Greek imagery. Yet the South itself was commonly orientalized in the period's fiction. See Hortense Spillers, "Changing the Letter: The Yokes, the Jokes of Discourse: or Mrs. Stowe and Mr. Reed," in *Slavery and the Literary Imagination*, ed. Deborah McDowell and Arnold Rampersad (Baltimore: Johns Hopkins Univ. Press, 1988), 25–61.

24 Sander L. Gilman, "Black Bodies, White Bodies: Toward An Iconography of Female Sexuality in Late Nineteenth-Century Art, Medicine, and Literature," in *'Race,' Writing, and Difference*, 228.

25 Gilman, 251.

26 Hortense J. Spillers, " 'The Tragic Mulatta': Neither/Nor—Toward An Alternative Model," in *The Difference Within: Feminism and Critical Theory*, ed. Elizabeth Meese and Alice Parker (Philadelphia: J. Benjamins, 1989), 168.

27 Gilman, 251.

28 The quadroon in *The Awakening* also brings to mind the infamous quadroon balls of New Orleans, still held with some regularity in the 1890s. The *plaçages* or liaisons (often more like common-law marriages) between wealthy white men and these much-courted quadroons and octoroons might have seemed appealing to a white woman questioning traditional marital and sexual arrangements. For a discussion of the *plaçage*, see John W. Blassingame, *Black New Orleans, 1860–1880* (Chicago: Univ. of Chicago Press, 1973); see also George Washington Cable, *Madame Delphine* (New York: Charles Scribner's Sons, 1893), 5–6, for his reverence for these women whom he saw, paradoxically, as "chaste sirens."

29 In Chopin's fiction, explicit allusions to class relations and the need to preserve social hierarchies are often made by "mulattoes." In *The Awakening*, for instance, the mulatta Madame Pouponne wishes to "discuss class distinctions" (110) with Edna; in *Athénaïse*, the quadroon, Sylvie, believes "firmly in maintaining the color line, and would not suffer a white person, even a child, to call her 'Madame Sylvie,'—a title which she exacted religiously, however, from those of her own race" (245). In New Orleans in the 1880s and 1890s, intraracial discrimination was common, but because in Chopin's fiction blacks—and almost never whites—conspicuously support the class hierarchies based on color, they deflect attention from white discrimination. Like the nannies and servants in *The Awakening*, Sylvie and Madame Pouponne become representatives of status quo class relations even though Sylvie, for instance, is associated with sexual experimentation.

30 After having run from her husband's sexual attentions, Athénaïse is revealed to herself after a chat about life's facts with the "very wise" (257) quadroon: "She stayed . . . quite stunned, after her interview with Sylvie. . . . Her whole being was steeped in . . . ecstasy. When she finally arose . . . and looked at herself in the mirror, a face met hers which she seemed to see for the first time, so transfigured was it with wonder and rapture" (257).

Sylvie is "knowing," perhaps, because she runs a "house" which caters to "discreet gentlemen" who wish an evening "outside the bosom of their families" (247)—men who want, like Athénaïse, to escape domestic confines. Sylvie's place, then, is a kind of border crossing where sexual enlightenment is a "discreet" possibility.

31 Patricia S. Yaeger, "'A Language Which Nobody Understood': Emancipatory Strategies in *The Awakening*" in *The Awakening* by Kate Chopin, ed. Nancy A. Walker, 285.

32 Wolff, 239. Although Arobin is Edna's lover, he similarly assumes an attitude of "subservience" (133) and dons a dust-cap to help Edna clean her pigeon-house (141).

33 George Steiner, *After Babel: Aspects of Language and Translation* (New York: Oxford Univ. Press, 1975), 392–93.

34 In the companion story, "At *Chênière Caminada*" (1894), for instance, Mme. Antoine is described as kind but with "coarse hands"; her son, Tonie, is a "rough fisherman" with a "bronzed" face and flesh as "hard as a horse's hoof" whose love for a mainland girl fires the "savage instinct of his blood." See also "At the 'Cadian Ball" (1892) and "The Storm: A Sequel to 'The 'Cadian Ball'" (1898). For a historical genealogy of the Acadian presence in the South and an account of the changing attitudes towards Acadians in the nineteenth century, see Carl A. Brasseaux, *Acadian to Cajun: The Transformation of a People, 1803–1877* (Jackson: Univ. Press of Mississippi, 1992).

35 Such homes, seen also in Chopin's novel *At Fault*, are represented as an open invitation to the white women. For a discussion of the nostalgia among white women in particular for this romanticized interracial sisterhood, see Elizabeth Fox-Genovese, *Within the Plantation Household: Black and White Women of the Old South* (Chapel Hill: Univ. of North Carolina Press, 1988).

36 Dimock, *Empire for Liberty*, 20.

37 Edna's "most authentic act of self-definition" (30), according to Gilbert, offers a similar example of strategic occupation without conflict. At the *coup d'état* of her dinner-party, Edna is enthroned in and thus usurps the patriarchal seat at the head of the table. But her husband's seat is already vacant since he is out of town on a business trip; hence she stages the "spectacle" (173) of her self-ordination without the effort of direct confrontation.

38 Spillers, "Tragic Mulatta," 173.

39 Gilbert, 25.

40 Frederick Stielow, "Grand Isle, Louisiana and the 'New' Leisure Class, 1866–1893," *Louisiana History* 23 (1982): 243.

41 *The Life and Letters of Lafcadio Hearn*, 2 vols., ed. Elizabeth Bisland (Boston, 1906), 1:87; quoted in Stielow, 243. See also Hearn's mention of the island in his novel *Chita: A Memory of Last Island* (New York: Harper & Brothers, 1889), 11.

42 For a discussion of the idealization of the plantation as a utopian social and economic model, see Richard Slotkin, *The Fatal Environment: The Myth of*

the Frontier in the Age of Industrialization, 1800–1890 (Middletown, Conn.: Wesleyan Univ. Press, 1985), 141–46.

43   For an insightful discussion of the interdependence of race and gender in the cult of true womanhood, see Hazel V. Carby, *Reconstructing Womanhood: The Emergence of the Afro-American Woman Novelist* (New York: Oxford Univ. Press, 1987), 20–39. As Carby makes clear, the interdependencies of race and class make gender identification alone an insufficient (at the very least an inconsistent) basis for political resistance.

44   George Washington Cable, *The Grandissimes: A Story of Creole Life* (New York: Penguin, 1988), 71.

45   Calvin Hernton, *Sex and Racism in America* (New York: Doubleday, 1965), 50–51.

46   For an analysis of the relationship between Freudian constructions of (white) female sexuality and race, see Gilman, 256–57.

47   Critics have pointed out the contrast between sexual expectations for white women and women of color, especially black women, in the nineteenth century and in Chopin's fiction. See Wendy Martin, "Introduction," *New Essays on The Awakening* (New York: Cambridge Univ. Press, 1988), 16; and Carby, *Reconstructing Womanhood*, xxv. For works which more extensively examine the role of race in Chopin's fiction, see Elfenbein, 117–158, and Helen Taylor, *Gender, Race, and Region in the Writings of Grace King, Ruth McEnery Stuart, and Kate Chopin* (Baton Rouge: Louisiana State Univ. Press, 1989), 138–203. Elfenbein and Taylor criticize Chopin's racial stereotyping, while Emily Toth argues that Chopin appropriates racial stereotypes in the service of a broader social critique, in "That Outward Existence Which Conforms: Kate Chopin and Literary Convention" (Ph.D. diss., Johns Hopkins University, 1975). This essay hopes to move beyond the question of stereotyping in order to examine some of the stranger satisfactions race affords Edna, and the ways in which Edna's sexuality works in conjunction with—and not despite—troubling constructs of racial difference. For a discussion of the need to reconsider the role of "race" in biographical studies of Chopin, see my review essay, " 'The Rogue in Porcelain': Feminism, Race, and the Representation of Kate Chopin," *Genre* 24 (Winter 1991): 461–67. For a critique of white feminist theory which points up the necessity to factor race into analyses of gender relations, see bell hooks, *Ain't I A Woman: Black Women and Feminism* (Boston: South End Press, 1981).

48   Hernton, 51.

49   Elfenbein suggests that, for Edna, "Mariequita appears stereotypically dark and carefree" (149), but that her reinforcement of Victor's romanticized image of a "mythic Edna" means that Mariequita remains "untouched by Edna's awakening" (157). Like other "dark" women in the novel, Mariequita is not elevated by Edna's "awakening"; in fact, by reinforcing the representation of Edna as a social belle ("who gave the most sumptuous dinners in

America"), she is represented as complicit with the social expectations Edna seeks to evade.

50 See W. E. B. Du Bois, "Of Our Spiritual Strivings" in *The Souls of Black Folk* (New York: Library of America, 1986), 364; hereafter cited in text. Although I see Edna's double-vision as both vertiginous and appropriative, Chopin is praised for her representation of a similar mode of "seeing" in other novels, for her adoption of the "point of view of [New Orleans] working-class men—one white, one black—into whose consciousness a decorous lady like Chopin herself might not have been expected to enter" (Gilbert, 16), and for being a "daughter of slave owners" who looked on "the thoughtless white world through the eyes of a woman of color" (Toth, *Kate Chopin*, 222).

51 For arguments linking the United States' imperialist discourse with domestic policy regarding the "race question," see Hazel V. Carby, "'On the Threshold of Woman's Era': Lynching, Empire, and Sexuality in Black Feminist Theory," in *'Race,' Writing and Difference*, 301–17, and C. Vann Woodward, *The Strange Career of Jim Crow* (New York: Oxford Univ. Press, 1974), 72–75.

52 Toni Morrison, "Unspeakable Things Unspoken: The Afro-American Presence in American Literature," *Michigan Quarterly Review* 28 (1989): 11.

53 Calixta figures both in the companion story, "At the 'Cadian Ball" (1892) from which this quote is taken, and in "The Storm" (unpublished in Chopin's lifetime) where her hair is "kinked more stubbornly than ever" (282).

54 Elfenbein, 141. Indeed, Calixta's act would only be considered liberatory if she is a (vicariously) "white" woman; as a "dark" woman, her sexual passion would be viewed as commonplace. Elfenbein argues that the "story suggests more about the limitations of bourgeois marriage" than about sexual antitheses, although I suggest that it is this dialectic which forms the very basis of a critique of white middle-class marriage.

55 Clearly, the politics of race in *The Awakening* need not have complete explanatory force throughout the novel, nor does it exhaust the reasons for Edna's death; it does, I suggest, reframe the controversy surrounding it.

56 Morrison, *Playing in the Dark: Whiteness and the Literary Imagination* (Cambridge: Harvard Univ. Press, 1992), vii. Morrison further points out that examining the ways in which constructions of racial or cultural difference "ignite critical moments of discovery or change or emphasis in [white-authored] literature" (viii) helps us understand "'literary whiteness'" as well as "'literary blackness'" (xii).

57 See Anna Julia Cooper, *A Voice from the South* (1892; reprint, New York: Oxford Univ. Press, 1988). Writing in 1892, Cooper offers a scathing critique of legislation based on perceived differences between white and black women, citing as an example the segregation of public toilets labeled "For Women" and "For Coloureds."

Part IV

Barbara Ladd

"The Direction of the Howling": Nationalism and the Color Line in *Absalom, Absalom!*

Although stories of the slaveholder's mixed-race children were immensely popular prior to the Civil War, most were written, as one might expect, by northern writers intent on, or at least not opposed to, stirring public sentiment against slavery. The white southern writer tended to avoid the subject. After the Civil War, however, mixed-blood characters began to appear with some frequency in the work of white southern writers like George Washington Cable, Joel Chandler Harris, Grace King, Kate Chopin, Mark Twain and, later, William Faulkner. The issue of passing was of particular interest to many of these writers; they often depicted characters traditionally classified as "quadroons" or "octoroons," not solely to indicate that these characters had more white ancestry than black, but also to suggest their origins in the colonialist slave cultures of the Deep South and the Caribbean where they were associated with a distinct caste of free persons of mixed blood relatively unknown in the slaveholding areas of the Upper South—creoles of color. Consistent with this cultural legacy, in many of these Deep South texts the octoroon is initially attributed not with an African origin, but with a European, that is, a French or Spanish, one; the figure seldom carries any telltale sign of African ancestry. It is well into *The Grandissimes*, for instance, before the young German American Joseph Frowenfeld learns that his dark and elegant landlord Honoré Grandissime is anyone other than a white creole. Nor, to take another example, is Armand's ancestry known until the very end of Chopin's "Désirée's Baby." In Alice Morris Buckner's *Towards the Gulf,* we are never sure if the innocent young wife carries the "fatal drop" or not. And William Faulkner's Charles Bon is taken for a white creole for a long time before he is "reconstructed."

This "mistake" in identifying the octoroon as a French or Spanish creole is strategic and points to questions and anxieties that the white southerner had about his or her own future in a nationalistic and increasingly imperialistic United States.

The most salient feature of the octoroons as they are constructed in these texts is their capacity to delineate the political and cultural repressions and displacements, the submerged or forgotten history that underlies the dream of U.S. national unity. In so many of these texts, the personal history of the octoroon—his or her origin in a slave culture, alienation from the father, even the memory of a dead, sometimes anonymous, or monstrously rendered mother—is a psychologized recapitulation of the nationalist narrative; the octoroon's tragic fate, typically death or exile to Europe, is the destiny that always attends the past in any dream of U.S. redemptive nationalism. In most of these texts the figure is inscribed with the threatening characteristics of the displaced colonialist culture—he or she is almost always "aristocratic," a true product of a European-style and colonial class system, often superfluous both economically and politically, completely unsuited to the economic and political life of the American republic. The presence of the octoroon, as sign of transgression of American racial as well as cultural ideology, is associated with the southern white protagonist's review, critique, and confirmation of his or her own political and cultural entitlements. In the octoroon, the white author creates alternative political and cultural selves, selves that for one reason or another have to be rejected, scapegoated, or otherwise silenced, but versions, nevertheless, of the postbellum white southerner in terms of the political and cultural history of the Deep South.[1] One of the most profound achievements of *Absalom, Absalom!* is its power of commentary on this (and at times its own) use of the creole of color. In *The Grandissimes*, for example, lying beneath the scapegoating of unacceptable legacies in the exile of the quadroon woman and the suicide of the octoroon man, one discerns a faint suggestion that the white heroes might someday once again have to face their own troublesome history of slavery. It is a suggestion that becomes reality in *Absalom, Absalom!*, where the economy of American national innocence is itself thematized and the economy of the text is one of historical reclamation. That Charles Bon should, in following his American father (and Martinican grandfather) into the frontier wilderness of Mississippi, be transformed from "Charles Good, Charles Husband-Soon-to-be" into decadent white creole, into brother, into "the nigger that's going to sleep with your sister"; and that he should then eventuate in the figure of Jim Bond, the "one nigger Sutpen left," whose howling in that wilderness has no direction, cannot be traced toward New Orleans, toward the West Indies, nor finally eastward toward Europe—a howling traceable nowhere, in fact, except inward—is the final reclamation of a damning history by Quentin Compson, as he himself lies displaced, and shivering, in a "cold known land."[2]

■ ■ ■

The reasons for the assignment of a French or Spanish origin to the octoroon stem directly from the history of colonization and miscegenation in the Deep South (especially Louisiana, which is this figure's site of origin in so many of these works) and particularly from the very different methods of classifying the offspring of Anglo- or Euro-African liaisons there. Prior to the Louisiana Purchase in 1803, racial classification in the creole Deep South was much more complex than in the Anglo Upper South, where the status of a mixed-blood child followed that of the mother from the very beginning of the eighteenth century. Consequently, in the Upper South, the figure of the mixed blood was classed officially and metaphorically as part of the race that was defined as "slave," a legal/political nonentity. In the Deep South, however, traditions were different. Until the Louisiana Purchase, racial classifications were based, in some ways, upon the status of the father. Children of white fathers were more easily manumitted in the Deep South, and fathers acknowledged those children more frequently than in the Upper South. Children could inherit from the white father's estate more easily. Furthermore, legalized marriages between white men and black women were possible, if rare. Throughout the West Indies (including New Orleans), these children of European colonists and African women constituted a separate caste and were recognized, by law as well as by sentiment, as bearing some legitimacy as carriers of European "blood" or "culture." They could, and often did, fight against slaves during insurrections. Many identified, strongly, with the European homeland, sometimes being sent to France to be educated, and in many cases, emigrating to France where they bore even less of the stigma of African descent, it having been decreed at one point that any slave or former slave who once set foot in the French homeland would be forever free.[3] The consequence is that the mixed blood possessed some power of economic and political agency in these cultures and often exercised a considerable economic and political role with respect to the colony's relationship to the homeland.

The cession of colonialist Louisiana to the nationalistic U.S. in 1803 overturned this system of race and caste in the Louisiana Territory. The biggest difference between France and the United States with respect to racial policies derived from the fact that the French government, like many colonialist governments, found it useful to pursue a policy of assimilation between its own agents on distant frontiers and other populations. This practice had produced an intermediate black creole caste which provided the home government (as well as white creoles, or white persons born in the colonies) with assistance in the acculturation of alienated populations—that is, slaves and natives—in the colony, but because of the distance between the homeland and the colony (and for other reasons) did not threaten the "integrity"—the status quo—of the colonialist government. Yet the U.S. was not acquiring a new colony. The nationalistic U.S. was acquiring the Louisiana Territory to be a part of its expanding nation; the racist ideology of American nationalism (like many other nationalisms) had never been particularly hospitable to amalgamation. What happened was the attempted replacement of an assimilationist colonial policy with respect to racial relationships by a segregationist and nationalist policy which demanded that one prove title as white in order to be assimilated to any degree whatsoever into the redemptive New World nation.[4]

Initially, creoles of color seem to have had some hopes that the new American government in Louisiana would augment their status, but the segregationist ideology of the U.S. not only prevented any such thing from happening, but tended to eradicate the distinctions of caste already in existence. Creoles of color were in a difficult situation. They negotiated with Governor Claiborne and his successors for a number of years in an effort to preserve some of their traditional rights of caste, but the segregationist U.S. had no place for them except as "free blacks" or (to use the legal term) "free men/women of color"—a class of persons the U.S. was already, in the 1820s, beginning to persecute in various ways. Many creoles of color emigrated to France during this period.

Whereas white racial purity had been an important commodity prior to the cession, afterwards it became absolutely essential to upper-class creoles intent on maintaining their status. Creoles had to insist on it if they could do so—and they would do so, vehemently. "Creolism," or the worship of the supposedly "pure" European inheritance of the creole elite, originated in the West Indies in the revolutionary years of the late eighteenth century when blacks and mulattoes rebelled against slavery and French rule. Ironically, it seems to have functioned as a means of legitimation. Because Europeans as well as Americans had doubts about the capacities of mixed races for self-government, the reputation of a creole as "white" thus carried with it an important kind of cultural validation. But creolism increased in Louisiana during the years following the cession. Members of the creole elite began to insist that the word itself, where capitalized, always referred to the white descendant of a French or Spanish colonist, with the emphasis on "white." In actuality, "creole" (capitalized or not) had long been used in both North and South America in several different ways to classify various groups of people (as well as to classify plants, architecture, language, art, religion, political authority, and just about everything else) with respect to their place via New World colonies and Old World powers. In France's Caribbean holdings (which included Louisiana and much of the Deep South) during the seventeenth and eighteenth centuries, the word was used irrespective of race to designate someone (or something) born in the colonies rather than in the French or Spanish homeland.[5] And it makes sense, of course, that in an outlying colony, where the government of the homeland finds it useful to pursue a policy of assimilation, the possession of wealth by members of the intermediate racial caste would in some instances work to break down taboos regarding intermarriage between whites and certain members of that caste. Under the new American government, however, assumptions about race, culture, and politics were vastly different.

Despite the insistence of some creoles upon white racial purity (and despite the fact that many were "white" even by U.S. standards), the association of "creole" with suggestions of colonialist race mixing persisted in the American context. As late as 1854, some American politicians in Louisiana attempted to ensure their victory by charging that their creole opponents possessed African ancestry, a charge that was by that time a de facto basis for political disfranchisement. Alexander Dimitry, one of the oldest and most "elite" of New Orleans creoles, found his own son-in-law, George Pandely, removed from office because of a supposed trace of African inheritance.[6] But the association of creoles with the slave population was not always so exclusively focused on biological "traces and taints." More often it seems to have derived from the tendency of Anglo-Americans (many of whom were already uncomfortable with the presence of slavery in the U.S.) to associate creoles—regardless of whether they believed those creoles to be biologically "tainted" or not—with the colonialist site of slavery, miscegenation, and political and cultural degeneration. As Europeans, as Roman Catholics, and even as victims of slave insurrections and of seizures of property and torture, creoles were carriers of "traces and taints" that Americans feared as challenges to their own redemptive mission in the New World. At one point, during Thomas Jefferson's reelection campaign in 1800, U.S. Congressman Robert Goodloe Harper wrote home to South Carolina that the antislavery French were about to launch an invasion of the southern states from bases in St. Domingo—an indication that the creole threat was not solely based on the specter of black revolution.[7] For a time, Americans, terrified of the effects on their own slaves of contact with refugees from the black and mulatto revolutions of the West Indies, prohibited immigration into ports at Charleston and New Orleans. It was not only black creoles who were feared, but white ones as well; the latter carried servants with them but even if servants were prohibited from entering the ports, these white refugees would talk of what they themselves had experienced. It was sometimes the fear of the effects of rumor, of talk, that made Americans distrust even white creoles. They too carried "news" that might threaten the supposed peace of the U.S. slave states. John Rutledge in 1787 reported to the Fifth Congress on the insurrectionary activities of West Indian slaves, concluding in righteous American fashion—"sufficient for the day is the evil thereof"—and advising that southern states "shut their door against any thing which had a tendency to produce the like confusion in this country."[8]

There is no doubt something biblical about Rutledge's style, but there is something equally biblical about the general American fear of rumor, of news from either "senile" Europe or "savage" Haiti. That is because there was something biblical about the way the New World nation envisioned itself as redemptive, as innocent, as untouched (or "unconfused") by history. The ethos of national innocence made it perfectly logical to link white creoles and black as constituting an intricately interconnected challenge to the mission of the United States. In 1804, while debating the kind of government most appropriate to the newly acquired Louisiana Territory, disagreement hinged on the effect of granting a republican form of government to subjects of European monarchy. If they were not ripe for liberty, the consequences for the U.S. could be dire. An exchange between Benjamin Huger, a U.S. representative from South Carolina, and John Jackson, from Virginia, demonstrates very clearly exactly what those consequences were imagined to be. Huger, arguing that creoles were unfit to rule themselves, asserted that they "ought to be looked upon as a certain portion of people among us [slaves] and treated as such." Jackson objected to the analogy, but took the opportunity to issue a plea for freedom: "I believe," he said "that man is the same, whether born in the United States or on the banks of the Ganges, under an African sun or on the banks of the Mississippi, and that a love of liberty is implanted in his nature."[9] This is no doubt an instance of one of the early skirmishes in the American debate over southern slavery, but it is more relevant to this argument that black slaves would be implicated in that debate as rhetorical surrogates in what was supposed to be a discussion of the fitness of white creoles for republican self-rule.

Black surrogacy makes sense, of course; it was supposed at this time that the white creole created the man of mixed blood, educated him, gave him rights withheld from men of African descent, and in that way paved the way toward the terrifying revolutions that eventually replaced white with supposedly degenerate mulatto governments in Haiti. (Similar suppositions would be made with respect to the relationship between the white American slaveholder and the slave during the mid- and late-nineteenth centuries in the United States.) Under the circumstances, it is no wonder that white Americans like Huger feared Europe's presence in the New World—Europe was seen as the source of those mulatto governments since it was presumably French Revolutionary idealism and the political pressure of France, as well as Great Britain, to abolish slavery in the Caribbean colonies that had led to those governments. Both France and Great Britain even went so far as to recognize the mulatto government of Haiti, the second independent Republic in the New World (the first being the United States itself). For slaveholders and speculators, for whom manifest destiny, the Monroe Doctrine, and the "benevolent institution" of slavery were concepts essential to the understanding of America's messianic mission, such recognition may have been only one more example of Old World complicity with African insurrectionists in a threat against the political and economic integrity of the United States. It is within this context of anxiety that we should perhaps understand the speed with which the coming of Claiborne and the United States government into the Louisiana Territory resulted in a redefinition of the mixed blood as part of the "black," hence "slave," population. In other words, this redefinition of the creole of color was an attempt to supplant a long tradition of assimilationism which enabled those descendants of white fathers to "aspire" (but probably never to attain) to something resembling the status of the European colonist.

■ ■ ■

This particular historical and discursive context exerted a real fascination for postbellum southern writers. In it they found the same issues that would reappear in the discourse surrounding the reconstruction of the South in their own eras—race and nationalism, assimilation and segregation, black surrogacy or the moral "contamination" of the slaveholder by the slave, as well as the cultural effects of racial hybridization or amalgamation versus what might be termed racial purity, homogeneity, or (even more insidiously) "integrity." In Cable's postbellum generation—and perhaps largely through Cable's work and influence—there developed a tendency to represent the defeated South as "creole," to attempt to read the reconstruction of the postbellum white southerner in terms of the nationalization of white creoles during the cession years. On their surfaces, texts like *The Grandissimes* or the stories of *Old Creole Days* are optimistic reconciliation tales where white creoles become American or are displaced by those who do. But the complexity of the historical discourse about "creoles"—"real" or metaphoric creoles, political or literary discourse—in the American context, the very indeterminacy of the word "creole" itself especially where its racial referents were concerned, permits what Foucault might term the excavation of a counternarrative, a narrative that ran submerged in the story Cable may have wanted to tell of our nation's progress toward redemptive unity, toward a kind of political millennium wherein history would be transcended. It is a counternarrative of division and recalcitrance and defeat by history. Faulkner's *Absalom, Absalom!* will pursue this counternarrative with as much diligence as Cable's texts pursue the reconciliationist dream of reunification and transcendence of tragic history.

As I have already suggested, the term creole has operated as a kind of traveling (and changeable) stage upon which the national drama of race and nationalism in the Deep South is enacted. When Cable appropriated the term in the 1870s in order to define the South's own complex relationship to colonialism, to slavery, and to U.S. ahistorical nationalism, he seems to have been unprepared for the outrage his characters would elicit from the elite creoles of New Orleans who were concerned not only about what they perceived as caricatures of themselves but by Cable's suggestions of race mixing among the creole elite, a suggestion it had long been essential to deny. Hence Cable's scrupulous acknowledgement in *The Creoles of Louisiana* that Creoles (capitalized) define themselves as the *white* descendents of European colonists. But the mere necessity for such insistence belies its problems, as Cable concedes when he writes that "there seems to be no more servicable definition of the Creoles of Louisiana than . . . that they are the French-speaking, native portion of the ruling class." He is even more direct about this in an entry written for the ninth edition of the *Encyclopedia Brittanica*, where he says that the "better class" of creole in New Orleans appears to be white although "the name they [Louisiana creoles] have borrowed . . . [from the West Indies] does not necessarily imply, any more than it excludes, a departure from a pure double line of Latin descent."[10]

The newly intensified debate in the 1880s and afterwards over the definition of *creole* reminds us that once again, in the post-Civil War era, the question of who might be or become an American had resurfaced, and the implicit racism of the United States national mission made it once again necessary that the color line be reaffirmed. The speed with which Claiborne and the U.S. government divested creoles of color of their hopes for citizenship after the Louisiana Purchase (which took a couple of decades) is outdone by the speed with which the U.S. divested freedmen of their hopes after the Civil War. It took less than one decade to decide that the freedman would not become an active participant in national life except through the mediation of former white masters. The cultural debate about the capacities of the former slaveholder continued, however, in much the same fashion as the debate over the capacities of the white creole during the years following the cession. The questions were the same: the impact of slavery on the moral fiber of the former slaveholder, the slaveholder's fitness for self-government, and the impact of the former slaveholder's assimilation upon the body politic. An editorialist for the *New York Tribune* summed up a too-familiar argument: "Wherever slavery existed, there the moral sense was so blunted and benumbed that the white people as a whole is to this day incapable of that sense of honor which prevails elsewhere."[11]

Despite the persistence of some suspicion that the former slaveholder was, like the creole who so often represented him in the discourse, tragically compromised—morally if not genetically—by his intimacy with the savage and the senile, the rhetoric of southern redemption was largely inspiriting. In an 1882 address to the graduating class at the University of Mississippi, Cable called for southerners to transcend the past, to put history behind them. In this talk, he objected to the phrase "New South," suggesting that we aim for the "No South": "Does the word sound like annihilation? It is the farthest from it. It is enlargement. It is growth. It is a higher life."[12] Yet neither the reality of political and economic life in the South nor the literature of the period bears out the promise of Cable's optimistic rhetoric. The white southerner's return to the reunified nation during the significantly named Redemption Era that followed Reconstruction was less a transcendence of southern history in a redemptive national body than a return to the white southerner of the rights to reconstitute, or attempt to reconstitute, a racial order which imitated, in some respects, that of antebellum years. And, predictably enough, it was less a redemption from than a renewal of certain racist assumptions about the proper relationship between black and white in the United States. It also revealed the continuing assumption that it was the white southerner's particular history and nature that would fit him to deal with the dangerous African American. There is in this assumption something of the idea that Emerson had attributed to the abolitionist: that "the negro [and] the negro-holder are really of one party."[13]

It might have been expected that the fundamental racism of the American culture would result in a "redemption" that amounted to the return of the African American to a semi-slave status and the return of the white South to a marginal status with respect to a national mission imagined in terms of its capacity to transcend history. Certainly the politics of the Redemption Era returned the southern white man to power in the South but also led to the South's increasing political, economic, and cultural isolation and to a growing—because related—southern hysteria about the dangers of "amalgamation." This hysteria seems to have developed from the white southerner's awareness, at least on some level, that the color line was little more than a reflection of the political, cultural, and economic alienation of selected populations, that he himself was, in some respects, alienated by that very color line from the U.S. national mission, and that to be alienated in the U.S. was, whatever the color of your skin, to be "black."

Lest this sound a bit extreme, we might recall that it is the putative "blackness" of the mysterious stranger who appears white that preoccupied the white southern writer, as it preoccupied the United States court system during these years.[14] This preoccupation was based on the belief that political and economic equality for the freedman would inevitably lead to "social equality," to the "contamination" of white bodies with black

blood, to the "degeneration" of white civilization in the South. These terrors themselves reflected doubts—on the part of the white southerner
as well as the rest of the nation—about the white southerner's capacity
to accomplish the transcendence of history that was required before he
could be effectively redeemed. They also reiterated the issues of assimilation versus segregation that had preoccupied the nation during the
original cession of the Louisiana Territory to the U.S. and echoed against
a new reality, the reality of imperialism, which ironically placed the white
American abroad in the same position in which the white southerner had
been placed on the domestic front.

This complex history of cultural displacement is of particular relevance
to *Absalom, Absalom!*, where the creole becomes the means through
which post–Civil War white southerners dramatize their own recalcitrance. In a sense, *Absalom, Absalom!* will eventually appropriate the
figure of the creole of color as he is constructed by earlier white writers
like Cable, but Faulkner's text also transfigures the construction in ways
that result in a stronger, more deliberate and less qualified critique of
the ahistorical nationalism that would seek to deny or transcend United
States complicity with Europe and with Africa in the development of a
New World nation. In *Absalom, Absalom!*, unlike so much of the earlier
literature, there is not even the illusion of a happy ending—no marriage,
no dynasty, no legitimate offspring.

In this work, the hubris of an American innocent, Thomas Sutpen, creates a retributive agent in the figure of Charles Bon, a mystery whom we
never see, who never speaks except through the mouths of those who
tell his story, who has no identity independent of their projections.[15] The
fact remains, however, that the significance of Charles Bon—like that
of the dark Honoré in *The Grandissimes*—evolves from the relationship
between the history of the Deep South with respect to United States
nationalistic expansion in the early nineteenth century and the political,
rhetorical situation of the white southerner in the years after the Civil
War. It is also important to note that the construction and reconstruction
of Charles Bon recapitulates the construction and reconstruction of the
creole Deep South as site of the struggle between an ahistorical ideology of American transcendence of history and American history itself. In
other words, the issue of race mixing and the effort to keep the mixed
blood out of the white family (or nation) in *Absalom, Absalom!* is a return,
through the medium of psychological family drama, to the issue of assimilation versus segregation of the creole as it was defined and discussed

in the political discourse of American nationalism between 1803 and the beginning of the Civil War.

Charles Bon, that "durn French feller" (133), appears suddenly in the middle of frontier Mississippi. He comes—at least initially we are told he comes—from New Orleans, the site of the colonialist culture represented by so many of the octoroons in U.S. literature. And like so many of them he possesses a fatal (and fatalistic) creole sophistication and later, much later, for some speakers (and only for some speakers), the "taint" of African ancestry—a detail that is considered fact by most Faulkner scholars and probably comes as close to fact as any other detail concerning Bon, which is to say not very close at all. The real fact, of course, is that the conversation that supposedly reveals Bon as black is not included in the text, which leaves open the possibility that Quentin might have misconstrued, or invented, such a conversation for his own purposes. The reason for the murder of Charles Bon by Henry Sutpen in 1865 becomes one of the novel's central mysteries—as central as the mystery of Thomas Sutpen's character to which that murder is intricately tied—and the need to create a satisfactory explanation for that murder becomes an obsession for each speaker.

We, as readers, do not know exactly why Henry Sutpen killed Charles Bon. All we can be sure of is that, for all of the speakers except Miss Rosa, Henry was driven by some necessity for preserving his family's (and the nation's) purity. In fact, what we are more than likely meant to know is that the story of the murder constructed by each speaker is remarkably representative of that speaker's sense of his own defeat within a specific historical context. In other words, whether the "purity" that Henry is seen as protecting is constructed in terms that are nationalistic, familial, or racial depends upon who the speaker is, or rather *when* he is. Repeatedly Faulkner warns us that the story is "invented" (335) by the tellers of the tale, and "true enough" to boot, but that the telling of the story is a matter of "hearing and sifting and discarding the false and conserving what seemed true, or fit the preconceived" (316). Under the circumstances Faulkner's decision to embed the truth in the drama of performance, to bind information so tightly to interpretation leads the reader to ask not only who or what Charles Bon was—whether he was black or white, possible son or would-be husband—but to ask who and what the speakers are with respect to the Charles Bon they construct. And it is clear that who and what they are has everything to do with history as it happened in the Deep South in the years between the cession of the Louisiana Territory and the early twentieth century. It is the relationship of two postwar generations—represented by Jason Compson and his son Quentin, respectively—to that history (which in this text takes the form of the "preconceived") that makes the tale. The final irony is that whatever the rationale, the murder itself did happen and, instead of releasing the Sutpens and those whom they represent from the tragedies of their own history, serves to accelerate their decline into that history. In this sense, *Absalom, Absalom!* is as much a novel about the return of a tragic history to the American South—in the guises first of white creole decadence, then of blackness and in the form of retributive justice—as *The Grandissimes* and other, earlier "octoroon" stories are stories of the attempted (and often failed) expulsion of history in the exile of the man of mixed blood and extranational loyalties.

There is little doubt that Faulkner wrote *Absalom, Absalom!* out of a deep familiarity with the political and cultural situation in both New Orleans and in Haiti, especially as it was perceived by and important to nineteenth- and early twentieth-century southerners such as the ones upon whom Jason and Quentin Compson were modeled. Faulkner's familiarity with this context should not be surprising, given his Deep South origins; the arrival of his own most famous ancestor, William Clark Falkner, in the southwestern frontier during the first half of the nineteenth century when Mississippi was still very much frontier and creole New Orleans was a newly acquired southern terminus (hardly sixty miles south); and his own time in the French Quarter of New Orleans and in France in the mid-1920s.

Thomas Sutpen lives in French Haiti from the early 1820s to 1833. He serves for a time as overseer on a sugar plantation owned by a French planter; he "subdues" an uprising of Haitian slaves who threaten the planter with their Voodoo in what is probably one of the many skirmishes that made up the long and bloody Haitian revolution of the late eighteenth and nineteenth centuries; he marries Eulalia, the planter's daughter by a Spanish creole; his son, Charles Bon, is born in 1829; and Sutpen makes the "discovery" that causes him to repudiate Eulalia in 1831, two years before he arrives in Yoknapatawpha County and not long before his spurned wife arrives, with their son, in New Orleans—still a logical destination for a West Indian creole at this time.

That a man like the young Sutpen, obsessed with his redemptive design, should end up in the West Indies is probable. Despite the U.S. refusal to recognize the mulatto government of Jean Pierre Boyer, Haiti, of all the West Indian islands, was of great economic importance to the United States. The Caribbean was the logical theater for dreams of American expansion in the pre–Civil War era (as it would be once again in Quentin Compson's era) since the desire for expansion had certainly not been exhausted by the acquisition of the Louisiana Territory. What did happen between that time and the years preceding the Civil War was the development of a more articulate ideology of expansion in which the idea of the design as redemptive was more pronounced and more intricately entangled with the ideology of race and slavery. Throughout the pre–Civil War era, dreams of worldly wealth for white Americans and dreams of a millennial civilization, or terrestrial paradise, where even the enslavement of the darker races could be seen as a step toward lifting them out of such darkness and into the light of God's righteous millennium, were united in that rhetoric. By extension, it was of great importance to preserve the American nation from contamination by decadent Europe and its leveling influence, already visible in the formation of Haiti as the first mulatto government in the New World. The question of course— the same question that Americans put to themselves in their debate over national assimilation of white creoles—was whether such preservation was possible. It was a question that would be readily appropriated by the postbellum white American as a way to explain the South's defeat as somehow preordained. Just as importantly it was a question that would be readily appropriated by William Faulkner as the key to the construction and reconstruction of Charles Bon and the means through which Faulkner might explore the implications of his own generation's imperialist designs.

In the light of Faulkner's critique of millennialist ideology, it is certainly of some ironic import that the architect for Sutpen's mansion should be a colonialist Frenchman from Martinique, because in so many ways the slave culture that the Anglo planter in the Deep South inherited (if not the slave culture he envisioned) was established upon a West Indian, predominantly French and Spanish, foundation. During the time that Sutpen's mansion is going up, the architect, "in his formal coat and his Paris hat and his expression of grim and embittered amazement lurked about the environs of the scene with his air something between a casual and bitterly disinterested spectator and a condemned and conscientious ghost— amazement . . . not at the others and what they were doing so much as at himself, at the inexplicable and incredible fact of his own presence" (38).

Later, Charles Bon will share not only a French cultural identification but also the Frenchman's spectral relationship to the American slaveholder:

> from the moment when he [Bon] realized that Sutpen was going to prevent the marriage if he could, he (Bon) seems to have withdrawn into a mere spectator, passive, a little sardonic, and completely enigmatic. He seems to hover, shadowy, almost substanceless, a little behind and above all the other straightforward and logical, even though (to him) incomprehensible, ultimatums and affirmations and defiances and challenges and repudiations, with an air of sardonic and indolent detachment like that of a youthful Roman consul making the Grand Tour of his day among the barbarian hordes which his grandfather conquered. (93)

Bon, like the French architect (who may be, at least rhetorically and symbolically, the "grandfather" referred to) is a ghostly spectator who seems condemned to haunt the site of a former life. Despite the intricate historical relationships among New World slave cultures, the expansion of the United States during the early nineteenth century placed the colonialist cultures of Europe in just this position with respect to the developing nation in the New World, a nation that defined itself as the working out in a New World wilderness of a Providential design impossible in the corrupt atmosphere of Europe. That this French architect should so clearly prefigure Charles Bon suggests that Faulkner was well aware of the inevitable persistence of the displaced in any design which sought to transcend a historical relationship among various cultures and peoples.

It is the persistence of history in the New World—in the discourse of New World speakers—and its capacity to undermine official American innocence that seems most to interest Faulkner. His rich historicism is strikingly apparent in his handling of the voices that construct and reconstruct the story of Charles Bon, constructing and reconstructing themselves in the process. According to Rosa Coldfield, who came of age in the antebellum South—and for whom the Civil War is a consequence rather than a cause—Bon's murder is inexplicable except as the inevitable consequence of Sutpen's—the American innocent's—own demonic nature (15). For Rosa, Bon is "Charles Good, Charles Husband-Soon-To-Be," an unseen prince who is nothing less than a miracle, a civilized man on the Mississippi frontier. Thus for Rosa, the marriage between Judith and Bon is "forbidden without rhyme or reason or shadow of excuse" (18). But according to those speakers who came of age after the

Civil War, including Jason Compson and his son Quentin, the murder is made necessary by Bon's nature, not by Sutpen's—at least that is the kind of motivating cause these speakers pursue with greatest energy. Not surprisingly, these are the speakers for whom the Civil War has become a kind of originary moment wherein the Sutpens, like their textual descendants the Compsons, find their motive and rationale.

Jason and Quentin Compson are nevertheless quite different as speakers and their stories of Bon—of the South's (and of America's) repressed history—diverge, especially insofar as race figures into the stories, chiefly because for Faulkner they represent two distinct generations whose understanding of the United States and of their own relationship to the U.S. and to the history of slavery and race in the Deep South is very different. Although both imagine Bon as a creole possessed of the expected creole decadence and capable of corrupting the innocence of Sutpens, it is only in Quentin's narrative that Bon is constructed as black. For Jason—whose understanding of Bon and of the South's defeat seems to have developed free of the impact of U.S. imperialism and radical racist ideas of race and culture (which became popular only in the late 1880s, long after Jason would have first heard of Bon and begun to formulate his own understanding)—Bon is simply "the curious one" in this American frontier, "apparently complete, without background or past or childhood," a man who invades an "isolated puritan country household" and seduces both brother and sister in a way more inevitable than deliberate (93). For Jason, preoccupied with the scene of a colonizing and corrupting European empire and its impact on the American Deep South, the white creole Bon is representative of a retributive power perceived as culminating in his inheritance of the French architect's ability to "curb the dream of grim and castlelike magnificence" (38) toward which Sutpen aims. The difference between Jason and his antebellum forbears, of course, is that the postbellum Jason Compson identifies *himself* more closely with the white creole Bon than with the Sutpens. Charles Bon is, in Donald Kartiganer's words, Jason Compson "writ large," a man "equipped with a cynicism that rivals Mr. Compson's own" and, fundamentally, a man who shares with Jason Compson the kind of cultural superfluity that results from having inherited, like the French aristocrats in Faulkner's early manuscript *Elmer*, "an old and splendid thing worn out with time." [16] It is difficult to resist Kartiganer's reading, for the South's defeat in the Civil War has left Jason in the very position he constructs for Bon, as "complete [yet] without background . . . a mere spectator" (93). Jason's heroic ancestors are separated from him not only by time or death but by a kind of political legitimacy he, like the white creole, can no longer aspire to; unlike him, they are "not dwarfed and involved but distinct, uncomplex who had the gift of loving once or dying once instead of being diffused and scattered creatures drawn blindly limb from limb from a grab bag and assembled, author and victim too of a thousand homicides and a thousand copulations and divorcements" (89). In this passage Jason reveals his own sense of confused and violent origins as well as the alienation of the southerners whom he represents from the ordering power of a nationalistic discourse, an alienation traceable to 1865 and, in this text, to the murder of Bon.

When Jason attempts to explain that murder, he resorts predictably to the terms of his own compelling narrative of the encounter of the nationalistic American and the colonizing European. Henry Sutpen, the "legitimate" ("puritan") son of Thomas Sutpen, might have found that Bon had to be killed for the fatal French assimilationism which allowed him to maintain, in a semblance of legitimacy, an octoroon woman and their son (100)—a story which recapitulates the response of the segregationist U.S. to the existence of the intermediate caste of creoles of color in the Caribbean and reflects, in terms of domestic/sexual history, American distrust of the French as authors of the black revolutions in the Caribbean. In murdering Bon, then, Henry (according to the logic of Jason Compson's version of events) may have been attempting to preserve Thomas Sutpen's vision of order and hierarchy from the example of Europe. That Bon maintained a black family and perhaps even carried their pictures with him must have seemed to Henry a violation of the very terms upon which civilization must be established. One must note, however, that for Jason the threat (and the seductive promise) of "race-mixing" is situated in the female octoroon, whom he imagines as a creature utterly powerless to challenge or threaten the white estate except as a tool of the colonist. The relish with which Jason describes her home in New Orleans, closed and hidden, its crumbling walls and old doorkeeper like a figure from a French woodcut, confines her threat within the displaced colonialist culture—far removed by the ideologies of race, gender, and nation from any possibility of a serious claim to the white estate, except through the agency of the European colonist (112–13).

It is, however, Quentin's appropriation and deployment of this horror of confused and violent origins in his reconstruction of Charles Bon himself as "white nigger" that is of greater significance. It is, after all, Quentin Compson as "commonwealth" (12), as heir of southern history, its final dying original, who completes—and is himself completed by—the story begun by Rosa Coldfield and continued by Jason. It should not be surprising that a white southerner of Quentin's generation, caught between a history that associates him with Africa and with Europe and a political rhetoric that would assimilate him to a nationalistic, increasingly imperialistic, and racist ideal, would dramatize his situation with respect to the very best representative of that situation, the creole man of mixed blood.

Central to Quentin's reconstruction of Bon are the preoccupations of his own turn-of-the-century South with questions of white racial purity and the American mission. In his revision, black Haiti replaces white creole New Orleans as the locus for Bon, who eventually becomes a representative of that troubled "mulatto nation"—as well as a harbinger of America's own assimilation to a like future through the inevitable "amalgamation" that racists of Quentin's generation felt would result from any recognition of blacks as equal citizens of the United States. The extent and the nature of this cultural hysteria are most visible in the work of radical racists like Thomas Dixon Jr. and Robert Lee Durham. There is little question that in the work of these writers the octoroon has been characterized very differently than by Cable and other Deep South writers of his generation. In these explicitly racist fictions, the octoroon figure is marked by an inclination to sexual excess and violence associated with images of "African" savagery, his or her white skin nothing more than a mask to hide the destructive fires associated with the heavily sexualized "dark continent," a place that ostensibly exists prior to history and political order and the site of a radical chaos which is presented as a danger to the American redemptive mission. Of course Quentin's narrative eventually does work its way around to this sexualized vision of an African Bon, but the development of this Bon as part of a longer historical process of "inventing" Bon serves as a means of textual containment and commentary on that vision. As a matter of fact, it is really not very far, in terms of metaphorical development, from Jason's creation of Bon (and by extension of himself) as cynical or fatalistic European charged with the seduction of the South through the unveiling of the white negro—the beautiful octoroon woman or "apotheosis of chattelry" (112)—to Quentin's creation of Bon (and by extension of *himself*) as the white negro, a man who has inherited both the violence and the illegitimacy, and whose blood demands vengeance. Both Jason's and Quentin's accounts are dramatizations of the white southerner's sense of his own construction by postbellum history. By extension one might also note that Bon's capacity to contain all of history in this new role of "nigger" (corrupt European and dispossessed elder brother as well as "nigger")—as if the "white nigger" is indeed the "supreme apotheosis" not only of chattelry but of all of history—offers us some sense of the extremity of Quentin's position as both American and as southern heir to a past he cannot transcend.

Equally important to the reconstruction of Bon is the context of U.S. imperialism. What Theodore Roosevelt called New Nationalism may have been the logical outcome of the reunion of North and South after Reconstruction, but by the end of the century, nationalism had become imperialism—at the very least, what Benedict Anderson calls "official nationalism" had become useful rhetorically for the agenda of empire. At the turn of the century the imperialistic designs of the U.S. tapped the same racist ambitions and anxieties in white Americans that the expansionist designs of slaveholders had tapped half a century before.[17] The concurrent rise of U.S. imperialism abroad and radical racism inside the U.S., the latter holding that blacks—freed from the civilizing influences of slavery—were retrogressing into savagery and would eventually die out in the competition with whites, was no coincidence. One might, in fact, read the hysteria of radical racism as an appropriation, on the domestic front, of the imperialistic agenda of redemption, the burnings and dismemberments of black bodies a dramatization on the physical body of the effects of colonization on the black cultural bodies of Cuba, Puerto Rico, and the Philippines, acquired by the U.S. in the Spanish-American War. The U.S. agenda was quite clear. Albert Beveridge may have said it best:

> God has not been preparing the English-speaking and Teutonic peoples for a thousand years for nothing but vain and idle self-contemplation and self-admiration. No. He made us master organizers of the world to establish system where chaos reigned. He has given us the spirit of progress to overwhelm the forces of reaction throughout the earth. He has made us adept in government that we may administer government among savage and senile peoples. Were it not for such a force as this the world would relapse into barbarism and night. And of all our race He has marked the American people as His chosen nation to finally lead in the redemption of the world.[18]

Beveridge made this speech to the U.S. Senate at the turn of the century, marshalling in only a few lines the kind of rhetoric that William Faulkner would conjure with in his development of Quentin as both victim and agent of such imperialist ideology.

Quentin's narrative begins in the winter following his discovery of Henry Sutpen in the old mansion. What this means is that it begins after he has supposedly learned that Bon was black. Nevertheless, Quentin does not reveal this putative solution to the text's various mysteries until very late in the story, allowing the detail of miscegenation to seem to be arrived at by a process of deduction from the premise of Bon's origins in a colonialist slave culture—a process that recapitulates the psychopolitical drama of the white southerner in the novel, whose own origins in a colonialist slave culture eventually lead to his defeat and alienation. At first, we know only that Charles Bon is a mysterious French Creole, but as Quentin's story unfolds, Bon is transformed from colonialist creole into Thomas Sutpen's elder son into "the nigger that's going to sleep with your sister" (358). In other words, Quentin's narrative transforms Charles Bon from a man who had, at a prior stage of history (Jason Compson's), some—albeit negligible—claim upon the white estate (a claim to assimilation) into someone who cannot possibly, according to the conventional logic of American radical racism, sustain any such claims.

It is here that the extent of Quentin Compson's own alienation from the ordering power of the nationalist discourse becomes most evident. Quentin's Charles Bon—Quentin Compson "writ large"—wants the father's recognition more than he wants his father's daughter. Bon's lawyer (never mentioned in Jason's story and certainly more believable as a product of the imaginations of two turn-of-the-century college students than as a realistic representation of antebellum legal counsel) is more intent on pressing the claims of the (at this point) white and creole Bon on the American father's estate than in pressing his suit of love. In fact, the *"daughter? daughter? daughter?"* (309) is hardly more than a means for acquiring some portion of entitlement to that estate. Bon's ultimatum, implicit but nevertheless clear enough, requires either recognition by the American father and all it entails or incestuous marriage to the daughter. It is also implicit, but clear enough, that the ultimatum is designed to lead to the father's recognition of Bon and not to Bon's marriage to Judith. What it does lead to, as Quentin imagines it, is Thomas Sutpen's revelation to Henry that Bon is not white, a revelation that changes everything. Bon's claims to the white estate are rendered absolutely monstrous and Bon is transformed from alienated son into "the nigger who's going to sleep with your sister," an agent for the destruction of the white estate.

It is here that the post-1890 context out of which Quentin constructs his story becomes most evident. The phrase that Bon uses during his final confrontation with Henry—"the nigger that's going to sleep with your sister"—would not likely have been used in the South of 1865, when Charles Bon is supposed by Quentin Compson to have uttered it, although it had become a racist rallying cry by the turn of the century when Quentin Compson constructs this imaginary scene. (It is indeed fascinating that Quentin attributes that line to Charles Bon himself, as if giving the character an opportunity to comment, somewhat prematurely, upon his own development as a construct.) In Quentin's South, a South growing more and more isolated from the rest of the country, the terms "black" and "brother" became just reconcilable enough in the rhetoric of radical racism which claimed that the black man wanted nothing so much as the white woman, just possible enough to function as the white southerner's ultimate nightmare of alienation. As African, as "black beast," as "the nigger that's going to sleep with your sister," and yet as brother nonetheless, Charles Bon represents all that the post-1890 white southerner most feared: the gradual usurpation of political, familial, and economic purity—legitimacy, recognition by the national body or by the father—by a mulatto brother or brother-in-law, a usurpation almost always associated with the degeneration of a proud civilization into a "mongrel" future.

What this substitution of "nigger" for "brother" suggests is the existence in Quentin's narrative of a perceived necessity, played out in a rhetorical maneuver, of denying the Fifteenth Amendment, of denying, in effect, that one can be *both* black and brother. In 1913, Senator James K. Vardaman spoke directly to this point: "I unhesitatingly assert that political equality for the colored race leads to social equality. Social equality leads to race amalgamation, and race amalgamation leads to deterioration and disintegration."[19] What Vardaman and those for whom he spoke reveal in such statements is the fear of the degeneration of their own lines, political as well as familial. Under the circumstances, it is relatively easy to see that what the white racist is attempting to protect by refusing to acknowledge a black man as brother or "social equal"—the purity of the family line as a kind of metaphor for citizenship and rights to govern—is, in *Absalom, Absalom!*, exactly what such a policy does not protect, precisely because of the possibility that an unrecognized (and unrecognizable) black son might, through passing unknown into the white family, violate laws against miscegenation as well as incest. Ironically, Thomas Sutpen's refusal to acknowledge his mulatto son, to give him the father's name which would "place" him with respect to his lineage (a placing that had been possible in the Caribbean cultures that preceded the coming of Americans like Sutpen into the Deep South), is exactly what precipitates the dual threats of incest and miscegenation.

If we recall, for a moment, Quentin's often discussed obsession with his sister Caddy—the incestuous desires that lead him in *The Sound and the Fury* to transform his own virginity into the sign of incest consummated and reified—the nexus of issues of racial (familial) purity and national legitimacy in the novel becomes clearer as the site of the white southerner's own struggle for cultural redemption, for an escape from history into the millennial New World nation of the United States. Bon is Quentin himself "writ large" in the language of his own defeat as a construct who almost, but not quite, gets away with the incest Quentin imagines that he has committed, longs to have committed, and fears desperately that he has committed—an incest that, as John Irwin has suggested, operates as a metaphor for origination and authority in Quentin Compson but also carries with it the threat, as well as the promise, of death.[20]

"Amalgamation is incest," wrote one Mississippian as early as 1854: "Impurity of race is against the law of nature. Mulattoes are monsters. The law of nature is the law of God. The same law which forbids consanguinous amalgamation forbids ethnical amalgamation. Both are incestuous."[21] It is a powerful equation when read in terms of Quentin's narrative of race and sex, where the monster who must be destroyed, the figure who "owns the terror," is both black and brother—despite the rhetoric that would deny that relationship—in other words a dramatization of the white racist's most nightmarish vision of his own future under the new dispensation. If the "supreme apotheosis" of slavery is the octoroon woman, the supreme apotheosis of emancipation, in the mind of a radical racist, may be the "white nigger." It is particularly important in this reading of Quentin Compson's paradoxical desire for and rejection of the "black" brother that this is a phrase used at this time not only to refer to the octoroon but also to describe certain kinds of traitorous whites who exhibited what was perceived as "morally black" behavior—incest, for example.[22] Quentin's incestuous desires are thus not only configured as the logical outcome of his own loss of cultural legitimacy which could effectively "name" and thereby "place" him (in a parallel of the black creole's loss of such legitimacy during the cession years), but they do indeed redefine him as a "white nigger," as "morally black"; they make him, in a sense, "the nigger that's going to sleep with your sister." As a matter of fact, Shreve McCannon, Quentin's audience and co-creator for the story, suggests this very thing. "You've got . . . one nigger Sutpen left," he tells Quentin at the end of *Absalom, Absalom!*: "I think that in time the Jim Bonds are going to conquer the western hemisphere. Of course it won't quite be in our time and of course as they spread toward the poles they will bleach out again like the rabbits and the birds do, so they won't show up so sharp against the snow. But it will still be Jim Bond; and so in a few thousand years, I who regard you will also have sprung from the loins of African kings" (378). The subtext, of course, is that Quentin himself has already, in some sense, "sprung from the loins of African kings." Shreve's prophecy makes it apparent that, already, through a process of constructing the story in terms of the most deadly fear, assimilation/amalgamation, it is the white southerner himself who finally and ironically "owns the terror" (369–70) because he has been transformed (or has transformed himself), through the rhetoric of defeat as it is used in a racist and nationalistic culture, into the victim, into the European and African ghosts the U.S., obsessed with its own ahistorical uniqueness, fears so intensely. In other words, when a nation envisions itself in ahistorical and millennialist terms, as new and as redemptive, it denies its relationships to the past, even to the history of its making. The consequence for a white southerner who had been prior to his defeat by the United States at the very center of a southern nationalism that envisioned itself in terms remarkably similar to those of the United States (as redemptive) is that—by the logic of his own rhetoric—he has become through his defeat the inheritor of history as well as the bearer of prior displacements in his own.

In the climactic scene between Henry Sutpen and Charles Bon at the gate to Sutpen's mansion, the segregationist ideal is enforced. No marriage takes place between Charles Bon and Judith Sutpen. By all the lights of radical racist ideology, this is preservation, the laying of foundations for a sunny future. But in Faulkner's text, the segregationist dream is subverted into its own nightmare. Instead of progress, redemption from the sins of the fathers, and transcendence of history, we are left with degeneration, damnation, and submergence into history. The fact is that Quentin fails. It is not so much that he fails to penetrate the mysteries of the past—that failure is inevitable. The more significant failure is that he reconstructs Charles Bon in the same terms, according to the same economy of exclusion that his fathers had used in their construction of America on the preposterous ideal of transcendence of history. Like his fathers, Quentin is incapable of reading his own kinship with those populations alienated by New World ideology as anything other than a sign of his own degeneracy. Quentin's is a failure of imagination, an inability to rewrite the old stories. Quentin solves no mystery of Charles Bon; he solves no murder. Bon remains invisible; the murder remains unexplained; and Quentin remains as much a victim of the past as his many fathers.

But if Quentin's status as a victim of history makes him a compelling representation of the southerner of Faulkner's generation, it also makes him equally as compelling as a representation of Faulkner's future American. Certainly Shreve's metaphor of migration suggests that the implications of amalgamation are not exclusively for that region of the U.S. known as the "South," although one has to acknowledge that the alienated status of the American South at this period is essential to the story. The reality of implication suggests, instead, that in *Absalom, Absalom!* the South is not only a discrete region within the geographical borders of the U.S., but a phase within the narrative of nationalism, a tropic site wherein that narrative originates and from which it flees. The power of *Absalom, Absalom!* is to be found in its capacity to subvert, on southern terrain, those rhetorical strategies the U.S. has used to constitute itself as a coherent and culminating entity, distinct from its colonialist past and slavery. Carolyn Porter observes of *Absalom, Absalom!* that "by the time we find out what is going on, we are already implicated in it."[23] For all of its engagement with the alienating discourses of racial, national, and regional divisions, *Absalom, Absalom!* is a study in implication.

Notes

1   I am focusing on the construction of this figure in the work of white writers. African American writers have used the figure of the creole of color often, and in ways very different from those devised by whites. Certainly, in African American literature as in Anglo-American literature, the octoroon is an alienated figure; however, in much African American literature, he or she is also an index of racial progress and the drama often moves the character from an alienated condition to an identification with and commitment to the African American community. For a good discussion of the use of the mixed blood figure in African American literature, see J. Dickson Bruce's *Black American Writing from the Nadir: The Evolution of a Literary Tradition, 1877–1915* (Baton Rouge: Louisiana State Univ. Press, 1989), 11–55.

Furthermore, it is important to acknowledge that in Anglo-American literature, the submergence (not to be mistaken for the complete eradication) of Africa as site of the octoroon's origins may be evidence of an anxiety around the issues of race that is deeper than any political anxieties associated with the Old World. Be that as it may, neither Cable's Honoré Grandissime, free man of color, nor William Faulkner's Charles Bon possesses any of the expected tags of African ancestry—strange shiverings around slaveyards, uncanny resemblances to black characters, and so on. It is the meaning of the characteristics the figure does possess that is of primary interest in this study.

2   William Faulkner, *Absalom, Absalom!* (New York: Random House, 1936), 148, 358, 378, 250. All further quotations from *Absalom, Absalom!* are from this edition and cited in parentheses in the text.

3   Gwendolyn Midlo Hall's recent *Africans in Colonial Louisiana: The Develop-ment of Afro-Creole Culture in the Eighteenth Century* (Baton Rouge: Louisi-ana State Univ. Press, 1992), especially her chapter "The Pointe Coupee Post: Race Mixture and Freedom at a Frontier Settlement," is invaluable for an understanding of race mixing and passing on the French colonialist frontier.

For discussions of the traditions of classifying children of black/white liai-sons in the Deep South and the West Indies and the political and economic consequences of the cession of the Louisiana Territory to the United States, see also Ira Berlin, *Slaves Without Masters: The Free Negro in the Antebellum South* (New York: Random House, 1974), 97–98; Carl Degler, *Neither Black Nor White: Slavery and Race Relations in Brazil and the United States* (New York: Macmillan, 1971), 226–45; Laura Foner, "The Free People of Color in Louisiana and St. Domingue," *Journal of Social History* 3 (summer 1970): 406–30; Winthrop Jordan, *White Over Black: American Attitudes Toward the Negro, 1550–1812* (New York: Norton, 1977), 167; James Kinney, *Amalga-mation!: Race, Sex, and Rhetoric in the Nineteenth-Century American Novel* (Westport, Conn.: Greenwood Press, 1985); John G. Mencke, *Mulattoes and Race Mixture: American Attitudes and Images, 1865–1918* (Ann Arbor: UMI Research Press, 1979): 1–36; and H. E. Sterkx, *The Free Negro in Antebel-lum Louisiana* (Rutherford, N.J.: Fairleigh Dickinson Univ. Press, 1972).

The following discussions focus specifically upon the coming of the United States into the Louisiana Territory: Alice Dunbar Nelson, "People of Color in Louisiana" (Parts I and II), *The Journal of Negro History* 1 (1916): 361–76, and 2 (1917): 51–78; Donald E. Everett, "Emigrés and Militiamen: Free Per-sons of Color in New Orleans, 1803–1815," *The Journal of Negro History* 38 (1953): 377–402; Thomas Marc Fiehrer, "The African Presence in Colonial Louisiana," in *Louisiana's Black Heritage*, ed. Robert R. MacDonald, John R. Kemp, and Edward F. Haas (New Orleans: Louisiana State Museum, 1977); and Charles Barthelemy Rousseve, *The Negro in Louisiana* (New Orleans: Xavier Univ. Press, 1937), 47–48, especially the speech by Robespierre included in the appendix and entitled "Speech on the Condition of the Free Men of Color in the French Colonies," 173–74, and a series of documents under the heading "Legislation Restricting Free People of Color," 175–78.

4   For a discussion of the different policies of nationalist and colonialist expansion, especially as worked out in the Deep South context, see Arnold R. Hirsch and Joseph Logsdon, *Creole New Orleans: Race and Americanization* (Baton Rouge: Louisiana State Univ. Press, 1992), especially the essays by Joseph G. Tregle Jr., "Creoles and Americans," and Gwendolyn Midlo Hall, "The Formation of Afro-Creole Culture." The introduction to "Part II: The American Challenge" is also useful. For a discussion of nationalism and its connections to ideas of "race" as well as for a good discussion of race in the creole New World, see Benedict Anderson's *Imagined Communities: Reflections on the Origin and Spread of Nationalism*, rev. ed. (New York: Verso, 1991).

5   Hirsch and Logsdon, *Creole New Orleans*, 60, 98, 132ff.

6   Hirsch and Logsdon, *Creole New Orleans*, 98.

7   Jordan, *White Over Black*, 388.

8   Jordan, *White Over Black*, 388.

9   Jordan, *White Over Black*, 389–90.

10   George Washington Cable, *The Creoles of Louisiana* (New York: Scribner's, 1885), 41, 42. *Encyclopedia Brittanica*, 9th ed., s.v. "New Orleans."

11   *New York Tribune*, 30 August 1879.

12   George Washington Cable, "Literature in the Southern States," in *The Negro Question: A Selection of Writings on Civil Rights in the South*, ed. Arlin Turner (New York: Doubleday, 1958), 44.

13   *The Journals and Miscellaneous Notebooks of Ralph Waldo Emerson*, vol. 13, 1852–1855, ed. by Ralph H. Orth and Alfred R. Ferguson. (Cambridge: Harvard Univ. Press, 1977), 198.

14   See Eric Sundquist's discussion of the *Plessy v. Ferguson* case and its impact on American literature of the era in "Mark Twain and Homer Plessy" in his *To Wake the Nations: Race in the Making of American Literature* (Cambridge: Harvard Univ. Press, 1993).

15   In calling Sutpen an "American innocent," I follow critics like Cleanth Brooks and Carolyn Porter for whom Sutpen is, in Porter's words, "no less American for being Southern, and no less Southern for being American" (*Seeing and Being: The Plight of the Participant Observer in Emerson, James, Adams, and Faulkner* [Middletown, Conn.: Wesleyan Univ. Press, 1981], 209). See also Cleanth Brooks's important discussion of the character of Thomas Sutpen in *William Faulkner: The Yoknapatawpha County* (New Haven: Yale Univ. Press, 1963), 11ff, and 296.

16   Donald Kartiganer, *The Fragile Thread: The Meaning of Form in Faulkner's Novels* (Amherst: Univ. of Massachusetts Press, 1979), 81–82; William Faulkner, "Elmer," *The Mississippi Quarterly* 36 (summer 1983): 410.

17   Anderson, *Imagined Communities*, 83–111.

18 Quoted in Ernest Lee Tuveson, *Redeemer Nation: The Idea of America's Millennial Role* (Chicago: Univ. of Chicago Press, 1968), vii.

19 Quoted in Joel Williamson, *The Crucible of Race: Black-White Relations in the American South Since Emancipation* (New York: Oxford Univ. Press, 1984), 379.

20 John Irwin, *Doubling and Incest/Repetition and Revenge: A Speculative Reading of Faulkner* (Baltimore: Johns Hopkins Univ. Press, 1975), 64, 82–94.

21 Henry Hughes, *A Treatise on Sociology: Theoretical and Practical* (Philadelphia: Lippincott, Grambo, and Company, 1854), 31.

22 Williamson, *The Crucible of Race*, 466.

23 Porter, *Seeing and Being*, 49.

Ramón
Saldívar

Border Subjects and Transnational Sites:
Américo Paredes's *The Hammon and
the Beans and Other Stories*

Américo Paredes's fame rests on his foundational
work in the nineteen-fifties and sixties on the ballads, legends, and everyday folklife of Mexican Americans and on his subsequent elaboration of
that work during the seventies and eighties. Among his most recently
published works, a novel, *George Washington Gómez* (1990), and a book
of poetry, *Between Two Worlds* (1991), have added a literary dimension to
the imposing array of Paredes's contestational work in historical, ethnographic, and theoretical realms. These imaginative works address the
predicaments of contemporary Chicano/a cultural politics, identity formation, and social transformation. Given the modernity of their concerns,
it is startling to learn that Paredes's literary creations are not contemporary pieces, nor even products of the fifties and sixties. They are works
from the thirties and forties, decades before Paredes's groundbreaking
scholarly work. As products of an era and of literary formations different
from those currently in vogue, the literary texts belie their postmodern,
post–Chicano Movement thematics and publication dates.

Together with the later scholarly work, the novel and the poetry can
now be seen as part of a larger imaginative project to invent a figural
discourse of transnational epic proportions appropriate to the construction of a new narrative of modern American social and cultural history.
For Paredes, this new, *pan*-American history is not limited by imaginary
geopolitical borders and symbolic security checkpoints or customs and
immigration offices, but transcends these to include cultures and peoples
that traverse national boundaries and inhabit the fluid borderlands of
culture.

The new Mexican American consciousness that Paredes underwrites in his novel and poetry—a consciousness that resides in the cognitive, social, and political-economic space "between two worlds" and speaks a bicultural tongue—also emerges triumphantly in a new collection of short stories. The narrative voices of *The Hammon and the Beans and Other Stories* [1] contest other discourses for the authority to assign meaning and direction to everyday Mexican American reality. Functioning as discursive constructions of collective identity, Paredes's poetry and fiction serve as narrative sites of struggle for the privilege of representation, showing how a subaltern population might stave off dependency in the realm of cultural production. And while contesting the unqualified racism of Anglo-American representations of Mexican American reality, these works simultaneously resist the tendencies of both the progressivist modernity of New Deal rhetoric and the assimilative, pluralistic ideology of other Mexican American reformers of the day in order to renew the possibility of an "imagined community" of socio-cultural coherence. [2] Composed for the most part in the period between 1940 and 1953, Paredes's stories strike out in a direction markedly different from that of other border narratives of the day, anticipating analytical formations and discursive strategies that lay decades in the future.

Already in the thirties and forties, Paredes had grasped the notion that, in Edward Said's phrase, "culture serves authority, and ultimately the national State, not because it represses and coerces but because it is affirmative, positive, and persuasive." [3] Concerning the cultural construction of the American West during the first decades of this century, Warren I. Susman has noted that "the most characteristic use of the frontier in this period was the largely sentimental effort to retain what was considered to be the picturesque glamour and glory of the Old West." [4] Paredes's literary project participates in a critique of the prevailing mode of representation, offering instead an unsentimental and antipicturesque view of the Mexican borderlands. Unlike J. Frank Dobie, Walter Prescott Webb, and other official state intellectuals whose mythopoeic renderings of the American West and Southwest sought to legitimize one particular vision of American culture, and unlike even oppositional Mexican American writers who sought to pluralize that legitimacy, Paredes sought instead precisely to *de*-legitimize this vision by showing the production of a modern American "nation-space" in process, half-made, and "caught in the act of 'composing' its powerful image" [5] on a regional and hemispheric scale, and by demonstrating that its modernity was liable to a critical reproduction.

Speaking in another colonial context, Homi Bhabha has noted: "The marginal or 'minority' is not the space of a celebratory, or utopian, self-marginalization. It is a much more substantial intervention into those justifications of modernity—progress, homogeneity, cultural organicism, the deep nation, the long past—that rationalize the authoritarian, 'normalizing' tendencies within cultures in the name of the national interest or ethnic prerogative."[6] In the same vein, Said has noted that the main battle in imperialism is surely over land, "but when it came to who owned the land, who had the right to settle and work on it, who kept it going, who won it back, and who now plans for the future—these issues were reflected, contested, and even for a time decided in narrative."[7] Clearly, this is the sense in which Bhabha has suggested that nations are narrations and that addressing them from the perspective of narrative "will establish the cultural boundaries of the nation so that they may be acknowledged as 'containing' thresholds of meaning that must be crossed, erased, and translated in the process of cultural production."[8] Now these cultural boundaries and epistemological crossings, the border checkpoints of cultural production, are the very barriers that Paredes crosses and translates in many of his finest short stories. His interventions into the ideological justifications of American modernity remap the cultural space of the American West and make powerful additions to the ongoing critical revision of the entire narrative of American cultural nationalism and its place in mid-twentieth-century global politics. They constitute what Fredric Jameson, in a related idiom, has called the "cognitive mappings"[9] of the new type of collective social space and social practice where resistance to forces of domination might be effectively marshalled and enacted.

■ ■ ■

Américo Paredes's first stories are set, significantly, in his home region, the South Texas border country. By the mid-1930s when Paredes began to write, many farms and ranches in that region, which had been for generations small, family-owned, or family-tenanted, held and worked in common, were being taken over by large, corporate, agribusiness interests, organizing production for a newly developing competitive global market.[10] As a result of this shift from family to corporate relations of production, from collective to capitalist structures of socio-political organization, Mexican Americans were increasingly being displaced onto smaller and smaller parcels of land which they worked primarily through contract sharecropping, thus "ensuring the availability of cheap resident labor throughout the year."[11] Already in the late 1910s, with the coming of new irrigation and large-scale farming technologies, ranch land bought cheaply from native Texas Mexicans (*Tejanos*) was being "resold dearly as farmland—all on the basis of water."[12] As Anglo investors, speculators, and settlers arrived in large numbers in the South Texas region during a land speculation boom that changed the cultural and ethnic character of the region from Mexican to Anglo-American, even sharecropping became less profitable for white landowners, because they could make more money by hiring Mexicans as wage laborers than by leasing to them. Especially at harvest times, agricultural work came to be handled by a migratory workforce that was controlled, as Montejano points out, by various economic and legal means (wage-fixing, mobility restrictions, vagrancy laws, and so on). These labor controls amounted to a program of labor repression and legalized discrimination. Since 1848, American efforts to dominate the region had proceeded apace. By the late nineteenth and early twentieth centuries these efforts had produced a new socio-spatial, cultural, and geopolitical reality in the former Mexican territories, resulting in communities experiencing the development of new forms of social modernity.

In the face of growing oppression, overt deterritorialization, and forced transformation of the traditional Texas Mexican social formation, many *Tejanos* sought ways of expressing their frustration and outrage. Historian James A. Sandos has shown how the anarchist politics that were influencing sectors of the contemporary revolutionary movement in Mexico and that were being heard in the United States through radical media outlets such as Ricardo Flores Magón's newspaper *Regeneración* offered some natives of the South Texas region a strategy of resistance. Floresmagonista anarchist thought was disseminated throughout the region and "became progressively more militant about the need for direct action to redress the wrongs done to Mexicans and Tejanos on both sides of the river."[13] The anarchist program of "direct action" (a code phrase for revolutionary praxis) came to mean for some Texas Mexican sympathizers of Mexican anarchist revolutionary thought the reclaiming of the land Mexico lost between 1836 and 1848 through an armed uprising against the United States.

By late 1914 conditions seemed ripe for such "direct action." In January 1915 a tiny group of Floresmagonistas based in San Diego, Texas, a small, border ranching community in Duval County, scripted a plan for action.

Following the dictates of the Plan of San Diego, a manifesto outlining the structure and strategy for revolutionary direct action in support of social justice, a plot for a full-blown rebellion against American imperial domination of former Mexican territories was set in motion. According to the broadsides announcing the manifesto, Plan supporters, marching under a red banner, would reclaim all of the former Mexican territories now constituting the American West and Southwest and proclaim a multi-ethnic, social revolutionary Border Republic. Its political and social agenda clear, the Plan offered membership only to "the Latin, the Negro, or the Japanese race." Moreover, American Indians were offered a promise that "their ancestral territory would be restored to them in return for their support." In a later revision, the revolutionary cast of the Plan was even more pronounced, as it now called for a complete social revolution, "decried the exploitation of land and labor by whites and denounced their racist discrimination against people of color."[14] Finally, the Plan pronounced the establishment of "the Social Republic of Texas."[15]

Following the principles outlined in this anarchist-inspired, ideally conceived blueprint for revolution, armed Mexican irregulars crossed the Rio Grande on 4 July 1915 and attacked Anglo ranches, burned railroad bridges, cut telegraph wires, and killed several Americans. Reprisals followed quickly, and over the next two years Texas Rangers and other law enforcement agencies set out with vigor to obliterate the rebellion by putting into final effect "the long-standing Ranger practice of ridding [the] area of Mexican 'undesirables.'"[16] As one contemporary Anglo Texan observer put it: "A Ranger can shoot a poor peon with impunity, and he is scarcely even asked to put in the usual plea of self-defense, which is as a general rule an untrue one anyway. No race, however ignorant or downtrodden, is going to submit to this for long without feeling an overwhelming sentiment, not only against the rangers themselves, but against the race from which they come."[17] South Texas residents coined a new word—"rangering"—to describe the summary execution of Mexican Americans suspected of participating in, or even sympathizing with, the rebellion.[18] In the Brownsville vicinity alone, long-standing racial antagonism vented in vigilante tactics and arbitrary action on the part of the Rangers led to the killing of as many as three hundred Mexican Americans, "many in 'cold blood.'"[19]

Instead of inspiring fear, however, the bloody Texas Ranger terror following the rebellion of 1915 provoked further anger and retaliation on the part of Floresmagonista sympathizers like *Tejanos* Luis de la Rosa, a former deputy sheriff of Cameron County, and Aniceto Pizaña, a respected rancher from the Brownsville vicinity. Over the next year, de la Rosa and Pizaña, subscribers to the anarchist newspaper *Regeneración* and adherents to the Plan of San Diego, attacked the implements of the Anglo Texan modern system of production: their ranches, irrigation pumping stations, railroad trains and depots, and automobiles. Using guerrilla tactics, they burned bridges and railroad trestles, cut telegraph and telephone wires, ambushed Ranger and U.S. Army patrols, and even struck "the major symbol of Anglo domination, the enormous King Ranch."[20] The Seditionists, as they came to be called in a contemporary *corrido* (anonymous folk ballad) about the rebellion, performed what they conceived as acts of war, intending to reclaim land taken from Mexico by the United States, reject the changes wrought by the Anglo capitalist mode of production in the Rio Grande Valley, and establish a new Border Republic.[21] The upshot of revolutionary action was that "by the fall of 1915, south Texas was on the verge of a race war," as an Anglo "backlash of massive proportions" created a reign of terror aimed at virtually eliminating the Mexican American population of South Texas.[22]

■ ■ ■

In "Theses on the Philosophy of History," Walter Benjamin argues that "to articulate the past historically does not mean to recognize it 'the way it really was.'. . . It means to seize hold of a memory as it flashes up at a moment of danger. . . . Only that historian will have the gift of fanning the spark of hope in the past who is firmly convinced that *even the dead* will not be safe from the enemy if he wins."[23] Benjamin's words fittingly capture Paredes's mission "to articulate the past historically." His stories seize just such a moment of historical memory as it flashes in a moment of danger—the danger of cultural eradication—by concretizing it in the reality of regional space. In instance after instance, the rhetorical tone of *The Hammon and the Beans* is that *"even the dead"* are not safe from the enemy when the social history of the region is obliterated from the narrative of American history. (Indeed, by the time I was growing up in Brownsville in the sixties, all mention of Mexican American resistance had been erased from our Texas history lessons.)

Paredes's title story, "The Hammon and the Beans," and a number of those that follow fan the spark of hope in the past by remembering the Plan of San Diego, its revolutionary creed, and the racial hatred and tension that has persisted to the present in South Texas in the aftermath of the bitter fighting, the "border troubles," of 1915 to 1917. In Paredes's fiction we are not immediately concerned with that revolutionary struggle. Instead, the focus is on the effects of struggle and on the end of the heroic past of Mexican American armed resistance to Anglo American hegemony. His stories look forward to the beginning of a new stage of Mexican American resistance in the realm of culture and ideology. Paredes's narratives underscore brilliantly the difficult dialectic between a Mexican past and an American future for Texas Mexicans living on the border at the margin of modernity and modernization.

The immediate past is represented by the Plan of San Diego rebellion of 1915–17. With its links to the Mexican Revolution, international anarchism, socialism, and the heroic resistance struggle of the Flores Magón brothers, the rebellion represents the phase of "direct action," now part of the legendary past. The future is represented in the stories of the troubled children who must cross the ever-present border between their parents' Mexican past and an as-yet-unspecified American future. Squeezed between what has been and what might be, between necessity and freedom, the represented present often seems retrospectively to the stories' narrators a series of moments of pathos and diminished possibility.

"The Hammon and the Beans" is set in the lower Rio Grande Valley of South Texas, the region of the most intense border conflict.[24] Paredes's first-person narrator re-creates the mood of life on the border in the nineteen-twenties, a historical moment when the heroic resistance of men like the *corrido* hero Gregorio Cortez and even of the Plan of San Diego revolutionaries Luis de la Rosa and Aniceto Pizaña is already fading into the hazy and unhistoricized past. Brownsville, Paredes's hometown, is depicted in the story as "Jonesville-on-the-Grande," a place of diminished heroic quality with the feel of a town suffering under the occupation of a victorious foreign army. The narrator reminds us that "it was because of the border troubles, ten years or so before, that the soldiers had come back to old Fort Jones" (4).

"Fort Jones" serves in the story as both a metaphor for the paternal presence of the occupying army and a literal reminder of the power behind that presence. With that power came the prerogative to write history. The "high wire fence that divided the post from the town" (4) is an objective correlative of the political and cultural distance that separates the occupying army from the Mexican American citizens of Jonesville: "We stuck out our tongues and jeered at the soldiers," continues the narrator.

"Perhaps the night before we had hung at the edges of a group of old men and listened to tales about Aniceto Pizaña and the 'border troubles,' as the local paper still called them when it referred to them gingerly in passing" (4). However, the oral histories of the old men must compete for the children's allegiance with the official histories of revolutionary resistance they are learning from the books in their American schools: stories not about the Plan of San Diego but "about George Washington . . . and Marion the Fox and the British cavalry that chased him up and down the broad Santee" (4).

In ideological terms, what the scene of everyday life offers is an ongoing dramatization of the conflicts between the residual elements of the child's traditional community and the ideals and forces of the newly dominant American culture, a battle for the hearts and minds of the Mexican American children. That ideological power struggle—whose outcome is already painfully obvious—seen through the eyes of the child-narrator, is precisely what the story is about: "And so we lived, we and the post, side by side with the wire fence in between" (5).

The separation between the two is not as absolute as the initial scenes of the story lead us to believe. Every evening a child named Chonita would enter the forbidden grounds "to the mess halls and [press] her nose against the screens and [watch] the soldiers eat" (5). "Ever since the end of the border troubles there had been a development boom in the Valley, and Chonita's [supposed] father was getting his share of the good times." The "good times" amount to "six dollars a week," notes the narrator wryly (6). Returning from her nightly forays into the fort with the leftovers from the soldiers' meals for her family, Chonita, who "was a poet too" (6), would amuse her friends by mimicking the soldiers' cries as they "call[ed] to each other through food-stuffed mouths: 'Give me the hammon and the beans!' . . . 'Give me the hammon and the beans!' " (6).

Her mimicry and her daring are the instruments of her poetry. On the evening of Chonita's death, we learn that her biological father had died earlier during the "border troubles," "shot and hanged from a mesquite limb" for working too close to the tracks the day the "Olmito train was derailed" (8). The reference to Plan of San Diego action identifies him as one of the victims of the Texas Ranger terror following the rebellion of 1915. Away from the adult conversations that he has been overhearing, the boy drowsily muses over what he has heard and only half understood concerning the heroic acts of men who lived and died before he was born. As his mind drifts among contradictory thoughts, all of a sudden he hears "the cold voice of the [post] bugle [that] went gliding in and out of the dark like something that couldn't find its way back to wherever it had been" (9). The stark loneliness of the bugle's homeless notes brings him back to poor Chonita, who according to his mother is "in Heaven now" (7): "I thought of Chonita in Heaven, and I saw her in her torn and dirty dress, with a pair of bright wings attached, flying round and round like a butterfly shouting, 'Give me the hammon and the beans!' " (9). In another age, the fragile, malnourished "butterfly" might have found life not in a deferred vision of a plentiful afterlife or by begging scraps from the army kitchens but in radical politics or collective action, demanding social justice on the picket lines with her oppressed sisters and brothers: "In later years," says the narrator, "I thought of [Chonita] a lot, especially during the thirties when I was growing up. Those years would have been just made for her. Many's the time I have seen her in my mind's eye, in the picket lines demanding not bread, not cake, but the hammon and the beans" (7). Her poetry might have been radical rather than mimicry. "But it didn't work out that way" (7), the narrator admits. The past age of heroic direct action, "with pistols in hand," seems as distant from present reality as a future time of collective organization. Envisioned in the narrator's imagination as a forerunner of Paredes's own childhood heroine, the great Depression era labor organizer and secretary of the Communist Party of Texas, Emma Tenayuca, Chonita represents the noble possibility of revolutionary social action, deferred. But since it is deferred, there can be no falsely victorious ending, as the narrator in later life realizes. His night of mourning for Chonita is the source of his memorial to her: the story of her brief life of poverty. That written monument is one that might help create the conditions for a reawakening of the spirit of direct action and eliminate the possibility of other little girls having to suffer Chonita's fate. The text of the story thus becomes, like the *corridos* the narrator overhears, an occasion for the expression of a symbolic solution to the determinate contradictions of history.

"Macaria's Daughter," composed about 1943, is perhaps Paredes's most gripping attempt to imagine a social revolution tied not to anarchist direct action or to cultural or symbolic action but to gender and feminine consciousness. The story tells a woefully familiar tale of the murder of a young Mexican American woman (who "looked like Hedy Lamar") by her singularly unappealing husband. But what distinguishes Paredes's treatment of this plot is the bitter irony that allows readers to view simultaneously—through a complex, multitemporal narrative frame—both the young wife's naively ambiguous desires and her husband's growing murderous desperation. The young wife, Marcela (who is known throughout the story simply as "Macaria's daughter"), has been constructed by her mother's identity. Marcela's identity is confused by the mother's intimacy with an American man. Marcela's mixed Anglo-Mexican blood (her father is an Anglo door-to-door drummer), her resemblance to the illusory figures of the Hollywood silver screen, and even more powerfully the limitations enforced upon Mexican women by a harsh and merciless patriarchal culture describe a subjective space as constricted as the *barrio* she inhabits and as arbitrary as the boundaries between nation-states. In the tableau-like ending of the story, a plaster image of the Virgin of Guadalupe, the Mother Protectress of all Mexican peoples, with "its brown Indian face," stares down upon the murdered woman from the altar in a corner of their shabby shack, that is, from the feminized space of prayer and supplication. The young wife's mutilated body becomes a symbol of women's victimization and an abject mark of the terrible power of abstract male ideology. Even though the young husband agonizes over the murder, he feels the community's unvoiced ethical imperative: in response to his wife's marital transgression, he *must* kill her in order "to keep being a man."

Frida Kahlo's approximately contemporaneous painting, *Unos Cuantos Piquetitos!* (A few small nips) (1935), depicting not the symbology but the reality of male terror and woman's blood, might well serve as emblem to "Macaria's Daughter." Kahlo's painting of a woman gruesomely murdered in her bed was inspired in part by Guadalupe Posada's turn-of-the-century illustrations of brutal murders and ghastly accidents and in part by a contemporary newspaper account of a vicious murder of a woman by her husband.[25] The multitemporal vividness of Paredes's narrative echoes the violence of Posada's visual narratives and Kahlo's indictment of male pornographic fantasies, linking male violence and female sexuality in disturbing imagery drawn from the Mexican popular imagination. The difference, however, is that in Paredes's story the awesome callousness of Kahlo's perpetrator is partially displaced from the Chicano husband onto the Anglo policemen who, investigating the crime, policing the borders of the Mexican *barrio* to contain its violence and its despairs, see not Marcela but only a Mexican woman's exposed, torn body and reflect on its sensual beauty. In both Kahlo and Paredes, to be sure, the issue is the shocking brutality of male power suavely condoned, indeed compelled, by traditional community values.

The "Gringo" of Paredes's 1952–53 story is a fair-skinned, blue-eyed Texas Mexican boy caught in the midst of historic events. His story forms part of the narrative of nineteenth-century American nation formation as Paredes situates us within the developing discourses of nation, region, and political allegiance. "The Gringo" is a vignette of historical romance set in the opening days of the U.S.-Mexican War. In February 1846, after Texas had sought annexation to the United States, U.S. President James K. Polk ordered General Zachary Taylor to lead part of his forces to the border of the disputed trans-Nueces River area, some two hundred miles north of the Rio Grande. Claimed by both the Republics of Texas and Mexico after the Texas Rebellion of 1836, the region between the Nueces River to the north and the Rio Grande to the south had remained during that ten-year period disputed space, culturally Mexican even if geopolitically indeterminate. When U.S. army units patrolling in the area were engaged by guerrilla forces of resisting Texas Mexicans, Polk declared that "American blood had spilled on American soil"[26] and ordered Taylor to move into the occupied territories of the north bank. Taylor's move south toward the Rio Grande was tantamount to an act of war and was countered by a corresponding northward movement of a Mexican force led by General Pedro Ampudia to Matamoros, Mexico, across the Rio Grande from Brownsville.[27]

Having been wounded by real gringos in an earlier ambush in which his father and brothers were killed and he was spared when mistaken for an American because of his white skin, "the Gringo" (named Ygnacio) is nursed back to health by the daughter of one of the Americans. The minor action in which he has participated represents the first act of resistance to the enactment in the coming months of the grand design that John L. O'Sullivan, editor of *United States Magazine and Democratic Review*, would in 1844 term "Manifest Destiny." These skirmishes signaled U.S. hemispheric and global imperial goals. When Ygnacio comes to and attempts to speak to the woman who is tending him, she warns him not to because she has already divined his identity and understands that a certain lynching will follow the revelation. Appropriately named Prudence, the young woman tends Ygnacio's wounds, attempts to teach him English, and even tries to convince her father that Ygnacio is "white" and can thus be taught to be "a real Christian" (53). By portraying the source of the Americans' hatred as Ygnacio's status as a Spanish-speaking Mexican— rather than his skin color—Paredes is clearly interested in the dynamics of American ethnophobia and the procedures by which one may pass as a

Gringo. Like other minority intellectuals of the inter-war period, Paredes sees racism as motivated at times by racial phenotypes that are never absolutely clear and distinct and at others by socio-cultural factors that test the boundary between what is acquired and what is essential. On the border, racism was but one form of prejudice—religion, class, language, and other cultural gestures being others. The indeterminacy of racist attitudes aside, the fact remains that such distinctions are made and acted upon. Thus, at a hint of a romantic attachment between the daughter and a culturally Mexican white man, the "gringo" is transformed in the Anglo father's eyes into just another "greaser," fair skin or no. With Prudence's help, Ygnacio manages to escape across the Nueces River toward the Rio Grande.

In Matamoros, on the Mexican side of the border, wearing identifiably American clothing and armed with the brace of "horse pistols" given to him by the American woman, "the Gringo" experiences the reverse of the initial "passing," as he is now taken for an American spy, especially when he warns about the might of Taylor's approaching army. Just as his cultural and linguistic traits set him at odds with the Americans, his fair features and hybrid cultural ways mark him for suspicion among Mexican nationals. The representational spaces of style of dress, speech gestures, and skin color overlap to construct a doubly ambiguous positionality for the oddly composite figure, the Mexican Gringo. At issue here is the recognition on the part of the trans–Rio Grande Mexicans of Ygnacio's subtle but real difference as a transcultured, Mexican American gringo. The disputed river boundary, once a unifying focus of regional life, now becomes a symbol of separation, transforming formerly homogeneous Mexican space into overdetermined sites of conflicting racial, ethnic, and political American identities.

At story's end, facing the weaponry of American technology and its commerce of war, the newly invented rapid-firing revolver, and armed only with a broad, heavy machete, a weapon and tool indicative of decidedly pre-capitalist modes of social organization, "the Gringo" charges headlong into history as "the guns of Palo Alto went off inside his head" (56). In the last instant of his life, Ygnacio opposes what must surely seem like the massively unstoppable force of American historical destiny, the taking of the trans-Nueces region of South Texas serving as mere prelude to the seizure of all northern Mexican territories in the present U.S. West and Southwest. In the various thematic strands combined at story's end, Paredes articulates the disjunctures between the socio-spatial levels and social practices of race, nationalism, gender roles, and the developing implications of U.S. expansionism.

Other stories in the collection take us out of the geographical, if not the social, space of early twentieth-century South Texas and into the World War II Pacific theater of operations and the opening days of the Korean War. In these selections, the issues remain, as in the Jonesville stories, the intersections of race, power, and conquest. But now Paredes moves from the socio-spatial practices of the family and the local South Texas region to the hemispheric and global level of transnational sites. At this macro-level Paredes attempts to account for the extraordinarily fierce Manichean nature of the war in Asia by linking domestic American racism with the conduct of its armed forces during the war and the postwar occupation of Japan. What is at issue now is the global nature of the idioms of racism and their role in the construction of an American national subject, as Paredes suggests how expressive forms of race hate encountered on the border became imbricated with the effects of colonialism and imperialism in Asia during World War II.

Writing in September 1939 in *The Socialist Appeal*, the Socialist Workers Party newspaper, C. L. R. James posed the question people of color faced at the onset of the war: "Why should I shed my blood for Roosevelt's America, for Cotton Ed Smith and Senator Bilbo, for the whole Jim Crow, Negro-hating South, for the low-paid, dirty jobs for which Negroes have to fight, for the few dollars of relief and the insults, discrimination, police brutality, and perpetual poverty to which Negroes are condemned even in the more liberal North?"[28] Because non-whites were denied the core protections of democracy as formulated in the Fourteenth and Fifteenth Amendments or as expressed in Roosevelt's famed "four freedoms,"[29] the World War II experiences of Mexican Americans, African Americans, Native Americans, Asian Americans, and other American people of color exposed the hypocrisy of American critiques of Nazi and Axis racism.

To demonstrate how racism and reactions to racism influenced the conduct of the war in the Pacific, Paredes takes us, in a story entitled "Little Joe," to infantry basic training at Camp Robinson, Little Rock, Arkansas.[30] An Anglo narrator named Watson reflects on the curious experiences of a fellow trainee, Little Joe, who hails from the Texas-Mexico border. Watson and the other white recruits cast Little Joe in the role of a knife-wielding killer, like all of his kind, genetically endowed with the bloodthirsty impulses of a savage cutthroat; that is, he is seen as a being possessed of special powers of non-human evil. "One must remember," notes Paredes, "that in the 1930s supposedly scholarly studies still were being published in Texas depicting Mexicans as treacherous and cowardly, a degenerate product of miscegenation between Spaniard and Indian."[31] Here, Little Joe's fellow recruits have constructed such an exaggerated and blatantly racist image of him that even the biggest man in the squad, a Minnesotan named Great Big Johnson, is petrified whenever Little Joe cleans his bayonet: "That little guy, he don't look like much, but don't cross him. I'd hate to do that" (112). The reality is that Little Joe is a neat, quiet, polite South Texas boy, not a cold-blooded killer.

In contrast to the Mexican of American popular culture, notoriously portrayed as a knife-wielding killer during the Zoot Suit Riots of 1942–43 and symbolically presented as a brutal primal force in World War II novels such as Norman Mailer's *Naked and the Dead*, Paredes's Little Joe is not a man primordially linked to the harsh power of uncivilized savagery but simply a decent person attempting to live under the constraints of the prevailing Jim Crow, segregationist, white supremacist American racial policies.

Mailer's caricature of a Texas Mexican in *The Naked and the Dead*, Sergeant Julio Martinez, regularly represented through exaggerated metaphors of animal panic, is described at one point as reacting like Pavlov's dog in conditioned terror to the sounds of combat, or at another as having the *"poise and grace of a deer . . . nervous and alert as if he were thinking of flight."*[32] Derisively called "Mex" and "Japbait" by the other characters, Mailer's Mexican American speaks an infantile English, acts "instinctively," understands "intuitively," and cringes with "inferiority . . . when he talked to . . . White Protestant(s)."[33] Like the metaphors linking him to hunted prey, these descriptions reflect the extent to which Mailer's Mexican American is grouped in the same category of the Other that Americans usually reserved for the Japanese enemy. Paredes's Mexican American soldiers, by contrast, serve as implied critiques of the Manichean dimension of caricature. They are reflective, doubting, amusing figures, active agents of their own fate, illustrating far more complex versions of the experience of the racialized combat in the Pacific than does Mailer's Julio Martinez.

The U.S. Occupation force in Japan is the subject of "When It Snowed in Kitabamba."[34] Captain Meniscus, an unabashed idolizer of Douglas MacArthur obsessed with neatness and order, sees his duty as Occupation Forces chief of Kitabamba to transform the Japanese into Americans. He keeps the motto of his pragmatic obsessions framed underneath a portrait of MacArthur: "The shortest distance between two points is a straight line" (130). In his zeal to represent the superiority of American ways and to impress the Japanese with the precision of American methods, the captain has turned the delivery of the daily mail from Tokyo into an intricate, arcane ceremony, complete with martial music, rows of MPs lining his route toward the mail train, and his own march of high solemnity.

From such pompous solemnity only a fall can result. And so indeed, one day when an unexpected snow falls on Kitabamba, the Captain's dogged short march between two points is sidetracked when he slips and falls awkwardly in the snow, turning his exalted ritual into ridiculous farce. His MPs laugh with disdain at his discomfiture. The gathered Japanese are more gentle with their conqueror; at first they too are mildly amused by his comic comedown. However, their amusement quickly turns into something else as "with sadness in their eyes" (147) they recognize something deeper than the pathos of a petty tyrant's stumble. In "On the Essence of Laughter," Baudelaire notes that "the power of laughter resides with the one who laughs, never with the object of laughter. It is not he who falls who laughs at himself, unless he is a philosopher, someone who has acquired, by habit, the ability to reflect upon himself (*se dédoubler*) and attend like a disinterested spectator upon the phenomena of his *I*." [35] Paul de Man argues that such a reflective capacity, within consciousness, between two moments of the self, is not an intersubjective relation at all but is in fact essential to the nature of irony. However, the laughter of the witness to the fall is to the fallen surely a mark of intersubjective difference, denoting the superiority of one subject over another, "with all the implications of will to power, of violence, and possession which come into play when a person is laughing at someone else—including the will to educate and to improve." [36] In Meniscus's tumble, the superiority implicit in the laughter of his MPs is clear: they disdain his pretensions and mark their distance from him with it. Meniscus himself is hardly philosophical enough to "reflect upon himself." The gentle laughter of the Japanese, however, does tend toward a Baudelarian *dédoublement*, as it designates less hierarchies of superiority and inferiority than an implicit recognition of their *own* separation from themselves. In laughing at Meniscus, they implicitly lament their own newly fallen state. From this fallenness they can pity Meniscus's fall, express "fellowship" with his humiliating comedown, and force him to contemplate the shallowness of his own understanding of those over whom he has lorded as a stand-in for the haughty Supreme Commander, Douglas MacArthur. Their laughter and their philosophic detachment, like the name "Meniscus" itself,[37] ironically subvert MacArthur's truism about "the shortest distance between two points."

"Ichiro Kikuchi," also predicated on a peculiar turn of irony, is based on an actual experience of a young friend of Paredes's wife, Amelia.[38] In the story, Ichiro Kikuchi is the son of a Japanese father and a Mexican mother. Born and raised in Cuernavaca and baptized Juan Guadalupe, he grows to young adulthood raising flowers on his Japanese father's and Mexican uncle's farm. At his father's insistence, Ichiro travels to Japan to maintain his Japanese identity and finds himself unable to return to Mexico after Pearl Harbor. The young Japanese Mexican is eventually drafted, sent into action, and immediately captured by Americans in the Philippines. By 1945, the Japanese army is a far cry from the proud, disciplined, able force it once was. Ichiro's unit of old men and schoolboys, ordered to fight to the death, surrenders instead, tragically misjudging the good faith of the American army. Contrary to the notion that it was only the Japanese who wantonly killed their prisoners, the fact is that the war in the Pacific was "a war without mercy" for both sides: "No quarter, no surrender. Take no prisoners. Fight to the bitter end. These were everyday words in the combat areas, and in the final year of the war such attitudes contributed to an orgy of bloodletting that neither side could conceive of avoiding." Many Japanese fighting men did die rather than surrender, but they did so in part because of "the disinterest of the Allies in taking prisoners."[39] Ernie Pyle, war correspondent of near folk-hero status, having transferred to the Pacific from Europe in February 1945, offered a partial explanation for this "disinterest" by noting in one of his first dispatches that "in Europe we felt that our enemies, as horrible and deadly as they were, were still people." He continues, "But out here I soon gathered that the Japanese were looked upon as something subhuman and repulsive; the way some people feel about cockroaches and mice."[40] Ichiro, about to be executed with his entire unit, is digging his own grave when a GI, a Mexican American sergeant assigned to kill the prisoners, notices the medallion of the Virgin of Guadalupe Ichiro wears. Symbol and icon of a national and racial unity of faith, the Guadalupe medallion tears Ichiro from the propaganda narrative of Japanese dehumanization and re-inserts him in the discourse of greater Mexican identity. For the Mexican American GI, the medallion identifies the "Japanese" infantryman not only as a fellow Catholic but also as a fellow Mexican. When Ichiro responds in

Spanish to the shaken GI's hailing, he only confirms what the icon has already revealed.

Later in Tokyo, after the war, the shock of having partially seen himself in the demonized Japanese Other proves too much for the Mexican American GI: he turns away from Ichiro, who attempts to thank him for the gift of his life. Race hate bred at home, displaced in combat onto a vicious and odious enemy, appears at this moment uncomfortably close. By turning away, the Mexican American GI declines to acknowledge the extent to which he too, at home and in Japan, straddles binary oppositions as he stands in the position of the reified and objectified racial Other. Here again, Paredes masterfully represents the situation that C. L. R. James suggested Americans of color would face in World War II and anticipates the contradictions posed for them by other postcolonial struggles in Korea and Vietnam. In the Manichean struggle between seemingly incompatible antagonists, with merciless extermination the goal of each side's efforts, the defining line between "war crimes" and justifiable action becomes as blurred and ambiguous as the line between fortune and fate. The supreme irony and double-jeopardy of racism, its destructive force whether one expresses it or receives it, remains the issue of Paredes's stories.

"The American Dish" is a broad farce narrated in a parodically picaresque style by a roguish, salacious character named Johnny Picadero.[41] It is part of what was intended to be a series of stories featuring this anti-hero. "Passing" is again the issue, but in this case the satire is aimed at American venture capitalists looking for sleazy opportunities in postwar Latin America who think they can pass as Mexicans because they know how to order "chile con carne," an American dish. The roguish Johnny encounters "spies," the delectable Miss Ross (another American dish) and the shady operatives of a fly-by-night American film company attempting to steal Mexican cultural capital by illegally filming "the tribal dances of the Culomula Indians" (229). As with the punning names of the fictional Indian tribe[42] and the picaresque main character, Paredes's intent here is not to diminish the sting of his earlier satires of American racist norms but to extend the critique into the realms of comedy, burlesque, and caricature.

As in "When It Snowed in Kitabamba," laughter is the ironic medium through which the philosophic detachment necessary for the recognition of mistaken, mystified assumptions about superiority and inferiority, and even the acknowledgment of difference, can occur. Related to the comedic spirit that Paredes would later celebrate in *Uncle Remus con Chile*, a collection of jests, oral histories, legends, and anecdotes from South Texas, the Johnny Picadero stories explore the vernacular rhetorical modes available to revisionary and contestatory history as it seeks to correct the narrative of American nationhood at the borderlands of culture. For Chicanos, as for African Americans, sometimes the only escape from brutality and shattered hopes in a land uneasily pledged to "inalienable rights" is wit, paradox, and laughter.[43] In each of the stories, however, whether in the mode of tragedy, comedy, or realistic narrative, the guiding rhetorical force of the narrative is ironic wisdom, the self-knowledge that glimpses the discontinuity and plurality of levels within a subject caught between two worlds who comes to know itself by what it is not.

■ ■ ■

Positioned by difference, Paredes's border subjects acknowledge the social dimensions of difference and its limitations and contradictions. Repeatedly, this acknowledgment occurs aesthetically, in the shapes and nuances of a variety of oral forms, gestures, expressions, and styles— that is, in the formulaic patterns that disguise and sometimes reveal the limits of community. In an essay of 1983 Paredes asked pointedly about the construction of future communities: "What will this new community be like? It must be something more than personal relationships and a strong sense of values because those have existed [and not sufficed] in the past."[44] Perhaps the answer is implicit in the vernacular forms his writings use. These forms are a Chicano version of the aesthetic of cognitive mapping to which I referred earlier, that is, "a pedagogical political culture which seeks to endow the individual subject with some new heightened sense of its place in the global system."[45] This cultural geography describes a place that remains crosscut by sedimented layers of conflicting history and contradictory struggles.

And yet, in the midst of the present hysteria concerning undocumented Mexican immigration and the renewed ethnophobia stirred up during the debate over the North American Free Trade Agreement (NAFTA), and the passage in California of the anti-immigrant Proposition 187, the new, pan-American history that Paredes narrates offers a significant alternative version of life in the borderlands. Paredes's symbolic representations of life in the transnational social and political sites of the nation indicate as clearly as do other contemporary studies that persons of Mexican-origin communities, whether of early or recent vintage, are as likely as any other immigrant group to experience the conflicted and stratified entry into American social space. Indeed, his writings urge us to interrogate what constitutes American social space—as an arena of polity, of race, and of gender. It is here, surely, that Paredes's virtuosity as a storyteller and clearsighted critic of contemporary vernacular ethnic culture and its historiography is most powerfully present. His version traverses imaginary borders and immigration checkpoints to document the undocumented imaginative styles and lived realities that make up Chicano struggles for social justice and economic equality. In no uncertain terms, Paredes's work displays the power of culture to configure the imaginative borders of the modern American nation and to shape the subject within the nation. Creating a new historiographical space while critiquing the process of history-making itself, *The Hammon and the Beans and Other Stories* is the latest evidence of Américo Paredes's centrality as an artist and scholar of the American ethnic vernacular imagination.

Notes

1   Américo Paredes, *The Hammon and the Beans and Other Stories* (Houston: Arte Público Press, 1994).
2   For a full elaboration of Paredes's participation in the critique of Roosevelt's New Deal liberalism, see R. Saldívar, "Bordering on Modernity: Américo Paredes's *Between Two Worlds* and the Imagining of Utopian Social Space," *Stanford Humanities Review* 3, (Winter 1993): 54–66; and "Modernity, the Nation, and Chicano Subject Formation: Américo Paredes's *Between Two Worlds*," in *Minority Discourse*, ed. Abdul JanMohamed (forthcoming). My reference to "imagined communities" alludes of course to Benedict Anderson's *Imagined Communities: Reflections on the Origin and Spread of Nationalism*, rev. ed. (London: Verso, 1991).
3   Edward Said, "Reflections on American 'Left' Literary Criticism," in *The World, the Text, and the Critic* (Cambridge, Harvard Univ. Press, 1983), 171.
4   Warren I. Susman, "The Frontier Thesis and the American Intellectual," in *Culture as History: The Transformation of American Society in the Twentieth Century* (New York: Pantheon, 1984), 30.
5   Homi K. Bhabha, *Nation and Narration* (New York: Routledge, 1990), 3.
6   Bhabha, *Nation and Narration*, 4.
7   Edward Said, *Culture and Imperialism* (New York: Knopf, 1993), xii–xiii.
8   Bhabha, *Nation and Narration*, 4.

9   Fredric Jameson, *Postmodernism, or, The Cultural Logic of Late Capitalism* (Durham: Duke Univ. Press, 1991), 53–54.

10   David Montejano, "Frustrated Apartheid: Race, Repression, and Capitalist Agriculture in South Texas, 1920–1930," in *The World-System of Capitalism: Past and Present*, ed. Walter L. Goldfrank, Vol. 2, Political Economy of the World-System Annuals (Beverly Hills: Sage Publications, 1979), 133.

11   Montejano, "Frustrated Apartheid," 138.

12   James A. Sandos, *Rebellion in the Borderlands: Anarchism and the Plan of San Diego, 1904–1923* (Norman: Univ. of Oklahoma Press, 1992), 70.

13   Sandos, *Rebellion in the Borderlands*, 72–73, 74.

14   Sandos, *Rebellion in the Borderlands*, p. 81, 83.

15   Charles H. Harris III and Louis R. Sadler, "The Plan of San Diego and the Mexican–United States War Crisis of 1916: A Reexamination," *Hispanic American Historical Review* 58 (1978): 385.

16   Sandos, *Rebellion in the Borderlands*, 91.

17   Tracy Hammond Lewis, *Along the Rio Grande* (New York: Lewis Publishing Co., 1916), 178, cited in Sandos, *Rebellion in the Borderlands*, 92.

18   Sandos, *Rebellion in the Borderlands*, 92.

19   Colin M. MacLachlan, *Anarchism and the Mexican Revolution: The Political Trials of Ricardo Flores Magón in the United States* (Berkeley: Univ. of California Press, 1991), 57. MacLachlan is citing a contemporary report by U.S. Secret Service agent Edward Tyrell.

20   Harris and Sadler, "The Plan of San Diego," 386, 387.

21   See "Los Sediciosos," in Américo Paredes, *A Texas-Mexican Cancionero: Folksongs of the Lower Border* (Urbana: Univ. of Illinois Press, 1976); and my discussion of the ballad in *Chicano Narrative: The Dialectics of Difference* (Madison: Univ. of Wisconsin Press, 1990), 30–31. Paredes's *'With His Pistol in His Hand': A Border Ballad and Its Hero* (Austin: Univ. of Texas Press, 1958) is of course the classic study of the *corridos* of border resistance.

22   See Harris and Sandler, "The Plan of San Diego," 390–92; Sandos, *Rebellion in the Borderlands*, 108–10; and Frank C. Pierce, *A Brief History of the Lower Rio Grande Valley* (Menasha, Wis.: George Banta Publishing Co., 1917), 114–15.

23   Walter Benjamin, "Theses on the Philosophy of History," in *Illuminations*, ed. Hannah Arendt (New York: Schocken Books, 1969), 255.

24   For the publication history and a fuller close reading of "The Hammon and the Beans," see *Chicano Narrative*, 48–60. Page numbers refer to *The Hammon and the Beans and Other Stories*.

25   Sarah M. Lowe, *Frida Kahlo*, Universe Series on Women Artists (New York: Universe Publishing, 1991), 83–84.

26   James K. Polk, presidential address, 1846.

27   Pierce, *A Brief History of the Lower Rio Grande Valley*, 26–27.

28 C. L. R. James, et al., "Why Negroes Should Oppose the War," in *Fighting Racism in World War II* (New York: Monad Press, 1980), 28.

29 See Paredes's scathing poem of that title in *Between Two Worlds*; also my discussion, "Bordering on Modernity," 54–66.

30 Written in Japan, soon after Paredes landed there in 1945 with the Occupation Army. "Done while my memories of basic training in Arkansas were still fresh on my mind." Paredes, personal correspondence, 13 December 1992.

31 Paredes, *Uncle Remus con Chile* (Houston: Arte Público Press, 1993), 11. Paredes adds that J. Frank Dobie in *The Flavor of Texas* "defends the Mexican by switching stereotypes, from treacherous knife-stabber to kindly Uncle Remus."

32 Norman Mailer, *The Naked and the Dead* (New York: Rinehart & Co., 1948), 18, 63.

33 *The Naked and the Dead*, 591, 592, 691.

34 Done in Japan between 1946 and 1950. Paredes, personal correspondence, 13 December 1992.

35 Charles Baudelaire, "On the Essence of Laughter," in Paul de Man, *Blindness and Insight: Essays in the Rhetoric of Contemporary Criticism* (Minneapolis: Univ. of Minnesota Press, 1983), 211–12. My translation.

36 De Man, *Blindness and Insight*, 212.

37 *OED, s.v.* "meniscus": denoting a non-linear figure of crescent shape formed by the juncture of concave and convex surfaces.

38 In personal correspondence, 13 December 1992, Paredes notes that this story, composed between 1948 and 1949, was "based on an experience to a young friend of [Amelia's] family. He was not half Mexican but had been born in Mexico. Like many Nisei, he was caught in Japan by the war. It was a crucifix he was wearing on a chain around his neck when he was digging his own grave along with other members of his platoon. There were plenty of 'war crimes' committed by U.S. forces long before Vietnam and My Lai. Yet we executed the Japanese leaders as war criminals because Japanese soldiers also committed the same kind of atrocities."

39 Dower, *War Without Mercy*, pp. 10–11, 11.

40 Ernie Pyle, *Last Chapter* (New York: Henry Holt & Co., 1945), 5.

41 "Picadero," derived from *picar* (to prick), suggests various puns in the Spanish, including *pícaro* (traditional knavish adventurer of Spanish fiction), *picador* (horseman who pricks the bull's neck muscles in the bullfight), *picardía* (Mexican oral lore of pungent word-play). Both stories were begun during the first few months that Paredes arrived in Occupation Japan as *Stars and Stripes* correspondent at the 11th Replacement Depot near Okazaki. From personal correspondence, 13 December 1992.

42 *Culomula* might be crudely rendered as "mule's ass."

43 Lawrence W. Levine, "Laughing Matters," review of *On the Real Side:*

394   Ramón Saldívar

Laughing, Lying, and Signifying—The Underground Tradition of African-American Humor that Transformed American Culture, from Slavery to Richard Pryor, by Mel Watkins (New York: Simon & Schuster, 1994), in *The New York Times Book Review*, 27 February 1994, 1, 27–28.

44   Américo Paredes, "Nearby Places and Strange-Sounding Names," in *The Texas Literary Tradition: Fiction, Folklore, History*, ed. Don Graham et al. (Austin: The College of Liberal Arts and the Texas State Historical Association, 1983), 132.

45   Jameson, *Postmodernism*, 54.

**Lori
Askeland**

Remodeling the Model Home in
Uncle Tom's Cabin and *Beloved*

> One hundred years later, the Negro is still languishing in the
> corners of American society and finds himself an exile in his
> own land.—Martin Luther King Jr., "I Have A Dream"

Within the labels "structuralism" and "poststruc-
turalism" resides an architectural view of language and meaning. Even
when such views are deconstructive ones, building and dwelling metaphors inevitably inhabit these critical discourses—as it simultaneously
becomes more difficult to establish clear boundaries and build firm walls.
Thus, not surprisingly, the critical theories being debated and reworked
in English departments also wormed their ways into the walls and offices
of architecture departments. Amos Rapoport, for example, became one
of the founders of environment-behavior studies during the 1960s and
1970s, helping to broaden the study of architecture to include "vernacular" (or "folk") architecture as well as the canon of buildings designed and
conceived by professional architects. Rapoport finds that as social and cultural institutions buildings are related to language because "both express
the cognitive process of making distinctions, reflecting the tendency of
the human mind to impose an order on the world through schemata and
naming." He insists that "One can, therefore, look at built environments
as physical expressions of schemata and cognitive domains: *environments
are thought before they are built.*"[1]

As proponents of the "Cult of Domesticity" during the mid-nineteenth
century, Harriet Beecher Stowe and Catharine Beecher were clearly
aware of the power of ordering that comes from the creation of a model

home. Hence, in their "textbook" for young homemakers, *The American Woman's Home*, the sisters argue that the "employments" of housewives are not only difficult and deserving of "honor and remuneration," but also compose the "sacred duties of the family state."[2] As females, however, they were conscious of the vulnerability of Victorian women, whose employments were usually uncompensated and whose domains were always conceived, designed, and owned by males. This double awareness fits with Arthur C. Danto's recent reflection on the linguistic roots of the words we use to describe our dwelling places. He notes that the word "domain" shares a root with a family of English terms that refer back to the Latin *domus* and asserts that through these words "the house speaks to us precisely as the symbol of rulership, ownership, mastery, power." Rapoport's "cognitive domain," then, views the built environment only as an expression of human domination, looking beyond the all too human need for shelter, which Danto relates to the Old English root of the word "house." This root, *hus*, was "cognate with *huden*—to hide, shelter, conceal, cover"—which shows us "the fragile, threatened, exposed side of our self-image as dwellers: beings that need protection, a place to crawl into . . . and our walls announce our vulnerability."[3] Thus, by conceiving of a location as being "ours," we cognitively create a domain, an area of power, while in the back of our minds we may have "housed" the knowledge of how arbitrary and fragile that power always is. For the Victorian woman, this fragility was emphasized by the fact that she did not even own the walls she needed for shelter, let alone power.

By using what power women did have, Stowe and Beecher desired to increase the individual power and status of women, mothers in particular, and thereby to increase the strength of the family by creating a "family state," that is, a domain as big as the country. Numerous critics have discussed the influence of the ideology of domesticity on *Uncle Tom's Cabin*, with most viewing it as a method of female empowerment. As Elizabeth Ammons puts it, Stowe's radical version of the domestic ideal converts "essentially repressive concepts of femininity into a positive (and activist) alternative system of values in which woman figures not merely as the moral superior of man, his inspirer, but as a model for him," while she remains in a separate domestic sphere.[4] The vulnerability of this domain, however, must not be overlooked; the house remains a sheltered "feminine" space, that is, a *hus* for true spiritual growth, which by virtue of its enclosure in the "masculine" domain of materialism and commercialism, always remains in danger of being invaded and corrupted by it.

Beginning in the Beecher sisters' era, Gwendolyn Wright's *Moralism and the Model Home: Domestic Architecture and Cultural Conflict in Chicago, 1873–1913* traces housing reform movements across the country and explains the importance of "schemata and cognitive structures" for the Victorian American culture she is confronting. She notes that "the word 'model' evokes an abstract, artificial construction, following ideal laws, against which ambiguous and complex social situations are judged," yet argues that Victorian reformers "envisioned their model homes as one means for bringing order and control to what seemed dangerously volatile social conditions."[5] Implicitly, then, the "model home" represented both shelter from and dominance over the chaos of the world. As several scholars have noted, the kitchen was one place where Stowe and Beecher in particular believed that order and control could be brought to bear on society's problems.[6] Wright, in fact, calls *The American Woman's Home* "[t]he most important book" for rationalizing kitchen work-space, and praises it for featuring "revolutionary approaches to housework and layout." Yet, despite the widespread popularity of the book and attempts by middle-class housewives to achieve the sisters' ideal of the "selfless, self-sufficient housewife," Wright notes that "builders did not follow through on the innovative proposals of the two authors."[7] Thus, because their domain was always undermined by their need for shelter in the larger masculine domain, Victorian women were often forced to enact the reverse of Rapoport's dictum: to "think" their domain, create a mental ideal of it, after it had already been built, and thereby remodel as best they could.

It is my contention that Toni Morrison's *Beloved* sets itself up as a remodeling of *Uncle Tom's Cabin* that examines this ideology and revises it in a way that avoids reification of a patriarchal power structure. The parallels in the texts are numerous. *Beloved* is set in part in the same place and during the same period as *Uncle Tom's Cabin*: Sweet Home's northern Kentucky must be near the location of the Shelby plantation, and both novels' initial action represents a response to the Fugitive Slave Act. Moreover, *Beloved*'s main action takes place near Cincinnati in 1873, which was the Beechers' home from 1832–1849—a significant factor in Stowe's writing of *Uncle Tom's Cabin*, since it was there that she gained first-hand experience of recently "freed" slaves. The mid-1870s also saw both the waning of the housing reform movements in the North as houses served more and more materialistic goals and the "reconstruction" of the patriarchal structure of the South. Finally, both novelists use and remodel traces of slave history to create narratives that will also remodel the ideologies that dominate the country's power structure. Yet both novels remain haunted by the figures that represent that power.

The epigraph to chapter thirty-two of *Uncle Tom's Cabin* provides what is to be our introduction to Simon Legree's house: "The dark places of the earth are full of the habitations of cruelty."[8] As Theodore Hovet has noted, the fall from spirituality to materialism could not be better symbolized in *Uncle Tom's Cabin* than by Simon Legree's significantly kitchenless, utterly materialistic "anti-home."[9] Moreover, the enigmatic, ghostly character of Cassy as the haunter of this house has also recently received careful treatment from a number of readers. In her study of "The Haunted Houses of Lyman Beecher, Henry Ward Beecher, and Harriet Beecher Stowe," Karen Halttunen suggests that Stowe's application re-models her father's and brother's ghostly metaphors by focusing on the psychological haunting suffered by evildoers like Legree, while incorpo-rating her ideal of domestic social reform.[10] Halttunen's reading builds on Gilbert and Gubar's paradigm of the "madwoman in the attic" and sug-gests that Cassy both reforms and is reformed by her environment— which is exactly the dream of the housing reform movement. In the lan-guage of my paradigm, then, because Cassy exploits the madwoman in the attic story to suit her needs, she is empowered to remodel the attic into a "model home," centered on a motherly love for Emmeline. We see her transformed from a madwoman capable of murdering her chil-dren into a woman who can transform a *hus*, her temporary shelter from the wrath of Legree, into a matriarchal *domus*—complete with make-shift kitchen, sitting room, and bed—by which she gains power over her utterly masculine, materialistic "master."

Regardless of this power, however, Cassy's domain remains in the cor-ner of a house owned by white men and in a religion controlled by white men.[11] Just as "a vestige of the rough logs" of Uncle Tom's cabin can always be seen beneath its be-flowered exterior, so a vestige of slavery and male-dominated culture can be seen beneath even the most idyllic utopias in the book. Stowe dreams of reforming society, and even the world via George Harris's African mission, on the basis of Rachel Halli-day's model home—the center of a utopian Quaker community where men are peripheral figures who are at their best when off "in the corner, engaged in the antipatriarchal operation of shaving" (146). Yet this ideal community is only a very small corner of the slave-holding union; like Cassy's attic in Simon Legree's house, this community represents for the slaves a safe but only temporary shelter from the domain of the larger community. It houses an idealized matriarchal domain, but a domain that has its boundaries drawn for it by the larger culture—boundaries it admittedly haunts and subverts by its presence. Further, although Rachel's "Hadn't thee better?" is obeyed as a command, one wonders if the domain that she has created is tied up in her existence as primary power in the home. That is, if "everything rests on her presence," as it does on Mr. Garner's in *Beloved's* Sweet Home, is a matriarchy all that different from a patriarchy?

Likewise, although George Harris is supposed to employ Stowe's ideas on a global level to lift Africa out of the corners and into the living room of the house that is humanity, one cannot help wondering if Africa is but another, more faraway corner of this male-dominated society and Stowe's matriarchal world, a corner that does not reform the house because, as William L. Andrews asserts, it "reconcile[s] black progress with black alienation without threatening the white status quo." [12] Instead it becomes a place to send a strong, fighting black man who doesn't fit with Stowe's "romantic racialism," a perspective that makes Africans, by virtue of race, "affectionate, magnanimous, and forgiving" (446)—just as women are, by virtue of gender. [13] One mustn't ignore the importance of Stowe's feminized remodeling of Christianity, as Elizabeth Ammons's recognition and appreciation of the ideal of the feminized Christ in Tom and Eva has demonstrated. Nevertheless, a trace of the Christian father-God pervades the Quaker community, George's plans for Africa, and the language of the entire book, and continues to evoke the patriarchal ideal of church as bride to the masculine God. George, and even Africa itself, require an "essentially Christian" development; his self-sufficient, inventive, and rebellious "Anglo" self must be claimed by God and subjected to his magnanimous "African" self.

The progressive transformations of Cassy's threatening power and pride further demonstrate the delimiting power of this trace of patriarchal Christianity on the characters of Africans and women. First, to make a woman who has murdered her children "safe" for this Christian and domestic perspective, she must be portrayed as slightly mad. Hence, although she has the power and strength of a male field hand, that power is ascribed to "the debil and all his angels," as Sambo and Quimbo put it (363). She must operate "by magic," and her eyes must be "wildly," as well as "mournfully," despairing (360). Then, in the chapter entitled "The Quadroon's Story," Cassy plays a combination Good Samaritan and

Mary Magdalene to Tom's Jesus—he, wounded, accepts her ointments gratefully and listens to her tale of woe without casting any stones. In this role, Cassy, like the biblical prostitute, considers herself a "lower" slave than Tom can ever be, because of the sexual and maternal fall that she describes in her subsequent slave narrative.[14] In that story, even to justify her very motherly violence against the men taking away her son, she must say that "something in [her] head snapped" (374). When she concludes her story with the murder of her own son, her voice is full of a "beguiling" force that affects even the pure, wounded Tom—and an "insane light glance[s] in her heavy black eyes" as she plots the murder of Legree (376). Just as George's natural "African" qualities have been possessed by the aggressive "Anglo" ones, making him too dangerous for Stowe's vision, so Cassy's natural, domestic female self has been "possessed" by slavery and made strong and mad.

But this possession does not end with slavery. When Cassy is united with and enabled to "sink into the bosom of the family," Eliza's "steady, consistent piety" must transform even the strong maternal force that Cassy redeveloped in the attic with Emmeline into the "gentle, trusting" love of a grandmother. Her maternal love might still be judged too powerful, or "too thick,' as Paul D will put it to Sethe in *Beloved*. After all, like Sethe's, Cassy's motherlove has led to the attempted murder of a white man and to the murder of her own child. Thus her "shattered and weary mind" must be so weakened by Eliza's mothering that Cassy is able to "[yield] at once, and with her whole soul, to every good influence, and bec[o]me a devout and tender Christian" (443). This Christianity, however, has a masculine force reminiscent of Cassy's old masters who "can do anything with a woman when [they've] got her children" (374). Her claim to herself has been taken once again by a God whose benevolent force haunts *Uncle Tom's Cabin* like the ghost of Simon Legree.

The trace of God's patriarchal power is made most overt at Tom's death. Although George has "come to buy" Tom and "take him home," God is, at least in part, the traditional big slaveholder in the sky, who, Tom says, " 's bought me and is going to take me home,—and I long to go. Heaven is better than Kintuck" (429). Heaven is here another, if better, slave-holding state than Kentucky, presided over by a more benevolent and more permanent master than George or Arthur Shelby. At the end of the novel, George Shelby remains a lesser version of God as "The Liberator," even though he operates in the domestic, feminine scheme of his mother's moral, familial suasion. He now will teach his newly-freed slaves what it means to be free, and he re-appropriates Uncle Tom's cabin as a symbolic reminder for the slaves of what it means to be a good Christian servant (451). A double realm of masculine domination surrounds Stowe's brave movement toward the increased "global" power of domesticity: the ever-present power of the masculine state that has infiltrated even some of her ideal matriarchies, with which the even more overarching power of God's slave-owning kingdom operates in complicity.

Although parts have been remodeled, the house is ultimately owned and haunted by a patriarchal figure who cannot be easily overcome, even while He, like Simon Legree, is invaded, subverted, and haunted by memories of a feminine, domestic ideal of motherhood and spirituality. Stowe's scheme still depends on racial and gender distinctions that cannot stand up to the strength of a character like George, who must be shipped off to an African corner, or Cassy, whose character (like George's) must be quickly subverted and made into the docile domain of a patriarchal God whose claim problematizes the philosophy upon which *Uncle Tom's Cabin* is founded. Ultimately, because it still maintains the metaphor of being "bought," privileges white slaveowners as a class over their slaves, and exalts the duty of self-sacrifice, Stowe's Christianity, in the words of Harriet A. Jacobs, will be "too much like slavery" for *Beloved*'s Baby Suggs. It cries out for her further remodeling.

Beloved offers an exemplary Victorian model home, Sweet Home, as a critique of a system covered with the "bignonias" of the domestic ideal but built of the "rough logs" of slavery. Mrs. Garner is presented as a self-sacrificing, motherly woman. She works hard, humming alongside the quiet Baby Suggs without complaint. Admittedly, the crippled, elderly Baby Suggs, having already seen the worst of slavery, still recognizes it as "a special kind of slavery," but slavery just the same: "It's better here, but I'm not."[15] Sethe, however, was young and motherless when she arrived. She loves Mrs. Garner like a mother, so that even after eighteen years of "freedom" she can insist: "I tended her like I would have tended my own mother if she needed me . . . I couldn't have done more for that woman than I could my own ma'am . . . and I'd have stayed with her until she got well or died" (200).[16] The limits of the True Woman's domain, however, become clear upon Mr. Garner's death: a "decent" white woman cannot live alone on a farm with no one but slaves. Worse still, her loving, Rachel-Halliday-like intercession on behalf of the sexually abused Sethe results in the severe beating that puts the tree on Sethe's back. The familial unity and love she shares with Sethe, like that advocated by the Beecher sisters, has difficult impediments to surmount because everything still rests on the male head of the household.

After all, like Arthur Shelby, Mr. Garner is a "man of humanity" who allows his slaves to be "men": to make decisions, use guns, and, in Halle's case, to buy his mother's freedom. His death, however, reveals the fragility of the male slaves' "domain" on Sweet Home, and indeed that of all such domains—especially those dependent upon the benevolence of a master. Paul D wonders "how much difference there really was between before schoolteacher and after," noting that "Garner called and announced them as men—but only on Sweet Home, and by his leave. Was he naming what he saw or creating what he did not?" (220). The limits of their domain and the degree to which they had been isolated in Mr. Garner's "wonderful lie" become clear in Paul D's question. They were, under Mr. Garner as under schoolteacher, simply "the defined" as men, and never the definers of themselves.

Moreover, despite its northern locale, 124 Bluestone is haunted as much by the "patriarchal institution" of slavery as by the ghost named Beloved, who is seemingly Sethe's murdered baby.[17] When we first encounter 124 Bluestone it is "spiteful," and Sethe and Denver are the only ones able to carry on life there.[18] But as with Cassy's haunting of Simon Legree, the overt haunting—the tables that move, the sound of a baby crawling up the stairs, and the fight with the house that Paul D seems to win upon his arrival—overshadows the presence of the benevolent, but nonetheless white, male owner of the space, Edward Bodwin, whose presence is for the most part covert.

But near the end of the novel we enter Bodwin's mind as he drives his carriage towards 124. He has not been to the house since he was three years old, but he remembers a few things—"that the cooking was done behind the house, the well was forbidden to play near, and that women died there: his mother, grandmother, an aunt and an older sister before he was born" (259). These women, who probably gave him such rules about where to play and did at least part of the cooking, and who were probably strong, domestic women who had a certain amount of rule in the home and the kitchen in the back, all died, inexplicably, in this strange house. Morrison leaves this enigmatic fact unexplained and undeveloped. Was it their deaths that forced the men to move away while one young daughter, herself eventually a spinster, was left? Is that why they now rent it out to "negroes"? Why does this haunted house use up women like Simon Legree uses up and throws away slaves?

More substantial than these questions, however, is Bodwin's seeming indifference to their deaths. They cling to his re-memory, but, despite the disturbing nature of this loss—the dissolution of the female core of the family—he still feels something "deeper and sweeter" about the house than about the surrounding farmland. His main concern is now remembering where he once buried things there: "Precious things he wanted to protect. As a child every item he owned was available and accountable to his family. Privacy was an adult indulgence, but when he got to be one, he seemed not to need it" (259). Bodwin developed this love for the place not through his mother's love and sacrifice but by appropriating certain long-forgotten spaces. The housing reformers believed it important that children develop such a sense of "home-feeling." Historian Clifford E. Clark, for example, quotes one reformer supporting an argument for separate rooms: "satisfying this home-feeling will also contribute immensely to [the children's] love of the homestead. Without it, it is only their *father's* home, not theirs. . . . But by giving them their own apartment, they themselves become personally identified with it." [19] As a result of his burying the toys, 124 was no longer just Bodwin's father's house, as it could easily have been to a motherless child who moved away at age three. It was, and is, his—cognitively and literally.

This ownership subverts, however, Bodwin's claim that he no longer needs privacy. Ever since that childhood dependency, his privacy has been continually guaranteed. As a white male landowner he has never had Baby Suggs's experience of having "them" come in his yard—that is, those who, like schoolteacher and Bodwin himself, already have power and privacy, for whom the entire world seems part of their domain. In fact, the glimpses we get of his yard and home are in keeping with the domestic ideal as it allied itself with the nineteenth-century beginnings of the movement toward suburbia. Clark describes this movement by quoting landscape architect Frederick Law Olmsted, who argued that, much like a kitchen, the "essential quality of suburbia is domesticity," whereas in the inner city there can be "no feeling of privacy, no security from intrusion." [20] Bodwin's is just such a suburban home, "right in the center of a street full of houses and trees"—a quiet, white neighborhood that protects his home from all invasion and separates it from the rapidly developing industrial city (143). The black people who come for his benevolence enter his back door and sit in the kitchen—hidden also, in keeping with the domestic ideal, at the back of the house. Meanwhile he entertains white slave owners (whom he doesn't "hold with—even

Garner's kind") in the front (145). It is unlikely that he does not "need" privacy, any sort of a *hus*, but rather that he does not see that in his domain, privacy and shelter are a given. His vulnerability is so imperceptible that he does not even realize it exists, so he has never lost faith in the philosophy that Baby Suggs shared with him and his father until the Misery: "human life is holy, all of it" (260).

Before the Misery, Baby Suggs had literally remodeled the cast-aside house that Bodwin had "given" her as a place to live. In so doing, she remodeled the ideal of the model home. Denver mentions the literal remodeling in her narrative to Beloved: "The room we sleep in upstairs used to be where the help slept when whitepeople lived here. They had a kitchen outside, too. But Grandma Baby turned it into a woodshed and toolroom when she moved in. And she boarded up the back door that led to it because she said she didn't want to make that journey no more. She built around it to make a storeroom, so if you want to get in 124 you have to come by her" (207). Clearly, Baby Suggs associates servanthood with a back door and a corner bedroom, and this is all tied to the placement of the kitchen. Although by the 1870s the domestic norm stipulated a kitchen inside—but at the back of the house—both Gwendolyn Wright and Clifford Clark comment on the reason for this suggestive placement. The front rooms of the house were, in the ideal, reserved for family gatherings in keeping with the ideal of creating and protecting the unified family. Not surprisingly, however, these front rooms usually became excuses for "lavish and prominent display" of the (male) owner's wealth as the materialistic realm asserted its power over the "female" spiritual domain.[21] Rather than the spiritual gathering places the idealists dreamed of, these front rooms became the kind of place you could show off to Southern slave-owning aristocrats that you don't hold with, while their freed slaves would sit in the kitchen.

To protect this ideal/materialistic space, the ideal kitchen had to be kept far to the back. As Clark describes it: "It was important, said the advocates of housing reform, that the kitchen and other service aspects of the house be hidden from the eyes of any visitors. . . . If servants were hired, a back staircase was put in to give them access to the kitchen and keep them out of sight."[22] Despite Stowe's ideal of the value and worth of women's work (cf. Ophelia's New England home where the work is unobtrusively "done up" without servants by the mother and her girls), even in *The American Woman's Home* kitchens are relegated to the back of the house in the suggested floor plans. As Wright sees it, such designs suggest that in the model home, "the kitchen area was planned as the hired woman's territory," despite the fact that fewer and fewer homeowners could afford hired help. Thus, " 'Queen Anne in the front, and Mary Anne in the back,' was a quip of the time, referring to a typical house plan. By this account, the lady of the house gave all her time and attention to the front parlor, where she reigned amidst her fashionable English splendor, while her servant . . . was hidden away in the back kitchen." [23] The ideal became, then, to separate the woman who worked from the True Woman who reigned on the pedestal of her front parlor, without a hair out of place.

Baby Suggs confronts this alignment of kitchen placement with servanthood and remodels her house to avoid it. Thus the Bodwins' servants' quarters become a bedroom for the family, and no one ever has to make the servant's "journey" into the house again. Moreover, Denver's statement that whoever wanted to come into 124 had to get by Baby Suggs's scrutiny suggests that, although Baby Suggs had a clear understanding that her house could be invaded, she trusted in her strength as ruler over her domain, as a working "queen" of her kitchen. And, as further testimony to the strength of her will, she accomplishes this remodeling despite apparent criticism from the outside: "Said she didn't care what folks said about her fixing a two-story house like a cabin where you cook inside. She said they told her visitors with nice dresses don't want to sit in the same room with the cook stove and the peelings and the grease and the smoke. She wouldn't pay them no mind, she said" (207). Baby Suggs does not want to create a separate domain for community and spirituality; it is located in her kitchen where there is no pretense of servants, lavish displays, or of life lived without the real work of living. Even kitchen life is holy.

So holy, in fact, that under this philosophy 124 was able to become known as "a way station." Not a temporary one, as the Quaker settlement, Garner's Sweet Home, and Stowe's America itself were for the black community, but a communal center:

. . . 124 had been a cheerful, buzzing house where Baby Suggs, holy, loved, cautioned, fed, chastised and soothed. Where not one but two pots simmered on the stove; where the lamp burned all night long. Strangers rested there while children tried on their shoes. Messages were left there, for whoever needed them was sure to stop in one day soon. Talk was low and to the point—for Baby Suggs, holy, didn't approve of extra. "Everything depends on knowing how much," she said, and "Good is knowing when to stop." (86–87)

Rather than trying to shut itself off in the privacy of suburbia, consistent with the ideal, this remodeled, lively house with a life-giving kitchen at its heart creates a communal domain. Simultaneously, this center gives Baby Suggs the kind of power that allows her to lay down the rules in her axiomatic expressions of Quakerly simplicity and balance. Like the Halliday home, her home functions as both *domus* and *hus* for herself and the community—a place of shelter from the larger society as well as an expression of their communal power, such as it is, in the face of that society.

Moreover, the religion that binds this community upholds the philosophy that "human life is holy." It does not center on a benevolent patriarchal God, but on an ex-slave female who does not tell the others that they are "the blessed of the earth, its inheriting meek or its glorybound pure" (88). That would be to preach that they are best out of power and that they need to be patient so they can go to the big plantation in the sky, keeping themselves in the self-sacrificing mentality that even haunts the Quaker settlement—the true mentality fit for women and "negroes." Baby Suggs knows that this part of Stowe's religion is not what they need to hear. Rather, they need to be commanded to a bit of selfishness: to love their "flesh that weeps, laughs; flesh that dances on bare feet in grass," because "Yonder they do not love your flesh. They despise it" (88). In Baby Suggs's philosophy, it is this hatred of black flesh that allows white people to claim it. They are able to take the self it encloses for their domain, as Sethe realizes: "anybody white could take your whole self for anything that came to mind. Not just work, kill, or maim you, but dirty you. Dirty you so bad you couldn't like yourself anymore. Dirty you so bad you forgot who you were and couldn't think it up" (251). Even Stowe's use was in some ways a "taking" of their bodies, then, a recreating of black selves in an ideal that also would not threaten "the white status quo," despite her own strong examples to the contrary in George and Cassy. Baby Suggs knows that before being fit for any more self-sacrifice, an ex-slave community living in alien territory needs this love of their own flesh. For that alone will allow her people to claim ownership of themselves, as Sethe does in her twenty-eight days of freedom: "Bit by bit, at 124 and in the Clearing, along with the others, she had claimed herself. Freeing yourself was one thing; claiming ownership of that freed self was another" (95).

When Paul D leaves Sethe, he sees her claim as the community did: "more important than what Sethe had done was what she claimed" (164). Sethe's claim of love for herself and for her children makes her love "too thick" according to Paul D. Like Cassy's, her motherlove goes beyond what the community can bear: "This here Sethe talked about love like any other woman . . . but what she meant could cleave the bone. This here Sethe talked about safety with a handsaw. This here new Sethe didn't know where the world stopped and she began" (164). Paul D, like the community, wants to be able to draw a clear line between self and the world, but Sethe's love of her children makes that difficult. Ella, for instance, "understood Sethe's rage in the shed twenty years ago, but not her reaction to it, which Ella thought was prideful, misdirected, and Sethe herself too complicated" (256). Everything about Sethe's situation is complicated. Not even Paul D can tell her what "better" options she may have had, but he and the community do not want to see these lengths of the love that Baby Suggs preached. They want Sethe just to talk love, like Baby Suggs's feast, her love is too overwhelming in the flesh. Like Stowe, they want her to be simply crazy and then tamed—not a proud woman who resents their lack of understanding and who can hold a job and get on without them. This communal resentment is voiced again by Ella: "When she got out of jail and made no gesture toward anybody, and lived as though she were alone, Ella junked her" (256).

Hence, although Paul D "knew exactly what she meant: to get to a place where you could love anything you chose—not to need permission for desire—well now, that was freedom," in the same conversation he condemns her for not remembering that she has two feet (162). Sethe refuses the only seeming alternatives to her love: Paul D's suggestion to "love small" and Ella's advice "don't love nothing" (92). She had reclaimed her freedom to love; she could no longer allow schoolteacher to invade, contaminate, and claim the selves of her children, "her best thing," seemingly the only thing she had left that was pure. As she sees it, she was doing her first duty as a mother: "to know what is [as opposed to 'what's worse'] and to keep them away from what I know is terrible" (165).

When faced with schoolteacher's hat, Sethe felt the invasion of Baby Suggs's domain, her own *hus*. He, by sanction of the Fugitive Slave Act, was trying to take away the freedom she had tried to claim as a result of Ohio's domain as a free state. So her reaction to the Fugitive Law was to stop the man by putting her children "on the other side," beyond the domain claimed by whitemen: "I took and put them where they'd be safe" (164). Her pride comes from a triumph over the whiteman's domain. This is not, however, to forget that Sethe's was "a rough choice" that even Baby Suggs "cannot approve or condemn" (180). The nature of her claim is still problematic: did she have the right to the bodies of her children? She sees her action as claiming a domain over herself, but where does "the world stop and she begin"? Good, after all, is knowing when to stop. By killing her children, even out of love, was she staking a claim that was too wide, or just as wide as the Baby Suggs ideal allowed it to be? Most frighteningly, was that act of love crossing the boundary into the acts of hate that were committed by the owners of the slaves' bodies? Her loving action also may be haunted by the presence of Simon Legree and schoolteacher, and for most of the book we do not have the "comforting" knowledge that she is simply another crazy Cassy—and neither does she. In the clearing Sethe observes: "Other people went crazy, why couldn't she?" (70).

Yet if Sethe's action has scarred her, then it also makes us see Ella, again representative of the whole community, as scarred another way. Ella also killed a child, one she was forced to have by "the lowest yet," by refusing to feed it. She killed it out of hatred; it was a "hairy, white thing" that bespoke her violation. Yet her equally understandable decision not to love at all anymore is symptomatic of the community's unwillingness to accept Baby Suggs's love freely. Hence, when "they"—the whitemen— come into the yard of 124, Baby Suggs's belief in the amazing grace that seemed to make her home overflow in a feast for five thousand (that turns out to be a "last supper") disappears. As she stands in the field, sensing the town's disapproval, she feels she has broken her own rule of "knowing when to stop": "And then she knew. Her friends and neighbors were angry at her because she had overstepped, given too much, offended by excess" (138). This refusal of her love marks Ella and the community as being unable to claim the freedom to love, just as Sethe's marks her as one who has overstepped. Everything depends on knowing how much.

But what Baby Suggs sees and what Stamp Paid is beginning to see is that "the heart that pumped out love, the mouth that spoke the Word," all those things that Baby Suggs had been working to get the community to love in themselves seemingly "didn't count. They came in her yard anyway. . . . The whitefolks had tired her out at last" (180). The whitemen seem to have claimed every living domain on the land, and every soul in it. Thus, when Sethe argues against her on the side of the whitemen, saying, "They gave you this house," Baby Suggs answers, "Nobody gave me anything" (244). The whitemen's invasion has made Baby Suggs aware that her communal domain never mattered, never was a given. More disturbingly, not even a claim to one's self is a given in a society that justifies slavery. Like Simon Legree's mansion, 124 has always been haunted by the ownership of whitemen—both by Edward Bodwin's literal ownership and the broader political ownership that allowed the men to invade her home in the name of the law, "at the very hour when everyone stopped dropping by" (163).

As with Rachel Halliday's Quaker settlement, the spiritual unity of the town seems to have rested on Baby Suggs's shoulders, and the community refused to go where she was leading them. Particularly after Baby Suggs's death, the family within 124 struggles to create a self-sufficient unity devoid of outside community and entrapped by the memory and haunting of slavery in the form of Beloved. Even Paul D's banishment of the ghost lasts only long enough for Sethe to go out and re-establish a nodding acquaintance with the community. She just becomes able to imagine the solidity of the three hand-holding shadows that she sees as she, Paul D, and Denver walk home from the carnival, when Beloved appears.[24] After that, Beloved demands unity with Sethe alone, Denver with Beloved, and Paul D with Sethe, who, however, still seems to want to mother and love everyone; she wants the three hand-holding shadows as a model family for 124 because that kind of unity represents the binding claim of her motherlove.

Deborah Horvitz does well to remind us that Beloved does "give by taking," by demanding that "Sethe reveal memory and story about her life before Sweet Home, memory about her African-speaking, branded mother and her life right after Sweet Home when she cut Beloved's throat."[25] She does, thereby, help forge links between Sethe, her lost mother, grandmother, and Beloved herself, as Horvitz argues, as well as being the memory tyrant who refuses to share Sethe. This tyrannical aspect of Beloved's haunting is clarified by a connection to the Gothic tradition of ghosts on which both of the novels draw. Karen Halttunen notes that Cassy's "haunting" of Simon Legree in the form of his mother played off and satirized the tradition of ghosts in nineteenth-century Gothic novels; Legree "haunts himself" as the ghost becomes to him the outward realization of his fears and guilt regarding his lost mother and his own lost innocence.[26] So Beloved seems to embody the insecurities of each of the residents of 124: the pervasive, tyrannical memory of the "patriarchal institution" that continues to sap their ability to claim freedom. Because of this memory, her "tyranny" has strong overtones of slavery's patriarchal force. She moves Paul D out of the house and further weakens his manhood by compelling him to have sex with her against his will—like the slave owner Baby Suggs describes as "studding his boys." Importantly, this "violation" takes place in the coldhouse, the house away from the communal flame of the kitchen. In her quasi-patriarchal possession of the house, Beloved even convinces the fiercely independent Sethe that her womanly place, in fact the only domain, is in the house: "Whatever is going on outside my door ain't for me. The world is in this room. This here's all there is and all there needs to be" (183).

Ultimately, Denver realizes that this "possession" has gone too far, but she too has been virtually convinced by her years of seclusion that "the world beyond the edge of the porch" will swallow her up (243). And, as a representative of the community, Stamp Paid recognizes the unintelligible voices that form a noose around 124 as the voices of enslavement—voices that we know ring with "She mine." Beloved has become, at least in part, the embodiment of slavery's patrimony to Sethe and her daughter: a conscience who refuses to understand and forgive the ambiguity of Sethe's simultaneously loving and cruel response to the mock freedom granted by the Fugitive laws. Beloved's presence calls forth from Sethe a boundless retribution that fills up the house and drives all three women to the edge of sanity: "If the whitepeople of Cincinnati had allowed Negroes into their lunatic asylum, they would have found candidates in 124" (250). Although Sethe has seemingly been broken down into a "safe" madwoman like Cassy, she has become so only after having her claim to herself taken away by this ghost that demands to be her only "best thing." Such a theft of claim represents the epitome of patriarchal possession.

Denver, Stamp Paid, and Ella ultimately lead the rest of the community in a movement of reconciliation that continues to the end of the novel. Denver recognizes the danger of Beloved's possession and determines to seek outside help, even though the world outside of 124 might eat her up. The community, in turn, finds in Denver's expression of need the ties forged by Baby Suggs. Beloved has fulfilled and surpassed the community's vengeful anger at both Sethe's and Baby Suggs's dangerous, boundless loves. In the end the women led by Ella do what they refused to do at Sethe's arrest; they form a "cape of sound" to wrap around her "like arms to hold and steady her on her way" (152). Upon making this effort they see the ghosts of their young selves on the lawn, with Baby Suggs "laugh[ing] and skipp[ing] among them, urging more" (258). They see themselves happy in her bountiful last supper, "not feeling the envy that surfaced the next day" (258). Baby Suggs's ghost once again teaches the wideness of love, and they are now ready to carry her love on.

Yet, at the very moment when everyone starts dropping by again, we are reminded that these women are still the madwomen in Mr. Bodwin's attic as his presence returns to haunt 124 and the community with his power, and Sethe with the memory of schoolteacher's return twenty years earlier. Her passion cannot be broken down like Cassy's; mother-love for her is still a killer. But this time she does not strike her own child. She strikes Bodwin, the good-intentioned whiteman who still carries in him the ghosts of the patriarchal institution—the ghost of "the man without skin" in Beloved's vision who has a whip in his hand, and those of the ghostly men who run the slave ship of her narratives, pushing the dead into the sea (215). When Beloved sees this whiteman looking at Sethe, and Sethe running towards him, she disappears; the more permanent possessor/ghost has returned to his domain, and her possession simply doesn't match up. She does not own the walls of 124. When Sethe directly attacks him—the "real" ghost of patriarchal ownership—the ghostly embodiment of her enslavement can disappear.

Yet Morrison provides us with hints of Bodwin's vulnerability, too. Unaware of Sethe with her deadly ice pick, Mr. Bodwin is a seventy-year-old man having "thoughts of mortality" that are "not new" but which "still ha[ve] the power to annoy" (260). He is a fragile being who must, after all, be saved by a girl—Denver. His two houses—the one a secluded nest in town, the other a possessed two-story house in the black community—announce his vulnerable, human need for shelter as well as his need for a material domain. Of course, in the end the community still recognizes their dependence on his benevolent power. As with Mr. Garner, "everything rests on him": "He somebody never turned us down. Steady as a rock. I tell you something, if she had got to him, it'd be the worst thing for us" (265). But they also have a new kind of communal strength established by the reciprocal movements out of and towards 124.

Because of this strength, at the very end of the novel we are given a slightly precarious hope that Paul D, Denver, and Sethe will make it there anyway. They will remodel this home and Baby Suggs's ideal in keeping with their love for and mutual dependence on one another—despite Miss Bodwin's desire to get rid of 124 and Mr. Bodwin's feeble resistance. Denver may be growing up and out of the house, but she has been reconciled to Paul D; she no longer sneers at him. She and Paul D have, in fact, worked out a reciprocal, loving relationship to the ill Sethe: "Denver be here in the day. I [Paul D] be here in the night. I'm a take care of you, you hear?" (272). Their model home is being built in a remodeled patriarchal space that only needs painting. Paul D no longer jealously wishes to be the "head" of the family, or for Sethe to be only "the woman he wanted to protect" (132, 127). That is the domestic ideal, the patriarchal ideal that has always haunted the house. This nonpatriarchy does not mean that Paul D is emasculated in the way that readers have complained of or have praised Stowe's Uncle Tom for being.[27] Rather, manhood, too, is redefined; he can still be empowered as a male in this culture. He doesn't need to be sent to Africa or any such safe, faraway corner of the world. He will, of course, protect Sethe in her current weakness and nurture her back to health. But he will also lay his story next to hers, in an equal reciprocity, so that together they can try to create "some kind of tomorrow" out of their pasts. They are not looking forward to a big plantation in the sky. Rather their story wants to preach Baby Suggs's, holy, self-love story, which will allow Sethe to reclaim herself: "You your best thing, Sethe. You are" (273). And the "present" of this is, indeed, a story to pass on and create a future with.

Stowe and Morrison share an acute awareness of the power of the patriarchal culture ostensibly to offer the home as woman's *domus* and *hus* while remaining always threatening and able to invade that domain and shatter its security. Both authors, however, optimistically offer alternative visions to this patriarchal control. Stowe began the remodeling by using the domestic ideal as a new form of global female empowerment. But her matriarchal ideal does not finally alter the basic structure of the patriarchy—as a true remodeling must. It shifts power into the hands of a female head of the household who continues operating under the ultimate control of a patriarchal, slave-owning God. By setting up her text as a conscious parallel to *Uncle Tom's Cabin*, Morrison re-entered this structure to continue the remodeling and demonstrated how to alter irreversibly the power structure of the patriarchal home. She suggests a space where a warm, communal center could be made out of the working place of the home: a space where women and men can share themselves in the form of their stories without fear of their stories being claimed by someone else's labels of them as being wrong—animalistic, bad, unwomanly, or unchristian; where painful stories can be made bearable because they are shared by more than one person and accepted by the community; where that community can learn to love anything they choose and claim themselves in the domain of that love. If they indeed accomplish this loving claim, as we are given to hope at the end of *Beloved*, then the ghosts of the patriarchy may finally cease to have power over, if not to cease haunting, the houses of women's fiction.

Notes

1   Amos Rapoport, "Vernacular Architecture and the Cultural Determinants of Form," in *Buildings and Society: Essays on the Social Development of the Built Environment*, ed. Anthony D. King (London: Routledge, 1980), 284.

2   Harriet Beecher Stowe and Catharine Beecher, *The American Woman's Home* (1869; rpt., Watkins Glen, N.Y.: Library of Victorian Culture, 1979), 13. In his introduction to this edition, Joseph Van Why notes that this book was essentially a revision of Catharine Beecher's *Treatise on the Domestic Economy for the Use of Young Ladies at Home and at School* to which Stowe's famous name was attached, although she may have contributed some thoughts from her own series of essays *House and Home Papers*, first published in the *Atlantic Monthly* in 1864. On the differences between the Beecher sisters regarding the domestic ideal, see Jeanne Boydston, Mary Kelley, and Anne Margolis, *The Limits of Sisterhood: The Beecher Sisters on Women's Rights and Woman's Sphere* (Chapel Hill: Univ. of North Carolina Press, 1988); and Gillian Brown, who finds that Stowe seeks a "utopian rehabilitation" of the traditional ideals of domesticity more closely allied with her sister Catharine, in "Getting in the Kitchen with Dinah: Domestic Politics in *Uncle Tom's Cabin*," *American Quarterly* 36 (1984): 503–23.

3   Arthur C. Danto, "Abide/Abode," in *Housing: Symbol, Structure, Site*, ed. Lisa Taylor (New York: Cooper-Hewitt Museum, 1990), 9.

4   Elizabeth Ammons, "Heroines in *Uncle Tom's Cabin*," *American Literature* 49 (1977): 161–79; rpt. in *Critical Essays on Harriet Beecher Stowe*, ed. Ammons (Boston: G. K. Hall, 1980), 153. Among others, see also Ammons's "Stowe's Dream of a Mother-Savior: *Uncle Tom's Cabin* and American Women Writers Before the 1920s," in *New Essays on "Uncle Tom's Cabin,"* ed. Eric J. Sundquist (New York: Cambridge Univ. Press, 1986), 155–95; Gillian Brown, "Getting in the Kitchen with Dinah"; and Jane Tompkins, "Sentimental Power: *Uncle Tom's Cabin* and the Politics of Literary History," in *Sensational Designs: The Cultural Work of American Fiction, 1790–1860* (New York: Oxford Univ. Press, 1985), 122–47.

5   Gwendolyn Wright, *Moralism and the Model Home: Domestic Architecture and Cultural Conflict in Chicago, 1873–1913* (Chicago: Univ. of Chicago Press, 1980), 2.

6   See especially Gillian Brown, "Getting in the Kitchen with Dinah," and Theodore Hovet, *The Master Narrative: Harriet Beecher Stowe's Subversive Story of Master and Slave in "Uncle Tom's Cabin" and "Dred"* (Boston: Univ. Press of America, 1989).

7   Wright, 37.

8   Harriet Beecher Stowe, *Uncle Tom's Cabin, or Life Among the Lowly*, ed. Kenneth S. Lynn (Cambridge: Harvard Univ. Press, 1962), 350. Subsequent references to this edition will be incorporated parenthetically into the text.

9   Hovet, 23.

10   Karen Halttunen, "Gothic Imagination and Social Reform: The Haunted Houses of Lyman Beecher, Henry Ward Beecher and Harriet Beecher Stowe," in *New Essays on "Uncle Tom's Cabin,"* 107–34.

11   Brown concludes her article by noting that, although "men as we know them" cannot exist in Stowe's matriarchal utopia, Stowe's retention of "the name of the male God throughout her matriarchal design suggests that her imagination of a feminized world still requires the sanction of male authority" (523).

12   William L. Andrews, *To Tell a Free Story* (Urbana: Univ. of Illinois Press, 1986), 180.

13   On the use of the term "romantic racialism," see George M. Fredrickson, "Uncle Tom and the Anglo-Saxons: Romantic Racialism in the North," in *The Black Image in the White Mind: The Debate on Afro-American Destiny, 1817–1914* (New York: Harper, 1971), 97–130.

14   In the *Key to "Uncle Tom's Cabin"* (London: Clarke, Beeton, 1853), Stowe does not offer a specific parallel for Cassy's narrative, but she does include a clipping from a newspaper article that describes a slave mother's murdering of her own children and subsequent suicide, and the owner's befuddled reaction (273). Later, Stowe also includes a letter from a freed slave whose mother's desire to "fix [him] so they'd never get [him]" reminded him of Cassy (304).

15   Toni Morrison, *Beloved* (New York: Knopf, 1987), 140. Subsequent references to this edition will be incorporated into the text parenthetically.

16   See Karen E. Fields on Morrison's exploration of this possibility of love even between slave and master, in "To Embrace Dead Strangers: Toni Morrison's *Beloved*," in *Mother Puzzles: Daughters and Mothers in Contemporary American Literature*, ed. Mickey Pearlman (New York: Greenwood, 1989), 159–70, 166 in particular.

17   On the complex nature of Beloved's ghostly character, see Deborah Horvitz, "Nameless Ghosts: Possession and Dispossession in *Beloved*," *Studies in American Fiction* 17 (1989): 157–67.

18   Marilyn Chandler does an especially fine job of discussing Denver's relation

to 124 Bluestone in her recent comparison of *"Housekeeping* and *Beloved*: When Women Come Home," in *Dwelling in the Text: Houses in American Fiction* (Berkeley: Univ. of California Press, 1991), 291–319.

19 Clifford E. Clark Jr., "Domestic Architecture as an Index to Social History: The Romantic Revival and the Cult of Domesticity in America, 1840–1870," *Journal of Interdisciplinary History* 7 (1976): 33–56; quotation from 50 (emphasis his).

20 Clark, 41.

21 Wright, *Moralism and the Model Home*, 35.

22 Clark, 50.

23 Wright, 35–36.

24 On the importance of the number three in Morrison's earlier fiction, see Susan Willis, "Eruptions of Funk: Historicizing Toni Morrison," in *Black Literature and Literary Theory*, ed. Henry Louis Gates Jr. (New York: Routledge, 1990), 263–84.

25 Horvitz, "Nameless Ghosts," 160.

26 Halttunen, "Gothic Imagination and Social Reform," 123–24. I would also like to thank Elizabeth Schultz for her insights on this point.

27 Ammons is one of the foremost admirers of the feminization of Tom, finding that Tom's equation with mothers and Eva/Christ "indicts masculine ethics" and calls for a redefinition of masculinity along more feminine lines, towards a reformation of society as a whole. See especially "Stowe's Dream of a Mother-Savior." She argues, of course, against the anger of such critics as James Baldwin, who asserts that Tom "has been robbed of his humanity and divested of his sex" in "Everybody's Protest Novel," *Partisan Review* 16 (1949): 578–85, rpt. in *Critical Essays on Harriet Beecher Stowe*, ed. Elizabeth Ammons (Boston: G. K. Hall, 1980), 92–97. The quotation appears on 94.

Siobhan   A Zuni Raconteur Dons the
Senier   Junco Shirt: Gender and Narrative Style in
the Story of Coyote and Junco

In her introduction to *The Sacred Hoop*, Paula Gunn Allen criticizes Western anthropological accounts of Native American cultures that "discount, degrade, or conceal gynocratic features or re-contextualize those features so that they will appear patriarchal."[1] Such studies, she maintains, belong to a long tradition of efforts to project Western patriarchy's worst features onto a thoroughly woman-centered culture in order to justify the obliteration of that culture.[2] The charge is a sobering one for a European-American student trying to sort out gender dynamics in Native American oral literature; indeed, in Gunn Allen's view, it seems that any discussion of "patriarchal" features in tribal culture is tantamount to an "unstated but compelling rationale for genocide."[3]

It is with some trepidation, then, that I offer what might look, in part, like a "patriarchal" reading of a Zuni version of the story of Coyote and Junco, as told by Andrew Peynetsa and recorded in Dennis Tedlock's *Finding the Center*.[4] This comic narrative, in which Old Lady Junco pulls a fast one on Coyote, who is trying to bully her into giving him her song, does contain features that can be seen as distinctly gynocratic. At the same time, though, an especially brief narration by Peynetsa and the comic mode itself appear in some ways to suppress those elements—or at least to deny them fuller fruition—even as they produce them. I would thus like to ask why the tale is gendered and relayed as it is in *Finding the Center*, and to speculate as to what kind of impulses this narration might be reinforcing or subverting. It is not that I want to suggest that Zuni culture is a patriarchy, or that this Coyote tale is an undoubtedly subversive (or undoubtedly not subversive) moment in a uniformly oppressive context. Rather, it may be that Zuni culture and Zuni stories are, like most cultures and stories, somewhat more complicated than either purely patriarchal or fully feminist accounts allow. Resistance, then, may be part and parcel of whatever power relations are in place; it may be both suppressed and allowed at once, or constituted in the very presence of suppressed features.

Inquiring into the effects of Peynetsa's version implicitly raises the question of what other possibilities exist for the telling of this tale. I will examine some of the alternate versions here, including that by Hopi raconteur Helen Sekaquaptewa, whose performance of the story (titled "I'isau and the Birds") appears on a video produced by Larry Evers.[5] Comparing different versions of the "same" story can be at once illuminating and frustrating, because it raises a tangle of issues surrounding the way we interpret a literature that is "different" both in content and form. It also brings us back to and beyond Gunn Allen's problem with "patriarchal" readings. The final question may be not whether a reading should fall on one "side" (masculinist or feminist, oppressive or subversive) or another, but whether it is appropriate at all to draw broad conclusions about the function of these stories' gendered figures in their cultures.

■ ■ ■

Finding the Center raises the question of whether we can claim, as Gunn Allen has claimed, that tribal cultures are "never" patriarchal.[6] For example, Tedlock's introduction tells us that, in Zuni culture, storytelling is a male privilege: men are usually the ones who perform formal storytelling, and the stories themselves are largely the property of older men.[7] The same is true among Hopis, according to Sekaquaptewa's ethnoautobiography; moreover, she reveals, origin stories are told only to men.[8] In addition, Zuni stories (in Tedlock's anthology as well as in earlier collections) seem to contain their fair share of culpable or dangerous women. In one story in *Finding the Center*, a woman's adultery brings famine and tragedy on a Hopi community. In other Zuni narratives, female or feminized figures renege on their roles as caregivers with disastrous results: a young girl leaves her (*tom*) turkeys to go dancing and they punish her for it;[9] a mother abandons her infant, and (in some versions) the child's relatives condemn her and/or later kill and eat the deer mother who took in the child. Still more brutally, when a group of women end a game with the warrior Payatamu by cutting off his head (a term to which he had agreed), he wreaks his vengeance by summoning beasts to rape them and then brings the women back to his village for humiliation at the hands of his more "domestic" kinswomen. Further abuse of female figures can be found in a variety of Zuni narratives, such as one in which twin war gods, playing their rain-making game, drown grandmothers, or another in which women are beheaded by Coyote, again in a game. And then there is the series of tales, noted by Ruth Benedict, that manifest male anxiety about female sexuality: sometimes newly married men misunderstand and fear their wives, or innocent young boys are pursued by voracious women (including one with a toothed vagina).[10]

It is difficult as a European-American feminist not to see blame of women and the making monstrous of their sexuality here, but it is not my project to try to prove that these stories are overtly or essentially sexist. Indeed, if they do betray any patriarchalism, they are also interesting for the way they problematize that ideology. Zuni stories are seldom totalizing—Peynetsa's version of the Hopi famine tale, for example, gives voice to both the betrayed husband who censures his wife and to the Hopis who blame her lover as well as her. Zuni stories are also not static. As another example, Peynetsa's version of the deer story seems to enlist some sympathy for the "natural" mother while the versions collected by Ruth Bunzel show her community condemning and punishing her.[11] Nevertheless, it is difficult to reconcile the account of Payatamu's actions—against a group of women who, perhaps not incidentally, live apart from his village in a community of only women—with the idea of a wholly gynocratic culture or text. We do not need to take *Finding the Center* (or, indeed, any group of oral narratives) as a paradigm of Zuni culture— the stories themselves and the way they are transcribed are, after all, largely the choices of a white Western male. But again, it is useful to ask why certain figures in these stories might be gendered as they are, to ask why men in this culture tell stories of this kind to other men. Perhaps we should be as wary of suppressing patriarchal features in the name of feminist readings as we are of writing them in.

■ ■ ■

It is against this wholly provisional and ostensibly paternalistic backdrop of *Finding the Center* that I would like to look at "Coyote and Junco." Like many Western literary scholars working with Native American texts, I turned to ethnographic research on the subject of women's status in Zuni culture. Zuni is a matrilineal culture, with the mother's household traditionally the domain of economic activity.[12] Though not without their differences, anthropologists from the pre-World War I generation of Matilda Coxe Stevenson to contemporary researchers including M. Jane Young generally agree that men and women's roles in Zuni, though different, are equitable and complementary. Stevenson addresses Zuni women's institutionalized exclusion from religion by recording those rare instances of female membership in some of the religious societies and esoteric fraternities.[13] Contemporary writers like Young, Will Roscoe, and Barbara Tedlock observe that many women play essential symbolic roles in religion (for instance, in the feeding of kachina masks), and that, where excluded, they find ingenious ways to make their participation and presence felt: Young describes women leaving their handprints when they plaster the walls of the kivas, where women do not gather, and Barbara Tedlock finds that while only Zuni men "officially" know how to paint kachina masks, women do paint them, with the tacit acceptance of the community.[14] Zuni women also have had specialized areas of knowledge, as in the grinding and storing of corn, the making of purgatives, and the designing of pottery; older women in particular, according to Young, receive special respect.[15]

"Coyote and Junco" seems in many ways to fit this picture in that its vanquishing figure, the one whose wisdom prevails, is a small female finch. As Peynetsa tells it, Old Lady Junco is at home winnowing when Coyote approaches her to demand that she teach him her winnowing song. Although clearly annoyed with his aggressiveness,[16] Junco sings it for him, but Coyote forgets it almost as soon as he leaves her and returns to ask her to repeat it. The two reenact this encounter four times; in the final instance Junco vows not to sing for him again and puts her "junco shirt" over a rock. Coyote threatens the disguised stone for a bit before biting "her" and breaking his teeth.

This very brief, very funny story would seem to reinforce the notion of Zuni culture as matrilineal and matriarchal. Unlike some other older female figures in Zuni stories (the aforementioned abused grandmothers, for instance), Junco clearly gets the last laugh. She does so despite her small size. And perhaps more interesting is the reason she finally decides to thwart Coyote: while on one level she clearly wants to get rid of this pesky visitor, it is tempting to read her final gesture as a move to preserve her space and her song as her own. Admittedly, the issue of motivation is complicated in Native American texts, which may be more driven in this regard by cultural and narrative conventions than by Western notions of psychology and interiority. Nevertheless, Junco is the only female figure in Tedlock's anthology to mark out her territory in this way or this successfully; speech may be considered here a private act, even an act of power, and (in the Zuni oral performance tradition anyway) that act is a privilege limited mainly to men.

However, certain details work against reading the story as a simple battle of the sexes in which the woman emerges the victor. For one thing, if "Old Lady" maintains the effect of the Zuni term as well as Dennis Tedlock claims it does,[17] then that term undercuts Junco. Her age, gender, and size seem to diminish her too, if we compare her with some of the healthy, warrior-like male heroes of the other narratives. This is not to undervalue the importance of the so-called woman's sphere, nor to impose a very Western interpretation on the tale by seeing Old Lady Junco as weaker than Payatamu simply because she is elderly, small, and female. But the contrast is unmistakable: what Junco can inflict on Coyote—a few broken teeth—hardly compares with another Coyote's beheading of his grandmother or with the humiliation that Payatamu inflicts on the women who sever his head.

Comparing Junco and Coyote as gendered figures reveals the acute tension between "gynocratic" and "patriarchal" readings. First of all, Junco works alone. It may be that the Zunis revere older women, yet—again—she is called "Old Lady," suggesting something of the spinster, or perhaps an object of ridicule. On the other hand, there is the equally interesting possibility that "Old Lady" really is supposed to be an analogue of "Old Man." According to William Bright, agricultural tribes often used this term to underscore the archaic nature of the trickster.[18] Peynetsa's story may, then, be reversing or complicating the trickster role, with Junco competing for that capacity. This idea is further supported by the possibility that everyone (Junco, narrator, audience) understands that Coyote's attempts to learn the song are only a ruse finally to eat the bird, yet such chicanery is not the trickster's only capacity. Bright lists a wide variety of roles for Coyote, including that of the "loser," and indeed, Andrew Peynetsa's nephew Joseph remarks, "These Coyote stories make it sound like he's an outcast and nobody thinks too much of him." [19] There is some slippage, then, between Junco's diminishment and aggrandizement.

Secondly, Junco is winnowing, which seems important, but she is winnowing pigweed and tumbleweed, which would have dubious results. Meanwhile, Peynetsa puts Coyote out hunting for food for his children, which is arguably a more productive, even "nurturing" endeavor, unless that sense is absolutely overwhelmed by a shared cultural understanding of Coyote as a scavenger and a dupe.[20] It is difficult to say which figure is being privileged where—the venerable bird engaged in the seemingly redundant activity or the "outcast" Coyote as provider. According to Young, however, this kind of ambiguity is pervasive in Zuni thought, art, and ritual, all of which eschew binary oppositions or rigid boundaries between conceptual categories and instead create paradox and interrelationships through "intentional . . . creative and playful manipulation of ideas."[21] Moreover, there may be gendered ambiguity in a male Coyote's taking up the role of feeder, which in Zuni is the domain of women.[22] Yet this, too, is in keeping with Zuni thought. In *The Zuni Man-Woman*, for instance, Will Roscoe argues for the berdache as a genuine third gender that, at least years ago, helped multiply the possibilities for gendered behavior and interaction in Zuni culture. "One's identity as a Zuni," says Roscoe, "could never be reduced to a fixed gender"; indeed, the Zunis understand gender to be acquired (specifically, through social norms and symbolic rituals), not innate, and they see it as "situationally determined" by a variety of factors (like work preferences) beyond mere sexual preference or biological attributes.[23] Appropriately, then, one of the most interesting moves in "Coyote and Junco" is the way in which it genders its figures and then "de-genders" them, a point I will return to near the end of this essay.

If attempted "patriarchal" and "gynocratic" readings of this tale keep blurring, one thing that is less ambiguous is its tone; this conflict is a good deal less "serious" than others in Tedlock's anthology that pit feminine against masculine figures. In many ways, this seems to come down to narratorial choice: Peynetsa makes this story funny and quick. He learned it, according to Tedlock, from someone who told "only very short stories." Also, as Tedlock notes in the preface to a retranslation, stories featuring animals tend to be much shorter than those featuring humans.[24] Even so, the brevity of the narrative seems to have as much to do with a comparatively laconic kind of performance as it does with the conventions that might surround it. "Coyote and Junco" generates ample opportunity for the kind of long repetitive passages that appear in stories like "The Women and the Man," but Peynetsa doesn't seize these opportunities for repetition and elaboration. For example, Coyote demands that Junco repeat her story four times, but Peynetsa only sings it through once. Actually repeating the entire song might have highlighted Junco's building frustration or even anger. At the very least, it might have reinforced her performance of a culturally valued activity. But such a strategy seems somehow at odds with the story, or with Peynetsa's vision of it.

As Tedlock's transcriptions suggest, that vision seems focused on the hilarity of each of Coyote's failures. For example, Peynetsa eschews detail in describing Coyote's thwarted attempts to sing. In one of these episodes he raises his voice as "BLACKBIRDS FLEW UP," vocalizing that incident through Coyote and making the distraction ludicrously melodramatic. And the emphasis he puts on the pushy prairie wolf's "ONE . . . TWO . . . THREE" as he waits for a faux Junco to yield builds to ever greater heights of silliness, until the storyteller is pointing at his own molars and laughing as he sums up the story's "meaning" ("Because this was lived long ago, Coyote has no teeth here"). What we have, then, could be read as a story whose content appears to hold at least the possibility of a conflict in which gender is a factor and in which the feminine figure emerges triumphant, but also in which various features of the narration appear, for whatever reasons, to work to foreclose or at least suppress that possibility.

"Coyote and Junco" *is* funny and it is precisely the humor that I find so significant here; in addition to asking why this story is gendered at all, I think we can ask why, when a story with this kind of gender dynamic comes along, it is laughed off. One factor might well be generic: "Coyote and Junco" belongs to the *telapnaawe* (tales), which, according to Tedlock, Zunis see as more fictional than stories of "The Beginning," or *chimiky'ana'kowa*.[25] Thus, Joseph Peynetsa remarks, "[The story] just teaches how the coyote is being very foolish. It doesn't teach anything like a human being might do."[26] Andrew Peynetsa seems similarly dismissive, even in the context of the anthology's other telapnaawe (all of the stories I cited early in this essay belong to that genre). Like Junco blocking off Coyote's access to her ritual chant, then, this particular story, this narration, seems to be drawing a line in front of the inquisitive and usurping audience. Almost as quickly as it opens up a possibility it re-conceals it, burying in action and drowning out through laughter a gendered meaning that it refuses to probe too deeply.

■ ■ ■

We get quite a different approach from Helen Sekaquaptewa. Comparisons involving versions that come from different storytelling communities and that are translated in widely divergent modes do pose problems, to say nothing of the difference in media here (video and versified transcription). For example, in the six versions of the Coyote story that Andrew Wiget lists in his performance analysis of the Sekaquaptewa video, we find a wide range of transcription practices that would hinder comparisons on something like the repetition of a song.[27] One older written translation, H. R. Voth's transcription of an Oraibi version, is widely considered to be reductive;[28] indeed, many of the older collections omit devices like repetition in the interest of "getting the basic story." Alternately, fieldworkers sometimes put rather too much of their own elaborations into their translations.[29] And then the matter of the "basic story" is a problem: Wiget lists a Moencoepi story, "Coyote and the Dancing Birds," as the closest comparison to Sekaquaptewa's, for example, but a related story—"Turtle's Crying Song"—looks even closer because it also includes a song. Or is it closer? What can comparisons based on "story," or narrative content (as opposed to "discourse," or narrative style) tell us?

The Sekaquaptewa version might be the most useful in pointing up the choices made in the Zuni narration, if only because the video and the Tedlock transcription seem to provide the most detailed information about individual performances. It is important to note, however, that the content (still a sticky term) of the two versions is radically different. For one thing, the gender dynamic—if such it can be called—that I observed in the Zuni version is "gone" because Sekaquaptewa uses a flock of birds instead of Old Lady Junco. Indeed, the figures vary widely not only across cultures—a Shumopovi variant uses Grasshopper instead of Junco in one version and a she-coyote in another; a Moencopi version uses a turtle and again a female coyote—but within Zuni: a version of the tale in Alvina Quam's *The Zunis: Self-Portrayals of the Zuni People* has "old lady Coyote" confronting a male grasshopper.[30] Also, if Peynetsa's version is about one figure's attempted appropriation of another's song, Sekaquaptewa's has a song less integral to the storyline, even though she incorporates so many repetitions of it. In fact, Coyote learns the song without any trouble in Sekaquaptewa's telling, so when the storyteller does sing it, she must do so with other motivations, as I will discuss in a moment. The primary "joke" in Sekaquaptewa's version involves both Coyote's feigned desire to fly, which the birds later say is just a ruse to devour them, and the way the birds trick him into flying by first lending him their feathers and then pulling them off him in midair.[31]

Wiget warns against comparisons based on content; he believes that they reflect a misguided privileging of a story's structure over narratorial style and the storytelling situation.[32] Indeed, the major revelation of comparing content is perhaps that these tales are not reducible to any kind of "hypothesized base tale."[33] Structuralist readings that reduce the scenario to one figure trying to usurp another's "natural" role hardly get at the "meaning" of the tale. As Wiget suggests, neither does speculation about what the raconteur intended, like worrying the idea that Sekaquaptewa is trying to highlight the Hopi work ethic by punishing a lazy I'isau who, unlike Peynetsa's Coyote, is lazily scavenging while the birds work hard. Instead, as Wiget says, meaning is created by the narrator and the audience in each situation; it is something that is neither fixed nor fixable. When we note that Sekaquaptewa (or her community) chooses a flock of birds rather than Old Lady Junco, we point to the possible significance of the way Peynetsa (or his community) does gender Junco. Similarly, the Hopi storyteller's pointed characterization of the trickster as a scavenger can redirect us to Peynetsa's situating of Coyote as out hunting for his children. My point is not that one version is "right" and the other "wrong," nor do I wish to indulge in what Wiget correctly criticizes as meaningless speculation about "why" a raconteur "departs" from some sort of hypothesized "correct" version. I am asking, rather, what effect each narrative choice might have, given that other choices could have been made.

The Sekaquaptewa and Peynetsa versions differ in their styles of narration as well as in their content. Part of this difference relates directly to the business of repeating the song; in fact, as I suggested above, Sekaquaptewa seems on this occasion to take every opportunity to sing it through, even though the actual "plot" of her rendition does not depend on these repetitions. The video reveals that at times the children listening to the story smile and at least one sings along. We might, then, read this repetition as functioning like any chorus—a mental or verbal hook, a point of identification, participation, inclusion.[34] Again, I ask what the effect might be when Peynetsa proceeds without seizing such moments. And, while like her Zuni colleague Sekaquaptewa clearly sees this story as immensely funny, she uses very different methods to capitalize on that humor.

One result of Sekaquaptewa's use of repetition for humor is that her telling is lengthy. At the end of the story, she comments (in English) that "it is quite long," as though she is surprised that it turned out this way. As many writers have observed, the performance situation often generates a different kind of telling than the storyteller originally planned. Sekaquaptewa tells the story for members of her family, which might explain why her performance seems more drawn out and open than Peynetsa's, though given the presence of cameras and microphones this can hardly be said to be a "spontaneous" or "authentic" performance (if indeed there is such a thing).[35] Unlike Peynetsa, the Hopi storyteller makes many verbal gestures to include the audience: she describes the birds as "sitting here as you are" and includes rhetorical questions like "You know that rock, Oirabi?" At several points, she even touches members of the audience, enacting the placing of feathers on Coyote, for example. Wiget calls this "dangerous," noting that such moves can destroy the story frame if the storyteller does not execute them successfully.[36] In the case of the I'isau story, he sees the audience being "taken in." One could use a slightly different metaphor, though, and read this precisely as a fragmented story frame, an incipient dissolution of the boundaries between fiction and "reality," storyteller and listener, text and participant.

In the Zuni version, even though Peynetsa does make obvious gestures (to his own teeth, for instance), there appears to be a certain tendency to want to maintain the story frame and have done with the tale. It is a little more difficult to answer questions about audience interaction with his version; as detailed as Tedlock's written transcription is, it cannot provide as many of the kind of details that a video does for interpreting a performance. We do know, however, that Peynetsa and fellow storyteller Walter Sanchez had a fairly long working relationship with Tedlock and his tape recorder, and that Peynetsa told "Coyote and Junco" as part of an evening of storytelling among these three men and the machine. Such factors surely do their work on the final speech event and may themselves account for some of the brevity of the Zuni performance. Without praising one version over the other, we can say that Sekaquaptewa achieves a comic mode that seems to blur the boundaries between storyteller and listener, while Peynetsa's seems to demarcate and reinforce those lines. The contrast between the laconic and the generous, the "closed" and the open, makes Sekaquaptewa's version much more interactive, Peynetsa's more speaker-centered.

■ ■ ■

I should here make explicit some of my discussion's approaches to contextualization. One is a more traditional view of context as a kind of itemized list of extranarrative elements that appear to impinge on the actual speech event: the presence of recording equipment, the relationships among participants, a culture's values regarding gender relations. Another approach looks at the way the world outside of the particular narrative gets worked into the story—thus my interest in looking at different versions. We may rightly understand narrative as shaped by its context, or even "tradition," but recent research has begun to consider narrative in a more active light—as giving something back to that context, reshaping it, in dialogue with it.[37] In this vein, T. C. S. Langen has argued that whenever we deal with folktales or stories we must consider their "collections"—the cycles of versions and episodes from which each individual performance derives. In Langen's words:

> Each version is a realization of the possibilities provided by the collection; any version may add to the collection; no one version is an isolate, either for the storyteller or the audience, but resounds against the knowledge of the collection held by each person present at the performance; no storyteller ever tells the whole collection or ever knows the whole collection, but she always knows more than she tells in any one performance or perhaps in all the performances she ever gives; no person's knowledge of the collection is the same as any other person's. The collection, then, is protean in the ways in which it is apprehended.[38]

Thus when Peynetsa performs his Coyote story, he implicitly calls up its other versions. When he chooses elements like a female junco, a male coyote, and a struggle over a song—when he makes that story a short and fast comedy—he creates something new, overturns something old, at once reinforces and re-informs participants' existing knowledge and experience. The "collection," of course, is as mutable and contestable as the idea of a contained "tale." Peynetsa's version of "Coyote and Junco," then, must be interpreted as one particular combination of details, deployed at a particular moment, in a specific manner; it must also be seen as partaking of a kind of dialogue with other forms of the story, and with participants' experience of those forms. Our interpretations should perhaps be as "protean" as the stories themselves.[39]

One reading could be, as I suggested earlier, that "Coyote and Junco" works as a kind of suppression of feminine power. In some of the other pieces in *Finding the Center*, conflicts between gendered figures (with masculine victors) are gruesome, violent, even sexually explicit. In this story, where the winner is marked as female, that conflict is downplayed. So it may be that a conflict of this kind is somehow threatening; if we recall what may be a more or less "male" realm—storytelling—within a matriarchal culture, the story may be somehow compensatory. In *The Beautiful and the Dangerous*, Barbara Tedlock describes some interesting moments in her encounters with the Zunis where men displayed some anxiety about discussions of women's activities or power: one man acted as if "he thought he might lose his importance if his wife or daughters talked with us [Barbara and Dennis Tedlock], even half as much as he did"; others "chuckled at the thought of being supported by women."[40] Of course such things happen among European-Americans, who are not renowned for their fair treatment of women, but Tedlock's evidence does suggest a possibility for reading gendered conflicts in Zuni oral narratives. Reading "Coyote and Junco" in this vein, we see that the story might provoke anxious laughter over the very issue of power and gender, along with the exhilarating kind of laughter induced by the bad guy (here indeed a guy) getting his comeuppance.

On the other hand, if we consider again "the collection," the very presence of this gendered conflict may in itself be a radical move, especially among the other *telapnaawe* that demonize or punish female figures. In keeping with what Young and others say about female strategies for seizing power even where they do not "officially" have it, the story may thus constitute a kind of resistance—to male usurpation, to female deprivation or disempowerment. This doesn't imply that Peynetsa intended this move—or that he didn't—nor does it imply resistance in the form of an isolated rebellion to some monolithic, wholly patriarchal context (even one within a larger, matriarchal context). Instead, we may be seeing a kind of fissure or gap. The comic mode may ensure that this account of feminine victory has a kind of life; it may generate that victory even as it undercuts it.

As I stated at the beginning of this paper, the Zuni stories collected by Tedlock might have tendencies that look patriarchal, but they also contain other possibilities. It would be reductive to read "Coyote and Junco" solely as either a subversive narrative of female victory or as evidence of the suppression of this narrative by masculine conventions or practice. Furthermore, it could be troublesome to maintain that Zuni stories promote a particular ideology of gender, even a highly complex one, especially in light of Roscoe's findings that the Zunis see gender as "situational." It seems unlikely that gender "means nothing" in these stories, but then, as I have shown, the tales vary enormously from community to community. If a continually retold story like Cinderella has a rigid and virtually unmistakable "gender agenda," "Coyote and Junco"'s implications for gender are revised with each narration.[41] That in itself could reflect quite a different attitude toward gendered subjectivity— and toward meaning-making in narrative—than is often found in Western traditions.

This reading, one that is finally suspicious about what it really "means" that Coyote is male and Junco female, brings us (through the rather Western "sense of an ending") to the story's end, for it is there "Coyote and Junco" raises the question of gender and meaning itself. As I mentioned before, Coyote is hunting ("man's work") but also seems to have responsibility for feeding ("women's work"). In the story's second to last line, he goes home to find his children are dead: it is as though his error is compounded by his failure to fulfill a role as nurturer and caregiver. But this revelation comes amidst all the jocularity over his losing his teeth, so again the telling downplays something potentially gender-charged and sobering. "Coyote and Junco" describes a conflict between two poles, yet it blurs those poles. The gendered conflict happens, but perhaps on a more mutable, local level than we are used to seeing in many Western texts. Continually, Peynetsa's narration tries to make us self-conscious about assigning meaning or identity. Coyote's fatal move, after all, was mistaking Junco's image for the real thing.

Notes

I would like to thank Bob Parker and Larry Danielson for their careful reading, suggestions, and encouragement.
1   Paula Gunn Allen, *The Sacred Hoop: Recovering the Feminine in American Indian Traditions* (Boston: Beacon, 1986), 4.
2   For example, Gunn Allen cites the familiar portrayals of "Indians as hostile savages who capture white ladies," adding that "allied with the view of the Indian as the hostile savage is the common practice . . . of proving that Indians mistreat women brutally and [that they therefore] deserve extermination" (5).
3   Gunn Allen, 5.
4   Dennis Tedlock, *Finding the Center: Narrative Poetry of the Zuni Indians* (Lincoln: Univ. of Nebraska Press, 1978), 75–84.
5   *I'isau and the Birds*, produced and directed by Larry Evers (Univ. of Arizona, 1976). Both the video, part of a series called *Words & Place*, and a useful transcript are available from Norman Ross Publishing Co. Inc., 330 West 58th Street, New York, New York 10019.
6   Gunn Allen, 2.
7   *Finding the Center*, xvi. But in Zuni, at least, the question of who tells the stories and who hears them is rather more complicated. The Zunis evidently share stories in a variety of contexts, among men, women, and children; see, for instance, Tedlock's notes in *Finding the Center* or his "Ethnography as Interaction" in *The Spoken Word and the Work of Interpretation* (Philadel-

phia: Univ. of Pennsylvania Press, 1983). Also, older collections including Ruth Bunzel's *Zuni Texts* (Publications of the American Ethnological Society, 15 [New York, 1933]) seem to contain stories from just as many female informants as male, though such limited selections do not prove that an equal number of women and men tell or have told the stories. Another contemporary collection, *The Zunis: Self-Portrayals by the Zuni People*, translated by Alvina Quam (Albuquerque: Univ. of New Mexico Press, 1972), like Tedlock's, appears to include the work of only male raconteurs.

8   Helen Sekaquaptewa, *Me and Mine*, trans. Louise Udall (Tucson: Univ. of Arizona Press, 1969), 228.

9   This tale is a variation on the Cinderella story and so titled in Stith Thompson's *Tales of the North American Indians* (Cambridge: Harvard Univ. Press, 1929), 225–31. The Zuni ending of punishment, as opposed to rescue, makes for an interesting comparison.

10   Ruth Benedict, *Zuni Mythology*, 2 vols., (New York: Columbia Univ. Press, 1935), 1:xxi–xxii. See also 1:xlff. for Benedict's interesting discussion of some differences in storytelling among male and female informants.

11   Bunzel, 97–123.

12   Fred Eggan, *Social Organization of the Western Pueblos* (Chicago: Univ. of Chicago Press, 1960), 188.

13   Matilda Coxe Stevenson, *The Zuni Indians: Their Mythology, Esoteric Fraternities, and Ceremonies*, 23rd Annual Report of the Bureau of American Ethnology for the Years 1901–02 (Washington, D.C., 1904), 1–634.

14   Will Roscoe, *The Zuni Man-Woman* (Albuquerque: Univ. of New Mexico Press, 1991), esp. 18–22; Barbara Tedlock, *The Beautiful and the Dangerous: Encounters with the Zuni Indians* (New York: Viking, 1992), 51, 96; and M. Jane Young, "Women, Reproduction, and Western Puebloan Society," *Journal of American Folklore* 100 (1987): 436–45.

15   M. Jane Young, *Signs from the Ancestors: Zuni Cultural Symbolism and Perceptions of Rock Art* (Albuquerque: Univ. of New Mexico Press, 1988), 15.

16   This is a good example of how Dennis Tedlock's transcriptions, with their indications of pause, pitch, volume, and gesture, capture the storyteller's art; Junco's pauses before she actually answers Coyote betray her disgust, as Tedlock himself explains in "On the Translation of Style in Oral Narrative" in *The Spoken Word and the Work of Interpretation*, 59–60.

17   *Finding the Center*, xxix. The term translated as "old lady" is "okyattsik'i," a "slightly substandard" one according to Tedlock, and different from what Alfred Kroeber describes in *Zuni Kin and Clan* (New York: American Museum of Natural History, 1917): "the suffixes '-lacci' and '-ts'anna' are . . . freely added to any and all terms, and often bring out seniority or juniority within the limits of one generation" (79).

18   William Bright, "The Natural History of Old Man Coyote," in *Recovering the Word: Essays on Native American Literature*, ed. Brian Swann and Arnold Krupat (Berkeley and Los Angeles: Univ. of California Press, 1987), 372.

19 Bright, 339–87; *Finding the Center*, 84.

20 I keep using these qualifying phrases because, as much as I have tried to learn about Zuni or the trickster, I think it's important to keep foregrounding my "outsiderness." Writers like Barre Toelken argue, quite sensibly, that people outside a culture can never have full access to the meaning of a folk story; see his *The Dynamics of Folklore* (Boston: Houghton Mifflin, 1979), 212.

21 M. Jane Young, "Ambiguity and Metaphor in Ceremonialism and Daily Life," *Southern Folklore* 48 (1991): 167. Toelken makes a similar observation about the circular and interrelated nature of the Native American (specifically, Navajo) "worldview" in *Dynamics of Folklore*, 236.

22 Roscoe, 19; Young, "Women, Reproduction, and Western Puebloan Society," 437.

23 Roscoe, 144.

24 Andrew Peynetsa, "Coyote and Junco," translated by Dennis Tedlock in *Coyote Stories*, ed. William Bright (Chicago: Univ. of Chicago Press, 1978), 171. Readers might also enjoy Bright's *A Coyote Reader* (Berkeley and Los Angeles: Univ. of California Press, 1993), an eclectic and fascinating collection of pieces ranging from Mark Twain's sketch of the "real" coyote to Coyote narratives, both traditional and contemporary.

25 *Finding the Center*, xvi.

26 *Finding the Center*, 84.

27 Andrew Wiget, "A Performance Analysis of a Hopi Coyote Story," in *Recovering the Word*, 297–336. See also Elsie Clews Parsons, *Tewa Tales*, Memoirs of the American Folklore Society 19 (Philadelphia, 1926): 161–62 and 283–85. Wiget's citation (see his note 6) of the other versions is a little misleading, since he goes by text number and the Parsons volume is in two sections, which doubles some text numbers. There is also a version from Parsons in the *Journal of American Folklore* 31 (October–December 1918): 221–25. In addition, Franz Boas has an untranslated version of the tale in *Keresan Texts* (Publications of the American Ethnological Society, 1928); Leslie Marmon Silko includes a short version in *Storyteller* (New York: Little Brown, 1981), 255; there is a version in Quam's *The Zunis*, 117–19; another in Frank Cushing's *Zuni Folk Tales* (New York: G. P. Putnam's, 1901), 255; and Ruth Benedict includes a version that uses an old woman instead of Old Lady Junco in *Zuni Mythology* 2:220.

28 See, for instance, Harold Courlander, *Hopi Voices: Recollections, Traditions, and Narratives of the Hopi Indians* (Albuquerque: Univ. of New Mexico Press, 1982), xviii; and Parsons, *Tewa Tales*, 6, note 3.

29 Frank Cushing is an extreme example of a translator who adds too much elaboration. Dennis Tedlock writes a scathing critique of Cushing and other translators in "On the Translation of Style" in *The Spoken Word and the Word of Interpretation*, 31ff. Jesse Green offers a small defense of Cushing in *Zuni: Selected Writings of Frank Hamilton Cushing* (Lincoln: Univ.

of Nebraska Press, 1979), 334–36. For an interesting debate among Karl Kroeber, Toelken, and others about the hazards and benefits of comparing different translations of the "same" tale, see the *Journal of the Folklore Institute* 18 (May–Dec. 1981): 99–156.

30 Wilson D. Wallis, "Folktales from Shumopovi, Second Mesa," *Journal of American Folklore* 49 (1936): 50–53; Courlander, 229–31; Quam, 117–19.

31 Ruth Benedict has an interesting discussion of various versions and combinations of the Coyote stories in *Zuni Mythology*, 2:310.

32 Wiget, "A Performance Analysis," 312.

33 Wiget uses this term in "A Performance Analysis," 313.

34 Sekaquaptewa mentions the importance of repetition as a mnemonic device in *Me and Mine*, 230.

35 See Susan Hegeman, "Native American 'Texts' and the Problem of Authenticity," *American Quarterly* 41 (June 1989): 265–83.

36 Wiget, "A Performance Analysis," 324.

37 This research is undertaken in the ethnography of communication, and interested readers will find a good introduction to contextualization in *Rethinking Context: Language as an Interactive Phenomenon*, ed. Alessandro Duranti and Charles Goodwin (New York: Cambridge Univ. Press, 1992). "Tradition" is a good example of a "rethought context"; where earlier writers viewed it as a kind of quantifiable range of narrative elements that predetermined a storyteller's art, current theorists see it as something continually sustained and re-imagined by those performers.

38 T. C. S. Langen, "Estoy Eh-Muut and the Morphologists," *Studies in American Indian Literatures* 1 (Summer 1989): 6.

39 I refer readers again to Hegeman's article. Questioning our colonizing impulse to seek the "authentic" translation or rendition of Native American narratives, she argues that we should maintain multiple translating methods for Native American materials. We might similarly ask what we are after when we try to interpret Native American texts—the "authentic" Zuni reading? Clearly these texts will do very different kinds of cultural work as they are admitted into the so-called mainstream canon than they do in American Indian cultures, just as they do different kinds of cultural work at different moments in different Native American settings.

40 *The Beautiful and the Dangerous*, 5, 60.

41 I refer to the Golden Book/Walt Disney version of Cinderella with which European-Americans are perhaps most familiar.

Kristin Carter-Sanborn

"We Murder Who We Were":
Jasmine and the Violence of Identity

> Now, i am not only given the permission to open up and talk,
> i am also encouraged to express my difference. My audience
> expects and demands it; otherwise people would feel as if they
> have been cheated: We did not come to hear a Third World
> member speak about the First (?) World, We came to listen
> to that voice of difference likely to bring us *what we can't have*
> and to divert us from the monotony of sameness. . . . Eager
> not to disappoint, i try my best to offer my benefactors and
> benefactresses what they most anxiously yearn for: the pos-
> siblity of a difference, yet a difference or an otherness that
> will not go so far as to question the foundation of their beings
> and makings.
> —Trinh T. Minh-ha, *Woman, Native, Other*

The narrator of Bharati Mukherjee's *Jasmine* implic-
itly positions herself early in her own text in terms of narratives already
abandoned. At age seven, Jyoti is the star pupil of Masterji, "the oldest
and sourest teacher in our school": "I was a whiz in Punjabi and Urdu, and
the first likely female candidate for English instruction he'd ever had. He
had a pile of English books, some from the British Council Library, some
with USIS stickers. . . . The British books were thick, with more long
words per page. I remember *Great Expectations* and *Jane Eyre*, both of
which I was forced to abandon because they were too difficult."[1] By thus
locating her novel in the space circumscribed by two classic texts of Victorian education and identity, Mukherjee signals to the reader the generic
continuity between her *bildungsroman* and these earlier narratives. Like
Jane's and Pip's stories, Jyoti's is told retrospectively, this time from the

point of view of a young woman about to light out for the territory, having already experienced a whirlwind series of transformative events. After witnessing her mentor Masterji's death at the hands of Sikh militants, who will later murder her husband, Jyoti flees her native Punjab, "phantom[s her] way through three continents" (91), and arrives with forged papers on the Gulf Coast of Florida. From there she travels to Queens, Manhattan, and then to a small town in Iowa, metamorphosing on the way into Jasmine, Jazzy, Jase, and Jane. The America she encounters is, in its endemic violence, not unlike the Punjab she left behind. Indeed, the latest influx of immigrants to the United States has transformed it into an "archipelago of ghettos seething with aliens" (124); or, as one reviewer put it, a "new Third World."[2]

The contemporary complexities of "first" and "third" world relations foregrounded by *Jasmine* return us to *Great Expectations* and *Jane Eyre*, the mention of which must also invoke for us the Victorian imperial project in which their production was situated. Both of these earlier novels are indeed "thick" with the voice of an ostensibly progressive colonial authority addressing issues of gender and class formation. The fact that Jyoti abandons the deciphering of that voice as "too difficult" will signal to us that, as Homi Bhabha suggests, the site of that authority is vexed, compromised, "agonistic."[3]

Although the literary voice of colonial authority hardly gets a hearing in Jyoti's Punjab village, the very dismissal of Brontë's book is coincident with its introduction as a structuring "presence" in *Jasmine*.[4] I would like to use this framing presence as a starting point for my discussion of the postcolonial concerns of *Jasmine*, even as I too eventually abandon it in favor of a more general examination of the dynamics of subjectivity in Mukherjee's novel.

Jyoti's rejection of *Jane Eyre* only begins to suggest the complex relationship between the colonialist subtext of Brontë's novel and the "multicultural" implications of *Jasmine*'s narrative. Jyoti leaves off reading *Jane Eyre* in Hasnapur only to take the Christian name of that novel's protagonist once she reaches Iowa; her character's development also echoes and revises Jane Eyre's in other ways, as we will see. And just as we must consider whether Jane Eyre, in her search for a new female domestic identity, is implicated in the violent repression of colonial subjectivity as figured by Bertha Mason,[5] we also need to ask whether Jyoti-Jasmine-Jane's "discovery" of an American selfhood covers up a similar complicity in the elision of the "third world" woman Mukherjee's narrator purportedly speaks as and for. More generally, we must question whether *Jasmine* is implicated in the neo-imperialist demands of the Western reader as they are described by Trinh in the epigraph to this essay—demands for "what we can't have," for an exotic diversion from the "monotony of sameness."[6]

This question is especially critical in light of the novel's mainstream and academic popularity—it was received with acclaim in nearly every major review publication[7] and has been increasingly taught since then in women's studies, ethnic studies, and contemporary American literature courses. I would argue that the novel's appeal can be traced in part to its readers' complicated investment in the racial and cultural otherness of the narrator (and, of course, her author). Beginning with Richard Eder's laudatory notice in the *Los Angeles Times Book Review*, the arrangement and selection of popular reviews on the back of the Fawcett Crest paperback edition foreground a simultaneous interest in both Jasmine's alterity and her suitability for naturalization to an "American" way of life:

> ARTFUL AND ARRESTING . . . BREATHTAKING . . . A Hindu woman flees her family's poverty, and the Sikh terrorism that bloodies her village. . . . After a time in New York—*only a foreign eye could fix the world of the Upper West Side with such hilarious and revealing estrangement*—she moves to a small town in Iowa. In corn and hog country—now prey to farm foreclosures and despair—she marks with unsparing brilliance the symptoms of a new Third World.[8]

Subsequent blurbs reproduce the fascination with the estranged "foreign eye" of Eder's assessment (a fascination less evident, it should be noted, in sections of the review not quoted by the publisher). Helping us (that is, mainstream U.S. readers) to see "ourselves as others see us," the "uncanny third eye of the artist [that] forces us to see our country anew"[9] reveals itself to be the uncanny eye of the third *world* artist for these reviewers. But at the same time it embodies the mystical insight of the Other, Jasmine's "third eye" represents a way of seeing that is ultimately transformed, in the mini-narrative of the book blurb, from the myopia of a backward "Indian village girl, whose grandmother wants to marry her off at 11," into the enlightened vision of "an American woman who finally thinks for herself."[10] The book's selling power seems, then, to stem from its simultaneous exoticism and domesticability, its existence as a sort of pop multiculturalist prop not much different from the one envisioned by Trinh. This observation is not to suggest that *Jasmine* has no place on our course reading lists. On the contrary, its difficulties may provide us with more paths than obstacles to understanding the exigencies of representing "third world experience." I offer this critique of the novel in the hope that it may help us and our students reexamine our expectations regarding textual authenticity and ethnicity in the literature classroom.

We might consider these expectations in light of Trinh's assessment of the ends and means of the anthropological "dialogue." Essentially a "conversation of 'us' with 'us' about 'them,'"[11] "the conversation [the anthropologist-nativist] aspires to turns out to be rather intimate: a chatty talk, which, under cover of cross-cultural communication, simply superposes one system of signs over another."[12] Gayatri C. Spivak further complicates this conversational dynamic. Commenting on her own discussion of the suicide of a young Indian woman, Bhuvaneswari Bhaduri, in Calcutta in 1926 she remarks,

> What I was doing with the young woman who had killed herself was really trying to analyze and represent her text. She wasn't particularly trying to speak to me. I was representing her, I was reinscribing her. To an extent, I was writing her to be read, and I certainly was not claiming to give her a voice. So if I'm read as giving her a voice, there again this is a sort of transaction of the positionality between the Western feminist listener who listens to me, and myself, signified as a Third World informant.[13]

In the context of the "transaction" detailed in Spivak's and Trinh's descriptions, certain questions about Mukherjee's novel arise. Does the text in fact ask to be read as speaking the "subaltern" voice through Jasmine's first-person narrative? Or is such an assumption merely a function of the misguided expectations of what Spivak calls "cardcarrying listeners"?[14]

The expectations of others—readers, listeners, lovers, and entire communities—do in fact provide one of the most important structural matrices on which *Jasmine* is plotted. When he first glimpses Jasmine, Bud Ripplemeyer tells her, *"It felt as if I was a child again, back in the Saturday-afternoon movies. You were glamour, something unattainable"* (177, author's emphasis). By renaming her Jane, her lover has something much more exotic and erotic in mind than the "Plain Jane" the narrator and her Victorian namesake would more readily identify with. "Me Bud, you Jane. I didn't get it at first," she reflects. "He kids. Calamity Jane. Jane as in Jane Russell" (22). Her "genuine foreignness" frightens the relatively staid Midwestern banker, however (22), and as Jane to his crippled Rochester-Tarzan, the narrator can assuage Bud's fears only by settling into the role of domesticated exotic. Earlier, having abandoned the village of her father for her "city man" husband Prakash Vijh (69), she even more readily settled into the "small and sweet and heady" role of "Jasmine," Vijh's modern wife and business partner—a "new kind of city woman" whom he can show off to friends (70). And between Jasmine and Jane, she becomes "Jase," exoticized domestic and au pair to Manhattan professionals Wylie and Taylor Hayes. The narrator's ability to "shuttle . . . between identities" (70), to accept another's interpellation with little difficulty, is explicated in the text as a symptom of the liminality of the "third world" subject. The quick-changes she accomplishes reflect Jasmine's self-imposed mandate, expressed early in the novel, to "murder who we were so we can rebirth ourselves in the images of dreams" (25).

The "images of dreams" . . . but of whose dreams? This ambiguous phrase, central to our understanding of Mukherjee's project, opens up a number of possible readings, all of which compete for primacy in the text. We might compare Jasmine's "suicides" and "rebirths" to the revolutionary process of decolonization as described by Frantz Fanon in *The Wretched of the Earth*: "National liberation, national renaissance, the restoration of nationhood to the people, commonwealth: whatever may be the headings used or the new formulas introduced, decolonization is always a violent phenomenon. . . . Without any period of transition, there is a total, complete, and absolute substitution."[15]

Jasmine's violent substitution of self, then, could be recognized as a move constituting part of the ethnic nationalist repertoire, a liberatory gesture which achieves "that kind of *tabula rasa* which characterizes at the outset all decolonization," and which institutes a "new language and a new humanity."[16] In this context the significance of "rebirth . . . in the images of dreams" is that "it is willed, called for, demanded"—the dream is a conscious hope, an aspiration or goal, an object of rational desire that determines anticipatory behavior.[17] Most important, the dream and the program which follows from it are acts of agency, and in fact grant agency: "[T]he 'thing' which had been colonized becomes man during the same process by which it frees itself."[18] Jasmine's agenda could offer a counterdiscourse or model of resistance to those who would name and thus control her. She is a "tornado, a rubble-maker, arising from nowhere and disappearing into a cloud" (214), destroying all in her path as she chooses, including her old selves; her dream is a will to power.

But in the context of Mukherjee's representation of certain Hindu beliefs, the "images of dreams" take on a more spiritual dimension. With those dreams she may mean to invoke some kind of cataclysmic return of the repressed, in which consciousness or agency is subjected to an actor's own intuitive (and uncontrollable) dream-knowledge of who she "essentially" and unconsciously is. This "regression" may seem counter to the notion of rebirth. But the constellation of beliefs surrounding the birth-death cycle that the narrator invokes early in the novel, in addition to Jasmine's own "theoretical" belief in reincarnation (112) and reliance on other traditional Hindu cultural forms, obliges us at least to investigate this particular shading of "dreams."

Reincarnation is figured in Jasmine's narrative as the shattering of fleshly vessels that had given only temporary shape to an essentially ephemeral spirit. Recounting the story of Vimla, a young woman who douses herself with kerosene and sets herself on fire after the death of her husband, Jasmine recalls that "[t]he villagers say when a clay pitcher breaks, you see that the air inside it is the same as outside" (12). Vimla commits *sati* "because she had broken her pitcher; she saw there were no insides and outsides. We are just shells of the same Absolute. In Hasnapur," she adds, "Vimla's isn't a sad story" (12). In fact, it is a triumphant one, guaranteeing for her as it does liberation from the cycle of transmigration and a return to an originary "Absolute." Anthropologist Michael M. J. Fischer has tried to articulate the "absoluteness" of ethnicity itself in language strikingly similar to that of the villagers, reading the "epiphanic" moments of ethnic autobiography as "revelations of traditions, re-collections of disseminated identities and of the divine sparks from the breaking of the vessels."[19] Here an ethnic absolute or essence functions (quite problematically, I believe) like a neurosis "that manifests itself through repetition of behavioral patterns and that cannot be articulated in rational language but can only be acted out," fearfully and anxiously, through the mechanism of transference or "the return of the repressed in new forms."[20] This inarticulate "acting out" of ethno-spiritual essence seems to have affinities with both Vimla's act of self-violence and Jasmine's generalization about the compulsive and metaphorically murderous process of "shuttl[ing] between identities."

At various points the novel asks to be read according to one of these glosses. It seems to me, however, that the first—decolonizing, ethnic nationalist—insufficiently explains what is going on in the text as a whole; the second—reincarnation—may in fact disguise the imperial subject dreaming of and violently remaking its "third world" Others to fit those dreams. In other words, it may disguise the dynamic of what Edward Said calls "Orientalism" (one form of which is manifested in Trinh's "conversation of 'us' with 'us' about 'them'"): "Orientalism is the discipline by which the Orient was (and is) approached systematically, as a topic of learning, discovery, and practice. But in addition I have been using the word to designate that collection of dreams, images, and vocabularies available to anyone who has tried to talk about what lies east of the dividing line. These two aspects of Orientalism are not incongruent, since by use of them both Europe could advance securely and unmetaphorically upon the Orient."[21] Bud, Taylor, and even her first husband Prakash, whom Jasmine characterizes as a type of Professor Higgins (70), call upon these vocabularies in order to speak the narrator's name and thus remake her in the shape of their own fantasies. And, as we will see, these fantasies are sometimes very unmetaphorically acted out on Jasmine's body. When Jasmine reflects that "there are no harmless, compassionate ways to remake oneself," then, she may actually be invoking a process in which change is predicated on pain wrought from without. Although one might expect Mukherjee to demonstrate some ironic distance on this construction of the transformative process, the author's own emphatic "yes," when asked by interviewers if she indeed saw violence as necessary to the metamorphosis of character reveals this not to be the case: "And I can see that in my own case it's been psychic violence. In my character Jasmine's case it's been physical violence because she's from a poor farming family."[22] This response (the theoretical implications of which I will take up later) further confounds our efforts to locate agency in Jasmine's model of self-transformation.

To move closer to an understanding of this model, I would like to explore the ways in which Mukherjee has herself addressed key questions of agency and subjectivity in other essays, where those seem to be topics of some concern. In an early autobiographical collaboration with her husband Clark Blaise, Mukherjee has described herself as "a late-blooming colonial who writes in a borrowed language (English), lives permanently in an alien country [Canada at the time], and publishes in and is read, when read at all, in another alien country, the United States. My Indianness is fragile; it has to be professed and fought for, even though I look so unmistakably Indian. Language transforms our ways of apprehending the world; I fear that my decades-long use of English as a first language has cut me off from my *desh*."[23] Here the author describes a consciousness that is characterized mainly by its liminality and sense of exile in a field where borders of identity are repositioned and fixed by language itself. In later work, however, Mukherjee seems to abandon the idea that in her current milieu she is somehow exiled or cut off from her "Indianness." Writing now as a recently naturalized U.S. citizen, she exhorts her fellow immigrant writers to "cash . . . in on the other legacy of the colonial writer, and that is his or her duality. From childhood, we learned how to be two things simultaneously; to be the dispossessed as well as the dispossessor. . . . History forced us to see ourselves as both the 'we' and the 'other.'"[24]

Such a split subjectivity, Mukherjee asserts, can and must be brought to bear on the literary production of minority and immigrant writers. The "fluid set of identities" thus made available to the artist can broaden her range of materials and the perspectives that she may represent in her fiction.[25] Her training as a "third-world" subject gives the artist the ability "to 'enter' lives, fictionally, that are manifestly not [her] own. . . . over and across the country, and up and down the social ladder," without sacrificing authenticity.[26] In interviews, Mukherjee has schematized this fluidity in terms of psychological transformation, self-reinvention, or, as in *Jasmine*, murder and rebirth—a "shuttling" and shuffling of selves. Such reinvention, as I noted before, is always violent and, it seems, imperative in the context of emigration, particularly for women. The Asian man, Mukherjee argues, "comes for economic transformation, and he brings a wife who winds up being psychologically changed. . . . The men have a sense of accomplishment. They have no idea of staying here. The idea is saving money and going. But they don't realize the women have been transformed."[27] Here the man transforms, the woman is transformed, and as positive as her transformation might be, it results from the opposition of violence to agency, of active force to passive object. The male postcolonial nurtures his American dream; with that dream he wields the power that will violently "rebirth" the wife.

On a purely theoretical level, Mukherjee's idea of the gendered colonial "ethnic" subject has easily recognizable affinities with the critique of colonial discourse elaborated in the work of Fanon and, more recently, of Homi Bhabha and Gayatri Spivak, although I would argue that the theoretical positions of the latter two ultimately undermine Mukherjee's argument. Obvious parallels can be found between Mukherjee's manipulation of the concept of cultural dualism or "simultaneity" and Bhabha's more labored articulation of the "hybridization" enacted at the site of native oppression. For Bhabha, hybridity represents "that ambivalent 'turn' of the discriminated subject into the terrifying, exorbitant object of paranoid classification—a disturbing questioning of the images and presences of authority."[28] The ambivalence thus revealed "turns the discursive conditions of dominance into the grounds of intervention": the discriminated subject, incompletely contained by the power and paranoid knowledge invested in its constitution, participates in, confronts, and unsettles that very power.[29]

Jasmine does take as one of its main subjects the authoritative "ambivalence" or uncertain promise of U.S. cultural space, itself described by the narrator as a "third world" or postcolonial field barely distinguishable, in its tortured and violent landscape, from Mexico, from Haiti, or from Jasmine's own Punjab.[30] The lost promise of this place is at once a disappointment, a force of oppression, and a field of opportunity for the immigrant. "In America," the narrator muses, "[N]othing lasts. I can say that now and it doesn't shock me, but I think it was the hardest lesson of all for me to learn. We arrive so eager to learn, to adjust, to participate, only to find the monuments are plastic, agreements are annulled. *Nothing is forever, nothing is so terrible, or so wonderful, that it won't disintegrate"* (160; my emphasis). The author would have her immigrant characters negotiate this hard lesson using the resources of "simultaneity" they have already learned at home; ideally, Mukherjee's protagonists would be able to tap into what Gloria Anzaldúa has called the *"mestiza* consciousness," a "tolerance for contradictions, a tolerance for ambiguity"[31] like that demonstrated by Jane's adopted son Du, a young refugee who has established a "delicate thread of . . . hyphenization" (200). The balance he has struck prevents his identity as a Vietnamese from being effaced by the dominant culture.

But in fact, for Gayatri Spivak the duality of which Mukherjee speaks is evidence of the colonial project's success in effacing the female subaltern subject.[32] In the argument over the status of *sati*, or widow immolation, in modern Indian culture,[33] an exchange emblematic of the collusion between elite nativist and colonial interests, "the figure of the woman disappears, not into a pristine nothingness, but into a violent shuttling which is the displaced figuration of the 'third-world woman' caught between tradition and modernization."[34] Rather than speaking as both the woman-in-patriarchy and the woman-in-imperialism, Spivak asserts, she can speak as neither, precisely because she is constituted as both, and therefore subject to a "violent shuttling" that enacts a steady erasure of being, rather than a series of progressively triumphant rebirths.[35]

I would argue, then, that Mukherjee's theorization of the gendered postcolonial self most closely follows the colonialist fantasy itself, described here by Fanon: "[I]t is implicit that to speak is to exist absolutely for the other. The black man has two dimensions. One with his fellows, the other with the white man. . . . That this self-division is a direct result of colonialist subjugation is beyond question. . . . The colonized is elevated above his jungle status in proportion to his adoption of the mother country's cultural standards. He becomes whiter as he renounces his blackness, his jungle."[36] Implicit in Fanon's description is the assumption that the settler's fantasy (elsewhere outlined by Said) has in fact determined reality, enacting a "Manichean" world of "them or us."[37] But this Manichean logic ultimately "leaves the native unshaken," for as we have already seen, he "has practically stated the problem of his liberation in identical terms. . . . For the native, [the violence of the settlers] represents the absolute line of [liberationist] action."[38] The "simultaneity" which Mukherjee celebrates in essays and interviews is proposed but ultimately dismantled in her novelistic work: fluidity in *Jasmine* is theorized not as hybridity but as a perpetual gesture toward absolute otherness. The trajectory of Jasmine's meteoric transformation traces that of Fanon's theory of change in form only, which is to say that it ends up tracing a fairly traditional colonial itinerary, not without important consequences for the postcolonial "ethnic" gendered subject.

To act, for Jasmine, is to become entirely other. In an interesting inversion of the colonial project sketched by Bhabha, Jasmine can authoritatively impute the idea of "multiplicity" to her own character only retrospectively (again we are reminded of Jane Eyre's own retrospective identity-building), from the perspective of a woman with an all-seeing "third eye." She can look back and reflexively assert her difference from herself as the narrator of the text: "Jyoti of Hasnapur was not Jasmine, Duff's day mummy and Taylor and Wylie's *au pair* in Manhattan; *that* Jasmine isn't *this* Jane Ripplemeyer having lunch with Mary Webb at the University Club today. And which of us is the undetected murderer of a half-faced monster, which of us has held a dying husband, which of us was raped and raped and raped in boats and cars and motel rooms?" (114; author's emphasis). In cataloging her selves Jasmine is able to conjoin them in the overarching "multiple" consciousness of the narrative. But in the very construction of that consciousness there is no "simultaneity" or even continuity to be found. The narrator is not the widow *and* the *au pair*; the Iowa wife *and* the undetected murderer. The continuity between one of these states and any other is either obscured or destroyed, her implicit argument goes, by the violence of the transformative moment. She abandons agency in this moment to her theoretical Other, and it is this Other who determines and delivers her into new forms. Far from maintaining a "critical difference from [her]self," an ambivalent and non-unified, hybrid subjectivity, Jasmine's self-making insists on fixing "the differences made *between* entities comprehended as absolute presences."[39] Having rejected the demands of a patriarchal nativism which (in the person of her father and the Sikh terrorist group, the Khalsa Lions) violently seeks to limit her cultural mobility, she turns to America and picks up the colonial "text" we thought she had set aside for good. Her flirtation with "multiplicity" ironically resolves itself into a domestic and domesticated fantasy, a classic American dream of assimilation. Disguised as a call for a revolution in our very understanding of the processes of identity in contemporary America, the narrative's lessons reveal a desire to invest American identity itself with presence and authority. Thus the novel may more than anything demonstrate the very impossibility of an integrated subjecthood in the framework of Western notions of independence and individual accomplishment.

At the time of its publication, Mukherjee said of *Jasmine*, "[I]t's not a realistic novel. It's meant to be a fable."[40] The imaginative license Mukherjee thus allows herself enables her to elaborate a plot in which questions of gender, racial, and cultural identity are skirted through recourse to cultural icons and stereotypes (both Indian and American) and a broad indulgence in fictional extremes.[41] In her novel, as in the Victorian dream of the "Orient" described by Said, the Punjab and even the U.S. itself become places "of romance, exotic beings, haunting memories and landscapes, remarkable experiences."[42] In this charmed landscape, selfhood and identity are mystified. Many of these mystifications are quite powerful, and indeed might be said to participate in the cultural work of myth-building.[43] I will not attempt to argue against the liberating potential of mythification in general terms; however, I do believe that the specific instances of exoticism in *Jasmine* serve to reify subaltern identity rather than to liberate it.

This reification is accomplished in the context of a particular notion of rebirth or transformation that is, as we have seen, metaphorically if not literally violent. The ways in which *Jasmine* moves between the metaphorical violence of identity transformation, the notion of representation itself as violence, and the fact of empirical violence raise a number of theoretical and methodological difficulties. If we indulge too fully the Derridean play between the "violence of the letter" and violence in the social field, or if we define as violent the very forces of psychic transformation, we obviously run the risk of derogating material violence—the physical violation of living bodies—and any political motivation one might have for wanting to represent it textually. This happens when Mukherjee herself starts making comparisons, with little apparent irony, between the "psychic violence" she experienced as the daughter of a wealthy factory owner growing up in Calcutta and the actual physical violence someone like Jasmine might face: "I had to personally experience a great deal of labor violence and unrest. There were many times when I went to school with what we used to call 'flying squads.' Military policemen in vans in front, special policemen in vans in back, our car, with chauffeur and bodyguard in between so we could, the three sisters, take part as pretty maidens in . . . Gilbert and Sullivan light operas."[44] While certainly the fear and psychic trauma associated with the threat of violence must have had very real effects on the young Mukherjee, there is obviously an incommensurable difference between the anxiety felt by a girl cradled in a "flying squad" and the kind of bodily oppression "labor" was experiencing at the same time, a difference Mukherjee only partially acknowledges.

As Spivak has noted, "The narrow epistemic violence of imperialism gives us an imperfect allegory of the general violence that is the possibility of an episteme."[45] Imperfect but not arbitrary—it is imperative that we understand violence in its discursive articulation if we *are* to detail the real effects of material violence beyond the physical. These effects might include a community's or individual's self-description as circumscribed, limited, and defined in daily life by violence, for instance, which may in turn result in nonviolent interventionary practice in the realm of legal or social discourse. In any case, I am aware of the many difficulties involved in any negotiation of "literal" and "metaphoric" social practice. I will try to acknowledge carefully those difficulties as I explore the ways in which Mukherjee's text does in fact "allegorize" psychological violence and the representation of male and female empirical violence, as each extends, comments on, ironizes, and complicates the other.

In *Jasmine*, "textual" or metaphoric violence is generalized from the postcolonial experience to the immigrant and "minority" experience in the United States. More significantly, Mukherjee makes it contiguous with the very constitution of American identity, broadly construed to include dominant as well as "ethnic" cultural forms. As Edward Said has acknowledged, there is nothing "especially controversial or reprehensible" about the *fact* that "cultures impose corrections upon raw reality," including encounters with other cultures, in order to make sense of them;[46] but the *way* those "corrections" are imposed can obviously have serious implications and consequences. Mukherjee's move to represent mainstream American culture in terms of "third world" identity must stand in problematic relation to a feminist or "third world" politics of difference. This becomes apparent when we examine the ways in which Jasmine adapts traditional Hindu doctrine, which argues for the contiguity of the human soul with an eternal *atman*, and which has historically been used to maintain a rigid caste system. Jasmine attempts to transplant this hierarchical doctrine onto the modern American idiom of class mobility and individual opportunity. It is as if she travels to America in order to radically, violently accelerate the evolution of her soul:

> What if the human soul is eternal—the swamis say of it, fires cannot burn it, water cannot drown it, winds cannot bend it—what if it is like a giant long-playing record with millions of tracks, each of them a complete circle with only one diamond-sharp microscopic link to the next life, and the next, and only God to hear it all?
> I do believe that. And I do believe that extraordinary events can jar the needle arm, rip across incarnations, and deposit a life into a groove that was not prepared to receive it. (113)

Here, "Fate" still maintains its hold on Jasmine's understanding, and as an idea, if not an actual force, it does in fact determine her plot. A confluence of "extraordinary events" replaces the inexorable propulsion of human life along a predetermined track, and as we shall see, Jasmine's syncretic adaptation of sacred Hindu and secular American beliefs collapses under the weight of what it must support: an impossible negotiation between destiny and opportunity, between unwilled necessity and the willed, private revolution of the "self-made man." As in the debate over *sati* detailed by Spivak, the figure of the subaltern woman is erased in a proliferation of arguments over her place within feudal patriarchy on the one hand and capitalist patriarchy on the other, both of which posit an evanescent equality of opportunity.

The impossibility of Jasmine's project is not readily apparent in the opening pages of the novel. As a seven-year-old girl, she is foretold of her widowhood and exile by an astrologer and refuses vehemently to believe in her "fate." " 'Suit yourself,' the astrologer cackled. 'What is to happen will happen.' Then he chucked me hard on the head," upon which the young girl falls down and a sharp stick punctures a hole in her forehead (1). This act of violence seems to inaugurate in Jyoti's life what Spivak has called a "discursive displacement"—a shift of perspective which can "only be operated by the force of a crisis," political or social.[47] Such a shift or "functional change in sign-systems" can make the objects of historiography into the subjects of their own history, as in the work of the Subaltern Studies group about which Spivak writes. This collection of scholars has tried to demonstrate how the "criminality" of a rebellious subaltern group is transformed by them into "insurgency," the label of "bondsman" traded in for the radically charged category of "worker."[48] Brought to crisis by the astrologer's prediction, Jyoti can thus assert to her family that her wound is in fact a "third eye," and she, a newly-born sage (2). A new way of seeing provides her with an intuitive rubric for knowing "what I don't want to become" (3).

Later, on her morning trip to the outhouses with the other women of the village, Jyoti must confront a mad dog which she somehow knows "had come for me, not for the other women. It had picked me as its enemy." However, even as she recognizes "fate" in the terrifying form of the rabid jackal she resists that doom: "I wasn't ready to die" (49). On the way to the outhouse she had picked up a thorny staff cast off by one of the Khalsa Lions and felt a "buzz of power" as her hand closed on it (47); this "buzz" now translates to action, and she kills the dog in mid-leap with the club. Jyoti's grandmother attempts to defuse Jyoti's moment of triumph over fate—"All it means is that God doesn't think you're ready for salvation. Individual effort counts for nothing" (50)—but it seems in fact that against the violent forces of Sikh gangs, crazy astrologers, and mad dogs, individual effort is all, and holiness without significance.

Mukherjee describes the landscape of contemporary America in similarly violent terms, painting a picture of a state in economic, social, and political crisis: "Last week in Dalton County, a farmer dug a trench all around his banker's house with stolen backhoe equipment. On TV he said, 'Call it a moat of hate.' Over by Osage a man beat his wife with a spade, then hanged himself in his machine shed" (138). Stable bonds of family and community seem to have dissolved, leaving behind only "Monster Truck Madness"; televised INS raids; farmers shooting bankers who foreclose on them; and the constant threat and reality of rape which first Jyoti, then Jasmine, then Jane and other immigrant women must constantly negotiate. As Jasmine muses, "Something's gotten out of hand in the heartland" (138). The vertiginous violence of change in the American landscape unsettles and even nauseates the narrator: "I feel at times like a stone hurtling through diaphanous mist," she tells us, "unable to grab hold, unable to slow myself, yet unwilling to abandon the ride I'm on. Down and down I go, where I'll stop, God knows" (123).

Between this moment and the one in which Jyoti describes the "buzz of power" she feels as she handles the thorned club, the text of *Jasmine* has accomplished a subtle displacement of agency. Jyoti has gone from being the subject to being the object of transformation, and it is violence itself which has displaced her on that positional continuum. Exactly at that instant when Jasmine desires to break the "diamond sharp links" from one state of being to another, she allows her own (not so peculiar) notion of female subjectivity to confirm her position as it stands, even as she is repositioned in terms of plot. The mysteriously accomplished shift recalls Mukherjee's description, in the interview excerpted earlier, of the passive "transformation" of the Indian women who trail after ambitious husbands seeking economic and educational riches here in the States. And indeed, even the language Jyoti uses to describe her confrontation with the mad dog is strangely passive: "I took aim and waited for it to leap on me. The staff crushed the dog's snout while it was still in mid-leap. Spiny twigs hooked deep into its nostrils and split them open. I saw all this as I lay on the winter-hard ground" (49). It is as if the staff has leaped out of Jyoti's hands and done its work alone; she describes the scene from the point of view of prone and helpless observer.

A similar displacement of agency occurs as the narrator confronts another attacker, after she arrives on U.S. shores. Jasmine's killing of the rapist Half-face constitutes a defining moment in the complex articulation of violence and gendered subjectivity that I have begun to sketch. In this moment Jasmine clearly reveals her complicity in an assimilative imperial and patriarchal practice, the primal scene of which, ironically, is the scene of Othering. The narrator's complicity is crystallized not in her act of violence, but in her figuration of that violence—the way in which the act is discursively deployed. Thus I am emphatically *not* making the argument that any material act of violence implicates its executor in the perpetuation of imperialism or patriarchy.[49] Rather, it is the way in which the narrator makes the act of violence intelligible to herself and to her witness, the reader, that is significant. The framework in which she enacts violence is one in which that act is seen only as a symptom of the greater epistemic violence of modern subjectivity, "first world" as well as "third world." Jasmine reinforces the colonizer's project by figuring her activity as assimilation or commutation to her Other—the "duality" she (and, implicitly, Mukherjee) has figured as power resolving itself into assimilation.

When Half-Face takes Jasmine to his motel room, several levels of violence—epistemic, metaphoric, and literal—are collapsed. Even as he drags her into the room she observes that "[h]is leg flew waist-high in a show-offy kick and the door thumped closed" (99)—that is, his violence is stylized, it has meaning, and thus operates at the level of discourse. He forces himself on her and she, not surprisingly, refuses his advance. But Half-Face is surprised. "I thought you'd be different from the others. A spark, you know?" (99). Something about her categorical difference, her "Indianness" has intrigued him. "You don't like white men, that it?" he asks (99). Jasmine here represents to Half-Face the inaccessible "exotic"—not in terms of her sexual availability, which he easily enforces, but in terms of her "inscrutability," her unknowability, her otherness. Angered by her suggestion that her life in India was not that much different from his life in the motel room—she looks at his television and notes that her husband had been a whiz repairman of such objects—Half-face must recapitulate epistemic violence at the literal level. "Don't tell me you ever *seen* a television set. Don't lie to me about no husbands and no television and we'll get along real good" (100; author's emphasis), he yells, even as he slams her head over and over into the set. His violence enacts his dream of the Other, in which he will be the one to painfully introduce the native to the requirements and perquisites of culture, assuming as he does that culture itself is unknown to her: "I got things I can do for you and you got something you can do for me, and I got lots of other things I can do *to* you, understand?" (100; author's emphasis).

Once he has raped her, Jyoti, in turn, enacts her own "dream" of violence, destroying in the same instant both Half-Face and her former self. Significantly, she plans to kill herself in order to purify her soul after the rape—she asserts, in fact, that she has already left her earthly body and would soon be joining her father's and husband's souls (104), even before she puts her knife to her own throat. As she hides in the motel bathroom, the "murkiness of the mirror" into which she looks "and a sudden sense of mission" stay her literal suicide (105). At the very moment, in other words, that she loses sight of her "self," she is subjected to a mandate spoken by an authority from *elsewhere*. Jyoti implicitly acknowledges this splitting of her subjectivity by symbolically slicing her tongue with the knife she will then use to slit Half-Face's throat. In doing so she becomes Kali of the bloody tongue, the destroyer goddess, "walking death. Death incarnate" (106). Only in this dissociative state can she do what she has to do. It is important to note that even as Mukherjee figures the act as one of agency rather than reactive self-defense—after all, Jasmine leaves Half-Face and *upon reflection* returns to murder him—she makes the murderer not Jasmine, but Kali. Where before she had stood before him a naked, vulnerable young girl, she would now return to stand over him with her "mouth open, pouring blood, [her] red tongue out," in the classic pose of the vengeful goddess (106). When it is over, the narrator still feels that her "body was merely the shell, soon to be discarded" (108); in the wake of this violent birth into America, she can only look forward to future rebirths, a perpetual "revolution" of the soul which begs the question of its own existence.

As Mukherjee represents her, the "third world" woman cannot be violent without recourse to some original mythic, mystic "presence" (in this instance, the Bengali Hindu goddess Kali) that ironically blocks access to agency. As I stated earlier, the invocation of cultural heroes is not automatically disempowering—it can be a valuable tool for amassing spiritual strength and focus. But in Jasmine's case, Kali's presence overcomes and effaces Jasmine and the personal history which has brought her to this point. Kali, the "Goddess *ex machina*"[50] appears and positions herself as a kind of midwife in the "rebirthing" process, an intermediary between one Jasmine and another. (The flesh-and-blood Lillian Gordon and Mother Ripplemeyer serve the same function in other instances. They each arrive on the scene just in time to pluck her from a dangerous situation and arrange for her a new "position.") Rebirth is a violent event, then, but this violence does not secure agency, as it does for Fanon. Rather, Jasmine's "act" of violence is an "act" of de-selfing, much like *sati* itself. Literal violence, in this case, murder, stands in for, even numbs, the pain of individual transformation. This violence of identity in turn replaces or masks the discursive violence Jasmine is subjected to as a "third world" gendered subject objectified by the "first world," represented here by her own author, Bharati Mukherjee.[51]

The central problematic for any radical theory of change, according to Spivak, is that "the possibility of action lies in the dynamics of the disruption of the [continuous sign-chain constituting the socius], the breaking and relinking of the [semiotic] chain. This line of argument does not set consciousness over against the socius, but sees it as itself also constituted as and on a semiotic chain. It is thus an instrument of study which participates in the nature of the object of study. *To see consciousness thus is to place the historian in a position of irreducible compromise.*"[52] The tangle of metaphorical and empirical violence itself has brought Jasmine to this same "irreducible" position, never interrogated and always abandoned, only to make its violent return again and again.

As the novel ends, we find Jane, pregnant with her Rochester's child, facing once again the "promise" of America and preparing herself for the next transformation. This time around it is at the hands of Taylor, once her employer and now her lover. "I realize I have already stopped thinking of myself as Jane," she tells us. " 'Ready?' Taylor grins. I cry into Taylor's shoulder, cry through all the lives I've given birth to, cry for all my dead" (214). In these few minutes, she seems finally to begin acknowledging the strength of her former "attachments"—but the mourning period is brief, and "then there is nothing I can do" (214). In the final moments of the book, then, the narrator abdicates agency once again, scrambling forward to meet a fate and a frontier already "pushing indoors" (214), she hopes, to embrace and assimilate her.

Notes

1   Bharati Mukherjee, *Jasmine* (1989; reprint, New York: Fawcett Crest-Ballantine, 1991), 35. Subsequent quotations from the novel are from this edition and are cited parenthetically.

2   Richard Eder, "Resisting the Pull of Tradition," review of *Jasmine*, by Bharati Mukherjee, *Los Angeles Times Book Review*, 17 September 1989: 3.

3   Homi K. Bhabha, "Signs Taken For Wonders: Questions of Ambivalence and Authority under a Tree Outside Delhi, May 1817," in *"Race," Writing, and Difference*, ed. Henry Louis Gates Jr. (Chicago: Univ. of Chicago Press, 1986), 171. Bhabha constructs his theory of colonial discourse around what he calls the process of "ambivalence" inherent in its major discursive strategy, the stereotype. The stereotype is "a form of knowledge and identification that vacillates between what is always 'in place,' already known, and something that must be anxiously repeated." (Homi K. Bhabha, "The Other Question . . . The Stereotype and Colonial Discourse," *Screen* 24, no. 6 [1983]: 18). Bhaba asserts that, "As a signifier of [the authority which avows this stereotype], the English book acquires its meaning *after* the traumatic scenario of colonial difference, cultural or racial, returns the eye of power to some prior, archaic image or identity. Paradoxically, however, such

an image can neither be 'original'—by virtue of the act of repetition that constructs it—nor 'identical'—by virtue of the difference that defines it. Consequently, the colonial presence is always ambivalent, split between its appearance as original and authoritative and its articulation as repetition and difference." ("Signs Taken For Wonders," 168–69; author's emphasis.)

4   *Great Expectations* doesn't bear as significant a relationship to *Jasmine* as Brontë's novel, although it does make an oblique appearance in Mukherjee's text. Watching Monster Truck Madness on television with her partner Bud and her adopted son Du, the narrator sees "[h]elmeted men giv[ing] me victory signs. They all plan on winning tonight. Nitro Express, Brawling Babe, Insane Expectations. Move over, I whisper" (17).

5   See Gayatri Chakravorty Spivak, "Three Women's Texts and a Critique of Imperialism," in Gates's *"Race," Writing, and Difference*, 262–80; and the introduction to Patrick Brantlinger's *Rule of Darkness: British Literature and Imperialism, 1830–1914* (Ithaca: Cornell Univ. Press, 1988) for a fuller explication of this dynamic.

6   Trinh T. Minh-ha, *Woman, Native, Other* (Bloomington: Indiana Univ. Press, 1989), 88.

7   See for example reviews by Eder, above; Douglas Foster, "No Place Like Home," *Mother Jones*, December 1989: 43–44; Marvin Gazzaniga, *Vogue*, September 1989: 512; Steven G. Kellman, *USA Today Magazine* 118 (May 1990): 96; Rhoda Koenig, "Passage from India," *New York*, 25 September 1989: 132; *Publishers Weekly*, 7 July 1989, 48.

8   *Jasmine*, back cover, emphasis added.

9   *Jasmine*, back cover.

10 *Jasmine*, back cover.

11 Trinh, 65. Or, in the case of Jane Eyre, the conversation is one of "us" with "us" *despite* "them."

12 Trinh, 67–68.

13 Gayatri Chakravorty Spivak, *The Post-Colonial Critic: Interviews, Strategies, Dialogues*, ed. Sarah Harasym (New York: Routledge, 1990), 57.

14 Spivak, 60.

15 Frantz Fanon, *The Wretched of the Earth*, trans. Constance Farrington (1961; reprint, New York: Grove Press, 1963), 35.

16 Fanon, 35, 36.

17 Fanon, 35.

18 Fanon, 36–37.

19 Michael M. J. Fischer, "Ethnicity and the Post-Modern Arts of Memory," in *Writing Culture: The Poetics and Politics of Ethnography*, ed. James Clifford and George E. Marcus (Berkeley and Los Angeles: Univ. of California Press, 1986), 198.

20 Fischer, 204, 207.

21 Edward Said, *Orientalism* (1978; reprint, New York: Vintage Books, 1979), 73.

22   Bharati Mukherjee, "An Interview with Bharati Mukherjee," *The Iowa Review* 20, no. 3 (1990): 8.

23   Clark Blaise and Bharati Mukherjee, *Days and Nights in Calcutta* (Garden City, New York: Doubleday & Co., 1977), 170.

24   Bharati Mukherjee, "Immigrant Writing: Give Us Your Maximalists!" *New York Times Book Review*, 28 August 1988: 29.

25   Mukherjee, "Immigrant Writing," 29.

26   Mukherjee, "Immigrant Writing," 29.

27   Mukherjee, "An Interview," 16.

28   Bhabha, "Signs Taken For Wonders," 174.

29   Bhabha, "Signs Taken For Wonders," 172–73.

30   Novels like *Jasmine* demonstrate the importance of postcolonial discourse theory to any understanding of contemporary American literature engaged with issues of color and class. While American ethnicity may differ in very real ways from postcolonial identity, the novel reveals the extent to which these two have become imbricated in late twentieth-century U.S. culture.

31   Gloria Anzaldúa, *Borderlands*/La Frontera: *The New Mestiza* (San Francisco: Spinsters/Aunt Lute, 1987), 77, 79.

32   Gayatri Chakravorty Spivak, "Can the Subaltern Speak?" in *Marxism and the Interpretation of Culture*, ed. Cary Nelson and Lawrence Grossberg (Urbana: Univ. of Illinois Press, 1988), 287.

33   For a complete history of the debate, see Lata Mani, "Contentious Traditions: The Debate on *Sati* in Colonial India," in *Recasting Women: Essays in Colonial History*, ed. Kumkum Sangari and Sudesh Vaid (New Delhi: Kali For Women, 1989), 88–126 (reprinted in *The Nature and Context of Minority Discourse*, ed. Abdul R. JanMohammed and David Lloyd [New York: Oxford Univ. Press, 1990]).

34   Spivak, "Can the Subaltern Speak?" 306. Spivak's representation of *sati* itself forms a striking parallel to Fanon's description of the process of decolonization. While in Fanon's formula, the " 'thing' which had been colonized becomes man during the same process by which it frees itself" (*Wretched*, 37), in Spivak's final analysis, the *sati* by which the "woman" colonized by both tradition and modernity can be said to "free" herself can be occasionally constructed as an "unemphatic, ad hoc, subaltern rewriting of the social text of *sati*-suicide" ("Subaltern," 308).

35   Benita Parry has observed that Spivak's deconstruction of the dual colonial subject is perhaps too readily or prematurely accomplished: "[W]hat are the politics of projects which dissolve the binary opposition colonial self/colonized other, encoded in colonialist language as a dichotomy necessary to domination, but also differently inscribed in the discourse of liberation as a dialectic of conflict and a call to arms?" ("Problems in Current Theories of Colonial Discourse," *Oxford Literary Review* 9 [1987]: 29).

36   Frantz Fanon, *Black Skin, White Masks*, trans. Charles Lam Markmann (1952; reprint, New York: Grove, 1967), 17–18.

37 Fanon, *Wretched*, 84.
38 Fanon, *Wretched*, 85.
39 Trinh, 90; author's emphasis.
40 Mukherjee, "An Interview," 8.
41 In one of the few negative reviews of *Jasmine*, Uma Parameswaran writes, "[W]hat enrages the discerning South Asian reader is Mukherjee's repeated pulling down of symbol to stereotype, but in a way that non-South Asians in the West and non-Americans elsewhere would not identify and therefore tend to accept unquestioningly. . . . The life and routine of Indo-Americans emerge as unrelentingly trivial, and the novel seems to establish that Jasmine-Jane fulfills herself only because she washed her hands of her fellow Indians" (*World Literature Today* 64, no. 4 [1990]: 699).
42 Said, 1.
43 Compare, for instance, Anzaldúa's embracing of the archetypal "Coatlicue state" in Chapter 4 of *Borderlands*.
44 Mukherjee, "An Interview," 8.
45 Spivak, "Can the Subaltern Speak?" 287.
46 Said, 60, 67.
47 Gayatri Chakravorty Spivak, *In Other Worlds: Essays in Cultural Politics* (New York: Routledge, 1987), 197.
48 Spivak, *In Other Worlds*, 197.
49 Teresa de Lauretis in fact makes such a claim: "For the subject of violence is always, by definition, masculine; 'man' is by definition the subject of culture and of any social act" ("The Violence of Rhetoric: Considerations on Representation and Gender," in *The Violence of Representation: Literature and the History of Violence*, ed. Nancy Armstrong and Leonard Tennenhouse [London: Routledge, 1989], 250). This definition seems to me a skirting of the (nonlinguistic) issues surrounding the female embodiment of violence.
50 Sarah Curtis, "All American Indian," review of *Jasmine*, by Bharati Mukherjee, *Times Literary Supplement*, 27 April 1990: 436.
51 Inevitably, in the sense that Spivak is inevitably complicit (despite greater self-consciousness than Mukherjee about her positionality) in the erasure of the young Indian woman she writes about in "Can the Subaltern Speak?" (see note 13).
52 Spivak, *In Other Worlds*, 198; my emphasis.

**Lauren
Berlant**

The Queen of America Goes to
Washington City:
Harriet Jacobs, Frances Harper, Anita Hill

For many readers of Harriet Jacobs, the political un-
canniness of Anita Hill has been a somber and illuminating experience.
These two "cases" intersect at several points: at the experience of being
sexually violated by powerful men in their places of work; at the experience of feeling shame and physical pain from living with humiliation; at
the use of "going public" to refuse their reduction to sexual meaning,
even after the "fact" of such reduction; at being African American women
whose most organized community of support treated gender as the sign
and structure of all subordinations to rank in America, such that other
considerations—of race, class, and political ideology—became both tacit
and insubordinate.[1] In these cases, and in their public reception, claims
for justice against racism and claims for justice against both patriarchal
and heterosexual privileges were made to compete with each other:
this competition among harmed collectivities remains one of the major
spectator sports of the American public sphere. It says volumes about
the continued and linked virulence of racism, misogyny, heterosexism,
economic privilege, and politics in America.

In addition to what we might call these strangely non-anachronistic
structural echoes and political continuities, the cases of Hill and Jacobs
expose the unsettled and unsettling relations of sexuality and American
citizenship—two complexly related sites of subjectivity, sensation, affect, law, and agency. The following are excerpts from Frances Harper's
1892 novel *Iola Leroy*, Jacobs's narrative, and Hill's testimony. Although
interpretive norms of production, consumption, and style differ among
these texts, each author went public in the most national medium available to her. For this and other reasons, the rhetorical gestures that rhyme

among these passages provide material for linking the politics of sex and the public sphere in America to the history of nationality itself, now read as a domain of sensation and sensationalism, and of a yet unrealized potential for fashioning "the poetry of the future" from the domains where citizens register citizenship, along with other feelings:[2]

> [Iola Leroy:] "I was sold from State to State as an article of merchandise. I had outrages heaped on me which might well crimson the cheek of honest womanhood with shame, but I never fell into the clutches of an owner for whom I did not feel the utmost loathing and intensest horror.". . . [Dr. Gresham:] "But, Iola, you must not blame all for what a few have done." [Iola:] "A few have done? Did not the whole nation consent to our abasement?" (Frances E. W. Harper, *Iola Leroy* [1892])[3]

> I have not written my experiences in order to attract attention to myself; on the contrary, it would have been more pleasant to me to have been silent about my own history. Neither do I care to excite sympathy for my own sufferings. But I do earnestly desire to arouse the women of the North to a realizing sense of the condition of two million of women at the South, still in bondage, suffering what I suffered, and most of them far worse. . . . [My] bill of sale is on record, and future generations will learn from it that women were articles of traffic in New York, late in the nineteenth century of the Christian religion. It may hereafter prove a useful document to antiquaries, who are seeking to measure the progress of civilization in the United States. (Harriet A. Jacobs, *Incidents in the Life of a Slave Girl* [1861])[4]

> It is only after a great deal of agonizing consideration, and sleepless— number of—great number of sleepless nights, that I am able to talk of these unpleasant matters to anyone but my close friends. . . . As I've said before, these last few days have been very trying and very hard for me and it hasn't just been the last few days this week.
>
> It has actually been over a month now that I have been under the strain of this issue. Telling the world is the most difficult experience of my life, but it is very close to having to live through the experience that occasioned this meeting. . . .
>
> The only personal benefit that I have received from this experience is that I have had an opportunity to serve my country. I was raised to do what is right and can now explain to my students first hand that despite the high costs that may be involved, it is worth having the

truth emerge. (Anita Hill, *New York Times*, 12 October 1991; 15 October 1991)[5]

On the Subject of Personal Testimony and the Pedagogy of Failed Teaching

When Anita Hill, Harriet Jacobs, and Frances Harper's Iola Leroy speak in public about the national scandal of their private shame, they bring incommensurate fields of identity into explosive conjunction. Speaking as private subjects about sexual activities that transpired within the politically charged spaces of everyday life, their testimony remains itself personal, specifically about them, their sensations and subjectivity. We hear about "my experiences," "my own suffering," "unpleasant matters"; we hear of desires to return to silence, and of longings to be relieved of the drive to consign this material to public life, which requires the speaker to re-experience on her body what her rhetoric describes. But since their speech turns "incidents" of sexuality into opportunities for reconstructing what counts as national data—that is, since these sexual autobiographies all aim to attain the status of a *finding*, an official expert narrative about national protocols—the authors must make themselves representative and must make the specific sensational details of their violation exemplary of collective life. It is always the autobiographer's task to negotiate her specificity into a spectacular interiority worthy of public notice. But the minority subject who circulates in a majoritarian public sphere occupies a specific contradiction: insofar as she is exemplary, she has distinguished herself from the collective stereotype; and, at the same time, she is also read as a kind of foreign national, an exotic representative of her alien "people" who reports to the dominant culture about collective life in the crevices of national existence. This warp in the circulation of identity is central to the public history of African American women, for whom coerced sexualization has been a constitutive relay between national experience and particular bodies.

Hence the specifically juridical inflection of "personal testimony." This hybrid form demarcates a collectively experienced set of strains and contradictions in the meaning of sexual knowledge in America: sexual knowledge derives from private experiences on the body and yet operates as a register for systemic relations of power; sexual knowledge stands for a kind of political counterintelligence, a challenge to the norms of credibility, rationality, and expertise that generally organize political culture; and yet, as an archive of injury and of private sensation, sexual knowledge can have the paradoxical effect of *delegitimating* the very experts who can represent it as a form of experience. As the opening passages show, these three women produced vital public testimony about the conditions of sexuality and citizenship in America. Their representations of how nationality became embodied and intimate to them involve fantasies of what America is, where it is, and how it reaches individuals. This requires them to develop a national pedagogy of failed teaching: emerging from the pseudo-private spaces where many kinds of power are condensed into personal relations, they detail how they were forced to deploy persuasion to fight for sexual dignity, and how they lost that fight. They take their individual losses as exemplary of larger ones, in particular the failure of the law and the nation to protect the sexual dignity of women from the hybrid body of patriarchal official and sexual privilege. They insist on representing the continuous shifting of perspectives that constitutes the incommensurate experience of power where national and sexual affect meet. They resist, in sum, further submission to a national sexuality that blurs the line between the disembodied entitlements of liberal citizenship and the places where bodies experience the sensation of being dominated. For all these verbs of resistance, the women represent their deployment of publicity as an act made under duress, an act thus representing and performing unfreedom in America. These three narrators represent their previous rhetorical failures to secure sexual jurisdiction over their bodies, challenging America to take up politically what the strongest individualities could not achieve.

Anita Hill is the most recent in a tradition of American women who have sought to make the nation listen to them, to transform the horizons and the terms of authority that mark both personal and national life in America by speaking about sexuality as the fundamental and fundamentally repressed horizon of national identity, legitimacy, and affective experience. That these are African American women reflects the specific sexual malignity black women have been forced to experience in public as a form of white pleasure and a register of white power in America. In this sense the imagination of sexual privacy these women express is a privacy they have never experienced, except as a space of impossibility. Anita Hill situated her own testimony not as a counter to the sexual economy of white erotics but in the professional discourse of an abused worker. Therefore, in Hill's testimony, two histories of corporeal identity converge. In both domains of experience, before sexual harassment became illegal, it was a widespread social practice protected by law. Invented as a technical legal category when middle-class white women started experiencing everyday violations of sexual dignity in the workplace, it has provided a way to link the banality and ordinariness of female sexualization to other hard-won protections against worker exploitation and personal injury.[6] It has also contributed to vital theoretical and policy reconsiderations of what constitutes the conditions of "consent" in the public sphere, a space which is no longer considered "free," even under the aegis of national-democratic protections.

What would it mean to write a genealogy of sexual harassment in which not an individual but a nation was considered the agent of unjust sexual power? Such an account of these complaints would provide an incisive critique of the modes of erotic and political dominance that have marked gender, race, and citizenship in America. It would register the sexual specificity of African American women's experience of white culture; it would link experiences of violated sexual privacy to the doctrine of abstract national "personhood," making America accountable for the private sexual transgressions of its privileged men and radically transforming the history of the "public" and the "private" in America; it would show how vital the existence of official sexual underclasses has been to producing national symbolic and political coherence; finally, and more happily, it would provide an archive of tactics that have made it possible to reoccupy both the sexual body and America by turning the constraints of privacy into information about national identity. I take the texts which I have quoted—Harriet Jacobs's slave narrative *Incidents in the Life of a Slave Girl*, Frances E. W. Harper's novel *Iola Leroy*, and the testimony of Anita Hill—as my sensorium of citizenship. The women in these texts each determine, under what they perceive to be the pressure or the necessity of history, to behave as native informants to an imperial power, that is, to mime the privileges of citizenship in the context of a particular national emergency. These national emergencies are, in chronological order, slavery, reconstruction, and the nomination of Clarence Thomas to the Supreme Court. They respond to these emergencies, these experiences of national sexuality, by producing what might be read as a counterpornography of citizenship. For the next two sections I will locate the history of gesture and sense that characterizes this genre in readings of the nineteenth-century texts, and then shift historical perspective to Anita Hill in section four. Senators without pants, lawyers without scruples, and a national fantasy of corporeal dignity will characterize this story.

A Meditation on National Fantasy, in which Women Make No Difference

These texts provide evidence that American citizenship has been profoundly organized around the distribution and coding of sensations. Two distinct moments in the nineteenth-century texts crystalize the conditions and fantasies of power motivating this affective domination, and so represent the negative space of political existence for American women in the last century. It may not appear that the sexual and affective encounters I will describe are indeed national, for they take place intimately between persons, in what look like private domains. The women's enslavement within the sensational regime of a privileged heterosexuality leads, by many different paths, to their transposition of these acts into the context of nationality. Even if sexual relations directly forced on these women mark individuals as corrupted by power, the women's narratives refuse to affirm the private horizon of personal entitlement as the cause of their suffering. America becomes explicitly, in this context, accountable for the sexual exploitation it authorizes in the guise of the white male citizen's domestic and erotic privilege.

Incidents in the Life of a Slave Girl registers many moments of intense corporeal stress, but one particular transitional gesture measures precisely on Harriet Jacobs's body the politics of her situation: hers is a hybrid experience of intimacy and alienation of a kind fundamental to African American women's experience of national sexuality under slavery. A mulatta, she was thought by some whites to be beautiful, a condition (as she says) that doubles the afflictions of race. She writes that the smallest female slave child will learn that "If God has bestowed beauty upon her, it will prove her greatest curse. That which commands admiration in the white woman only hastens the degradation of the female slave" (28). Racial logic gave America a fantasy image of its own personal underclass, with European-style beauty in the slave population justifying by nature a specific kind of exploitation by whites, who could mask their corporeal domination of all slaves in fantasies of masculine sexual entrapment by the slave women's availability and allure. For dark-skinned "black" women this form of exploitation involved rape and forced reproduction. These conditions applied to mulatta women too, but the lightness of these women also provided material for white men's parodic and perverse fantasies of masking domination as love and conjugal decorum.[7] Theatrically, they set up a parallel universe of sexual and racial domestic bliss and heterosexual entitlement: this involved dressing up the beautiful mulatta and playing white-lady-of-the-house with her, building her a little house that parodied the big one, giving her the kinds of things that white married ladies received, only in this instance without the protections of law. Jacobs herself was constantly threatened with this fancy life, if only she would consent to it.

This relation of privilege, which brought together sexual fantasy and the law, disguised enslavement as a kind of courtship, and as caricature was entirely a production of the intentions and whims of the master. Harriet Jacobs was involved in an especially intricate and perverse game of mulatta sexual guerilla theater. One of *her* moves in this game was to become sexually involved with a white man other than her owner, Dr. Flint. (This man's *nom de théatre* is "Mr. Sands," but his real name was Samuel Tredwell Sawyer and he was a United States Congressman, a status to which I will return in the next section.) Jacobs reports that Mr. Sands seemed especially sympathetic to her plight and that of their two children, and when he is introduced in the narrative's first half he seems to represent the promise of a humane relation between the sexes in the South—despite the fractures of race and in contrast to the sexual and rhetorical repertoire of violences with which Dr. Flint tortures Jacobs and her family. But the bulk of *Incidents* finds Jacobs in constant psychic torture about Sands himself. Her anxiety about whether he will remember her when she is gone, and remember his promises to free their children, makes her risk life and limb several times to seek him out: "There was one person there, who ought to have had some sympathy with [my] anxiety; but the links of such relations as he had formed with me, are easily broken and cast away as rubbish. Yet how protectingly and persuasively he once talked to the poor, helpless, slave girl! And how entirely I trusted him! But now suspicions darkened my mind" (142). No longer believing that Sands is a man of his word, Jacobs at length decides to escape—not at first from the South, but from Dr. Flint, following an intricately twisted path through the swamps, the hollow kitchen floors, and the other covert spaces of safety semi-secured by the slave community.[8] This spatial improvisation for survival culminates in a move to her grandmother's attic, where she spends seven years of so-called freedom, the price of which was lifelong nervous and muscular disruptions of her body. On the last day of her transition from enslavement, which was also the end of her freedom of movement, Jacobs's final act was to walk the public streets of her home town (Edenton, North Carolina) in disguise, one that required perverse elaborations of the already twisted epidermal schema of slavery. In her traveling clothes she does not assume white "lady's" apparel but hides her body in men's "sailor's clothes" and mimes the anonymity of a tourist, someone who is passing through; second, in this last appearance in her native town she appears in blackface, her skin darkened with charcoal. A juridically black woman whose experience of slavery as a mulatta parodies the sexual and domestic inscription of whiteness moves away from slavery by recrossing the bar of race and assuming the corporeal shroud of masculinity. This engagement with the visible body fashions her as absolutely invisible on the street. Moving toward escape, she passes "several people whom [she] knew," but they do not recognize her. Then "the father of my children came so near that I brushed against his arm; but he had no idea who it was" (113).

When Mr. Sands does not recognize Jacobs, though he sees her and touches her body, it becomes prophetically clear how specific his interest in her was. He desired a mulatta, a woman who signifies white but provides white men a different access to sexuality. Dressed as a man, she is invisible to him. With a black face, she is invisible to him, no longer an incitement to his desire. Touching him she thinks about other kinds of intimacy they have had—she calls him the father of their children— but in a certain sense her body registers what is numb to his *because* he is privileged. He has the right to forget and to not feel, while sensation and its memory are all she owns. This is the feeling of what we might call the slave's two bodies: sensual and public on the one hand; vulnerable, invisible, forgettable on the other. It is not surprising in this context that until Jean Fagan Yellin performed her research, the scholarly wisdom was that Harriet Jacobs could not have produced such a credible narrative. Her articulate representation of her sensational experience seemed itself evidence for the fraudulence of her authorship claims.[9]

If Jacobs experiences as a fact of life the political meaninglessness of her own sensations, Harper represents the process whereby Iola is disenfranchised of her sensations. In the following passage Iola discovers that she is a slave, politically meaningful but, like Jacobs, sensually irrelevant. Harper meticulously narrates Iola's sustained resistance to the theft of her senses by the corporeal fantasies of the slave system.[10] This resistance is a privilege Iola possesses because of the peculiar logic of racial identity in America, which draws legal lines that disregard the data of subjectivity when determining the identity of "race." Iola is a mulatta raised in isolated ignorance of her mother's racial history. Her mother Marie was a Creole slave of Eugene Leroy's, manumitted and educated by him before their marriage. Against Marie's wishes, the father insists that the children grow up in ignorance of their racial complexity, the "cross" in their blood. He does this to preserve their self-esteem, which is founded on racial unselfconsciousness and a sense of innate freedom (84). When the father dies, an unscrupulous cousin tampers with Marie's manumission papers and convinces a judge to negate them. He then sends a lawyer to trick Iola into returning South and thus to slavery. Her transition between lexicons, laws, privileges, and races takes place, appropriately, as a transition from dreaming to waking. She rides on the train with the lawyer who will transport her "home" to the slave system, but she is as yet unknowing, dreaming of her previous domestic felicity:

> In her dreams she was at home, encircled in the warm clasp of her father's arms, feeling her mother's kisses lingering on her lips, and hearing the joyous greetings of the servants and Mammy Liza's glad welcome as she folded her to her heart. From this dream of bliss she was awakened by a burning kiss pressed on her lips, and a strong arm encircling her. Gazing around and taking in the whole situation, she sprang from her seat, her eyes flashing with rage and scorn, her face flushed to the roots of her hair, her voice shaken with excitement, and every nerve trembling with angry emotion. (103)

When, like the Prince in a debauched *Sleeping Beauty*, the lawyer kisses Iola, he awakens her and all of her senses to a new embodiment. At first Iola dreams of life in the white family, with its regulated sexualities and the pleasure of its physical routine. Feeling her father's arms, kissing her mother, hearing the servants, snuggling with mammy: these are the idealized domestic sensations of white feminine plantation privilege, which provides a sensual system that is safe and seems natural. This is why Iola does not understand the lawyer's violation of her body. Since he already sees her as public property, authorized by a national slave system, he feels free to act without her prior knowledge, while she still feels protected by white sexual gentility. Thus the irony of her flashing-eyed, pulsating response: to Iola this is the response of legitimate self-protectiveness, but to the lawyer the passion of her resistance actually increases her value on the slave market. Her seduction and submission to the master's sexuality would reflect the victory of his economic power, which is a given. Her sensations make no sense to the slave system; therefore they are no longer credible. Her relation to them makes no difference. This is the most powerful index of powerlessness under the law of the nation.

Slavery, Citizenship, and Utopia: Some Questions About America

I have described the political space where nothing follows from the experience of private sensation as a founding condition of slave subjectivity, a supernumary nervous system here inscribed specifically and sexually on the bodies and minds of slave women. We see, in the narratives of Jacobs and Iola Leroy, that the process of interpellating this affective regime was ongoing, and that no rhetoric could protect them from what seemed most perverse about it, the permission it seemed to give slave owners to create sexual fantasies, narratives, masquerades of domesticity within which they could pretend *not* to dominate women, or to mediate their domination with displays of expenditure and chivalry.

But if this blurring of the lines between domination and play, between rhetorical and physical contact, and between political and sexual license always worked to reinforce the entitled relation to sensation and power the master culture enjoyed, both *Incidents* and *Iola Leroy* tactically blur another line—between personal and national tyranny. In the last section I described the incommensurate experiences of intimacy under slavery. Here I want to focus on how these intimate encounters with power structure Jacobs's and Harper's handling of the abstract problem of *nationality* as it is experienced—not as an idea, but as a force in social life, in experiences that mark the everyday. For Jacobs, writing before Emancipation, the nation as a category of experience is an archive of painful anecdotes, bitter feelings, and precise measurements of civic failure. She derives no strength from thinking about the possibilities of imagined community: hers is an anti-utopian discourse of amelioration. In contrast, Harper writes after the war and enfranchisement. These conditions for a post-diasporic national fantasy provide the structure for her re-imagination of social value and civic decorum in a radically reconstructed America. The felt need to transform painful sexual encounters into a politics of nationality drove both of these women to revise radically the lexicon and the narratives by which the nation appears as a horizon both of dread and of fantasy.

Jacobs's *Incidents* was written for and distributed by white abolitionists whose purpose was to demonstrate not just how scandalous slavery was but how central sexuality was in regulating the life of the slave. Yet the reign of the master was not secured simply through the corporeal logics of patriarchy and racism. Jacobs shows a variety of other ways her body was erotically dominated in slavery—control over movement and sexuality, over time and space, over information and capital, and over the details of personal history that govern familial identity—and links these scandals up to a powerful critique of America, of the promises for democracy and personal mastery it offers to and withholds from the powerless.

Jacobs's particular point of entry to nationality was reproductive. The slave mother was the "country" into which the slave child was born, a realm unto herself whose foundational rules constituted a parody of the birthright properties of national citizenship. Jacobs repeatedly recites the phrase "follow the condition of the mother," framed in quotation marks, to demonstrate her only positive representation in the law, a representation that has no entitlement, a parodically American mantra as fundamental as another phrase about following she had no right to use, "life, liberty, and the pursuit of happiness."

But the technicalities of freedom were not enough to satisfy Jacobs that America had the potential to fulfill its stated mission to be a Christian country. To gain free, unencumbered motherhood would be to experience the inversion of the sexual slavery she has undergone as a condition of her noncitizenship: at the end of the text, her freedom legally secured, she considers herself still unfree in the absence of a secure domestic space for her children.[11] But if Jacobs's relation to citizenship in the abstract is bitter and despairing, her most painful nationally authorized contact was intimate, a relation of frustrating ironic proximity.

I have characterized her sexual and reproductive relation with Mr. Sands, the United States Congressman Samuel Tredwell Sawyer. A truly sentimental fiction would no doubt reveal something generous about Congressman Sawyer, about a distinguished political career that might have included, somehow, traces of the influence Jacobs had on Sawyer's consciousness, revealed in a commitment to securing legal consensus on the humanity of slaves; and it would be simply trivial to note that issues of the *Congressional Globe* from 1838 reveal him in another universe of political consciousness, entirely undistinguished (he seems concerned with laws regulating duelling). More important, *Incidents* establishes that his rise to national office directly correlated with his increasing disregard for his promises to emancipate their children and her brother, both of whom he had bought from Flint in isolated acts of real empathy for Jacobs. Like many liberal tyrants, Sawyer so believes that his relative personal integrity and good intentions place him above moral culpability that he has no need to act morally within the law. Indeed, the law is the bar to empathy. When Harriet's brother William escapes from him, Sawyer says petulantly, "I trusted him as if he were my own brother, and treated him as kindly. . . . but he wanted to be a free man. . . . I intended to give him his freedom in five years. He might have trusted me. He has shown himself ungrateful; but I shall not go for him, or send for him. I feel confident that he will soon return to me" (135–36).

Later, Jacobs hears a quite different account from her brother, but what's crucial here is that the congressman whose sexual pleasure and sense of self-worth have been secured by the institution of slavery is corrupted by his proximity to national power. Yet Jacobs speaks the language of power, while Sawyer speaks the language of personal ethics; she looks to political solutions, while his privilege under the law makes its specific constraints irrelevant to him. Under these conditions Jacobs concludes three things about the politics of national sexuality. One is borne out by the performative history of her own book: "If the secret memoirs of many members of Congress should be published, curious details [about the sexual immorality of official men] would be unfolded" (142). The second she discovers as she returns from a trip to England where she has found political, sexual, racial, and spiritual peace and regeneration: "We had a tedious winter passage, and from the distance spectres seemed to rise up on the shores of the United States. It is a sad feeling to be afraid of one's native country" (186). Third, and finally, having established America as a negative space, a massive space of darkness, ghosts, shame, and barbarism, Jacobs sees no possibility that political solutions will ameliorate the memory and the ongoing pain of African American existence—as long as law marks a border between abstract and practical ethics. By the end of *Incidents* national discourse itself has become a mode of memorial rhetoric, an archive of dead promises.

I have identified thus two kinds of experience of the national for Jacobs: the actual pain of its practical betrayals through the many conscriptions of her body that I am associating with national sexuality and a psychic rage at America for not even trying to live up to the conditions of citizenship it promises in law and in spirit. After emancipation, in 1892 when

Frances Harper is writing *Iola Leroy*, speaking at suffrage conferences, at the National Congress of Negro Women, and at the Columbian Exposition, she imagines that citizenship might provide a model of identity that ameliorates the experience of corporeal mortification that has sustained American racisms and misogyny.[12] Harper argues that "more than the changing of institutions we need the development of a national conscience, and the upbuilding of national character," but she imagines this project of reconstruction more subtly and more radically than this kind of nationalistic rhetoric might suggest.[13] She refuses the lure of believing that the discourse of disembodied democratic citizenship applies to black Americans: she says, "You white women speak here of rights. I speak of wrongs. I, as a colored woman, have had in this country an education which has made me feel as if I were in the situation of Ishmael, my hand against every man, and every man's hand against me."[14] But Jacobs's solution to the enigma of social life under racism and misogyny—to privatize social relations—was not the only solution to this violent touching of hands. In contrast to Jacobs's narrative, Harper's *Iola Leroy* seizes the scene of citizenship from white America and rebuilds it, in the classic sense, imagining a liberal public sphere located within the black community.[15] More than a critical irritant to the white "people," the text subverts the racially dominant national polity by rendering it irrelevant to the fulfillment of its own national imaginary. Harper's civic and Christian black American nationality depends not only on eliding the horizon of white pseudo-democracy; she also imagines that African American nationalism will provide a model of dignity and justice that white American citizens will be obliged to follow.

A double movement of negation and theorization transforms the condition of citizenship as the novel imagines it. Harper's critical tactic banishes white Americans from the utopian political imaginary activity of this text. The initial loss of white status is performed, however, not as an effect of African American rage but rather as an act of white political rationality. A general in the Northern Army, encountering the tragedy of Iola's specific history and the detritus of the war, disavows his own identification as an American: he thinks, "Could it be possible that this young and beautiful girl had been a chattel, with no power to protect herself from the highest insults that lawless brutality could inflict upon innocent and defenseless womanhood? Could he ever again glory in his American citizenship, when any white man, no matter how coarse, cruel, or brutal, could buy or sell her for the basest purposes? Was it not true that the cause of a hapless people had become entangled with the lightnings of heaven, and dragged down retribution upon the land?" (39). This repudiation envelops national, racial, and gendered self-disenfranchisement, and clears the way for a postpatriarchal, postracist, Christian commonwealth. Its ethical aura hovers over the novel's postwar narrative as well: Iola's experience of racism and misogyny in the metropolitian and commercial spaces of the North induces more pronouncements by whites about the unworthiness of white people to lead America in official and everyday life, since it is white national culture that has transformed the country from a space of enlightenment to a place of what she calls shadows and foreshadowing.

Such political self-impeachments by whites make it possible for Harper to reinvent a truly African American–centered *American* citizenship. In this sense, race in *Iola Leroy* is not solely a negative disciplinary category of national culture but becomes an archive of speech and life activities recast as a political arsenal. The originary form for African American insurgent community building derives from the subversive vernacular practices of slave life—from, as the first chapter title suggests, "The Mystery of Market Speech and Prayer Meetings." The narrative opens in the marketplace, where the slaves are shown to use an allegorical language to communicate and to gossip illegally about the progress of freedom during the Civil War. Just as the white masters travel, "talking politics in . . . State and National capitals" (7), slaves converse about the freshness of butter, eggs, and fish: but these ordinary words turn out to contain covert communication from the battlefield (7–8). In addition to exploiting the commercial space, the slave community performs its political identity at prayer meetings, where more illegal communication about the war and everyday life under slavery also transpires in allegory and secrecy.

The internal communications and interpretations of the community become public and instrumental in a different way after the war, when the place where the community met to pray to God and for freedom is transformed into a site where families dispersed by slavery might recombine: "They had come to break bread with each other, relate their experiences, and tell of their hopes of heaven. In that meeting were remnants of broken families—mothers who had been separated from their children before the war, husbands who had not met their wives for years" (179). These stories demonstrating kinship locate it not, however, in memories of shared lives or blood genealogies but rather in common memories of the violence of familial separation and dispersal. Under the conditions of legal impersonality which had governed slave personhood, the repetition of personal narratives of loss is the only currency of identity the slaves can exchange. The collective tactic here after slavery is to circulate self-descriptions in the hope that they will be repeated as gossip and heard by relatives, who will then come to the next convention and recite their own autobiographies in the hope that the rumor was true, that their story had an echo in someone else's life.

The collective storytelling about the diasporic forces of slavery is re-invented after the migration north, in salons where what Harper calls *conversazione* take place. Habermas and Landes have described the central role of the salon in building a public sphere.[16] Its function was to make the public sphere performatively democratic: more permeable by women and the ethnic and class subjects who had been left out of aristocratic privilege and who learn there to construct a personal and collective identity through the oral sharing of a diversity of written ideas. Harper explains at great length how conventions and *conversazione* transformed what counted as "personal" testimony in the black community: the chapter "Friends in Council," for example, details papers and contentious conversations about them entitled "Negro Emigration," "Patriotism," "Education of Mothers," and "Moral Progress of the Race," and a poem written by Harper herself entitled "Rallying Cry." All of these speeches and the conversations about them focus on uplifting the race and rethinking history; and the conditions of uplifting require imagining a just America, an America where where neither race nor sexuality exists as a mode of domination. As Iola's friend, Miss Delaney, says, "I want my pupils to do all in their power to make this country worthy of their deepest devotion and loftiest patriotism" (251). Finally, after these face-to-face communities of African Americans seeking to transform their enslaved identities into powerful cultural and political coalitions are established, a literary tradition becomes possible: Iola herself is asked to serve the race by writing the story of her life that is this novel. Harper, in the afterword to the novel, imagines a new African American literature, "glowing with the fervor of the tropics and enriched by the luxuriance of the Orient." This revisionary aesthetic will, in her view, fill the African American "quota of good citizenship" and thus "add to the solution of our unsolved American problem" (282). In sum, the transmission of personal narrative, inscribed into the interiority of a community, becomes a vehicle for social transformation in *Iola Leroy*, recombining into a multicultural, though not multiracial, public sphere of collective knowledge. In so reconstructing through mass-circulated literature the meaning of collective personhood, and in so insisting on a "quota system" of good citizenship based not on racial assimilation but on a national ethics, the African American community Harper imagines solves the problem of America for itself.

Diva Citizenship

When you are born into a national symbolic order that explicitly marks your person as illegitimate, far beyond the horizon of proper citizenship, and when your body also becomes a site of privileged fantasy property and of sexual contact that the law explicitly proscribes but privately entitles, you inhabit the mulatta's genealogy, a genealogy of national experience. The national body is ambiguous because its norms of privilege require a universalizing logic of disembodiment, while its local, corporeal practices are simultaneously informed by that legal privilege and—when considered personal, if not private—are protected by the law's general proximity. The African American women of this narrative understood that only a perversely "un-American" but nationally addressed text written from the history of a national subculture could shock white citizens into knowing how compromised citizenship has been as a category of experience and fantasy, not least for the chastised American classes.

This question of sexual harassment is thus not just a "woman's" question. A charged repertoire of private domination and erotic theatricality was licensed by American law and custom to encounter the African American women of whom I have written here, and many others, whose locations in hierarchies of racism, homophobia, and misogyny will require precisely and passionately written counter-histories. In twentieth-century America, anyone coded as "low," embodied, or subculturally "specific" continues to experience, with banal regularity, the corporeal sensation of nationality as a sensation over which she/he has no control. This, in the broadest sense, is sexual harassment. These texts break the sanitizing silences of sexual privacy in order to create national publics trained to think, and thus to think differently, about the corporeal conditions of citizenship. One of these conditions was the evacuation of erotic or sexual or even sensational life itself as a possible ground of personal dignity for African American women in America. As the rational, anti-passional logic of *Incidents* and *Iola Leroy* shows, the desire to become national seems to call for a *release* from sensuality—this is the cost, indeed the promise, of citizenship.

But the possibility of a revitalized national identity flickers in traces of peculiar identification within these texts. I call this possibility Diva Citizenship, but can only describe, at this point, the imaginable conditions of its emergence as an unrealized form of political activity. Diva Citizenship has a genealogy too, a dynastic, dignified, and pleasuring one. It courses through a variety of media forms and public spheres— from the Old Testament through CNN, through the works of bell hooks, Donna Haraway, Wayne Koestenbaum, and others.[17] For Haraway, cyborg citizenship replaces the "public/private" distinction as a paradigm for political subjectivity; hooks similarly derives the potential politics of the "third world diva girl" from the everyday forms of assertive and contesting speech she absorbed among "Southern black folk." These forms of speech are lived as breaches of class decorum between and among white, Third World, and African American feminists who discipline the ways women take, hold, use, respect, or demonize public authority: hooks sees the transgression of these decorums as central to liberation politics. For Koestenbaum, the Diva's public merging of "ordinariness touched by sublimity" has already been crucial to the emergence of a "collective gay subcultural imagination," where the public grandiosity of survival, the bitter banality of negotiating everyday life, generates subversive gossip about icons that actually works to create counterculture. "Where there is fever," he writes, "the need for police arises." Crossing police barricades and the civilizing standards of public life, Diva Citizenship takes on as a national project redefining the scale, the volume, and the erotics of "what you can [sincerely] do for your country."

One strategy of slave literature has been its royalist strain.[18] In *Iola Leroy*, Harper locates the promise of Diva Citizenship in the Biblical story of Queen Esther. Marie, Iola Leroy's mother, makes an abolitionist speech, executing a performance of refracting ironies. Marie speaks as a Creole slave woman to a free white audience on the day she graduates from the "finishing" school that will enable her to pass as the white wife of Albert Leroy: "Like Esther pleading for the lives of her people in the Oriental courts of a despotic king, she stood before the audience, pleading for those whose lips were sealed, but whose condition appealed to the mercy and justice of the Nation" (75). The analogies between Marie and Esther are myriad: forced to pass as a Persian in the court of Ahasuerus, the King and her husband, Esther speaks as a Jew to save her people from genocide. She mobilizes her contradictions to unsettle the representational and political machinery of a dominant culture that desires her. It is not only in the gesture of special pleading that Marie absorbs Esther, but in the analogy between the mulatta woman and the assimilated Jew. Esther's capacity to pass likewise not only made her erotic masquerade the default activity of her everyday embodiment but also gave her sexual access to power—which she used not in a prevaricating way but under the pressure of a diasporic ethics. Purim, Queen Esther's holiday, is offered as a day of masquerade, revelry, and rage at tyranny—although as a story additionally about a wronged Queen (Vashti) and a holocaust, its status as an origin tale of domestic and imperial violence cannot be glossed over.[19] But Queen Esther stands in Harper's text as another foreign national separated at birth from the privileges of nationality, and also as a slave to masterly fantasies of sexual hierarchy and sensational excess who learned to countertheatricalize her identity and to wield it against injustice.

Jacobs's contribution to this monarchical fantasy politics deploys the Queen not as a figure of tactical self-distortion and instrumental sexual intimacy but as a figure of superior power who remakes the relations between politics and the body in America. She represents the "state of civilization in the late nineteenth century of the United States" by showing a variety of indirect and noncoherent ways the nation came into deliberate contact with slaves—through scandalous and petty torture. In turn, Jacobs shows how the slaves misrecognize, in potentially and sometimes strategically radical ways, what constitutes the nation. This passage takes place in an extraordinary chapter titled "What Slaves Are Taught to Think of the North." Jacobs describes at great rageful length the relation between the sexual brutality of masters to slaves and their lies, what she calls "the pains" masters take to construct false scenarios about "the hard kind of freedom" that awaited freed or escaped slaves in the North. She argues that these slaves, so demoralized by the impossibility of imagining political freedom, become actively complicit in the local scene of sexual savagery—actually sneaking "out of the way to give their masters free access to their wives and daughters" (44)—because sexuality is the only exchange value the slaves pseudo-possess. Jacobs takes the example of these relations of misrecognition and affective distortion and turns them back on the nation:

> One woman begged me to get a newspaper and read it over. She said
> her husband told her that the black people had sent word to the queen

of 'Merica that they were all slaves; that she didn't believe it, and went to Washington city to see the president about it. They quarrelled; she drew her sword upon him, and swore that he should help her to make them all free.

That poor ignorant woman thought that America was governed by a Queen, to whom the President was subordinate. I wish the President was subordinate to Queen Justice. (45)

Let us suppose it were true that the Queen of America came down to Washington and put the knife to the President's throat. Her strategy would be to refute his privilege, and that of citizens like him, to be above the sensational constraints of citizenship. The Queen of America educates him about his own body's boundaries with a cold tip of steel, and he emancipates the slaves. But Jacobs, never one to give the nation credit for even potentially recognizing its excesses, closes this anecdote not advocating violence on this individual President but subversively transferring the horizon of national identity to its illiterate citizens. She does this in order to counter what Donna Haraway has called "the informatics of domination":[20] using the misrecognitions of everyday life as the base of her national archive, Jacobs shows how national consciousness truly cuts a path through gossip, deliberate lies of the masters, the national press, the President of the United States who lives in Washington, the Queen of America who is dislocated from any specific capital, and the Queen of Justice who rules, perhaps in a universe parallel to that of the other Queen, and who has no national boundaries. In so creating this genealogy, this flow chart of power whose boundaries expand with every sentence written about America, Jacobs dislocates the nation from its intelligible forms. She opens up a space in which the national politics of corporeal identity becomes displayed on the monarchical body, and thus interferes with the fantasy norms of democratic abstraction; in so doing, she creates an American history so riddled with the misrecognitions of mass nationality that it is unthinkable in its typical form, as a narrative about sovereign subjects and their rational political representation. For no American president could be subordinate to any Queen—of America or of Justice. Bracketing that horizon of possibility, it becomes imperative to take up the scandalous promise of Jacobs's strategy, which is to exploit a fantasy of cutting across the space that doesn't exist, where abstract and corporeal citizenship come into contact not on the minoritized body but on *the body of the nation*.

It is this phantasmatic body that the Anita Hill/Clarence Thomas hearings brought to us in the delusional week before the vote. It was alluded to in the corporeality of Thomas himself: in his alleged exploitation of personal collegiality in federal workspaces; in the racist fantasies that he evoked to account for his victimization by Hill and on the Hill; in the aura of the minority stereotype black authority represents as a "token" on the Supreme Court. The national body is signified in Hill's own body as well, which displayed all of the decorums of bourgeois national polity while transgressing the veil between official and private behavior that grounds the erotic power of the state. Finally, the body of the nation was configured in the images of senators sitting in judgment and in the experts they brought in to testify to the law and to issues of "character" and "appearance."[21]

What I want to focus on is a displaced mediation of the national embodiment Hill and Thomas produced, in a television sitcom about the activities of a white and female-owned Southern business: the episode of *Designing Women* entitled "The Strange Case of Clarence and Anita" that aired shortly after the vote. In many ways, this episode reproduces the legitimacy of masculine speech over feminine embodiment in the political public sphere, most notably by contrasting news clips of speaking powerful men to clips that represent Hill only in tableau moments of demure silence before the Senate Judiciary Committee. Thus in one light the show's stifling of Hill reproduces a version of the imperial fantasy Gayatri Chakravorty Spivak describes, in which white women "heroically" save brown women from brown *and* white men. But while Hill herself demonstrated respect for national decorums and conservative ideologies of authority, her *case* substantially disrupted norms of embodiment of the national space and, indeed, revealed and produced disturbances in what counts as the national space itself.[22]

In this episode, the characters share private opinions about Thomas and Hill, along with painful personal memories of sexual harassment; but under the pressure of historical circumstance, the ordinary space of intimacy they share comes into contact with a media frenzy: tee shirts they buy at the mall that say "He did it" or "She lied" turn their bodies into billboards, which they flash angrily at each other; opinion polls that register the micro-fluctuations of "public sentiment" generate conversation about linguistic bias and motivate assertions of their own superiority to the numerically represented "people"; CNN, reinstated as the source of national identity, transforms the undifferentiated stream of opinions from all over the country into national data as "official" as that emanating from

Washington itself; the television set focuses the collective gaze, such that domestic and public spheres become merged, as do news and entertainment (the character Julia Sugarbaker, for example, suggests that Thomas belongs not on the Supreme Court, but in the National Repertory Theatre); and, in the climactic moment, a local television reporter tapes an interview with Suzanne Sugarbaker, a Thomas supporter, and Mary Jo Shively, a self-described "feminist," right in their living room. What's striking about the condensation of these media forms and forms of embodied political intimacy is how close so many different and overlapping American publics become—and in the context not of a soap opera but of a situation comedy that refuses, this time, to contain the "situation" within the frame of its half-hour. Judge Thomas and Professor Hill turn into "Clarence" and "Anita" in this situation, like TV neighbors having a domestic row; and the diverse, incorrect, passionate, and cynical range of opinions that flow in the room take on the status of personal and political gossip. Not just gossip about judges or senators without pants but about the intimate details of national identity.

At one point Mary Jo explodes in rage at Senator John Danforth's claim, shown on CNN, that Anita Hill suffered from a delusional disease in which she confused her own desire for power with the power of Thomas's sexual desire. Hearing Danforth's pleasure in this pop-psych diagnosis rouses Mary Jo to call his office in Washington. But she is frustrated in this desire because the line is busy. I myself wanted to call Washington during Hill's testimony or to testify in any way to my own banal/expert knowledge of the nonconsensual erotics of power we code as "harassment." The desire for contact sometimes took the phantasmatic form of a private letter to a senator, or one to a newspaper, sometimes a phone encounter, sometimes a fantasy that a reporter from the national news or "Nightline" would accost me randomly on the street and that my impromptu eloquence would instantly transport me to the televisual realm of a Robert Bork, where my voice and body would be loud, personal, national, and valorized.

In my view this ache to be an American diva was not about persuasion. It derived from a desire to enter a senator's body and to dominate it through an orifice he was incapable of fully closing, an ear or an eye. This intimate fantasy communication aimed to provoke sensations in him for which he was unprepared, those in that perverse space between empathy and pornography that Karen Sánchez-Eppler has isolated as constitutive of white Americans' interest in slaves, slave narratives, and other testimonials of the oppressed.[23] And in so appealing to a senator's authority over the terms in which I experience my (theoretically impossible) sexualized national being, I imagined making him so full and so sick with knowledge of what he has never experienced officially that he would lose, perhaps gratefully, his sensual innocence about—not the power of his own sexuality—but the sexuality of his own power, and . . .

This is where my fantasy of swearing out a female complaint would falter, stop knowing itself and what it wanted. The desire to go public, to exploit the dispersed media of national life, became my way of approximating the power of official nationality to dominate bodies—a motive which, in a relation of overidentification, I and many others had mapped onto Hill's majestic and courageous citizenship. It also suggested to me that the fantasy of addressing the nation directly, of violating the citizen's proper silence about the sensations of citizenship, is a fantasy that many Americans live.[24]

The horizon of critical possibility lies, however, not in orchestrating mass culture and mass nationality through the pseudo-immediacy of "electronic town halls," currently offered as a solution to the problem of recovering representational politics as a kind of collective decision making in the United States. Diva Citizenship reminds us that the legal tender of contemporary politics is no longer calibrated according to a gold standard of immediacy, authenticity, and rationality; the bodily distortions and sensual intimacy of national media degrade representations of political agency and therefore bleed into a space of surprise where political experiments in re-imagining agency and critical practice itself can be located, perhaps among the kinds of queenly gestures and impulses toward freedom I have recorded here.

To close: the final narrative image of *Designing Women*, which merges a radical embodied female citizenship with the aura of the star system. Annie Potts, who plays Mary Jo Shively, wears Bette Davis drag. Dixie Carter, who plays Julia Sugarbaker, masquerades as Joan Crawford. Having come directly from a dress rehearsal of a local theatrical adaptation of *What Ever Happened to Baby Jane?* they sit on the couch, exhausted. They are not exhausted from the rehearsal, but from the rage they have expended on what they call this "day of [national] infamy." Meanwhile, their friends slow dance the night away, like pre-adolescents at a slumber party. Bette asks Joan to dance with her. They get up and look at each other. "Who should lead?" asks Bette Davis. "Well, Bette," says Joan Crawford, "considering who we are, I think we both should."

And who are they? As Joan says to Bette in an earlier moment, "two of the toughest talking big-shouldered broads ever to live in this country."

Notes

Special thanks to Gordon Hutner, Miriam Hansen, and audiences at Rutgers, the University of North Carolina, Chicago State, and the MLA for insightful and impassioned critical responses.

1   The most incisive overview of the feminist, as opposed to class- and race-based, interpretations of the Hill-Thomas events is by Nancy Fraser, in "Sex, Lies, and the Public Sphere: Some Reflections on the Confirmation of Clarence Thomas," *Critical Inquiry* 18 (Spring 1992): 595–612. Fraser sees this event as a symptom of transformations of and contestations over definitions of public and private, publicity and privacy. See also Rosemary L. Bray, "Taking Sides Against Ourselves," *The New York Times Magazine*, 17 November 1991, 56–97. Two volumes have recently emerged that perform repeatedly the adjustments between gender, race, class, and ideological identity categories I am describing here, with much emphasis on the "problem" of articulating "gender" not only with "race" but also with the political movements that make these categories contested and unstable ones in the political public sphere. *The Black Scholar* has assembled *Court of Appeal: The Black Community Speaks Out on the Racial and Sexual Politics of Thomas vs. Hill*, ed. Robert Chrisman and Robert L. Allen (New York: Ballantine, 1992), from which the following essays are directly germane: Calvin Hernton, "Breaking Silences," 86–91; June Jordan, "Can I Get a Witness," 120–24; Barbara Smith, "Ain't Gonna Let Nobody Turn Me Around," 185–89; Rebecca Walker, "Becoming the Third Wave," 211–13. In Toni Morrison's edited volume, *Race-ing Justice, En-gendering Power: Essays on Anita Hill, Clarence Thomas, and the Construction of Social Reality* (New York: Pantheon, 1992), see especially Kimberlé Crenshaw, "Whose Story Is It Anyway? Feminist and Antiracist Appropriations of Anita Hill," 402–40; Christine Stansell, "White Feminists and Black Realities: The Politics of Authenticity," 251–68; Cornel West, "Black Leadership and the Pitfalls of Racial Reasoning," 390–401.

2   The word "experience" is important in the texts I am addressing and in the one I am writing here, and requires some explication. The category "experience" is not meant to refer to self-evident autobiographical data over which the experiencing person has control: the experience of being dominated, for example, is subjective, and therefore incompatible descriptions of it might engender legitimate contestation. But I take experience here more fundamentally to be something produced in the moment when an activity becomes framed as an event, such that the subject enters the empire of quotation

marks, anecdote, self-reflection, memory. More than a category of authenticity, "experience" in this context refers to something someone "has," in aggregate moments of self-estrangement. Jacobs, Harper, and Hill are aware of the unreliability of experience as data both in their own perceptions and in their drive to produce convincing evidence to buttress their arguments for social change or informed consciousness. For a strong summary of the current historicist argument over the evidentiary use of experience, see Joan W. Scott, "The Evidence of Experience," *Critical Inquiry* 17 (Summer 1991): 773–97; and, more critically, Mas'ud Zavarzadeh and Donald Morton, "Theory Pedagogy Politics: The Crisis of 'The Subject' in the Humanities," in their collection *Theory/Pedagogy/Politics: Texts for Change* (Urbana: Univ. of Illinois Press, 1991), 1–32; and Chris Weedon, "Post-Structuralist Feminist Practice," in the same volume, 47–63. The phrase "the poetry of the future" comes, famously, from Karl Marx, *The 18th Brumaire of Napoleon Bonaparte.*

3   Frances E. W. Harper, *Iola Leroy; or, Shadows Uplifted* (1892; rpt., College Park, Md.: McGrath, 1969), 115–16. All further references will be contained in the text.

4   Harriet A. Jacobs, *Incidents in the Life of a Slave Girl: Written by Herself* (edited by Lydia Maria Child), ed. Jean Fagan Yellin (Cambridge: Harvard Univ. Press, 1987).

5   Anita Hill, *New York Times*, 12 October 1991, sec. 1; 15 October 1991, sec. 1.

6   For the myriad transformations in legal theory and practical juridical norms regulating what counts as "injury" and "harm" to women, see *At the Boundaries of Law: Feminism and Legal Theory*, ed. Martha Albertson Fineman and Nancy Sweet Thomadsen (New York: Routledge, 1991); and *Feminist Legal Theory: Readings in Law and Gender*, ed. Katharine T. Bartlett and Roseanne Kennedy (Boulder: Westview, 1991).

7   There is a large outstanding bibliography on this subject. It includes Hazel Carby, *Reconstructing Womanhood* (New York: Oxford Univ. Press, 1987); P. Gabrielle Foreman, "The Spoken and the Silenced in *Incidents in the Life of a Slave Girl* and *Our Nig*," *Callaloo* 13 (Spring 1990): 313–24; Jane Gaines, "White Privilege and Looking Relations: Race and Gender in Feminist Film Theory," *Screen* 8 (Autumn 1988): 12–27; Hortense J. Spillers, "Notes on an Alternative Model—Neither/Nor," in *The Difference Within: Feminism and Critical Theory*, ed. Elizabeth Meese and Alice Parker (Philadelphia: John Benjamins, 1989), 165–87 and "Mama's Baby, Papa's Maybe: An American Grammar Book," *Diacritics* 17 (Summer 1987): 65–81.

8   See Valerie Smith, "'Loopholes of Retreat': Architecture and Ideology in Harriet Jacobs's *Incidents in the Life of a Slave Girl*," in *Reading Black, Reading Feminist*, ed. Henry Louis Gates Jr. (New York: Meridian, 1990), 212–26.

9   See Jean Fagan Yellin, "*Written by Herself*: Harriet Jacobs's Slave Narrative," *American Literature* 53 (1981): 479–86.

10 I adapt this notion of "theft" from Harryette Mullen's work on orality and writing in *Incidents in the Life of a Slave Girl*. See "Runaway Tongue: Resistant Orality in *Uncle Tom's Cabin, Our Nig, Incidents in the Life of a Slave Girl*, and *Beloved*," in *The Culture of Sentiment: Race, Gender, and Sentimentality in Nineteenth-Century America*, ed. Shirley Samuels (New York: Oxford Univ. Press, 1992), 244–64.

11 On the counternational politics of gender and kinship in *Incidents*, see Spillers, "Mama's Baby, Papa's Maybe."

12 To place *Iola Leroy* in the context of Harper's complex political activities, see Carby, *Reconstructing Womanhood*, 63–94. Carby's chapter on Harper emphasizes the race/gender axis of her concerns, and provides crucial support to my thinking about nationality. See also Frances Smith Foster's Introduction to Frances Ellen Watkins Harper, *A Brighter Coming Day: A Frances Ellen Watkins Harper Reader* (New York: Feminist Press, 1990), 3–40.

13 Frances Ellen Watkins Harper, "Duty to Dependent Races," in *Black Women in Nineteenth-Century American Life: Their Words, Their Thoughts, Their Feelings*, ed. Bert James Loewenberg and Ruth Bogin (1891; rpt., University Park: Pennsylvania State Univ. Press, 1976), 245.

14 Harper, *A Brighter Coming Day*, 218.

15 The argument that nationality can overcome the fractures of race operates throughout Harper's speeches and poems as well. Perhaps the most condensed and eloquent of these was delivered at the Columbian Exposition. See "Woman's Political Future," in *The World's Congress of Representative Women*, ed. May Wright Sewall (Chicago: Rand, McNally, 1894), 433–38.

16 Jürgen Habermas, *The Structural Transformation of the Public Sphere: An Inquiry into a Category of Bourgeois Society*, trans. Thomas Burger (Cambridge: Harvard Univ. Press, 1989), 31–43; Joan B. Landes, *Women and the Public Sphere in the Age of the French Revolution* (Ithaca: Cornell Univ. Press, 1988), 22–31.

17 Donna Haraway, "A Manifesto for Cyborgs," in *Simians, Cyborgs, and Women: The Reinvention of Nature* (New York: Routledge, 1991), 162; bell hooks, "Third World Diva Girls," in *Yearning: Race, Gender, and Cultural Politics* (Boston: South End, 1990), 89–102; Wayne Koestenbaum, "The Codes of Diva Conflict," chap. 3 of *The Queen's Throat: Opera, Homosexuality, and the Mystery of Desire* (New York: Poseidon, 1993). See also Laura Kipnis, "(Male) Desire and (Female) Disgust: Reading *Hustler*," in *Cultural Studies*, ed. Lawrence Grossberg, Cary Nelson, and Paula Treichler (New York: Routledge, 1992), 373–91; Miriam Hansen, "The Return of Babylon: Rudolph Valentino and Female Spectatorship (1921–1926)," part 3 of *Babel and Babylon: Spectatorship in American Silent Film* (Cambridge: Harvard Univ. Press, 1991); Andrew Ross, *No Respect* (New York: Routledge, 1989);

Carole-Anne Tyler, "Boys Will Be Girls: The Politics of Gay Drag," in *Inside/ Out: Lesbian Theories, Gay Theories* (New York: Routledge, 1991), 32–71; and Patricia J. Williams, "A Rare Case Study of Muleheadedness and Men," in Morrison, *Race-ing Justice, En-gendering Power*, 159–71.

18 Barry Weller, "The Royal Slave and the Prestige of Origins," *Kenyon Review* 14 (Summer 1992): 65–78.

19 I focus here on the analogy Harper seems to make between Esther's complicated ethnic masquerade and Marie's racial one, and on the conditions for political speech that ensued. The *Book of Esther* as a whole tells a far more complex story. On the one hand, it might have provided Harper, and us, with a less patriarchalized model of feminine power: Queen Vashti, whose refusal to display her royal beauty to a banquet of drunken courtiers provoked Elizabeth Cady Stanton's *The Woman's Bible* to name her "the first woman recorded whose self-respect and courage enabled her to act contrary to the will of her husband. . . . [in] the first exhibition of individual sovereignty of woman on record. . . . true to the Divine aspirations of her nature" (86–88). On the other hand, the *Book of Esther* is a story about holocausts, a Jewish one averted and a Macedonian one revengefully executed by the Jews themselves (Elizabeth Cady Stanton and the Revising Committee, *The Woman's Bible* [1898; rpt., Seattle: Coalition Task Force on Women and Religion, 1974]).

20 Haraway, 161.

21 See especially Waneema Lubiano, "Black Ladies, Welfare Queens, and State Minstrels: Ideological War by Narrative Means," in Morrison, 321–63.

22 The original sentence, describing the mentality of "imperialist subject-production," is "White men are saving brown women from brown men" (Gayatri Chakravorty Spivak, "Can the Subaltern Speak?" in *Marxism and the Interpretation of Culture* [Urbana: Univ. of Illinois Press, 1988], 296).

23 Karen Sánchez-Eppler, "Bodily Bonds: The Intersecting Rhetorics of Feminism and Abolition," *Representations* 24 (Fall 1988): 28–59.

24 The fantasy of diminishing the scale of America to make the nation a place one might encounter has a long history in American letters. See Lauren Berlant, *The Anatomy of National Fantasy: Hawthorne, Utopia, and Everyday Life* (Chicago: Univ. of Chicago Press, 1991); Jody Berland, "Angels Dancing: Cultural Technologies and the Production of Space," in Grossberg, Nelson, and Treichler, 39–55; and John Caughie, "Playing at Being American," *Logics of Television: Essays in Cultural Criticism*, ed. Patricia Mellencamp (Bloomington: Indiana Univ. Press, 1990), 44–58.

**Karla F. C.   The Body Politic
Holloway**

There was precedent, two hundred years earlier, for Professor Anita Hill's 1991 testimony before the skeptical members of the United States Senate Judiciary Committee. Although Phillis Wheatley was only a teenager in 1772, when she sat in a New England courthouse before her Boston jury, there are striking visual parallels between the two scenes that encourage a comparison. The austere chambers of law and politics housed both events. Professor Hill was separated from her interlocutors by a strip of federal green cloth that symbolized the judiciary. It is my guess that because green was a common draping for the courtroom tables of eighteenth-century New England, a similar piece of fabric also separated Phillis Wheatley from her panel of judges. In addition to the likely visual parallels, skepticism, outright disbelief, and implied derision surrounded both events, and the powerful presence of the judiciary stalked both the margins and the centers.

Thomas Hutchinson, the governor of the Boston colony, led the inquisition of Wheatley, "a young Negro girl." She had had the audacity to claim she was the author of a thin volume of poems—that they had been, as the title claimed, "written by herself." Her examination, "by some of the best judges," would finally lead to their attestation that she had indeed been the source of the words in her book.[1]

Two centuries later, law professor Anita Hill would also find herself nearly encircled by a panel of white males who would listen to her assert the legitimacy of her words. Legitimacy in Hill's case was more a matter of accuracy than of authorship. Hill's testimony before a gathering of senators who would decide on the viability of Judge Clarence Thomas's candidacy for a position on the Supreme Court was to verify both the words she had submitted on a sworn affidavit and the experiences those words described. Her character, intellect, and spirit were derisively abused during that hearing. We can imagine that similar emotional devastation was Wheatley's experience in the 1772 hearings. Any private identity Anita Hill had prior to those hearings would be reinvented by the public rehearsal of her testimony and the senators' public and political posturing.[2]

In both cases words—spoken and written—were at the center of a conflict over credibility, scripting, as it were, a rhetorical parallelism that united the two events. Both women's testimony was labeled incredible, and both women attempted a negotiation of racial and gender politics within which neither had a stable or legitimized presence. Anita Hill's claim of sexual harassment was certainly different in kind, but not in degree, from Phillis Wheatley's claim to authorship. The material of both events was a visual transliteration that recalls the simulation Baudrillard notes as the *desert of the real itself.* Baudrillard argues that the simulation is a substitution for the real—a hyperreal cover-up of a deserted territory where the actual once reigned. Legislative language and processes intended to make the democratic ideal real and available to a common U.S. populace are the "disappeared" reality that the simulation has replaced. The senatorial interrogation of Hill and the examination of Wheatley allowed justice to vanish behind the veil of their dark bodies, which shadowed any presence other than their own. In these cases the territory of justice's blind geography was displaced by the simulacrum's dark and female visual assault. This assault challenged the discursive historico-cultural ground of United States politics. The legitimacy of both women's testimony was determined in courts of public and political opinion that had prejudged the likelihood of their credibility on the basis of their gender and ethnicity. In a fair forum, the "external" evidence confronting the judges—Wheatley's and Hill's female bodies and their African color—would have been absolutely irrelevant; but because of the racist and sexist history of cultural politics in the United States, we know that gender and color were considered absolutely essential factors and clearly relevant to the witnesses' credibility.

Both events led to a crisis of identity within the body politic. The gendered and ethnic identities of the white male judges gave them titular power and control over these hearings. How they thought about and behaved toward black women created and enforced the cultural politics of their eras. These judicial bodies were supposed to behave in a manner consistent with the ethical codes of jurisprudence—which call for a blind justice, unaffected by privately held notions of culturally invested superiority. However, the conflict of representation that the black and female bodies would initiate challenged notions of judicial restraint. This confusion of subject and object irrevocably compromised the processes.

The ethical issues that the Senate panel was gathered to debate hinged directly upon the ethnicity of those who testified before it.[3] The ethical puzzle that Wheatley and Hill placed before their white examiners challenged these men's ability to visualize the witnesses' claims and words without regard to ethnicity. These panels had to judge in a color-blind way by rendering the identities of Wheatley and Hill invisible and their claims visible. It was a catch-22 position. The 1772 jury admitted by its presence that the only reason they had gathered was that Phillis Wheatley was an African woman. The 1991 jury might as well have confessed the same.

In addition to the specular features of these encounters, the place that language occupies within both events is of considerable interpretive significance. Language offers itself as a code by which we might interrogate with some consistency the territorial coordinates of these visual events. Anita Hill's testimony claimed sexual misconduct by her former employer. It was a claim that immediately compromised the males of the Senate Judiciary because it created a conflict between privately gendered empathies and public political postures. It may be, however, that if we look closely at the conduct of these linguistic codes we will find that the sworn affidavit and the volume of poetry—the texts of these two events—behaved in similar ways. Both were written documents brought to an oral forum. Word as script and word as voice were placed in a central position within the text of these events. The situation was inherently problematic, because both Hill's and Wheatley's testimony came from black women, and theirs were the very bodies that political and legal systems in the United States had worked hard to render passive and silent. Consider, for a moment, how this reality contradicts what Lyotard describes as a narrative of freedom, wherein the State receives its legitimacy not from itself, but from the people. The status of *person*hood is immediately made unstable by the bodies of these women. One escaped only by territorial accident the legislative label of slave (although the geographical border could not erase her body's politics). The other's personhood was assaulted—not confirmed—by the State. Legitimacy for Hill was not the outcome of this encounter with the State. The State was instead an antagonistic provocateur.

If Hill and Wheatley could face each other, we might imagine their encounter as a mirrored contemplation. A mirror would indicate the self-reflective potential within their mutual gaze. And it would allow us to speculate on the nature of the relationship I am interrogating here, between private identities and public reconstructions of those identities within the racial and gendered frames of American cultural history. For black women, a mirrored image encourages confrontation with the racialized and sexualized image that the United States has chosen as its exotic Other. Without this reflective confrontation, black women's linguistic codes—as spoken or written texts—exist without the requisite attention to or acknowledgment of the socially constructed Other that grounds the realities of racism and sexism. Absent the mirrored image, language is blind to the other-identified self, and this critical, albeit displaced, awareness has no opportunity to inform language. It's a socially blind conversation—one in which black women engage at considerable risk.

I've chosen this mirrored speculation as a provocative metaphor for my discussion because the mirror both engages and disrupts and because identity politics never fails to inscribe its biotext onto a specular event. Between Anita Hill and Phillis Wheatley, there is no ideal coextensivity in the specular (the phrase is Baudrillard's); but there is instead something akin to a liquidation of essentials producing not the miniaturizations of Baudrillard's project but what I will discuss as mimetic disorientation.

This essay will explore the literary representation of the black woman's body as it recognizes its publicly constructed figuration and as it makes this recognition a moment of active linguistic engagement. My thesis will consider the consequences of this location in self as a process that foregrounds sexual differences—what Hélène Cixous calls *reparage en soi*. It's my sense that this disruptive process contributes to the image's perversion (or distortion) and that the language which scripts this recognition and frames the event captures the critical moments of the visual disorientation. Finally, in these juridical moments especially, the way in which the spoken text of a female's experience does or does not embody a perception of physical identity, as it is negotiated by the often dangerous and diminishing cultural politics of the era, becomes a textual starting point.

Close examination of the literature of twentieth-century African American women writers makes clear the self-reflective ways in which black women's bodies metaphorically represent the conflicted presence of gender and race within America's cultural history. In a consistent fashion, narrative passages in these works construct some configuration of the body politic's culturally enforced stereotypes. Literary representations become places where the consequences of this shift from the public domain of cultural and social history to the private domains of the black woman's body are linguistically negotiated. Black women writers have contextualized the experience of recognition through the linguistic strategies of their narratives. However creative and imaginative the twentieth-century characterizations of black women have become, the one factor that continues to mediate intertextually, and that collects these works into a tradition, is the conduct of their words *within* the codes of the narratives that are rehearsed by black women's bodies.

Paradoxically, in a contemporary literature that is often discussed critically in terms of the crisis of psychological and/or spiritual identity, the essential feature in this struggle is actually quite superficial —it is black women's bodies—not their selves. The tragic loneliness these women consistently face as they stand before judges—sometimes white, but sometimes black; sometimes male, but sometimes female — is heart-wrenching. I focus on the mirrored image as a figurative and literal moment that duplicates the trauma imposed by racism and sexism. This shifting gaze—targeting blackness or femaleness or both— is a consistently disabling and often tragically disfiguring assault. The mirrored image reveals to these women their contradictory identities as *blackwomen*—contradictory because the design of prejudice is to reduce identity to a simplifying visual. Blackwomen challenge the simplemindedness of prejudice. Their black and female bodies complicate the visual image. A destructive confusion results from this complication, and its perverse consequence powerfully enables the already potent destructiveness of racism and sexism. Blackwomen constantly cross racial and gendered boundaries; their bodies visually assault the systems designed to identify neatly and easily the unempowered. Sexism alone targets women. Racism's targets are the ethnic Other. Blackwomen deconstruct the formal stability of those prejudices and challenge the politically and socially legislated impermeability of those boundaries.

As varied as their stories are, it seems that at some point most African American women writers force their female characters to confront the confounding physical reality presented by their black and female bodies.

This moment of confrontation is so critical to black women's psyches, and so frequently rehearsed in contemporary literature, that it argues for a cultural and gendered identity in this particular framing of story.

> "No wonder," she said at last. . . . "No wonder. . . . Look at how I look."—Toni Morrison, *Song of Solomon*

Regardless of a black female character's stature in her community or her place within a relationship, there comes an essential moment when she acknowledges that one of the elements out of (her) control is purely physical. How she looks—the impact of her color and gender on whatever situation she confronts—becomes a linguistic configuration of "informed consent," an acknowledgment that reconfigures the moment of interpretive significance as the character moves from private and passive anguish to a public and active response. When she sees herself—her body—as others see her, the confrontational gaze is both dark and clear. Because this moment of vision is often enabled by a mirror, the character vibrantly enacts both clauses of the scriptural passage "Now we see as through a glass, darkly; but then face to face."

In Toni Morrison's *Song of Solomon*, Hagar's moment of body-discovery throws her into a panic of frenzied and pitiful shopping to correct the image she understands to be the barrier to Milkman's love.[4] Her anguish is palpable as she moves from store to store in a frenetic search that "could not let go until the energy and busyness culminated a beauty that would dazzle him." At home, she strips herself naked, garnishes herself with every brand-name cosmetic imaginable, and covers her face with "sunny glow," "Mango tango," and "baby clear sky light." Ultimately, Hagar is forced to the realization that her enterprise will not effect the change she feels is essential. Her melancholy over this discovery eventually destroys her, and death is the only silence Hagar can bear.

Now, an unsympathetic reader may see her action as the ultimate "shop-'til-you-drop" episode; however, I find a more resonant and thoughtful comparison in a poem by Dudley Randall, "Ballad of Birmingham."[5] In Randall's poem, a mother who dresses her child for Sunday school—"she has combed and brushed the nightdark hair,/ and bathed rose petal sweet"—subtextually dresses the dead body of this child who will be killed in a bomb blast during the morning's services. Reba and Pilate, too, have seen their child's final dressing. Nothing is left for them but her connection to her mother and grandmother: "'My baby girl.' Moving back down the aisle, she told each face turned toward her the same piece of news. 'My baby girl. . . . ' Conversationally she spoke, identifying Hagar, selecting her away from everybody else in the world who had died" (322).

If we recall Hélène Cixous's explication of equivoice (a voice mixed with milk), we've an analogy that makes clear the privilege of the feminine voice in women's writing. Up to this point in the story, Hagar's behavior has been pathetically ineffective. She could do little to force her cousin Milkman to return the wildly possessive love she felt for him. Her only moment of real action—the frenzied search through the stores for the right look, the one that would change her body enough so that Milkman could love her—came immediately after a telling glimpse in a mirror. The issue for me is not whether her gaze was sane. Instead, I want to indicate only that this gaze and the words it elicited preceded the one moment of significant, self-initiated behavior in her life, and that this behavior resulted in her death. Prior to this moment, image and language were detached, so consciousness was only partial and speech was diminished by this lack. Cixous argues that the privilege of voice in women's writing defends the logic of the author's discourse with her body—here paral leled by the mother's voice—in a metaphorical association that makes her "flesh speak true."

In contemporary black women's literature this fleshly moment of facing foregrounds the physical, giving narrative substance to Roland Barthes's argument that the text is an anagram, irreducible to the physiologic needs of an essentially erotic body. The characters' critically significant encounters with their black and female bodies determine the conduct of the narrative as it brings speech to a cultural awareness of the body it represents. It illustrates and anticipates the reader's voyeuristic complicity in these episodes, whose physical empowerment provokes a climactic (and my word choice is absolutely intentional) resolution.

Consider Janie in Hurston's *Their Eyes Were Watching God*.[6] After Jody dies, humiliated by Janie's withering judgment of his masculinity (or lack thereof),[7] Janie goes to a bedroom mirror where she "starched and ironed her face and came set in the funeral behind her veil" (136). Tea Cake forces her away from her dim, starched gaze and prompts her to "go tuh de lookin glass" (157) where she takes "a good look at her mouth, eyes and hair" (160). Her glimpse initiates "the beginning of things" (163)— the relationship with Tea Cake that forces this story's conclusion.[8]

And, in Gloria Naylor's *Linden Hills*, Willa Nedeed struggles desperately for a privilege of recognition similar to Janie's. She knows the source of her incarceration in a basement lies somehow within her own body, but deprived of light and sense for so long, she can no longer trust her touch: "She reached her hand up and began to touch her own face, her fingers running tentatively across the cheeks and mouth. . . . She tried to place the curves and planes, the shape of the jutting cheekbones and texture of her hair. . . . But it was difficult to keep it all in position. When she returned with the curve of her ear, the chin had shifted and melted up toward the mouth; the nose dissolved before she could bring back the lips."[9] Frustrated, "she . . . closed her eyes and used both hands, *trying to form a mirror* between her fingers, the darkness, and memory—but she needed to be sure." Willa's lack of surety makes her improvise a mirror using the shiny surface of an aluminum pot: "Holding the pot as still as she could, she found that an image would form . . . a dim silhouette. Rimmed by light, there was the outline of her hair, the shape of the chin . . . the profile of her nose and lips. . . . No doubt remained—she was there" (267–68). Once she was sure, "now that she had actually seen and accepted reality . . . she could rebuild" (268). This event immediately precedes the "December 24th" section of Naylor's novel where the two planes of its existence, the submerged and the surface, meet in a dramatic and fiery conclusion. Willa's words frame the moment that will fracture the fragile generations of the Nedeed clan: "Luther . . . your son is dead" (299).

Black women's literatures indicate ways in which we must critically interrogate the relatively orthodox Western theories of progressive and culturally austere stages of reflection (Lacan) as well as those who would suggest that women hold responsibility for framing the patriarchal unconscious (Mulvey). When black women in literature face themselves, the immediate panic the reflection provokes elides the luxury of a progression through neatly patterned stages. It also gives resonance and depth to the comparatively meager notion of a decisive moment. Also, black women's bodies do not frame issues of law and language for any patriarchal order, as Laura Mulvey would argue, since they exist chaotically—outside of order and despite the color-blind democratic equity promised in legal language.

> There is no respect or wonder for her silence.—Patricia Williams's reflection on the rape of Tawana Brawley

Legal scholar Patricia Williams must have an intimate understanding of Willa Nedeed's fear of dismemberment. Gloria Naylor's imaginative rendering of Willa's fear of fracture and invisibility, cited in the section from *Linden Hills* quoted above, is echoed in Williams's words from *The Alchemy of Race and Rights*: "There are moments in my life when I feel as though a part of me is missing. Those are the times when my skin becomes gummy as clay and my nose slides around on my face and my eyes drip down to my chin. I have to close my eyes at such times and remember myself. . . . When all else fails, I reach for a mirror and stare myself down until the features reassemble themselves" (229).[10] Lacan argues that dreaming during especially stressful times makes manifest a fragmented body—a "fragilization" that defines the anatomy of phantasy.[11] However, Patricia Williams's experience is not a dream—it's a daytime reality. For black women, the kind of stress Lacan associates with the unconscious is not buried at all. In fact, such episodes do not merely express the anatomy of imaginative (phantasmagoric) discourse, they are descriptive as well of the dismembering nature of racism, which some would argue also reaches eerily into the realm of the fantastic.

Williams makes an impassioned plea to be recognized, culminating in one instance in her hissed rebuke to a gang of white male athletes who jostled and pushed her off of what should have been their common ground (a sidewalk): "Don't I exist for you? See me! And deflect, godammit!" Her reprimand allows her to "pursue her way, *manumitted back into silence*" (235, 236). The intentional allusion to manumission recalls the legal fiction of black women's rights in the United States.

Our bodies—black and female—have historically constituted both implicit and explicit contracts within our legal, political, and cultural systems. These contractual identities have been complicated by the tension that comes from (enforced) silence and have consequently been exploited by our vocal constraint. In *The Color Purple*, Alice Walker's Celie is told upfront, on page 1, in the first line and in italics: "*You better not never tell nobody but God.*"[12] Williams reminds her reader that commercial transactions work in similarly confining ways, constraining "the lively involvement of [contractual] signatories by positioning enforcement in such a way that parties find themselves in a passive relationship to a document" (224). Recall that her rebuke was "hissed," not shouted.

The positions of the black and female body in literature and in contemporary cultural politics reinforce notions of constraint and the conflicted nature of our silence. Even some who believed Anita Hill's testimony found her guilty of speech: she should have kept quiet, they argued, rather than tell on a black man and fracture the fragile unity of the African

American community. Similar allegations met Robin Givens and Desiree Washington—both victims of fighter Mike Tyson's explosive violence and both accused of having some motive other than truth-telling in their public recitations of his abuse. In contrast, Tawana Brawley, a fifteen-year-old black girl who was found nearly naked, streaked with feces, burned and otherwise brutally abused, has never spoken out about her trauma. The price of her silence has been a criminal conspiracy to call into question the facts of her appearance.[13] Words like "seemingly," "allegedly," and "contradictory" began to surround this child. Others who spoke for her— her mother, her lawyers, her counselors—were subjected to an abusive media attack on their credibility. But Tawana Brawley never spoke of her kidnapping "on the record," perhaps and understandably further and more deeply traumatized into silence by the spectacle of what was happening around her. Speaking out is a dangerous practice for black women.

In literature we understand the correctness of this interpretation, because it is not until silence is broken and the body is activated and acknowledged that stasis is interrupted. Willa Nedeed ascends from her basement, Hagar resolves the dilemma of her life, Janie moves from the storeroom to the porch, and Celie discovers *jouissance* through body and self as the intimate reward of self-seduction. However, there is no necessary narrative consonance in these evocative moments.

Morrison's Pecola (*The Bluest Eye*) has less success fighting the fracture of racism and abuse. Her effort to escape her parents' horrific battles are directed toward invisibility and fracture, not away from it. " 'Please, God,' she whispered. . . . 'Please make me disappear'. . . . Little parts of her body faded away. . . . Her fingers . . . her arms . . . her feet. . . . The face was hard. . . . Only her tight, tight eyes were left. They were always left" (39). Pecola sat "long hours . . . looking in the mirror, trying to discover the secret of the ugliness".[14] We might easily bring Lacan's notion of fragilization as an aspect of the schizoid into our critical perspective as we gaze at Pecola's gaze. Fracture and invisibility were her inheritance, and her silence is not overcome by her prayer. Instead, an inverted use of the mirrored and voiced metaphors of empowerment, activation, and self-recognition forces Pecola into a muddled and mad silence where no one ever speaks to her and where "her inarticulateness made us believe we were eloquent" (159). Pecola Breedlove is Tawana Brawley's literary sister.

In contrast to the failed voices of Tawana and Pecola, Walker's Celie does reap benefits from her mirrored gaze and her articulation of its vision. When Celie looks at her "naked self in the looking glass," the powerfully etched contrasts of her black and female body confront her gaze. "My hair is short and kinky. . . . My skin dark. My nose just a nose. My lips just lips. My body just any woman's body going through the changes of age." Note that Celie's specular moment is inscribed by her voice. The narrative continues, "I talk to myself a lot, standing in front of the mirror" (220). An earlier scene of Celie's mirrored empowerment occurs at Shug's initiation and illustrates the critical dimensions of my argument that the "site" of women's bodies is a negotiated space of exchange, confrontation, and positionality: "Here, take this mirror and go look at yourself down there. . . . I stand there with the mirror. . . . I lie back on the bed and haul up my dress. Yank down my bloomers. Stick the looking glass tween my legs . . . my pussy lips be black . . . inside look like a wet rose. . . . I haul up my dress and look at my titties. . . . I touch it with my finger. A little shiver go through me. . . . just enough to tell me this the right button to mash" (69, 70). As she experiments with masturbation for the first time, this sensual moment gives Celie her first experience with sexual pleasure. The mirror displaces the phallus here, although the descriptive context encourages its trace on the narrative— she "stick[s]" it between her legs. It's a moment that supports those who take issue with Lacan's privileging the phallus as a governing signifier and that not only makes clear the way in which the failure to consider race and class undermines theory but also illustrates what Anthony Appiah labels theory's often meager evidential terrain. In this instance, the phallic privilege loses its structure (I consciously signify on the signifier), because rather than the mirror's thrust bringing any gendered identity to this moment, Celie's voice—her language—and its engagement with the language of her body inscribe the occasion. In each of these structures (I take, I stand, I lie, I haul, I stick), Walker avoids copulative verbs— instantiating an indirect but nevertheless poignant displacement of the phallus as signifier. Consequently, this event does not engage *jouissance* beyond the phallus (Lacan); it is instead *jouissance* despite the phallus. The shiver *tells* Celie that she's found the right spot. Her words have empowering substance. This desire—not *for* the Other but *as* the Other— allows her to be so generously disposed toward Shug for encouraging her to discover her sensuality that she gives Shug permission—she *tells* her she can sleep with Mister: "'I don't care if you sleep with him,' I *say*. Shug take me at my word. I take me at my word too." Her word and her body become her own, and the masturbatory release from fingering her "little button" and stroking her "titties" give her sexual pleasure. There is an implicit contractual exchange here. Her body, commodified, is the exchangeable item. Its commercial intimacy is a value she will claim rather than lose, as most diasporan women do. The critical difference is one of control and initiative—she has negotiated this contract. The pleasure she has learned to extract from her body is paired with the empowerment of her words.

I want to underscore that this trajectory is not consistent or linear. The argument I make in *Moorings and Metaphors*—that fracture and shift articulate the spiraling narratives of black women's literatures—is evidenced in the mirror episodes discussed here.[15] In these situations, the mirror's connection to voice is severed when the socio-political glare across the gaze successfully disrupts the effort that language makes to negotiate the space of its vision.

In American culture, and in the imaginative representations of that culture in literature, our compromised environments often allow publicly constructed racial and sexual identities to supersede private consciousness. The result may be a negative dialectic—an "enabled" activity (or language) that dangerously rehearses the dynamics of racism and sexism. We saw this dialectic in practice when Anita Hill faced the fourteen senators of the Judiciary Committee. With little difficulty, we suspect this discourse was also a factor in the Wheatley hearings of 1772. Angela Davis reminds us of the pervasiveness of the abuse of black women in American history: "Throughout Afro-American women's economic history sexual abuse has been perceived as an occupational hazard. In slavery, Black women's bodies were considered to be accessible at all times to the slave-master. In 'freedom' there is ample documentation that as maids and washerwomen, Black women have been repeatedly the victims of sexual assault."[16] Davis's recitation of abuse leads a critical reader to question the motivation of Wheatley's slavemaster. Why would he come to the impassioned defense of his seventeen-year-old house slave? Davis suggests that we remember the direct relationship of sexual violence "as it is mediated by racial, class, and governmental violence and power" (47). The positions of Wheatley and Hill—enslaved and employed by powerful white men and then surrounded in *oral* (I *do* intend this double-entendre) examination by a gathered body politic—gain a disturbing dimension.

The intersections formed by the plurality of texts that script themselves onto our contemporary politics in various ways are impressive: Anita and Phillis; Hagar, Celie, and Willa Nedeed; Desiree, Robin, and

Tawana; Julie Dash's Yellow Mary and Trula from *Daughters of the Dust* and Audre Lorde's autobiographical inscription of *Zami*—a West Indian word for women who work together as friends and lovers. All subvert and challenge the cultural biotext of legislative racism. These women, both fictive and compellingly real, have insisted themselves into the subject position in cultural theories of blackwomen's identities. Essential and actual images within our public and private cultures oblige our attention to women who rap or who are our culture's most abused objects: women and their children; women whose dying and disease from AIDS and madness or the madness that is AIDS threatens the seeming equilibrium of our spiritual conscience; and women whose bodies are their texts. Recall that in 1993, Pennsylvania law professor Lani Guinier was not even allowed to speak before the Senate Judiciary Committee in defense of her troubled nomination to a post in the Justice Department. Not to be similarly silenced, and rather than run the risk of losing control over their image-making power, the media fixed us on her body (especially her hair) and grotesquely manipulated her words out of their contexts in her legal writings. These writings (all we had as evidence of her speech) were so distorted and her image so caricatured—with her hair as the identifying mark—that rescuing the two (language and body) was a hopeless task that even her appearance on Ted Koppel's *Nightline* could not accomplish.

The metaphor of the mirrored body—the self facing its blackness and femaleness by gazing at the image seen by others—gains dimensionality when it reneges on the contractual silence of its politicized position. Once it gives voice and language to its story from the discrete positionality that cultural and gender politics have enforced within the dimensions of our literary and cultural histories, the code of silence is broken. As the contemporary literature of African American writers provocatively indicates, and as the historical and contemporary experiences of African American women have consistently documented, the cost of voice remains high. In the imaginative vision these spaces are negotiated with great variety and great skill by the diverse and courageous bodies of black women who live the fictive legacy of America's cultural politics.

Notes

1   Eighteen white men—churchmen, merchants, politicians, the governor and lieutenant governor among them—gathered for this examination of Wheat-

Karla F. C. Holloway

ley. They described themselves as "some of the best judges" in the preface to her volume. Their "Attestation" assured the world that "Phillis, . . . brought an uncultivated Barbarian from Africa," had authored the poems in the book (*Phillis Wheatley: Poems on Various Subjects* [New York, 1985], vii).

2   The flag-waving, anti-intellectual, and knee-jerk support accorded David Brock's *The Real Anita Hill: The Untold Story* (New York: Free Press, 1993) by the conservative right (Rush Limbaugh and Tony Brown are two embarrassingly public examples) attests to the fearful hysteria Hill's bravery aroused. In personal correspondence, my colleague Cathy Davidson asks a series of relevant and hard-hitting questions about this book: "Why would anyone feel compelled to trash a witness? To write a whole book about her? And why would it become a bestseller?" The sub-text of this repulsive book is clearly articulated in Brock's (now publicly retracted) one-liner—that Hill is "a little nutty and a little slutty." The real story is preserved on video. It clearly indicates that in the face of the cameras and the white males of the Senate Judiciary Committee, Hill's bravery, articulateness, intelligence, honesty, unwavering dignity, and heroism had to be deconstructed.

3   The fact of color certainly did not escape the text of the hearing. Thomas himself understood it to "play to the worst stereotypes about black men in this country." Commentators evoked legions of history's black women so that the legacy of color was not lost on the reading public. Commentator Nancy Gibbs called Hill "the poised daughter of so many [abused] generations of black women," naming her as the legatee of Harriet Tubman, Sojourner Truth, and Rosa Parks ("An Ugly Circus," *Time*, 21 October 1991, 35.) In the same issue, columnist Jack White recalled sexist reactions to Alice Walker when *The Color Purple* became a national phenomenon and to the incredulity that met Tawana Brawley's statements. White noted that "black women's complaints about sexist behavior are taken even less seriously than white women's" ("The Stereotyping of Race," 66). Sidney Blumenthal wondered aloud whether then President Bush's "trump card on race" (Clarence Thomas) could be played "when the game is sexual politics" ("The Drifter," *The New Republic*, 11 November 1991, 24).

4   Toni Morrison, *Song of Solomon* (New York: Signet, 1977). All citations will be from this edition.

5   Dudley Randall, "Ballad of Birmingham," in *Understanding the New Black Poetry*, ed. Stephen Henderson (New York: Morrow, 1973), 233.

6   Zora Neale Hurston, *Their Eyes Were Watching God* (1937; rpt. Urbana: Univ. of Illinois Press, 1978).

7   In Hurston's novel, Janie says to her dying husband, "When you pull down yo' britches, you look lak de change uh life" (123).

8   For an extended discussion of the mirror's imagery and its intimate connection to voice in this book, see Karla Holloway, "Holy Heat: Rituals of the Spirit in Hurston's *Their Eyes Were Watching God*," *Journal of Religion and Literature* 23 (Autumn 1991): 127–41.

9   Gloria Naylor, *Linden Hills* (New York: Penguin, 1985), 267. Parenthetical page references are to this edition.

10 Patricia Williams, *The Alchemy of Race and Rights* (Cambridge: Harvard Univ. Press, 1991), 229.

11 Jacques Lacan, "The Mirror Stage," in *A Critical and Cultural Theory Reader*, ed. Antony Easthope and Kate McGowen. (Toronto: Univ. of Toronto Press, 1992), 74.

12 Alice Walker, *The Color Purple* (New York: Harcourt Brace Jovanovich, 1982), 3. Parenthetical page references are to this edition.

13 An especially clear-sighted discussion of this incident can be found in the chapter "Mirrors and Windows" in Williams's *Alchemy*. See esp. 169–78. I am indebted here to Williams's powerful discussion of Tawana Brawley's trauma.

14 Toni Morrison, *The Bluest Eye* (New York: Washington Square Press, 1970), 39.

15 See Karla Holloway, *Moorings and Metaphors: Figures of Culture and Gender in Black Women's Literature* (New Brunswick: Rutgers Univ. Press, 1992), esp. chapter 2, "The Novel Politics of Literary Interpretation."

16 Angela Y. Davis, *Women, Culture, and Politics* (New York: Random House, 1984), 45.

Index